The Selected Lectures of Ralph Waldo Emerson

The Selected Lectures of

RALPH WALDO EMERSON

Edited by Ronald A. Bosco & Joel Myerson

THE UNIVERSITY OF GEORGIA PRESS *Athens and London*

© 2005 by The University of Georgia Press

Athens, Georgia 30602

All rights reserved

Set in Minion by Bookcomp, Inc.

Printed and bound by Maple-Vail

The paper in this book meets the guidelines for permanence and
durability of the Committee on Production Guidelines for
Book Longevity of the Council on Library Resources.

Printed in the United States of America

09 08 07 06 05 C 5 4 3 2 1

09 08 07 06 05 P 5 4 3 2 1

Library of Congress Cataloging-in-Publication Data

Emerson, Ralph Waldo, 1803–1882.

[Speeches. Selections]

The selected lectures of Ralph Waldo Emerson /
edited by Ronald A. Bosco and Joel Myerson.

p. cm.

Includes bibliographical references and index.

ISBN 0-8203-2644-5 (alk. paper) —

ISBN 0-8203-2733-6 (pbk. : alk. paper)

1. Speeches, addresses, etc., American.   I. Bosco, Ronald A.
II. Myerson, Joel.   III. Title.

PS1616.B673 2005

813'.3—dc22   2005008675

ISBN-13: 978-0-8203-2644-3 (alk. paper)

ISBN-13: 978-0-8203-2733-4 (pbk. : alk. paper)

British Library Cataloging-in-Publication Data available

Contents

Preface

The appearance of our edition of *The Later Lectures of Ralph Waldo Emerson, 1843–1871* in 2001 continued an extraordinary cycle of recovery and publication from manuscript of primary sources from the hand of the individual who is arguably the foremost intellectual architect of American culture. That cycle began in 1939, when Ralph L. Rusk published the first six volumes of Emerson's letters. Joseph Slater added *The Correspondence of Emerson and Carlyle* in one volume in 1964, and Eleanor M. Tilton added an additional four volumes of letters between 1990 and 1995. The cycle continued with a generation of editors who in the 1950s turned their attention to Emerson's early lectures and journals. Emerson's early lectures, edited by Stephen E. Whicher, Robert E. Spiller, and Wallace E. Williams, appeared in three volumes between 1959 and 1972, and his journals and miscellaneous notebooks, under the chief editorship first of William H. Gilman and then of Ralph H. Orth, appeared in sixteen volumes between 1960 and 1982. After the completion of the edition of Emerson's journals and miscellaneous notebooks, the cycle continued with a new generation of editors who had been recruited by Mr. Gilman and Mr. Orth to carry on the work of the first generation of Emerson editors, many of whom had passed away by the 1980s. Under Mr. Orth's chief editorship, that new generation of editors, several of whom had worked on the journals and miscellaneous notebooks, prepared the one-volume edition of Emerson's poetry notebooks for publication in 1986 and the three-volume edition of his topical notebooks, which appeared between 1990 and 1994. Finally, under the chief editorship of Albert J. von Frank, *The Complete Sermons of Ralph Waldo Emerson* was published between 1989 and 1992 in a four-volume edition.

This extraordinary cycle of recovery and publication would never have been possible without the care with which, early on, Emerson's children and first editors—Ellen and Edward Waldo Emerson along with James Elliot Cabot, Emerson's literary executor—preserved the manuscripts on which these editions have been based and with which, under the agency of the Ralph Waldo Emerson Memorial Association, the manuscripts were subsequently collected and preserved at the Houghton Library of Harvard University and made available to scholars. While numbers alone cannot tell the whole story of the genesis of these editions or the extent to which they sustained scholarly inquiry into Emerson's mind and legacy as they increasingly became available in print, the numbers are impressive with respect to the cycle of recovery. Over the past sixty years more than thirty editors crossing multiple generational lines have produced a magnificent archaeology of Emerson's thought and an outpouring of scholarly, biographical, and textual studies that is unprecedented for an American author.

We gratefully acknowledge the Ralph Waldo Emerson Memorial Association and the Houghton Library of Harvard University for permission to publish Emerson's lectures as a selected volume. The staff of the Houghton Library extended to us the usual splendid courtesies with which they have supported Emerson editors over several decades; for these courtesies we would like to thank Leslie A. Morris, curator of manuscripts, and Susan Halpert, Denison Beach, Tom Ford, Jennie Rathbun, Virginia Smyers, and Emily Walhout.

All scholarship is collaborative; as the record of Emerson editions published over the past six decades suggests, scholarly collaboration has been a necessary condition of all editorial work on Emerson's manuscripts, and it has always been graciously offered by specialists in the study of Emerson, by textual specialists, and by archival specialists. We have already expressed our gratitude to those many individuals who assisted our work in editing Emerson's later lectures in those volumes (see *Later Lectures*, 1:x–xii).

Mr. Bosco thanks Gareth Griffiths, chair of the Department of English, and Joan Wick-Pelletier, dean of the College of Arts and Sciences, for their support of this edition and gratefully acknowledges President Karen R. Hitchcock and Provost Carlos E. Santiago of the University at Albany, State University of New York, for providing him with the intellectual space to complete work on this edition.

Mr. Myerson thanks Steven Lynn, chair of the Department of English of the University of South Carolina, for his continued support of this and other Emerson projects. Chris Heafner assisted with the research and proofreading of this volume.

Both editors thank Nancy Grayson of the University of Georgia Press for her continuous support of our editions of Emerson's lectures and for making them a reality.

We are very grateful to Bernadette M. Bosco and Greta D. Little for allowing Emerson to intrude into their lives yet once again.

Ronald A. Bosco
Concord, Massachusetts
and
Joel Myerson
Edisto Beach, South Carolina

Works Frequently Cited

Cabot, *A Memoir*   James Elliot Cabot. *A Memoir of Ralph Waldo Emerson.* 2 vols. Boston and New York: Houghton Mifflin, 1887.

CEC   *The Correspondence of Emerson and Carlyle.* Edited by Joseph Slater. New York: Columbia University Press, 1964.

Complete Sermons   *The Complete Sermons of Ralph Waldo Emerson.* Albert J. von Frank, chief editor; Ronald A. Bosco, Andrew H. Delbanco, Wesley T. Mott, and Teresa Toulouse, editors; David M. Robinson, Wallace E. Williams, and Douglas Emory Wilson, contributing editors. 4 vols. Columbia: University of Missouri Press, 1989–92.

CW   *The Collected Works of Ralph Waldo Emerson.* Alfred R. Ferguson, Joseph Slater, and Douglas Emory Wilson, general editors; Robert E. Burkholder, Jean Ferguson Carr, Philip Nicoloff, Barbara L. Packer, Robert E. Spiller, and Wallace E. Williams, editors. 6 vols. to date. Cambridge, Mass.: Harvard University Press, 1971–.

Early Lectures   *The Early Lectures of Ralph Waldo Emerson.* Edited by Stephen E. Whicher, Robert E. Spiller, and Wallace E. Williams. 3 vols. Cambridge, Mass.: Harvard University Press, 1959–72.

Emerson Chronology   Albert J. von Frank. *An Emerson Chronology.* New York: G. K. Hall, 1994.

Emerson's Antislavery Writings   *Emerson's Antislavery Writings.* Edited by Len Gougeon and Joel Myerson. New Haven, Conn.: Yale University Press, 1995.

Emerson's University Lectures   Ronald A. Bosco. *"His Lectures Were Poetry, His Teaching the Music of the Spheres": Annie Adams Fields and Francis Greenwood Peabody on Emerson's "Natural History of the Intellect" University Lectures at Harvard in 1870. Harvard Library Bulletin,* n.s., 8, no. 2 (Summer 1997).

JMN   *The Journals and Miscellaneous Notebooks of Ralph Waldo Emerson.* William H. Gilman and Ralph H. Orth, chief editors; Linda Allardt, Ronald A. Bosco, George P. Clark, Merrell R. Davis, Harrison Hayford, David W. Hill, Glen M. Johnson, J. E. Parsons, A. W. Plumstead, Merton M. Sealts Jr., and Susan Sutton Smith, editors; Ruth H. Bennett, associate editor. 16 vols. Cambridge, Mass.: Harvard University Press, 1960–82.

Later Lectures *The Later Lectures of Ralph Waldo Emerson, 1843–1871.* Edited by Ronald A. Bosco and Joel Myerson. 2 vols. Athens: University of Georgia Press, 2001.

Letters *The Letters of Ralph Waldo Emerson.* Edited by Ralph L. Rusk (vols. 1–6) and Eleanor M. Tilton (vols. 7–10). New York: Columbia University Press, 1939, 1990–95.

PN *The Poetry Notebooks of Ralph Waldo Emerson.* Edited by Ralph H. Orth, Albert J. von Frank, Linda Allardt, and David W. Hill. Columbia: University of Missouri Press, 1986.

TN *The Topical Notebooks of Ralph Waldo Emerson.* Ralph H. Orth, chief editor; Ronald A. Bosco, Glen M. Johnson, and Susan Sutton Smith, editors; Douglas Emory Wilson, consulting editor. 3 vols. Columbia: University of Missouri Press, 1990–94.

W *The Complete Works of Ralph Waldo Emerson.* Edited by Edward Waldo Emerson. Centenary Edition. 12 vols. Boston and New York: Houghton Mifflin, 1903–4.

Introduction

Emerson as Lecturer

Grace Greenwood tells of an interesting afternoon in the Old Corner Bookstore in Boston, when [Bayard] Taylor, in a weary and a somewhat petulant mood, dissuaded her from lecturing, saying that it was an occupation full of misery, that he himself detested it, and that an audience seemed to him no other thing than a collection of cabbage-heads. A few minutes later Mr. Emerson congratulated her upon the thought of lecturing, saying that there was recompense for all the hardships of the work in the kind words and the smiling faces and the bright eyes of the audience. —Albert H. Smythe, *Bayard Taylor* (Boston, 1896), 103

[T]he sermon I heard from Mr Finney [in 1829 or 1830] was in Park Street Church . . . from the text "The wages of sin is death[.]" . . . He [later] came to Boston & I took courage & went. His text was, "The wages of sin is death," and I recognized in succession all the topics & treatment. . . . It was twenty five years later, . . . when I next saw Mr Finney, soon after his return from London, that I found myself on a Sunday in Rome, New York, & learned that he was to preach there. I went, & his text was "The Wages of sin is death" & the sermon in the main & I suppose in all the particulars the same. . . . It was plain that he was as bad as a hack lecturer like myself. —Ralph Waldo Emerson to Edward Everett Hale, 30? June? 1870?, *Letters*, 6:123

When I handed him a check for twelve hundred dollars for his six lectures, "What a swindle!" was his exclamation. —William Henry Furness, "Random Reminiscences of Emerson," *Atlantic Monthly* 71 (March 1893): 348

Until recently, there have not been many studies of Emerson as a lecturer. The reasons for this neglect, we believe, have been fourfold. First, until 2001, when our edition of Emerson's later lectures appeared and brought the record of his career as a lecturer forward from the 1840s through the 1870s, only sixty-five of his surviving lectures from 1833 to 1842 had been published as *The Early Lectures of Ralph Waldo Emerson*, the last volume of which was published in 1972. Second, the manuscripts of Emerson's lectures after 1843 exist in varying stages of disarray that make it impossible to reconstruct the complete texts of more than fifty of what were well over one thousand lecture deliveries by Emerson from 1843 through the end of his career in the 1870s. Third, there are so many accounts of Emerson's lecturing in major and minor newspapers that the idea of tracing his platform career through a search of these sources has typically proved so daunting to scholars that they have preferred to study other aspects of Emerson's career in depth. Fourth, as the remarks by Emerson and others printed above suggest, the information known about him as a lecturer is often so contradictory that scholars have preferred to work with aspects of his career that are more straightforward.

The biographical and intellectual gaps in our knowledge of Emerson caused by the lack of studies of his career as a lecturer are now being filled. This is very fortunate for Emerson's reputation and, more importantly, for our understanding of how he emerged in the middle of the nineteenth century as the foremost architect of American intellectual culture and as America's most prominent man of letters. Emerson spent more than half a century in front of public audiences sharpening his ideas and his style, so that if, as Bliss Perry has so famously stated, his journals were the "savings bank" into which he deposited the ideas for his essays and other writings, then his lectures were where he first gave public expression to these ideas once he had withdrawn them from his account.[1] Again and again we see Emerson's writings develop from a variety of journal entries devoted to a particular topic, to a lecture revised over multiple deliveries, to a published work. Indeed, a number of his lecture series became books, such as *Representative Men* (1850), *English Traits* (1856), and *The Conduct of Life* (1860), while several of his lecture series on philosophy provided the basis for a posthumous work, *Natural History of Intellect* (1891), first edited, if not actually created, by his literary executor, James Elliot Cabot, and then supplemented by his son, Edward Waldo Emerson, Cabot's successor.[2]

But Emerson tried out not only his ideas and his style on the lecture platform, he tried out "Ralph Waldo Emerson," the public persona he both adopted for and was forced into by his audiences. We know that Emerson attempted a number of careers in his life, including minister, lecturer, Concord gentleman landowner, family man, author, publishing agent, editor, traveler, and, finally, one of the most famous men in America. He also took on a number of formal personae, going through turns as "Ralph" to his family and friends (before becoming "Waldo"), as the anonymous author of *Nature* (1836) and of articles and poems in the *Dial* (1840–44), as "R. Waldo Emerson" in formal correspondence, and as "Ralph Waldo Emerson" on the title pages of his books and pamphlets, a signature that soon became interchangeable with his image as the Sage of Concord. Significantly, while he worked through these various public and formal personae, Emerson worked through his most important ideas and extensive statements on subjects such as abolitionism, woman's rights, and temperance on the lecture platform, not on the printed page. His career as a lecturer thus provided an integral component to his constant reinvention of his public self and his service to society as a public intellectual. As Stephen Railton argues, the lecture platform was necessary not only for Emerson's continual self-invention but also for its ability to provide him with a constant reminder of his success in doing exactly that: "[While] the thematic goal of Emerson's oratory was to announce the omnipotence of each listener's self, the dramatic goal of each such performance was to confirm his own."[3]

Scholars usually assume that Emerson spent so much time as a lecturer because he needed the money and was well paid for his efforts. In some ways the statistics might bear them out, as in this summary by Robert D. Richardson Jr. of Emerson's lecturing career:

> Over his active career of four decades, Emerson gave some 1,500 public lectures. Lecturing was a major part of his life and a major source of income. For twenty-five years he was out and away from home lecturing for four, five or even six months out of each year, every year. He traveled as far west as St. Louis, Des Moines, Minneapolis, and eventually California; he gave 17 lectures in Canada but almost none south of the Ohio River. He delivered the great majority of his lectures in Massachusetts. He gave 157 lectures in New York state. He gave more lectures in Maine than in New Hampshire (35 to 27) and many more in Illinois (49), Ohio (56), Pennsylvania (42), and Wisconsin (29) than in Connecticut, . . . where he spoke only 18 times in his entire career.[4]

Yet although Emerson was dependent on lecturing for his (and his family's) livelihood during his early life, after the settlement of his first wife's estate in the mid-1830s and because of his early profits as a lecturer and as an author as well as his shrewd investment of his monies his finances became so secure that in 1851 he was listed in *The Rich Men of Massachusetts* as possessing $50,000.[5] And after he changed his publishers in 1860 to Ticknor and Fields, the most prestigious Boston firm of the time, his royalty income increased markedly.

To Emerson, then, lecturing was significantly more than just a means to obtain money, more than a financially driven alternative career. At the same time there is no denying that lecturing provided him with a substantial income, and as the following remarks he entered in his journal suggest, he was more than willing to endure certain inconveniences to maintain that income:

> 'Twas tedious the obstructions & squalor of travel. The advantage of their offers at Chicago made it needful to go. It was in short this dragging a decorous old gentleman out of home, & out of position, to this juvenile career tantamount to this: "I'll bet you fifty dollars a day for three weeks, that you will not leave your library & wade & freeze & ride & run, & suffer all manner of indignities, & stand up for an hour each night reading in a hall:" and I answer, "I'll bet I will," I do it & win the $900.[6]

And should the "winning" sum in nineteenth-century as opposed to twenty-first-century dollars seem an exaggeration, consider that during the early years of his career Emerson netted, for example, $200.00 from a lecture series on English literature that he delivered in 1835, $571.00 for ten lectures in a *Human Culture* series in Boston in 1837, and $461.92 for ten lectures in a *Human Life* series in Boston in 1838–39. In terms of the value of these amounts relative to the value of U.S. dollars in 2002, $200.00 equals $4,050.00, $571.00 equals $10,600.00, and $461.92 equals $8,870.00. By the 1850s and 1860s, with his reputation firmly established, Emerson was routinely offered or commanded fees on the order of $1,166.34 (or $24,800.00 in 2002 U.S. dollars) for six lectures in a *Topics of Modern Times* series in Philadelphia in 1854, $883.08 (or $19,100.00) for six lectures in a *Natural Method of Mental Philosophy* series in Boston in 1858, and $1,655.75 (or $20,800.00) for six unconnected lectures before a private audience in Boston in 1868.[7]

Although Emerson was known to his contemporaries primarily as a lecturer, he comes down to us today primarily through his published writings, through works such as *Nature*, "The American Scholar," "The Divinity School Address," "Self-Reliance," "The Poet," "Experience," "Fate," and the biographical essay "Thoreau," all of which have introduced him in anthologies of American literature to generations of students and kept him before the general public for well over one hundred years. But to understand Emerson's writings we must first see him at work as a lecturer. This role was crucial to Emerson, as he himself readily admitted:

> I look on the Lecture Room as the true Church of the coming time, and as the home of a richer eloquence than Faneuil Hall or the Capitol ever knew. For here is all that the true orator will ask, namely, a convertible audience,—an audience coming up to the house, not knowing what shall befall them there, but uncommitted and willing victims to reason and love. There is no topic that may not be treated, and no method excluded. *Here*, everything is admissible, philosophy, ethics, divinity, criticism, poetry, humor, anecdote, mimicry,—ventriloquism almost,—all the breadth and versatility of the most liberal conversation, and of the highest, lowest, personal, and local topics—all are permitted, and all may be combined in one speech. It is a panharmonicon combining every note on the longest gamut, from the explosion of cannon to the tinkle of a guitar. . . .
>
> . . . Here is a pulpit that makes the other chairs of instruction cold and ineffectual with their customary preparation for a delivery: the most decorous with fine things, pretty things, wise things, but no arrows, no axes, no nectar, no transpiercing, no loving, no enchantment. Here, the American orator shall find the theatre he needs; here, he may lay himself out utterly large, prodigal, enormous, on the subject of the hour. Here, he may dare to hope for the higher inspiration and a total transfusion of himself into the minds of men.[8]

Thus, by examining his lectures and how they were delivered, we can look into the laboratory of Emerson's intellectual and compositional processes and see his published writings gestating. And perhaps the most important thing to remember in reading Emerson's lectures is that we need to study not just the words but the manner in which they were delivered.

As a minister, Emerson liked preaching far more than his technical or pastoral ministerial duties. There was something about appearing before an audience that appealed to him, and something in him, too, that recognized the importance of language and, as his contemporaries reported it, of an "earnest and magnetic" presence as the means to move an audience by moral suasion. Emerson's language and presence were the sources of his authority both in the pulpit and at the lectern, and they were easily acknowledged by all, including his lifelong friend Elizabeth Palmer Peabody, who remarked after his death that Emerson was

> always pre-eminently the preacher to his own generation and future ones, but as much—if not more—out of the pulpit as in it; faithful unto the end to his early chosen profession and the vows of his youth. Whether he spoke in the pulpit or lyceum chair, or to friends in his hospitable parlor, or *tête-à-tête* in his study, or in his favorite walks in the woods with chosen companions, or at the festive gatherings of scholars, or in the conventions of philanthropists, or in the popular assemblies of patriots in times and on occasions that try men's souls,—always and everywhere it was his conscious purpose to utter a "Thus saith the Lord."[9]

As John McAleer astutely observed more recently, "Rather than being a preacher who came before his audiences in the guise of a lecturer, Emerson had begun his career as a lecturer who came before his congregations in the guise of a preacher."[10] In effect, then, Emerson's transition from the traditional pulpit to the emerging—and increasingly public and fashionable—lecture platform was virtually seamless.[11] And being a lecturer not only allowed Emerson to spread his doctrines and to work on his writings, it also gave him opportunities to pursue his lifelong task of personal growth. As Barbara Packer has shown, Emerson's early public performances were "mediated through institutions—the church, the lyceum, or the speaker's platform at some ceremonial occasion." But when he went out on his own as a lecturer, "Emerson for the first time found himself speaking to an audience whose only reason for coming was to hear *him* and whose only reason for staying was that they were interested in what they heard."[12] What this meant, according to Stephen Railton, was that "henceforward he would meet his potential congregation as Ralph Waldo Emerson, not as a minister." Finding himself now viewed as a person and not a type, standing without "a commissioned role, with no institutional authority to speak from, with neither Bible nor liturgy to refer to, he took it upon himself— his presence and his language—to work out the terms of a public identity. The people who filled the hall met only on the common ground that Emerson could supply in his text for the evening."[13] It is by looking at Emerson's platform performances as described by his contemporaries that we can better understand what Packer and Railton are describing.

Emerson's first biographer, George Willis Cooke, has left a general description of Emerson's lecturing habits that is worth quoting at length:

> On the lecture platform Emerson seems to be unconscious of his audience, is not disturbed by interruptions of any kind, by hisses, or by the departure of disappointed listeners. He always reads his lectures, though he is not always confined to his manuscript; while he often misplaces his sheets, and stumbles over the chirography. He usually begins in a slow and spiritless manner, in a low tone; and he is not fluent of speech, or passionate in manner. As he proceeds, he becomes earnest and magnetic; while the thrilling intensity of his voice deeply affects and rivets the attention of his audience. He is full of mannerisms in expression and in bodily attitude, seldom makes a gesture, and has little variation of voice. He secures the interest of his hearers by the simple grandeur of his thought, the inspiration of his moral genius, the conviction and manliness which his words express, and by the silvery enchantment of his voice. The glow of his face, the mobile expressiveness of his features, the charm of his smile, add to the interest created by his thought. It is the quality of his ideas, however, which attracts his hearers. His thought often rises to the heights of the purest eloquence. Such passages are sure to command the closest attention. It is the glowing faith and the moral intensity of the seer which gives them their power.[14]

Here we see the basic elements of Emerson's posture as a lecturer: he ignores the audience, he shuffles the pages of his manuscript, his voice is not impressive, and his physical gestures are negligible, yet the audience follows him with rapt attention and goes away inspired. What is happening here? How can Emerson be the subject of such comments as this one from the *Boston Post* in 1849: "It is quite out of character to say Mr. Emerson lectures—he does no such thing. He drops nectar—he chips out sparks—he exhales odors—he lets off mental skyrockets and fireworks—he spouts fire, and conjurer-like, draws ribbons out of his mouth. He smokes, he sparkles, he improvises, he shouts, he sings, he explodes like a bundle of crackers, he goes off in fiery eruptions like a volcano, but he does not *lecture*"?[15]

Lecturing styles in the mid-nineteenth century were classical in origin, formal in practice, Latinate rather than Saxon in word choice, and long in delivery. Elocution, not ideas, was the standard of the day, and Emerson was always dubious of its value. The historical process by which American oratory was changed from neoclassical to popular models was timed perfectly for Emerson's own beliefs, for this was a man who wrote, "Ought not the scholar to convey his meaning in terms as short & strong as the truckman uses to convey his?"

> The language of the street is always strong. . . . I feel too the force of the double negative, though clean contrary to our grammar rules. And I confess to some pleasure from the stinging rhetoric of a rattling oath in the mouth of truckmen & teamsters. How laconic & brisk it is by the side of a page of the North American Review. Cut

these words & they would bleed; they are vascular & alive; they walk & run. . . . It is a shower of bullets, whilst Cambridge men & Yale men correct themselves & begin again at every half sentence.[16]

Writing critically in 1828 about his brother Charles, who had just delivered the valedictory oration to his class at Harvard College, Emerson states that "the vice of [Charles's] oratory lies here—he is a *spectacle* instead of being an *engine*; a fine show at which we look, instead of an agent that moves us." By concentrating solely on the technical aspects of his presentation, Charles was like someone who has "chalked around him a circle on the floor & within that he exhibits these various excellences to all the curious." The result is, therefore, that instead of "feeling that his audience was an object of attention from him, he felt that he was an object of attention to the audience." This, Emerson says, is "the reverse of what it should be. Instead of finding his audience . . . an angry master who is to be pacified, or a sturdy master who is to be cajoled,—&, in any case, one whose difficult regard is to be won,—[Charles] takes it for granted that he has the command." And in his final lesson drawn from the example of Charles's oratory, Emerson also criticizes one of the best-known orators of the day, Edward Everett: "Let him feel his situation. Let him remember that the true orator must not wrap himself in himself, but must wholly abandon himself to the sentiment he utters, & the multitude he addresses;—must become their property, to the end that *they may become his*. Like Pericles, let him 'thunder & lighten.' Let him for a moment forget himself, & then, assuredly, he will not be forgotten."[17]

Contemporary accounts indicate that Emerson himself took the advice he had given to Charles. After all, it was natural for the man whose 1837 address "The American Scholar" called for a truly American literature to call for an indigenous American oratory. But this lack of flash and spectacle has led some scholars to ask why Emerson *was* successful; as one modern critic concludes in puzzlement, "He never altered his manner on the platform and as he relied on no gimmicks, physical or oratorical, his ability to captivate an audience remains somewhat mysterious."[18]

The accounts of Emerson as a lecturer that were published over half a century parallel those judgments of his printed works set forth over the same period of time: he goes from being attacked as a radical whose writings have no discernible organizing principles to, in his middle and especially later years, being praised as a great American whose ideas and brilliancies transcend a style that is often difficult to follow. And just as the radical print Emerson became standardized and, in that sense, tamed in later years as his books went through numerous reprintings and showed up in leather-bound volumes in America's best homes, so audiences attempted to tame the radical lecturer. The reformer Sallie Holley recalled an occasion when the "hall was crowded with the beauty and chivalry of Rochester[, New York]. How queerly fashion regulates some things in the world! Here was a man of the most ultra radical views, a Garrisonian abolitionist, a Unitarian minister of the worst heretical stamp, a disunionist, a transcendentalist, etc., etc. Yet the very sanctity, piety, patriotism, and boated conservatism were all present, dressed in their most good-humoured smiles!"[19] However, commentators on Emerson's articles and books could not see his writing process at work: they did not have access to the thirty published volumes of his journals, topical notebooks, and letters that modern scholars are able to consult today. The audiences for Emerson's lectures, on the other hand, could gather in his appearance and delivery firsthand evidence as to how his work was being created in front of a future group of readers. In general, echoing Cooke's description, they note that Emerson did not make much of a physical impression; he shuffled and searched his papers during his presentation; he spoke in a discontinuous, even abrupt, fashion; and he puzzled his audience by delivering lectures they did not consider to be logically organized.

Emerson's physical presence on the platform was unimposing. Many accounts note his plain black—almost clerical—garb, often commenting on its old-fashioned cut or on how poorly it fit him. He possessed no flamboyant gestures, but he did demonstrate two oddities that audiences noticed. One was "the motion of the left hand at his side, as if the intensity of his thought were escaping, like the electricity of a battery at that point," or, as another person described it, he used the hand "with unconscious earnestness in driving imaginary stakes."[20] This was combined with a "rocking motion" that "originated in Emerson's unconscious habit of periodically lifting himself up on his toes, as a form of emphasis."[21] The elder Henry James was able to notice that this unprepossessing appearance had a purpose:

> His deferential entrance upon the scene, his look of inquiry at the desk and chair, his resolute rummaging among his embarrassed papers, the air of sudden recollection with which he would plunge into his pockets for what he must have known had never been put there, for his uncertainty and irresolution as he arose to speak, [became] his deep relieved inspiration as he got well from under the burning glass of his auditor's eyes, and addressed himself at length to their docile ears instead.[22]

Clearly, then, Emerson's lack of physical gestures and flourishes forced the audience to concentrate on his words, not his performance.

Numerous commentators noted how Emerson shuffled his manuscripts. This was in large part due to the way in which the lectures were written after the mid-1840s; in later years it was due both to Emerson's declining eyesight and to the gradual decline of his memory.[23] Although the pages of a few of his lecture manuscripts from the 1840s, 1850s, and 1860s are sewn together and appear reasonably neat and finished, the vast majority of lecture manuscripts from these decades consist of heavily emended unsewn leaves. With numerous revisions undertaken on pages worn thin by repeated use, with new prose added on relatively fresh pages of varying paper stocks interleaved among the worn pages, and with multiple sequences of page numbers, these manuscripts survive as concrete evidence that Emerson created lectures incrementally and by organizing them around discrete thoughts occasionally strung together with transitional prose.

Most auditors considered Emerson's shuffling through his manuscripts to be a fault: even old friends like Bronson Alcott commented on "his perilous passages from paragraph to paragraph of manuscript, [that] we have almost learned to like." [24] Others were more astute and found a method to Emerson's apparent confusion: "His peculiar manner of reading a few pages, and then shuffling his papers, as though they were inextricably mixed, was embarrassing at first, but when it was found that he was not disturbed by it, and that it was not the result of an accident, but a characteristic manner of delivery, the audience withheld its sympathy and rather enjoyed the novelty and the feeling of uncertainty as to what would come next." [25] As an analogical rather than an analytical thinker, Emerson, too, seemed to enjoy "the novelty and the feeling of uncertainty" as to where he would finally take a given lecture. More than once he warned the members of his audience that if they had come to hear a finished and formally developed discourse, then they were likely to be disappointed. Describing his compositional method, style of delivery, and suspicion of systematic metaphysicians in a lecture on the intellect that James Elliot Cabot eventually mined for the essay "Powers and Laws of Thought," Emerson said,

> I write anecdotes of the intellect; a sort of *Farmer's Almanac* of mental moods. I confine my ambition to true reporting of its play in natural action. . . .
>
> I cannot myself use that systematic form which is reckoned essential in treating the science of the mind. But if one can say so without arrogance, I might suggest that he who contents himself with dotting a fragmentary curve, recording only what facts he has observed, without attempting to arrange them in one outline, follows a system also,—a system as grand as any other, though he does not interfere with its vast curves by prematurely forcing them into a circle or ellipse, but only draws that arc which he clearly sees, or perhaps at a later observation a remote curve of the same orbit, and waits for a new opportunity. . . .
>
> I confess to a little distrust of that completeness of system which metaphysicians are apt to affect. [26]

The disorganization of and constant searching through his manuscripts exacerbated the problem many found with Emerson's delivery, that of speaking in a discontinuous, even abrupt, fashion. Not everyone appreciated his "peculiar, emphatic, abrupt, sharp, impressive and oracular" elocution, and few would agree with John Jay Chapman that "in some of Emerson's more important lectures the logical scheme is more perfect than in his essays. . . . [I]n the process of working up and perfecting his writings, in revising and filling his sentences, the logical scheme became more and more obliterated."[27] The comments of the *Marietta Register*'s reporter are more representative of the problems auditors had with the organization of Emerson's lectures: "The Lecturer could begin in the middle, and work forward or backward; or go to the end first, and take his beginning last; or strike this paragraph or that one, this or that sentence—go through or between, above or below—and the Lecture be as complete in any case, even though the half were left out, or more patched on."[28] Another midwestern reporter describes the problem in this fashion:

> Ralph Waldo Emerson's lecture on Eloquence reminded us of the way it is said vessels are built on the St. Lawrence—by the mile, and then cut off to suit orders. Mr. Emerson turns over about six sheets where he reads one, and it is of no consequence where his turning over stops; one place to splice on, or to leave off, is just as good as another. His lecture, called "On Eloquence," or by any other name, would pass as well, while, no doubt, from that cord of manuscript before him, he could extract any required number of lectures, on any required subjects, just as a magician can draw all sorts of liquors, on demand, from the same bottle.[29]

Emerson's friend Convers Francis, the minister and Harvard Divinity School professor, had similar reservations:

> His style is too fragmentary and sententious. It wants the requisite words or phrases of connection and transition from one thought to another; but has unequalled precision and beauty in single sentences. This defect, and his habit of expressing a common truth in some uncommon (is it not sometimes slightly fantastic?) way of his own, are the reasons perhaps why it is so difficult to retain and carry away what he says. I find that his beautiful things are *slippery*, and will not stay in my mind.[30]

And, as occasionally happened, a reporter's or a friend's polite reservations about Emerson's lecturing style sometimes underestimated the sense of outrage that other auditors felt at paying good money for a lecture they could not understand. Speaking for those disaffected folk, an unnamed reporter writing for the New York periodical the *Knickerbocker* in 1865 dubbed Emerson "roaring Ralph" and mercilessly satirized his ideas, his language, and his overall style of delivery. According to this reporter, Emerson, "our flighty friend," "speaks vigorously, yet says nothing" through "metaphorical beauties" that are "bewildering, astounding and incomprehensible"; the reporter adds that just as "no thought can fathom his intentions," for "his finished sentences" are "bottomless," so too Emerson's "show business," "high-heeled, knock-kneed logic, [and] *au fait* dexterity in concocting flap-doodle mixtures" that he calls lectures deliver unwary listeners into the lecturer's own strange realm of "gin and bitters, or opium discourses on—delirium tremens."[31]

Even Emerson himself, in complaining about newspaper reports of his lectures, wrote that the "fault of the reporters is doubtless owing to the lecture itself
which lacks any method, or any that is easily apprehensible."[32] But others found
his delivery, while initially problematic, finally to be crafted with a purpose. Abigail
May (Mrs. Bronson) Alcott wrote after hearing Emerson lecture: "He is abrupt—
disjointed fragmentary but you are arrested by a truth which like a cut diamond
sparkles and radiates—you forget the rubbishy stuff which covered it in its normal state—the transition from Scenes of Misery to the Banquet of Beauty was too
much—my brain reeled with it."[33] Oliver Wendell Holmes was less dramatic but
equally favorable. Commenting on how Emerson's slow delivery was the result of
his careful choice of words, he praised "the delicate way [Emerson] steps about
among the words of his vocabulary—if you have ever seen a cat picking her foot-
steps in wet weather, you have seen the picture of Emerson's exquisite intelligence,
feeling for his phrase or epithet."[34]

Some commentators were able to appreciate Emerson's presentation as a whole.
A reporter for the *Milwaukee Sentinel* notes that the

> style of the speaker is that which is frequently observed in great thinkers—a cer-
> tain nervousness of expression, now rapid in motion, now impressively—almost
> painfully—slow; paying little or no regard to customary punctuation, grammatical
> or rhetorical; now carrying out a word with great care before he lets it fall, and now
> splintering them off with much greater rapidity; and in this being governed not at all
> by the importance of the words, but rather by the motions of his own thoughts.[35]

A Baltimore reporter complains that Emerson "goes fumbling through his manuscript picking out a page here and there, and making an awkward pause till he
finds it," but as he does, then, when he "takes off his eye-glasses and extemporizes
a sentence or two[,] he has the air of a careful apothecary who is compounding a
prescription behind a pair of delicate scales."[36] And in one of the more intriguing
reports of Emerson's success as a lecturer that also contained a warning to reporters
to beware of criticizing his performance too harshly, Nathaniel Parker Willis, who
had personally witnessed Emerson's evolution from a New England preacher to
a lecturer with an international audience, stands back in awe at the authority he
wields from the lectern. In his "Second Look at Emerson," a review of Emerson's
delivery of "The Spirit of the Times" before the Mercantile Library Association of
New York City on 29 January 1850, Willis characterizes Emerson as "our Prophet of
the Intuitive" and states that his audience comes "selectively out, like steel filings
out of a handfull of sand to a magnet," knowing full well that he "has climbed above
the atmosphere of this world and kicked away the ladder—holding no deferential
communication . . . with any of the intermediate ladder-rounds." Alluding to Sir
Henry Wotton's classic dismissal of critics, Willis remarks, "That 'critics . . . are
brushers of noblemen's clothes,' one feels very sensibly and reprovingly, in turning

a pen to write any comment on Emerson. He says so many . . . wonderfully true and good things . . . in one of his Delphic lectures, that, to find any fault with him, seems like measuring thunder by its echo down a back alley."[37]

Again, George Willis Cooke shows himself to be a perceptive observer of Emerson's lecturing style when he describes what he considers to be the basis for Emerson's platform demeanor:

> He hesitates for words, and seems to find it difficult to secure the precise expression he desires. He speaks on the lecture-platform much as he converses. . . . In his conversation, there is the same antithesis and abrupt transition to be found as in his books. He does not think continuously; he does not in conversation follow a subject through, but hesitates, skips intervening ideas, is unable, apparently, to hold his mind to all the links of thought. It is not natural for him to do so. He does not think logically, but intuitively, sees and seizes at a glance, in bold generalizations, but is unable to follow and arrange the intervening steps from premise to conclusion.[38]

What Cooke describes as Emerson's conversational style is something that has also been seen in his published works: a loose, apparently disorganized presentation that nevertheless invites in the listener or reader to follow the author's own thought processes as he works toward his conclusions. Indeed, it is a style that Emerson quite self-consciously projected, as he himself admitted in 1870 while looking back at the success of his career as a lecturer and writer:

> The reason of a new philosophy or philosopher is ever that a man of thought finds he cannot read in the old books. I can't read Hegel, or Schelling, or find interest in what is told me from them, so I persist in my own idle & easy way, & write down my thoughts, & find presently that there are congenial persons who like them, so I persist, until some sort of outline or system grows. 'Tis the common course: Ever a new bias. It happened to each of these, Heraclitus, or Hegel, or whosoever.[39]

Emerson was a genius in creating a sense of spontaneity on the platform; James Russell Lowell claims to have seen "how artfully (for Emerson is a long-studied artist in these things) does the deliberate utterance, that seems to wait for the first word, seem to admit us partners in the labor of thought, and make us feel as if the glance of humor were a sudden suggestion; as if the perfect phrase lying written there on the desk were as unexpected to him as to us!"[40] Lowell put this more succinctly another time: "He somehow managed to combine the charm of unpremeditated discourse with the visible existence of carefully written manuscript lying before him on the desk."[41] By inviting his audience to join with him in the pursuit of ideas, he became, as one reporter noted, "the personification of 'man thinking.' The angular gestures, the awkward poses, the shuffling pages—all these were forgotten the moment the audience felt that it was in the presence of ideas in process of creation. Here, fresh from the depths of a great mind, was thought taking form before one's very eyes."[42]

One reason for Emerson's spontaneity was that his lectures were nearly always in the process of becoming. He once wrote that he regretted staying with a friend while lecturing, "in spite of my almost uniform practice of choosing the hotel when I read lectures, for the reason that my lecture is never finished, but always needs a super-final attention."[43] Not only were the lectures constantly being written under deadline, they were rewritten throughout Emerson's career as well for multiple deliveries, for wholesale revision and incorporation into other lectures, and for practice as what would become book chapters. Emerson's first stage of composition always occurred in his journals and notebooks, where he recorded everything, including his waking thoughts, texts copied from his voluminous readings, passages translated from his favorite classical and modern writers, snippets of correspondence received from select friends, and modest prose drafts that were either original with him or syntheses—"assimilations," to use his term—drawn out of one or more of the foregoing sources. Out of those entries Emerson constructed lecture prose, virtually sentence by sentence. Throughout his career the major portion of Emerson's actual lecture-writing time was devoted first to his creation of elaborate indices to journal and notebook sources on specific topics and then to his adaptation of extant journal and notebook prose appropriate to the topics for use at the lectern. This was his version of process writing, and as his second stage of composition it yielded freestanding lectures on individual topics as well as lectures on related topics for series. Whether freestanding or parts of series, Emerson's lectures grew in length with repeated reading and became increasingly sharpened in thesis and scope with each successive delivery. They were then revised again, in much the same way, for publication.[44]

Small wonder, then, that Emerson disliked having his lectures reported on by the newspapers. "These new lectures are rather studies than finished discourses," he wrote one newspaperman, "and I hope, one day, to complete, revise, & print them, or the substance of them."[45] "I am exceedingly vexed," he wrote the editor of the *Boston Commonwealth*, "by finding in your paper this morning, precisely such a report of one of my lectures, as I wrote to you a fortnight since to entreat you to defend me from." "My lectures are written to be read as lectures in different places," Emerson explained, "& then to be reported by myself. Tomorrow, I was to have read this very lecture in Salem, & your reporter does all he can to kill the thing to every hearer, by putting him in the possession beforehand of the words of each statement that struck him, as nearly as he could copy them." Emerson did not want to be a censor, but he did wish to maintain his intellectual and financial property rights to his words: "Abuse me, & welcome, but do not transcribe me."[46] And to a third editor he complained, "This particular lecture was read in a most unfinished state[,] its statements all crude & not properly connected[,] some veiled sketches of private persons whose modesty would be painfully wounded could they be read in print."[47]

Some reporters agreed that they did Emerson a disservice by putting down the texts of his lectures in print. According to one, Emerson's lecture is "not to be reported—without his own language, his manner, his delivery it would be little— to essay to reproduce it, would be like carrying soda-water to a friend the morning after it was drawn, and asking him how he relished it."[48] Even Franklin Benjamin Sanborn, a newspaperman and longtime acquaintance, confessed, "I have always thought the reports of Mr. Emerson's lectures most unsatisfactory, and I find my own no exception. The truth is, in listening one perceives a coherence of thought lying back of the isolated statements—like a vast encircling dome where lamps hang; in Mr. Emerson's presence one feels the great dim curve which surrounds all—but afterwards it is only the separate glancing lights one recalls."[49]

But Emerson had more than artistic reasons for not wanting to be reported. Put simply, if people could read his lectures for free, they would be less likely to pay to hear him in person. A main reason why Emerson wrote so many newspaper editors to forbear printing transcriptions of his lectures was to convince them all to agree to the practice; whenever one refused, responses such as this were typical:

> Mr. Emerson delivered his lecture at Horticultural Hall yesterday in the very earnestly expressed "hope" that it might not be reported. Had there been a reasonable probabil- ity that this wish would command universal acquiescence from the press, we should cheerfully have acceded to the request, at the cost of disappointing our own readers, and making our columns so far an incomplete record of the noteworthy public utter- ances of the day. But repeated experience has showed that the result of such appeals has been that while we, in common with other Boston papers, have respected the wishes of fastidious speakers, the press outside the city has utterly disregarded them, published such grossly imperfect reports as to deserve all the detestation which Mr. Emerson feels for them, and then sneered at the "lack of enterprise" of the local jour- nals. We have therefore thought that we should best meet the spirit of the eminent philosopher's desire in the matter by making our report as faithful and accurate as possible, in the space at our disposal.[50]

In his later years Emerson's lectures became harder to report because they used more and more quotations from other sources. Just as Emerson had earlier ar- gued that we should "read for the lustres," now his lectures consisted more and more of personal "lustres" or individual aphorisms and quotations.[51] In writing to someone organizing a private class for him, Emerson comments, "I fancy that, like every old scholar, I have points of rest & emphasis in literature. I know what books I have found unforgetable, & what passages in books. It will be most agreeable to me to indicate such. I should like, in poetry, especially, to mark certain authors & certain passages which I prize, & to state on what grounds I prize them."[52] As usual, perhaps the best statement of Emerson's compositional desires and habits comes from him. In his introduction to "Genius and Temperament," written especially for a delivery before a regular audience at Meionaon Hall, Boston, in 1861, he says:

> I cannot tell you with how much satisfaction I meet once more this company. In all other audiences, I have a painful sense of my deficiencies,—real enough, and everywhere to be deplored,—but forced on my own attention elsewhere by the necessity of meeting the expectation and general average of an assembly to whom I am partially known. But here I have no such embarrassment. The company,—substantially the same persons for so many years,—know what to look for and what to pardon, when they come to the class, and do not demand of me,—what they might of another,—a more formal and precise external method,—but are content that I should use my own, knowing that I value a thought or a scientific law, for itself, without insisting that it should stand in a syllogism. They know that a scholar loves any piece of truth better than the most coherent system, because he well knows that every truth is one face of the world.
>
> A scholar is a diamond merchant, and, when he has got from old caskets, or from the mine, a true gem, is not very careful to set it in a coronet, or in a jewel-case. It shows its light very well in a wooden box, or in your hand.

Still, Emerson knows that he has been asked to appear for a purpose, and though in "the best company, good sense is taken for granted, and we are contented not to shine," he recognizes that, of course, "I wish to justify the inviting of a class, by offering you thoughts and facts which may have struck my own mind with force in the late months; but I shall think I pay my audience a just compliment if I state them carelessly and incidentally, so only that I state them, as knowing that they will detect fast enough what is important, without too much pains to give it perspective." [53]
While audiences who saw blandness and disorganization in Emerson's platform style left disappointed, those who saw originality and subtle interconnectedness went away inspired, including Henry Clay Folger, who heard Emerson lecture on Shakespeare and afterward devoted his life to putting together the greatest collection of Shakespeareana in the world, now housed in the library bearing his name in Washington, D.C. In a comparative treatment of the merits of Margaret Fuller, Henry Thoreau, and Emerson as inspiring teachers and public intellectuals, their friend Bronson Alcott reserved his choicest praise for Emerson's accomplishments:

> Mr. Emerson has certainly been a university to our people. Think of his value as a lecturer. For thirty years every winter he has travelled from East to West, and been heard by select audiences. Now no lecture-course in any State of intelligence is thought to be perfect without at least one lecture from Mr. Emerson for those who wish it and can enjoy it; because the best things are not enjoyed by all. I think we may say he made the lecture. The lyceum is Emerson's work really, since he began lecturing

earlier than any one and holds his place as no other lecturer has. A great many of the lecturers have fallen away, but Emerson is still a bright star, and sought after. . . . He is as wholesome as spring. With him it is all fair weather, all out of doors. . . . His is a grand mind . . . pretty nearly divinized.[54]

And, finally, in one of the most moving tributes to Emerson's enduring impact on his friends as well as on the strangers who sat in his audiences, Annie Adams Fields, who in her "Glimpses of Emerson" admits that he was her model for the "perfect consistency of a truly great life, where inconsistencies . . . appear at once harmonized by the beauty of the whole," states that Emerson stands among those rare individuals who "warm and cheer us with something of their own beloved and human presences."[55] After hearing Emerson deliver an academic lecture on the laws of the mind in his *Natural History of the Intellect* course at Harvard in 1870 during which he completely lost control of his subject, Fields, who attended the lecture with Henry Wadsworth Longfellow, wrote the following description of the setting and her ultimately sympathetic reaction to Emerson's plight:

> There are laws of the mind, there are powers and analogies which we shall consider. First among them stands . . . Identity, then follow Metamorphosis, Flux——
>
> Here the papers became inextricably tangled and we were left in a kind of mist.
>
> I walked away with Mr. Longfellow, who could not resist a kindly smile of sympathy with me over something in this lecture. . . . But no one could fail to be stimulated by [Emerson's] suggestion which was various and endless. It was indeed poetic seed-grain.[56]

Emerson's success as a lecturer was due in part to a major reason why he is still a popular author today: both auditors and readers find in Emerson's works resonances of their own ideas and beliefs as well as opportunities to expand on them by virtue of Emerson's suggestiveness—the "poetic seed-grain" that contemporaries such as Fields discovered in his prose and spoken words and that so piqued their own intellects and imaginations. As a preacher and as a lecturer during the 1830s and 1840s at the height of criticism of his religious views, Emerson could appear to the conservatives in his audience as a dangerous radical and to the liberals as a sweet voice of reason—and this would be at the same sermon or lecture.[57]

Modern scholarship has provided us with various means with which to evaluate Emerson's effect upon his audiences, and it comes to pretty much the same conclusions as did his contemporaries. Writers employing reader-response criticism, for example, argue that Emerson's lectures gained meaning not so much through his own intentions as through what his audiences made of them. Writing about Emerson's western New York lectures, Sallee Fox Engstrom suggests that "the text, delivery, and reputation of Emerson as lecturer were dialogic in nature, so that his known views supporting individualism, anti-traditionalism, and, most recently, social reform combined with his presence here to create a symbiotic relationship with audiences in this place at this time." The philosophy of Emerson's message brought "something elevating" into the lives of his audience that "they were eager to hear, something that matched the fervor of individualism already present in the reforming spirit of these communities, even if they did not fully comprehend what they were hearing."[58] Others heard in Emerson's calls for self-reliance and individualism just the opposite: a justification for growing capitalism as the century progressed. As Mary Kupiec Cayton notes, the basis for Emerson's lectures was "the radically idealist cosmology sketched out in *Nature* and further elaborated in the spoken and published lectures of the early period," and whatever language or analogies he employed to reach his audience, "he saw himself as preaching a message of moral reform whose warrant was a unique spiritual understanding of nature and nature's laws." However, his audience often "heard the warrant to be a set of already familiar, pragmatic, common-sense rules for attaining individual financial and social success. The Emerson whose anecdotes and aphorisms are understood but whose larger method is not becomes the epitome of the commercial values prized by the audiences who invited him."[59]

Those contemporaries who truly appreciated Emerson's appearance as a lecturer would have agreed with this description by John Jay Chapman that, we believe, succinctly states the reasons for Emerson's genius and his appeal:

> It was the platform which determined Emerson's style. He was not a writer, but a speaker. On the platform his manner of speech was a living part of his words. The pauses and hesitation, the abstraction, the searching, the balancing, the turning forward and back of the leaves of his lecture, and then the discovery, the illumination, the gleam of lightning which you saw before your eyes descend into a man of genius—all this was Emerson. He invented this style of speaking.[60]

And, we might add, Emerson helped to invent this style of reading, for just as his lectures urged audiences to participate intellectually in his oral discussions, so too do his writings invite us to interact with the bases and the development of ideas and thoughts found there. Emerson the lecturer whom we are just now beginning to appreciate, then, is worthy of study not only himself but also because he serves as the midwife to Emerson the essayist whom, we believe, we know so well.

Reading Emerson's Selected Lectures

This edition of *The Selected Lectures of Ralph Waldo Emerson* is the first and only comprehensive selection of Emerson's lectures. It includes twenty-five complete lectures that collectively provide a representative overview of the style, content, and occasions of the lectures for which Emerson was famed during his life. Included here are lectures from his very earliest days on the speaker's platform to his last days as a public presence in America. These lectures have been drawn from series of lectures on related topics and from lectures independent of series that Emerson delivered along America's eastern corridor, across the settled regions of the country, and in the British Isles from 1833 to 1871. In these selections Emerson speaks on science, literature and aesthetics, history, philosophy, education, politics and reform, American nationalism, Anglo-Saxon culture, individualism, nineteenth-century concepts of "progress," and social issues such as abolitionism, woman's rights, and his ideal of reconstruction following the Civil War. Given their timeliness and their rich range of reference, these lectures underscore the justice of Bronson Alcott's remark quoted earlier to the effect that, over the four decades of his public career, Emerson had "certainly been a university to our people."[61]

The Emerson with whom most readers of this volume will already be acquainted is the author whose essays *Nature*, "The American Scholar," "The Divinity School Address," "Self-Reliance," "The Poet," "Experience," "Fate," and "Thoreau" are routinely reprinted in anthologies of American literature and social or intellectual history. The lectures included in this edition are natural complements to these familiar works because they reveal Emerson in substantial discourse on all of his important themes and concerns. They also disclose previously unexplored connections between his performances on the speaker's platform and the evolution of those themes and ideas that we associate with him but have thus far approached only through essays that he published in his own time. Here, for example, in lectures such as "Genius," "The Poet," "Poetry and English Poetry," "Powers of the Mind," and "The Scholar" we recognize for the first time Emerson's lifelong preoccupation with the challenge that he and members of his generation faced in theorizing and then executing a literature that was both national and universal and that could define and then represent an aesthetics and a creative process that were truly American. Here, too, in early lectures such as "The Uses of Natural History" and "Humanity of Science" and in later lectures such as "The Tendencies and Duties of Men of Thought" and "Country Life—Concord" we recognize that Emerson's explorations of the natural world and that world's metaphoric relation to humanity's social, moral, and intellectual growth were serious lifelong concerns, not merely the introductory note to Emerson's career, as they appear to be in many introductions to *Nature*. Reading these same lectures along with the later lectures "Perpetual Forces" and "Resources" we also come to appreciate how Emerson was very much an intellectual of his time for whom science was not a passing interest but an integral component of his lifelong commitment to philosophic idealism. Indeed, late in life Emerson remarked that neither humankind nor he had anything to fear from the rapid advancements and startling discoveries being made on an almost daily basis by those working in the various departments of scientific research. "I do not know," he wrote in 1871 in a journal passage that may strike today's readers as unexpectedly modern,

> that I should feel threatened or insulted if a chemist should take his protoplasm or mix his hydrogen, oxygen & carbon, & make an animalcule incontestably swimming & jumping before my eyes. I should only feel that it indicated that the day had arrived when the human race might be trusted with a new degree of power, & its immense responsibility; for these steps are not solitary . . . but only a hint of an advanced frontier supported by an advancing race behind it.[62]

Even if it is not the entire focus of a particular lecture, Emerson's growing sense of himself as a social observer and, especially, as a social reformer is evident in numerous lectures printed in this volume. In early lectures such as his introductory piece for the *Human Culture* series he delivered in 1837–38 and in midcareer and later lectures such as "The Spirit of the Times," "The Anglo-American," "Reform," "Essential Principles of Religion," and "The Rule of Life" Emerson reveals himself not only as a socially aware individual but also as a public intellectual who conceives his role as a lecturer to be that of an agent who, by increasing the public's critical awareness of the pressing social and ethical issues of the time, effects meaningful change, first at the level of the individual and then at the level of society at large. Lectures such as these, as well as his "Address to the Citizens of Concord on the Fugitive Slave Law," "Address at the Woman's Rights Convention," and "Fortune of the Republic" that more overtly address slavery, woman's rights, and the ideals he believed a victorious North needed to follow during the period of reconstruction after the Civil War, show Emerson to be shrewd in his sense of the most important ethical and social issues facing his mid-nineteenth-century American audiences. They also anticipate those questions raised about gender, race, and class that are central to today's literary scholarship and broadly construed classroom discussions in the field of cultural studies.

A Note on the Texts

Two major editions of Emerson's lectures have been produced since 1959. *The Early Lectures of Ralph Waldo Emerson*, edited by Stephen E. Whicher, Robert E. Spiller, and Wallace E. Williams, appeared in three volumes from 1959 to 1972, and our own edition of *The Later Lectures of Ralph Waldo Emerson, 1843–1871* appeared in two volumes in 2001. Between them, these editions print—on the whole for the first time—the 114 complete lectures that survive in manuscript from Emerson's forty-year career as a lecturer. This number is remarkably small considering the fact that Emerson is known to have appeared at more than 1,500 lecture engagements during his career. The following three reasons account for the discrepancy between the number of lectures that survive in manuscript and are printed in these editions and the number of occasions on which Emerson is known to have lectured. First, neither of these editions reprints lectures from series that Emerson himself revised for publication as essays in *Representative Men* (1850), *English Traits* (1856), and *The Conduct of Life* (1860). Second, apart from the lectures that became essays in these three books and the 114 lectures included in the editions of Emerson's *Early Lectures* and *Later Lectures*, the remainder of Emerson's lectures exist, at best, only as fragmentary manuscripts that defy reconstruction and publication as complete lectures (or essays). Third, the fragmentary manuscripts of Emerson's later lectures that come down to us are, at best, of marginal value for two reasons. Emerson himself took the most important and coherent passages in these fragments and incorporated them into lectures that do survive in complete manuscript form (and are thus included in the editions cited above) or into essays that he eventually published. Also, James Elliot Cabot and, later, Edward Waldo Emerson "arranged" essays for publication under Emerson's name during his last years or after his death by drawing published texts from various lecture manuscripts.[63]

Full and complete descriptions of manuscript sources, statements of editorial rationale, and policies governing the preparation of lecture texts for inclusion in both *Early Lectures* and *Later Lectures* have been published by the editors of those volumes.[64] This edition of *The Selected Lectures* prints seven lectures that appeared in *Early Lectures* and eighteen lectures that appeared in *Later Lectures*. Although the copy-texts for all lectures printed in both editions were the manuscripts deposited in the Houghton Library of Harvard University by the Ralph Waldo Emerson Memorial Association, a fundamental difference of editorial approach between our preparation of Emerson's later lectures and our predecessors' preparation of his early lectures has caused us to return to the seven manuscript sources of lectures that they originally printed and edit those lectures completely anew. The lectures in question are the first seven that appear in this volume: "The Uses of Natural History," "Humanity of Science," "Ethics," "An Address Delivered at Providence, Rhode Island, on the Occasion of the Opening of the Greene Street School," "*Human Culture*: Introductory Lecture Read at the Masonic Temple in Boston," "Genius," and "The Poet." The remaining eighteen lectures in this volume are printed as they appeared in *Later Lectures*.

Because the editors' manuscript sources were relatively stable texts (i.e., their source for an individual lecture was generally a straightforward gathering of manuscript pages that were sometimes sewn together), the editors of *Early Lectures* believed they could reconstruct the first delivery of a given lecture by Emerson by rejecting most of his substantive authorial revisions in a manuscript as belonging to a later delivery. However, because our manuscript sources were far more fluid in their evolution and, as loose and unsewn collections of manuscript pages, unstable in their preserved manuscript state than were the texts collected in *Early Lectures*, we approached every text in *Later Lectures* in the belief that what we were editing was Emerson's last delivery of a lecture that he *always* construed as a work in progress. Whereas, like the editors of *Early Lectures*, we might have reason to assume that in presenting the text of a lecture that Emerson delivered only once we are close to or are exactly representing the state of the lecture's earliest delivery, in practice, given Emerson's and his executors' extraordinarily casual, almost cavalier, treatment and arrangement of the manuscript pages of his lecture texts both before and after their delivery, we do not believe that we or anyone else can with certainty claim to restore Emerson's lectures to their earliest delivery. Consequently, our practice throughout *Later Lectures* and in our editing anew from manuscript the seven lectures included in the present volume that were previously printed in *Early Lectures* has been to assume that we are editing the latest version of Emerson's delivery of a lecture, and we have treated our sources accordingly. Unless we possess evidence (i.e., evidence that is internal to the manuscript and entirely in Emerson's own hand) that leads us to assume otherwise, we have consistently prepared all lecture texts included in this volume as they were last delivered by Emerson.[65]

As they are printed here, then, all lectures follow Emerson's final level of inscription and emendation of copy-text; this is, all lectures follow Emerson's text and have been prepared by following his own insertions, cancellations, variants, and transpositions in the manuscripts. But as we explain and illustrate in great detail in the statement of editorial policy governing our preparation of texts in *Later Lectures*, because we understand Emerson's lectures as works in progress, not as finished texts that he was ready to submit for publication, as editors we have had to walk a fine line between overregularization of texts Emerson prepared for oral delivery and underregularization of texts that, because they betray a host of idiosyncrasies that result from both the rushed conditions under which Emerson wrote them and his own inconsistent stylistic practices, would be difficult, if not in some cases impossible, to read.[66]

Many of Emerson's practices we let stand; for instance, we preserve his erratic use of capitals following colons and semicolons and following commas, colons, and semicolons followed by a dash. We also preserve his inconsistent use of British and American forms of words as well as all of his unusual but typical word constructions, including his use of what would today be regarded as unacceptable forms for plural nouns, verbs, the comparative and superlative forms of adjectives and adverbs, and terms improvised from science, other disciplines, or languages other than English. However, for the sake of grammar, style, sense, or context we have editorially emended other of Emerson's practices according to these guidelines:

inserting a word or short phrase needed to complete a thought;

deleting sentence fragments that represent the false start of a sentence or a passage, a word or words accidentally left uncanceled by Emerson within a larger canceled passage, and Emerson's accidental doubling of words;

silently regularizing Emerson's use of proper names in a text and his occasionally erratic use of numerals, uppercase and lowercase, punctuation, and paragraph forms;

silently supplying periods, question marks, exclamation points, commas, colons, semicolons, and dashes where they are unquestionably needed, as at the end of sentences, inside closing quotation marks, to separate items in a series, to introduce quotations, and to set off appositional or subordinate phrases and clauses;

silently expanding abbreviations and ampersands;

regularizing various forms of "etc." as "and so forth";

and, when necessary, regularizing Emerson's use of apostrophes to show possession or to make clear his use of one in a contraction.

We have followed the manuscripts for compound and hyphenated words, but we have regularized Emerson's use of underlining as italicization, left the titles of books, journals, newspapers, poems, and plays as Emerson wrote and punctuated them as long as he either underlined them or enclosed them within single or double quotation marks, and silently supplied punctuation for titles he left unpunctuated. We have regularized Emerson's inconsistent practice with long quotations thus: quoted passages of 100 or more words are printed as block quotes; otherwise, quotes are left as Emerson inscribed them in his own narrative. Finally, except in the body of lectures, throughout this edition we have regularized dates to day, month, year order.

In this volume of selected lectures a lecture title is typically the one last used by Emerson, if he gave the lecture a title at all; all additional titles given to a lecture by Emerson are reported in the headnote to each lecture. The date or dates following each lecture title report the lecture's year or range of years of delivery. Immediately following each lecture's title and date(s), headnotes introduce readers to the occasion(s) surrounding Emerson's composition and delivery or deliveries of a lecture. We also direct readers to substantial draft passages of the lecture that they may wish to review in the volumes of Emerson's journals and miscellaneous notebooks, topical notebooks, or letters. At the conclusion of each headnote we direct readers to adaptations of the lecture in whole or in part in publications by Emerson or by his literary executors. Throughout, footnotes to Emerson's lectures identify his allusions to persons, places, occasions, quotations, and books; universally known figures such as Shakespeare have not been identified.

Finally, we would recommend the following research sources to readers of Emerson's *Selected Lectures* who wish to perform detailed analyses of the texts printed here or who may desire more extensive evidence of Emerson's compositional practices than is represented in his creation of these lectures. In our estimation the Harvard editions of Emerson's early lectures and journals and miscellaneous notebooks, the Georgia edition of his later lectures (including the electronic textual notes available at http://www.emersonsociety.org), the Missouri editions of his complete sermons and topical notebooks, the Columbia edition of his letters, and Len Gougeon's and Joel Myerson's edition of Emerson's antislavery writings are indispensable to both enterprises. To these we would add four recent publications: Ronald A. Bosco's treatment of Emerson's university lectures, Albert J. von Frank's *An Emerson Chronology*, and the *Biographical Dictionary of Transcendentalism* and the *Encyclopedia of Transcendentalism*, both edited by Wesley T. Mott.[67]

Notes

1. Bliss Perry, "Emerson's Savings Bank," *Nation*, 24 September 1914, 371–73.

2. The editors of Emerson's collected works (*CW*) have been scrupulous in documenting his creation of published essays from journal, notebook, and lecture sources. For instance, they note 108 journal and lecture sources for passages ranging in length from a few lines to several paragraphs for his essay *Nature*, and they note eighty-five such sources for "The Poet" (see *CW*, 1:270–74 and 3:268–70, respectively). Between 1835 (near the beginning of his career as a lecturer) and the late 1860s Emerson created numerous notebooks and topical indexes that he regularly used as resources during his preparation of lectures. Eight such notebooks and one index have been edited and published in *JMN*, 12. Two such notebooks (one devoted to poetics and entitled by Emerson "PY—Theory of Poetry" and another entitled by Emerson "PH—Philosophy") have been edited and published in *TN*, 2:256–329 and 330–84, respectively.

3. Stephen Railton, *Authorship and Audience: Literary Performance in the American Renaissance* (Princeton, N.J.: Princeton University Press, 1991), 32.

4. Robert D. Richardson Jr., *Emerson: The Mind on Fire* (Berkeley: University of California Press, 1995), 418–19.

5. A. Forbes and J. W. Greene, *The Rich Men of Massachusetts* (Boston: V. V. Spencer, 1851), 101.

6. Emerson, 15 February 1865, *JMN*, 15:457.

7. The sums Emerson received have been drawn from his "Account Books" at the Houghton Library of Harvard University (see bMS Am 1280 H112a–j). We are currently editing the "Account Books," which Emerson kept from 1828 to 1872. Extreme variations in the relative value of nineteenth-century dollars (e.g., the decline of the value of the dollar between 1854 and 1868) are explained by inflation and the depreciation of the value of the dollar during the post–Civil War years.

8. See "New England: Genius, Manners, and Customs," in this edition.

9. Elizabeth Palmer Peabody, "Emerson as Preacher," in F. B. Sanborn, ed., *The Genius and Character of Emerson: Lectures at the Concord School of Philosophy* (Boston: James R. Osgood, 1885), 146–47.

10. John McAleer, *Ralph Waldo Emerson: Days of Encounter* (Boston: Little, Brown, 1984), 487.

11. See Wesley T. Mott, *"The Strains of Eloquence": Emerson and His Sermons* (University Park: Pennsylvania State University Press, 1989), and Susan L. Roberson, *Emerson in His Sermons* (Columbia: University of Missouri Press, 1995), for thorough studies of Emerson's preaching style. For Emerson's ease of transition from the pulpit to the speaker's platform see David Robinson, *Apostle of Culture: Emerson as Preacher and Lecturer* (Philadelphia: University of Pennsylvania Press, 1982), which remains the authoritative treatment of this subject.

12. Barbara L. Packer, "The Transcendentalists," in Sacvan Bercovitch, ed., *The Cambridge History of American Literature* (Cambridge: Cambridge University Press, 1995), 2:394.

13. Railton, *Authorship and Audience*, 29.

14. George Willis Cooke, *Ralph Waldo Emerson: His Life, Writings, and Philosophy* (Boston: James R. Osgood, 1881), 258–59.

15. *Boston Post*, 25 January 1849, 2.

16. For the first quotation see *TN*, 2:149, and for the second, dated June 1840, see *JMN*, 7:374. For more on the changes in American oratory during Emerson's time see Kenneth Cmiel, *Democratic Eloquence: The Fight over Popular Speech in Nineteenth-Century America* (New York: William Morrow, 1990).

17. Emerson to Charles Chauncy Emerson, 15 July 1828, *Letters*, 1:238–40.

18. Alfred F. Rosa, "Emerson and the Salem Lyceum," *Essex Institute Historical Collections* 110 (April 1974): 77.

19. Letter of 10 February 1850, in John White Chadwick, ed., *A Life for Liberty: Anti-Slavery and Other Letters of Sallie Holley* (New York: Putnam's, 1899), 68.

20. *Cincinnati Daily Times*, 28 January 1857, quoted in David Mead, *Yankee Eloquence in the Middle West: The Ohio Lyceum 1850–1870* (East Lansing: Michigan State College Press, 1951), 43; John Townsend Trowbridge, *My Own Story with Recollections of Noted Persons* (Boston: Houghton Mifflin, 1903), 348.

21. McAleer, *Ralph Waldo Emerson*, 492.

22. Henry James Sr., "Emerson," *Atlantic Monthly* 94 (December 1904): 741.

23. In his later years Emerson was quite explicit in directions to his hosts on how he wished his platform lighted to accommodate his declining eyesight. For instance, he wrote to Samuel Longfellow, "My manuscript should be well lighted for my old eyes; for I sometimes find immoveable gas burners two or three feet from the desk" (28 January 1868?, *Letters*, 9:303–4). Between February and April 1871 Emerson gave his last major lecture series in public, a series of seventeen lectures delivered under the title *Natural History of the Intellect* at Harvard (see Emerson's *University Lectures*). Although he continued to deliver occasional lectures as late as 1880, his failing eyesight and his failing memory required him to secure the assistance of his daughter, Ellen, who served her father by helping him to turn the pages of his manuscripts and by prompting him whenever he lost his place during his delivery. Julian Hawthorne, Nathaniel Hawthorne's son, who remembered Emerson in his last years as possessing the face of "one who dreams awake," "resigned . . . to the care of his daughter" and "tended affectionately by her, like an angel half asleep," found Emerson's decline "touching and in no respect a painful spectacle" ("Personal Glimpses of Emerson," *Booklovers Magazine* 1 [February 1903]: 164).

24. A. Bronson Alcott, *Concord Days* (Boston: Roberts Brothers, 1872), 26.

25. A description of Emerson lecturing in 1871 by Charles A. Murdock in *A Backward Glance at Eighty* (1921), quoted in William Hawley Davis, "Emerson the Lecturer in California," *California Historical Society Quarterly* 20 (March 1941): 4.

26. "Powers and Laws of Thought," *W*, 12:11–12.

27. The first quotation is from the *Cincinnati Daily Times*, 28 January 1857, quoted in Mead, *Yankee Eloquence*, 43; the second is from John Jay Chapman, "Emerson, Sixty Years After," *Atlantic Monthly* 79 (January 1897): 34.

28. *Marietta Register*, 21 March 1867, quoted in Mead, *Yankee Eloquence*, 57–58.

29. *Morning Cleveland Herald*, 5 December 1867, quoted in Mead, *Yankee Eloquence*, 58.

30. Convers Francis, journal entry, 16 February 1837, quoted in Joel Myerson, "Convers Francis and Emerson," *American Literature* 30 (March 1978): 24.

31. "Ralph Waldo Emerson," *Knickerbocker* 65 (June 1865): 545–47. For a recent account of this episode that includes the complete text of the review see Cameron C. Nickels, " 'Roaring Ralph': Emerson as Lecturer," *New England Quarterly: A Historical Review of New England Life and Letters* 76 (March 2003): 116–23.

32. Emerson to James Bradley Thayer, 16 December 1864, *Letters*, 5:394.

33. Abigail May Alcott, journal entry (January 1848), Houghton Library of Harvard University, *59M-311 (2), folder 4.

34. Quoted in Edward Waldo Emerson, *The Early Years of the Saturday Club 1855–1870* (Boston: Houghton Mifflin, 1918), 477.

35. *Milwaukee Sentinel*, 24 January 1865, quoted in Hubert H. Hoeltje, "Ralph Waldo Emerson in Minnesota," *Minnesota History* 11 (June 1930): 152.

36. *Baltimore American*, 2 January 1872, quoted in *Mr. Emerson Lectures at the Peabody Institute* (Baltimore, Md.: Peabody Institute Library, 1949), 10–11.

37. "Second Look at Emerson" (1850), reprinted in N. Parker Willis, *Hurry-Graphs; or, Sketches of Scenery, Celebrities and Society, Taken from Life* (New York: Charles Scribner, 1851), 175, 177, 178. Emerson's "The Spirit of the Times" is printed in this edition.

38. Cooke, *Ralph Waldo Emerson*, 264.

39. *JMN*, 16:189.

40. James Russell Lowell, "Mr. Emerson's New Course of Lectures," *Nation*, 12 November 1868, 389–90, quoted in Cooke, *Ralph Waldo Emerson*, 260, as from *My Study Windows* (Boston: James R. Osgood, 1871).

41. Quoted in Richard Garnett, *Life of Ralph Waldo Emerson* (London: Walter Scott, 1888), 170.

42. *Milwaukee Sentinel*, 24 January 1865, quoted in Hoeltje, "Ralph Waldo Emerson in Minnesota," 153.

43. Emerson to W. H. Furness, 10 February 1875, *Letters*, 10:153.

44. As reported in note 2, the editors of Emerson's collected works (*CW*) have extensively documented the evolution of his published writings from journal, notebook, and lecture sources. Of the projected ten volumes in this series, six have appeared, including *Representative Men, English Traits*, and *The Conduct of Life*. Information contained in those volumes under the category "parallel passages" (that is, passages in Emerson's printed writings that can now be traced back to their sources in his printed journals [*JMN*], notebooks [*TN*], or lectures [*Early Lectures* and, more recently, *Later Lectures*]) provides the basis for entirely new and exciting studies of Emerson's compositional practices.

45. Emerson to Epes Sargent, 13 January 1849, *Letters*, 7:203.

46. Emerson to Elizur Wright, 7 January 1852, *Letters*, 4:272–73.

47. Emerson to John Russell Young, 27 October 1868, *Letters*, 9:322.

48. *Cincinnati Daily Times*, 28 January 1857, quoted in Mead, *Yankee Eloquence*, 43.

49. [Franklin Benjamin Sanborn], "Emerson at Horticultural Hall—The Problem of Reporting Him," *Springfield Daily Republican*, 10 April 1869, 2.

50. *Boston Daily Advertiser*, 13 March 1871, 2.

51. "Nominalist and Realist," *Essays: Second Series, CW*, 3:137.

52. Emerson to James Bradley Thayer, 22 November 1868, *Letters*, 6:43.

53. "Genius and Temperament," *Later Lectures*, 2:200–201.

54. "Fuller, Thoreau, Emerson. Estimate by Bronson Alcott. The Substance of a 'Conversation,' " *Boston Commonwealth*, 6 May 1871, 1–2.

55. Annie Adams Fields, "Glimpses of Emerson," *Harper's New Monthly Magazine* 68 (February 1884): 457.

56. Emerson's *University Lectures*, 42.

57. For more on how auditors and readers saw different versions of Emerson in the same text see Sarah Ann Wider, *Anna Tilden: Unitarian Culture and the Problem of Self-Representation* (Athens: University of Georgia Press, 1997), and Joel Myerson, ed., *Emerson and Thoreau: The Contemporary Reviews* (New York: Cambridge University Press, 1992).

58. Sallee Fox Engstrom, *The Infinitude of the Private Man: Emerson's Presence in Western New York, 1851–1861* (New York: Peter Lang, 1997), 3, 86–87.

59. Mary Kupiec Cayton, "The Making of an American Prophet: Emerson, His Audiences, and the Rise of the Culture Industry in Nineteenth-Century America," *American Historical Review* 92 (June 1987): 614. For how Emersonian ideas have been misappropriated see Howard Horwitz, "The Standard Oil Trust as Emersonian Hero," *Raritan* 6, no. 4 (Spring 1987): 97–119, expanded in his *By the Law of Nature: Form and Value in Nineteenth-Century America* (New York: Oxford University Press, 1991), 171–91.

60. Chapman, "Emerson, Sixty Years After," 36.

61. "Fuller, Thoreau, Emerson," 1–2.

62. See *JMN*, 16:232.

63. For discussions of the mining of Emerson's manuscripts either by Emerson himself or by Cabot and Edward Waldo Emerson see *Later Lectures*, 1:xxxviii–xli; Emerson's *University Lectures*, 14–18; and

Nancy Craig Simmons, "Arranging the Sibylline Leaves: James Elliot Cabot's Work as Emerson's Literary Executor," in Joel Myerson, ed., *Studies in the American Renaissance 1983* (Charlottesville: University Press of Virginia, 1983), 335–89.

64. For their respective statements of editorial policy see the editors' textual introductions in *Early Lectures*, 1:xxii–xxvii, 2:xv–xx, and 3:xvii–xxiv; and *Later Lectures*, 1:xxxii–lxii.

65. We make the point here that we accept only evidence in a lecture manuscript as to the time and place of its delivery that is entirely in Emerson's hand (as opposed to the hands of either Cabot or Edward Waldo Emerson) because it has been our consistent policy in editing Emerson's lectures as well as other of his writings to reject any and all intrusions into manuscript sources by his literary executors and other early editors.

66. See *Early Lectures*, 1:xxii–xxvii, 2:xv–xx, and 3:xvii–xxiv; and *Later Lectures*, 1:xxxii–lxii.

67. See *Emerson's Antislavery Writings*; *An Emerson Chronology*; Wesley T. Mott, ed., *Biographical Dictionary of Transcendentalism* (Westport, Conn.: Greenwood, 1996); and Wesley T. Mott, ed., *Encyclopedia of Transcendentalism* (Westport, Conn.: Greenwood, 1996). Other works have been previously identified.

The Uses of Natural History

(1833–1835)

"The Uses of Natural History" is the first lecture Emerson delivered after deciding upon his new "callings" as lecturer and naturalist. He read this lecture twice, first on 5 November 1833 before the Natural History Society at the Masonic Temple in Boston and then two years later on 9 November 1835 in Lowell, Massachusetts. Emerson drew a significant portion of the body of the lecture from journals in which he had reported his travels in Europe throughout most of 1833. During those travels he visited Italy, France, England, and Scotland, but the experiences that most influenced his decision to become a naturalist were the hours he spent examining objects on display in the Cabinet of Natural History at the Jardin des plantes in Paris, attending lectures on science at the Sorbonne, and observing the seminars of Jean-Baptiste Biot, Dominique-François Arago, Antoine-Laurent de Jussieu, and Louis-Jacques Thénard, who were then France's leading men of science. During a visit on 13 July 1833 to the Cabinet of Natural History, as he studied case after case of specimens preserved in the museum, Emerson achieved the profound insight that would serve as the unifying vision of his philosophy from this day through the end of his life. Here Emerson witnessed for the first time the relational nature of all things in the universe, so that hereafter he would respect nature as large and thoroughly organic (see especially *JMN*, 4:198–200).

In accepting the invitation with which the Directors of this Society have honored me to introduce the Course, I have followed my inclination rather than consulted my ability. My time has been so preoccupied as to prevent any particular course of reading or collection of novel illustrations of the subjects treated, which I should gladly have proposed to myself. I shall therefore say what I think on the subject of this Lecture according to such imperfect general information as I already possessed.

It seems to have been designed, if anything was, that men should be students of Natural History. Man is, by nature, a farmer, a hunter, a shepherd and a fisherman, who are all practical naturalists and by their observations the true founders of all societies for the pursuit of science. And even after society has made some progress, so that the division of labor removes men into cities, and gives rise to sedentary trades and professions, every man who is fortunate enough to be born in circumstances that require him to make any exertion to live, is compelled to pick up in his own experience, a considerable knowledge of natural philosophy,—as, an acquaintance with the properties of water, of wood, of stone, of light, of heat, and the natural history of many insects, birds and beasts.

And as if to secure this end in the constitution of all men, the eye is so fitted to the face of nature or the face of nature to the eye that the perception of beauty is continually awakened in all places and under the most ordinary circumstances. The beauty of the world is a perpetual invitation to the study of the world. Sunrise and sunset; fire; flowers; shells; the sea—in all its shades, from indigo to green and gray, by the light of day, and phosphorescent under the ship's keel at night; the airy inaccessible mountain; the sparry cavern; the glaring colours of the soil of the volcano; the forms of vegetables; and all the elegant and majestic figures of the creatures that fly, climb, or creep upon the earth—all, by their beauty, work upon our curiosity and court our attention. The earth is a museum, and the five senses a philosophical apparatus of such perfection, that the pleasure we obtain from the aids with which we arm them, is trifling, compared with their natural information.

It is frequently observed how much power the influence of natural objects gives to the sentiment of love of country which is strongest in the most wild and pic-turesque regions. It deserves notice also as it is this which not only heightens but creates the charm which hunting has for many persons who would start at being thought to have any poetry in their constitution.[1] If the running down a fox or hare were performed under cover, or in a street, it would soon lose its noble name, but great bodily exertion made along the mountain side, upon fields glittering with a million beads of dew, or in the shades of a wood—which always seem to say something, we cannot well make out what;—exhilarated by the fragrant scents, and cheered on by the trumpet of all the winds,—it is not strange that a man should learn to love these scenes, though he err in thinking he loves to kill his game.

Yielding ourselves to the same pleasant influences, let us inquire what are the advantages which may be expected to accrue from the greater cultivation of Natural Science.

They are in my judgment great and manifold, and probably more than can be now enumerated. I do not think we are yet masters of all the reasons that make this knowledge valuable to us. They will only disclose themselves by a more advanced state of science. I say this because we have all a presentiment of relations to external nature, which outruns the limits of actual science.

I lately had an opportunity of visiting that celebrated Repository of Natural Curiosities, the Garden of Plants in Paris; and except to Naturalists, I might hesitate to speak of the feelings it excited in me.[2] There is the richest collection in the world

---

1. Emerson inadvertently included the word "only" in a canceled passage; it is editorially restored here.

2. Emerson's visit to the Jardin des plantes in Paris on 13 July 1833 fundamentally changed the way he looked at nature (see *JMN*, 4:187–200, 405–6).

of natural curiosities arranged for the most imposing effect. The mountain and morass and prairie and jungle, the ocean, and rivers, the mines and the atmosphere have been ransacked to furnish whatever was rich and rare; the types of each class of beings—Nature's proof impressions;—to render account of her three kingdoms to the keen insatiable eye of French Science.

In spacious grounds skilfully laid out, and shaded with fine groves and shrubberies, you walk among the animals of every country, each in his own paddock with his mates, having his appropriate food before him,—his habits consulted in his accommodation. There towers the camelopard nearly twenty feet high, whose promenade and breakfast attract as much attention as the king's; the lions from Algiers and Asia; the elephants from Siam—whose bath is occasionally performed with great applause from the boys;—our own countrymen, the buffalo and the bear from New Hampshire and Labrador.[3] All sizes and all stripes of tygers, hyenas, leopards, and jackals; a herd of monkeys; not to mention the great numbers of sheep, goats, llamas, and zebras, that sleep, browse, or ruminate in their several country fashions, as much at ease as in their own wilds, for the amusement of the whole world in the heart of the capital of France.

Moving along these pleasant walks, you come to the botanical cabinet, an inclosed garden plot, where grows a grammar of botany—where the plants rise, each in its class, its order, and its genus, as nearly as their habits in reference to soils will permit, arranged by the hand of Jussieu himself.[4] If you have read Decandolle with engravings, or with a *hortus siccus*, conceive how much more exciting and intelligible is this natural alphabet, this green and yellow and crimson dictionary, on which the sun shines, and the winds blow.[5]

The Cabinet of Natural History is contained in a large stone edifice in the centre of the grounds. It is a prodigality to visit in one walk all the various halls in this great gallery of Nature. The ornithological chambers require an entire day: For who would mix and confound so fine and delicate sensations? This house of stuffed birds is a finer picture gallery than the Louvre. The whole air is flushed with the rich plumage and beautiful forms of the birds. The fancy coloured vests of those elegant beings make me as pensive as the hues and forms of a cabinet of shells have done before. They fill the mind with calm and genial thought. Some of the birds have a fabulous beauty that seems more appropriate to some Sultan's garden in the Arabian Nights Entertainments than to a real tangible Scientific Collection.[6] You see the favourites of nature,—Creatures in whose form and coat seems to have been a design to charm the eye of cultivated taste. Observe that parrot called *Psittacus*

3. A camelopard is a giraffe; Siam was the name of Thailand in Emerson's time.
4. Antoine-Laurent de Jussieu (1748–1836), French botanist who helped devise the modern system for classifying plants.
5. Either Augustin-Pyrame de Candolle (1778–1841) or his son Alphonse-Louis-Pierre-Pyrame de Candolle (1806–93), both Swiss botanists; a hortus siccus is a herbarium or collection of dried plants.
6. A reference to the collection of ancient Persian-Indian-Arabian traditional tales called *The Arabian Nights' Entertainments* or *A Thousand and One Nights* (1450), originally in Arabic.

Erythropterus. You need not write down his name for he is the beau of all birds and you will find him as you will find a Raffaelle in a gallery.[7] Then the humming birds so little and so gay—from the least of all, the *Trochilus Niger* not so big as a beetle—to the *Trochilus Pella* with his irresistible neck of gold and silver and fire; and the *Trochilus Delalandi* from Brazil whom the French call the magnificent fly or glory in miniature.

The birds of Paradise are singularly delicate and picturesque in their plumage. The manucode or royal Paradisaea from New Guinea, the red Paradisaea, and the Paradisaea Apoda, seem each more beautiful than the last and each, if seen alone, would be pronounced a peerless creature. I watched the different groups of people who came in to the gallery, and noticed that they picked out the same birds to point to the admiration of their companions. They all noticed the Veuve à épaulettes— the widow with epaulettes—a grotesque black fowl called Emberiza Longicauda with fine shoulder ornaments and a long mourning tail, and the Ampelis Cotinga. All admired the *Phasianus Argus,* a pheasant that appeared to have made its toilette after the pattern of the peacock, and the *Trogon pavoninus,* called also the Couroucon. But it were vain to enumerate even the conspicuous individuals in the parti-coloured assembly. There were black swans and white peacocks, the famous venerable ibis come hither to Paris out of Egypt,—both the sacred and the rosy; the flamingo with a neck like a snake; the Toucan, rightly denominated the rhinoceros; and a vulture whom to meet in a wilderness would make the flesh creep, so truculent and executioner-like he stood.

The Cabinet of birds was a single and even small part of that noble magazine of natural wonders. Not less complete, scarcely less attractive is the collection of stuffed beasts, prepared with the greatest skill to represent the forms and native attitudes of the quadrupeds. Then follow the insects, the reptiles, the fishes, the minerals. In neighboring apartments is contained the collection of comparative anatomy, a perfect series from the skeleton of the *balaena* which reminds everyone of the frame of a schooner, to the upright form and highly developed skull of the Caucasian race of man.[8]

The eye is satisfied with seeing and strange thoughts are stirred as you see more surprizing objects than were known to exist; transparent lumps of amber with gnats and flies within; radiant spars and marbles; huge blocks of quartz; native gold in all its forms of crystallization and combination, gold in threads, in plates, in crystals, in dust; and silver taken from the earth molten as from fire. You are impressed with the inexhaustible gigantic riches of nature. The limits of the possible are enlarged, and the real is stranger than the imaginary. The universe is a more amazing puzzle than ever, as you look along this bewildering series of animated

7. Raphael (1483–1520), Italian painter whose works adorn the Vatican; also called "Raphaelle" or "Raphaello" by Emerson.
8. *Balaena* is the genus of the Greenland whale.

forms, the hazy butterflies, the carved shells, the birds, beasts, insects, snakes, fish, and the upheaving principle of life every where incipient, in the very rock aping organized forms. Whilst I stand there I am impressed with a singular conviction that not a form so grotesque, so savage, or so beautiful, but is an expression of something in man the observer. We feel that there is an occult relation between the very worm, the crawling scorpions, and man. I am moved by strange sympathies. I say I will listen to this invitation. I will be a Naturalist.

Under the influence of such thoughts, I say that I suppose many inducements to the study of Natural History will disclose themselves as its secrets are penetrated. Besides that the general progress of the Science has given it a higher and higher place in the public estimation is there not every now and then some inexplicable fact or new class of relations suggested which for the time seems not so much to invite as to defy scientific solution? For example, what known laws are to classify some of the astounding facts embodied in the Report of the Committee of the French Institute in 1830 upon the subject of Animal Magnetism—a committee too, considering the persons and the circumstances, who might be regarded as a picked jury of the most competent scientific persons on earth?[9] But not to venture upon this dangerous ground, the debateable land of the sublime and the ridiculous, let me confine my attention to the enumeration of certain specific advantages easily marked and understood which may serve as the commendation of the objects of this society.

First. It is the lowest and yet not a bad recommendation of the occupations of the Naturalist that they are serviceable to the health. The ancient Greeks had a fable of the giant Antaeus, that when he wrestled with Hercules, he was suffocated in the gripe of the hero, but every time he touched his mother earth, his strength was renewed. The fable explains itself of the body and the mind. Man is the broken giant, and in all his weakness he is invigorated by touching his mother earth, that is, by habits of conversation with nature. It is good for the body exhausted by the bad air, and artificial life of cities, to be sent out into the fresh and fragrant fields, and there employed in exploring the laws of the creation. The study of Botany deserves the attention of those interested in Education, for this, if for no other cause. The wild rose will reflect its hues upon the cheek of the lover of nature. It is well known that the celebrated Wilson was led to the study of Ornithology for the benefit of his enfeebled health, and in his enthusiastic rambles in the wilderness his constitution was established whilst he enlarged the domain of science.[10]

The mountain minerals will pay their searcher with active limbs and refreshed spirits: And he who wanders along the margin of the sounding sea for shellfish or marine plants, will find strength of limb and sharpness of sight and bounding

9. Animal magnetism is a type of hypnosis.
10. Alexander Wilson (1766–1813), American ornithologist born in Scotland.

blood in the same places. Dig your garden, cross your cattle, graft your trees, feed your silkworms, set your hives—in the field is the perfection of the senses to be found, and quiet restoring Sleep,—

His poppy grows among the Corn.[11]

Second. In the second place, the main advantage to be proposed from the study of natural history is that which may seem to make all further argument needless; to be itself the manifest ground on which the study stands in the favor of mankind, I mean the direct service which it renders to the cultivator and the world, the amount of useful economical information which it communicates. The proof of this assertion is the history of all discoveries, almost the history of civilization itself. Who is not indebted for the comforts and accommodations of every day to the investigations which have been carried into every kingdom of nature?

It is the earth itself and its natural bodies that make the raw material out of which we construct our food, clothing, fuel, furniture, and arms. And it is the Naturalist who discovers the virtues of these bodies and the mode of converting them to use. In the most refined state of society, these are most accumulated; but these are now so numerous and the subdivision of labor has removed each process so far out of sight, that a man, who by pulling a bell can command any luxury the world contains, is in danger of forgetting that iron came out of a mine, and perfume out of a cat.

You sit in your parlor surrounded by more proofs of the cultivation of Natural Science than books or cabinets contain. The water that you drink was pumped up from a well by an application of the air pump. The well ventilated chimney which every mason can build, derived its hint from Franklin and Rumford.[12] The sugar in your dish was refined by the instruction given by a modern chemist on the adjustment of temperature for the crystallization of syrup; the brasses, the silver, the iron, the gold, which enter into the construction of so many indispensable articles, and indeed the glass, the cloth, the paints and dyes, have employed the philosopher as well as the mechanic.

There is scarcely any manufacture whose processes are not assisted or directed by rules and principles derived from the observations of Naturalists, apart from the consideration that all the foreign fabrics, drugs, fruits, and condiments, which are as familiar as salt, were transported hither across the sea by the aid of that map of the stars and the Record of the predicted places of the sun and the earth, which

---

11. Quoted from "Of Greatness" (1668) by Abraham Cowley (1618–67), English poet, in a translation from the Roman poet Horace (65–8 B.C.).

12. Benjamin Franklin (1706–90), American statesman, author, printer, editor, and inventor of, among other things, a stove that held its heat well; Benjamin Thompson, Count Rumford (1753–1814), British scientist and philanthropist born in Massachusetts, developed a type of fireplace that bears his name.

the lovers of nature from the Chaldean Shepherd to Laplace and Bowditch have aided in bringing to perfection.[13]

The history of modern times has repeatedly shown that a single man devoted to Science may carry forward the mechanic arts and multiply the products of commerce more than the united population of a country can accomplish in ages wherein no particular devotion to scientific pursuits exists. This is forcibly illustrated by the historical fact of the influence produced in France by the appointment of the celebrated Duhamel to the professorship of the School of Mines.[14] In 1822 it was stated to the Academy by its Secretary

that from the appointment of M. Duhamel to the time of his death, the products of iron in France were quadrupled; the mines of this metal opened near the Loire in the region of coal, and in the midst of combustible matter, were about to yield iron at the same price as in England. Antimony, manganese, which we formerly imported, are now exported in considerable quantities. Chrome, discovered by one of our chemists, is also the useful product of one of our mines. Zinc and tin have already been extracted from the mines on the coast of Brittany. Alum and Vitriol, formerly almost unknown in France, are collected in abundance. An immense mass of rock-salt has just been discovered in Lorraine, and all promises that these new creations will not stop here. Doubtless it is not to a single man, nor to the appointment of a single professorship that all this may be attributed but it is not the less true that this one man, this one professorship has been the primary cause of these advantages.

But the advantages which Science has presented to human life are in all probability the least part of her possessions. To the powers of science no limit can be assigned. All that has been is only an accumulated force to act upon the future. The prospective power, the armed hand, the learned eye are worth more than the riches they have acquired. It is a maxim in philosophy that a general truth is more valuable than all the particular facts which it has disclosed.

The natural history of water is not studied with less diligence or advantage at this moment than when Watt and Fulton made it a day laborer for mankind.[15] It is but the other day that our countryman, Mr. Jacob Perkins, noticed the small bubbles that are formed on the sides and bottom of a vessel in which water is heated, and most rapidly on the hottest parts, and discovered that these bubbles operate as a screen between the fire and the body of water in the vessel, preventing the rise of the temperature within in any proportion to the increase of the temperature on the

13. The Chaldeans of early Babylon were known for their study of astronomy; Pierre-Simon de Laplace (1749–1827), French astronomer and mathematician; Nathaniel Bowditch (1773–1838), American mathematician and astronomer.

14. Jean-Pierre-François Guillot Duhamel (1730–1816), French scientist and inspector of mines.

15. James Watt (1736–1819), Scottish engineer who harnessed steam power; Robert Fulton (1765–1815), American civil engineer and inventor of the steamboat.

outside.[16] He found especially that in the boilers of steam engines great inconvenience and danger frequently resulted from this cause because when the engineer quickened his fire it consumed the coats of the boiler more rapidly without making a proportionate expansion of the steam. This observation led to the thought that a strong circulation in the water might be caused which should continually rush against the sides of the vessel and break or remove these air bubbles. This thought he has recently executed in the machine called the Circulators and which has already been adopted in three of the locomotives on the Liverpool and Manchester Railroad with the best success and is about being introduced into all. And this may serve for a hundred examples of the benefit resulting from these observations.

Third. But it is high time to enumerate a third reason for the cultivation of natural history which is the *delight which springs from the contemplation of this truth,* independent of all other considerations. I should be ashamed to neglect this good, in too particular a showing what profit was to accrue from the knowledge of nature. The knowledge itself, is the highest benefit. He must be very young or very sordid who wishes to know what good it will do him to understand the sublime mechanism on which the stability of the Solar System and the faithful return of the seasons depend. What good will it do him? Why, the good of knowing that fact. Is not that good enough?—

Moreover, is it not disgraceful to be served by all the arts and sciences at our tables, and in our chambers and never know who feeds us, nor understand the cunning they employ? I cannot but think it becoming that every gentleman should know why he puts on a white hat in summer, and a woolen coat in winter; and why his shoes cannot be made until the leather is tanned. Better sit still than be borne by steam, and not know how; or guided by the needle and the quadrant through thousands of miles of sea, without a mark in the horizon, and brought to a little dent in the shore on the other half of the globe, as truly as if following a clew in the hand—and never ask how that feat is accomplished.

Bias was asked what good, education would do for a boy;—"When he goes there," pointing to the marble seats of the theatre, he replied, "that he might not be a stone sitting upon a stone."[17] Every fact that is disclosed to us in natural history removes one scale more from the eye; makes the face of nature around us so much more significant. How many men have seen it snow twenty or forty winters without a thought being suggested beyond the need of stout boots, the probability of good sleighing, and the country trade; until some kind philosopher has drawn our attention to the singular beauty of that phenomenon, the formation of snow; and shown us the texture of that self-weaving blanket with which the parts of the globe

---

16. Jacob Perkins (1766–1849), American inventor of a technique for printing banknotes.
17. Bias of Priene (sixth century B.C.), Greek writer known for his apothegms.

exposed to cold, cover themselves in pile proportioned to their exposure, at the time when the animated creation on the same side of the earth whiten and thicken their fleeces. We cannot see again without new pleasure what the Latin poet calls the thick fleece of silent waters—

densum tacitarum vellus aquarum.[18]

You cannot go out when the snow is falling in a calm still air and catch the little hexagon upon the palm of your hand and measure the invariable angles of the radii of the star without a finer delight than ever sprang from the consideration of the convenience of the general railroad with which it covers the country for the woodcutter and the farmer. The snowstorm becomes to your eye a philosophical experiment performed in a larger laboratory and on a more magnificent scale than our chemists can command.

To the naturalist belongs all that keen gratification which arises from the observation of the singular provision for human wants that in some instances, requiring ages for its completion, was begun ages before the use of it was shown.

The science of Geology which treats of the structure of the Earth has ascertained that before the period when God created man upon the earth very considerable changes have taken place in the planet. It is made probable that the various rocks that are now found broken upon it, as granite, slate, chalk, and so forth, covered it as so many concentric crusts or coats, like the coats of the onion, one without the other. But the soils which now cover it are formed by the decomposition of these stones, so that in this position of them that mixture of them which is essential to the production of vegetable life could never have been affected. By internal volcanoes, or other means, these several strata have been broken and raised and are now found lying as may be seen in mountain countries in oblique and perpendicular instead of horizontal layers so as to yield their various treasures to man and to the soil.

This is yet more striking in the case of coal, so important to old countries, and recently to this, and has naturally attracted the particular attention of British naturalists.

It is well known how vastly the great development of the commerce of Great Britain and thence of the great civilization of that country is indebted to the boundless abundance of coal in its mines. In consequence of the abundance and accessibility of this mineral in that island, and its opportune association with beds of iron ore, and the invariable contiguity of limestone employed to flux the iron, the English have been enabled to surpass all other nations in the cheapness of machinery and thence in the extent of their manufactures.

---

18. "[T]hickly the still fleecy shower [flows down]" (see *JMN*, 4:61n). Quoted from *Epigrams* 4.3 by Martial (ca. 40–ca. 103), Roman poet born in Spain.

But the discoveries of geologists have shown that the coal which is undoubtedly a vegetable formation is the relic of forests which existed at an unknown antiquity before the era of the creation of mankind, and by the overflowing of the sea and other changes of the surface had been buried below the surface at too great a depth to be reached by man. But before the creation of our race Earthquakes or other convulsions of enormous force have lifted up these mineral beds into ledges so that they are found extending from one thousand feet above the level of the ocean, to unknown depths below it. And so it happens that these vast beds of fuel so essential to man's comfort and civilization, which would have been covered by the crust of the globe from his knowledge and use, are thus brought up within reach of his little hands; and a great work of Nature in an antiquity that hath no record—namely the deposit and crystallization of Antediluvian forests, is made to contribute to our pleasure and prosperity at this hour.

Thus knowledge will make the face of the earth significant to us: it will make the stones speak and clothe with grace the meanest weed. Indeed it is worth considering in all animated nature what different aspect the same object presents to the ignorant and the instructed eye. It only needs to have the eye informed, to make everything we see, every plant, every spider, every moss, every patch of mould upon the bark of a tree, give us the idea of fitness, as much as the order and accommodation of the most ingeniously packed dressing box. For, every form is a history of the thing. The comparative anatomist can tell at sight whether a skeleton belonged to a carnivorous or herbivorous animal—to a climber, a jumper, a runner, a digger, a builder. The conchologist can tell at sight whether his shell were a river or a sea shell, whether it dwelt in still or in running waters, whether it were an annual or a perennial covering, and many the like particulars. And this takes away the sense of deformity from all objects; for, every thing is a monster till we know what it is for. A ship, a telescope, a surgical instrument, a box of strange tools are puzzles and painful to the eye, until we have been shown successively the use of every part, and then the thing tells its story at sight, and is beautiful. A lobster is monstrous to the eye the first time it is seen, but when we have been shown the use of the case, the color, the tentacula, and the proportion of the claws, and have seen that he has not a scale nor a bristle, nor any part, but fits exactly to some habit and condition of the creature, he then seems as perfect and suitable to his sea-house, as a glove to a hand. A *man* in the rocks under the sea, would indeed be a monster; but a lobster is a most handy and happy fellow there. So there is not an object in nature so mean or loathsome, not a weed, not a toad, not an earwig, but a knowledge of its habits would lessen our disgust, and convert it into an object of some worth; perhaps of admiration. Nothing is indifferent to the wise. If a man should study the economy of a spire of grass—how it sucks up sap, how it imbibes light, how it resists cold, how it repels excess of moisture, it would show him a design in the form, in the color, in the smell, in the very posture of the blade as it bends before the wind.

There is an excellent story in one of our children's books called "Eyes and No Eyes."[19] A dull, dumb, unprofitable world is this to many a man that has all his senses in health. But bring under the same arch of day, upon the same green sod, under the shadow of the same hills Linnaeus or Buffon or Cuvier or Humboldt and the sea and the land will break forth into singing, and all the trees of the field will clap their hands.[20] The traveller casts his eye upon a broken mountainside, and sees nothing to detain his attention a moment. Let Cuvier regard the same thing; in the rough ledges, the different shades and superposition of the strata, his eye is reading as in a book the history of the globe, the changes that were effected by fire, by water, by pressure, by friction in ages long prior to the existence of man upon the planet; he is hearkening to the infallible testimony of events whereof is no chronicle but in the memory of God, and taking down minutes of the same for the guidance and confirmation of future inquirers.

It has been felt by their contemporaries as a public calamity when such an observer who knew the value of his senses has been deprived of their use. One of the most touching incidents in biography is the affliction that befel Galileo, who, after announcing in rapid succession to the world his splendid discoveries, made by the aid of the telescope, namely, the uneven surface of the moon; the spots on the sun by which the revolution of that body was proved; that Venus was horned like the moon; the satellites, and the belt of Jupiter; the ring of Saturn;—was bereaved of sight.[21] His friend Castelli wrote to one of his correspondents, "The noblest eye is darkened that nature ever made; an eye so privileged, and gifted with such rare qualities, that it may with truth be said to have seen more than all of those which are gone, and to have opened the eyes of all which are to come."[22]

These men have used their senses to such good purpose, led on by the mere pleasure of observation, the high delight which they found in exploring the works of nature.

Fourth. There is a fourth good purpose answered by the study of Natural History which deserves a distinct enumeration. I refer to its salutary effect upon the mind and character of those who cultivate it. It makes the intellect exact, quick to discriminate between the similar and the same, and greedy of truth.

Moreover, I hope it will not be thought undue refinement to suppose that long

19. "Eyes and No Eyes; or, The Art of Seeing" was published in *Evenings at Home* (1792–96), edited by John Aiken (1747–1822), English essayist and physician, and his sister, Anna Letitia Barbauld (1743–1825), English poet and editor.

20. Carolus Linnaeus (1707–78), Swedish botanist, is considered one of the founders of modern systematic botany; Georges-Louis Leclerc de Buffon (1707–88), French naturalist; Georges Cuvier (1769–1832), French naturalist and comparative anatomist; Alexander von Humboldt (1769–1859), German traveler and scientist.

21. Galileo Galilei (1564–1642), Italian physicist and astronomer indicted as a heretic by the Catholic Church.

22. Benedetto Castelli (1578–1643), Italian scientist.

habits of intimate acquaintance with nature's workmanship, which is always neat, simple, masterly, accustoms her scholars to think and work in her style. All our ideas of sublimity and beauty are got from that source. Our contrivances are good but will not bear comparison with hers.

An orrery is esteemed an ingenious and elegant machine to exhibit the relative motions of the bodies of the solar system, but compare it with nature's own orrery, as it would appear to the eye of an observer placed above the plane of the system. He should see the beautiful balls moving on, self-poised in empty space: no rods reaching from them to the sun—no wires fastening the moons to their planets, but all bound by firm but invisible cords, that never entangle, nor crack, nor wear, nor weigh, namely, those threads of attraction, that join every particle in creation to every other particle.

Or to take a much lower instance in an object at our feet of the simplicity of the means by which important ends are effected. Who are those that hoe and harrow the surface of the ground to keep it in a state of looseness fit for tillage, and to make the fallow land penetrable to the roots of the grasses, and to the germination of forest trees? The Earthworms.

It has been observed by the entomologist that Worms promote vegetation by boring, perforating, and loosening the soil, and rendering it pervious to rains, and to the fibres of plants; by drawing straws and stalks of leaves and twigs into it; and most of all by throwing up such infinite numbers of lumps of earth called Worm-casts which manure the grain and grass.[23] Without the incessant aid of these little gardeners and farmers, the earth would soon become cold, and hardbound, and void of fermentation.

Thus Nature keeps the surface of the soil open; but how does she make the soil? Who are the strong and skilful architects that build up the solid land from the bottom of the sea? A little insect, the coralline, the madrepore, almost too small for sight, possessing the power of extracting lime from the sea water, builds up the coral reefs from the bed of the ocean to the surface, and these make in the course of ages the broad floor, on which by the agency of the marine vegetation, and of the birds, and the accidents of drift timber, a coat of soil is gradually laid, and a new land opened for the accommodation of man.

There are numberless examples in the economy of bees, the celebrated discovery of Reaumur relative to the angles of the cells, the observations of Huber upon the simplicity of the means by which the hive is ventilated, that are too long and too well known to be detailed.[24]

---

23. Quoted from *Natural History and Antiquities of Selborne* (1789) by Gilbert White (1720–93), English naturalist.

24. René-Antoine Ferchault de Réaumur (1683–1757), French naturalist and inventor of a thermometer that bears his name; François Huber (1750–1831), French naturalist specializing in the study of bees.

Can the effect be other than most beneficent upon the faculties dedicated to such observations?—upon the man given

> To reverend watching of each still report
> That Nature utters from her rural shrine.[25]

Moreover, the state of mind which nature makes indispensable to all such as inquire of her secrets is the best discipline. For she yields no answer to petulance, or dogmatism, or affectation; only to patient, docile observation. Whosoever would gain anything of her, must submit to the essential condition of all learning, must go in the spirit of a little child. The naturalist commands nature by obeying her.

And this benign influence passes from the intellect into the affections and makes not only the judgment sound but the manners simple and the whole character amiable and true. Fontenelle, who wrote the lives of the members of the French Academy of Sciences, a society of natural philosophers and mathematicians, takes notice of the amiable simplicity of their manners which rather seemed common to that class of men of letters than peculiar to any individual. D'Alembert, who wrote the lives of the Members of the Academy—a society of poets and fine writers— nowhere pretends to represent this amiable quality as characteristic of this class of men of letters.[26]

Indeed I think that a superiority in this respect of truth and simplicity of character extends generally to people resident in the country whose manner of life so nearly resembles that of the professed naturalist. That flippancy which is apt to be so soon learned in cities is not often found in the country. Nor are men *there* all ground down to the same tame and timid mediocrity which results in cities from the fear of offending and the desire of display. But the peculiarities of original genius stand out more strongly which are the results of that framework which the hand of God has laid for each man and which it behoves every man to respect as it constitutes the only plan according to which his particular structure can ever rise to greatness. These peculiarities in the resident of the country are the effects no doubt of silence and solitude, and of constant familiarity with calm and great objects. Though this influence is often exaggerated, yet I believe none of us are quite insensible to it, as every man may prove who goes alone into a picturesque country. I apprehend that every man who goes by himself into the woods, not at the time occupied by any anxiety of mind, but free to surrender himself to the genius

25. Quoted from "Written upon a Blank Leaf in 'The Complete Angler'" (1819), ll. 5–6, by William Wordsworth (1770–1850), English poet and, with Samuel Taylor Coleridge, founder of the romantic movement.

26. Bernard Le Bovier de Fontenelle (1657–1757), French philosopher and author; Jean Le Rond d'Alembert (1717–83), French mathematician; the contrasting view of the two writers is attributed to *Theory of Moral Sentiments* (1759; Philadelphia, 1817), 213, by Adam Smith (1723–90), Scottish political economist and moral philosopher, by Emerson in a note in the manuscript.

of the place, feels as a boy again without loss of wisdom. In the presence of nature he is a child.

One thing more under this head of the effect of these studies upon the mind and character. It generates enthusiasm, the highest quality, say rather, the highest *state* of the character. It has been the effect of these pursuits and most conspicuously upon the first class of minds to absorb their attention. What was sought at first as a secondary object, to satisfy an occasional curiosity, or amuse a rainy day, gradually won upon their interest, excluding every former occupation, until it possessed itself of the whole man.

They have felt the interest in truth as truth which was revealed to their inquiries. The story of Archimedes running as a madman, around the streets of Syracuse, after discovering the mode of determining the specific gravity of bodies, crying out as he ran, "I have found it," is familiar to children.[27] Scarce less notorious is that trait recorded of Newton, that, when after the new measurement of a degree of the earth's surface, he renewed his comparison of the earth's attraction of the moon, to the earth's attraction of a falling apple,—and saw, in the progress of the calculation, that he was approaching the result he had formerly anticipated, he was so much agitated by the grandeur of the fact about to be disclosed, that he was unable to go on, and was obliged to call in a friend to finish the computation.[28] As they say, the soldier who dies in hot blood never feels the wound, it is remarked of several physiologists, that they have continued their observations into the very doors of death. It is recorded of Haller, the celebrated Swiss physiologist, that he continued his observations in his last illness upon the progress of his disease with perfect calmness; taking note of the successive alterations in his system, and keeping his hand upon his own pulse,—until at last he exclaimed to his physician, "My friend, the artery ceases to beat," and expired.[29]

And it is related of John Hunter that he retained the habit of critical observation to the last pulse, and said to a friend who sat beside him, "I wish I had power of speaking or writing that I might tell you how pleasant are the sensations of dying."[30]

These are the heroes of science who have an instinctive preference of the value of truth, and who think that man has no nobler vocation than to watch and record the wonders that surround him. Hence the high prophetic tone which they have sometimes assumed, speaking as with the voice of time and nature.

When Kepler had discovered the three harmonic laws that regulate the motion of the heavenly bodies, he exclaims,

At length, after the lapse of eighteen months, the first dawn of light has shone upon me; and on this remarkable day, I have perceived the pure irradiation of sublime

---

27. Archimedes (ca. 287–212 B.C.), Greek mathematician and engineer.
28. Sir Isaac Newton (1642–1727), English natural philosopher and mathematician.
29. Albrecht von Haller (1708–77), Swiss scientist and poet.
30. John Hunter (1728–93), British surgeon and physiologist born in Scotland.

truth. Nothing now represses me: I dare yield myself up to my holy ardor; I dare insult mankind by acknowledging, that, I have turned worldly science to advantage; that I have robbed the vessels of Egypt to erect a temple to the living God. If I am pardoned, I shall rejoice; if blamed, I shall endure it. The die is cast; I have written this book:—whether it be read by posterity or by my contemporaries, is of no consequence: it may well wait for a reader during one century since God himself during six thousand years has waited for an observer like myself.[31]

The biography of chemists, botanists, physicians, geometers abounds with the narrative of sleepless nights, laborious days and dangerous journeyings. There is no hazard the love of science has not prompted them to brave; no wilderness they have not penetrated; no experiment suggested, which they have not tried. And with all my honour for science, so much greater is my respect for the observer Man, than for any thing he observes, that I esteem this development of character—this high unconditional devotion to their cause, this trampling under foot of every thing pitiful and selfish in the zeal of their pursuit of nature,—to be worth all the stars they have found, all the bugs or crystals or zoophytes they have described, all the laws how sublime soever, which they have deduced and divulged to mankind.

Fifth. I have spoken of some of the advantages which may flow from the culture of natural science: health; useful knowledge; delight; and the improvement of the mind and character. I should not do the subject the imperfect justice in my power if I did not add a fifth. It is in my judgment the greatest office of natural science, and one which as yet is only begun to be discharged, to explain man to himself. The knowledge of the laws of nature,—how many wild errors—political, philosophical, theological, has it not already corrected. The knowledge of all the facts of all the laws of nature will give man his true place in the system of being. But more than the correction of specific errors by the disclosure of particular facts, there yet remain questions of the highest interest which are unsolved and on which a far more profound knowledge of Nature will throw light.

The most difficult problems are those that lie nearest at hand. I suppose that every philosopher feels that the simple fact of his own existence is the most astonishing of all facts. But I suggest the question, with great humility, to the reason of everyone present, whether, the most mysterious and wonderful fact, after our own existence, with which we are acquainted, be not, the power of *expression* which belongs to external nature; or, that correspondence of the outward world to the inward world of thoughts and emotions, by which it is suited to represent what we think.

There is more beauty in the morning cloud than the prism can render account of. There is something in it which reflects the aspects of mortal life, its epochs, and its fate. Is the face of heaven and earth—this glorious scene always changing—

31. Johannes Kepler (1571–1630), German mathematician and astronomer.

yet always good—fading all around us into fair perspective,—over-hung with the gay awning of the clouds,—floating themselves as scraps of down under the high stars, and the ever lasting vault of space,—is this nothing to us but so much oxygen, azote,[32] and carbon of which what is visible is composed? Is there not a secret sympathy which connects man to all the animate and to all the inanimate beings around him? Where is it these fair creatures, in whom an order and series is so distinctly discernible, find their link, their cement, their keystone, but in the Mind of Man? It is he who marries the visible to the Invisible by uniting thought to Animal Organization.

The strongest distinction of which we have an idea is that between thought and matter. The very existence of thought and speech supposes and is a new nature totally distinct from the material world; yet we find it impossible to speak of it and its laws in any other language than that borrowed from our experience in the material world. We not only speak in continual metaphors of the morn, the noon and the evening of life, of dark and bright thoughts, of sweet and bitter moments, of the healthy mind and the fading memory; but all our most literal and direct modes of speech—as right and wrong, form and substance, honest and dishonest, and so forth, are, when hunted up to their original signification, found to be metaphors also. And this, because the whole of Nature is a metaphor or image of the human Mind. The laws of moral nature answer to those of matter as face to face in a glass. "The visible world," it has been well said, "and the relations of its parts is the dial plate of the invisible one."[33] In the language of the poet,

> For all that meets the bodily sense I deem
> Symbolical, one mighty alphabet
> For infant minds.[34]

It is a most curious fact that the axioms of geometry and of mechanics only translate the laws of ethics. Thus,

A straight line is the shortest distance between two points;

The whole is greater than its parts;

The smallest weight may be made to lift the greatest, the difference of force being compensated by time;

Reaction is equal to action;

and a thousand the like propositions which have an ethical as well as a material sense. They are true not only in geometry but in life; they have a much more exten-

32. Azote, a type of gas that is fatal when breathed, is another name for nitrogen.

33. Attributed to Samuel Sandels, "Emanuel Swedenborg," *New Jerusalem Magazine* 5 (July 1832): 437, by Emerson (*JMN*, 4:33).

34. Quoted from "The Destiny of Nations: A Vision" (1817), ll. 18–20, by Samuel Taylor Coleridge (1772–1834), English poet and philosopher and, with William Wordsworth, founder of the romantic movement.

sive and universal signification as applied to human nature than when confined to technical use. And every common proverb is only one of these facts in nature used as a picture or parable of a more extensive truth; as when we say, "A bird in the hand is worth two in the bush," "A rolling stone gathers no moss," " 'Tis hard to carry a full cup even," "Whilst the grass grows the steed starves."— In themselves these are insignificant facts but we repeat them because they are symbolical of moral truths. These are only trivial instances designed to show the principle. But it will probably be found to hold of all the facts revealed by chemistry or astronomy that they have the same harmony with the human mind.

And this undersong, this perfect harmony does not become less with more intimate knowledge of nature's laws but the analogy is felt to be deeper and more universal for every law that Davy or Cuvier or Laplace has revealed.[35] It almost seems as if according to the idea of Fontenelle, "We seem to recognize a truth the first time we hear it."

I look then to the progress of Natural Science as to that which is to develop new and great lessons of which good men shall understand the moral. Nature is a language and every new fact we learn is a new word, but it is not a language taken to pieces and dead in the dictionary, but the language put together into a most significant and universal sense. I wish to learn this language—not that I may know a new grammar but that I may read the great book which is written in that tongue. A man should feel that the time is not lost and the efforts not misspent that are devoted to the elucidation of these laws; for herein is writ by the Creator his own history. If the opportunity is afforded him he may study the leaves of the lightest flower that opens upon the breast of Summer, in the faith that there is a meaning therein before whose truth and beauty all external grace must vanish, as it may be, that all this outward universe shall one day disappear, when its whole sense hath been comprehended and engraved forever in the eternal thoughts of the human mind.

35. Sir Humphry Davy (1778–1829), English chemist who advanced an electrical theory of chemical affinity.

Humanity of Science

(1836–1848)

Emerson first delivered "Humanity of Science" on 22 December 1836 as the second in a series of twelve private lectures on the philosophy of history at the Masonic Temple in Boston.
Other lectures in this series included "Literature," "Manners," "The Present Age," "The Individual," and "Ethics." (See *Early Lectures*, 2:55–68, 129–42, 157–72, and 173–88, respectively;
"Ethics" is printed in this edition.)

After delivering "Humanity of Science" at the Masonic Temple in 1836 Emerson apparently set the lecture aside for a number of years; he returned to it in the late 1840s as one of
the lectures he revised for use during his tour of the British Isles in 1847 and 1848. The revisions Emerson made in the lecture for later deliveries are easily traced to two specific events.
First, the reference he makes to the blind fish dwelling in Mammoth Cave in Kentucky was
added after he toured that site in 1843 and wrote home about his experiences there (see
Letters, 3:123–24). Second, he incorporated information on Louis Agassiz that he gleaned
from an article by James Elliot Cabot in the *Massachusetts Quarterly Review* (see *Emerson
Chronology*, 225). There is some evidence that Emerson delivered "Humanity of Science" in
England in November or December 1847 at the Mechanics' Hall in Manchester, and there is
definite evidence that he delivered it in Sheffield in January 1848 (see *Letters*, 3:431n, 4:8–9).

Along with his remarks in "The Uses of Natural History" (printed in this edition) and
in "On the Relation of Man to the Globe" (1834; see *Early Lectures*, 1:28–49), in "Humanity
of Science" Emerson identifies very early in his career his fascination with and devotion
to science. Although he rarely presented lectures entirely on science after the late 1840s,
"Humanity of Science" establishes the dominant themes and interests Emerson brought to
his public remarks on science for the remainder of his life. In fact, it is fair to say that a
rough outline he prepared for this lecture anticipates his use of science in later lectures,
beginning with his three lectures on "intellect" in his *Mind and Manners of the Nineteenth
Century* series (1848–49) and ending with his two university lecture courses, *Natural History
of the Intellect*, at Harvard in 1870 and 1871 (see Emerson's *University Lectures*). Outlining
"Humanity of Science" in his journal for 1836, Emerson wrote:

> Here are two or three facts respecting Science. 1. The tendency to order & classifica-
> tion in the mind. 2. The correspondent Order actually subsisting in Nature. 3. Hence

the humanity of science or the naturalness of knowing; the perception that the world was made by mind like ours; the recognition of design like ours; the seeing in the brutes analogous intelligency to ours.— Otherwise

Man puts things in a row

Things belong in a row

The showing of the true row is Science.

History teaches

1. The presence of Spirit.

2. The antecedence of Spirit[.]

3. The humanity of Spirit[.]

Corollary

Science must be studied humanely. (*JMN*, 5:168–69)

It is the perpetual effort of the mind to seek relations between the multitude of facts under its eye, by means of which it can reduce them to some order. The mind busies itself in a perpetual comparison of objects to find resemblances by which those resembling may be set apart as a class. Of those resembling it seeks to abstract the common property; which it compares again with another common property of another resembling class, to derive from these two, a still higher common property. This is Method, Classification.

The child puts his playthings in a circle or in a row; he builds his blocks into a spire or a house; he aims still at some intelligible arrangement. A man puts his tools in one place; his food in another; his clothes in a third, his ornaments in a fourth. Woman is an angel of system. Her love of order is a proverbial blessing. A house is her classification. The art of bookkeeping is a striking example of the pleasure and the power of arbitrary classification. A state, an army, a shop, a school, a post-office are others.

The first process of thought in examining a new object is to compare it with known objects and refer it to a class. The mind is reluctant to make many classes or to suppose many causes. This reduction to a few laws, to one law, is not a choice of the individual. It is the tyrannical instinct of the mind.

This act of classifying is attended with pleasure, as it is a sort of unlocking the spiritual sight. I am shown a violet, the hearts ease, for example. If I have never seen a plant of the sort, I fasten my attention on the stem, leaves, and petals, of this; and I do not easily believe in the existence of any other sort of violet, than that I see. But another is shown me,—the white; then the round-leaved; then the yellow. I see each with a livelier pleasure, and begin to see that there exists a violet family, after which type all these particular varieties are made. I experience the like delight in being shown each of the tribes in the natural system of Botany, as the liliaceous, the papilionaceous, the mosses, or the grasses.

There is great difference between men in this habit or power of classifying. Some men unite things by their superficial resemblances, as if you should arrange a company by the color of their dress, or by their size, or complexion. Others by occult resemblances, which is the habit of wit; others by intrinsic likeness, which is Science. The great moments of scientific history, have been the perception of these relations.

Newton sees an apple fall, and cries—"the motion of the moon is but an apple-fall; the motion of the earth is but a larger apple-fall: I see the law of all nature"—and slow observation makes good this bold word.[1] It happened in our time that a German poet beholding a plant and seeing, as we may see in a pond-lily, a petal in transition from a leaf, exclaimed, And why is not every part of a plant a transformed leaf? A petal is a leaf, a fruit is a leaf, a seed is a leaf, metamorphosed, and slow-paced experiment has made good this prophetic vision,[2] that is, it may be demonstrated that a flower is analogous in its structure to a branch covered with leaves,—is a branch of metamorphosed leaves.—This is shown by proving a bract to be a modification of a leaf; a sepal of a bract; a petal of a sepal; a stamen of a petal; the carpel of a leaf; the ovule of a leaf-bud, a view now accepted by the English and French botanists.

The same gifted man walking in the Jews' burying ground in the city of Venice saw a sheep's skull on the ground and was struck with the gradation by which the vertebrae passed into the bones of the head. Instantly he said to himself, the vertebra of the spine is the unit of anatomy; all other parts are merely metamorphoses, degradations, abortions, or enlargements of this. The head was only the uppermost vertebra transformed. "The plant goes from knot to knot, closing at last with the flower and the seed. So the tapeworm, the caterpillar, goes from knot to knot, and closes with the head. Man and the higher animals are built up through the vertebrae, the powers being concentrated in the head." He is the author of a beautiful theory of colors beginning to be studied in which the prismatic hues are reckoned simply mixtures of darkness and light.[3]

The system of Lamarck aims to find a monad of organic life which shall be common to every animal, and which becomes an animalcule, a poplar-worm, a mastiff, or a man, according to circumstances.[4] It says to the caterpillar, "How dost thou, Brother! Please God, you shall yet be a philosopher." In the like spirit of audacious system another physiologist concludes that the monad becomes animal or plant only according to the element of darkness or light in which it unfolds. These

---

1. Sir Isaac Newton (1642–1727), English natural philosopher and mathematician.
2. This definition is attributed to Johann Wolfgang von Goethe (1749–1832), Germany's most famous writer, by Emerson (*JMN*, 5:220).
3. Goethe published a study of optics in 1810.
4. Jean-Baptiste de Lamarck (1744–1829), French naturalist and forerunner of Darwin in evolutionary theory, classified animals into vertebrates and invertebrates.

are extreme examples of the impatience of the human mind in the presence of a multitude of separate facts, and the energy with which it aims to find some mark on them according to which they can all be set in some order.

Classification is one of the main actions of the intellect. A man of great sagacity divides, distributes, with every word he speaks. And we are always at the mercy of a better classifier than ourselves.

Every system of faith, every theory of science, every argument of a barrister, is a classification, and gives the mind the sense of power in proportion to the truth or centrality of the traits by which it arranges. Calvinism, Romanism, and the Church of Swedenborg, are three striking examples of coherent systems which each organize the best-known facts of the world's history, and the qualities of character, into an order that reacts directly on the will of the individual.[5] The success of Phrenology is a lively proof of the pleasure which a classification of the most interesting phenomena gives to the unscientific.[6]

Whilst we consider this appetite of the mind to arrange its phenomena, there is another fact which makes this useful.

There is in nature a parallel unity, which corresponds to this unity in the mind, and makes it available. This methodizing mind meets no resistance in its attempts. The scattered blocks with which it strives to form a symmetrical structure, fit. This design following after, finds with joy that like design went before. Not only man puts things in a row, but things belong in a row. The immense variety of objects is really composed of a few elements. The world is the fulfilment of a few laws.

Hence, the possibility of Science. When one considers the feeble physical nature of man, how disproportionate to the natures which he investigates, he may well ask, How to such an animal, of seventy inches, walking and in the earth, is the solar system measurable and the nature of matter universally? Because a straw shows how the stream runs, and the wind blows; because as falls the apple, so falls the moon; because as grows one inch of one vegetable in a flowerpot, so grow all the forests; and as one animal of one species is formed, so are formed all animals of all species; because in short the wide universe is made up of a few elements and a few laws; perhaps of one element and one law.

Nature works unique through many forms. All agents—the most diverse—are pervaded by radical analogies, so that music, optics, mechanics, galvanism, electricity, magnetism are only versions of one law. The study of one natural object is like the study of a book in a foreign language. When he has mastered that one book, the learner finds with joy that he can read with equal facility in ten thousand books.

5. John Calvin (originally Jean Cauvin) (1509–64), French Protestant reformer and theologian; "Romanism" refers to Roman Catholicism; Emanuel Swedenborg (1688–1772), Swedish scientist, theologian, and mystic.

6. Phrenology is a way of reading a person's character through the configuration of his or her skull.

A half inch of vegetable tissue will tell all that can be known on the subject from all the forests; and one skeleton or a fragment of animal fibre intimately known is a zoological cabinet.

But whilst the laws of the world coexist in each particle, they cannot be learned by the exclusive study of one creature. A man shall not say, I will dedicate my life to the study of this moss, and through that I will achieve nature. Nature hates cripples and monomaniacs. All her secrets are locked in one plant; but she does not unlock them in any one. She shows one function in a tree, and another function in a seaweed. If the spiral vessels are exposed in a hyacinth, the vesicles are seen in a chara; the stomata in [blank];[7] the pila in a mullein; and chromule in sage; and to show all the parts of one plant, she leads you round the whole garden.

She writes every obscure and minute fact in colossal characters somewhere. Our microscopes are not necessary. They are a pretty toy for chamber philosophers, but nature has brought every fact within reach of the unarmed eye somewhere. It is difficult in the most level country or on the highest mountain to appreciate the outline of the earth, but on the seashore the dark blue sea line reveals at once the true curve of the globe. The question was once vexed whether mineral coal was of vegetable origin. Playfair found the bough of a tree which was perfect wood at one end, and passed through imperceptible gradations to perfect mineral coal at the other.[8]

In the old fossil fishes, the earliest creation, the vertebrae of the back are not divided; but an unbroken cord or bone runs from the head to the tail. Modern science has discovered one or two fishes yet existing, in which the vertebral column is still undivided; thus bringing to the eye of the anatomist the reality of this antique and fabulous structure, and connecting it with the living races. Again; the utmost attention has been given by modern physiologists to microscopic observations of the changes of the egg, especially in fishes and reptiles. It is now found that the order of changes in the egg determines the order of the strata containing remains. Each of the temporary states through which the young animal passes in the egg, is the type of a great class of animals which existed in that form on the earth for thousands of years, and when doubt existed as to the priority of two strata, it has been determined by reference to the living egg.

A peat bog may show us how the coal mines were formed. A shower of rain in the mountains may explain the diluvial and alluvial formations; the frost shooting on the windowpane, the process of crystallization; the deposit of sediment in a boiling pot, is a small Vesuvius; as Vesuvius is a small Himalaya.[9]

7. Between "the stomata in" and the semicolon there occurs a short blank space in the manuscript; as late as 1853 Emerson was undecided as to what word to use in the phrase "the stomata in [blank]" (JMN, 13:229).

8. John Playfair (1748–1819), Scottish natural philosopher and geologist.

9. Mount Vesuvius in Italy erupted in A.D. 79, burying Pompeii and two other cities; it continues to be an active volcano, last having a major eruption in 1944.

Science is the arrangement of the phenomena of the world after their essential relations. It is the reconstruction of nature in the mind. This is at once its ideal and its historical aspect.

The most striking trait of modern science is its approximation towards central truths. On all sides it is simplifying its laws and finding one cause for many effects. Unexpected resemblances in the most distant objects betray a common origin. It has been observed in earthquakes that remote countries were shaken at the same hour, showing that the explosion was far within the globe, and the vibrations communicated through vast hollows radiating from a deep centre to equidistant points on the surface, but points very distant from each other. In like manner, from a common law at the foundation of terrestrial natures may spring a great variety of surface actions. This is the theory of comparative anatomy. One grand idea hovers over a wide variety of forms. Look at the skeleton of man, with legs and arms. Then look at the horse or the ox, and you see the same skeleton with some variations. Occasionally, the type comes out conspicuously, when five fingers are severed, usually bound up in a hoof. In a bird, you see the same radical skeleton, but whilst the legs remain of the same use, the arm is deprived of the hand, is covered with feathers and made a wing. In the whale the forearm is a flipper to swim the sea. By insensible gradations, this one type may be detected in fishes and insects. It is so conspicuous, that Camper, the physiologist, was wont to draw on his blackboard the man, and by a few strokes transform him into a horse, then into an ox, into a bird, into a fish.[10]

In like manner see how the type of a leaf is present and creative in all leaves. It was once supposed that the various forms of leaves required each a new theory for its form. A leaf was a body originally undivided which owing to some unintelligible action became cut into segments in different ways so as to acquire at last a lobed form. But more accurate botanists showed that at a certain distance from the stem the stalk of the leaf follows the analogy of the tree and begins to branch; each branch carrying with it its green coat of parenchyma. If these branches remain distinct we have the simplest form of leaf with many threadlike claws, such as occurs in some species of the ranunculus. If these claws should grow together at their edges, a more entire leaf is formed; if still more, a leaf more perfect like the wild geranium; then a fivefinger like the passion flower; and when the green web quite joins the claws, a round leaf like the plane tree or lime tree is at last produced.

The phenomena of sound and of light were observed to be strikingly similar. Both observed the same law of reflection and of radiation. Both were subject to the same law of interference and harmony. That is, two rays of light meeting, cause darkness; two beats of sound meeting, cause silence. Whenever the eye is affected by one prevailing color, it sees at the same time the accidental color; and in music,

---

10. Pieter Camper (1722–89), Dutch physician and comparative anatomist.

the ear is sensible at the same time to the fundamental note and its harmonic sounds.

It was then observed that the same laws might be translated into the laws of Heat; that all the principal phenomena of heat might be illustrated by a comparison with those of sound. The analogy is followed out, and Light, Heat, Sound, and the Waves of fluids are found to have the same laws of reflection, and are explained as undulations of an elastic medium.

This analogy is followed by others of deeper origin. Light and Heat are analogous in their law to Electricity and Magnetism. Magnetism and Electricity are shown to be identical,—the spark has been drawn from the magnet and polarity communicated to the needle by electricity. Then Davy thought that the primary cause of electrical effects and of chemical effects is one and the same,—the one acting on masses, the other on particles.[11] The phenomena of Crystallization resemble electric laws. The famous experiment of Chladni demonstrates a relation between harmonic sounds and proportioned forms.[12] Finally the sublime conjecture sanctioned by the minds of Newton, Hooke, Boscovich, and now of Davy, that the forms of natural bodies depend upon different arrangements of the same particles of matter; that possibly the world shall be found to be composed of oxygen and hydrogen; and that even these two elements are but one matter in different states of electricity;—all these, whether they are premature generalizations or not, indicate the central unity, the common law that pervades nature from the deep centre to the unknown circumference.[13]

Chemistry, Geology, Astronomy, surprise all the time, and the appointed way of man from infancy to omniscience, is through an infinite series of pleasant surprises.

In a just history, what is the face of science? What lesson does it teach? What wisdom will a philosopher draw from its recent progress?

A lesson which science teaches, unanimous in all her discoveries, is the omnipresence of spirit. Life, creation, and final causes meet us everywhere. The world is saturated with law. Beautifully shines a spirit through all the bruteness and toughness of matter. Alone omnipotent it converts all things to its own end. The adamant streams into softest but precise form before it. The same ponderable matter which lay yesterday in a clod of earth, today takes the form of a grain of wheat, and tomorrow, in fine nourishment, enters the stomach of man, replenishes the waste of the day, and sparkles in the humors of the eye, or grasps, pulls, or pushes

11. Sir Humphry Davy (1778–1829), English chemist who advanced an electrical theory of chemical affinity.

12. Ernst Florens Friedrich Chladni (1756–1827), German physicist and authority on acoustics, invented the euphonium.

13. Robert Hooke (1635–1703), English scientist and experimental philosopher; Ruggiero Giuseppe Boscovich (originally Rudjer Josip Bošković) (1711–87), Croatian mathematician and physicist active in Italy.

in the fingers of the hand. Life refuses to be analysed. The best studies of modern naturalists have developed the doctrines of Life and of Presence, of Life conceived as a sort of guardian genius of each animal and vegetable form which overpowers chemical laws, and of Presence whereby in chemistry atoms have a certain restraining atmospheric influence where they do not chemically act. Behind all the processes which the lens can detect, there is a *Life* in a seed, which predominates over all brute matter, and which irresistibly forces carbon, hydrogen, and water, to take shape in a shaft, in leaves, in colors of a lily, which they could never take themselves. More wonderful is it in animal nature. Above every being, over every organ, floats this predetermining law, whose inscrutable secret defies the microscope and the alembic. The naturalist must presuppose it, or his results are foolish and offensive. As the proverb says, "he counts without his host who leaves God out of his reckoning," so science is bankrupt which attempts to cut the knot which always spirit must untie.

In monsters there is never a new thing, but merely the joining of two normal forms that do not belong together; one being developed, the other not yet developed, as part fish, part man: it is right things out of place. "This we learn if from nothing else from malformations and monsters. If we never saw anything but what followed a known law, we should think there was a necessity for this thing; it could not be otherwise. But deviations, degradations, monsters, teach us that the law is not only firm and eternal, but is also alive; that the creature can turn itself, not indeed out of itself into somewhat else, but, within its own limits, into deformity; always however being holden back as with bit and bridle by the inexorable masterdom of the law."[14]

This spiritual presence which awes us in the phenomena of life is not inactive elsewhere; for every step of Science is to find measures, checks, adaptations. There is no outlaw, no forgotten or useless matter in the globe. Nowhere is death, deformity, immoveableness; but as the ivy creeps over the ruined tower, and grass over the new-made grave, so, over the spoils of a mountain chain, shivered, abraded, and pulverized by frost, rain, and gravity, and brought down in ruins into the sea, a new architecture is commenced and perfected in darkness. Under the ooze of the Atlantic, she builds her basalts and pours melted granite like warm wax into fissures of clay and lime and when the deposits of a thousand rivers have strewn the bed of the ocean with every year a new floor of spoils, she blows her furnaces with a gas and lifts the bed of the ocean above the water and man enters from a boat, kindles a fire in the new world, and worships God thereon, plants a field and builds a school.

The ameliorating presence of spirit, using to great ends what is base and cheap, teaches in a very impressive manner. The order of the world has been wisely called

14. Attributed to Goethe (*Early Lectures*, 2:30n).

"an open secret."[15] And it is true that Nature's mode of concealing a law is in its very simplicity; she hides facts by putting them next us.[16] Where is that power not present? Where are the crypts in which Nature has deposited her secret and notched every day of her thousand millenniums? In facts that stare at us all day; in the slab of the pavement, the stone of the wall, the side of the hill, the gravel of the brook. In these pages every strong agent has written his name: the whirlpool, the lake, the volcano, and the wind. The facts are capable of but one interpretation, as the rings on the tree or on the cow's horn record every year of their age. No leaps, no magic, eternal, tranquil procession of old familiar laws, the wildest convulsion never overstepping the calculable powers of the agents; the earthquake and boiling geyser as accurate results of known laws as the rosebud and the hatching of a robin's egg. The irresistible destroyers of the old are all the time strong builders of the new—the irresistible destroyers who have rent and shivered the planet being now as near and potent as ever, nay the beautiful companions and lights of man's daily walk, mountain and stream, cloud and frost, sun and moon. "In the economy of the world," said Hutton, "I can find no traces of a beginning, no prospect of an end."[17]

The permanence and at the same time endless variety of spiritual nature finds its fit symbol in the durable world, which never preserves the same face for two moments. All things change; moon and star stand still never a moment. Heaven, earth, sea, air, and man are in a perpetual flux. Yet is all motion circular, so that, whilst all parts move the All is still.

The two sciences of astronomy and geology have been explored with wonderful diligence in these times, and have bestowed splendid gifts on men. Astronomy, which seems to be geometry exemplified in the glorious diagrams of the sidereal heavens, is the most appeasing influence to the agitations of human life and is our symbol of material grandeur exhausting in its realities the straining conception of possible power, size, and duration.[18]

But in all this extent our little globe and its friendly globes or globules that attend it, farther or nearer, are a sufficient guide and index. Far as we rove in observation or induction, we never come into new laws. We can go nowhere into a foreign country, though we run along the vast diameters of the sidereal spaces.

In Geology, again, we have a book of Genesis, wherein we read when and how the worlds were made, and are introduced to periods as portentous as the distances of the sky. But here too, we are never strangers; it is the same functions, slower performed; the wheel of the clock which now revolves in the life of our species, once took the duration of many races of animals on the planet to complete its circle. The

15. Attributed to Goethe by Emerson (*JMN*, 5:139).
16. Emerson's "he" has been editorially emended to "she" to match subsequent text.
17. James Hutton (1726–97), Scottish geologist and naturalist.
18. Sidereal, relating to the stars.

world was newer; the blood was colder; life had not yet so fierce a glow; or rather, the vast chart of being which lay in outline already, was to be prospectively and symmetrically consummated; an immense unity of plan we infer from these old medals of deluges and conflagrations, which has never been departed from, and can never: a plan successively realized and the now existing types were in view at the beginning.

Yet in all the multitude and range of spawning life, there is no unrelated creature, and the laws so firm and so apprehensible, that Cuvier not long since from a fragment of a fossil bone succeeded in restoring correctly the true skeleton and outline of a saurian; and Agassiz, in these very days, from a single scale of one fossil fish, undertook to determine the form of the perfect fish, and when, soon after, a specimen of the fish was found in the strata, it did not differ materially from the professor's drawing.[19]

The presence and the antecedence of spirit are impressively taught by modern science. Step by step with these facts, we are apprised of another, namely, the Humanity of that spirit; or, that nature proceeds from a mind analogous to our own.

Nature proceeds from a mind congenial with ours. Nature is overflowed and saturated with humanity. All things solicit us to know them by obscure attractions which we call the beauty of nature. We explore them and learn their law; straightway we find the discovery an exalting influence. So that I may say, we more fully possess ourselves for our new possession. A certain enthusiasm, as all know, has attended the great naturalists. As we learn more, we see that it is natural to know. Each discovery takes away some deformity from things, and gives them beauty; or takes away a less beauty, which hid a greater. There is nothing in nature disagreeable, which science does not bereave of its offence. Anatomy and Chemistry awake an absorbing interest in processes and sights the most tedious and revolting to the ignorant, so that it is observed at universities that of all the liberal professions it is only students of medicine who work out of study hours.

As we advance in knowledge we learn that all wears this great countenance of wisdom. Nothing is mean. It speaks to the noblest faculties. It conspires with piety: it conspires with poetry. It is the work of a perfect mind but of one which he can follow and evermore become. The reason which in us is so dim a ray, is a conflagration of light in Nature. Man sees that it is the measure of his attainments, for so much of nature as he is ignorant of, just so much of his own mind does he not yet possess.

Reason finds itself at home in nature and everything fits man and is intelligible to him. My mind is not only an inlet into the human mind but into the inferior intelligences that surround us in the field and stall. To this point let me quote a

19. Georges Cuvier (1769–1832), French naturalist and comparative anatomist; Louis Agassiz (1807–73), Swiss-born American naturalist and zoological explorer, began in 1859 the collections now at the Harvard Museum of Comparative Zoology.

passage from the works of an acute observer, the eminent historian of the Anglo-Saxons.

> If I could transfer my own mind divested of all the human knowledge it has acquired, but with its natural faculties unimpaired into the body of any fowl, and could give it the ideas and memory which their organs and habits have acquired—should I in the exercise of my judgment on such sensations as theirs act otherwise than they do? When I have put the question to myself I have not been able to discern that I should. They seem to do all the things they ought, and to act with what may be called a steady common sense in their respective situations. I have never seen a bird do a foolish thing for a creature of its powers, frame, and organs. Each acts with a uniform propriety, nothing fantastic, absurd, inconsistent, maniacal, or contradictory appears in their simple habits or daily conduct. They seem to have mental faculties and feelings like mine up to a certain extent, but to that they are limited. They have not the universality, the diversifying capacity, nor the improvability of the human intellect.[20]

Whilst this analogy exists in the animated creation the inanimate is so far pervaded by a homogeneous design that the human reason is its interpreter and its prophet; for in how many instances has the sagacity of men of science anticipated a late discovery.

A very curious and sublime subject of speculation is the identity of nature's mind, and man's. We always confide that there is a reason for every fact in the order of nature, which, whenever we hit upon it, will justify the arrangement to our judgment also. I have seen certain fishes found in the waters of the Mammoth Cave of Kentucky, which have no eyes, nor any rudiments of eyes; for they are born in darkness, and live in the dark.[21] It is an example of the eternal relation betwixt power and use, and such as we should expect beforehand. Indeed, man may well be of the same mind as nature, for he too is a part of nature, and is inundated with the same genius or spirit. He lives by some pulsations of her life.

Man's wit is secondary to nature's wit. He applies himself to nature to copy her methods, to imbibe her wisdom. The art of the surgeon limits itself to relieving the dislocated parts from their false position, putting them free;—they fly into place by action of their own muscles. The art of medicine is in removing and withholding causes of irritation. On this art of nature, all our arts rely. The correction of the refraction of glass, was borrowed from the use of two humours in the eye.

> For nature is made better by no mean
> But nature makes that mean.[22]

---

20. Attributed to Sharon Turner (1768–1847), English historian, in Emerson's note in the manuscript.

21. Emerson wrote his wife, Lidian, describing Mammoth Cave in Kentucky (*Letters*, 4:211–14).

22. William Shakespeare, *The Winter's Tale*, 4.4.89–90.

One can feel that we are brothers of the oak and of the grass, that the vegetable principle pervades human nature also. The old Norsemen represented the power of life by the tree Ygdrasil, which groweth out of Mimir's spring, where knowledge and wit are hidden.[23]

It grows when we sleep. It is observed that our mental processes go forward, even when they seem suspended. Scholars say, that, if they return to the study of a new language, after some interruption, the intelligence of it seems to have grown in their mind. A subject of thought to which we return from month to month, from year to year, has always some ripeness, of which we can give no account. Hence we say, the book grew in the author's mind.

And we are very conscious that this identity extends far wider than we know,— that it has no limits, or none that we can ascertain; as appears in the language men use in regard to men of extraordinary genius. For the signal performances of great men seem only the same art of nature applied to toys or puppets. Thus in Laplace and Napoleon, is the old planetary arithmetic now walking in a man; in the builder of Egyptian or in the designer of Gothic piles a reduction of nature's great aspects in caverns or forests to a scale of human convenience.[24] And there is a conviction in the mind that some such impulse is constant, that if the solar system is good art and architecture, the same achievement is in our brain also, if only we can be kept in height of health, and hindered from any interference with our great instincts. The current knows the way to be realized in some distant future. Something like this is the root of all the great arts; of picture, music, sculpture, architecture, poetry. And the history of the highest genius will warrant the conclusion, that, in proportion as a man's life comes into union with nature, his thoughts run parallel with the creative law.

The history of science in the last and the present age teems with this truth. The multitude of problems; the stimulated curiosity with which they have been pondered and solved, the formation of societies, the expeditions of discovery and the surveys, the gifts which science has made to the domestic arts are signs that the human race is in sympathy with this omnipresent spirit and in a perception of its rights and duties in regard to external nature.

Hence arises a corollary which every page of modern history repeats; that is, that science should be humanly studied. It will publish all its plan to a spirit akin to that which framed it. When science shall be studied with piety; when in a soul alive with moral sentiments, the antecedence of spirit is presupposed; then humanity advances, step by step with the opening of the intellect and its command over nature. Shall the problems never be assayed in a feeling of their beauty? Is not

---

23. Yggdrasill in Norse mythology is an ash tree that binds earth, hell, and heaven together; Mimir, a water demon, is the Scandinavian god of wisdom; Mimir's Well (Mimisbrunner) is under the roof of Yggdrasill.

24. Pierre-Simon de Laplace (1749–1827), French astronomer and mathematician; Napoléon Bonaparte (1769–1821), born in Corsica, general and later emperor of the French as Napoléon I.

the poetic side of science entitled to be felt and presented by its investigators? Is it quite impossible to unite severe science with a poetic vision?

Nature's laws are as charming to Taste and as pregnant with moral meaning as they are geometrically exact. Why then must the student freeze his sensibilities and cease to be a man that he may be a chemist and a physiologist?

I know the cry which always arises from the learned at this expectation. It is like Bonaparte who charged Lafayette and every lover of freedom with being an ideologist.[25] They tax us directly with enthusiasm and dreamers.

It is certainly true that the tendency of imaginative men is to rash generalization and to the confounding of intuitive perception with conjecture. Conscious of good-meaning the poet leaps to a conclusion which is false. Whilst he is thus swift, Nature is not; she holds by herself; and he must be brought back from his error by a faithful comparison of the facts with his premature anticipation.

On the other hand, not less dangerous is the tendency of men of detail to distrust final causes, and the generous sovereign glances of the soul over things, and to cling to the cadaverous fact until Science becomes a dead catalogue, and arbitrary classification. Then, when facts are allowed to usurp the throne of the mind, and the naturalist works as the slave of nature, and loses sight of its origin in spirit connate, yea identical with his own, then is wrong done to human nature, science is unhallowed and baneful; as happened signally in philosophic France; and has often befallen individuals.

And just so far as the fear of theory and the idolatry of facts characterises science, just so far must it lack the sympathy of humanity. The great men, the heroes of science, are persons who added to their accuracy of study a sympathy with men, a strong common sense, and an earnest nature susceptible of religion, as Kepler, Galileo, Newton, Linnaeus, and in our days Davy, Cuvier, Humboldt.[26] For it certainly must be, that not those parts of science which here and there a virtuoso may love, as the reckoning of logarithms or minute and merely curious chemical compositions, are the most attractive to the great naturalist, but those which catch the eye and fire the curiosity of all men: the discovery of a new planetary system, the discovery of a new analogy uniting great classes of hitherto sundered facts, the decomposition of diamond and the earths.

It is a characteristic of the present day that public education has advanced so far as to create a great number of books, lectures, and experiments having for their object to acquaint the people with the elements of the sciences. This was at first

25. Marie-Joseph-Paul-Yves-Roch-Gilbert du Motier, the marquis de Lafayette (1757–1834), French military leader and a hero of the American Revolution.

26. Johannes Kepler (1571–1630), German mathematician and astronomer; Galileo Galilei (1564–1642), Italian physicist and astronomer indicted as a heretic by the Catholic Church; Carolus Linnaeus (1707–78), Swedish botanist, considered one of the founders of modern systematic botany; Alexander von Humboldt (1769–1859), German traveler and scientist.

ridiculed, and undoubtedly a large deduction is to be made from the apparent result. What did it all signify? The Mechanics' Institutes had acquainted a few laboring men with the order of oolitic series or the habits of the kangaroo.[27] But here is the benefit. It will be the effect of the popularization of science to keep the eye of scientific men on that human side of nature wherein lie grandest truths. The poet, the priest must not only receive an inspiration, but they must bring the oracle low down to men in the marketplace. And why not Newton and Laplace? The education of the people forces the savant to show the people something of his lore which they can comprehend, and he is taught by their taste to look for what humanity yet remains in his science, and now calls to mind, seeing how it is valued, much that he has forgotten. It lets in good sense upon it, which is to laboratories and telescopes what the air of heaven is to dungeons or the hot chamber of the sick.

Any reader of history will see this clearly in comparing the science of antiquity with that of the present day, that the modern science is pervaded with good sense. In antiquity a great man was allowed to give currency to a silly opinion; as we read in Plutarch's *Placita Philosophorum* the grave nonsense of Empedocles and Anaxagoras about astronomy and physics.[28] It could not happen otherwise; it was the influence of genius when science was confined to a few. But now the effect of National Education and of the Press is that great numbers of men are directly or indirectly parties to the experiment of the philosopher and judges of it; So that the great instincts of mankind, and indeed the verdict of the Universal mind has an irresistible check upon the whims and spirit of system of the individual. But it is only the morning of the day. The philosopher and the philanthropist may forebode the time when an interest like that which now is felt in scientific circles in the wonders opened by Faraday, Ampere, and Oersted, in Magnetism and Electricity; a finger-pointing at laws and powers of unrivalled simplicity and extent,—shall take the place in the general mind of contemptible questions concerning persons and interests which now divide men into parties and embitter and degrade the mind of millions.[29]

The highest moral of science is the transference of that trust which is felt in nature's admired arrangements, light, heat, gravity,—to the social and moral order. The first effect of science is to stablish the mind, to disclose beneficent arrangements, to remove groundless terrors. Once we thought the errors of Jupiter's

27. An oolite is a rock consisting of small grains, usually calcium carbonate, cemented together.

28. Plutarch (ca. 46–ca. 120), Greek historian best known for his series of "lives," or character studies, arranged in pairs in which a Greek and a Roman are compared; Empedocles (ca. 490–430 B.C.), Greek poet, statesman, and philosopher who believed that he possessed magic powers; Anaxagoras (ca. 500–428 B.C.), Greek philosopher whose work predicts atomic theory.

29. Michael Faraday (1791–1867), English chemist and physicist, known for his experiments with electromagnetism; André-Marie Ampère (1775–1836), French physicist who discovered the relationship between magnetism and electricity; Hans Christian Ørsted (1777–1851), Danish physicist and chemist who worked with electricity.

moons were alarming; it was then shown that they were periodic. More recently mankind have been frighted with news of a resisting medium in the celestial spaces which threatens to throw all things into a lump. Men of science conversant with these unerring agents, with stars, with acids, with plants, with light, heat, gravity, are observed to grow calm and simple in their manners and tastes, the calm and security of the order of nature steals into their lives, and the contrast between them and the irritability of poetic genius appears to all and one may easily believe that a man of lifelong habit of observation of nature in the laboratory or the observatory who should come into politics, or into courts of justice, or into trade, and see the meanness and the falsehood which are so busy in these places, would conceive an impatience and disgust at this lawless and confused living. Let Newton or Cuvier or Laplace, peaceful with beholding the order of planets and of strata, come into senates or bureaus, and see some pert boy with some conceited proposition which he wishes to impose as a civil law on the millions of subjects of an empire: and indeed the whole history of states has been the uncalled for interference of foolish, selfish persons with the course of events. They might well wish to fly,—as the old hermits, to their desart and cell;—so these to their alembic and thermometer. Indeed, if they could entertain the belief that these rash hands really possessed any power to change the course of events, men would wish to rush by suicide out of the door of this staggering Temple.

But the survey of nature irresistibly suggests that the world is not a tinderbox left at the mercy of incendiaries. No outlaw, no anomaly, no violation, no impulse of absolute freedom is permitted to exist; that the circles of Law round in every exception and resistance, provide for every exigency, balance every excess. The self-equality in the birth of the sexes is constant; so is the relation of the animal to his food; so is the composition of the air in all places. The same symmetry and security is universal; and the inference is inevitable that the same Law extends into the kingdom of human life, and balances these refractory parties one against the other, and from age to age carries forward by war as well as by peace, by selfishness and ignorance and cheating, as well as by honour and love, the general prosperity and education of souls.

Ethics

(1837–1840)

Emerson first delivered "Ethics" on 17 February 1837 as the tenth in a series of twelve private lectures on the philosophy of history at the Masonic Temple in Boston. In the opening paragraph of the lecture he alludes to some of the other lectures he delivered in this series: "Art," "Literature" (or "Letters"), "Politics" (or "States"), "Religion," and "Manners" (or "Customs") (*Early Lectures*, 2:41–54, 55–68, 69–82, 83–97, and 129–42, respectively). Emerson also delivered "Ethics" on 29 January 1840 as the eighth in a series of ten private lectures entitled *The Present Age* at the Masonic Temple in Boston and on 29 April 1840 as the seventh in a series of nine lectures with the same title before the Concord Lyceum in Concord, Massachusetts.

"Ethics" is the first lecture included in this edition from which Emerson or his literary executor, James Elliot Cabot, drew substantial passages for inclusion in published essays. In this instance Emerson used portions of this lecture in his essays "Self-Reliance," "Compensation," and "Spiritual Laws" (*CW*, 2:25–51, 52–73, and 75–96, respectively).

In the preceding lectures, we have been considering one after another, the elements of history, and have seen of each, that they are only the dealings of the soul of man with the external world that all these grave forms of which books and laws make so much, viz. Art, Letters, States, Religion, Customs, are only signs more or less near of the human will. History is ever inferring the hidden nature of the human soul from these gigantic and remote effects. What is that we explore with so much curiosity in all these conspicuous departments of study? Man is the game we hunt. Man is the mystery we unveil. There are nearer manifestations of this interesting being—in the walls of his house, in the walls of his flesh. The same phenomena which the world illustrates in capitals the house illustrates in small letter. To the clock of history the movement and mechanism is the same whether we read upon its face seconds, minutes, and hours or years, centuries, and millenniums.

The history of a man is the history of the world, and if we would rightly understand our subject, we must not always view it in the gross but sometimes also in the particular. A single house, said the Roman poet, will show all that is done and suffered in the world.[1]

I cannot feel that we have explored all the divisions of our subject until some essay has been made to unfold a part of philosophy very little treated in formal systems, and only treated, as far as I know, in the proverbs of all nations, and yet, a subject the most engaging and sublime we can study and which for want of a more exact title may stand under the name of Ethics. It is that we mean by the phrase that goes current in all men's mouths, the Nature of things. The law of all action which cannot yet be stated, it is so simple, of which every man has glimpses in a lifetime and values that he knows of it more than all knowledge, which whether it be called Necessity or Spirit or Power is the law whereof all history is but illustration, is the law that sits as pilot at the helm and guides the path of revolutions, of wars, of emigrations, of trades, of legislation. And yet private life yields more affecting examples of irresistible nature of the human spirit than masses of men or long periods of time afford us. In the present lecture I wish to offer you some sketches of the appearance of this law in various parts of life, all suggesting the importance of the instincts, that the simplest, the instinctive action is ever the part of the wise man.

The moment the act of reflection takes place in the mind, that is, the moment we look at ourselves in the light of thought, we discover that our life is embosomed in beauty. Behind us, as we go, all things assume pleasing forms as clouds do far off. Not only things familiar and stale, but even the tragic and terrible are comely, as they take their place in the pictures of memory. Even the corpse that has lain in the chambers has added a solemn ornament to the house. If in the hours of Clear Reason we should speak the severest truth we should say that we had never made a sacrifice. That which the mind is in these sane hours seems so great, that nothing can be taken from us that seems much. All loss, all pain is particular; the Universe remains to the heart unhurt. Distress never trifles, never abates our trust. No man ever stated his griefs as lightly as he might. Allow for exaggeration in the most patient and most sorely ridden hack that ever was driven. For it is only the finite that has wrought and suffered; the infinite lies stretched in smiling repose.

And as in action the most despised life has this beauty in perspective, so his intellectual life or his opinions may be kept clean and healthful if he will live the life of nature and not import into his mind difficulties which are none of his. No man need be perplexed in his speculations. Let him keep his mind healthy and by doing and saying what strictly belongs to him, though very ignorant of books, his nature shall keep him free from any intellectual embarrassment.

It is quite another thing that he should be able to give account of his faith,

---

1. Attributed to Juvenal (ca. 55–ca. 127), Roman satirist and rhetorician, from *Satura* 13.159–60 (*Early Lectures*, 2:144n).

to represent to another the theory of his self-union and freedom. This requires rare gifts. Our progress is always concentrical: the man may move now in his first and narrowest rings, and no ray shoot out to the far circumferences he shall hereafter attain, yet there need be no obliquity or death in that which he is. A few strong instincts and a few plain rules suffice us. Some young people are diseased with speculations, for example, the theological problems of original sin, origin of evil, predestination and the like. These never presented a practical difficulty to any man,—never darkened across any man's road, who did not go out of his way to seek them. These are the mumps and measles and whooping coughs of the soul. And those who have not caught them, cannot describe their health nor prescribe the cure.

And whilst thus the health and the satisfaction of the soul are in its nature secured, not less provision has been made for its acquisition. Always it goes forth to the conquest of the world. Always we are learning the nature of things. Nothing is so carefully secured as this, that whilst we live, we shall learn.

Why should we fret at particular events? For every thing you have missed, you have gained something else; and for every thing you gain, you lose something. Our education goes on, whether we dig or saw or read. And even sleep reflects the image of action as water the trees and mountains on the banks. When you act, you lose no time from your book, because you still study and still learn, so that you have a right mind and a right heart. If not, you still learn though all is mislearned. What is a grown man but a knower of laws? What is a good judgment but a knowledge of laws in that particular province in which the praise is attributed, got by experience in that province? Or can a man forget anything which he truly knows? No, for a man knows no more to any purpose than he practises, and that which he knows, that is he. The more knower, the more man. We learn as we advance to correct our first estimates of the value of time and to reckon those hours and days often at the very highest rate which we had set at the least. At the close of a day, at the close of a week, we are scarce yet competent to say if it have been well or ill spent. Often when we have least to show for our time, no accounts settled, no contracts made or discharged, no books read, we have yet philosophised best, and arrived at solid conclusions that become conspicuous thoughts in the following months and years.

And the only true economy of time seems to be to rely without interval on your own judgment. Keep the eye open to all impressions, but deepen no impression by effort. Keep the upright position. Resign yourself to your thoughts and then every object will make that mark, that modification of your character which it ought. All the time will be lived; the journey; the meal; the waiting in antechambers, will not need to be subtracted. The ship beating at sea gains a small commission of miles for her true course on every tack: So in life our profession, our amusements, our errors even give us with much parade, or with our own blushes, a little solid wisdom. Amidst them all a few days and hours,—the days and hours of Reason,—

shine with steady light as the life of life, and all the other days and years appear as hyphens to join these.

But to proceed from life to the laws of life,—One fact all just observation will teach,—the absolute self-sufficiency of the mind.

The laws of the mind transcend all positive rules and take effect themselves. The mind wants nothing but to be aroused from sleep. Its checks are complete. Wake the mind and it will be vocation, ear, judge, apology, guard, physician, prophet, paradise unto itself. Let me make a few steps into this region of absolute nature, that we may see how short and sublime are its laws, how closely they resemble each other. Let me select a few phenomena of the deep principles of which, as they underlie all nature, every man sees some and every man different features.

The endless mistake of unwise men is to govern too much, to endeavor on the authority of a poor individual will to impose laws on the life and mind of man, but that which first engages our attention, is, the absolute inviolability of the laws of man,—not written upon vellum or brass,—not enforced by pursuivants and sheriffs,—but which execute themselves all around us.

We are to learn that the mind is its own measure; that the true call is the talent; true progress is conforming the life to the thought; true gratitude is to do what you can; true economy of time is fidelity to yourself; true pertinence is depth of thought; that there is no defect but is lucrative; that utterance is place enough; that your own praise is praise enough; that the like minded are society enough.

To specify some of the ways in which this self-sufficiency of the mind appears:— Each man has his own vocation.

All men are but several porches into one mind. Each man has his own calling, which is determined by his peculiar reception of the Common Reason. There is one direction to every man in which unlimited space is open to him. He has faculties silently inviting him thither to endless exertion. He finds obstruction on all sides but one. On that side all obstruction is taken away and he sweeps serenely over God's depths into an infinite sea. His call to do any particular work, as to write poems, to invent models, to go supercargo to Calcutta, or missionary to Serampore, or pioneer to Michigan, is, his fitness to do that thing he proposes.[2] And this results from his peculiar organization, or the mode in which the general soul is incarnated in him. Therefore, whoever is genuine, his ambition is exactly proportioned to his powers. The height of the pinnacle is determined by the breadth of the base. Any thought that he has another call than this,—a summons by name and date and diploma,

> Signs that mark him extraordinary,
> and not in the roll of common men,

2. Serampore is a town in India where Baptist missionaries established a college in 1818.

is fanaticism, and denotes obtuseness in perceiving that there is one mind in all the individuals and no respect of persons therein.

A true man can never feel rivalry. All men are ministers to him, servants to bring him materials, but none nor all can possibly do what he must do. He alone is privy, nor even is he yet privy to his own secret. They can never know until he has shown them what it is. Let them mind their own.[3]

And as the mind makes its own call so always it makes audience and occasion for itself. True pertinence is deep thought. The superficial man is always impertinent, the profound man never. Poor Tom never knew the time when the present occurrence was so trivial that he could tell what was passing in his head without being checked for unseasonable speech. But let Bacon speak, and wise men would rather listen though the revolution of kingdoms was going on.[4]

A like realism pervades all teaching or communication of truth. Solus docet qui dat, et discit qui recipit.[5] There is no teaching until the child is brought into the same place, state, principle in which you are. A perfect transfusion takes place: he is you and you are he; then is a perfect teaching and by no chance unfriendly or bad company, can he ever quite lose the benefit. But your propositions run out of one ear as they ran into the other. So it seems to me, is Christianity the famous name, the moral sentiment, the nut of truth.[6]

That which engages our attention is the absolute inviolability of its laws which are not anywhere recorded in words but which execute themselves all around us with a precision and energy of which the laws of matter are only faint symbols. These are the laws which cannot be added or detracted from. Man is ever led by his material nature to attempt to limit and elude this spiritual nature and ever in vain. But any man who sees that all men are but several porches into one mind will see how futile must be all attempts at the dissembling or concealing of character or opinions.

If a teacher have any opinion which he wishes to conceal, his pupils will become as fully indoctrinated into that, as into any that he publishes. If you pour water into a vessel ever so twisted into coils and angles, it is in vain for you to say, I will pour it only into this or that; it will find its level in all. Men feel and act the consequences of your doctrine without being able to show how they follow. Show us an arc of the curve and a good mathematician will find out the whole figure. We are always

3. This entire paragraph is inserted here in accordance with Emerson's direction to himself in the manuscript: "Insert here, that, the true man can have no rival, [Journal] D. [p.] 57" (JMN, 7:42).

4. Francis Bacon (1561–1626), English essayist, statesman, and philosopher.

5. "He alone teaches who gives, and he who receives, learns," from The Select Works of Robert Leighton (1823) (JMN, 5:408).

6. This entire paragraph, drawn from a page inserted in the manuscript but never sewn together with the remainder of the manuscript, is inserted here in the place Emerson marked for it. With the exception of the Latin quotation, the paragraph comes from a journal passage that Emerson dated May 1837 (JMN, 5:504).

reasoning from the seen to the unseen. Hence the perfect intelligence that subsists between the wise men of remote ages. A man cannot bury his meanings so deep in his book but time and like-minded men will find them. Plato had a secret doctrine, had he?[7] What secret can he conceal from the eyes of Bacon, of Montaigne, of Kant?[8]

And as you publish all that you strive to conceal, so another property of your nature is that what you have within that only can you see without.

What can we see, read, acquire but what we are? You have seen a skilful man reading Plutarch. Well, that author is a thousand books to a thousand persons. Take the book into your two hands and read your eyes out. You will never find there what the other finds. If the wise man would have a monopoly of the wisdom or delight he gets, he is as secure now the book is Englished as if it were imprisoned in the Pelews' language.[9] Or do you think you can possibly hear and bring away from any conversation more than is already in your mind born or ready to be born?

It is with a good book as it is with good company. Introduce a base person among gentlemen. It is all to no purpose; he is not their fellow. Every company protects itself. The company is perfectly safe and he is not one of them though his body is in the room.

No man can learn what he has not preparation for learning, however much the object is before him. A chemist may tell his most precious secrets to a carpenter and he shall be never the wiser,—the secrets he would not utter to a chemist for an estate. Thus God screens us evermore from premature ideas. Our eyes are holden and we cannot see things that stare us in the face; until the hour arrives when the mind is ripened,—then we behold them, and the time when we saw them not, is like a dream.

Another property of the soul is that like fire it will not be hidden, but evermore it publishes its nature through action, word, countenance. A power quite superior to his private will forces every man to hang out his colors, to give a tongue in every action to his ruling thoughts; so sung old Gower,

> The privates of man's heart
> They speken and sound in his ear
> As though they loud winds were.[10]

If you would not be known to do anything, never do it. A man may play the fool in the drifts of a desert, but every grain of sand shall seem to see. He may be a solitary eater but he cannot keep his foolish counsel; a broken complexion,

7. Plato (ca. 428–348 B.C.), the most famous of the Greek philosophers.

8. Michel Eyquem de Montaigne (1533–92), French essayist and philosopher, usually identified with skepticism; Immanuel Kant (1724–1804), German philosopher.

9. Pelew or Palau, a group of about one hundred islands that are part of the Caroline Islands in the Pacific Ocean southeast of Manila.

10. Quoted from *Confessio amantis* 1.2806–8 by John Gower (ca. 1330–1408), English poet and friend of Chaucer.

a swinish look, ungenerous acts, and the want of due knowledge—all blab. Can a cook, a Chiffinch, an Iachimo be mistaken for a Seneca?[11] Confucius exclaimed, "How can a man be concealed? How can a man be concealed?"[12]

And as you cannot read in the same book what your friend reads there; as you cannot see anything that you have not within; as you cannot be in a company where you do not belong; as you cannot conceal any *thing*, so the relation which you sustain to other men is not to be determined by the will; but the mind of your companion and your own determine the character of the connexion by their intrinsic nature. They refuse to abide by any covenant: day by day they make their own. That mood into which a friend can bring us is his dominion over us. To all the thoughts of that state of mind, he has a right. All the secrets of that state of mind he can compel. There is no need of professions: there is no need of promises: you know what impression you have made on any man by considering how superficial or how sincere are the communications he has made to you.

Thus in all ways the human soul goes forth to make its law and refuses to accept any influence than spiritual. Foolish men encumber life with artificial forms and weave evermore the web of pretension and hypocrisy. The Soul substitutes always being for seeming, as in petrifaction a particle of stone replaces a particle of wood. But all the art of the plausible is vain. Manner never did the work of matter. "What hath he done?" is the divine question which searches men and transpierces the paper shield of every false reputation. A fop may sit in any chair of the world nor be distinguished for his hour from Homer and Washington; but there can never be any doubt concerning the respective ability of human beings when we seek the truth.[13] Pretension may sit still, but cannot act. Pretension never feigned an act of real greatness. Pretension never wrote an Iliad; nor drove back Xerxes; nor Christianized the world; nor abolished slavery.[14]

The obvious inference from these laws is the one maxim which makes the whole Ethics of the Mind, Self-Trust. Self-Trust, that is, not a faith in a man's own whim or conceit as if he were quite severed from all other beings and acted on his own private account, but a perception that the mind common to the Universe is disclosed to the individual through his own nature. Ascend a mile where you will and the barometer indicates the same levity of air. Rise to a certain height of thought and you behold and predict that which is true for all men in all times. Nothing is sacred but the integrity of one's own mind. Absolve you to yourself and you shall have the

---

11. Chiffinch, one of the 108 characters in the novel *Peveril of the Peak* (1822) by Sir Walter Scott (1771–1832), prolific Scottish novelist; Iachimo, a character in Shakespeare's *Cymbeline*; Seneca the Elder (ca. 55 B.C.–A.D. 39), Roman writer and rhetorician born in Spain.

12. Confucius, or K'ung Ch'iu (551–479 B.C.), Chinese philosopher.

13. Homer (ninth–eighth century B.C.), Greek poet, presumed single author of the *Iliad* and the *Odyssey*.

14. Xerxes I (ca. 519–465 B.C.), king of Persia (486–465 B.C.) who launched an unsuccessful invasion of Greece in 480 B.C.

suffrage of the world. Stick by yourself and mankind shall leap and run to be of your opinion. Speak your privatest thought and it shall be the universal sentiment, for always the inmost becomes the outmost, and our first thought the Last Judgment. That statement only is fit to be made public which you have got at in attempting to satisfy your own curiosity. The place where you are is your workyard. The work you can do is your office. The friend you love is your ordained yokefellow. Insist on yourself; never imitate. For your own gift you can present every moment with all the force of a lifetime's cultivation, but can sustain it on the basis of the world; but of the adopted talent of another, you have only an extemporaneous half possession.

Be true to yourself. I have seen boys in their play put a shovel under the feet of one of their mates and trip him up. The boy standing on the shovel resembles the man's state who does not rely upon himself. The sincere man who does without second thought that which he is prompted to do, stands upon the basis of the world; he is not an individual so much as he is the hands and the tongue of nature itself. Could he be wholly of this mind he would be strictly omnipotent because his will conspiring with the divine will, his will being the mere effluence of the Reason, he would behold what he willed done.

To believe your own thought,—to believe that what is true for you, in your private heart, is true for all men,—that is genius. Familiar as the voice of the mind is to each, the highest merit we ascribe to Moses, Plato, and Milton, is, that they set at nought books and traditions, and spoke not what other men, but what they thought.—[15] Yet this principle, in practical life as arduous as in the intellectual, may serve for the whole distinction betwixt men. It is the harder because you will always find those who think they know what is your duty better than you know it yourself. It is easy in the world to live after the world's opinion. It is easy in solitude to live after our own. But the great man is he who in the midst of the crowd keeps with perfect sweetness the independence of solitude.

Whilst thus the sufficient rule of all Ethics is comprised in the Stoical precept, Reverence Thyself, explained by Christianity that in the heart of man, is the sanction and reward that goes along with it, is the perfect system of Compensation which pervades nature, and which though too subtle and simple to be reduced to a science and formally taught, yet finds utterance in a thousand proverbs, in old oracles, in fables, and in history.[16]

An eye for an eye; a tooth for a tooth; blood for blood; measure for measure; love for love. Give and it shall be given you. He that watereth shall be watered himself. "What will you have?" quoth God; "Pay for it and take it." Who doth not work, shall not eat. Nothing venture, nothing have. It is written on the tomb of

---

15. John Milton (1608–74), English poet and political writer, best known for his poem *Paradise Lost* (published in 1667 in ten books).

16. Stoicism, a philosophical school founded in Athens in 308 B.C., was inspired by the teaching of Socrates. Stoics stressed duty and were known for their belief in calmly submitting to necessity.

a Shah of Persia, "Thou shalt be paid exactly for what thou hast done; no more; no less."—[17] Curses are chickens that come home to roost.— Thefts never enrich, Alms never impoverish, and Murder will speak out of stone walls. Self-abasement is self-exaltation. Giving is receiving. The lover is loved.

A perfect compensation adjusts itself through all the parts of material and of moral nature. Darkness answers to light, heat to cold, ebb to flow, reaction to action.

In brute nature no creatures are favorites but a certain compensation balances every gift and every defect. A surplusage given to one part is paid out of a reduction from another part. If the head and neck are enlarged the body and extremities are cut short. "Economical nature has prescribed to herself a Civil list, a budget in whose single chapters she reserves to herself entire freedom, but in the sum total ever remains true to herself since if on one side too much is given she immediately subtracts it on the other and in the most decided manner makes all square."[18] All things are administered under the same law.— Every faculty which is a receiver of pleasure has an equal penalty put on its abuse: it is to answer for its moderation with its life.

Human life is an endless exhibition of this law of balance or compensation. All things are double, one against another. "Harm watch, harm catch;" says the proverb. And again, "for every grain of wit that a man hath, is there a grain of folly." No man had ever a point of pride that was not injurious to him and no man had ever a defect that was not somehow made useful to him. The stag in the fable admired his horns and blamed his feet but when the hunter came, his feet saved him, and, afterwards, caught in the thicket, his horns destroyed him.[19] Every man in his lifetime needs to thank his faults. As no man thoroughly understands a truth until first he has contended against it, so no man has a thorough acquaintance with the hindrances or talents of men until he has suffered from the one and seen the triumph of the other over his own want of the same.

The world is not the product of manifold power, but of one will, of one mind, and that one mind is everywhere, in each ray of the star, in each wavelet of the pool, active, and whatever opposes that will, is everywhere baulked and baffled, because things are so made and not otherwise. This doctrine in numberless ways the ancients expressed. This is their doctrine of Nemesis who keeps watch in the universe and lets no offence go unchastised.[20] "The Furies," they said, "are attendants on Justice and if the Sun in Heaven should transgress his path would punish

---

17. Attributed to an inscription on the tomb of the Persian king Nushirvan or Chosroes I (531–79) by Emerson (*JMN*, 6:215).

18. Attributed to Goethe (*Early Lectures*, 2:153n).

19. See "The Stag at the Pool," one of the fables by Aesop, a legendary Greek fabulist of the sixth century B.C.

20. Nemesis, a female Greek deity who is the personification of righteous anger. She was referred to as the daughter of night or of justice.

him."²¹ The poets related that brute walls and iron swords and leather thongs forgot not the wrongs of their owners; that the belt which Ajax gave Hector, dragged the Trojan over the field at the wheels of the car of Achilles; and the sword which Hector gave Ajax was that on whose point Ajax fell.²² They recorded, that, when the Thesians erected a statue to Theagenes, a victor in the games, one of his rivals went to it every night, and endeavored to throw it down by repeated blows, till, at last, he moved it from its pedestal, and was crushed to death beneath its fall.²³

Authentic history and biography, and the walls of every house testify the same thing. The modern historian has remarked that the Emperor Charles V always dissembled and never was believed.²⁴

They have remarked that "the pretensions to miraculous power lent the Catholic clergy extensive aid for which they were one day to pay a high price in the general unbelief to which these pretensions gave rise."

They have testified that that came to pass in our times which was anciently spoken, that when you put a chain around the neck of a slave, the other end fastens itself around your own.

What can be more sublime than this doctrine that the soul of the world does impregnate every atom and every spirit with its omnipotent virtue, so that all things are tuned and set to good. Evil is merely privative not absolute. It is like cold which is the privation of heat. All evil is so much nonentity, so much death. Benevolence is absolute and real. So much benevolence as a man hath, so much life hath he. For all things proceed out of this same spirit which is differently named love, justice, temperance in its different applications just as the ocean receives different names on the several shores which it washes. All things proceed out of the same Spirit and all things conspire with it. Whilst a man seeks these ends he is strong by the whole strength of nature. In so far as he roves from these ends, he bereaves himself of power, of auxiliaries; his being shrinks out of all remote channels and he disuniversalizes and he individualizes himself—and becomes all the time less and less, a mote, a point, until absolute badness is absolute privation. Pure badness therefore could not subsist. It is annihilation.

Observe *how* man is strong. His entire strength consists not in his properties but in his innumerable relations. There is nothing in the world that does not correspond to properties in him. If you embrace the cause of right of your country, of mankind, all things work with and for you,—the sun and moon, stocks and stones. The virtuous man, the seeker of truth, finds brotherhood and countenance in so far forth in the stars, the trees, and the waters. All Nature cries to him, All Hail! The

21. Quoted from Plutarch, "Of Banishment," *Moralia* 3.57.
22. Ajax, a hero of the Trojan War; Hector, in the *Iliad*, was slain by Achilles at Troy.
23. Theagenes was a tyrant who ruled the Greek city of Megara in the late seventh century B.C.
24. Charles V (1500–1558), Holy Roman emperor (1519–56) and king of Spain (1516–56) as Charles I, grandson of Ferdinand and Isabella.

bad man finds opposition, aversation, death in them all. All mankind oppose him. No whisper from secret beauty or grandeur cheers him. The world is silent: the heaven frowns. What is that star to him whose beam called out a sentiment of love in the hero? A white point. And being not in the current of things, but an outlaw, a stoppage, the wheels of God must grind him to powder in their very mission of charity.

The bearing of these general views of human nature upon actual history is direct and practical. These make the consolation of the mind under all that dejecting load of wrongdoing, public and private, which always gives a dubious or melancholy character to the news of the day. At this moment, the desponding patriot says, the present is full of fear; but in all ages the present is full of fear. In all ages, the majority of society are young men. In all ages the complaint has been, "the majority are wicked." The voice of equity is drowned by the clamor of interest. The virtuous few are outvoted by the misled many. The good law is postponed; the reckless party triumphs. Meantime, the misdeeds which agitate so many true and patriotic hearts with fear and shame; the coarse malignity which they do not hide; the barefacedly selfish legislation which is palmed upon the world; which seems at the moment to threaten society with tyranny and a flood of depravity, is as short-lived and shorter-lived than the agents. They twist ever a rope of sand. Being contravened by time and nature, by the heart and mind, their house has no foundation; it is no man's interest to keep it; it crumbles, it shrivels, it fleeth away. Where is the great empire which Napoleon built,—and every stone of whose foundation and superstructure was laid in the fear and foreboding of the nations?[25] All gone, not a wreck remaining; here and there a plank stamped with his name floats vagabond on the waves. Contrast it on the other hand with the labors of Paul of Tarsus, the tentmaker.[26] See what a tent he built of which the world will assuredly never see the downfall, for every star in heaven shone auspiciously on a pure and beneficent design and it hath a friend in the bottom of the heart of every man. Destroy as often as you will, the superstructure, yet Paul built his tent directly upon the human nature and so it always reappears.

And so it always is, the good institution, statute, or action which you project now must meet the brunt of passion and ignorance, but slowly it shall find friends, and when you are not in the earth it shall survive and be owned by good and bad alike and according to what sincere benefit is in it, shall flourish and multiply and nations repose in its shade. Sufficient unto the brave good man is his own purpose and his own superiority to the hostility of the world.

25. Napoléon Bonaparte (1769–1821), born in Corsica, general and later emperor of the French as Napoléon I.

26. Saint Paul (died between 62 and 68 A.D.), born a Jew in Tarsus, trained as a rabbi and a tentmaker, converted to Christianity on the road to Damascus.

An Address Delivered at Providence, Rhode Island, on the Occasion of the Opening of the Greene Street School

10 June 1837

Emerson's address given at the opening of the Greene Street School in Providence, Rhode Island, was delivered only once, on 10 June 1837. The editors of the *Early Lectures* titled the piece "Address on Education" (2:194); here we have followed the title Emerson wrote at the top of the first page of the manuscript. Emerson accepted an invitation to speak at the dedication ceremonies from Hiram Fuller, the popular principal of this new progressive school that was modeled on Bronson Alcott's experimental Temple School in Boston. In this address Emerson first gives voice to his ideas on education, especially his conviction that education had to nurture self-trust and self-reliance in the individual and respect for what Emerson would later define as "the infinitude of the private man" (1840; *JMN*, 7:342).

This address anticipates some of the themes of the many discourses on education that Emerson delivered over the course of his career before school and college audiences. These discourses include "The American Scholar" (*CW*, 1:52–75), which he delivered at the Phi Beta Kappa Day ceremonies at Harvard two months after he spoke at the Greene Street School; "Discourse Read Before the Philomathesian Society of Middlebury College in Vermont, 22 July 1845" and "Discourse Read Before the Philorhetorian and Peithologian Societies of Wesleyan College in Connecticut, 6 August 1845" (*Later Lectures*, 1:81–100); "An Address to the Adelphic Union of Williamstown [now Williams] College, 15 August 1854" and "An Address to the Social Union of Amherst College, 8 August 1855" (*Later Lectures*, 1:348–66); "Celebration of Intellect: An Address at Tufts College, 10 July 1861" (*Later Lectures*, 2:240–52); and "The Scholar," read first at Dartmouth College in New Hampshire and then at Waterville (now Colby) College in Maine in 1863 (printed in this edition). James Elliot Cabot drew substantially from this address to create the essay "Education," which he printed in *Lectures and Biographical Sketches* (1883; *W*, 10:123–59).

I congratulate the patrons of the School upon the completion of their house, and the very favorable auspices with which the institution is now to begin its work. A great liberality in adverse times demonstrates your conviction of the supreme importance of good instruction. All men must feel an interest in your enterprise. All men are so united, that the commonwealth is benefitted by every new amount of wisdom and virtue that is added to any individuals. And so, let the doors of the new edifice be opened with high hopes and pure wishes, and let all that pass by, feel the omen of a good cause, and draw some inward strength from beholding a temple dedicated to Wisdom.

The occasion has been offered me as a fit one for inviting the attention of the friends of the School to a consideration of the subject of Education. In yielding to the wish of my friends I ought to admonish them that I fear the views I am accustomed to take of this subject are of too abstract and purely theoretic a character to be esteemed by them as judicious hints for the determination to be given to a school such as this large community will demand and approve for their children. I shall nevertheless offer you my thoughts upon the defects that show daily more glaring in our systems of teaching and upon the true direction which the nature of man indicates for its culture. Yet why should I say *I fear*? I know the place where I stand. I know and honor, as the history of my country teaches me, the first asylum of religious liberty in the world: And I will not so far wrong the living citizens of this famous town, as to doubt their readiness to hear every sincere opinion, whether they approve or whether they reject it.

It even seems to me that the peculiar aspects of the times draw new attention to the subject of Education. They seem to advertise us of radical errors somewhere. They afford, as great calamities often will, rare facilities to the philosopher in his inquiries. If one would know somewhat of the ground plan and interior architecture of Society, let him study it when a commercial or political revolution has shattered its frame. In exploring the relations of social man at a period of calamity and alarm, I seem to learn geology the morning after an earthquake.

As the student of strata learns fast on the ghastly diagrams of the cloven mountain and upheaved plain and the dry bottom of the sea,—so the philanthropist reads plain and clear the signs of the times, when convulsions uncover the roots of institutions, and show how far they run, and rend away that which is artificial from that which is eternal.

The disease of which the world lies sick, is, the inaction of the higher faculties of man;—the usurpation by the Senses of the entire practical energy of individuals, and the consequent prevalence of low and unworthy views of the manly character.

Amid the swarming population how few men! If one go into the Exchange or into the professions, or to the farms to search for individuals who satisfy the idea of Man, he will scarce find any. The old gibe of Diogenes with his lantern, is still good.[1] He will find here a strong arm, and there, cunning fingers; he will find a stout soldier; a ready writer; a shrewd banker,—he will find parts and beginnings, but no whole. There are no men. Men are subject to things. They are overcrowed by their own creation. A man is not able to subdue the world. Is he learned? He does not use learning as an instrument, but he looks upon learning as an established thing of good fame in society, and passively acquires all that is reputed such. So he regards Wealth; and so a profession, and the offices of power,—they are the goods which he is to get; *they* are absolute value; *he* is only valuable as he may have skill to win these; and so thinking, he becomes not their master but their slave. He is a Lexicon. He is a money chest. He is the treadle of a factory-wheel. He is a tassel at the apron string of society. He is an appendage to a great fortune or a legislative majority or to the Revised Statutes or to some pretending Institution, Association, or Church. But the deep and high and royal man is not parasitic upon time and space, upon traditions, upon his senses, or his organs, or his fortunes, but the master of them,—who does not slide into the vacant places of the last generation abdicating all discretion to change them, but who, out of a central hope, affirms with a voice of sovereignty— "I also am a man,"—we are not, and when he comes, we hoot at him, "Behold this dreamer cometh."[2]

Is there not even at this time, a more than usual torpidity in the high ideal faculties whence always the life, the regeneration of Society proceeds? An immense prosperity,—*an immense activity*, that is, *of the Senses*, and devotion to the senses, has taken place, without example in history. The riches of nature, the whole active faculty of man, civil or savage, under every clime, have been strained to serve them. In the flush and astonishment of these results, all men shared. In the extent of new countries opened to the population; the magical facilities of transportation, the prodigies of mechanical invention, the creation of property, the dazzling products of the economic arts begot new desire, new industry, new skill in the merchant to possess them. They overpowered in the farmer the still religious tendencies of his primitive employment and drew him to the fever of the market. They infected even the brain of the scholar and the clerk and tinged the removed dreams of the poet with some hope of the realization of his aims out of mechanical force. Under the din and glitter of this excessive sensual life, men did not see that sleep was creeping over the soul, that justice and love were sacrificed to appetite, that priest after priest withdrew from the temple of Truth to be hewers of wood and drawers of water and that the worst plague—namely the degradation of man—impended amid the shouts and congratulations of cities and nations.

In England and America, who have taken the lead in this triumph of the Senses,

1. Diogenes (ca. 412–323 B.C.), Greek Cynic philosopher, advocated voluntary poverty and self-sufficiency, subject of the legend that he once went through the streets with a lantern, seeking an honest man.

2. Genesis 37:19.

there has ensued great hollowness in literature, politics, and religion, notwith-standing the immense vital energy of the Saxon race. A desperate conservativism clings with both hands to every dead form in the schools, in the state, in the church. A timid political tithe paying and church going zeal takes the place of religion. That utter unbelief which is afraid of change, afraid of thought, supervenes. The liter-ature feels it. It is factious or it is imitative or it is low and economical. No new work of the human mind of a commanding sort, no creation has for many years appeared. There is neither desire for such nor energy to create such.

Society feels it. The old wear no crown. Life does not to many offer attractions enough for its preservation. At times the land smells with suicide. Young men have no hope. The educated class stand idle in the streets. No man calleth them to labor. Even the thoughtful and prudent, perhaps the best men in society, find no employ-ment, no object of ambition, and waste on trifles a godlike strength. Perhaps it is true that the greatest men are not known, that they who preserve the pure fire, find so little encouragement in the face of society that they suppress their spirit and go to the grave unthought of.

Is it asked on what authority we judge thus severely the actual state of society? Is it asked whether the like charges might not be laid against existing institutions even during the most fortunate times? I reply, These are the judgments of the very highest authority which no man can gainsay or resist and which no time, no expe-rience can countervail. It is the voice of the pure Reason.

We are necessitated to judge by our constitution which evermore suggests to man an ideal perfection. The Universal Soul dwelling within the soul of all par-ticular men, does ever yield the idea of the Good, of the Perfect. Do what we can, we can never quite undo and abolish this fountain. All particular truth that ex-ists embodied in the world is only a drop scooped from this mighty water. This is the principle of replenishment and repairs to all the decays of time and vice. Out of this proceeds evermore every correction of opinion, every reform in religion, every melioration in manners. And the affirmations of this inward oracle are so peremptory that we should still be compelled to accept and believe them, though not only no community, but no individual on the face of the earth could be found whose life accorded with them.

This revelation of the perfect in the Soul of man reproduces in all times and places an inexhaustible hope.

> Hope is the paramount duty which Heaven lays
> For its own honor, on man's suffering heart,[3]

and out of that hope proceeds the effort for its own accomplishment.

3. Quoted from *Poems Dedicated to National Independence and Liberty* (1815), pt. 2, sonnet 33, ll. 5–6, by William Wordsworth (1770–1850), English poet and, with Samuel Taylor Coleridge, founder of the romantic movement.

This principle constrains us to expect new and better results from a new and better education. "I have hope," said the great Leibnitz, "that society may be reformed, when I see how much education may be reformed."[4] Our culture has truckled to the times,—to the senses. It is not manworthy. We teach boys to be such men as we are. We do not teach them to aspire to be all they can. We do not give them a training as if we believed in their noble nature. We scarce educate their bodies. We do not train the eye and the hand. We exercise their understandings to the apprehension and comparison of some facts, to a skill in numbers, in words; we aim to make accountants, attornies, engineers; but not to make able, earnest, greathearted men. Therefore, friends, the good and wise everywhere agree with a singular unanimity in an importunate call for a reform in our culture. Let at least, they say, in this great republic, no more generations rise with an entire famishing of Moral Sentiments. Let us form heroes and saints. Let our culture be directed toward the highest attributes of human nature. The great Idea in our breasts demands to be acknowledged in Education and that our discipline should be built on a basis so broad.

The great object of education should be commensurate with the object of life. It should be a moral one; to teach self-trust; to inspire the youthful man with an interest in himself; with a curiosity touching his own nature; to acquaint him with the resources of his mind and to teach him that there is all his strength and to inflame him with a piety towards the Grand Mind in which he lives. Thus would education conspire with the Divine Providence.

That I may the better show the claim of abstract against what are called practical views let me enter a little at length into the inquiry, What is the end of human life? It is not, believe me, the chief end of man that he should make a fortune and beget children whose end is likewise to make fortunes, but it is, in few words, that he should explore himself—an inexhaustible mine—and external nature is but the candle to illuminate in turn the innumerable and profound obscurities of the soul. Do we not see how cunningly for this end he is fitted to the world, to every object in which he hath relation?

As every wind draws music out of the aeolian harp, so doth every object in nature draw music out of his mind.[5] He is a harp on which all things play and every new influence brings a new melody therefrom. Is it not true that every landscape I behold, every friend I meet, every act I perform, every pain I suffer, leaves me a different being from that they found me? that poverty, love, authority, anger, sickness, sorrow, success, all work actively upon our being and unlock for us the concealed faculties of the mind? Whatever private and petty ends are frustrated, this end is always answered. Whatever he does or whatever befals him, opens an-

---

4. Gottfried Wilhelm Leibniz (1646–1716), German philosopher and mathematician.

5. An aeolian harp is a box-shaped string instrument that produces various tones when the strings are touched by the wind.

other chamber in his soul,—that is, he has got a new feeling, a new thought, a new organ. What else seeks he in the deep instinct of society, from his first fellowship— a child with children at play, up to the heroic cravings of friendship and love—but to find himself in another mind, to confess himself, to make a clean breast, to be searched and known, because such is the law of his being that only can he find out his own secret through the instrumentality of another mind? What else is a work of art but an experiment upon him educing the perception of beauty and the sublime? For this, he reads a novel or a poem; his fancy kindles, his tears stream, and he is conscious of new and delicious emotion for which discovery he must thank that idle tale. For this he goes to Faneuil Hall and lets himself be played upon by the enraged eloquence that is native there,—that he may learn with awe what terrific elements slumber within him.[6]

And what leads him to Science? Why does he track in the midnight heaven a pure spark, a luminous patch, wandering from age to age, but because he acquires thereby a majestic sense of power, learning that in his own constitution he can set the shining maze in order, and, finding and carrying their law in his mind, can, as it were, see his simple idea realized up yonder in giddy distances and frightful periods of duration.

And what is the charm which every ore, every new plant, every new fact touching winds, clouds, ocean currents, the secrets of chemical composition and decomposition possess for Humboldt?[7] What but that much revolving of similar facts in his mind has shown him that always the mind contains in its transparent chambers the means of classifying the most refractory phenomena, of depriving them of all casual and chaotic aspect and subordinating them to a bright reason of its own, and so giving to Man a sort of property, yea the very highest property in every district and particle of the globe. So that thus the heaven above, the earth beneath, and the waters under the earth become to him merely a kind of mnemonics or inventory of his inward kingdom.

Again why is it that this complex net of personal relations is woven round him? Why does he work with so many companions? Why must he face so many enemies? Why does he meet disaster, and redden with indignation? Why is he hindered by sickness, and tormented by doubt? Why, but to learn the laws of Ethics—the law of moral agents in the universe,—in other words, the moral constitution of his own mind?

Whilst thus the world exists for the mind, whilst thus the man is ever invited onward into shining realms of knowledge and power by the shows of the world which interpret to him the infinitude of his own consciousness, it becomes the office of a just education to awaken him to the knowledge of this fact. The continual

6. Faneuil Hall in Boston, first built in 1742, served as the city's town hall.
7. Alexander von Humboldt (1769–1859), German traveler and scientist.

tendency of the man, his great danger, is to overlook the fact that the world is only his teacher and the natures of sun and moon, plant and animal, only means of arousing his interior activity. Enamoured of their beauty, comforted by their convenience, he seeks them as ends, and fast loses sight of the fact that they have worse than no value—that they become noxious when he becomes their slave.

Thus a man may well spend many years of life in trade. It is a constant teaching of the laws of matter and of mind; no dollar of property can be created without some direct communication with nature and of course some acquisition of knowledge and practical force. It is a constant contact with the active faculties of men; an accumulation of power, a study of the issues of one and another course of action, and if the higher faculties of the individual be from time to time quickened, he will gain wisdom and virtue from his business. But if his pursuit degenerate into the mere love of money he dieth daily, he becomes no man but a money machine. The like is true of every sort of activity.

Somewhere in every society this redeeming influence should exist. For this reason we rear colleges, we crowd the churches, we establish schools, appointing therein a priesthood. For this reason it is essential to society that there should be a learned class—a clerisy—comprising, that is, the clergy, the literary men, the colleges, the teachers of youth as the fosterers of the superior nature of man and prompt to remind him of the mediate and symbolical character of things. Where there is no vision the people perish. I think it the most deplorable failure,—the causal bankruptcy, when lofty hopes, when worthy views of human life are buried in a pursuit of sensual good as ultimate, when the eye itself has become blind. When the teachers themselves of a land, whether in the pulpit or in the academy, lose sight of the capital secret of their profession, namely, to convert life into truth, or to show the meaning of events. Here is a man formally dedicated to the task of public instruction. To this end all conveniences and opportunities are furnished him. He has dwelt and acted with other men, he has ploughed and travelled, he has bought and sold, he has laughed and wept, eaten and drunken, he has read books and seen spectacles, been affrighted, and has been in love.

Yet is all this experience still aloof from his intellect. Not one single fact in it all has he yet imported into his doctrine, not one jot of it all has he yet converted into wisdom, and instead, he entertains the people with words. Herein he utterly fails in his office. For we learn nothing rightly until we learn the symbolical character of life. Any society of men can well afford to settle large incomes on learned men that they may enter into active life with advantage, that they may marry, buy, and sell, and administer their own goods,—if the practical lesson they thus learn they can translate into general terms and yield them its law and its poetry from week to week. For thus would he elevate their life which is contemporary and similar. Thus would they be consoled in misfortunes and calmed in hard times and sobered in success. The poorest drudge in the community would find his account in contributing of his earnings to the leisure and advantages of a man whose words made those labors light by the dignity he imparted to them and by the hope he showed within it.

This then is the office of a true Education, this the high point to which it should aspire. If it falls short of this, if it becomes mere routine, if it teach a little grammar and arithmetic, a little geography and logic, and there stop, it is false to its trust. It then makes no resistance to the torrent that is drowning the intellect and the soul. It then only arms the senses with a little more cunning to pursue their low ends. It makes only more skilful servants of mammon and puffs them up with a seeming wisdom. But what doth such a school to form a great and heroic character? What abiding Hope can such a school inspire? What Reformer will it nurse? What poet will it breed to sing to the human race? What discoverer of Nature's laws will it prompt to enrich us by disclosing in the mind the statute which all matter must obey? What fiery soul will it send out to warm a nation with his charity? What tranquil mind will it have fortified to walk with meekness in private and obscure duties, to wait and to suffer? Is it not manifest that our academic institutions should have a wider scope? that they should not be timid and keep the ruts of the last generation, but that wise men thinking for themselves and heartily seeking the good of mankind, and counting the cost of innovation should dare to arouse the young to a just and heroic life; that the moral nature should be addressed in the schoolroom; and children should be treated as the highborn candidates of truth and virtue?

In affirming that the moral nature of man is the predominant element and should therefore be mainly consulted in the arrangements of a school, I am very far from wishing that it should swallow up all the other instincts and faculties of man. It should be enthroned in his mind, but if it monopolize the man he is not yet sound, he does not yet know his wealth. He is in danger of becoming merely devout; and wearisome through the monotony of his thought. It is not less necessary that the intellectual and the active faculties should be nourished and matured. Give a boy accurate perceptions. Teach him the difference between the similar and the same. Make him call things by their right names. Pardon in him no blunder. Then he will give you solid satisfaction as long as he lives. To this end let him learn arithmetic, geometry, logic, chemistry. In like manner, strengthen his hands, sharpen his attention, form his active habits, make him temperate, punctual, laborious. Educate also his taste. Acquaint him with the face of Nature, and the creations of Art. And thus shall you send forth ardent, joyful, sincere, accomplished souls to run the race of humanity with a better hope than all who went before them.

I am aware, gentlemen, how easy it is to present these general views in comparison with the extreme difficulty of putting them in practice. I know that the time and labor and temper of the teacher must be expended chiefly on details, and in communicating particular methods, and enabling the pupil to classify particular facts. Yet I would have this new effort—commenced as I know it is with the purest will and prosecuted thus far with an admirable spirit,—signalized and hallowed by the very highest aspirations. I would that the Teachers and the Friends of this School might open its gates with whatever pious emotion and far-looking purpose can dilate the heart of man. I would that the heart might open to the reception of heaven's truth and heaven's will, so shall the highest welfare of the youth you shall rear, never be quite postponed and lost, so shall they catch from you the good contagion of magnanimity and love—their virtues shall make the house you have built, more beautiful within than it is without, and it shall be a temple which your country and all time shall thank you for,—a great light in the darkness of the world.

Human Culture:
Introductory Lecture Read at the
Masonic Temple in Boston

(1837–1838)

Emerson first delivered this introductory lecture on 6 December 1837 as the first in a series of ten private lectures on human culture at the Masonic Temple in Boston; other lectures in this series included "Doctrine of the Hands," "Being and Seeming," and "Heroism" (*Early Lectures*, 2:230–45, 295–309, and 327–39, respectively). Emerson delivered this introductory lecture three more times, twice in February 1838 in Cambridge and in Framingham, Massachusetts, when he used it to introduce two lecture series, each comprised of several lectures drawn from the *Human Culture* series, and again on 18 April 1838 as the first in a series of seven lectures on human culture before the Concord Lyceum in Concord, Massachusetts.

It is generally acknowledged by scholars that in the *Human Culture* series Emerson came into his own as a popular lecturer who would be known for his eloquent oratory, high tone, and capacity for appearing prophetic. In the privacy of his journals he self-consciously worked toward the comprehensive and idealistic definition of culture that informs this lecture, most other lectures in this series, and many other lectures on culture or self-culture that Emerson delivered over the course of his career. "It seems to me," he wrote two months before opening the *Human Culture* series at the Masonic Temple,

as if the high idea of Culture as the end of existence, does not pervade the mind of the thinking people of our community; the conviction that a discovering of human power to which the trades & occupations they follow, the connexions they form, and the motley tissue of their common experience are quite subordinate & auxiliary; is the main interest of history. Could this be properly taught, I think it must provoke and overmaster the young & ambitious, & yield rich fruits.

Culture in the high sense does not consist in polishing or varnishing but in so presenting the attractions of Nature that the slumbering attributes of man may burst their iron sleep & rush full grown into day. Culture is not the trimming & turfing of gardens, but the showing the true harmony of the unshorn landscape. (*JMN*, 5:410–11)

Emerson drew passages from this lecture for inclusion in his essays "Self-Reliance" and "The Poet" (*CW*, 2:25–51 and 3:1–24, respectively).

There is a historical progress of man. The ideas which predominate at one period are accepted without effort by the next age, which is absorbed in the endeavor to express its own. An attentive observer will easily see by comparing the character of the institutions and books of the present day, with those of any former period—say of ancient Judaea, or the Greek, or the Italian era, or the Reformation, or the Elizabethan age of England,—that the tone and aims are entirely changed.[1] The former men acted and spoke under the thought that a shining social prosperity was the aim of men, and compromised ever the individuals to the nation. The modern mind teaches (in extremes) that the nation exists for the individual; for the guardianship and education of every man. The Reformation contained the new thought. The English Revolution is its expansion. The American Declaration of Independence is a formal announcement of it by a nation to nations, though a very limited expression. The Church of Calvin and of the Friends have preached it ever.[2] The Missions announce it, which have girdled the globe with their stations "to preach the gospel to every creature." The Charity which is thought to distinguish Christendom over ancient paganism, is another expression of the same thought. The Vote,—universal suffrage—is another; the downfall of War, the attack upon Slavery, are others. The furious democracy which in this country from the beginning of its history, has shown a wish, as the royal governors complained, to leave out men of mark and send illiterate and low persons as deputies,—a practice not unknown at this day—is only a perverse or as yet obstructed operation of the same instinct,—a stammering and stuttering out of impatience to articulate the awful words I am. The servile statesman who once cried "Prerogative!" now on every stump and in every caucus has learned to snuffle "The Poor! the Poor!" Then science has been adopted at last by nations. War is turned out of the throne, and Wit is coming in. Instead of piratical voyages sent out by the English crown to hunt the Spanish Manilla galleon, the same crown visits Australasia with gifts, and sends its best blood—keen draughtsmen, post captains, and naturalists,—beyond the terminal snowbanks,—the farthest step to which mortal Esquimaux or wolverine dared approach the deadly solitude of the Pole. War subsides into Engineering.

1. Queen Elizabeth I (1533–1603) ruled England (1558–1603) during a golden age of politics and literature.
2. John Calvin (originally Jean Cauvin) (1509–64), French Protestant reformer and theologian; Society of Friends (Quakers), English sect founded in the seventeenth century known for its pacifism and belief in an inner spiritual voice.

The desperadoes go a-whaling or vent their superabundant activity on the bear and catamount-hunt of the frontier.[3] Men say, if there is any interest that is oppressed in large assemblies, it is that of the rich: and lastly, the word is forming, is formed, and is already articulated by legislatures,—Education.

Thus, in gross, the growth of the new Idea may be observed as it inscribes itself on modern history. Of course, in the mind of the philosopher it has far more precision, and is already attaining a depth and splendor which eclipse all other claims. In the eye of the philosopher, the Individual has ceased to be regarded as a part, and has come to be regarded as a whole. He is the World. Man who has been—in how many tedious ages—esteemed an appendage to a fortune, to a trade, to an army, to a law, to a state, now discovers that property, trade, war, government, geography, nay, the great globe itself and all that it inherits, are but counterparts of mighty faculties which dwell peacefully in his mind, and that it is a state of disease which makes him seem the servant of his auxiliaries and effects. He exists and the world exists to him in a new relation of subject and object, neither of which is valid alone, but only in their marriage have a creative life.

The new view which now tends to remould metaphysics, theology, science, law, trades and professions, and which, in its earnest creation, must modify or destroy the old, has as yet attained no clearer name than Culture.

His own Culture,—the unfolding of his nature, is the chief end of man. A divine impulse at the core of his being, impels him to this. The only motive at all commensurate with his force, is the ambition to discover by exercising his latent power, and to this, the trades and occupations men follow, the connexions they form, their fortunes in the world, and their particular actions are quite subordinate and auxiliary. The true Culture is a discipline so universal as to demonstrate that no part of a man was made in vain. We see men who can do nothing but cipher—dot and carry one;—others, who can only fetch and carry; others who can only write or speak; how many who hardly seem to have a right of possession to their legs, their shoulders, and who get the least service out of their eyes. So concentrated to some focal point is their vitality, that the limbs and constitution appear supernumerary. Scholars are noted to be unskilful and aukward. Montaigne says, that, "men of supercelestial opinions have subterranean manners."[4] Much oftener, we see men whose emotive, whose intellectual, whose moral faculties, lie dormant.

The philosopher laments the inaction of the higher faculties.

He laments to see men poor who are able to labor.

He laments to see men blind to a beauty that is beaming on every side of them.

He laments to see men offending against laws and paying the penalty, and calling it a visitation of Providence.

3. Catamount (short for *cat-a-mountain*), a wild cat such as a cougar living in the mountains.
4. Michel Eyquem de Montaigne (1533–92), French essayist and philosopher, usually identified with skepticism.

He regrets the disproportion so manifest in the minds of men. Cannot a man know the mathematics, and love Shakspear also? Cannot he unite an eye for beauty, with the ardours of devotion? Can he not join the elegant accomplishments of the gentleman, to the adoration of justice?

He laments the foreign holdings of every man, his dependence for his faith, for his political and religious estimates and opinions, on other men, and on former times.

And from all these oppressions is a wise Culture to redeem the soul.

Is it not possible to clear and disencumber a man of a thousand causes of unhappiness; to show him that he has but one interest in the world, that in his own character? Why should he sit groaning there at mischiefs he cannot help? Why should he be a dependant? Why should he be a pretender? Why should he seem and shuffle and apologize any longer, when there is nothing good, nothing lovely, nothing noble and sweet, that is not his own; when he himself is a commander; when with him he has reality; he only is rich; and when the universe is one choral invitation to him to put forth his thousand hands? Culture in the high sense does not consist in polishing and varnishing, but in so presenting the attractions of nature that the slumbering attributes of man may burst their sleep and rush into day. The effect of Culture on the man will not be like the trimming and turfing of gardens, but the educating the eye to the true harmony of the unshorn landscape, with horrid thickets, wide morasses, bald mountains, and the balance of the land and sea.

And what is the foundation on which so vast an ambition rests? How dare we in the face of the miserable world; in the face of all history which records nothing but savage and semi-savage life; in the face of the sensual nations, among whom no man puts entire confidence in the virtue of another, scarcely in the virtue of the pure and select souls; and where the heights of self-denial and benevolence are reached always by mixed motives and a winding stair—how can any observer hope so highly of man and reconcile his views with the faces and speech of the mob of men that you shall see pass, if you stand at the corner of a street; with the market and the jail?

I answer the basis of Culture is that part of human nature which in philosophy is called the Ideal. A human being always compares any action or object with somewhat he calls the Perfect: that is to say, not with any action or object now existing in nature, but with a certain Better existing in the mind. That Better we call the Ideal. Ideal is not opposed to Real, but to Actual. The Ideal is the Real. The Actual is but the apparent and the Temporary. Ideal justice is justice, and not that imperfect halting compensation which we can attain by courts and juries. The mathematicians say there is no perfect circle in nature and their reasonings are not true of any actual circle but only of the Ideal circle.

The universal presence of this vision of the Better in all parts of life is the characteristic of human nature. The lover enraptured with the new consent of a maiden's affection with his own is instantly sobered by observing that her living form detaches itself from the beautiful image in his mind. They never, never will unite and always in seeing her he must remark deficiency.

The patriot worshipping in his thoughts the pure Republic wherein every citizen should be free, just, and contented, strives evermore to realize his idea upon the green earth, upheaves the foundations of the state to build his own commonwealth. Instantly younger men see faults as gross in the new as he in the old and Reform is only a step to Reform.

The pious heart bewails the deadness of religion. Luther, Huss, Cobham, Knox, moved by this painful contrast of the actual with the ideal worship, shake down the churches of a thousand years; and already the youthful saint following the same eternal instinct sees the shortcomings of their reformation.[5]

The great works of art are unable to check our criticism. They create a want they do not gratify. They instantly point us to somewhat better than themselves.

In Nature it is no otherwise. No particular form of man or horse or oak entirely satisfies the mind. The physiologist sees ever floating over the individuals the idea which nature never quite successfully executes in any one form.

In human actions the man compares incessantly his deed with what he calls his duty; with the Perfect Action; and to the best action there is still in the mind a Better.

In human condition the Ideal suggests ever the pictures of Heaven.

In Character the mind is constrained ever to refer to a moral Ideal which we call God.

The fruit of this constitutional aspiration is labor. This aspiration is the centrifugal force in moral nature, the principle of expansion resisting the tendency to consolidation and rest. The first consequence of a new possession is a new want. The first fruit of a new knowledge is a new curiosity. Much will have more. We cannot go fast enough on our own legs, and so we tame the horse. The horse can no more equal the ideal speed, and so we forge and build the Locomotive. The ideal still craves a speed like a cannon ball, a speed like a wish, and the inventive and practical faculties will never cease to toil for this end.

Now what is the disclosure of the mind in regard to the state of Society? There is no part of society which conforms to its laws but rather, yawning chasms between. Man, upright, reasoning, royal man, the master of the lower world, cannot be found, but instead—a deformed society which confessedly does not aim at an

5. Martin Luther (1483–1546), German religious reformer, founder of Protestantism; Jan Hus (ca. 1372–1415), Czech religious reformer burned at the stake for heresy; Sir John Oldcastle, Baron Cobham (ca. 1378–1417), English soldier and follower of John Wycliffe (ca. 1330–84), whose writings inspired leaders of the Reformation; John Knox (1513–72), Scottish religious reformer and architect of the Scottish Reformation.

ideal integrity, no longer believes it possible, and only aims by the aid of falsehoods at keeping down universal uproar, at keeping men from each other's throats. The great endeavors of men are paralysed. Men do not imagine that they are any thing more than fringes and tassels to the institutions into which they are born. They take the law from things; they serve their property; their trade or profession; books; other men; some religious dogma; some political party or school of opinion that has been palmed upon them; and bow the neck and the knee and the soul to their own creation. I need not specify with accusing finger the unsound parts of our social life. A universal principle of compromise has crept into use. A Routine which no man made and for whose abuses no man holds himself accountable tyrannizes over the spontaneous will and character of all the individuals. A very nice sense of honor would be a very great inconvenience in a career of political, of professional, of commercial activity. A devotion to absolute truth would be unacceptable in the academy also. An asceticism built on the study and worship of Nature would be rude and harsh to the men of refinement.

The loss of faith is the greatest mischief. We are overpowered by this great Actual which by the numbers, by the extent, by the antiquity lost in darkness of its arrangements daunts our resolution and though condemned by the mind yet we look elsewhere in vain for a realized reform and we say, This is the way of the world, this is necessary, and we accept the yoke and accommodate our feet to the treadmill.

And what temerity is it that refuses this yoke, cries Society always to the aspirant? Art thou better than our father Jacob who gave us this well?[6] Alleviation is all we can expect, not health. "The best of life is just tolerable, it is the most we can make of it." What folly, "says Richard to Robin" and "says Every one," that one man should make himself wiser than the public, than the whole world.[7]

We reply that all the worth that resides in the existing men and institutions was the fruit of successive efforts of this absolute truth to embody itself, and moreover that this is the instinct of the Ideal, its antagonism to numbers, to Custom, and the precise mode of its activity.

There is a celebrated property of fluids which is called by natural philosophers the Hydrostatic Paradox, by reason of which a column of water of the diameter of a needle, is able to balance the ocean. This fact is a symbol of the relation between one man and all men.

A man may see that his conviction is the natural counterbalance of the opposite persuasion of any number of men or of all men. An appeal to his own Reason is good against the practice of all mankind. Numbers weigh nothing. The ideal of Right in our mind we know is not less peremptory authority though not an in-

6. John 4:12.

7. The child's "folk-chant" is documented in Iona Opie and Peter Opie, eds., *The Oxford Dictionary of Nursery Rhymes* (Oxford: Clarendon Press, 1951), 367–70.

dividual on the face of the earth obeyed its injunctions. Before the steady gaze of the soul, the whole life of man, the societies, laws, property, and pursuits of men, and the long procession of history do blench and quail. Before this indomitable soul ever fresh and immortal the aged world owns its master. There is not among the most frivolous or sordid a man who is not capable of having his attention so fastened upon the image of higher life in his mind that the whole past and the present state of society shall seem to him a mere circumstance—somewhat defective and ephemeral in comparison with the Law which they violate. And the clear perception of a single soul that somewhat universally allowed in society is wrong and rotten, is a prophecy as certain that sooner or later that thing will fall as if all creatures arose and cried out, It shall end.

This Ideal is the shining side of man. This is the bosom of discovery. This is the seed of revolutions. This is the Foresight that never slumbers or sleeps. This is the Morrow ever dawning, forgetting all the yesterdays that ever shone.

We say that the allegiance of all the faculties is the birthright of this. That the denial of its oracles is the death of hope, is the treason of human nature. That it has been made shamefully subservient to the Actual, which is as if the head should serve the feet. We say the great Reform is to do it justice, to restore it to the sovereignty. We say that all which is great and venerable in character is measured by the degree in which this instinct predominates. That there is always sublimity about even the least leaning to its suggestions. It breathes a fragrancy and grace over the whole manners and form. Finally we say that it is the property of the Ideal in man to make him at home everywhere and forever. It belongs to the inactive mind to honor only the Old or the Remote. He who can open his mind to the disclosures of the Reason will see that glory without cloud belongs to the present hour; for the Ideal is the presence of the universal mind to the particular.

And what are the Means of Culture?

The means of Culture is the related nature of man. He is so strangely related to every thing that he can go nowhere without meeting objects which solicit his senses, and yield him new meanings. The world treats him ever with a series of symbolical paintings whose moral he gradually finds out. He cannot do the most trivial act but a secret sense is smiling through it which philosophers and poets repeat. The light that shines on his shoes came from the sun and the entire laws of nature and the soul unite their energies in every moment and every place. There is no trifle in nature. No partiality in her laws. A grain of unregarded dust nature loves with her heart and soul. Out of it goes an attraction which leaps to the planets and from star to star. On it play light, heat, electricity, Gravity, Chemistry, Cohesion, Motion, Rest, so that the history of Physical Nature might be read from that grain.

So is it with the life of man. It is made up of little parts, but small details are dignified by this pervading relation which connects every point to the brain and the heart. Our culture comes not alone from the grand and beautiful but also from the trivial and sordid. We wash and purify every day for sixty years this temple of the human body. We buy wood and tend our fires and deal with the baker and fisherman and grocer and take a world of pains which nothing but concealed moral and intellectual ends of great worth can exalt to an ideal level.

Natural objects address him. If he look at a flower it awakes in him a pleasing emotion. He cannot see a stone, but his fancy and his understanding are attracted to the varieties of its texture and law of its crystallization, until he finds even this rude body is no stranger to him, and though it cannot speak, yet it is the history of the Earth down to the period of written history. He cannot see a star, but instantly this marriage begins of object and subject, of nature and man, whose offspring is power. In short, it is because of this universally cognate essence of man that science is possible. The obscure attractions which natural objects have for him are only indications of the truth which appears at last, that the laws of nature preexisted in his mind.

But his relation is not only intellectual to surrounding things. He is active also. He can hew the tree and hammer the stone and sow the barren ground. That is to say, he is so related to the elements that they are his stock, flexible in his hands; he takes the obedient mountain and puts his own will into it and it becomes a city, temples, and towers. His power is straitly hooped in by a necessity which by constant experiments he touches on every side until at length he learns its arc, which is learning his own nature. An hourly instruction proceeds out of his employment, his disasters, his friends, his antagonists. His life is a series of experiments upon the external world by every one of which a new power is awaked in his mind.

A countryman bred in the woods, cannot go into a crowded city, see its spectacles, and the manners of its inhabitants, and trade in its market and go back to his cabin the same man he left it. A man cannot enter the army and see service and bring home the mind and manners of a boy. He cannot follow the seas without a sea change. He cannot see a mob or hear music or be vexed or frightened; he cannot behold a cataract, a volcano, a meteor, without a new feeling, a new thought. He is as changeable as the face of a looking glass carried through the street, a new creature as he stands in the presence of new objects. Go into a botanical garden; is not that a place of some delight? Go to a muster-field where four or five regiments are marching with flags, music, and artillery; is not that a moving spectacle? Go to a dance, and watch the forms and movement of the youths and maidens; have they nothing of you in keeping? Go to a church where gray old men and matrons stand or sit with the young in serious silence. A new frame of mind. Climb the White Hills;—enter the Vatican; descend to the unburied Pompeii;—go hearken to the enraged eloquence of Faneuil Hall;—each of these shall make a new impression, shall enlarge the scope of the beholder's knowledge and power.[8]

8. By White Hills Emerson means the White Mountains in New Hampshire.

It will be seen at once that in the philosophic view of Human Culture, we look at all things in a new point of view from the popular one, viz. we consider mainly not the things but their effect on the beholder. And this habit of respecting things for their relation to the soul—for their intrinsic and universal effects,—it is a part of Culture to form.

It is the office of Culture to domesticate man in his regal place in nature.

A great step is made before the soul can feel itself not a charity boy, not a bastard or an orphan, not an interloper in the world which exists for it. To most men, a palace, a statue, or a costly book, have an alien and forbidding air, much like a gay equipage, and seem to say like that, Who are you, sir? A man is to know that they all are his; suing his notice, petitioners to his faculties that they will come out and take possession; born thralls to his sovereignty; conundrums he alone can guess; chaos until he come like a creator and give them light and order. My position in the world is wholly changed as soon as I see that a picture waits for my verdict and is not to command me but I am to settle its claims to praise. The arts are appeals to my taste. The laws to my Understanding. Religion to my Reason. Indeed it is a changed position. Now I come meek but well assured as a youth who comes to the College to be taught, not like an interloper who skulks whilst he gazes at the magnificent ornaments he has broken in to see. That popular fable of the sot who was picked up dead drunk in the street, carried to the duke's house, washed and dressed and put in the duke's bed, and then on his waking treated with all obsequious ceremony like the duke and assured that he had been insane, owes its popularity to the fact that it symbolizes so well the state of man, who is in the actual world a sort of sot and vagabond, but now and then wakes up, exercises his reason, and finds himself a true Prince.

This is the discipline of man in the degrees of Property. He learns that above the merely external rights to the picture, to the park, to the equipage, rights which the law protects,—is a spiritual property which is Insight. The kingdom of the Soul transcendeth all the walls and muniments of possession and taketh higher rights not only in the possession but in the possessor, and with this royal reservation, can very well afford to leave the so called proprietor undisturbed as its keeper or trustee.[9]

Therefore the wise soul cares little to whom belongs the legal ownership of the grand Monadnoc, of the cataract of Niagara, or of the Belvedere Apollo, or whatever else it prizes.[10] It soon finds that no cabinet though extended along miles of marble colonnade would suffice to hold the beautiful wonders it has made its own. It has found beauty and wonder progressive, incessant, universal. At last it discovers

9. Muniments are documents used to defend the title to an estate or a claim to rights.

10. Mount Monadnock in New Hampshire is popular with climbers; the Belvedere Torso, signed by the Greek sculptor Apollonius, dating from the first century B.C., and currently housed in the Vatican Museum, had a profound effect on Renaissance artists, including Michelangelo.

that the whole world is a museum and that things are more glorious in their order and home than when a few are carried away to glitter alone.

In viewing the relations of objects to the mind we are entitled to disregard entirely those considerations which are of great importance in viewing the relation of things to each other. For example, magnitude, number, nearness of place and time are things of no importance. The spiritual effect is all that concerns us. What moves the mind we are entitled to say was designed to move it, however far off in the apparent chain of cause and effect. Our being floats on the whole culture of the past, on the whole hope of the future. Men dead and buried now for some thousands of years affect my mode of being much more than some of my contemporaries. As things lie in my thought, as they recur to speech and to action—such is their value, and not according to time or to place. How can any thing die to the mind? To this end they all are alive.

To what end existed those gods of Olympus or the tradition so irresistibly embodied in sculpture, architecture, and a perdurable literature that the old names, Jupiter, Apollo, Venus, still haunt us in this cold, Christian, Saxon America and will not be shaken off?[11] To what end the ethical revelation which we call Christianity, with all its history, its corruption, its Reformation; the Revivals of Letters; the press; the planting of America; the conversion of the powers of nature to the domestic service of man, so that the ocean is but a waterwheel and the solar system but a clock? To what end are we distributed into electoral nations; half subject still to England through the dominion of British intellect and in common with England having not yet mastered or comprehended the astonishing infusions of the Hebrew Soul in the morning of the world?[12]

Why is never a local political arrangement made by a Saxon lawgiver for the getting justice in a market or keeping the peace in a village but it drafts a jury today in my county or levies a tax on my house? Why is never a pencil moved in the hand of Rembrandt or Raphael and never a pen in that of Moses or Shakspear but it communicates emotion and thought to one of us at the end of an age and across the breadth of half a globe?[13] Thus is the prolific power of nature to yield spiritual aliment over a period of three or four thousand years epitomized and brought to a focus on the stripling now at school. These things and all things are there for me, and in relation to me. It may not be strictly philosophical—it may be a little beyond strictness of speech to say these all were designed to teach us as they have, but we may affirm that this effect and this action meet as accurately as

11. Olympus was the home of the gods in Greek mythology; Jupiter was the supreme Roman god; Apollo was the Greek god of prophecy who, as the leader of the Muses, was the patron of poetry and music; Venus was the Roman goddess of love.

12. Emerson inadvertently included "having" in a canceled passage; it is editorially restored here.

13. Rembrandt van Rijn (1606–69), Dutch etcher and painter; Raphael (1483–1520), Italian painter whose works adorn the Vatican, also called "Raphaelle" or "Raphaello" by Emerson.

the splendid lights of morning and evening meet the configuration of the human eye and within that, the more subtle eye of taste.

Once begin to count the problems which invite our research, which answer each to somewhat in the unknown soul, and you find that they are coextensive with the limits of being. Boldly, gladly, the soul plunges into this broad element, not fearing but cheered by the measureless main.

Nothing is so old, nothing so mean, nothing so far but it has something for me. The progress of Science is to bring the remote near. The kelp which grew neglected on the roaring seabeach of the Orkneys now comes to the shops; the seal, the otter, the ermine, that no man saw but the Indian in the Rocky mountains, they must come to Long Wharf.[14] The seashells, strombus, turbo, and pearl, that hid a hundred fathoms down in the warm waters of the Gulf, they must take the bait and leave their silent houses and come to Long Wharf also: even the ducks of Labrador that laid their eggs for ages on the rocks, must send their green eggs now to Long Wharf.

So I think it will be the effect of insight to show nearer relations than are yet known between remote periods of history and the present hour. The Assyrian, the Persian, the Egyptian era now fading fast into twilight must reappear, and as a varnish brings out the original colors of an antique picture, so a better understanding of our own time and our own life, will be a sunbeam to search the faintest traces of human character in the first plantation of man. When we consider how much nearer in our own time Egypt, Greece, Homer, and Rome have come to us through Wolf, Niebuhr, Müller, Winckelmann, and Champollion we may believe that Olympus and Memphis, Zoroaster and Tubal Cain have not yet spoken to us their last word.[15]

Having spoken of the aim; the basis; the apparatus; and the scope; I proceed to speak of the Scale of Culture. What is the rule that is to introduce a just harmony in the universal school in which it seems we study? Where every being in nature addresses me shall I not be bewildered and without compass or chart?

Proportion certainly is a great end of Culture. A man should ask God morning and evening with the philosopher that he might be instructed to give to every being in the universe its just measure of importance. And it may be thought an obvious

14. The Orkney Islands are off the northeast coast of Scotland; Long Wharf is in Boston.
15. Homer (ninth–eighth century B.C.), Greek poet, presumed single author of the *Iliad* and the *Odyssey*; Friedrich August Wolf (1759–1824), German classicist and philologist, argued that the *Iliad* and the *Odyssey* are the work of several authors; Barthold Georg Niebuhr (1776–1831), German historian and critic; Johannes von Müller (1752–1809), Swiss public official and historian; Johann Joachim Winckelmann (1717–68), German antiquities expert; Jean-François Champollion (1790–1832), French historian and linguist who used clues from the Rosetta stone to decipher Egyptian hieroglyphics; Memphis, city south of Cairo, was the capital of ancient Egypt; Zoroaster (also known as Zarathushtra) (ca. 628–ca. 551 B.C.), Persian religious reformer and founder of Zoroastrianism; Tubal-cain, in the Bible, was a great-great-great-great-grandson of Cain and a forger of metal.

objection to views which set so high the hopes and powers of the individual that they foster the prejudices of a private soul which Bacon pointed out as one of the sources of error under the name of the idols of the Cave.[16]

But let it not be said that the only way to break up the idols of the cave is conversation with many men and a knowledge of the world. This is also distorting. State Street or the Boulevards of Paris are no truer pictures of the world than is a cloister or a laboratory.[17] The brokers and attorneys are quite as wide of the mark on one side as monks and academicians on the other.

There are two ways of cultivating proportion of character.

First. The habit of attending to all sensations and putting ourselves in a way to receive a variety, as by attending spectacles, visiting theatres, prisons, senates, churches, factories, museums, barracks, ships, hells, a thing impossible to many and except in merest superficiality impossible to any, for a man is not in the place to which he goes unless his mind is there.

But suppose a man goes to all such places as I have named and many more. Will he have seen all? What does he know about the miners of Cornwall or the lumberers of Maine?[18] Is he sure to allow all that is due to the Thugs of the Desert?[19] Does he appreciate Insanity? or know the military life of Russia? or that of the Italian lazzaroni?[20] or the aspirations and tendencies of the Sacs and Foxes?[21] The shortness of life and the limited walks in which most men pass it forbid any hope of multiplying particular observations.

Second. The other mode of cultivating gradation and forming a just scale is to compare the depth of thought to which different objects appeal. Nature and the course of life furnish every man—the most recluse—with a sufficient variety of objects to supply him with the elements and divisions of a scale. Looking back upon any portion of his life he will see that things have entirely lost the relative proportions which they wore to the eye at the moment when they transpired. The once dearest aims of his ambition have sunk out of sight and some transient shade of thought looms up out of forgotten years.

Proportion is not the effect of circumstances but a habit of mind. The truth is the mind is a perfect measure of all things and the only measure.

I acknowledge that the mind is also a distorting medium so long as its aims are not pure. But the moment the individual declares his independence, takes his life

---

16. In his *Novum Organum* (1620), the key to his system for a new systematic analysis of knowledge, Francis Bacon (1561–1626), English philosopher and author, wrote about how, in Emerson's paraphrase, each individual has "his own dark cavern or den into which the light is imperfectly admitted and to some error there lurking truth is sacrificed" (*Early Lectures*, 1:331).

17. State Street was the main commercial center of Boston.

18. Cornwall, a peninsula in the extreme southwestern part of England, is known for its tin mines.

19. Thugs were professional gangs of assassins and robbers in India.

20. Lazzaroni are homeless people in Naples, Italy, who live by begging and occasional work.

21. Sacs or Sauks and Foxes were Indian tribes in what is now Wisconsin.

into his own hand, and sets forth in quest of Culture, the love of truth is a sufficient gauge. It is very clear that he can have no other.

What external standard, what authority can teach the paramount rank of truth and justice but the mind's own unvarying instinct? Who shall tell it the claim of other things but Affection and Need and the incessant oracles of the overhanging Ideal? I confess my toleration does not increase to those who do not reverence their own mind. He is not a skeptic who denies a miracle, who denies both angel and resurrection, who does not believe in the existence of such a city as Thebes or Rome; but he is a skeptic who does not think it always an absolute duty to speak the truth, who pretends not to know how to discriminate between a duty and an inclination, and who thinks the mind itself is not a measure of things.

With such views of the aim, of the reason, of the apparatus, of Human Culture I have thought its transcendant claims should be laid before you. I think it the enterprize which out of the urn of God has fallen the lot of the present age. I think the time has come to ask the question, Why are there no heroes? Why is not every man venerable? Why should any be vulgar and vile? I wish that Education should not be trusted to the feeble hand of Societies but we should speak to the individual that which he ought to hear, the voice of faith and of truth. I wish him to perceive that his imitation, his fear, his dependency are child's clothes it is now time to cast off and assume his own vows. I wish him instead of following with a mendicant admiration the great names that are inscribed on the walls of memory, let him know that they are only marks and memoranda for his guidance, with which his own experience should come up. Let him know that the stars shone as benignantly on the hour of his advent as on any Milton or Washington or Howard.[22] There is no combination of powers that comes into the world in a child that is not new and that is not needed. No sign indicates beforehand that a great man—that is, that a true man, has been born. No faculty is marked with a broad arrow beforehand but every gift of noble origin is breathed upon by Hope's perpetual breath. Whoever is alive, may be good and wise. I wish him to adopt this end with a great heart and lay himself generously open to the influences of Heaven and earth. Let him survey in succession his instincts and faculties. Let him examine his senses and his use of them. Is a man's body to be regarded as a philosophic apparatus, a school of science, a generator of power, or is it designed only for the taste of sugar, salt, and wine and for agreeable sensations? Then let him contemplate the Intellect and ask if justice has been done it, if its great instincts have been observed. Let him explore the Active powers, and see if he is the able, self-helping, man-helping laborer or an afternoon man and a nuisance. Let him enter the enchanted ground of the Affections and know if he have appropriated their sweetness and health; let him explore the laws

22. John Milton (1608–74), English poet and political writer, best known for his poem *Paradise Lost* (published in 1667 in ten books); Charles Howard, Earl of Nottingham (1536–1624), lord high admiral of the successful British fleet against the Spanish Armada in 1588.

of Prudence. Let him learn the higher discipline of the heroic; and ascend to the study and practice of the Holy.

This great subject I desire to see laid before the American mind by all teachers. And whatever can be done by public teaching in our Lyceums done for this. Whatever topics are presented by the speakers in these institutions in our large towns let them be presented under the light of this great aim.

Into these depths I wish to drop my sounding line. Into the several districts of human nature I wish to cast the inquiring glances of one observer. I do not underestimate the difficulties of the task. I see the utter incompetency of a single mind to draw the chart of human nature. I have as much doubt as anyone of the value of general rules. There are heights of character to which a man must ascend alone—not to be foreshown,—that can only exist by the arrival of the man and the crisis. It is very far from being my belief that teaching can make a hero or that Virtue can be analysed in the lecture room and her deepest secret shown. I rely too much on the inexhaustible Ideal, whose resources always astonish. But I think and I feel that confidence may be inspired in the powers of the Will and in the aspirations of the Better by the voice and the faith of a believing man. I wish to inspire hope and shall esteem it the highest success if any ingenuous mind shall own that his scope has been extended; his conscience fortified and that more has been suggested than said.

Genius

(1839)

Emerson first delivered "Genius" on 9 January 1839 as the fifth in a series of ten private lectures on human life at the Masonic Temple in Boston; other lectures in this series included "Home," "Love," and "Tragedy" (*Early Lectures*, 3:24–33, 51–67, and 103–20, respectively). He delivered "Genius" two more times, first on 31 January 1839 in Plymouth, Massachusetts, as a lecture independent of the *Human Life* series, and then on 27 March 1839 as the second in a series of seven lectures on human life before the Concord Lyceum in Concord, Massachusetts.

Following the public's positive response to his *Human Culture* series during the previous winter, Emerson decided to extend but also to personalize the subjects he had addressed earlier in a new series. In "Doctrine of the Soul," the opening lecture of the *Human Life* series, Emerson said,

> I propose to continue the Course of Lectures delivered by me last winter . . . on Human Culture by a new series on such parts and topics in the problem of Human Life as are familiar to me. In approaching this subject I have been led into the great question of primary philosophy, Who lives? What is the Life? I shall endeavor in the present lecture to give some general account of . . . the Soul. . . . In subsequent lectures, I shall . . . consult better the taste of my audience as well as my own strength, in surveying [the Soul's] modified activity in the various domains of youth, of gaiety, of tenderness, of danger, of security as man marches with divine omens and guidance on his unknown road. (*Early Lectures*, 3:5)

Before he began to deliver the series Emerson thought he might be able to compose up to twelve lectures on human life; however, as he noted in "Demonology," the tenth and last lecture he delivered in the series at the Masonic Temple, ill health forced him to end the series early (*Early Lectures*, 3:170). Yet regardless of the state of his health, Emerson felt uneasy about the series' prospects and his ability to complete the series even before he began to deliver it. Writing to his brother William on 16 November 1838, he confessed, "I [am] drifting far & wide in the sea of 'Human Life' without port without chart & even with a glass so thick over the compass that it is only once in a while I can see sharply where it points" (*Letters*, 2:175). In the end, the fears that Emerson had for the *Human Life* series did not affect the public's positive response to it or the success either of his lecture on "Genius" or of the five essays to which it contributed: "History," "Self-Reliance," "Intellect," "Art," and "The Poet" (*CW*, 2:1–23, 25–51, 191–205, 207–18, and 3:1–24, respectively).

I n my last lecture I considered the subject of Love which diffuses a light so dazzling over the morning of life, whose heats and lustres subside however in all healthy minds into a calm day light and vital heat which are of the substance of the soul. Let us pass now to some analysis of the great brother element in the substance of the soul; from the enchantment of the affection to the enchantment of the intellect.

What is Genius? Genius—which in its various manifestations all men reverence, that which attracts from the interior of their soul wonder and joy and presentiments of still higher good, which constrains us to attribute to the possessor a rare and splendid nature,—to believe, that, as was said of Alexander, he had the eyes of a god and a fragrance as of flowers exhaled from his skin, so that when once known and acknowledged everyone—from the highest to the meanest in an entire nation,—delights in his name, feels a strict relation to him, welcomes him to all hospitality, gives him the freedom of institutions, houses, yea of the road, and the stage-coach, and begs a hair of him for memory; and when the clay which it animated, and made beloved and illustrious among men,—a mark and harbinger of respect and festivity wheresoever it went,—is forsaken by it, and the man departed to God, a still more deep and reverent hospitality awaits him among men.[1] All nations adorn their walls with his bust and picture. His name becomes a proverb in fair and learned mouths; and that he said or did thus or thus, is thought an argument for ages not only against the contrary opinion but even against the truth itself.

But with this external shew of honor there goes a finer compliment. The select souls of that man's nation and then in due time of other nations are stung by his words or works so that they cannot sleep and cannot sit. They talk with his ghost in solitude; they catch with hungry ear, every new opinion, practice, act, trait, that any book or stranger reports to them of this master and write it in light in their memories. These sing a sweet music in their brain. By these as fixed points they arrange all their knowledge; from these cardinal points map out the world of men and things in their memory; and from these recollections clustered into form, they measure men and things, and draw their estimate of life, and the possibilities of the soul. If you look over the pages of chronology, you will see that each nation has a few names that have long ago acquired an ideal brightness and have become indefinitely potent in forming the character of the succeeding generations, by constituting all that influence which every man concedes to authority.

---

1. Alexander the Great (356–323 B.C.), ruled as Alexander III of Macedonia (336–323), conqueror of the known civilized world.

The life of Moses, it will be admitted, was not without influence on the Hebrew people; the life of Numa, of Scipio, of Caesar, among the Romans; the life of Lycurgus, of Homer, of Socrates, Plato, Pericles, Alexander, among the Greeks.[2]

The Venetian, Florentine, and Roman masters do still as it were paint heads and landscapes through the hands and on the easels of other men, and in lands which they never saw. And why name the gods of our English Parnassus which outshine in our memory all foreign images?[3] These are the synonyms of Genius in our minds and by them we interpret that word. See the infinite pains with which every arm, head, or trunk mutilated and abraded by weather, ascribed to the hand of Phidias—is excavated, restored, modelled, copied in engravings, and exhibited in every museum of the world; and then for Shakspeare we have libraries of editors and commentators and illustrators and translators—an edition every year—his mulberry, his will, and the parish registers of London and Stratford; and now we have got so far that I see on the bookseller's counter a fair volume entitled "Insects Mentioned by Shakspeare."[4]

And what is this Genius whose hand is so strong, which pours this deep infusion into every man's cup of human life, so that he goes about the willing adorer of one or another of his fellows, dead or living, as if they were not his fellows but the inhabitants of some superior sphere? It is because they are his fellows and live from his own superior sphere that he pays them this respect. To speak somewhat paradoxically, they are more himself than he is. They hold of the Soul, as he also does, but they more.

The essence of Genius is Spontaneity. It is, as it were, the voice of the Soul, of the Soul that made all men, uttered through a particular man; and so, as soon as it is apprehended it is accepted by every man as a voice proceeding from his own inmost self.

It is wonderful into what deep considerations any definition will carry us of trivial things, as well of great and stately. It is an easy thing to say Spontaneity,—but not so easy to enter the dim infinity, which all spontaneous action implies. In all works, books, acts, manners, words, to which this sacred emphasis of Genius attaches, it is not mere man, but more than man that worketh. The energy is not

2. Numa Pompilius (ruled 715–673 B.C.), according to legend, the second king of Rome; Scipio Africanus, or Scipio the Elder (236–ca. 183 B.C.), Roman general; Gaius Julius Caesar (100–44 B.C.), Roman general and statesman; Lycurgus, according to tradition, was the ninth century B.C. lawgiver who imposed codes on Sparta designed to produce tough and able warriors; Homer (ninth–eighth century B.C.), Greek poet, presumed single author of the *Iliad* and the *Odyssey*; Socrates (ca. 470–399 B.C.), one of the most famous of the Greek philosophers, whose dialogic method of teaching gained many adherents; Plato (ca. 428–348 B.C.), the most famous of the Greek philosophers and a disciple of Socrates; Pericles (ca. 495–429 B.C.), Athenian statesman and orator.

3. Mount Parnassus in ancient Greece was sacred to Apollo and the Muses and thus was the seat of the arts.

4. Phidias (ca. 500–ca. 430 B.C.), greatest of the ancient Greek sculptors; *The Insects Mentioned in Shakespeare* (1838), by Robert Patterson (1802–72), Irish zoologist.

a knack, a habit, a skill of practice, a working by a rule, nor any empirical skill whatever; it is not anything the man can handle and describe and communicate, can even do or not do, but always a power which overawes himself, always an enthusiasm not subject to his control, which takes him off his feet, draws him this way and that, and is the master, not the slave.

But before we proceed further, it is proper to observe that this fact of Spontaneity is the link between the two established senses of the word Genius in our tongue.

First. Genius, a man's natural bias or turn of mind, as when we say, consult the boy's genius in choosing his trade or work; where it signifies the spontaneous turning of every mind to some one class of things and relates to practice. And, in like manner, we say the *Genius* of a certain institution, code of laws, or department of literature as history, the drama, and so forth, or of a tribe or nation of men, meaning thereby the spontaneous or unconscious quality by which quite above the intention of the author or authors or parties, the thing or class makes a certain impression on the mind.

Second. The second and popular sense of Genius is the intellect's spontaneous perception and exhibition of truth. Its subject is truth, its object a creation of truth without,—whether in a temple, a song, an argument, a steamboat, a Copernican system of astronomy.[5]

Genius is the spontaneous perception and exhibition of truth. Its object is Truth. They err who think Genius converses with fancies and phantoms; has anything in it fantastic and unreal. Genius is the truest soul; the most articulate, precise of speakers; hating all delusion and words; loving things. Common literature seems to be mere paraphrase and imitation, but when genius arrives the good human soul speaks because it has something to say. Genius seems to consist in trueness of sight, in using such words as show that the man was an eyewitness of the fact and not a mere repeater of what was told. Thus the poor girl who having overheard an account of the inclination of the axis of the earth to the plane of its orbit repeating the information in her own way said the earth was *a-gee*, evinced her perception not less than Lord Bacon when he calls exploding gun powder "a fiery wind blowing with expansive force."[6]

It evinces its realism or worship of truth by this, that it pauses never but gives new matter with every word. And it utters things *for the things*. There is no halfness about genius. It utters things for their own worthiness because they must be said: and what it saith therefore always justifies the saying.

But here is the reason why Genius is taxed with loving falsehood, playing with moonshine, and building air castles; namely, because its sight is piercing and

5. Nicolaus Copernicus (or Mikołaj Kopernik) (1473–1543), Polish astronomer credited with founding the science of modern astronomy, believed that the planets revolved around the sun.
6. Francis Bacon (1561–1626), English philosopher and author.

pauses not like other men's at the surface of the fact, but looks through it for the causal thought. Whilst other men give undivided heed to the fact Genius has been startled out of its propriety by perceiving the fact to be a mere appearance, a mask, and detecting eyes that peer through it to meet its own. It knows that facts are not ultimates. Through them it seeks the soul. A state of mind is the ancestor of every thing. Now common sense stops at a fact; to it a fact is sacred; it will not go behind this; and it reckons mad all who do. Yet *is* there somewhat higher than common sense.

There is at the surface infinite variety of things. At the centre, there is simplicity and unity of cause. How many are the acts of one man in which we recognize the same character. Let me illustrate this remark by adverting to the perfectness of our information in respect to the Greek genius. Thus at first we have the *civil history* of that people as Herodotus, Thucydides, Xenophon, Plutarch have given it to us: a very sufficient account of what manner of persons they were and what they did.[7] Then we have the same soul expressed for us again in their *literature*; in their poems, drama, and philosophy: a very complete form. Then we have it once more in their *architecture*:—the purest sensual beauty, the perfect medium never overstepping the limit of charming propriety and grace. Then we have it once more in *sculpture*; "the tongue on the balance of expression:" those forms in every action, at every age of life, ranging through all the scale of condition from god to beast, and never transgressing the ideal serenity, but in convulsive exertion the liege of order and of law.[8]

Thus we have for one remarkable people, a four-fold representation of the same genius in History, in Literature, in Architecture, and in Sculpture, the most various expression of one moral thing, and each of these do give back the same thought to the mind. Yet what is more unlike to the senses than an ode of Pindar and a marble centaur; the peristyle of the Parthenon and the last actions of Phocion?[9] Who then can doubt that these varied external expressions proceed from one spiritual cause?

In like manner, every one must have observed faces and forms which without any one resembling feature make yet a like impression on his mind. Further have you not found that a particular picture or copy of verses will awaken in your mind if not the same train of images yet superinduce the same frame of thought as some wild walk, perhaps into lonely and somewhat savage solitudes, although the resemblance is nowise obvious to the senses but is occult and out of the reach of

7. Herodotus (ca. 484–ca. 425 B.C.), Thucydides (ca. 460–ca. 401 B.C.), and Xenophon (ca. 431–ca. 352 B.C.), Greek historians, with Thucydides being the most famous of the three.

8. The quote is attributed to Johann Joachim Winckelmann (1717–68), German antiquities expert, as quoted by Friedrich von Schlegel (1772–1829), German author and critic, by Emerson (*JMN*, 5:18n).

9. Pindar (ca. 522–ca. 438 B.C.), the greatest of the Greek lyric poets; the Parthenon is the temple of Athena on the Acropolis in Athens, and a peristyle is an open space, enclosed by columns, surrounding a building; Phocion (ca. 402–318 B.C.), Athenian general and statesman and student of Plato who after the death of Alexander the Great ruled Athens but was executed on a false charge of treason.

the understanding? It is the spirit and not the fact that is identical. What is to be inferred from these facts but this; that, in a certain state of thought is the common origin of very diverse works; and that by descending far down into the depths of the soul, and not primarily by a painful acquisition of many manual skills, you shall attain the power of awakening other souls to a given activity. Thus it has been greatly said that, "common souls pay with what they do; nobler souls, with that which they are." And why? because a soul living from a great depth of being, awakens in us by its actions and words, by its very looks and manners, the same power and beauty that a gallery of sculpture or of pictures enkindles in me.

Truth is the subject of genius: not truth of facts, of figures, dates, measures,—which is a poor, low, sensual truth,—but Ideal truth, or, the just suggestion of the thought which caused the thing. Therein is the inspiration: there the dart that rankles, goads him with noble desire to express this beauty to men. That is what art aims ever to say—the truth of thought, and not a mere copy of the fact.

The sculptor sees hovering over all particular human forms a fairer and so a truer form than any actual beautiful person, and copies it with desire in marble: and so we have the Theseus; the Apollo; which with wonder all men allow, is truer than nature.[10]

In landscape, the painter's aim is not surely to give us the enjoyment of a real landscape; for, air, light, motion, life, heat, dampness, and actual infinite space, he cannot give us—but the suggestion of a better, fairer creation than we know. He collects a greater number of beautiful effects into his picture than coexist in any real landscape: the details—the prose of nature, he omits, and gives us only the spirit and splendor, so that we should find his landscape more exalting to the inner man, than any actual lake or hill-side.

And now having illustrated from these arts of design the object of genius let me indicate from them also the mystery of its subjective power. It is by its spontaneity that Genius is rich. And who knows the resources that lie in the vast bosom of the soul? That indeed beggars all description. If you would feel poor, reckon the things you have and those you can choose to do. If you would feel rich, resign yourself to Nature, and do its commandment. Not by any conscious imitation of particular forms are the grand strokes of the painter executed, but by repairing to the fountainhead of all forms in his mind. Consider who is the first drawing-master,—only in humble aid of whom our earthly drawing-master comes.

Whence had you those primary lessons in drawing,—the elements on which all practical skill must be based?—Without instruction we know very well the ideal

10. Theseus, in Greek legend, slew the Minotaur, conquered the female tribe of Amazons and had a son with their queen, Hippolyte, and later became king of Athens; "the Apollo" is probably a reference to the Belvedere Torso, signed by the Greek sculptor Apollonius, dating from the first century B.C., and currently housed in the Vatican Museum.

of the human form. A child knows at once if an arm or a leg be distorted in a picture, if the attitude be natural, be grand, or mean, though he has never received any instruction in drawing, nor heard any conversation on the subject, nor can himself draw with correctness a single feature of the body. A good form strikes all eyes pleasantly long before they have any science on the subject. And a beautiful face sets twenty hearts in palpitation prior to all consideration of the mechanical proportions of the features and head. We may owe to Dreams some light on the fountain of this skill; for, as soon as we let our will go, and let the Unconscious states ensue,—see what cunning draughtsmen we are. We entertain ourselves with wonderful forms of men, of women, of animals, of gardens, woods, and of monsters and the mystic pencil wherewith we then draw has no aukwardness or inexperience, has no meagreness and poverty. It can design well and group well, its composition is full of art, its colours are well laid on, and the whole canvas which it paints is lifelike and apt to touch us with terror, with tenderness, with desire, and with grief.

Genius is the activity which repairs the decays of things. Nature through all her kingdoms insures herself. Nobody cares for planting the poor fungus: so she shakes down from the gills of one agaric, countless spores, any one of which, being preserved, transmits new billions of spores tomorrow or next day. The new agaric of this hour has a chance which the old one had not. This atom of seed is blown into a new place not subject to the accidents which destroyed its parent two rods off.

She makes a man; and having brought him to ripe age, she will no longer run the risk of losing this wonder at a blow: but she detaches from him a new self, that the work may be safe from accidents to which the single individual is exposed. So when the soul of the poet has come to the ripeness of thought, it detaches from itself and sends away from it its poems or songs, a fearless, sleepless, deathless progeny which is not exposed to the accidents of the weary kingdom of time. A fearless, vivacious offspring, clad with wings, (such was the virtue of the soul out of which they came) which carry them fast and far and infix them irrecoverably into the hearts of men. These wings are the beauty of the poet's soul. The songs thus flying immortal from their mortal parent are pursued by clamorous flights of censures which swarm in far greater numbers and threaten to devour them; but these last are not winged. At the end of a very short leap, they fall plump down and rot, having unfortunately received from the souls out of which they came no beautiful wings. But the melodies of the poet ascend and leap and pierce into the deeps of infinite time.

Equally manifest in every form of art, of action, of speech it elevates and informs our life. The few memorable hours of life are the few strokes of genius that have been dealt upon us. Some Napoleon has struck the thunder strings which vibrate through the world; or some wise mechanic has thought out a toy coach to roll on a bar, and Europe and America are striped with iron roads; a poet in his walk has mused on the Supreme Cause and, written out, that shall be theology for the next age. Some chemist has detected a subtle affinity that instantly to his eye shoots its roots through nature. It is a few thoughts that carve out this vast business which the world so bustles in with endless craftsmen and clerks and books. A few men invented the works which all do.

Except in fortunate hours we do not even apprehend genius, much less exercise it. Our eye rests on the multiplicity of the details and does not pierce to the simplicity and grandeur of the Cause. Yet as soon as we do enter into the causes we sympathise with it; we see that it is aloof from everything artificial, low, and old: that it is pure and fresh as childhood and morning: its words and works affirm their own right to exist: in short, that it is allied to God. A tree, a flower, an animal, a mountain need no apology: their own constitution is the reason why they are. If we see a house, a boat, an implement we have no *a priori* reason why it should be. Experience is to make that good: but a work of genius, mechanical, plastic, literary, or active does in being vindicate itself. That is the prerogative of a masterpiece,— the kindred emotion which it awakens with that awakened by works of nature. That apprises us how deep in thought is its origin, how near to God it was. The identity of their origin at the fountain head, we augur with a thrill of joy.

And of this great pedigree whence these impulses come, another proof is furnished in the perfect analogy that is between Virtue and Genius. One is ethical; the other is intellectual creation. The work of genius implies and is a species of worship of the supreme Being,—an earnest of his favor and nearer communion, and, in like manner, the expression of the religious sentiment, wherever it is perfectly simple, strikes us with the same surprise and deep contentment as genius.

And proportionate to this dignity of its origin, is the date of its success. The work of genius is not perishable: it has immortal youth: it appeals to eternity. Verses that were made in the beginning of the world, we still read and imitate. Statues and buildings that were the earliest efforts of men at carving and building, are known to all the boys in the civilized world. We talk of old times; but the Apollo, the Venus, the Phidian marbles, are our emblems of youth; yet they are older than the oldest times that we know much of.[11] To this purpose let me read you a sentence of Sir Christopher Wren: "An architect ought to be jealous of novelties, in which fancy blinds the judgment and to think his judges as well those that are to live five centuries after him, as those of his own time. That which is commendable now for novelty, will not be a new invention to posterity, when his works are often imitated, and when it is unknown which was the original; but the glory of that which is good

---

11. The Venus de Milo, a statue now at the Louvre in Paris, was considered the epitome of female beauty soon after its discovery in Greece in 1829; Phidias carved many of the reliefs on the pediment of the Parthenon.

of itself, is eternal."[12] And the reason why the work of genius fits the wants of all ages, is because that which is spontaneous is not local or individual but flows from that internal soul which is also the soul of every man.

First. To analyze a little this wonderful energy—not to take it to pieces, for it is essentially one and whole, but to see successively features which in it are entire— and to enumerate a few of the conspicuous traits, I will say, first, Genius captivates us by its self-reliance. To believe your own thought,—that is genius. The voice of society sometimes, and the writings of great geniuses always are so noble and prolific that it seems justifiable to follow and imitate; but it is better to be an independent groom than to be the player of a king. In every work of genius, you recognize your own rejected thoughts. Here as in science the true chemist collects what every body else throws away. Our own thoughts come back to us in unexpected majesty. We are admonished to hold fast our trust in our instincts another time. What self-reliance is shown in every poetic description. Trifles so simple and fugitive that no man remembers the poet seizes and by force of them hurls you instantly into the presence of his joys.

Let me adorn my discourse with an example of the manner in which a poet seizes a circumstance so trivial that an inferior writer would not have trusted himself to detach and specify, from Wordsworth's picture of skating:

> So through the darkness and the cold we flew
> And not a voice was idle: with the din
> Meanwhile the precipices rang aloud;
> The leafless trees and every icy crag
> Tinkled like iron: while the distant hills
> Into the tumult sent an alien sound
> Of melancholy not unnoticed, while the stars
> Eastward were sparkling clear, and in the west
> The orange sky of evening died away.
>
> Not seldom from the uproar I retired
> Into a silent bay,—or sportively
> Glanced sideway, leaving the tumultuous throng
> To cross the bright reflection of a star,
> Image that flying still before me, gleamed
> Upon the glassy plain: and oftentimes
> When we had given our bodies to the wind,
> And all the shadowy banks on either side
> Came sweeping through the darkness, spinning still

12. Sir Christopher Wren (1632–1723), English architect, proposed plans for rebuilding London after the Great Fire (1666), including fifty-three churches, the best known of which is St. Paul's Cathedral (1675–1711).

The rapid line of motion, then at once
Have I, reclining back upon my heels,
Stopped short; yet still the solitary cliffs
Wheeled by me—even as if the earth had rolled
With visible motion her diurnal round.
Behind me did they stretch in solemn train
Feebler and feebler, and I stood and watched
Till all was tranquil as a summer sea.[13]

The reason of this trust is indeed very deep for the soul is sight, and all facts are hers; facts are her words with which she speaketh her sense and well she knoweth what facts speak to the imagination and the soul. For always the dignity is in the thought not in the thing; and an Assyrian empire, a kingdom of Britain, is a fact no more material to it than the tint of a fading violet. To the soul all facts are sacred as they are expressive. It is the senses that creep and measure with balances and yardsticks, and sidereal years.[14] To the soul Andes is not large nor is grass seed small and the only duration is the depth of the thought.

And well may the soul rely on itself and speak in a firm tone, assuring itself of a welcome in all hearts; for it asks nothing but welcome; it is rich, it is strong, it is good itself, and it leans on God. Rare indeed in this world is the voice of genius but when it cometh it can say all things. It raises immediately the apprehension of inexhaustible fertility. When thought is best, then is there most. When genius does arrive, it writes itself out in every word and deed and manner as truly and selfsame as in its elaborate masterpiece. In our purest hours nature appears to us one with Art: Art perfected: the work of genius and the fertility of both is alike. In nature a leaf in the forest or a field lily is a precious tablet on which the united energies of the creation have writ their perfect mind and if these two things were brought alone to the detached and hermit soul, would administer the same gratification and the same culture which we draw now from the treasuries of art and nature. But what a profusion of leaves in the vast forest!—of flowers, in the five zones! Not less opulent is genius. As many things as exist, so many things doth it ennoble; for what it looketh upon, instantly shines with wisdom. Let a man of lively parts and profoundness only name his subject and we begin to see it under his point of view. Its subtle infusions nothing can resist. Every work of genius makes us for the moment idealists. It dissipates this block of earth into shining ether.

Second. And being spontaneous, the work of genius is never predictable. It always surprises. It is the distinction of genius that it is always inconceivable: once

---

13. Quoted from "Influence of Natural Objects in Calling Forth and Strengthening the Imagination in Boyhood and Early Youth" (1809), ll. 38–63, by William Wordsworth (1770–1850), English poet and, with Samuel Taylor Coleridge, founder of the romantic movement.

14. Sidereal, relating to the stars.

and ever a surprise. Itself unsurprised,—itself doing the most natural thing in the world, it astonishes and exalts by every pulse. A strange influence! Michel Angelo in his seventh sonnet describing to his mistress the effect of her beauty on him speaks thus (if you will allow me to render into literal prose his mystic song):

> I know not if it be the reflected light of its author which the soul perceives, or if from the memory, or from the mind, any other beauty shines through into the heart; or if in the soul yet beams and glows a bright ray of its preexistence, leaving of itself I know not what burning, which leads me to complain. That which I feel, and that which I see, and that which guides me, is not with me; nor know I well where to find it in me, and it seems as if another showed it to me. This, lady, befel me when I first beheld you, that a bitter sweet, a yes and no moved me.[15]

This ambiguity which touches the springs of wonder in the soul at the contemplation of beauty; this feeling of *relationship* to that which is at the same time new and strange; this confusion which at the same time says It is my own and It is not my own—is not less remarkable in regard to the works of genius. Talent draws and experiments and the soul says, That is brave, but not right: you have great merit, no doubt, but I know you not: you help me not: you speak not to me. Genius grasps the pencil, and with sure audacity goes daring, daring on, new and incalculable ever, and the soul attentive greets each stroke with entire welcome, and says That is it: It is true; It is true. But O my friends! how knew the soul that it was true?

Its tone, its deed, its song none can predict, not even genius itself. Shakspeare we cannot account for. No history, no "life and times," solves the insoluble problem. I cannot slope things to him so as to make him less steep and precipitous; so as to make him one of many.

Inferior poets who give us pleasure, we can see, wrote things which we might and should also write, were we a little more favored by time and circumstance; a little cleverer. But Shakspeare, as Coleridge says, is as unlike his cotemporaries as he is unlike us.[16] His style is his own. And so is genius ever total, and not mechanically composable. It stands there, a beautiful unapproachable whole, like a pinetree or a strawberry, alive, perfect, yet inimitable, nor can we find where to lay the first stone, which given, we could build the arch. Phidias and the great Greeks who cut the Elgin marbles and the Apollo and Laocoon, belong to the same exalted category with Shakspear and Homer.[17]

Third. As one more sign of the deep aboriginal nature of genius and its perfect

15. Michelangelo (1475–1564), Italian painter, sculptor, and poet, quoted from sonnet 7 in Giambattista Biagioli, ed., *Rime de Michelangelo Buonorrati il vecchio* (1821).

16. Samuel Taylor Coleridge (1772–1834), English poet and philosopher and, with William Wordsworth, founder of the romantic movement.

17. Between 1801 and 1803 Thomas Bruce (1766–1841), seventh Earl of Elgin, as envoy to the Ottoman sultan brought a collection called the "Elgin marbles," including the Parthenon frieze, from the Acropolis to the British Museum. Laocoön, the Trojan priest of Apollo, tried to warn the Trojans of the trick

accord with all the highest elements of spirit, another trait is, its *love*. Genius is always humane, affectionate, sportful. Always it is gentle. It has been observed that there is always somewhat feminine in the face of men of genius. Hence the perfect safety we feel whenever genius is entrusted with political or ecclesiastical power. There is no fanaticism as long as there is the creative muse. Genius is a charter of illimitable freedom and as long as I hear one graceful modulation of wit I know the genial soul and do not smell fagots. The Bunyan, the Behmen is nearer far to Rabelais and Montaigne than to Bloody Mary and Becket and the Inquisition.[18] It is a just saying of Scaliger, "Never was a man a poet, or a lover of the works of poets who had not his heart in the right place."[19] They are not tainted by the worst company. Genius hath an immunity from the worst times and drawing its life from that which is out of time and place is serene and glad amid bigots and juntoes. I think if literary history be observed it will be found that the most devout persons are the freest speakers in reference to divine things, as Luther, Melancthon, More, Fuller, Herbert, Milton, whose words are an offence to the pursed mouths which make formal prayers; and beyond the word they are freethinkers also.[20] We trust genius; we trust its integrity. Its praise is praise; its religion, sincere. And so we prize the devotion, the moral sentiment which flames aloft even amid licence and nonsense in Chaucer, and in Shakspeare's broadest comedy.[21] I believe that we shall often find a covert unexpressed association in our own minds of names that minister to Faith, that would shock the squeamish ear of men that judge by appearance. And this will no wise appear strange to any one who considers what I may here affirm

---

of the Greek wooden horse and was then strangled, along with his two sons, by two sea serpents sent by Athena as punishment; their deaths are portrayed in a first century B.C. statue now in the Vatican.

18. John Bunyan (1628–88), English cleric and author of *The Pilgrim's Progress from This World to That Which Is to Come* (1678), an allegory in which Christian, the main character, leaves his home and family to journey to the Celestial City; Jacob Behmen (or Jakob Böhme) (1575–1624), German mystic, influenced romanticism and the Quakers; François Rabelais (ca. 1483–1553), French satirist and writer; Michel Eyquem de Montaigne (1533–92), French essayist and philosopher, usually identified with skepticism; Mary I or Mary Tudor (1516–58), daughter of Henry VIII and Catherine of Aragon, queen of England and Ireland (1553–58), led the Catholics against heretics, many of whom were executed; Thomas à Becket (ca. 1118–70), English prelate, archbishop of Canterbury under Henry II, murdered by four of his knights; Emerson may be thinking of either the Inquisition of the Roman Catholic Church against heretics during the thirteenth century in Italy and France or the Spanish Inquisition against Jews and Moors (1478–1835).

19. Joseph Justus Scaliger (1540–1609), Italian scholar, collected all available writings of classic Greek and Latin.

20. Martin Luther (1483–1546), German religious reformer, founder of Protestantism; Philipp Melanchthon (1497–1560), German reformer and religious scholar, collaborator with Luther; Sir Thomas More (1478–1535), English author and Christian humanist, best known for his *Utopia*, canonized in 1935; Thomas Fuller (1608–61), English cleric, poet, and historian, known for his posthumously published *History of the Worthies of England* (1662); George Herbert (1593–1633), English metaphysical poet; John Milton (1608–74), English poet and political writer, best known for his poem *Paradise Lost* (published in 1667 in ten books).

21. Geoffrey Chaucer (ca. 1342–1400), English poet, author of *Troilus and Criseyde* and *The Canterbury Tales*.

as the highest statement at which we can arrive concerning genius, that every work of pure genius will satisfy the demands of Taste, Virtue, and Science. Or, in other words, is charged with the elements of beauty, goodness, and truth. If it lack either of these elements so much genius does it lack.

Fourth. To add one more to these traits of this brave spontaneous life I may say that Genius is always representative. The men of genius are watchers set on the towers to report of their outlook to you and me. Do not describe him as detached and aloof: if he is, he is no genius. Genius is the most communicative of all things: the man of genius the most frank and sincere confessor of all his experience. The man of genius apprises us not of his wealth but of the commonwealth. And so I think all worthy men feel a warm brotherhood to the seers that are left in the land. If Collins, if Burns, if our American painter and our American poet is in the world we have more tolerance and more love for the changing sky, the mist, the rain, the bleak overcast day, the indescribable sunrise, and the immortal stars.[22] If we believed no poet survived on the planet nature would sometimes be tedious. The very highest merit of the poet is always his profounder sympathy with human nature than ours. The reason why he is alone; why we are slow to share his thought; is, because he deserts our customs and conventions to drink deeper of the thought which as yet we have hardly tasted. He commends it to our lips. When we have learned its wholesomeness and life, we shall do him justice. The true bard has always this consolation in his pursuits, that if they do not interest all men now, yet they will sooner or later. However alone, or in what small minority he may now stand, every man will, one day, recall his image with grateful and honorable remembrance. The best verse I think that Shelley has written is that which paints the sky lark:

> Like a poet hidden
> In the light of thought
> Singing hymns unbidden
> Till the world is brought
> To sympathy with hopes and fears it heeded not.[23]

Whose wit was Homer's? and whose Virgil's?[24] Whose was Bunyan's, Defoe's—and Cervantes' and Newton's?[25] Whose was it not? To whom in the swarming nations did not the joy and music and perception of these masters belong?

22. William Collins (1721–59), English lyrical poet whose neoclassical odes are considered preromantic; Robert Burns (1759–96), Scotland's most famous poet.

23. Quoted from "The Skylark" (1820), ll. 36–40, by Percy Bysshe Shelley (1792–1822), English romantic poet.

24. Virgil (or Vergil) (70–19 B.C.), Roman poet and author of the great epic of the founding of Rome, the *Aeneid* (30–19 B.C.).

25. Daniel Defoe (1660–1731), English journalist and novelist, best known for *Robinson Crusoe* (1719), a novel about a traveler stranded on a desert island; Miguel de Cervantes (1547–1616), Spanish

I know no more striking instance of the representative character of genius than we have in the rare fact of genuine eloquence. The orator masters us by being our tongue. By simply saying what we would but cannot say, he tyrannises over our wills and affections. The high exercises of this power are indeed rare; but a quite analogous example is familiar to us in our popular assemblies. As it was happily said of Sir James Scarlett, that the reason of his extraordinary success with juries was that "there were twelve Scarletts in the jury-box," so he who can say without hitch or hindrance that which is boiling in the bosom of all men, is the poet and master of the crowd.[26] We have all read this lesson at Faneuil Hall time and again. Join the dark, irregular, thickening groups that gather in the old house when fate hangs on the vote of the morrow. As the crowd grows and the hall fills behold that solid block of life—few old men, mostly young and middle aged, with shining heads and swoln veins. Much of the speaking shall no doubt be slovenly and tiresome but this excited multitude predominates; is all the time interlocutor; and the air grows electric; and the bucket goes up and down according to the success of the speaker. The pinched, wedged, elbowed, sweltering assembly, as soon as the speaker loses their ear by the tameness of his harangue, feel sorely how ill accommodated they are, and begin to forget all politics and patriotism, and attend only to themselves and the coarse outcries made all around them. Each man in turn is lifted off his feet as the press sways now this way, now that. They back, push, resist, and fill the hall with cries of tumult. The speaker stops. The moderator persuades, commands, entreats. The speaker gives way. At last the chosen man rises, the soul of the people, in whose bosom beats audibly the common heart. With his first words he strikes a note which all know; his word goes to the right place; as he catches the light spirit of the occasion his voice alters, vibrates, pierces the private ear of every one; the mob quiets itself somehow,—every one being magnetized,—and the house hangs suspended on the lips of one man. Each man whilst he hears thinks he too can speak; and in the pauses of the orator bursts forth the splendid voice of four or five thousand men in full cry, the grandest sound in nature. If a dull speaker come again, instantly our poor wedges begin to feel their pains and strive and cry.

And as the humblest hearer feels under that spell that he too could speak, so it is always the effect of genius to communicate its life to our torpid powers, to inspire a boundless confidence in the resources of the human mind. But for them we should be cowards and sleepers. To them we owe the great facts, and the laws, and the works of art, and the sweet and sublime songs that establish, instruct, and decorate this human life. Genius gave us astronomy, and navigation, the arts, and the bible. But to all her gifts genius adds one which makes all the rest of no esteem:

---

novelist best known for *Don Quixote* (1605, 1615); Sir Isaac Newton (1642–1727), English natural philosopher and mathematician.

26. Sir James Scarlett, first Baron Abinger (1769–1844), English jurist.

An infinite hope. Genius counts all its miracles poor and short. Its own idea genius never executed. The *Iliad,* the *Hamlet,* the Doric column, the Roman arch,
the Gothic minster, the Beethoven anthem, when they are ended, the master casts
behind him impatient and ashamed.[27] How sinks the song in the waves of melody
that the universe pours over his soul! Before that gracious infinite, out of which he
drew these few strokes, how poor and thin and dead they look, though the praises
of the world attend them. From the triumphs of his art the master turns with his
heart and soul to this greater defeat. Let those admire who will. With deep homage
and joy he sees himself to be capable of a beauty which eclipses all that his hands
have done,—all that human hands have done. Immense is now his ambition: immense his trust. What he did, was given him to do; he wist not of it; but lo! before
him, all Nature awaits, and will give itself unto him.

27. Ludwig van Beethoven (1770–1827), German composer, wrote many of his greatest works after
losing his hearing in 1798.

The Poet

(1841–1842)

Emerson first delivered "The Poet" on 16 December 1841 as the third in a series of eight private lectures entitled *The Times* at the Masonic Temple in Boston. Other lectures in this series included an introductory lecture, "The Conservative," "The Transcendentalist," "Manners," "Character," "Relation of Man to Nature," and "Prospects"; however, since only "The Poet" and "Prospects" survive as more than extremely fragmentary sections of former lecture manuscripts, we agree with the editors of the *Early Lectures* that it is difficult to speak definitively about this series. (For the editors' discussion of this series and for "Prospects" see *Early Lectures*, 3:335–45 and 366–82, respectively.)

In addition to delivering "The Poet" in *The Times* series at the Masonic Temple, Emerson may have delivered it as "Nature and the Powers of the Poet" on 3 November 1841 before the Concord Lyceum in Concord, Massachusetts, but since no evidence of the content of this lecture survives, we cannot say with certainty that Emerson read from "The Poet" on this occasion. He delivered "The Poet" twice in 1842, first on 12 February as the second in a series of five lectures entitled *The Times* at Franklin Hall in Providence, Rhode Island, and then on 5 March as the second in a series of six lectures entitled *The Times* before the Society Library of New York in New York City. In his capacity as a reporter for the *New York Aurora* Walt Whitman was present at Emerson's delivery of "The Poet" before the Society Library of New York. Whitman used his report as an occasion to poke fun at some of the types who were gathered in Emerson's audience and to lampoon Horace Greeley, Transcendentalist supporter and editor of the rival *New York Tribune*, but for Emerson he had only unqualified praise:

> The Transcendentalist had a very full house on Saturday evening. There were a few beautiful maids—but more ugly women, mostly blue stockings; several interesting young men with Byron collars, doctors, and parsons; Grahamites and abolitionists; sage editors, a few of whom were taking notes; and all the other species of literati. Greeley was in ecstasies whenever any thing particularly good was said, which seemed to be once in about five minutes—he would flounce about like a fish out of water, or a tickled girl—look around, to see those behind him and at his side; all of which very plainly told to those both far and near, that he knew a thing or two more about these matters than other men.

This lecture was on the "Poetry of the Times." He said the first man who called another an ass was a poet. Because the business of the poet is expression—the giving utterance to the emotions and sentiments of the soul; and metaphors. But it would do the lecturer great injustice to attempt anything like a sketch of his ideas. Suffice it to say, the lecture was one of the richest and most beautiful compositions, both for its matter and style, we have ever heard anywhere, at any time. (Walt Whitman, "Mr. Emerson's Lecture," *New York Aurora*, 7 March 1842)

Emerson's lecture "The Poet" bears virtually no relation to his famous essay "The Poet" (1844; *CW*, 3:1–24). Instead, Emerson apparently held the lecture in reserve for thirty years, during which he undoubtedly drew from it for other lectures on poetry that he delivered over the years. Late in life he used portions of his lecture "The Poet" in the essays "Poetry and Imagination" and "Eloquence" as they were finally arranged by James Elliot Cabot with the assistance of Ellen Emerson for inclusion in *Letters and Social Aims* in 1876 (*W*, 8:1–75 and 109–33, respectively).

I invite the attention of the audience to a consideration of the nature and offices of the Poet: to the power he exerts and the means and materials he employs; to the part he plays in these times, and is likely to play. I hope I shall not terrify any dear lover of poetry who regards it with a species of religion, and hears with alarm as a sort of sacrilege, that criticism so busy in these days threatens now at last to seize this mountain flower, and pick it to pieces with unhallowed fingers. Let me appease at once such apprehensions by declaring my persuasion, that the thing is impossible. If I were not, as I am, a devout lover of the Muse, I must still feel that its nature is not in danger from critics, that it is something not to be reached by criticism.

All books of Imagination endure, all which ascend to that power of thought that the writer sees Nature as subordinate to the soul and uses it as his language. Every sentence, every verse indicating this superiority or health is memorable and will take care of its own immortality. A man apparently foolish and helpless with nothing magnetic in him,—who is a churl in the drawing-room, an idiot in the legislature,—hides himself in his garret from the pride and pity of men, and writes a poem which, when at last it is published, is at first neglected, then hissed, and it pushes all potentates from their thrones, changes the course of affairs in a few years, and actually wipes out the memory of that triumphant state of things under which he suffered when he existed.[1]

---

1. Immediately after this paragraph in the manuscript Emerson listed in pencil the names of the following authors whose lives illustrated his point: Plato (ca. 428–348 B.C.), Greek philosopher; Aristophanes (ca. 450–ca. 380 B.C.), Athenian writer of comedies; Tyrtaeus, Greek elegiac poet who flourished in Sparta during the seventh century B.C.; Claude-Joseph Rouget de Lisle (1760–1836), French soldier and composer, wrote France's national anthem, "La Marseillaise" (1792); Jean-Jacques Rousseau

As one relates eagerly anecdotes of the youth or private life of an eminent person and collects minute particulars of his behavior, how he stood, how he looked, how he dressed, and does not thereby slake but inflame the curiosity of the hearer, so is it with the best analysis of poetry which we can make. You can tell me anecdotes of the Muse,—but there is no fear that you will exhaust or dispose finally of a subject so subtle and evasive.

I think of poetry as of that Angel which sits on the highest and most inaccessible cliff of all the mountain round which the hierarchies are ranged. It is a presence you cannot profane. On its person hands were never laid,—never can be laid. It bids defiance to the pursuer. If you come where it was, lo! it has departed and glitters in the distance like a planet; for its essence is inviolable, it is ever wild and new.

If then we proceed to inquire what we know of that element which is called Poetry, we shall find it to be no solitary fact, but one so intertwined with the nature of all things, that it is by no means easy to separate it, and say what is poetry, and what is not. Your definition is sure to be too large, or too small. Poetry finds its origin in that *need of expression* which is a primary impulse of nature. In nature there is no rest. All things are in perpetual procession, flow, and change. Every thought in man requires to be uttered, and his whole life is an endeavor to embody in facts the states of the mind. When he lays out a garden, or builds a house or a ship, when he frames a law, or plans a colony, or a war, or when he seeks to inform an individual or an assembly of his views, you see the need he stands in and the joy he finds in unbosoming himself, and contemplating his thought in a new form, on the face of the world, or in the minds of other men. When my thought has passed into a thing, I am one step farther on my way. To be unfolded, explained, expressed, that is the boon we crave of the Universe. The man is only half himself; the other half is his Expression, or the aggregate of his saying and doing. That man is serene who does not feel himself pinched and wronged by his condition but whose condition in general and in particular allows the utterance of his mind; and that man who cannot utter himself goes moaning all the day. Does happiness depend on "uninterrupted prosperity," as it is called? Oh no, but on Expression. Expression is prosperity. I must say what is burning here: I must do what I shall perish if I cannot do, I must appear again in my house, in my fortune, in my marriage, in my speech, or else I must disappear, and the brute form must crowd the soul out of nature. All possessions must obey and paint my thought, and, failing

---

(1712–78), French philosopher and one of the founders of romanticism; Niccolò Machiavelli (1469–1527), Italian statesman and political strategist; Voltaire (the assumed name of François-Marie Arouet) (1694–1778), French author and intellectual; Thomas Paine (1737–1809), American political philosopher and writer; Jonathan Swift (1667–1745), English churchman and satirist born in Dublin, Ireland; Martin Luther (1483–1546), German religious reformer, founder of Protestantism; François Rabelais (ca. 1483–1553), French satirist and writer; Muhammad (ca. 570–632), founder of Islam, born in Mecca; and Honoré-Gabriel Riqueti, comte de Mirabeau (1749–91), French statesman and orator, the most important figure during the first two years of the French Revolution.

this, all the aids and advantages you can add to me are mountains of aggravation and impediment.

That makes, and that only, the value of Old Age,—that it gives ample vent to all the parts and needs of the individual character.

That is the value of wealth, that it is external freedom, and allows the man to conform the general outline of his condition to his thought and to signify his bent and tendency in his house and lands, in his possessions, and the disposition of his time.

That is the esteem of Eloquence, that it is a wondrous power to report the inner man adequately to multitudes of men, and bring one man's character to bear on others.

All the facts of the animal and organic economy,—Sex, Nutriment, Gestation, Birth, Growth, are emphatic symbols of this eternal fact of the passage of the world into the soul of man to suffer there a change, and reappear a new and higher fact, another yet the same.

Expression;—all we do, all we say, all we see, is that, or for that. The reason for doing or avoiding anything is, that, in one fact I am represented,—in the other not. The love of nature, what is it, but that I find with wonder in the landscape certain high portraiture of my thoughts and emotions? For the same reason I follow particular persons: they do justice to my opinions and wishes. I love Guy, because he expresses my thought: I hate Jeffrey, because he does not. Am I warlike? Am I smitten with a rage for prodigious energy of action? I follow some Napoleon or Nelson as his shadow.[2] Am I bound to certain local or political objects? It is easy to see how the head of a party can draw my regard. Every artist draws me so. Taglioni must dance, and Paganini play.[3]

In every feat of genius the beholder feels his latent and slumbering powers vindicated. If Paganini "with three or four whips of his bow elicited points of sound as bright as the stars"; if it appeared to the audience that "he drew from the strings tones more than human which seemed to be wrung from the deepest anguish of a broken heart and in his hands the violin appeared to be some wild animal which he was endeavoring to quiet in his bosom, and which he occasionally lashes with his bow,—tearing from the creature the most horrid, as well as the most delightful tones,"—what is the origin of their enjoyment but an apprisal of their own power,—that the range of human articulation reaches higher and lower than they had yet found, and every hearer goes away to copy or appropriate to himself as far as he can the new art?

2. Napoléon Bonaparte (1769–1821), born in Corsica, general and later emperor of the French as Napoléon I; Horatio Nelson (1758–1805), English admiral, commanded the British fleet during the Napoleonic Wars.

3. Marie Taglioni (1804–84), member of a celebrated Italian family of ballet dancers, one of the first women to dance on the points of the toes; Niccolò Paganini (1782–1840), Italian composer and violinist.

The world runs to see some perfect dancer, some incomparable Taglioni or Bayadere, to admire the wisdom of the feet,—not certainly to see the leaps of the rope dancer, the impossible in attitude performed, but to rejoice in the grace of movement in wavelike form and action, in the fun of the coquetries, in the beautiful erectness of the body and the freedom and determination of her carriage, and in the perfect sympathy with the house, the mixture of deference with conscious superiority which puts her in perfect spirits and equality to her part.[4] When the fair creature curtsies, her sweet and slow and prolonged Salam which descends and still descends until she seems to have found new depths of grace and condescension, earns well the profusion of bouquets and flowers which are hurled on the stage. But what is her charm for the spectators other than this, that she dances for them, or they dance in her feet, not being,—fault of some defect in their forms or education,—able to dance themselves?

We must be expressed. In our wooden and prosaic ways of life, we seem to have lost our muscular vigor and alacrity, and still more we are bound up and pinioned in woolen and leather, in steel and india-rubber, so that we seem to walk with our feet alone and not with our whole person;—and to see the body in some graceful specimen as God made it, free for motion and delighting in the infinite variety of movement, is some indemnity and refreshment. Hence the cheer and exhilaration which the spectacle imparts and the intimate property which each beholder feels in the dancer.

If one considers the hunger with which men seek spectacles of every sort where anything strong and extreme in its kind is done, whether theatres, galleries, angry debates, the circus, the ring, land or naval battles; foreign cities, countries, savage tribes, men will seem to him a race of children running up and down for that end only,—to be gratified with the exhibition of a good deliverance of every fancy of the brain.

This need of expression is thus the cause of our action and of the love of spectacles or witnessing what is extraordinary in the action of others. But besides the need which every man has of doing something, and making his mark somewhere, which is the first result of the eternal impulse at the heart of things, it needs that not only his will, or the direction of his practical faculties should have this justice done it, but that his science or his perception of things in the intellect, should have an expression also.

To this need and desire the world or the face of nature very readily lends itself— so expressive, so changeable, so fruitful in names and methods and metres that it appears to be a sympathetic cipher or alphabet and to exist that it may serve man with a language.

All things are symbols. We say of man that he is grass, that he is a stream, a

4. Bayaderes were professional female dancers in India.

house, a star, a lion, fire, a day; and if we wish to accuse him at any time, we call him a snake, a baboon, a goat, a gull, a bat, an owl, a toad, and an infinity of names beside. These names are comparatively unaffecting in our ears, hearing them as we do merely caught by the ear from others and spoken without thought, but the man who first called another man Puppy or Ass was a poet, and saw at the moment the identity of nature through the great difference of aspect. His eye so reached to the thought and will of the wretch he beheld, that he could hear him bark or bray, with a bestial necessity under this false clothing of man.

We still feel this strong poetry whenever a powerful mind which disregards appearances signifies its sense in these metaphors. As when Napoleon says of the Bourbons, "They were a hereditary race of asses, whilst I made my generals of mud."[5] But everyone of these images and every other image may be applied to the world and the universe. There is no word in our language that can not become to us typical of nature by giving it emphasis. The world is an animal; it is a bird; it is a boat; it is a shadow; it is a torrent, a mist, a spider's snare; it is what you will, and the metaphor will hold, and it will give the imagination keen pleasure. Swifter than light the world converts itself into that thing you name, and all things find their right place under this new and capricious classification. Small and mean things serve just as well as great symbols. The meaner the type by which a spiritual law is expressed, the more pungent it is, and the more lasting in the memories of men, just as we value most the smallest box or case in which any needful utensil can be carried. The soul derives as grand a joy from symbolizing the Godhead and his Universe under the form of a moth or gnat as of a Lord of Hosts. Shall I call the heaven and the earth a maypole, a country fair with booths, an anthill, or an old coat, to give you the shock of pleasure which the imagination loves, and the sense of spiritual greatness? Call it a blossom, a rod, a wreath of parsley, a tamarisk crown, a cock, a sparrow, the ear instantly hears and the spirit leaps to the trope. A man must not, to be sure, go seeking for trivial or fantastic tropes, but every one is legitimate which occurs to any mind without effort or study.

It is related of Lord Chatham that he was accustomed to read in Bailey's *Dictionary* when he was preparing to speak in Parliament.[6] A similar fact has been related of other eloquent men. I think we may easily see how mere lists of words should be suggestive to a highly imaginative and excited mind.

It were a curious inquiry which one sees would lead at once into the heart of nature to ask what it is that so charms us in a symbol or trope. The fact I suppose

---

5. Bourbon was the name of the French royal family whose rule, which started in 1589 with Henry IV, was interrupted by the Napoleonic times between the reigns of Louis XVI (guillotined in 1793) and the restoration of the monarchy with Louis XVIII in 1814.

6. William Pitt, first Earl of Chatham (1708–78), English statesman and orator, twice virtual prime minister; Nathaniel Bailey (d. 1742), English lexicographer, first published in 1721 his *An Universal Etymological English Dictionary*, which not only defined words but contained instructions for pronouncing them as well.

is manifest enough of the extreme delight which all men take in symbols. See how fond of symbols the people are! See the great ball which they roll from Baltimore to Bunker Hill.[7] See in the political processions Lowell in a loom, and Lynn in a shoe, and Salem in a ship.[8] They fancy they hate poetry and they are all poets and mystics. Witness the striped pig, the cider barrel, the old Hickory, the log cabin, and all the cognizances of party.[9] See the national emblems, the star, the cross, the crescent, the lion, the eagle, or some similar figure on an old rag of bunting blowing in the wind on a fort in the ends of the earth make the heart beat and the blood tingle under the most civil and cultivated exterior. Hear our speech, see our dramatic exhibitions, see our dress, our furniture, our figure-heads, the ciphers on our seals and carriages, on the sleds of the children, the names of fire engines, of locomotives, and of ships. Hear the language of anger, of poetry, of love, and of religion.

What does all this love for these signs denote, if not that the relation of man to all these forms in nature is more intimate than the understanding yet suspects; and that perhaps the metamorphoses which we read in Latin or in Indian literature are not quite so fabulous as they are accounted? The soul passes through all forms. The same soul is at home in all, and ever seeks to rise from the lower to the next highest.

Who knows but more is meant than yet appears? Every gardener can change his flowers and leaves into fruit, and so perhaps is this man who astonishes the senate or the parlor by the splendor of his conversation, who seems to stride over all limits,—this genius who today can upheave and balance and toss every object in nature for his metaphor, capable in his next appearance in human nature of playing such a game with his hands instead of his brain. An instinctive suspicion that this may befall, seems to have crept into the mind of men. Genius may be dangerous. What would happen to us who live on the surface, if this fellow in some new transmigration should have acquired power to do what he now delights to say? He must be watched. Who shall set limits to the soul? Caius Gracchus dies imprecating slavery on the Romans, a prayer granted in no long time.[10] The soul goes forth to do what it prayed might be done.

7. The ceremonies for the laying of the cornerstone for the Bunker Hill Monument in Charlestown, Massachusetts, were on 17 June 1825, and the monument, which celebrated a battle during the American Revolution, was completed 17 June 1843; for the great ball that rolled from Baltimore to Bunker Hill see *JMN*, 7:379, 394.

8. Emerson refers to three Massachusetts towns: Lowell, famous for its textile mills; Lynn, at one time the women's shoe–manufacturing center of the world; and Salem, a major seaport.

9. *A History of the Striped Pig* (1838), a temperance pamphlet, describes the pig's death and post-mortem examination to show how the pig symbolized all drinking men; "Old Hickory" was the nickname of Andrew Jackson (1767–1845), seventh president of the United States (1829–1837); the cider barrel and the log cabin were campaign symbols, emphasizing his frontier origins, for William Henry Harrison (1773–1841), ninth president of the United States (1841, died of pneumonia after one month in office).

10. Gaius Sempronius Gracchus (153–121), Roman statesman, advocated limiting the power of the Roman Senate and courts in order to control corruption, committed suicide during a riot.

Meantime with all this passion and fury to be explained and expressed, and all this plastic world of objects yielding itself as a dictionary, adequate intellectual expression is very rare. Sufficient vent is got to prevent suffocation, we wriggle into some sort of nest or hole that will fit the body, into some mode of action that will employ our talent, get some grist between the stones to save the mill from grinding itself, but we do not get beyond serving the present distress, we do not attain to an example or universal picture and demonstration of the talent that is born with us to this time and to all time. Go into a senate or other assembly of public debate and listen to the speakers. It is easy to see that every man represents a new and perfect style of oratory, and each, if he speak long enough, and the matter is important enough to show his genius, will actually come to the verge of good deliverance;—comes so near that the professional poet or orator begins to feel himself quite superfluous:—What need of the deputy, when here the principal can state his own case? But neither of the speakers quite hits it, and none does, of thousands and thousands; and in a nation the one or two who do best, are separated by a whole length from all the rest. And this in the expression of right and wrong respecting their own affairs.

An obscure old instinct revives in the beholder, that this man who does what the beholder had panted in vain to do, or said what he was bursting to speak, is himself, himself with some advantages,—and he begins to love him as himself. We love, we worship the expressors of that which we have at heart. We forgive every crime to them. The head of a party can do no wrong. This is true of excellence in every department, of the genius in mechanics, in military command, in music, in dancing, in eloquence, in the fine arts, but most of all in intellect.

For whilst we are able to do some justice to our private thought upon those facts which concern private and particular duties, we find much more difficulty in giving any expression to their great, general, and universal relations. I know not how it is that we all should need an interpreter but so it happens that the great majority of men seem to be minors who have not yet come into possession of their own, cannot quite report the conversation we have had with nature. To no man is his position in the world, to no man are the sun and stars, the hills and waters quite indifferent objects, yet there seems a little too much phlegm in our constitution to allow them to make their due effect. Too feeble fall the impressions of our sense upon us to make us artists. Every touch should thrill. Now it is made with sufficient vivacity for knowledge but not for poetry or an adequate report. It would seem as if every man should be so much an artist that he could report in conversation what had befallen him.

Now the Poet is the person in whom these demands are answered, the person without impediment, who by the favor of God is sent into the world to see clearly what others have glimpses of, to feel richly what they suspect, to gaze with sound senses and responding heart at full leisure, and in a trance of delight, at the heavens and the earth; a soul through which the universe is poured,—into his eyes, and it comes forth not a blur, but a fair picture; into his ears, and it comes forth not a squeak nor a scream, but a song of rich and overflowing beauty: the complete man, who traverses the whole scale, who is at home in gaiety and in tears; in rich men's palaces and in poor men's huts; in the desarts of nature and the galleries of art;— the hospitable soul, which entertains in its spirit all travellers, tongues, kindreds, all employments, all eccentricities, all crimes even, in its vast charity and overcoming hope. Man knowing and man speaking is he. This is he whose speech is music; who gives name to whatever he beholds, and the name clings thenceforward: who announces news—the only teller of news, of news that never gets old—not in a thousand years. It is he who atones for all calamities and short comings, who gives a reason for the beauty of nature and revives hope in the heart. He adores the adorable: "He is the guardian of admiration in the hearts of the people;"[11] he is not free, but freedom; he is not tasteful, but he is taste: he is not the beneficiary but the benefactor of the world, and is the representative of man, in virtue of being the largest power to give and to receive. He is the man whose being soars higher and sinks deeper than another's, to a softer tenderness, a holier ardor, a grander daring. This is the man who makes all other men seem less, the very naming of whose name is ornamental and like good news, and the sound of his words for ages makes the heart beat quicker, and the eye glisten, and fills the air with golden dreams.

And Nature who gave to poets this high representative office and wished them to stand for the Intellect and not for the Will, did not make them blackhaired, hotheaded, and violent men, but of fair complexion and gentle manners: for she meant that they should not need any physical force or weapons to defend them, but that the love and pride of all mankind should shield and cherish them.

The universal knower and singer, he must have an universal experience. Nothing exists unrelated to him: he is covetous of sweet and of bitter things, of simple and of artificial experiences. He cannot spare any grief or pain or terror: he wants every rude stroke that has been dealt on his irritable texture: he hangs out his life like an Aeolian harp in a tree, where every wind from the northern tempest to the softest breath of southwestern air may play on it.[12] He needs his fear and his superstition as much as his purity and courage, as notes for the anthem which he is to compose. Pain has a new aspect for such a man. This wonderful gift of expression is a charmed life and turns bane to antidote. "Some god gave me the power to tell what I suffer," said a poet. This made the curse a benediction. Do not judge the poet's life to be sad, because of his plaintive verses and confessions of despair. Because he was able to cast off his sorrows into these writings, therefore went he

11. Attributed to Felicia Dorothea Hemans (1793–1835), English romantic poet, by Emerson (*JMN*, 7:154).

12. An aeolian harp is a box-shaped string instrument that produces various tones when the strings are touched by the wind.

onward free and serene to new experiences. You must be a poet also to draw a just inference as to what he was, from all the records, be they never so rich, which he has left. Did you hear him speak? His speech did great injustice to his thought. It was either better or worse. He gave you the treasures of his memory, or he availed himself of a topic rich in allusions to express hopes gayer than his life entertains, or sorrows lamented with an energy and religion which was an intellectual play, and not the habit of his character. You shall not know his love or his hatred from his speech and behavior. Cold and silent he shall be in the circle of those friends whom, when absent, his heart walks with and talks with evermore. Face to face with that friend who for the time is unto him the essence of night and morning, of the sea and land, the only equal and worthy incarnation of thought and faith, silence and gloom shall overtake him, his talk shall be arid and trivial. There is no deeper dissembler than the sincerest man. Do not trust his blushes, for he blushes not at his affection but at your suspicion. Do not trust his actions, for they are expiations and fines often, with which he has amerced himself and not the indications of his desire.[13] Do not conclude his ignorance or his indifference from his silence. Do not think you have all his thought when you have heard his speech to the end. Do not judge him worldly and vulgar, because he respects the rich and well bred, for to him the glittering symbol has a beauty it has not to other eyes, and his heart dances with delight in which no envy and no meanness are mixed. Him the circumstance of life dazzles and overpowers whilst it passes, because he is so delicate a meter of every influence. You shall find him noble at last, noble in his privacy, noble in his dealing.

Swedenborg had this vice that he nailed one sense to each image;—one and no more.[14] But in nature every word we speak is million faced or convertible to an indefinite number of applications. If it were not so we could read no book. For, each sentence would only fit the single case which the author had in view. Dante who described his circumstance would be unintelligible now.[15] But a thousand readers in a thousand different years and towns shall read his story, and find it a version of their story.

There is nothing which comes out of the human heart—the deep aboriginal region,—which is not mundane, thousand faced,—so that if perchance strong light falls on it, it will admit of being shown to be related to all things. The rose is a type of youth and mirth to one eye, of profound melancholy, of fever, of rushing fate to another. There is nothing in nature which is not an exponent of all nature.

The sense of nature is inexhaustible. You think you know the meaning of these tropes of nature, and today you come into a new thought, and lo! all nature converts

13. Amerced, to be fined at the discretion of a court.
14. Emanuel Swedenborg (1688–1772), Swedish scientist, theologian, and mystic.
15. Dante Alighieri (1265–1321), Italian poet, author of the *Divina commedia* (completed in 1321), which recounts the poet's journey through Hell, Purgatory, and Paradise.

itself into a symbol of that; and you see it has been chanting that song like a cricket ever since the creation. Nature is a tablet in which any sense may be inscribed, only not anything cunning, and consciously vicious. Draw the moral of the river, the rock and the ocean. The river, the rock and the ocean say "Guess again."

And what is the weapon which the poet wields? What the materials and means of his power? Verse or Metrical Language. Language, the half god, language, the most spiritual of all the works of man, yet language subdued by music—an organ or engine, it must be owned, scarcely less beautiful than the world itself, a fine translation into the speech of man of breezes and waves and ripples, the form and lights of the sky, the color of clouds and leaves. As the world is round, and not square,—as bodies have shadows; and sounds, echoes; and meeting balls a rebound; as there is beauty in a row of balls, or posts, or buildings, or trees, or statues, beyond their beauty as individuals, so is there a beauty in rhythm or metre, whereof rhyme is one instance, which has its origin in the pulse and constitution of man, and will never be quite absent from sane speech. Rhyme is one of its primary or rudest forms. The child sings or chaunts its first words, sings or chaunts before it talks, as we say. Poetry, in like manner, is found in the literature of all nations to precede prose. But the ear soon finds that there are finer measures than the coarse psalmody which tinkled in the nursery, and wondering it listens after that sweet beauty, as the eye pines over the colors of a gem, or the transparency of water or of glass. By and by it learns the secret, that love and thought always speak in measure or music,—that with the elevation of the soul, the asperities and incoherence of speech disappear, and the language of truth is always pure music. We are very far from having reached the term of our knowledge on this subject. How can we, unless we had reached the boundaries of thought and feeling? The finer poet, the finer ear. Each new poet will as certainly invent new metres as he will have new images to clothe. In true poetry, the thought and the metre are not painfully adjusted afterward, but are born together, as the soul and the body of a child. The difference between poetry and what is called "stock poetry," I take to be this, that in *stock poetry* the metre is given and the verses are made to it, and in poetry the sense dictates the tune or march of the words.

I think a person of poetical temperament cannot indulge his veins of sentiment without perceiving that the finest rhythms and cadences of poetry are yet unfound, and that in that purer state which his thoughts prophesy, rhythms of a faery and dreamlike music shall enchant us, compared with which the happiest measures of English poetry are psalm-tunes. I think even now, that the very finest and sweetest closes and falls are not in our metres, but in the measures of prose eloquence which have greater variety and richness than verse.

In the history of civilization, Rhyme may pass away, yet it will always be remembered as a consecrated and privileged invention possessing what I may call certain rights of sanctuary. Herein it resembles music, viz. in the privilege of speaking the truth,—not apparent but spiritual truth, which is not allowed to prose. Music is the uncultivated man's Parnassus.

With the very first note of the flute or horn, with the first strain of a song we quit the world of common sense and launch at once into the sea of ideas and emotions. Every note is an insult to all the common sense that has been droning in our ears all day. It gives it the lie. I seem to hear nothing but mocks and laughter in those tripping, lilting, faery sounds, which speak of love and moonlight, of wildness and dreams, and all audacious, extravagant, religious, and tender themes. Yet the sturdiest proser sits by and is silent. Say one half so much treason in articulate speech, and he would open his logic upon you by the hour. But the tune makes wild holiday. Well, the like allowance is the prescriptive right of poetry. You shall not speak truth in prose: You may in verse. In verse, you *may* treat the good Uncles and Aunts of this world and all the solemn matters that pass for so great in the street as pepper corns, and make them dance and sing again, and because it is poetry, no man shall forbid you.

This fact is by no means unimportant, as in this way poetry serves a great office to mankind in keeping before the mind of the most critical and unbelieving age those cardinal truths and ideas which make the religion of man, and which would be rejected and insulted, if stated in the newspaper, but when spoken in verse disarm criticism, and for the music's sake are allowed currency in the circles most committed to an opposite creed,—where they serve to mitigate and modify manners and laws, and keep the door open to a better knowledge. So that it has been well said by those who hope highest of the present time, that "the poetry of the Old Church is the philosophy of the New."

But the poet, as we intimated at the outset, is not to be painted in parts. When we have told all our anecdotes of detail, there yet remains the total wonder. We must add then the fact that no enumeration of particulars brings us nearer to an explanation; for poetry is always a miracle not to be explained or disposed of, a miracle to the hearer; a miracle to the poet; he admires his verses as much as you do, when they are the right inspiration; he cannot tell where or how he had them. The sign of genius is originality: its word cannot be guessed: it is new, yet tallies with all we know: it has an expected unexpectedness, a new oldness. The bee flies among the flowers and gets mint and marjoram and makes a new product which is not mint or marjoram but honey; and the chemist mixes hydrogen and oxygen to yield a new product which is not hydrogen or oxygen but water; and the poet listens to all conversations, and receives all objects of nature, to give back, not them, but a new, perfect and radiant whole. Whence the new proceeded, is the secret of nature. Only what is new delights us, for it is the last communication from God. I must know that the scholar who wrote, *only* wrote, and did not alter it: as I know a poet who had the honesty to say that he valued his poems not because they were his, but because they were not.[16]

We are a little afraid of poetry,—afraid to write and afraid to read it; are we not? We do not very willingly trust ourselves on the back of that wild winged horse of the Muses, ignorant whither he will carry us and where we shall alight.[17] Surprise and wonder always fly beside him. There is no poetry where they are not. Poetry ever descends like a foreign conqueror from an unexpected quarter of the horizon, carries us away with our wives and children, our flocks and herds, into captivity, to make us, at a later period, adopted children of the new land, and, in the end, to disclose to us, that this is really our native country.

And yet, as nothing so much concerns us as the question, if it can be a question, whether Poetry is possible in the present time.

Why not? What is poetry but the truest expression? and if the *thing* exists, so will its expression follow. It may not appear in quarters or in forms where we look for it; in such, namely, as it availed itself of in the last, or in earlier generations: for Nature does not repeat herself, but invents. How unlike is each to the last preceding! After Dante, and Shakspeare, and Milton, there came no grand poet until Swedenborg in a corner of Europe, hitherto uncelebrated, sung the wonders of man's heart in strange prose poems which he called "Heaven and Hell," the "Apocalypse Revealed," the "Doctrine of Marriage," "Celestial Secrets" and so on, and which rivalled in depth and sublimity, and in their power to agitate this human heart— this lover of the wild and wonderful,—any song of these tuneful predecessors.[18] Slowly but surely the eye and ear of men are turning to feed on that wonderful intellect, and severing the wheat from the chaff.

But nature never pauses. Whilst we admire and exaggerate one genius, and, perhaps, after a century or two, have learned to appreciate it, she throws into our neighborhood another and another to be the study and astonishment of other times and distant eyes.

We have suffered ourselves to live so sensually that we have defiled our own houses to that degree that they suggest to us places of indulgence and mere comfort or outward convenience, and not the residence of sacred and awful pleasures, so that when poetry and the joys of the imagination are spoken of, we instantly run

16. Attributed to Jones Very (1813–80), American poet and essayist, by Emerson (*JMN*, 8:52; *TN*, 3:64). Very wrote his most effective verse during an eighteen-month period beginning in the fall of 1838, when he felt himself infused with the Holy Spirit, making him a mere vehicle through which the Holy Word passed. Under Emerson's patronage Very published his poems in 1839.

17. The "wild winged horse of the Muses" is Pegasus.

18. John Milton (1608–74), English poet and political writer, best known for his poem *Paradise Lost* (published in 1667 in ten books); Swedenborg's *A Treatise Concerning Heaven and Its Wonders, and Also Concerning Hell* (1823), *The Apocalypse Revealed* (1836), *Love in Marriage* (1768), and *Arcana coelestia* (1749–56), which is sometimes translated as *A Disclosure of the Heavenly Depths in Sacred Scripture or the Word of the Lord.*

from home to seek for it; we run into memory, we run into futurity, into early youth, into cottages, into mines, into feudal keeps, or Arab tents, or Iceland huts underground. And yet the genius of Poetry is here. He worships in this land also, not by immigration but he is Yankee born. He is in the forest walks, in paths carpeted with leaves of the chestnut, oak, and pine; he sits on the mosses of the mountain; he listens by the echoes of the wood; he paddles his canoe in the rivers and ponds. He visits without fear the factory, the railroad, and the wharf. When he lifts his great voice, men gather to him and forget all that is past, and then his words are to the hearers, pictures of all history; and immediately the tools of their bench, and the riches of their useful arts, and the laws they live under, seem to them weapons of romance. As he proceeds, I see their eyes sparkle, and they are filled with cheer and new faith. Every achievement looks possible to them, and the evils of life are ebbing away. In strange, improbable places,—perhaps, as we said, not so much in metrical forms, as in eloquence,—we may detect the poetic genius.

You may find it, though rarely, in Senates,—when the forest has cast out some wild, black-browed bantling, some great boy, to show the same energy in the crowd of officials, which he had learned in driving cattle to the hills, or in scrambling through thickets in a winter forest, or through the swamp and river for his game. In the folds of his brow, in the majesty of his mien, nature shall vindicate her son; and even in that strange and perhaps unworthy place and company, remind you of the lessons taught him in earlier days by the torrent, in the gloom of the pine woods, when he was the companion of crows and jays and foxes, and a hunter of the bear.

Perhaps you may find it in some lowly Bethel by the seaside where a hard-featured, scarred, and wrinkled methodist whose face is a network of cordage becomes the poet of the sailor and the fisherman, whilst he pours out the abundant streams of his thought through a language all glittering and fiery with imagination.[19] A man who never knew the looking-glass or the critic; a man whom patronage never made, and whom praise cannot spoil; a man who conquers his audience by infusing his soul into them, and speaks by the right of being the person in the assembly who has the most to say, and so makes all other speakers seem puny and cowardly before his face. For the time his exceeding life throws all other gifts into deep shade, "philosophy speculating on its own breath," taste, learning, and all; and yet how willingly every man consents to be nothing in this presence, to share this surprising emanation, and be steeped and ennobled in the new wine of this eloquence. It instructs in the power of man over men! We feel that a man is a Mover,—to the extent of his being a Power, and in contrast with the efficiency thus suggested, our actual life and society appears a dormitory. We are taught that

19. Identified as Edward Thompson Taylor (1793–1871), American clergyman, chaplain of Seamen's Bethel Chapel in Boston, by Emerson (*JMN*, 7:359–60). He served as the original for Father Mapple in Herman Melville's *Moby-Dick*.

earnest, impassioned action is most our own, and invited to try the deeps of love and wisdom,—we who have been players and paraders so long.

But in purer forms than these will it rise—the poetic genius of the time,—in forms not unworthy of nature which it is to represent; in forms which shall not need, like these, to be praised with a grain of allowance, but which shall speak in tones that enrich and elevate those who hear. The Poet shall yet arrive—the fortunate, the adapted, the timely man, whose heart domesticated in Ideas sees them proclaimed in the face of the world of this Hour, in the men and women of today, and their institutions and covenants, their houses and shops;—who coupling what we do with what we are, the last effect with the first cause, shall search the heart and soul with every word he speaks, and in his lightest and gayest mood,—painting as if for idleness the creaking wagon or the poultry stepping round the farmhouse door,—scatters with every picture insights and presentiments, hopes and fears, and gives to the old dull track of daily life more than the blush and wonder of a lover's dream.

To doubt that the poet will yet appear is to doubt of day and night. Wherever there is a fact there must follow the expression of the same. Shall the grass grow with its wonted rankness; shall the water flow as silver-clear; and the light stream up the morning sky with no dimness in its ray,—and the higher life, which these things tend upward unto and predict, fail of its ripeness and advent? These are fears of the drowsy and the blind. New topics, new powers, a new spirit arise, which threaten to abolish all that was called poetry, in the melodious thunder of the new.

There is a great destiny which comes in with this as with every age, colossal in its traits, terrible in its strength, which cannot be tamed, or criticised or subdued. It is shared by every man and every woman of the time, for they are as leaves on this tree which bears them. In solid phalanx the generation comes on; the pattern of their features is new in the world: all wear the same expression, but it is that which they do not detect in each other. The Genius of the time is one Spirit, but of many operations. One and the same it ponders in the philosophers, drudges in the craftsmen, dreams in the poets, dilates in the love of woman. It is full of romance: the roughest Scythian or Troglodyte of old is not more rude with aboriginal force than this Spirit is.[20] It inspires every exertion that is made. It makes life sweet to all who breathe it. It is this which the ambitious seek power that they may controul: this they wish to be rich that they may buy; when they marry, it is out of love of this; when they study it is this which they pore after; this which they aim to read and write and carve and paint and build. It is new in the Universe: it is the attraction of time: it is the last work of the Creator: Calm and perfect it lies on the brow of the enormous eternity: and if in the superior recesses of nature there be

20. The Scythians were a tribe of nomadic people who lived in southeastern Europe during ancient times; Troglodytes were savages who lived in caves.

any abode for permanent spectators, what is there they would hang upon but this, the cumulative result, the new morning with all its dews, rich with the spoils of foregoing time? Is there not a strange folly to fear whilst the world stands here and we in it, that the day of poetry and creation is past? Is there not something droll to see the darlings of this age, those for whom a happy birth and circumstance and the rarest influences of Culture have done the most,—timid and querulous, ignorant of this mighty support which upbears them—ignorant of this resistless onward Fate, which makes the Individual nothing,—to hear them interrupt the awe and gladness of the time with their officious lamentations that they are critical and know too much? If ever anybody had found out how so much as a ryestraw was made! They seem to me torn up in a whirlwind, borne by its force they know not whence, they know not whither, yet settling their faces and their robes in the moment when they fly by me with this self-crimination of impertinent melancholy. But the grandeur of our life exists in spite of us—all over and under and within us,—in what of us is inevitable and above our control. Men are facts as well as persons, and the involuntary part of their life is so much, as to fill all their wonder, and leave them no countenance to say anything of what is so trivial as their private thinking and doing.

We are all poets at last, and the life of each has high and solemn moments which remind him of that fact in a manner he cannot choose but understand. Each of us is a part of eternity and immensity, a god walking in flesh, and the wildest fable that was ever invented, is less strange than this reality. Let us thank the poets as men who saw and celebrated this marvel whilst we slept.

New England:
Genius, Manners, and Customs

(1843–1844)

"New England: Genius, Manners, and Customs" was the most popular of five lectures associated with Emerson's *New England* series, which he delivered in Baltimore, Philadelphia, New York City, and Providence, Rhode Island, in 1843 and 1844. Typically, this lecture served as the third in the series, with "The Genius and National Character of the Anglo-Saxon Race" serving as the first lecture, "The Trade of New England" the second, "New England: Recent Literary and Spiritual Influences" the fourth, and "Tendencies" (or "Results and Tendencies") the fifth; with the exception of "Tendencies," all of these lectures survive (*Later Lectures*, 1:7–18, 19–38, and 57–70, respectively). However, Emerson routinely switched the order and the titles of his lectures on New England as he delivered the series from place to place, and he also routinely moved text from one lecture to another—even in the same delivery of the series. The complex genealogy of the *New England* series brings into stark relief the difference between Emerson's early and later lecturing practices. Whereas Emerson typically lectured from relatively stable texts up to and through 1842, the majority of lectures that he delivered between the mid-1840s and the close of his career as a lecturer in the 1870s show him engaged in the wholesale reworking of individual lectures and in rethinking and reordering lectures within and outside of series.

Emerson also read "New England: Genius, Manners, and Customs" as a lecture independent of the *New England* series, delivering it under titles such as "The Genius, Manners and Character of the New England People," "New England Character," "The Characteristics of New England," "New England," and "The New England Man." The title used for this lecture is taken from the title under which the lecture was advertised when Emerson delivered it on 17 February 1843 as the third lecture in a *New England* series at the New York Society Library. On that occasion this lecture followed "The Trade of New England," the theme of which Emerson references in his opening paragraph here as "the spirit of commerce which so strongly characterizes the English race in both hemispheres."

In my last lecture, I attempted to sketch some of the historical manifestations of the spirit of commerce which so strongly characterizes the English race in both hemispheres, and I enumerated the good results with their limitations which have flowed therefrom in New England. In the present lecture, I proceed to add some details that may still farther fill up the portrait of this race. Many of my remarks are of a miscellaneous character. I am not careful that they are not. A principal object with me is to name, (in any order), if I can, the chief facts in the recent literary and spiritual history of New England, believing that if we can rightly select those, we write the history of history: for it is to these that the mere recorder of facts must come at last. Neither is it to me of any importance to confine my sketches to a geographical section, for I am well aware that as soon as we say anything deep and true, it keeps no territorial limits. The heart is the citizen of every country, and so is strength of character. National characteristics, as soon as a man is well awake, give way to individual ones: as physicians say that fever in every new constitution is a new malady.

The national traits which have for ages distinguished the English race are for the most part very obvious in the New England character, only qualified by the new circumstances of a wide land, a sparse population, and a democratic government. The traits of the Englishman are found throughout America, so that to foreign nations it very naturally appears only an extension of the same people. In New England, where the population is most homogeneous and most English, they are very purely preserved, so as to give rise to the remark, that the Yankee is double distilled English. The British family is expanded, but not altered. The national traits are the same for centuries. We see at this moment only the demonstration of the thoughts which were already ripe in the beginning of the seventeenth century, when the Religious War drove the Puritans to America. The two main points by which the English nation was then distinguished, the two points by which they attached themselves to the heavens and the earth, to the mind and to matter, namely, Conscience and Common Sense, or, in view of their objects, the love of Religion and the love of Commerce,—Religion and Trade,—are still the two hands by which they hold the dominion of the globe.

I have elsewhere had occasion to speak at length of these two topics, the Religion and the Trade of New England; I shall not engage in their development this evening. My aim is to attempt some sketches of some remarkable particulars in the character and tendencies of the New England Man.

He is the old England man in a new place and new duties; and it is very easy to see the influence of his geographical position as a native of the seashore, and of a high latitude, in the modification of his character, distinguishing him not only from the European, but also from his fellow citizen of the interior and of the southern states.

A person of strong understanding, working to surround himself with defences against an extreme climate and a niggard soil, and gaining his victories over nature by successive expedients, as, by clothing, by warm building, by stove and furnace, and improved husbandry, his behaviour does not bely him. The Indian who puts out his fire, and hunts, eats, and sleeps in the snow; or the emigrant who quits a northern parallel and takes up his abode in a warmer clime,—these may be said each *at a single stroke* to relieve themselves of the long war with the elements, which the northern white man sustains. He, on the other hand, contests the field by inches, and his mind acquires the habit of detail, and his strength is that of caution, of forecast, of arithmetic, which accomplishes wonders, at last, by means of aggregation; builds a city, for example,—a noble and dazzling result, by a continual repetition of very easy acts. But the Indian who flings himself into the snow, or the Southerner who resigns himself to the grand influences of nature with boundless leisure to enjoy them, becomes more easily the home of great and generous sentiments. He is not accustomed to check his charitable or his romantic purpose by too narrow a computation of the methods, and he is a much more natural, graceful, and heroic actor, inasmuch as he is more impulsive. This contrast of character is exhibited very strongly every day wherever the Northerner and Southerner meet; not only in results—tabulated results of trade, manufactures, of civil and criminal legislation,—but especially where the races face each other, as in the northern colleges, where young men from different sections often meet; and, most of all, in the city of Washington, where they face each other full-grown, and these contrasts are seen in full breadth. The Southerner lives for the moment, relies on himself, and conquers by personal address. He is wholly there in that thing which is now to be done. The Northerner lives for the year, and does not rely on himself, but on the whole apparatus of means he is wont to employ, and is only half-present when he comes in person: he has a great reserved force which is coming up. The result corresponds. The Southerner is haughty, wilful, generous, unscrupulous,— who will have his way, and has it. The Northerner must think the thing over, and his conscience and his commonsense throw a thousand obstacles between him and his wishes, which perplex his decision and unsettle his behaviour. The Northerner always has the advantage of the Southerner at the end of ten years; and the Southerner always has the advantage today.

I am far from wishing to exaggerate the peculiarities of districts of the country; the grand principles of probity and of beauty are far deeper in man than that a line or two of latitude or a difference of employment will make any important change. They underlie the differences of habit I have spoken of, and the great ideas of modern times are equally honoured with slight differences of costume throughout the Republic.

The traits which I prefer to consider are those moral agents which have been of importance in the history of our people as restraints on the spirit of economy and commerce, which their position generated. The flagrant feature in our history down to a quite recent period, was its religious character, as indeed the planting of New England was the work of the most religious nation in their most religious epoch.

Beside the direct culture of the conscience and the general probity which this hereditary religious sentiment generates, I trace to this strong Calvinism other great and salutary results to the character of the New England people. First, namely, the culture of the intellect, which has always been found in the Calvinistic Church.[1] The religious are always disposed to give to their children a more liberal discipline of books, of schools, and of liberal conversation, a fact borne out by all history— but especially by the history of New England. The Colony was planted in 1620: In 1638, Harvard College was founded.

The General Court of Massachusetts in 1647, "To the end that learning may not perish in the graves of our forefathers, *Ordered*; that every township after the Lord had increased them to the number of fifty householders shall appoint one to teach all children to write and read; and where any town shall increase to the number of one hundred families, they shall set up a grammar school, the masters thereof being able to instruct youth so far as they may be fitted for the university." Many and rich are the fruits of that simple statute. The universality of an elementary education in New England is her praise and her power in the whole world.

To the school succeeds the village Lyceum, now very general throughout the country towns, where every week through the winter lectures are read and debates sustained which prove a college for the young farmer. Hence, it happens that young farmers and mechanics who work all summer in the field or shop, in the winter often go into a neighbouring town to teach the district school arithmetic and grammar. As you know, New England supplies annually a large detachment of preachers, and schoolmasters, and private tutors to the interior of the South and West. Great numbers less critically instructed, yet still with some smattering of letters, are employed by the Connecticut bookdealers as book agents to travel in the interior and vend their editions. And it sometimes happens that a poor man's son in Connecticut, whose intellect is superior, who would fain go to college, but has not money, escapes from hard labour for which his finer organization unfits him, finds someone to trust him with wares, and goes as a pedlar into Virginia and Carolina that so he may, at a small expense, see the world, converse with men, and by intercourse with more polished persons than his native village can exhibit, supply the defects of his limited and humble training. One of the most intellectual men I have ever seen had his training so.[2]

1. John Calvin (originally Jean Cauvin) (1509–64), French Protestant reformer and theologian; Calvinism was a major influence on Puritanism and the Presbyterian Church in Scotland.

2. This is Amos Bronson Alcott (1799–1888), American Transcendentalist, teacher, writer, and Emerson's longtime friend and Concord neighbor.

It is a remark frequently made by those who are conversant with New England that such is the high value universally attached to a superior education, that no political or religious prejudices are suffered to stand in its way. If the Catholics have a good school, or if the Unitarians have a good college, the most devoted adherents of other and conflicting sects will send their daughters or sons to these seminaries. It only needs a confidence that a superior culture is really to be had there, to bring as many pupils as are desired.

This is precisely the most agreeable picture which the Northern portion of the country has to show, the universality of a good elementary culture. If you ask me for the best result in this region, compared with the best advantages of other nations, I shall point you to a very common but always affecting spectacle,—the poor but educated family. Who can see unmoved the eager blushing boys discharging, as they can, their household chores, and hastening into the sitting-room to the study of tomorrow's merciless lesson: yet stealing time to read a novel hardly smuggled into the tolerance of father and mother: atoning for the same by some pages of Plutarch or Goldsmith; the warm sympathy with which they kindle each other in schoolyard or in barn and wood-shed.[3]

If in New England the climate and the commerce powerfully tended to generate that spirit of detail which is not grand and enlarging, but which goes rather to pinch the features and degrade the character, the religious spirit, always enlarging, firing man, prompting the pursuit of the vast, the beautiful, the unattainable, was especially necessary as an antidote. In the midst of our laborious, and economical, and rude, and awkward population, where is little elegance and no facility, with great accuracy in details, little spirit of society, or knowledge of the world, you shall yet not unfrequently meet that refinement which no education and no habit of society can confer, which makes the elegance of wealth look stupid, and which unites itself by natural affinity to the highest minds of the world, and nourishes itself on Plato and Dante, Michel Angelo and Milton; on whatever is pure and sublime in art, and I may say, which gave a hospitality in that country to the spirit of Coleridge and Wordsworth, and now to the music of Beethoven, before yet their genius had found a hearty welcome in Great Britain.[4]

I pass now to a topic not remotely related to the last,—to consider, namely, the

3. Plutarch (ca. 46–ca. 120), Greek historian best known for his series of "lives," or character studies, arranged in pairs in which a Greek and a Roman are compared; Oliver Goldsmith (1730–74), British writer, poet, and playwright born in Ireland.

4. Plato (ca. 428–348 B.C.), the most famous of the Greek philosophers; Dante Alighieri (1265–1321), Italian poet and Christian humanist; Michelangelo (1475–1564), Italian painter, sculptor, and poet; John Milton (1608–74), English poet and political writer, best known for his poem *Paradise Lost* (published in 1667 in ten books); Samuel Taylor Coleridge (1772–1834), English poet and philosopher and, with William Wordsworth (1770–1850), English poet, founder of the romantic movement; Ludwig van Beethoven (1770–1827), German composer, wrote many of his greatest works after losing his hearing in 1798.

taste for eloquence, native to every people, and in which every man is a competitor, but always favoured by the institutions of republics.

The thirst of our people for eloquence is often remarked, and in the cities of New England it finds every year more opportunities of gratification. Faneuil Hall is one of our best schools. Join the dark and closing groups that gather in the old house when fate hangs on the vote of the morrow. As the crowd grows and the hall fills, behold that solid block of life,—few old men, mostly young and middle aged, with shining heads and swollen veins. Much of the speaking shall no doubt be slovenly and tiresome. Then, the excited multitude predominates, is all the time interlocutor, and the air grows electric, and the multitude appear or disappear according to the success of the speaker. The pinched, wedged, elbowed, sweltering assembly, as soon as the speaker loses their ear, by the tameness of his harangue, feel sorely how ill accommodated they are, forget all politics and patriotism, and attend only to themselves and the coarse outcries which are made all around them. They back, push, resist, and fill the hall with cries of tumult. The speaker stops; the moderator persuades, commands, entreats; the speaker at length gives way. At last, the chosen man rises, the soul of the people, in whose bosom beats audibly the common heart. With his first words he strikes a note which all know. As he catches the light spirit of the occasion, his voice alters, vibrates, pierces the private ear of everyone: the mob quiets itself somehow,—everyone being magnetized, and the house hangs waiting on the lips of one man. Each man whilst he hears, thinks he too can speak, and, in the pauses of the orator, bursts forth the splendid voice of four or five thousand men in full cry,—the grandest sound in nature. If a dull speaker come again, instantly our poor wedges begin to feel their pains, and strive and cry.

New England is faithfully represented in her orators. The person most dear to the Yankees, of course, must be a person of very commanding understanding with every talent for its adequate expression. 'The American,' foreigners say, 'always reasons,' and their orator is the most American of the Americans. He should be a man of great good sense, always pertinent to time and place, with an eye to the simple facts of nature, the hour of the day, the neighborhood of the mountains or the sea, yet with sparing notice of these things, whilst he clings closely to the business-part of his speech; a man of gravity who trusts to his plain strength of statement for the attention of his assembly; a man of great fairness in debate, and who deserves his success by always carrying his points from his adversary by really taking higher ground than he: "I do not inflame, I do not exaggerate, I avoid all incendiary allusion."[5] He is one who is not at all magnetic, but the strongest intellect applied to business—intellect applied to affairs; the greatest of lawyers, and one who should rather carry points with the bench than with the jury or the caucus, and, therefore,

---

5. Emerson quotes Daniel Webster (1782–1852), American statesman and orator.

carries points with a New England caucus. He shall have no puerilities, no tricks, no academical play in any of his speeches, but as it was said of the orations of Demosthenes that they were soldiers, so the speeches of the Yankee orator should all be men of business.[6] No following shall this man have, no troop of friends except those whose intellect he fires. No sweaty mob will carry him on their shoulders. And, yet, all New England to the remotest farmhouse or lumberer's camp in the woods of Maine delights to tell and hear anecdotes of his forensic power.

But a new field for eloquence has been opened in the Lyceum, an institution not a quarter of a century old, yet singularly agreeable to the taste and habits of the New England people, and extending every year to the south and west. It is of so recent origin, that, although it is beginning already like the invention of railways, to make a new profession, we have most of us seen all the steps of its progress. In New England it had its origin in as marked a manner as such things admit of being marked, from the genius of one distinguished person, who, after his connexion with the University, read public courses of literary lectures in Boston. And as this was an epoch of much note in the recent literary history of all that portion of the country, I shall ask leave to pause a little on the recollection. That individual has passed long since into new employments, so that the influence he then exerted and which was a capital fact in the literary annals of the country, now fairly belongs to the past; and one of his old scholars will be indulged in recalling an image so pleasing.[7]

There was an influence on the young people from the genius of this eminent scholar which was almost comparable to that of Pericles in Athens. He had an inspiration which did not go beyond his head, but which made him the master of elegance. If any of my audience were at that period in Boston or Cambridge, they will easily remember, his radiant beauty of person, of a classic style; his heavy, large eye; marble lids, which gave the impression of mass which the slightness of his form needed; sculptured lips; a voice of such rich tones, such precise and perfect utterance, that, although slightly nasal, it was the most mellow, and beautiful, and correct of all the instruments of the time. The word that he spoke, in the manner in which he spoke it, became current and classical in New England.

He had in common with other distinguished members of his family, a great talent for collecting facts, and for bringing those he had to bear with ingenious felicity on the topic of the moment. Let him rise to speak on what occasion soever, a fact had always just transpired which composed with some other fact well known to the audience the most pregnant and happy coincidence. It was remarked that for a man who threw out so many facts, he was seldom convicted of a blunder.

He had a good deal of special learning, and all his learning was available for

6. Demosthenes (384–322 B.C.), Athenian statesman, regarded as the greatest Greek orator.
7. Emerson refers to Edward Everett (1794–1865), American Unitarian minister, Harvard professor, orator, and politician (*W*, 10:330).

purposes of the hour. It was all new learning, that wonderfully took and stimulated the young men. It was so coldly and weightily communicated from so command-ing a platform,—as if in the consciousness and consideration of all history and all learning,—adorned with so many simple and austere beauties of expression, and enriched with so many excellent digressions and significant quotations, that, though nothing could be conceived beforehand less attractive or, indeed, less fit for green boys from Connecticut, New Hampshire, and Massachusetts, with their unripe Latin and Greek reading, than exegetical discourses in the style of Hug, and Wolf, and Ruhnken on the Orphic and Ante-Homeric remains, yet this learning instantly took the highest place to our imagination in our unoccupied American Parnassus.[8] All his auditors felt the extreme beauty and dignity of the manner, and even the coarsest were contented to go punctually to listen for the manner, when they had found out that the subject matter was not for them. In the lecture room, he abstained from all ornament and pleased himself with the play of detailing eru-dition in a style of perfect simplicity. In the pulpit, for he was then a clergyman, he made amends to himself and his auditor for the self-denial of the professor's chair, and with an infantine simplicity still of manner, he gave the reins to his florid, quaint, and affluent fancy.

Then was exhibited all the richness of a rhetoric which we have never seen ri-valled in this country. Wonderful, how memorable were words made which were only pleasing pictures, and covered no new or valid thoughts. He abounded in sentences, in wit, in satire, in splendid allusion, in quotation impossible to forget, in daring imagery, in parable, and even in a sort of defying experiment of his own wit and skill in giving an oracular weight to Hebrew or Rabbinical words, as *Selah, Ichabod, Tekel, Mene, Upharsin,* and the like—feats which no man could better ac-complish, such was his self-command and the security of his manner. All his speech was music, and with such variety and invention, that the ear was never tired. Espe-cially beautiful were his poetic quotations. He delighted in Milton, more rarely in Byron, and sometimes in a verse from Watts, and with such sweet modulation, that he seemed to give as much beauty as he borrowed; and whatever he has quoted will be remembered by any who heard him with inseparable association with his voice and genius.[9] This eminently beautiful person was followed from church to church, wherever the fame that he would preach led, by all the most cultivated and intelli-gent youths with grateful admiration. He had nothing in common with vulgarity and infirmity, but speaking, walking, sitting was as much aloof and uncommon as

8. Johann Leonhard Hug (1765–1846), German biblical scholar; Friedrich August Wolf (1759–1824), German classicist and philologist, argued that the *Iliad* and the *Odyssey* are the work of several authors; David Ruhnken (1723–98), German classical scholar; Mount Parnassus in ancient Greece was sacred to Apollo and the Muses and thus was the seat of the arts.

9. George Gordon Byron, known as Lord Byron (1788–1824), English romantic poet; Isaac Watts (1674–1748), English theologian and hymn writer.

a star. The smallest anecdote of his behaviour or conversation was eagerly caught and repeated; and every young scholar could recite brilliant sentences from his sermons with mimicry good or bad of his voice. This influence went much farther; for he who was heard with such throbbing hearts and sparkling eyes, in the lighted and crowded churches, did not let go his hearer when the church was dismissed; but the bright image of that eloquent form followed the boy home to his bed chamber; and not a sentence was written in academic exercises, not a declamation attempted in the college chapel, but showed omnipresence of his genius to youthful heads. He thus raised the standard of writing and speaking in New England. This made every youth his defender, and boys filled their mouths with arguments to prove that the orator had a heart.

This was a triumph of Rhetoric. It was not the intellectual or the moral principles which he had to teach. It was not thoughts. When Massachusetts was full of his fame, it was not contended that he had thrown any truths into circulation. But his power lay in the magic of form; it was in the graces of manner, in a new perception of Grecian Beauty to which he had opened our eyes. And it was commonly said that he would be willing that every hearer should have a copy of his speech in his pocket: he would still be just as secure of their attention.

There was that finish about this person which is about women, and which distinguishes every piece of genius from the works of talent: that these last are more or less matured in every degree of completeness according to the time bestowed on them, but works of genius in their first and slightest form are still wholes. In every public discourse, there was nothing left for the indulgence of his hearer, no marks of late hours and anxious unfinished study, but the goddess of grace had breathed on the work a last fragrancy and glitter.

By a series of lectures largely and fashionably attended for two winters in Boston, this individual made a beginning of popular literary and miscellaneous lectures which in that region, at least, had important results. It is acquiring greater importance every day and becoming a national institution.

But a field for eloquence higher and deeper seems to me already opened in the Lyceum, an institution now in its infancy, yet growing every year into use and favor in the Atlantic cities, as our present meeting bears witness. It answers the purpose of a social meeting for both sexes in a very convenient manner, involving no expense, and no dissipation, and especially of giving an evening occupation to young men in the counting house, and so supplants the theatre and the ballroom. It gives an hour's discourse on some topic not far from the ordinary range, and by continually introducing new speakers, furnishes new topics to conversation with new means of comparison, every week. But these are the beginnings of its use. I set a higher value on it than amusement or the statement of valuable facts. I look upon it as a vent for new and higher communications than any to which we have been wont to listen. I see with pleasure that the first men in the country are put under contribution by this institution, for services which they cheerfully render, led, as I believe, by an instinct of its importance.

For this is precisely the most elastic and capacious theatre of eloquence,—absolutely unrestricted. Is it not plain that not in senates and courts, which only treat of a very narrow range of external rights, but in the depths of philosophy and poetry, the eloquence must be found that can agitate, convict, inspire, and possess us and guide men to a true peace? I look on the Lecture Room as the true Church of the coming time, and as the home of a richer eloquence than Faneuil Hall or the Capitol ever knew. For here is all that the true orator will ask, namely, a convertible audience,—an audience coming up to the house, not knowing what shall befall them there, but uncommitted and willing victims to reason and love. There is no topic that may not be treated, and no method excluded. *Here*, everything is admissible, philosophy, ethics, divinity, criticism, poetry, humor, anecdote, mimicry,—ventriloquism almost,—all the breadth and versatility of the most liberal conversation, and of the highest, lowest, personal, and local topics—all are permitted, and all may be combined in one speech. It is a panharmonicon combining every note on the longest gamut, from the explosion of cannon to the tinkle of a guitar.

It deserves the attention of such as have any truth to offer to men and will soon draw the best powers of the country to its aid. Let us, if we have any thought in our mind, try if Folly, Custom, Convention, and Phlegm cannot hear our sharp artillery. Here is a pulpit that makes the other chairs of instruction cold and ineffectual with their customary preparation for a delivery: the most decorous with fine things, pretty things, wise things, but no arrows, no axes, no nectar, no transpiercing, no loving, no enchantment. Here, the American orator shall find the theatre he needs; here, he may lay himself out utterly large, prodigal, enormous, on the subject of the hour. Here, he may dare to hope for the higher inspiration and a total transfusion of himself into the minds of men.

I please myself with the thought that this may yet be an organ of unparalleled power for the elevation of sentiment and enlargement of knowledge. Why should it not be capable of all the range whereof music is capable, and, as other nations have each their favorite instrument, as Spain her guitar, and Scotland her pibroch, and Italy a viol, and as we go eastward, cymbals and song, let the reasoning, fact loving, and moral American, not by nature a musician, yet with a hunger for eloquence, find his national music in halls opened for discourse and debate, the one leading to the other?[10] Will you let me say that I think the country will so give hospitality and hearing to its men of thought; and, as in former periods, the poet travelled as a harper from town to town, and from castle to castle, the bearer of thought and exhilaration, so now, in a manner fitting the habit of our institutions, the man of ideas and lover of beauty shall find a ready ear from his countrymen for those

---

10. Pibroch, a set of martial or mournful variations played on the Scottish Highland bagpipe.

secrets which in the solitudes of nature the muse whispered in his walks? The lover of men shall find his office foreshown by the master of English song:

> Before the starry threshold of Jove's Court
> My mansion is, where those immortal shapes
> Of bright aerial spirits live insphered
> In regions mild of calm and serene air,
> Above the smoke and stir of this dim spot
> Which men call Earth, and with low thoughted care
> Confined and pestered in this pinfold here
> Strive to keep up a frail and feverish being,
> Unmindful of the crown that virtue gives,
> After this mortal change, to her true servants
> Amongst the enthroned gods on sainted seats.
> Yet some there be, that by due steps aspire
> To lay their just hands on the golden key
> That opes the palace of eternity;
> To such my errand is.[11]

It will use less strict conventions than other assemblies or pulpits,—and invite, perhaps a bolder exercise of thought; for, with all deference to the lovers of precision and method, I think that the best method will always be a new one, new with each speaker, and proper to that which he has to say. There are, as I think, greatly higher merits than easiness of being reported. The great merit is power to excite the slumbering intellect, make it a party to the speaker's thought, and by hints and whispers even, if no more can be, from a great interior world, leave it with a renewed assurance that that world exists—and for him.

This institution, as a school of thought and reason, has vast importance as a check on the vices and insanities of the time. I have said that from the planting of New England down to a recent period, this country has been tinged with a religious spirit. But the boundless opportunity of labor and the rewards of labor opened before us have rapidly changed the genius of the people.

There is in the Anglo-Saxon race a great power of labor, and no country exhibits more results of incessant labor than New England. But is it climate, or is it hereditary temperament—the love of labour becomes usually in our people a certain fury, a storm of activity, and a necessity of excitement. Unhappily, the feature of the times seems to be a great sensualism, a headlong devotion to trade and to the conquest of the continent, and to each man as large a share of the same as he can carve for himself, and an extravagant confidence in our gregarious activity which becomes, whilst successful, a scornful materialism, but with the fatal fault of that

11. John Milton, "Comus," ll. 1–15.

habitude, of course, that it has no depth, no reserved force whereon to fall back when a reverse comes.

Our countrymen love intoxication of some sort. There is no repose in their character. All foreigners and we ourselves observe the sort of hunger, the voracity for excitement, which haunts us. Is it for food? Is it for news? Is it for money? Is it for stimulation in any form? One is drunk with rum, and one with politics, and one with barter, and one with impossible projects. Our trade is wild and incalculable. Our people are wide travellers; our steamboats explode; our ships are known at sea by the quantity of canvass they carry; our people eat fast; our houses tumble; our enterprizes are rash; our legislation fluctuating. The cases of insanity in this country are said greatly to outnumber the patients in Europe. The last President could not stand the excitement of seventeen millions of people, but died of the presidency in one month.[12] A man should have a heart and a trunk vascular and on the scale of the Croton Aqueducts or the Cloaca Maxima at Rome to bear the friction of such a Mississippi stream.[13]

We want steadiness and repose. We are too rash and sanguine to the verge of insanity. We are all resting our confidence on new arts which have been invented: on new machinery, on steam, on the glimpses of mechanical power to be derived from electricity or galvanism; on photogenic drawing, on india-rubber clothing, on lamps that shine without shadow, on stoves that burn without fuel; on clocks to be wound by the tide; on iron boats; and cast steel tools; on steam batteries, life-preservers, and diving bells.

This fury is heated by the peculiar skill and genius of the time. The great achievements that distinguish this age are its mechanical inventions. It is the age of tools. *Now*, the standing topic in all stage coaches and railroad cars, is the improved means of conveyance; and continual impatience is expressed at the slow rate of travelling; twenty five miles the hour is mere creeping; the travelling public will not long submit to such baggage-wagon pace, and wonderful are the plans of the projectors which fill the columns of the daily press.

The men and women shall be galvanically conveyed, or may be put in large quills and propelled across the Atlantic by the pressure of the atmosphere; or dressed in diving-suits manufactured (No. 6 Tremont Street, Boston) by the Roxbury Company, and conveyed by submarine siphons, and come up near Liverpool in fountains spouting men and women; or a tunnel may run under the sea, and they may go dry-shod. In order to avoid the danger of submarine volcanoes, strenuous measures are to be adopted by the countries abutting on the two ends of the canal. It is disgraceful that every few years an earthquake should be allowed from mere want

12. William Henry Harrison did die of pneumonia within a month of taking office.

13. The Croton Aqueduct (built 1834–42) extended from southeastern New York State into New York City and brought in approximately 70 million gallons of water daily; the Cloaca Maxima was the primary drainage system of ancient Rome.

of proper ventilation to swallow a town like a custard. It only needs timely and vigorous attention from the Congress of Nations. Every boy can take out the pulp and seeds of a pumpkin and make a useful lanthorn of the same. The earth should be properly bored with an artesian well of five hundred miles diameter at the mouth and running down to the depth of three thousand, then by means of steam excavator, the mephitic gases and whatever combustibles, should be brought to the surface and sold to the gas company. And a wholesome and agreeable circulation of air should be kept up.

It may hereafter be found best, when the structure of the human body is better understood and the science of anatomy is perfect, to take passengers to pieces and transport them in the air or under the sea *in parts* chemically packed to be put together by the Transportation Company on the other side at the depot, and the greatest care given to keep the packages *identical*. These marvellous expedients are but a specimen or symbol. In like manner, a certain hurry and impatience leads our people to short ways in every department of life: in short ways to science, to religion, to literature. The race of scholars, of laborious investigators will come to an end. Our people are insatiable readers of newspapers. What acres of these sheets they run through and spend several months of the year in that pastime. And so in their intellectual and scientific training. The vice of the American is that he is too easily pleased. A curious fact in the last ten or twelve years has been the dedication of this country to the study of phrenology, proved by its modification of the language and introduction into general use of as many words as the use of steam by land and water has added.[14] I do not think this is to be wholly attributed to the facility of our people and their deceivability, but partly to the fact that the system, however rudely and coarsely, was a return to a natural instinct; it brought observation to a noble and fit object, to which too much study cannot be given. It betrayed the instinctive belief that under all these dismal masks of men, masks which we wear and which we meet, the form of man was something sacred and beautiful which should yet appear; and it showed the thirst of men for a teaching nearer to their business and bosom than any they enjoyed. Had it confined itself to a reverent accumulation of the facts, it would have been a good hint, but would have had no world's renown; but now with its speedy ascent by one jump into the chair of science, it has become a symbol of the times. Is it that we have found quicker than others the real poverty at the bottom of all this seeming affluence of life; the headlong speed with which each seeing soul comes straight through all the thin masquerade on the old fact; is it the disgust at this indigence of nature which makes these raging livers drive their steeds so hard, in the fury of living to forget the soup maigre of life?[15]

---

14. Phrenology is a way of reading a person's character through the configuration of his or her skull.
15. *Soupe-maigre*, the French term for "soup-meagre," a broth made mainly from vegetables or fish.

Phrenology especially seems to have been invented for the American people with its swift and shallow mode of disposing of the sacred secrets of nature: a man shall be a mystery no more; let me put my hand on his forehead and his hindhead; give me a pair of dividers and a foot rule, and nature cannot hide his genius where I cannot find it by inches and seconds; the recesses of human power and probity are laid open to my fingers. Character is as easily read as a placard, and the fortunes of a man are reduced to an arithmetic problem. Genius is an inflammation of the brain and conscience, a secretion of the left lobe of the heart.

Yet phrenology was modest compared with the pretensions of mesmerism.[16] The ignorant are always on the watch how to cheat nature, and, if all the stories are true, here seemed a chance to occur. Mankind were no longer to labor to come at their ends, nor to abridge their labor by dexterous physical combinations, nor to overpower physical opposition by moral force, but by a third power, by gentle touching of the knuckles, and by persuasive passes, and by coaxing, beckoning, and ogling of fingers, we could hope to raise the state of man to rare and transcendant degrees. The most stupid and perverse man when awake, once get him fast asleep in his chair, shall become an angel of light, a learned physician, a surpassing astronomer, and a telegraph so subtle and swift that he is the Paul Pry of the universe.[17]

And this is the way we will outwit the laws of Nature. With unwashed hands, and our whole day's task unattempted before us, we are grasping after new powers like some Aesop's dog snatching at the shadow of our bone.[18] We would be magians and somnambulists and see with elbows, and know the architecture in Orion, and tunnel the earth to come into pagodas of Pekin.[19] And on the first hint of such powers being attained, we will enter heaven and enter hell, go to the poles and the antipodes so, and dodge the laws and the Fates, the powers of perseverance, the graces, the virtues, all angels, all heroes, all qualities, all gods, and pierce to the courts of power and light by this dull trick. The wise gods must needs laugh heartily this once.

That nature should have subtile compensations for infirmity, and morbid actions of natural organs, and even from all this profuse treasure house of power

16. Mesmerism, a word used for a type of hypnotism, although Franz Mesmer (1734–1815), the German physician who developed the theory of animal magnetism, did not use hypnotism with his patients.

17. Paul Pry, title character of a play (produced in 1825) by the English dramatist John Poole (ca. 1786–1872) whose name came to stand for a troublesome adventurer.

18. In Aesop's fable of the dog and the shadow a dog crossed a bridge over a stream with a piece of meat in his mouth, saw his own shadow in the water, and thought it another dog with a piece of meat double his own in size. Immediately letting go of his own and fiercely attacking the other dog to get his larger piece from him, the dog thus lost both pieces of meat, because the one in the water was a shadow and his own was swept away by the stream.

19. Orion, a constellation represented on charts by the figure of a hunter with a belt and sword; named after the giant hunter slain by Artemis, Greek goddess of wild animals.

and organization some overflowings of light and vitality into crevices and chinks, is not to be doubted; but for men to choose these exceptions and anomalies instead of the law, and prefer these haloes and meteors to the sun and moon, does not do them much honor. By Lake Winnepesaukee, a man lost his feet and learned to walk on his thumbs, and now all New Hampshire is learning to walk on its thumbs, and it will presently take a great genius to convince men that feet were made to walk with.

What is most noticeable is that men who never wondered at anything, who had thought it the most natural thing in the world that they should exist in this orderly and replenished world, have been unable to suppress their amazement at the disclosures of the somnambulist. The peculiarity of mesmerism is that it drew in as inquirers and students a class of persons never on any other occasion known as students and inquirers. Of course, the inquiry is pursued on low principles. Mesmerism peeps. It becomes a black art. The uses of the thing, the commodity, the power, at once come to mind and direct the course of inquiry. It seemed to open again that door which was open to the fancy of childhood: of magicians, and faeries, and lamps of Aladdin and travelling cloaks that were to satisfy the utmost wish of the senses without danger or one drop of sweat.[20] But as Nature can never be outwitted, as no man was ever known to get a cent's worth without paying in some form or other the cent, so this prodigious promiser ends always, and always will, as sorcery and alchemy have done before, in very small and smoky performance.

It is so wonderful that a man can see without his eyes, that it never occurs to the adept that it is just as wonderful that he should see with them. And that is ever the difference between the wise and the unwise: the latter wonders at what is unusual; the wise man wonders at the usual. Well, these things are only symptomatic of the disease of the people. That repose which is the ornament and the ripeness of man is not in New England, is not in America, but hurry, and partiality, and impatience are in its room.

The whole generation is discontented with the tardy rate of growth which contents every European community. America is, therefore, the country of small adventures, of short plans, of daring risks—not of patience, not of great combinations, not of long, persistent, close-woven schemes demanding the utmost fortitude, temper, faith, and poverty. Our books are fast changing to newspapers; our reformers are slight and wearisome talkers, not man-subduing, immutable—all attracting their own task, and so charming the eye with dread and persuading without knowing that they do so. We have no Duke Wellingtons, no George Washingtons, no Miltons, Bentleys, or Seldens among our rapid and dashing race, but

---

20. Aladdin and his lamp, which houses two genii, appear in the collection of ancient Persian-Indian-Arabian traditional tales called *The Arabian Nights' Entertainments* or *A Thousand and One Nights* (1450), originally in Arabic.

abundance of Murats, of Rienzis, of Wallers, and that slight race who put their whole stake on the first die they cast.[21] The great men bequeath never their projects to their sons to finish. These eat too much pound cake. Wordsworth said,

> 'Tis the most difficult of tasks to keep
> Heights which the soul is competent to gain,

and these lines are a sort of elegy on these times, and hardly less in the clerisy or scholastic class than in the practical.[22] If we read in the books of one of the great masters of thought, in Plato, in Aristotle, or in the great thinkers of the age of Elizabeth, we are astonished at the vigor and breadth of the performance.[23] Here is no short breath and short flight, but an Atlantic strength which is everywhere equal to itself and dares great attempts because of the life with which it feels itself filled.

See the impatience of our people to rush into the lists without enduring the training. The Americans are too easily pleased and remind us of what was said of the Empire of Russia: that it was a fine fruit spoiled before it had ripened. Our people are too slight and vain. They are easily elated and easily depressed. See how fast they extend the fleeting fabric of their trade, not at all considering the remote reaction and bankruptcy, but with the same abandonment to the moment and the facts of the hour as the Esquimaux when he offers to sell his bed in the morning. An old merchant said to me that he had learned that he could not learn by experience; for, ten times he had been taught by hard times not to extend himself again, yet always a new crisis took him by surprise, and he was as unprepared as ever. They act on the moment and from external impulse. They all lean on some other, and this superstitiously and not from insight of his merit. They follow a fact, they follow success, and not skill. Therefore, as soon as the success stops, fails, and the admirable man blunders, they quit him; already they remember that long ago they suspected his judgment, and they transfer the repute of judgment to the next prosperous person who has not yet blundered. Of course, this levity makes them as easily despond. It seems as if history gave no account of any society in which despondency came so readily to heart as we see it and feel it in ours. Young men at thirty, and even earlier, lose all spring and vivacity, and if they fail in their first enterprize, throw up the game.

I think we have no worse trait, as far as it is a national one, than this levity, than

21. Arthur Wellesley, first Duke of Wellington (1769–1852), British general and statesman born in Ireland, served in Britain's armies throughout the empire for nearly fifty years; Richard Bentley (1662–1742), English cleric and classical scholar; John Selden (1584–1654), English jurist, historian, and author; Joachim Murat (1771–1815), king of Naples and brother-in-law of Napoléon; Cola di Rienzo (1313–54), Italian popular leader and patriot; Sir William Waller (ca. 1597–1668), English general during the Thirty Years' War.

22. William Wordsworth, *The Excursion*, 4.138–39.

23. Aristotle (384–322 B.C.), Greek philosopher and scientist.

this idolatry of success, this fear to fail. We shall never have heroes, until we have learned that it is impossible to fail. Of course, this timidity about reputation, this terror of a disaster comes of looking at opinion as the measure of character, instead of seeing that character judges opinion. In the brave West, I rejoice to see symptoms of a more man-like sentiment than this timid asking leave to live of other men. The frank Kentuckian has a way of thinking concerning his reception by his friend that makes him whole: Here I am. If you do not appreciate me, the worse for you. And the great Indian sages had a lesson for the Bramin which every day returns to mind: "All that depends on another gives pain. All that depends on himself gives pleasure. In these few words is the definition of pleasure and of pain."[24] We must learn, too, failure is a part of success. Prosperity and pound cake are for very young gentlemen whom such things content: but a hero's, a man's success is made up of failures, because he experiments and ventures every day, and the more falls he gets, moves faster on: defeated all the time, and yet to victory born. I have heard that in horsemanship he is not the good rider who never was thrown, but that, rather, a man never will be a good rider until he is thrown; then, he will not be haunted any longer by the terror that he shall tumble, and *will ride,*—that is his business, *to ride,* whether with falls, or whether with none, *to ride unto the place whither he is bound.*

The noble Phocion, him of whom it has been so truly said, that, "Phocion haranguing the Athenian *Demos* was as solitary as a ship on the stormy Atlantic," was afraid of applause.[25] For a true man feels that he has quite another office than to tickle or flatter. He is here to bite and to stab, to inflict wounds on self-love and easy, prosperous falsehood, which shall not quickly heal. Demosthenes, when the people hissed him for his ragged and untuneable voice, cried out, "You are to judge players, indeed, by their sweet voices, but orators by the gravity and power of their sentences."

It would seem as if history were full of tributes to the unrivalled ascendency of personal qualities. He is the hero who conquers alone.

> In that immense crowd which throngs the avenues to power in the United States, I found very few men who displayed any of that manly candor and that masculine independence of opinion which frequently distinguished the Americans in former times, and which constitute the leading feature in distinguished characters wherever they may be found. It seems at first sight as if all the minds of the Americans were formed on one model, so accurately do they correspond in their manner of judging.

24. Attributed to *The Laws of Menu* (or *Manu*), Indian commentaries on religious laws and social obligations compiled between 200 B.C. and A.D. 200 (*TN*, 3:269).

25. Phocion (ca. 402–318 B.C.), Athenian general and statesman and student of Plato, after the death of Alexander the Great ruled Athens but was executed on a false charge of treason.

A stranger does indeed sometimes meet with Americans who dissent from these rigorous formularies; with men who deplore the defects of the laws, the mutability and the ignorance of democracy; who even go so far as to observe the evil tendencies which impair the national character and to point out such remedies as it might be possible to apply: but no one is there to hear these things beside yourself, and you to whom these secret reflections are confided, are a stranger and a bird of passage.[26]

Is not this tragic in so far as it is true, that this great country, hospitable to all nations, opened for the experiment of new ideas, now in the decrepitude and downfall of the old mythologies of church and state in Asia and Europe,—should be a country of dwarfs; cities and nations of democrats, and never an upright man? That our famous Equality should be a fear of all men; and our famous Liberty should be a servitude to millions; a despicable, skipping expediency; a base availableness, ducking with servile cap to the lowest and worst? I do not wonder that the well-disposed but slow of faith begin to look with wishful eyes to the decorum and police of monarchy, as the poetic and imaginative but drowsy mind is driven by the cold disputation of the Protestant to the stability and veneration of the Roman Church. Some of the most intelligent and virtuous foreigners who have been among us, and those who have surveyed us from afar, have expressed the feeling that the antidote to our excessive spirit of socialism must be found in a class of gentlemen or men of honor,—which, yet, they thought, our institutions did not go to form.

26. Alexis de Tocqueville (1805–59), French writer and politician, best known for his two-volume *De la démocratie en Amérique* (*Democracy in America*) (1835, 1840), written after a nine-month stay in the United States, from which Emerson quotes.

The Spirit of the Times

(1848–1856)

Emerson's lecture "The Spirit of the Times" has an extended genealogy. Its origin is in the lecture "Introductory," with which Emerson opened his *The Present Age* series in 1839 and 1840 and his *Human Life* series in 1840; he likely repeated the lecture under the individual titles "Analysis, the Character of the Present Age" and "The Character of the Present Age" in 1840. Late in 1847 he returned to the lecture "Introductory" as the basis for a new lecture that he called both "Genius of the Present Age" and "The Spirit of the Times" and read during his lecture tour in England in 1847 and 1848. In America he delivered the lecture as "The Spirit of the Times" throughout 1850. He then set it aside until 1856, when he delivered it under the title "Signs of the Times" in Boston.

Between leaving off "The Spirit of the Times" in 1850 and delivering it one more time in its original form in 1856, Emerson began to revise the lecture into a new one that he entitled both "Law of Success" and "Success" and first delivered in 1851. Indebted to "The Spirit of the Times" but through multiple revisions finally independent of it, Emerson's lecture on the topic of success became one of his staples on the lecture circuit from 1858 through 1869. Emerson eventually adapted his lecture manuscripts on success into the essay "Success," published in *Society and Solitude* in 1870 (*W*, 7:283–312), and he also drew from the ending of either "The Spirit of the Times" or its later adaptation as the "Law of Success" and "Success" for his series *Natural History of the Intellect* at Harvard in 1870 and in 1871 (Emerson's *University Lectures*).

We say the mind and manners of the Nineteenth Century, or the spirit of the times, a topic of universal pertinence. For what is the life of each one of us, but his own summary on the resources and tendencies of this Epoch? For what is the Age? It is what he is who beholds it. It is transparent in proportion to the powers of the eye. To one, the price current and the newspaper; another sees the roots of today in past centuries, and, beneath the past, in the Necessary and Eternal.

The age is not to be learned by the enumeration of all the traits; that were an inextricable miscellany; but by the eminency of some. No foregoing age but has left some residue and trace of itself; shall we therefore find in modern society no peculiar genius, but specimens of every mode of life and thought that has anywhere prevailed? Is modern society composed of the *débris* of the foregone structures of religion and politics, a mixed mass, just as the soil we till is made up of the degraded mountains of the elder world? No: but the age is to be described by those elements which are new and operative, and by their activity now detaching the future from the past, and exposing the decays of the corpse they consume,—and these are all that require attention.

In the confusion of figures, we have been accustomed to distinguish two parties, to one of which all men belong,—the party of the Past, and the party of the Future:—the movement, and the establishment.— This schism runs under the world, and appears in literature, philosophy, church, state, social customs; a war, it seems, betwixt Intellect and Affection. It is a crack in nature, which has split every church; Christendom, into Papal and Protestant; Calvinism, into old and new schools; Quakerism, into old and new; Methodism, into old and new; England, into Conserver and Reformer; America, into Whig and Democrat. It has reached into the immoveable East, and is renovating Constantinople and Alexandria and threatens China. It has reached into the Indian tribes of North America, and carries better politics of Democracy among the Red men.

If, in our inquiry, we fasten our regard on the second of these parties; if we can appreciate their activity and its causes, we can well spare all attention to the other class, except as illustrative of this.

This habit induces the consciousness of sufficiency in each man. The whole of modern history has an intellectual character. The former generations acted under the belief that a shining social prosperity was the beatitude of man, and sacrificed uniformly the citizen to the state. The modern mind believes that the nation exists for the individual, for the guardianship and education of every man, and speaks of itself, that men are reflective or intellectual.

This idea, which stands roughly written in all the revolutions and national movements, in the mind of the philosopher has far more precision, and is attaining a depth and splendour which win all the intellects of men to its party. In the eye of the philosopher, the individual is the World.

This perception is a sword such as was never drawn before. It divides and detaches bone and marrow, soul and body, yea,—almost the man from himself. It is the Age of Severance, of Dissociation, of Freedom, of Analysis, of Detachment. It is the Age of the first person singular. Every man for himself. The public speaker disclaims speaking for any other; he answers only for himself. The social sentiments are weak. The sentiment of Patriotism is weak. Veneration is low: The natural affections feebler than they were. People grow philosophical about native land, and parents, and relatives. There is an universal resistance to ties and ligaments once supposed essential to civil society. The new race is stiff, heady, and rebellious: they are fanatics in freedom; they hate tolls, taxes, turnpikes, banks, hierarchies, governors, yes,—almost laws. They have neck of unspeakable tenderness; it winces at a hair. They rebel against theological as against political dogmas, against mediation, or saints, or any nobility in the unseen. It tends to Solitude. The Association of the time is accidental, and momentary, and hypocritical: the detachment intrinsic and progressive. The Association is for power merely, for means; the end being the enlargement and independency of the individual. Anciently, society was in the course of things. There was a Sacred Band, a Theban Phalanx. There can be none now. College classes, military corps, or Trades Unions, may fancy themselves indissoluble for a moment, over their wine; but it is a painted hoop, and has no girth.

We say, the age is marked by a certain predominancy of the intellect in the balance of the powers. This has the most positive effects; the warm, swart earth-spirit, which made the strength of the past ages, mightier than it knew, with instincts instead of sciences; like a mother yielding food from her own breast, instead of procuring and preparing it through chemic and culinary skill; warm negro ages of sentiment and vegetation all gone; another hour has struck, and other forms arise. Instead of the social existence, which required no private strength,—by the emergence of the intellect, a slight interval is interposed between all the persons. No two are in contact. It is no longer possible to accept what all say, to accept Tradition,— such detachment has been made, that each is irrevocably solitary, and is driven to find all his resources, his hopes, rewards, society, and deity, within himself.

With this intellectual determination, the wants of man remain as they were, and enforce the direction of these fine energies on their supply. Instead of contenting himself like the first rude races with barbarous morsels got as a beast of prey from the nearest victims, or by main strength from a rude agriculture, he sails to other latitudes, and, by exchanging the products of his own, varies and refines his food. Commerce is the first fruit of the Intellect applied to Labor.

Every man must bear in his own person the badge of his time, grossly or spiritually. The sailor will find it in his boat, the scholar in his college, the statesman in parties. That which may be seen colossally traceable in the movements of masses, assumes another shape among the elegant and educated. And we hear more of it, because they know how to celebrate their wars; whilst the others strive and die unsung.

Among the cultivated is now an excess of the reflective habit, tendency to self-dissection, anatomizing of motives and thoughts, exultation in enfranchisement; reference of all persons and periods to our own. We run not to the cheerful world full of work, and the fraternity of a thousand labourers, but inward, and farther inward, to revolve the matter overmuch. Men are sick, ocular, vain, and vagabond.

The hour comes, when, to the mind of the man, the object disjoins itself from the mood of thought it awakens, and he sees that he owes a debt of emotion and thought to a person or thing, which, at the same time, he second-sees not fully to deserve the thought and emotion they have awakened, so that he loves, yet shrinks from marriage; he detests slavery, but his servant must not dare to be more than a servant; he burns with a wish to spread knowledge like water, but he will not serve in the school committee; he loves the state, but dislikes all the citizens; he transfigures a form of nature or art, and solidly proceeds with his theory of it, whilst he more than suspects that though his theory is sound, this actual form or object is unworthy of his praise; or that its emphasis to his imagination was quite accidental. He exposes with indignation the hollow charities of the day. He feels the education in vogue to be no education; the religion no religion. But he finds in himself no resources for the instruction of the people, when they shall discover that their present guides are blind. His criticism is too much for him. His wit has eaten his heart out. He excites others by thoughts, which do not move his own hand. The least effect of the oration is on the orator,—a slight recoil, a kick of the gun. He contrasts this coldness, with the healthy heart of the farmer and mechanic. In the Church, or public meeting, the rough farmers answer every call of sympathy: their faces soften, and their tears flow; but the old hardened sinners in black coats, the arid educated men and women, sit as dry as the bench. Napoleon, after reducing the sections of the city of Paris, under the Convention, had frequent occasion to harangue at the markets, in the streets, in the sections, in the *faubourgs*, and insisted that he always found the *faubourg* St. Antoine the most ready to listen to reason, and the most susceptible of a generous impulse.[1]

These are the distinctions we have been accustomed to draw in signalising the Century, which has now reached half its term. Before I proceed to trace with a little more precision some traits of our time, and connect them with the past and the future, I have to make the general remark that *all the traits or distinctions of any period co-exist in every period.* All the elements are ever co-present. What is once true is always true. Only what was background once, is foreground now. In truth you cannot banish any element of man. You say the religion is disappearing. I think there is as much now as ever there was; but it is there in new forms; it is there to modify and not to lead. We affirm the eminency or culmination of one quality; but the very exaltation of that element is sure to exasperate the antagonist element. For man is an exaggerator, and extreme reformers make conservatism extreme.

Many distinctions, solid or fanciful, may be set up in history. There are many methods of classifying the nations which have peopled our planet since men were wise enough to record their existence; and every distributor defends his own taste. But many of these civilizations are abortive.

1. Napoléon Bonaparte (1769–1821), born in Corsica, general and later emperor of the French as Napoléon I. The Convention nationale (National Convention, 1792–95), or governing assembly of the French Revolution, provided a new constitution for France after the overthrow of the monarchy. A *faubourg* is a suburb.

I do not easily distinguish but three periods, among those commonly accepted, as of deep and general significance.

First. The Greek Age, when, with very little science, man accepted nature, as it lay before his senses, and deified it, by only adding the human form to each of its elements. Jove was in the air; Neptune in the sea; Pluto in the mine; naiads in the fountain; faun and dryads in the wood; oreads on the mountain.[2] A happy, beautiful expression of his contentment and admiration of nature: which he simply obeyed in all his performances.

These people had bolder and completer senses than we: their art is inventive, yet so secure. We can only in a quite feminine way approve what they have done, owning that it is good as far as we can judge, and doubting not it is correct where we are not judges.

Second. When, now, the age of sensation, the age of the Gymnasium, of the chariot race, of dancing, of a music, and poetry, and history, addressed to the senses,— or, never overstepping a certain sensual limit, had been exhausted,—arrived the second or *Christian* Age.

The senses having been carried to perfection and exhausted, the moral sentiment, became pronounced, and made everything else sterile. The inexperienced soul made its sally into the absolute; craved a heaven out of nature, and above it; looking on nature now as an obstacle, an enemy, a snare. The powers that ruled the world, were held hostile to the Soul.

Here was a new and strange success; a triumph was achieved for the soul; an enlargement of region; and new resources were found in the sentiments,—for art, for architecture, painting, sculpture, poetry, and much more for the mind, for morals, for social life, for education, and the laws.

Christianity was culture and civilization to Europe, and, in its Asiatic imitation of Mahometism, to Asia and Africa. It had this distinction, that it made religion or the sentiment, the centre of all the institutions of Society. The throne, the laws, learning, and the arts rested on religion; in Romanism, in Anglicans and Presbyterian or Scottish Kirk.

The Greek and Roman age are the epoch of man, of virility, the Christian age the representation of Woman.

But this age exhausted itself also; ran into the excess or partialism of its own element,—too exclusively ideal, sentimental: fell into monkery, asceticism, formalism, and hypocrisy; departed too much from nature into unmanly melancholy, and, as is easy to see in looking back at the ecclesiastical ages, put man in a false and unreal position to nature, and his duties to the world.

Third. Now, lastly, arises the Modern Age, when the sentiments-become-

2. Jove or Jupiter, the equivalent of the Greek Zeus, was the central deity of the Roman religious world; Neptune (Greek Poseidon) was the Roman god of the sea; Pluto (Greek Hades) was the Roman god of the underworld.

sentimentalities of the Christian period force men to retrace their steps and return to Nature.

Nature which was looked upon as an enemy, and an obstacle,—is so regarded no more; but more sanely, as the proper home, and theatre, and means, of man's activity; his aim is now to convert the world into the instrument of right reason. He believes it to be a magazine of riches inexhaustible; it offers itself to him as the perfect means of executing his perfect will.

The first age was the Age of Man. The second age was the Age of Woman. The third is the Marriage of the mind to nature. This appears, in particulars, as the age of commerce, the age of tools, the age of natural science.

First. Age of Commerce.

I said in the outset that a highly intellectual development marked our times. This is the cause and effect of commerce. Commerce is the first fruit of intellect applied to labour. Commerce is at once the child and the nurse and tutor of the Understanding. Hence the perfection of the maritime nations in commonsense and acuteness. The Mediterranean Sea was the School of Europe; the Atlantic, of a still richer culture of the same faculties.

Commerce is only a single fruit of the new habit of thought. Yet such is the predominance that belongs to Trade and its consequences at the present day, that, viewed superficially, the Age might easily be designated as the age of commerce. Trade is the ascendant power, and government only a parachute to this balloon. The state is only one department of commerce, filled with virtual merchants, who are there to be rich, and, conscious of their parentage, or filled with the time-Spirit, Government is administered for the protection of trade. Law is interpreted and executed on the same principle, that a man's enjoyment of his estate is its main end. Education is degraded. It aims to make good citizens on this foundation. The one thing which the careful parent sees that his son shall be taught, is, Arithmetic. And Religion even, is a lever out of the spiritual world to work upon this. It is really commerce which broke the power of the Church; for though trade grew up under the shadow of the Church, and gave gifts, and won a kind of tolerance for itself, it is very easy to see that the merchant and the broker are not the men to exaggerate the sentiments; but Trade is the power which recalls man from the sentiments to earth, and occupies itself with arming him with more material weapons.

Among the marks of the age of cities, must be reckoned conspicuously the universal adoption of cash-payment. Once, it was one of many methods. People bought, but they also borrowed, and received much on various claims: of good-will, on hospitality, in the name of God, in the interest of party, of letters, of charity. Young men made essay of their talents for proof, for glory, for enthusiasm, on any reasonable call, nothing doubting, that, in one or another way, their hazarded bread would return to them after many days. But in the universal expansion of the city by railroads, the stock-exchange infects our country-fairs, and no service is thought reasonable which does not see a requital in money. Yet where is the service which can by any dodge escape its remuneration? For grandeur, at least, let us once in a while serve God.

Second. Age of Tools.

Commerce expresses the application of the intellect to the exchange of fruits and commodities; another great application of the understanding was mechanism, or the invention of tools. All truth is practical. No thought dawns on the intellect, but tends directly to become a mechanic power: and all these wonderful aids and means by which we live, were once simple and poetic acts. Every tool was a stroke of genius.

These tools they have invented,—screw, shears, clock, compass, ship, money, alphabet, decimal figures, the newspaper,—are effigies and statues of men also: their wit, their genius, perpetuated. And he that uses them, becomes a great society of men as wise as himself. All these tools think for us.

The effect of the analytic mind of the age has gone on making tools. But all tools are reagents. Mechanism mechanizes. It is a proverb in America, that the Union is holden by a cotton thread. These agents are absorbing and aggressive. The weaver becomes a web: the machinist, a machine. If you cannot command the tools, they command you; and the question that arises in the end, is, which is the tool?

It is too obvious that the tendency of the popular mind in this country, is, to rely on means provided by the understanding for the aid and defence of man and not on the simplest action of the man himself.

The life of a man in this country is clothed, fed, forwarded, amused, and, in every particular taken off its feet and supported on these secondaries. He is never suffered to touch the ground. He is superfluously served and prevented. He is cushioned, pampered, policed, coached, cabbed, steamed, and telegraphed, through the world. No mountain stops him, and no sea. The land is tunnelled; the water, bridged. He arrives at the seashore, and a sumptuous ship has floored and carpeted the stormy Atlantic for him, and made it a luxurious hotel amid the horrors of tempests; and steam has annihilated the head-wind. "It is the same to him who wears a shoe, as if the whole earth were covered with leather."[3] The same organising power has subsidized and reconstructed society for his use. The population seems to be all couriers, clerks, reporters, labourers or ministers of luxury for his behoof.

All things feel the encroachments of this iron hand. The social day has come to be divided and arranged by the time-tables of the Railway. See how the clocks of this country have been changed to astronomic-time, and all the sea submits to the invading thrills of the electric telegraph. The globe is now practically a moveable observatory to the astronomer; and the diameter of the solar system is the familiar

---

3. Quoted from *The Hĕĕtŏpădēs of Vĕĕshnŏŏ-Sărmā*, translated from Sanskrit by Charles Wilkins (Bath, 1787).

base of his triangles to compute the parallax of stars. The day is indebted to the penny post, the night to the gas-company. In London, lately, the new electric light puts out the gas light, as that had formerly put out the flame of oil: and the news-papers announce with some pathos, that there will be no more night in London; a state of things which has only this consolation, that a new lamp is a more effective guard against crime than twenty policemen.

Our disease, again, is indebted to ether and chloroform. The physician, the den-tist have learned to use the body as a piece of mechanism, and with ruder and robuster treatment than formerly. Nay more,—it is very plain that the musician, the churchman, the statesman, the socialist, begin to calculate on us; and, as we make tulips and dahlias to order, and breeds of cattle and swine, so Fourier and Owen are computing new combinations to be realized in human posterity.[4]

Yes, we prosper in point of tools. Things begin to mind us. The steam excavator carries off a hill as if we had a secret for making it liquid, and pumping or draining it. The engineer tunnels a mountain as a joiner puts a gimlet through a deal board. The world obeys, the cars roll, and nature is made a means to control nature.

The engineering is and continues admirable in what it achieves and in what it projects. The work of the world, the pendulum shall do. This idle gravitation, which offers itself everywhere to pull down,—a famous hand he is at pulling too,—pulls men, and stones, and trees, and planets, and suns down,—be a moth and a sluggard no longer, but shall pull to some useful purpose; and, since he has no living to get of his own, shall get a living for honest, walking, blushing men and women.

We have long ago learned to put brooks and rivers to a profitable industry. Not a stream dares to roar in the highlands of New Hampshire, but an ingenious gen-tleman hurries to the spot, and saves and sells every inch of the water at the price of wine. The sea, with his vast, unnecessary washing and flowing, hither and back, shall be taught something useful, and shall turn wheels, ring bells, and drive en-gines, and pay for his salt. The air, a chartered libertine, shall no longer be free; he must put on livery: he shall float as great a fleet of balloons and of flying carriages, as the sea now does of ships.

Why should all these fine, nameless energies of the summer-day be squandered? The railroad has turned all the citizens with all their brains full of traps and con-trivances like so many walking machine-shops, into the country, and they rack their wits how to extort out of these poor innocent pastures some dividend and brokerage. We will plant a few square miles of trees, that when the southwind blows, we shall not be warm in our own bodies only, but in ten-thousand limbs and ten-million leaves of blossoming trees, in orchard and forest. The wide-related

4. François-Marie-Charles Fourier (1772–1837), French social thinker whose doctrines guided the later period of the Brook Farm community, a utopian venture at West Roxbury, Massachusetts (1841–47); Robert Owen (1771–1858), Welsh social reformer and philanthropist.

planter in his groves feels the blood of thousands in his body, and his heart pumps the sap of all this forest of vegetation through his arteries.

Then again, he discovers, that, though he had plumed himself on his arts, he has really only taken the first steps. A few plants, like apple, wheat, cane, rice, tobacco, cotton, he has usurped and multiplied; and on a single plant, as, for instance, cotton, he has concentrated all his talent, arts, institutions, as if it were the tree of life; and empires breathe long or short, as the telegraph reports the worm, or blight, or bloom, of the crop in the sea-island:—*one plant*;—and, when he looks into his botanical manual, there are nearly 100,000 plants registered, each with virtues as precious as the cotton or the cane, on which, as yet, he has not experimented, and which are to characterise other civilizations, as cotton characterises this.

Our powers are great, and we seem to be on the edge of attaining greater. One might expect a great immorality from these suddenly developed powers, as from a pauper come unexpectedly into a great estate. It is a maxim, that all that frees talent without increasing self-command, is noxious. And, one thinks, if you have only armed the burglar and the assassin with more terrific agents, what have we gained? But in our experience, it turns out, that, as these arts are for all, they leave society where they found it.

Our powers are great, nor can it be denied that we seem to be on the eve of wonderful additions, through chemistry, magnetism, and, according to extraordinary rumours, through mesmerism also.[5] And yet to me it is very certain, that our hands will not be unbound, until our sanity is quite secure. There must be a relation between power and probity. We have now, no doubt, as much power as we can be trusted with. We seem to have more than we can be trusted with: and this must therefore be esteemed a preparation, I will not say, for a superior race, but for a higher civilization of the next centuries;—and is a higher omen of revolution than any other we have seen.

The new tools which we use, the steamboat, locomotive, and telegraph, are effecting such revolutions, as to induce new measures for every value, and to suggest a regret, which is daily expressed, that we who use them were not born a little later, when these agents, whose first machines we see prepared, should be in full play. We have been educated in stagecoach, spinning-wheel, and old tinder-box times, and we find ourselves compelled to accept new arts, new highways, new markets, and mend our old country-trot to keep up with these swifter-footed days.

These things well deserve all their fame, and their history is the history of this age.

Nor is there any chance in their appearance, but they came in the very point of time when they were due. When the man was ready, the horse was brought.

---

5. Mesmerism, a word used for a type of hypnotism, although Franz Mesmer (1734–1815), the German physician who developed the theory of animal magnetism, did not use hypnotism with his patients.

Thus, the timeliness of the invention of the locomotive must be conceded. It came just at the right moment, for America. The geography of America was in no other way to be subdued, the upward navigation of our great rivers; the dangerous navigation of inland seas. More than this, it is an eminent political aid. We could not, else, have held the vast North America together. It was already agitated seriously, the transfer of the seat of government to the west of the Alleganies. But the railroad, with the telegraph, is making it practicable to travel from the extremes of the Empire, without tedious journeys. The important consideration that the Federal Union takes away from its members is the power of declaring peace and war: and this is the main argument for annexation. So that, let Texas, and California, and Minnesota, and Oregon be never so quarrelsome, once in the Union their hands are tied. This gave vital importance to the new facilities of travel and intercourse.

What significance in all the particulars of this history? The course of national expansion and progress of races had just now made it plain that a road to the Pacific could not be postponed,—a railroad, a shiproad, telegraph,—complete communication in every manner for all nations.

See how it was secured: The World-Soul knows who and what it has to deal with, and employs cheap means for great effects. Suddenly, the Californian soil is spangled with a little gold dust, here and there, in a mill race,—in a mountain cleft; an Indian picks up a little; a farmer, a millwright, a soldier, each a little; the news flies here and there, to New York; to Maine; to London; and an army of sixty thousand volunteers, the sturdiest and keenest men that could be collected, embark for this desart, carrying tools, instruments, books, and framed houses, with them. Such a well-appointed Colony as never was planted before;—they arrive with the speed of sail and steam on these remote shores, carrying with them all these tools, as I say, the sum and upshot of all our old civilization,—and one weapon more, namely, that every colonist has taken his degrees in the caucus, town meeting, and county convention, at home; so that he knows the whole theory and practice of our politics, and is a walking American Constitution in the diggings of the Sacramento;— these all arrive bringing with them the necessity that their government shall at once proceed to make the road from Washington to San Francisco, which they themselves are all intimately engaged to assist.

I proceed to notice a very natural, but somewhat alarming, extension of this age of tools into the social relations.

Filled with wonder at our own success, in this delegation almost of human reason to our arts and instruments we say, "Come, let us make this dominion of art perfect." If tools have done so much, let us have nothing else. The world shall be as geometrical as a beehive, and the geometry, as with the bees, shall enter into the manners and wills of the population. It is but one step, and a very attractive step to bold and inventive heads, to apply the same engineering which they have found so effective on the face of the earth, to the earth-born,—and to employ men with the same precision and despotism, with which they have used shovels and wheels. Clearly, they say, things are very bad now. Every man is in a false position: how cruel, that, scholar and saint though he be, he should find himself in this most awkward relation to loaves of bread! And, as a civil engineer has proved so indispensable where wheat in the mountains, or lead or coal in mines, was to be brought to market,—so now we want a moral engineer who can dispose of these materials more refractory than granite, gravel, or conglomerate; can bring men up to their highest power, and reward them with the gratification of their legitimate desires. Stephenson, with his locomotive and road, executed the idea of the age in iron:—Who will do it in the social department?[6]

And, truly, I honour the generous ideas of the socialists, the magnificence of their theories, and the enthusiasm with which they have been urged.

They are the inspired men of the time. Mr. Owen has preached his doctrine of labour and reward, with the fidelity and devotion of a saint, to the slow ears of this generation.

Fourier,—almost as wonderful an example of the mathematical mind of France as Laplace or Napoleon,—has turned a truly vast arithmetic to the question of social misery, and has put men under the obligation which a generous mind always confers of conceiving magnificent hopes, and making great demands, as the right of man.[7] He took his measure of that which all should and might enjoy, from no soup-society or charity-concert, but from the refinements of palaces, the wealth of universities, and the triumphs of artists.

And when I consider how tragic are the evils to which these men addressed themselves, how grim and narrow the ways of life are grown in France, and in Europe generally, how expensive life is, and how many other calamities besides poverty, embitter it: when I consider how gigantic the problem is, I have no heart to make flippant objections to the plans of these reformers, least of all to assume the chair, and affect to decide the question. They who think and hope well of mankind, put all men under obligation. They who in times of gloom, perplexity, and danger, can pilot the ship into port, shall have the praise of the universe.

I regard these philanthropists as themselves the effects of the age in which we live, and, in common with so many other good facts, the efflorescence of the period, and predicting a good fruit that ripens.

They are not the creators they believe themselves; but they are unconscious prophets of a true state of society; one which the tendencies of nature lead unto; one which always establishes itself for the sane soul, though not in that manner in which they paint it: But they are describers of that which is really being done.

6. Emerson is likely referring to George Stephenson (1781–1848), English inventor and founder of railways, and Robert Stephenson (1803–59), his son and occasional assistant who constructed the first railway into London, completed in 1838.

7. Pierre-Simon de Laplace (1749–1827), French astronomer and mathematician.

The large cities are phalansteries; and the theorists draw all their argument from facts already taking place in our experience.[8] Especially are they to be heard as the proclaimers of the Gods' justice and love, which, they have courage to believe, will be fulfilled, come what may, in the world.

The socialist, I say, wished to mechanize society. I do not think it quite easy to seize the law which determines the legitimate action of this engineering. But it has its beneficent energy, and it has its limits. The world vegetates, like a bulb or an acorn; and everything in the world shares this vegetative quality. To machinery, also, the same pushing and progress is natural and inevitable. The vegetative quality runs into matter, runs into mind, runs into arts; they grow, too, and ramify, and subdivide, but always with the same tax.

The plant grows with less vigour as it leaves the ground, and passing into stem, leaves, flower, and fruit, arrives, with every step, at a new and finer production, becoming feebler all the time: and animal life, in the geologic ages, is, at first, slow and secular, requiring many thousands of years before an existing genus can modify its habit by developing a new organ, and forming a new species. In the fossil formations, it has cost ages to complete the changes through which the egg of a species will now pass in a few days. The world was then newer: the blood was colder: Life had not yet so fierce a glow.

Well; life is accelerated. That which Linnaeus called *prolepsis* or anticipation, takes place.[9] The species lives six days in one. The new races are more complex, finer, higher. In man it reaches its highest mark; but the term is proportionally shorter.

So is it with civility, and its arts and tools. They are only finer life, but the compensations appear. The giant size is reduced to a modest six feet. The antediluvian age, to a period far less alarming to insurance and annuity offices. Man has filled up his life with arts. Money, labour, is worth more, for there is more to buy. See how much more a dollar is worth in Massachusetts or New York than in Siberia;— or in Massachusetts or New York than in Wisconsin or Minnesota. There, it will buy bad bread, bad cloth, bad shelter, bad riding. Here, it will buy speed, comfort, luxury, books, and the neighborhood of sense, beauty, and refinement.

But one limit this power of arts and instruments has, only one limit to its benefit. You may extend it to any degree, so long as you keep it art and instrument: so long as it serves. Its antagonist force is the private reason and conscience of man; character; the moral sentiment; as it is manifested in the inspiration of each human mind. As the excess of Christianity had been asceticism and sentimentalism, so the excess of tools is the invasion of man, and converting man into tool, as Socialism does in the phalanx, as Government does in the tyranny of majorities, as public opinion does in newspaper and mob. The natural and eternal remedy is the reliance

8. Phalanstery, a Fourierist cooperative community.
9. Carolus Linnaeus (1707–78), Swedish botanist, is considered one of the founders of modern systematic botany.

on the private soul. This is that which alone is sacred, which alone is great. When this rules, all goes well. That which made the spring of the last period, is to make the regulator of this.

The aim, the determination must come from the Soul, and too much stress cannot be laid on this. Everything else is accidental.

Nothing is so subtle, and nothing so refractory, as what we call personal power; character and genius. It can use all these aids, or it can counterpoise them all. It rests on inspiration. We say, there exists in every man a privilege of obtaining an infallible verdict on all questions touching the conduct of life. And character or personal power has its strength from its obedience to that. The capital misfortune of Socialism is that when it asks for a verdict, the oracle is dumb. The oracle never answers to corporations, or legislatures, or masses; but only to the privacy of each mind.

I have long ago discovered that I have nothing to do with other people's facts. It is enough for me if I can dispose of my own. And I believe that whilst we see with joy the examples of the power of association, which are multiplying around us, and infer the new applications of a principle of such energy and benefit,—we must not prematurely add to them; we must not be bribed by the splendour of material results, to depart from our only safe guide.

The design is magnificent, but there is always a fatal fault in the execution. The economics which must be incidental come to be paramount. Nature's design is that there be men; a man; but, in execution, the philanthropist unmans them that they may have bread. Then the socialist incurably exaggerates his arrangements, and forgets that the virulence of personal qualities will neutralize all forms: as the King of Naples said, when a new uniform was proposed for his troops, "'T was no matter what dress you put on them, they were sure to run away."[10]

The members of the phalanx will be the same men we know. To put them in or out of a phalanx, will not so much mend matters. In the association, or out of it, it is very certain that a higher law will penetrate, which will make the powers and resources of the institution quite unimportant. It is certain that Nature will work in or out of the institution for the men as units, and by them as units. I suppose, it was not unconsidered, the sending of the youthful soul into this university of the world, and perhaps it must have this drastic treatment of famine and plenty, of insult and rapture, of wisdom and tragedy, of infernal and supernal society; in order to secure that breadth of culture which so long-lived a destiny needs. We talk sadly, but sometimes inconsiderately, of the suffering and starvation of the masses. But it could only be understood by the biographies of all the individuals.

"The evils of popular government seem greater than they are: there is compensation for them in the spirit and energy it awakens."

---

10. Joachim Murat (1771–1815), king of Naples and brother-in-law of Napoléon.

The knowledge of the particle is the key to the knowledge of the mass. In this age of mutations, every little while people become alarmed at the wrongs in society, and expect a revolution. There will be no revolution, none that deserves to be called so. There may be a scramble for money. But there will be no revolution, until there are revolutionists. As all the people we see, want the things we now have, and not better things, it is very certain that they will, under whatever change of forms, keep the old system. Whoever is skilful in heaping money now, will be skilful in heaping money again. When I see changed men, I shall look for a changed world.

When men say, 'These men occupy my place,' the revolution is near. But I never feel that any men occupy my place, but that the reason why I do not have what I wish, is, that I want the faculty which entitles. All spiritual power makes its own place. Revolutions of violence are scrambles merely.[11]

The importance of sound individuals cannot be overvalued. Whatever may be the cry in books of philosophy or in the public opinion of the hour against the dangers of egotism, the energy and wisdom of the universe express themselves through personalities. It is a power now in its beginning, and its power is not demonstrated. As every house that would be most solid and stable, must be built of square stones; so every society that can be depended on, must be composed of men that are themselves complete. It is vain to attempt anything without them. The communities that are quoted as successful, were nothing but the presence and influence of some superior man, and he owed nothing to the rules of his order.

In the judgment of Socrates, in *Gorgias*, "One wise man is better than ten thousand who are unwise."[12] And it is idle to attempt by any balance of rogues to educe honesty, or by combining follies to make wisdom.

The good town, the good state, quite naturally crystallizes round one healthy heart. Give us one, and the state seems to be redeemed. The majority carry the day because there is no real minority of one. If Lycurgus were here, the majority would not laugh any longer.[13] There is something in him which he cannot be laughed out of, nor argued out of, nor can he be terrified or bought off. I am afraid that in the formal arrangements of the socialists, the spontaneous sentiment of any thoughtful man will find that poetry and sublimity still cleave to the solitary house.

The arrangements of Owen and Fourier are enforced by arithmetic: but all the heroism and all the scope and play of thought cleave to the solitary house. The Spartan broth, the hermit's cell, the lonely farmer's life, are poetic; the phalanstery, the patent village, are culinary and mean. Forever we must say, the hope of the

11. Attributed to Charles-Maurice de Talleyrand-Périgord (1754–1838), French politician known for his lack of commitment to established principles, in a biography of him (*JMN*, 9:109).

12. Socrates (ca. 470–399 B.C.), one of the most famous of the Greek philosophers whose dialogic method of teaching gained many adherents and who is represented in Plato's dialogues, including the *Gorgias*.

13. Lycurgus, according to tradition, was the ninth century B.C. lawgiver who imposed codes on Sparta designed to produce tough and able warriors.

world depends on private independence and sanctity. Individualism never was tried. But now, when it is borne in like prophecy, on a few holy souls to go alone,— now, when a few began to think of such celestial enterprise, sounds this tin trumpet of a French phalanstery, and the newsboys throw up their caps, and cry, "Egotism is exploded, now for Communism!" But all that is valuable there comes of individual integrity. I have no wish to take sides, and make flippant criticisms, but sadly I think you must settle it in your hearts, that, when you get a great man, he will be hard to keep step with; he will not be a very supple member of any quadrangle. Spoons and skimmers may lie very well together, but vases and statues must have each its own pedestal.

Third. Age of Science.

I say the mind of the age is marked by a return to nature. Natural science is studied, and under the light of ideas. The English mind and the French mind are departmental. And they have long made science barren and repulsive by adding fact to fact superstitiously, and repudiating theory as dangerous. A revolution has come. Modern science, with all its tongues, teaches unity. All our new books trace analogy. Observe the titles of our books: Mrs. Somerville writes the *Connexion of the Sciences*; Humboldt writes the same thing under the name *Kosmos*. The *Vestiges of Creation* respects the same Unity.[14] Endless analogies are hunted out,—between the law that ranges leaves on the stem, and the distances of the planets from the sun; between the spinning of infusory eggs, and the planetary motions.

The phenomena of Sound and of Light were observed to be similar. Both observed the same law of reflection, of radiation, of interference, and of harmony. Two rays of light meeting cause darkness; two beats of sound meeting cause silence. When the eye is affected by one prevailing colour, it sees, at the same time, the accidental colour; and, in music, the ear is sensible, at the same time, to the fundamental note, and its harmonic sounds.

The same laws may be translated into the laws of Heat. Light, Heat, Sound, and the waves of fluids, have the same laws of reflection, and are explained as undulations of an elastic medium. Light and Heat are analogous in their law to Electricity and Magnetism. These are shown to be identical. Then, Davy thought the primary cause of electric and of chemical effects one and the same, one acting on masses, the other on particles.[15] Then, Chladni's experiment seems to me central.[16] He strewed

14. *The Connection of the Physical Sciences* (1834) by Mary Fairfax Somerville (1780–1872), Scottish writer on mathematics and physical science; *Kosmos* (1845–62) by Alexander von Humboldt (1769–1859), German traveler and scientist, is an account of the structure of the universe as then known; *Vestiges of the Natural History of Creation* (1844) by Robert Chambers (1802–71), Scottish publisher and evolutionist, proposed a theory of evolution.

15. Sir Humphry Davy (1778–1829), English chemist who advanced an electrical theory of chemical affinity.

16. Ernst Florens Friedrich Chladni (1756–1827), German physicist and authority on acoustics, invented the euphonium.

sand on glass and then drew musical tones from the glass, and the sand assumed symmetrical figures. With discords, the sand was thrown about. Orpheus, then, is no fable: Sing, and the rocks will crystallize; Sing, and the plant will organize.[17]

Newton, Hooke, Boscovich, Davy believed that the varied forms of bodies depend on different arrangements of the same particles of matter.[18] Possibly the world will be found to consist of oxygen and hydrogen, and even these two elements are one matter in different states of electricity.

Our own little globe is guide enough to the knowledge of all other globes far and near. We never come into new laws. We can go nowhere into a foreign country, though we run along the vast diameter of the sidereal spaces. History, in its largest sense embracing natural, civil, and psychical, is the biography of One Spirit. Swedenborg said that the societies in heaven appeared to him at a distance as one man. When he came near, he saw they were made up of multitudes.

We are struck in reading any continuous history, as of England and of France, with the almost biographical character it assumes. The chronicler is forced to treat the life of the nation as the life of one man. England is one Englishman. He has memory: carries all his past history in his head: remembers his laws: remembers the charters granted by his kings: knows all his rights, and when he is wronged, is always sure of his revenge, though it do not fully come until after a hundred years. Well, not less is the formation of the globe and of the races, the biography of one spirit. The lesson of geology is a method, a series, as continuous as the ripening of an apple or the growth of an animal. Geology shows the gigantic gropings of this embryo in the first plants, the first animals: the advance and refinement to complex organizations. The science of Cuvier, Oken, and Owen, shows one hand continuous in time, one thought in the variety of forms: a stupendous unity, which makes each figure convertible into the other, and all finding their key in the human mind; Man alone corresponding to, understanding, and using them all.[19]

The world is the body of the mind, the arm of the reason, and natural history and civil history are the life or biography of the Soul of the world; and all facts and all creatures are the proceeding of the Spirit into reality or into self-possession. The old way of representing it made us colonists, intruders, squatters; we were the accident of an accident; might have been dropped in Saturn or Mars, or the Sun, as well: and the powers in play here might prove an overmatch; the sea might drown, the earthquake swallow, the climate roast or congeal us; to use a common phrase, "We did not live, we only stayed;" and nothing indicated adaptation. No adoption

---

17. Orpheus, in the Greek myth, was given a lyre by Apollo. He played it so beautifully that he was able to make trees and rocks move and could charm wild beasts.

18. Sir Isaac Newton (1642–1727), English natural philosopher and mathematician; Robert Hooke (1635–1703), English scientist and experimental philosopher; Ruggiero Giuseppe Boscovich (originally Rudjer Josip Bošković) (1711–87), Croatian mathematician and physicist active in Italy.

19. Georges Cuvier (1769–1832), French naturalist and comparative anatomist; Lorenz Oken (1779–1851), German naturalist and philosopher.

of the planet as a home; no patriotism to it; no marriage. It was all experiment, and might easily be a failure.

To the eye of the Nineteenth Century, it looks differently. Thanks to the *hand* of science, the earth fits man. He does not ride on it, as a man rides on a horse; but as a man rides on his own legs. It does not fit him as a farm, or a cave, or a house fits him,—into which he accommodates himself, but as his body fits his mind; as his tongue obeys his thought; as his hands serve his eyes; as his eyes and ears serve his curiosity and his will.

There is not only a return to the study of nature, but to a natural method in the study. A return to nature from the superstition of facts. The people had been excluded. Science was costly, collegiate, with academies and laboratories; worst of all, there was no relation between its facts and the spirit in man.

But Democracy in our days had conquered the State. So humanity rushed into Science. The populace first broke in in Lavater's physiognomy, where the relation of the soul to form was shown: then, in Gall and Spurzheim's phrenology, shoving aside the gownsmen, laying a rough plebeian hand on the mysteries of animal and spiritual nature, and dragging down every sacred secret to a street show.[20] But the movement had much truth in it. It felt connection, where the professors denied it, and proved it by modifying the language, and forcing its phraseology into universal use.

Directly on the heels of this intruder, came mesmerism: like the Jacobins on the Girondists in the French Revolution; and with still more audacity pushed into the very shrines of the Soul; attempted the explanation of miracle and prophecy, as well as of creation.[21] What could be more revolting to the sober, patient, contemplative philosopher?

But a certain success attended it, against all expectation and probability. It was human, it was genial; it affirmed unity, and connection between remote points. While society remained in doubt between the indignation of the old school, and the audacity of the new, suddenly a higher note sounded: unexpected aid from high quarters came in to the mob. The German poet Goethe revolted against the science of the day,—against French science, against English science,—declared war against the great name of Newton, and proposed his own new and simpler optics.[22] Then in Botany he introduced his simple idea of metamorphosis; then he extended it into anatomy and animal life: and his views have been adopted into the orthodox science of Europe and America.

20. Johann Kaspar Lavater (1741–1801), Swiss poet and mystic, usually credited with founding the pseudoscience of physiognomy; the German physicians Franz Joseph Gall (1758–1828) and Johann Christoph Spurzheim (1776–1832), cofounders of the pseudoscience of phrenology, a way of reading a person's character through the configuration of his or her skull.

21. Members of the Jacobin Club promoted extreme radicalism and violence; the Girondists were moderates.

22. Johann Wolfgang von Goethe (1749–1832), Germany's most famous writer.

The Revolt became a Revolution; Schelling and Oken in Germany, and afterwards Hegel, introduced their ideal Natural-Philosophy. Hegel extended it to Civil History. Geoffroi Saint-Hilaire expounded it to France in natural science; Cousin in philosophy and history; Owen in anatomy explained it to England; and Agassiz to America.[23]

This science aimed at thoroughness to give a theory to elements, gases, earths, liquids, crystals, plants, animals, men; to show inevitable were all the steps; that a vast plan was successively realised; and that the last types were in view from the beginning, and were approached in all the steps; that each circle of facts, as, chemistry, astronomy, botany, repeated in a new plane the same law; that the same advancement which natural history showed on successive planes, civil history also showed; that event was born of event, that one school of opinion generated another; that the wars of history were inevitable; that victory always fell where it was due; no party conquered that ought not to conquer; for ideas were the real combatants in the field, and the truth was always advancing, and always victorious.

The idea of the age, as we say, was return to nature; conquest of nature; conversion of nature into an instrument; perfect obedience to nature, and thereby perfect command of nature; perfect representation of the human mind in nature.

This, of course, involves again the highest morals. Every immorality is a departure from nature, and is punished by a natural loss and deformity. The popularity of such books as Combe on the "Constitution of Man," (though a very humble book it is,) and the moral tone that appears in the most popular worldly and comic books,—in Dickens, Thackeray, Cruikshank, and in *Punch*,—betray the tendency that I mean, the growing feeling of mankind that the greatest of calamities is moral dereliction, and that moral justice can no more be defied or evaded than Gravitation.[24]

The gracious lesson taught by science to this Century is that the history of nature from first to last is *melioration*, incessant advance from less to more, from rude to finer and finest organisation, the globe of matter thus conspiring with the principle of undying Hope in man. Melioration in nature answers to Culture in man, and when he listens to the impulses of the heart, in him, and sees the progressive refinement in nature, out of him, he cannot resist the belief that every new race and moral quality impresses its own purpose on the atoms of matter, refines and

23. Friedrich Wilhelm Joseph von Schelling (1775–1854) and Georg Wilhelm Friedrich Hegel (1770–1831), German philosophers; Étienne Geoffroy Saint-Hilaire (1772–1844), French naturalist, propounded a theory of organic unity; Victor Cousin (1792–1867), French Transcendental philosopher; Louis Agassiz (1807–73), Swiss-born American naturalist and zoological explorer, began in 1859 the collections now at the Harvard Museum of Comparative Zoology.

24. *The Constitution of Man* (1828) by George Combe (1788–1858), Scottish phrenologist; Charles Dickens (1812–70) and William Makepeace Thackeray (1811–63), popular English novelists; George Cruikshank (1792–1878), English caricaturist and illustrator; *Punch*, the illustrated London satirical weekly, was started in 1841.

converts them into ministers of human knowledge and virtue; that cultivated bodies, instructed blood, ennobled brains shall yet address themselves to the work of the world, and shall obtain a new command of material elements, and obtain from willing nature more magnificent instrumentalities than have yet been suspected to run on errands still more magnificent.

The task appointed us, however special or humble, borrows the grandeur of the system of which it is a part. Modern Science teaches on a comparing of the ancient strata with the more perfect animal forms which accompany Man, "that there is a plan successively realized in nature, and the types now in existence were in view at the beginning." Is it less true that the ages are all necessary to each other, and that a slow but vast harmony unites the first and last members of this gigantic procession. Each has somewhat special assigned it, on which it lavishes the thought, and love, and lives of competing myriads. That done, the secret is lost; it is no longer doable; and for us remains that undone something which now hovers before and solicits all the leading minds.

To accept our own, is the truest wisdom. Beauty is in nature the pilot which leads us where health and fitness are found; and that work wherein we are most needed is that which is most desired by us.

It is all idle talking,—as if the motes on the stream should prate of the current that is bearing them on. Let us accept the immense beneficence we behold and share. Slower or faster it moves, the huge company;—suns, and earths, and the creatures that inhabit them,—without hurry, and without a pause. We can never intercalate an hour of respite to take breath, look about us, and form resolutions. This age is ours; is our world. As the wandering sea-bird which crossing the ocean alights on some rock or islet to rest for a moment its wings, and to look back on the wilderness of waves behind, and onward to the wilderness of waters before, so stand we perched on this rock or shoal of time, arrived out of the immensity of the past, and bound and road-ready to plunge into immensity again. What place is here to cavil or repine? What apology, what praise, can equal the fact that here it is; therefore, certainly, in the vast optimism, here it ought to be. Wondering, we came in to this watch tower, this broad horizon; but let us not go hence stupid or ashamed; and doubt never but a good genius brought us in, and will carry us out.

Besides, as I stand hovering over this gloom and deep of the Future, and consider earnestly what it forebodes, I cannot dismiss my joyful auguries. It is a reality arriving. It is also dear. I look not at the work of its hand; I follow ever.

The life of man is the true romance which, when it is valiantly conducted and all the stops of the instrument opened, will go nigh to craze the beholder with anxiety, wonder, and love. Wonderful powers are wrapped up under that coarsest of all mattings called Custom, and all wonder prevented. I have read in a German tale that in a gay company, who were amusing themselves on the lawn before a chateau, the master of the feast called for a telescope, and a silent, meagre guest put his hand into the breast-pocket of his grey taffeton coat, took from it a beautiful Dollond, and handed it with a bow to the entertainer.[25] Nobody seemed surprised that so large a machine should come from so tiny a pocket. But soon after, someone expressed a wish to have Turkey-carpets spread here on the turf which was growing damp, and the man in the grey coat, with modest and humble demeanour, began to draw out a rich, embroidered carpet twenty paces long, and ten broad. Nobody thanked him; only a young lady carelessly asked him if he had a marquee? He put his hand to his pocket, and drew forth canvass, bars, ropes, iron frame, in short, everything belonging to a sumptuous tent, which was erected by the help of the young men. In a little while, a ride was proposed, and he took from his pocket three noble riding horses all saddled and bridled.

Can you read the riddle?

Time is the little grey man who takes out of his breast-pocket first a pocket-book, then a telescope, then a Turkey-carpet, then saddled nags, and a sumptuous canvass tent. We are accustomed to Chemistry, and it does not surprise us. But Chemistry is a name for changes and developments as wonderful as those of this Breast-pocket: what then is *Animation*—this life which opens, and enlarges, and declines?

I have heard, and do sometimes remember, that I was a little chubby boy trundling a hoop on a sidewalk in Boston and spouting poetry at the Latin School. Time, the little grey man, has put away the city from me and taken out of his vest-pocket certain green fields and in a corner of them set a wooden house, in which I live; he has taken out of his pocket several full-grown and several very young persons and seated them close beside me. 'Tis wonderful how much we have to say to each other and how easily we act as if we had always known each other; then he has taken that boyhood and that hoop quite away and left here a lean person, a little grey man like himself. I am sure he has played, or is playing, tricks as extraordinary with each person who hears me. Is there nothing astounding in these changes, and are they only astounding when done fast?

The commonest life is made of miracles; for all the most valuable things in nature are on the highway, and not in rare and extraordinary fortunes. These are peculiarities of the time, but we are too much in the age to see them. Besides, all the peculiarities of any age are superficial: that which is deep and great belongs alike to all ages. As soon as we love, or think profoundly; or pray; or are rapt by music; or by grand works of imagination; or address ourselves to any task which absorbs the mind and heart; we are no longer related to our native village or to the current year and month, but are citizens of the world, and at home in all ages.

---

25. John Dollond (1706–61), English optician and inventor of the refracting telescope.

The Tendencies and
Duties of Men of Thought

(1848–1850)

"The Tendencies and Duties of Men of Thought" is associated with two lecture series that Emerson delivered in 1848 and 1849: *Mind and Manners of the Nineteenth Century*, which he delivered in six lectures in London in 1848 and in five lectures in Boston in 1849, and *Laws of the Intellect*, three lectures on the general subject of the natural history of the intellect, which he delivered before the Concord Lyceum in 1849. The other lectures on intellect that Emerson delivered in those series were "The Powers and Laws of Thought" and "The Relation of Intellect to Natural Science" (*Later Lectures*, 1:134–51 and 152–72). Emerson read "The Tendencies and Duties of Men of Thought" third in the London and Concord series and second in the Boston series; he also delivered versions of this lecture as "Instinct and Inspiration" in New York City and Philadelphia and as "Inspiration and Instinct" in Cincinnati when he delivered lecture series on unconnected topics in those cities in 1850.

Of the three lectures associated with his early construction of a "Natural History of the Intellect," Emerson and his literary executors, James Elliot Cabot and Edward Waldo Emerson, made the most use of "The Tendencies and Duties of Men of Thought." Emerson read from the manuscript of this lecture when he delivered "Conduct of the Intellect" in a series of six lectures he called *Philosophy for the People* in Boston in 1866, and he made extensive use of the manuscript in 1870 and 1871 in his two series entitled the *Natural History of the Intellect* at Harvard. At Harvard the manuscript provided text for "Conduct of Intellect" and "Relation of Intellect to Morals," which Emerson read in the 1870 version of the series, and for "Will and Conduct of the Intellect," "Conduct of the Intellect," and "Relation of Intellect to Morals," which he read in the 1871 version of the series (Emerson's *University Lectures*). He also turned to this lecture when he prepared text for the essays "Worship," first published in *The Conduct of Life* in 1860, and "Immortality," first published in *Letters and Social Aims* in 1876, a volume arranged by Cabot with the assistance of Emerson's daughter Ellen (*W*, 6:199–242 and 8:321–52). Finally, Edward mined "The Tendencies and Duties of Men of Thought" for the essay "Instinct and Inspiration," which, in the Centenary Edition of his father's works (1903–4), he added to Cabot's arrangement of the "Natural History of the Intellect" essay first published in *Natural History of the Intellect* in 1893. (For Edward's essay and notes on "Instinct and Inspiration" see *W*, 12:65–89 and 442–43.)

In reckoning the sources of our mental power, it were fatal to omit that one which pours all the others into mould:—that unknown country in which all the rivers of our knowledge have their fountains, and which by its qualities and structure determines both the nature of the waters, and the direction in which they flow. We have a certain blind wisdom, a brain of the brain, a seminal brain, which has not yet put forth organs, which rests in oversight and presence,—but which seems to sheathe a certain omniscience; and which, in the despair of language, is commonly called Instinct.

This is that which never pretends: Nothing seems less, nothing is more. Ask what the Instinct declares, and we have little to say; he is no newsmonger, no disputant, no talker. Consciousness is but a taper in the great Night; but the taper at which all the illumination of human arts and sciences was kindled. And in each man's experience, from this spark torrents of light have once and again streamed and revealed the dusky landscape of his life.

'Tis very certain that a man's whole possibility is contained in that habitual first look which he casts on all objects. Here alone is the field of metaphysical discovery, yes, and of every religion and civil order that has been or shall be. All that we know are flakes and grains detached from this mountain. None of the metaphysicians have prospered in describing this power, which constitutes sanity; and is the corrector of private excesses and mistakes; public in all its regards, and of a balance which is never lost, not even in the insane.

All men are, in respect to this source of truth, on a certain footing of equality; equal in original science, though against appearance, and 'tis incredible to them. There is a singular credulity which no experience will cure us of, that another man has seen or may see somewhat more than we, of the primary facts; as, for example, of the continuity of the individual; and, eye for eye, object for object, their experience is invariably identical in a million individuals. I know, of course, all the grounds on which any man affirms the immortality of the soul. Fed from one spring, the water-tank is equally full in all the gardens: the difference is in the distribution by pipes and pumps, the difference is in the aqueduct and fine application of it.

Its property is absolute science and an implicit reliance is due to it. Why should I hasten to solve every riddle which life offers me? I am well assured that the Interrogator who brings me so many problems, will bring the answers also in due time. Very rich, very potent, very cheerful Giver that he is! He shall have it all his own way for me. Why should I give up my thought, because I cannot answer an objection to it? Consider only whether it remains in my life the same it was.

All true wisdom of thought and of action comes of deference to this instinct, patience with its delays. We are to know that we are never without a pilot. When we know not how to steer, and dare not hoist a sail, we can drift: The current knows the way, though we do not. When the stars and sun appear, when we have conversed with other navigators who know the coast, we may begin to put out an oar, and trim a sail.

To make a practical use of this instinct in every part of life, constitutes true wisdom. And we must form the habit of preferring in all cases this guidance, which is given as it is used.

To indicate a few examples of our recurrence to instinct, instead of to the understanding: We can only judge safely of a discipline, of a book, of a man, or other influence, by the frame of mind it induces, as whether that be large and serene, or dispiriting and degrading. Then we get a certain habit of the mind as the measure, as Haydon found Voltaire's tales left him melancholy.[1] The eye and ear have a logic which transcends the skill of the tongue. The ear is not to be cheated. A continuous effect cannot be produced by discontinuous thought, and when the eye cannot detect the juncture of the skilful mosaic, the spirit is apprised of disunion, simply by the failure to affect the spirit.

Objection and loud denial not less prove the reality and conquests of an idea, than the friends and advocates it finds. One often sees in the embittered acuteness of critics snuffing heresy from afar, their own unbelief, and that they pour forth on the innocent promulgator of new doctrine, their anger at that which they vainly resist in their own bosom.

Again, if you go to a gallery of pictures, or other works of fine art, the eye is dazzled and embarrassed by many excellences. The marble imposes on us; the exquisite details impose; we cannot tell if they be good or not: but long after we have quitted the place, the objects begin to take a new order; the inferior recede and are forgotten; and the truly noble forms reappear to the imagination; as a strain of music is heard farther than the noise of carts and drays.

The Instinct begins at this low point at the surface of the earth, and works for the necessities of the human being; then ascends, step by step, to suggestions, which are, when expressed, the intellectual and moral laws.

And what is Inspiration?

It is this Instinct whose normal state is passive, at last put in action. We attributed power, and science, and good will to the Instinct, but we found it dumb and inexorable. If it would but impart itself!—To coax and woo the strong Instinct to bestir itself, and work its miracle, is the end of all wise endeavour. It is resistless, and knows the way, is the inventor of all arts, and is melodious, and, at all

---

1. Benjamin Robert Haydon (1786–1846), English painter of historical and biblical scenes; Voltaire (the assumed name of François-Marie Arouet) (1694–1778), French author and intellectual.

points a god. Could we prick the sides of this slumberous giant; could we break the silence of this oldest Angel, who was with God when the worlds were made! The whole art of man has been an art of excitation, to provoke, to extort speech from the drowsy genius. We ought to know the way to our nectar. We ought to know the way to insight and prophecy, as surely as the plant knows its way to the light; the cow and sheep, to the running brook; or the feaster, to his wine. We believe, the drop of blood has latent power and organs; that the rudest mind has a Delphi and Dodona,—predictions of nature and history in itself, though now dim and hard to read.[2] All depends on some instigation, some impulse. Where is the yeast that will leaven this lump? Where the wine that will warm and open these silent lips? Where the fire that will light this combustible pile?

Here are we with all our world of facts and experience, the spontaneous impressions of nature and men, and the original oracles,—all ready to be uttered, if only we could be set a-glow. How much material lies in every man!

A cold sluggish blood fancies it has not quite facts enough for the purpose in hand. But they who do speak and act, have no more,—have less. Heat, heat is all; heat, or freedom of motion, gives you all the power of the facts you have. That force or flame is alone to be considered; 'tis indifferent on what fuel it is fed. A snowflake will go through a pine board, if projected with more momentum.

Inspiration is the play of the powers at their highest health; it is the continuation of the divine Effort that built the man.

The same course continues itself in the mind which we have witnessed in nature, namely, the carrying on and completion of the metamorphosis from grub to worm, from worm to fly.

In human thought this process is so often arrested for years and ages. Who knows not the insufficiency of our forces, the solstice of genius? The star climbs for a time the heaven, but never reaches the Zenith; it culminates low, and goes backward whence it came. History of mankind is history of solstice, of arrested growth. The human faculty only warrants inceptions. Even those we call great men, build substructures, and, like Cologne Cathedral, these are never finished.[3] Lord Bacon begins; Behmen begins; Goethe, Fourier, Schelling, Coleridge, they all begin: we, credulous bystanders, believe, of course, that they can finish as they begun.[4] If you

2. In ancient Greece the cities of Delphi and Dodona had famous oracles who could predict the future; Delphi was dedicated to Apollo and Dionysus, and Dodona was dedicated to Zeus.

3. The cathedral in Cologne, or Köln, Germany, is the largest Gothic church in northern Europe.

4. Roger Bacon (ca. 1220–92), English philosopher and scientist; Jacob Behmen (or Jakob Böhme) (1575–1624), German mystic, influenced romanticism and the Quakers; Johann Wolfgang von Goethe (1749–1832), Germany's most famous writer; François-Marie-Charles Fourier (1772–1837), French social thinker whose doctrines guided the later period of the Brook Farm community, a utopian venture at West Roxbury, Massachusetts (1841–47); Friedrich Wilhelm Joseph von Schelling (1775–1854), German philosopher; Samuel Taylor Coleridge (1772–1834), English poet and philosopher and, with William Wordsworth, founder of the romantic movement.

press them, they fly to a new topic, and here, again, open a magnificent promise, which serves the turn of interesting us once more, and silencing reproaches, but they never complete their work.

Inspiration is vital and continuous. It is also a public or universal light, and not particular.

There is a conflict between a man's private dexterity or talent, and his access to the free air and light, which wisdom is; conflict too, between wisdom, and the habit and necessity of repeating itself, which belongs to every mind. Peter is the mould into which every thing is poured, like warm wax, and be it astronomy, or railroads, be it French revolution, or botany, it comes out Peter. But there are quick limits to our interest in the personality of people. They are as much alike as their pantries and barns and are soon as stupid and musty. They entertain us for a time. Therefore at the second or third encounter, we have nothing more to learn, and they have grown fulsome. But genius is as weary of his personality, as others are, and he has the royal expedient to thrust nature between him and you, and perpetually to divert attention from himself, by the stream of thoughts, laws, and images.

In the healthy mind, the thought is not a barren thesis, but expands, varies, recruits itself with relations to all nature, paints itself in wonderful symbols, appears in new men, in institutions, in social arrangements, in wood, in stone, in art, in books.

The mark and sign of it is newness. The divine energy never rests or repeats itself; but casts its old garb, and reappears, another creature; the old energy in a new form, with all the vigour of the earth; the Ancient of Days in the dew of the morning.

Novelty in the means by which we arrive at the old universal ends, is the test of the presence of the highest power, alike in intellectual and in moral action. How incomparable beyond all price, seem to us a new poem, (say Spenser), or true work of literary genius![5] In five hundred years, we shall not have a second. We brood on the words or works of our companion, and ask in vain the sources of his information. He exhibits an exotic culture, as if he had his education in another planet. The poet is incredible, inexplicable.

The poet works to an end above his will, and by means, too, which are out of his will. Every part of the poem is therefore a true surprise to the reader, like the parts of the plant, and legitimate as they. The Muse may be defined, *supervoluntary ends effected by supervoluntary means.* No practical rules for the poem, no working-plan was ever drawn up. It is miraculous at all points. The poetic state given, a little more or a good deal more or less performance seems indifferent. It is as impossible for labour to produce a journal of Milton, or a song of Burns, as Shakspeare's *Hamlet*; or the *Iliad*.[6] As we say on the railway, there is much loss in the stops, but the

5. Edmund Spenser (ca. 1552–99), English poet best known for *The Faerie Queene* (1590, 1596).
6. John Milton (1608–74), English poet and political writer, best known for his poem *Paradise Lost* (published in 1667 in ten books); Robert Burns (1759–96), Scotland's most famous poet.

running time need be but little increased, to add great results. One master could so easily be conceived as writing all the books of the world. They are all alike. For it is a power to convert all nature to his use. It is a taproot that sucks all the juices of the earth.

This is work which needs a frolic health to execute. In that prosperity, the artist is sometimes caught up into a perception of methods and materials, of fine machineries, and funds of poetic power, which were unknown to him, and which he can avail himself of, can transfer to mortal canvas, or reduce into iambic or trochaic, into lyric or heroic rhyme. These successes are not less admirable to the poet, than to his audience. He has seen something which all the mathematics and the best industry could never bring him unto: and, like Raffaelle or Michel Angelo, it only shows how near man is to creating.[7] To him, a man as other men, have come new circulations; the marrow of the world is in his bones; the opulence of forms begins to pour into his intellect; and he is permitted to dip his brush into the old paint pot, with which birds, flowers, the human cheek, the living rock, the ocean, the broad landscape, and the eternal sky were painted.

It is this employment of new means,—of means not mechanical, but spontaneously appearing for the new need, and as good as the end,—that denotes the inspired man. This is equally obvious in all the fine arts; and in action, as well as in fine arts. We must try our philanthropists so.

The reformer comes with many plans of melioration, and the basis on which he wishes to build his new world, a great deal of money. But what is gained? Certain young men or maidens are thus to be screened from the evil influences of trade by force of money. Perhaps that is a benefit; but those who give the money, must be just so much more shrewd, and worldly, and hostile, in order to save so much money. I see not how any virtue is thus gained to society. It is a mere transference. But he will instruct and aid us who shows us how the young may be taught without degrading the old; how the daily sunshine and sap may be made to feed wheat instead of moss and Canada thistle: and, really, the capital discovery of modern agriculture, is, that it costs no more to keep a good tree than a bad one.

But *how*, cries my reformer, is this to be done? *How* can I do it, who have wife and family to keep? The question is most reasonable,—yet proves that you are not the man to do the feat.[8] The mark of the Spirit, is, to know its way, to invent means. It has been in the universe before, of old, and from everlasting, oldest inhabitant, and knows its way up and down. Power is the authentic mark of Spirit. It can come at its ends. The mark of a great man, we say, is to succeed.

I may well say, this is divine, the continuation of the divine effort. Alas! It seems not to be ours, to be quite independent of us. What a revelation of power is music!

---

7. Raphael (1483–1520), Italian painter whose works adorn the Vatican; also called "Raphaelle" or "Raphaello" by Emerson; Michelangelo (1475–1564), Italian painter, sculptor, and poet.

8. Identified as Amos Bronson Alcott (1799–1888), American Transcendentalist, teacher, and writer and Emerson's longtime friend and Concord neighbor, by Emerson (*JMN*, 8:310).

Yet, when we consider who and what the professors of that art usually are, does it not seem as if music falls accidentally and superficially on its artists? Is it otherwise with poetry? Often, there is so little affinity between the man and his works, that we think the wind must have writ them. Here is a famous ode, which is the first performance of the British mind and lies in all memories as the high water mark in the flood of thought in this age. What does the writer know of that? Converse with him, learn his opinions and hopes: He has long ago passed out of it, and perhaps his only concern with it is some copyright of an edition in which certain pages so-and-so entitled are contained. When a young man asked old Goethe about *Faust*, he replied, "What can I know of this? I ought rather to ask you, who are young, and can enter much better into that feeling."[9] Indeed, I believe, it is true in the experience of all men,—for all are inspirable, and sometimes inspired,—that, for the memorable moments of life, we were in them, and not they in us. We found ourselves, by happy fortune, in an illuminated portion, or meteorous Zone, and passed out of it again; so aloof was it from any will of ours.

"How they entered into me, let them say if they can; for, I have gone over all the avenues of my flesh, and cannot find by which they entered," said St. Augustine.[10] And the ancient Proclus seems to signify his sense of the same fact, by saying, "The parts in us are more the property of wholes, and of things above us, than they are our property."[11]

Yes, this wonderful source of knowledge remains a mystery; and its arts and methods of working remain a mystery: it is untameable; the ship of heaven guides itself, and will not accept a wooden rudder.

It must be owned, that what we call Inspiration is coy and capricious; we must lose many days to gain one; and, in order to win infallible verdicts from the inner mind, we must indulge and humour it in every way, and not too exactly task and harness it.

Also its communication from one to another, follows its own law, and refuses our intrusion. It is in one, it belongs to all: yet how to impart it? This makes the perpetual problem of education. How shall I educate my children? Shall I indulge, or shall I controul them? Philosophy replies, Nature is stronger than your will, and, were you never so vigilant, you may rely on it, your nature and genius will certainly give your vigilance the slip, though it had *delirium tremens,* and will educate the children by the inevitable infusions of its quality.[12] You will do as you can. Why then cumber yourself about it, and make believe be better than you are? Our teaching is indeed hazardous and rare. Our only security is in our rectitude, whose influences

---

9. Goethe's play *Faust* (pt. 1, 1808) is the story of an old scholar who promises his soul to Mephistopheles in return for complete wisdom.

10. Saint Augustine of Hippo (354–430), early Christian Church father and philosopher.

11. Proclus (ca. 410–85), Greek Neoplatonic philosopher.

12. Delirium tremens refers to tremors caused by prolonged abuse of alcohol.

must be salutary. That virtue which was never taught us, we cannot teach others. They must be taught by the same schoolmaster. And, in spite of our imbecility and terrors, in spite of Boston and London, and universal decay of religion, and so forth, the moral sense reappears forever with the same angelic newness that has been from of old the fountain of poetry and beauty and strength. Nature is forever over education—our famous orchardist once more. Van Mons of Belgium, after all his experiments at crossing and refining his fruit, arrived at last at the most complete trust in the native power. "My secret is to sow, and sow, and resow, and in short do nothing but sow."[13]

It is not in our will. That is the quality of it, that, it commands, and is not commanded. And rarely, and suddenly, and without desert, we are let into the serene upper air. Is it, that we are such mountains of conceit, that Heaven cannot enough mortify and snub us,—I know not,—but there seems a settled determination to break our Spirit. We shall not think of ourselves too highly. Instead of a firmament, which our eyes ask, it is an eggshell which pens us in; we cannot even see what or where our stars of destiny are.

From day to day, for weeks, for months, the capital questions of human life are hidden from our eyes; suddenly, for a moment, they come to view, and, we think, how much good time is gone, that might have been saved and honoured, had any hint of these things been shown! A sudden rise in the road shows us the system of mountains, and all the summits, which have been just as near us, all the year, but quite out of mind. The inexorable Laws, the Ideas, the private Fate, the Instinct, the Intellect, Memory, Imagination, Fancy, Number, Inspiration, Nature, Duty.

'Tis very certain that these things have been muffled as under towels and blankets, most part of our days, and, at certain privileged moments, they emerge unaccountably into light. I know not why, but our thoughts have a life of their own, independent of our will.

We call genius, in all our popular and proverbial language, divine; to signify its independence of our will. Every man is a guest in the earth, a guest in his house, and a guest in his thought. Intellect is universal, not individual. Wisdom is like electricity. There is no permanent wise man, but men capable of wisdom, who, being put into certain company, or other favorable conditions, become wise, for a short time; as glasses rubbed acquire electric power for a while.

I think this pathetic,—not to have any wisdom at our own terms, not to have any power of organizing victory.

The only comfort I can lay to my own sorrow, is, that we have a higher than a personal interest, which, in the ruin of the personal, is secured. I see, that all beauty of discourse or of manners lies in launching on the thought, and forgetting ourselves; and, though the beatitude of the Intellect seems to lie out of our volition,

13. Jean-Baptiste Van Mons (1765–1842), Belgian horticulturalist.

and to be unattainable as the sky, yet we can take sight beforehand of a state of being wherein the will shall penetrate and controul what it cannot now reach. The old law of Science, "*Imperat parendo*," "*We command by obeying*," is forever true; and, by faithful serving, we shall complete our noviciate to this subtle art.

Yes, and one day, though far off, you will attain the controul of these states; you will enter them at will; you will do what now the Muses only sing. That is the nobility and high prize of the worlds.

And this reminds me to add one more trait of the inspired state, namely, incessant advance,—the forward foot.

For it is the curious property of truth to be uncontainable and ever enlarging. Truth indeed! We talk as if we had it, or sometimes said it, or knew anything about it:—that terrific re-agent. 'Tis a gun with a recoil which will knock down the most nimble artillerist, and therefore is never fired. The *ideal* is as far ahead of the videttes and the van, as it is of the rear. And before the good we aim at, all history is symptomatic, and only a good omen.

And the practical rules of literature ought to follow from these views, namely, that all writing is by the grace of God; that none but a writer should write; that he should write affirmatively, not polemically, or should write nothing that will not help somebody,—as I knew of a good man who held conversations, and wrote on the wall, "that every person might speak to the subject, but no allusion should be made to the opinions of other speakers;"— that we must affirm and affirm, but neither you nor I know the value of what we say, that we must be openers of doors and not a blind alley; that we must hope and strive, for despair is no muse and vigour always liberates.

The whole Ethics of Thought is of this kind, flowing out of reverence of the source, and is a sort of religious office. If there is inspiration, let there be only that. You shall not violate its conditions, but we will by all means invite it. It is a sort of rule in Art, that you shall not speak of any work of art except in its presence; then you will continue to learn something, and will make no blunder. It is not less the rule of this kingdom, that you shall not speak of the mount except on the mount; that there are certain problems one would not willingly open, except when the irresistible oracles broke silence.

He needs all his health and the flower of his faculties for that. All men are inspirable. Whilst they say only the beautiful and sacred words of necessity, there is no weakness, and no repentance. But, the moment they attempt to say these things by memory, Charlatanism begins. I am sorry that we do not receive the higher gifts justly and greatly. The reception should be equal. But the thoughts which wander through our mind, we do not absorb and make flesh of, but we report them as thoughts; we retail them as news, to our lovers and to all Athenians. At a dreadful loss we play this game; for the secret Power will not impart himself to us for tea-table talk; he frowns on moths and puppets, passes by us, and seeks a solitary and religious heart.

All intellectual virtue consists in a reliance on Ideas. It must be carried with a certain magnificence. We must live by our strength not by our weakness. It is the exhortation of Zoroaster, "Let the depth, the immortal depth of your soul lead you."[14] It was the saying of Pythagoras, "Remember to be sober, and to be disposed to believe; for these are the nerves of wisdom."[15]

Why should we be the dupes of our senses, the victims of our own works, and always inferior to ourselves. We do not yet trust the unknown powers of thought. The whole world is nothing but an exhibition of the powers of this principle, which distributes men.

Whence came all these tools, inventions, books, laws, parties, kingdoms? Out of the invisible world, through a few brains. Nineteen-twentieths of their substance do trees draw from the air. Plant the pitch-pine in a sandbank, where is no food, and it thrives, and presently makes a grove, and covers the sand with a soil by shedding its leaves. Not less are the arts and institutions of men created out of thought. The powers that make the capitalist are metaphysical: the force of method and the force of Will makes trade, and builds towns.

"All conquests that history tells of, will be found to resolve themselves into the superior mental powers of the conquerors:" and the real credentials by which man takes precedence of man, and lays his hand on those advantages which confirm and consolidate rank, are intellectual and moral.

The men are all drugged with this liquor of thought, and thereby secured to their several works. It is easy to see that the races of men rise out of the ground preoccupied with a thought which rules them, divided beforehand into parties ready armed and angry to fight for they know not what. They all share to the rankest Philistines the same belief.[16] The haberdashers, and brokers, and attorneys are idealists and only differ in the amount and clearness of their perception. Whether Whiggery, or Chartism, or Church, or a dream of Wealth, fashioned all these resolute bankers, merchants, lawyers, landlords who administer the world of today, as leaves and wood are made of air: an idea fashioned them, and one related to yours.[17]

A stronger idea will subordinate them. Yours, if you see it to be nearer and truer. A man of more comprehensive view can always see with good humour the seeming

14. Zoroaster (also known as Zarathushtra) (ca. 628–ca. 551 B.C.), Persian religious reformer and founder of Zoroastrianism.

15. Pythagoras (ca. 580–ca. 500 B.C.), Greek philosopher who raised mathematics to a science.

16. Philistines are people interested in materialism and disdainful of intellectual pursuits.

17. Whigs were conservative American politicians, often representing monied interests, who opposed Andrew Jackson; Chartists were English reformers who promoted better conditions for the working classes during the early to mid-nineteenth century.

opposition of a powerful talent which has less comprehension. 'Tis a strong paddy, who, with his burly elbows, is making place and way for him.[18] Trust entirely the thought. Lean upon it; it will bear up thee and thine, and society, and systems, like a scrap of down.

The world is intellectual; and the man is. Every man comes into nature impressed with his own polarity or bias, in obeying which, his power, opportunity, and happiness, reside. He is strong by his genius, gets all his knowledge only through that aperture. Society is unanimous against his project. He never hears it as he knows it. Nevertheless he is right; right against the whole world. All excellence is only an inflamed personality. If he is wrong, increase his determination to his aim, and he is right again.

What is the use of trying to be somewhat else? He has a facility, which costs him nothing, to do somewhat admirable to all men. He is strong by his genius, and happy also by the same. The secret of power is delight in one's work. He takes delight in working, not in having wrought. His workbench he finds everywhere, and his workbench is home, education, power, and patron. Whilst he serves his genius, he works when he stands, when he sits, when he eats, and when he sleeps. The dream which now or lately floated before the eyes of the French nation,—that, every man shall do that which of all things he prefers, and shall have three francs a day for doing that,—is the real law of the world; and all good labour, by which society is really served, will be found to be of that kind.[19]

All we ask of any man is to be contented with his own work. An enthusiastic workman dignifies his art and arrives at results. Him we account the fortunate man, whose determination to his aim is sufficiently strong to leave him no doubt.

I am aware that nature does not always pronounce early on this point. Many men are very slow in finding their vocation. It does not at once appear what they were made for. Nature has not made up her mind in regard to her young friend: and when this happens, we feel life to be some failure. Life is not quite desireable to themselves. It uniformly suggests in the conversation of men the presumption of continued life, of which the present is only one term. We must suppose Life to such is a kind of hybernation, and 'tis to be hoped that they will be very fat and energetic in the spring. They ripen too slowly than that the determination should appear in this brief life. As with our Catawbas and Isabellas at the eastward, the season is not quite long enough for them.[20]

This determination of Genius in each is so strong, that, if it were not guarded with powerful checks, it would have made society impossible. As it is, men are best and most, by themselves: and always work in society with great loss of power. They

---

18. Paddy, a nickname for Patrick, is an often offensive term for an Irishman.

19. Emerson is referring to the revolution in France that in 1848 replaced the monarchy with a republican form of government.

20. Catawbas and Isabellas are types of wine grapes.

are not timed each to the other: they cannot keep step; and life requires too much compromise.

Men go through the world each musing on a great fable dramatically pictured and rehearsed before him. If you speak to the man, he turns his eyes from his own scene, and, slower or faster, endeavours to comprehend what you say. When you have done speaking, he returns to his private music. Men generally attempt, early in life, to make their brothers, afterwards their wives, acquainted with what is going forward in their private theatre; but they soon desist from the attempt on finding that they also have some farce, or, perhaps some ear- and heart-rending tragedy forward on their secret boards, on which they are intent; and all parties acquiesce, at last, each in a private box, with the whole play performed before himself *solus*.

The source of thought evolves its own rules, its own virtues, its own religion. Its whole equipment is new, and it can only fight with its own weapons. Is there only one courage, one gratitude, one benevolence? No, but as many as there are men. Every constitution has its own health and diseases. A new constitution, a new fever, say the physicians. I think the reason why men fail in their conflicts, is, because they wear other armour than their own. Each must have all, but by no means need he have it in your form. Each must be rich, but not only in money or lands; he may have, instead, the riches of riches,—creative supplying power. He must be armed, not necessarily with musket and pike. Better, if, seeing these, he can feel that he has better muskets and pikes in his energy and constancy. To every creature its own weapon, however skilfully concealed from himself a good while.

His work, his work, is his sword and his shield. Let him accuse no one; let him injure no one. The way to mend the bad world, is to create the right world. The way to conquer the foreign workman, is, not surely to kill him; but every blow of the hammer, every blast of the forge in your own workshop, is conquest.

Within this magical power derived from fidelity to his nature, he adds also the mechanical force of perseverance. He shall keep the law which shall keep him. He shall work in the dark; work in gloom, and sorrow, and faintness. If he is insulted, he can be insulted. All his affair is, not to insult. In persistency, he knows the strength of nature and the immortality of man to lie.

A man must do the work with that faculty he has now. But that faculty is the accumulation of past days. That which you have done long ago, helps you now. No rival can rival backwards. What you have learned and done, is safe and fruitful. Work and learn in evil days, in barren days, in days of depression and calamity. "There is but one only liberator in this life from the daemons that invade us, and that is, Endeavour, earnest, entire, perennial endeavour." Partial activity and occasional impulses set free some part or limb for a short time.

Follow this leading, nor ask too curiously whither. To follow it, is thy part. And what if it lead, as men say, to an excess, to partiality, to individualism: Follow it still. His art shall suffice this artist, his flame this lover, his inspiration this poet.

The artist must be sacrificed. Take it sadly home to thy heart,—the artist must pay for his learning and doing with his life. The old Herschel must choose between the night and the day, and draw on his nightcap when the sun rises, and defend his eyes for nocturnal use.[21] Michel Angelo must paint Sistine ceilings, till he can no longer read, except by holding the book over his head. Nature deals with all her children so. See the poor flies, lately so wanton, now fixed to the wall or the tree, exhausted and presently blown away. Men likewise: they put their lives into their deed. What is a man good for, without enthusiasm, and what is enthusiasm, but this daring of ruin for its object? There are thoughts beyond the reaches of our souls. We are not the less drawn to them. The moth flies into the flame of the lamp; Archimedes, Socrates, Behmen, Bruno, Pascal, Swedenborg, must solve the problems, though they be crazed or killed.[22]

It is to be considered that the one secret of power intellectual or physical is concentration, and that all concentration involves a certain narrowness. It is a law of nature that he who looks at one thing must turn his eyes from every other thing in the universe. The horse goes better with blinders, and the man for dedication to his task. And if you ask what compensation is made for the inevitable narrowness: Why this, that, in learning one thing well, you learn all things. Things are coordinated.

There is a probity of the Intellect, which demands, if possible, virtues more costly than any Bible has consecrated. It consists in an absolute devotion to truth, founded in a faith in truth. You will say, this is quite axiomatic and a little too true. I do not find it an agreed point. Literary men, for the most part, have a settled despair as to the realization of ideas in their own times. There is in all students a distrust of truth, a timidity about affirming it, a wish to patronize Providence. We lie for the right. We affect a greater hope than we feel. We disown our debt to moral evil.

Society does not love its unmaskers. The virtue of the Intellect is its own, as its courage is of its own kind; and, at last, it will be justified, though for the time it seem hostile to that which it most reveres.

Truth is our only armour in all passages of life and death. The words you spoke are forgotten, but the part you took is organized into the body of the universe. I will speak the truth in my heart, or think the truth against what is called God.

Ignorant people confound the reverence for the intuitions with egotism. This confusion of thought in our vulgar theology argues great inexperience of that which is life to know. There is no confusion in the things themselves. True elevation

21. Sir William Herschel (originally Friedrich Wilhelm) (1738–1822), British astronomer born in Germany, discoverer of the planet Uranus.

22. Archimedes (ca. 287–212 B.C.), Greek mathematician and engineer; Socrates (ca. 470–399 B.C.), one of the most famous of the Greek philosophers whose dialogic method of teaching gained many adherents; Giordano Bruno (1548–1600), Italian pantheistic philosopher; Blaise Pascal (1623–62), French scientist, philosopher, and mathematician; Emanuel Swedenborg (1688–1772), Swedish scientist, theologian, and mystic.

of mind consists in the perception of law. Its dignity and joy consist in being under a law. Its goodness is the most generous extension of our private interests, the extension of our private interests to the dignity and generosity of ideas. Nothing seems to me so excellent as a belief in the laws. It communicates dignity and, as it were, an asylum in temples, to the loyal soul.

I confess that every thing connected with our personality fails. Nature never spares the individual. We are always baulked of a complete success. No prosperity is promised to that. We have our indemnity only in the sure success of that to which we belong. *That, that* is immortal, and we only through that.

One polarity is impressed on the Universe and on its particles. As the whole has its law, so each individual has his genius. Obedience to its genius, to speak a little scholastically, is the particular of faith; perception that the tendency of the whole is to the benefit of the individual, is the universal of faith.

The soul stipulates for no private good. That which is private, I see not to be good. "If Truth live, I live; if Justice live, I live," said one of the old saints, and the Chinese Confucius said, "Put men to death by the principles which have for their object the preservation of life, and they will not grumble."[23]

Do not truck for your private immortality. If immortality, in the sense in which you seek it, is best, you shall be immortal. If it is up to the dignity of that order of things you know, it is secure. The sky, the sea, the plants, the rocks, astronomy, chemistry, keep their word. Morals and the genius of humanity will also. In short, the whole moral of modern science is the transference of that trust which is felt in Nature's admired arrangements, to the sphere of freedom and of rational life.

But clear your notion of Immortality. Let the life you would continue into immensity, not be something you are ashamed of when it is only a few years long,—a few wearisome personalities, and dull trifles, repeated already much too often. It is a life a good man would not turn on his heel to save. What is called Religion effeminates and demoralizes; such as you are, the gods themselves could not help you. Men are too often unfit to live, from their obvious inequality to their own necessities; or, they suffer from politics, or bad neighbours, or from sickness,— and they would gladly know that they were to be dismissed from the duties of life. But the Intellect asks of these, How will Death help them? These are not dismissed, when they die. You shall not wish for death, out of pusillanimity. The weight of the Universe is pressed down on the shoulders of each slave to hold him to his task. The only path of escape known in all the world of God is performance. You must do your work, before you shall be released.

Men talk as if Victory were something doubtful. Work is Victory. Wherever work is done, victory is obtained. There is no chance, and no blanks: All draw prizes. You want but one verdict. If you have your own, you are secure of the rest.

23. Confucius (Latin name for K'ung Ch'iu) (551–479 B.C.), Chinese philosopher.

And yet, if witnesses were wanted, witnesses are near. I cannot see, without awe, that no man thinks alone, and no man acts alone; but the divine assessors, who came up with him into life, now under one disguise, now another, like a police in citizens' clothes, walk with him step by step through all the kingdom of time.

These studies seem to me to derive an importance from their bearing on the universal question of modern times, the question of Religion.

We live in a transition period, when the old faiths which have educated, and comforted, and legislated for nations, and not only so, but have made the nations, seem to have spent their force, and to be comparatively powerless on the public and the private mind of Europe and America. Society is full now of fancy faiths, of gentlemen and of nations in search of religions. It seems to me, as if men stood craving a more stringent creed than any of the pale and enervating systems to which they had recourse. The Turk who believes that his doom is written on the iron leaf on the moment when he entered the world, and that he cannot alter it, rushes on the enemy's sword with undivided will. The Buddhist who finds gods masked in all his friends and enemies, and reads the issue of the conflict beforehand in the rank of the actors, is calm. The old Greek was respectable, and we are not yet able to forget his dramas,—who found the genius of tragedy in the conflict between Destiny and the strong *should*, and not like the moderns, in the weak *would*. And the natural remedy against this miscellany of knowledge and aim, this desultory universality of ours, this immense ground-juniper falling abroad, and not gathered up into any columnar tree, is, to substitute realism, for sentimentalism; a recognition of the simple and terrible laws, which, seen or unseen—(seen as they are, or falsely, vicariously, and personally seen)—pervade and govern.

The religion which is to guide and satisfy the present and coming ages, whatever else it be, must be intellectual. The scientific mind must have a faith which is science. "There are two things," said Mahomet, "which I abhor, the learned in his infidelities, and the fool in his devotions."[24] Our times are very impatient of both, and specially of the last. Let us have nothing now which is not its own evidence. There is surely enough for the heart and the imagination. Our books are full of generous biographies of saints, who knew not that they were such; of men and of women who lived for the benefit and healing of nature. But one fact I read in them all,—that, there is a religion which survives immutably all persons and fashions, and is worshipped and pronounced with emphasis again and again by some holy person;—and men, with their weak incapacity for principles, and their passion for persons, have run mad for the pronouncer, and forgot the religion.

But there is surely enough for the heart and the imagination in the religion itself. Let us not be pestered with assertions and half-truths, with emotions and snuffle: "Surely all that is simple is sufficient for all that is good."

24. Muhammad (ca. 570–632), founder of Islam, born in Mecca.

There will be a new Church founded on moral science; at first, cold and naked, a babe in a manger, again; the algebra and mathematics of ethical law; the church of men to come; without shawms, or psaltery, or sackbut; but it will have heaven and earth for its beams and rafters; all science for symbol and illustration: it will fast enough gather beauty, music, picture, poetry. Was never Stoicism so stern and exigent as this shall be. It shall send man home to his central solitude, shame these social supplicating manners, and make him know, that, much of the time, he must have himself to his friend. He shall expect no cooperation; he shall walk with no companion. The nameless Thought, the nameless Power, the superpersonal Heart,—I wish him to repose alone on that.

He needs only his own verdict. No good fame can help, no bad fame can hurt him. The Laws are his Consolers: The good Laws themselves are alive: They know if he has kept them. They animate him with the consciousness of great duty and an endless horizon. Honour and fortune are to him who always recognizes the neighbourhood of the great, always feels himself in the presence of high causes. The joy of knowledge, the late discovery that the veil which hid all things from him is really transparent, transparent everywhere to pure eyes, and the heart of trust which every perception fortifies,—renew life for him. He finds, that events spring from the same root as persons; the Universe understands itself, and all the parts play with a sure harmony.

England

(1848–1852)

"England" ranks among Emerson's most significant and popular lectures. Emerson first visited England in 1833, and he visited it a third and final time in 1872–73, but his many renditions of "England" have their origin in his lecture tour of the British Isles during a second visit in 1847–48. While on that tour he delivered sixty-four lectures in twenty-five cities and towns in England and Scotland between November 1847 and February 1848 and six lectures as part of the series *Mind and Manners of the Nineteenth Century* at the Literary and Scientific Institution in London in June 1848. The importance of Emerson's British lecture tour to his national and international reputation as a lecturer, to the shaping of his ideas on English history, manners, and character, and to the fullest expression of his thoughts on England and the English in *English Traits*, published in 1856, cannot be overstated.

When Emerson returned home from his tour in 1848 American audiences were eager to hear about his experiences abroad and to receive his impressions of Anglo-Saxon culture and his judgment on the character of England's leading persons, many of whom he met and now counted among his favorite correspondents. He responded to his public's interest with "England," delivering the lecture nearly thirty times throughout New England and New York State and in Philadelphia, Cleveland, Cincinnati, Pittsburgh, and Montreal. Even though he had fairly well exhausted opportunities to deliver "England" to his regular audiences by 1852, Emerson continued to rely on the lecture for personal anecdotes and information about England as he gave lectures entitled "Characteristics of the English," "English Character and Influence," "English Influence on Modern Civilization," and "English Civilization" between 1854 and 1856.

The traveller on arriving in England is struck at once with the cultivation. On every side, he sees the triumph of labor. Man has subdued and made everything. The country is a garden. Under that ash-coloured sky, the fields are so combed and rolled, that it seems as if they had been finished with a pencil instead of a plough.[1] The structures that compose the towns, have been piled by

---

1. This description is drawn from the writings of Count Vittorio Alfieri (1749–1803), Italian dramatist, according to Emerson's note in the manuscript.

the wealth and skill of ages. Nothing is left as it was made. Rivers, hills, valleys, the sea all feel the hand of a master. The long habitation of a powerful and ingenious race has turned every rood of land to its best use, has found all the capabilities, all the short cuts, all the arable soil, all the quarriable rock, all the navigable waters; and the new arts of intercourse meet you everywhere, so that England itself is a huge mill, or hotel, or palais-royale, where all that man wants is provided within the precinct. Cushioned and comforted in every manner, the traveller rides everywhere, as on a cannon-ball, high and low, over rivers and towns, and through mountains, in tunnels of three miles and more, at twice the speed, and with half the shaking, of our trains, and reads quietly the *Times* newspaper, which, again, by its wonderful system of correspondence and reporting, seems to have machinized the world for his occasion.

If one remembers here Mr. Landor's exclamation, "Who would live in a new country, that can live in an old?",—especially, he recalls, in the old cities, where the question would find a more unanimous affirmative,—no familiarity or long residence can exhaust the advantages of London, because the past as well as the present are always filling the basket faster than any diligence can empty it.[2] Every age since Julius Caesar has left some trace of itself in the building of old King Lud's town, and a certain civility and conservative instinct has kept all in repair.[3] The railway excavations, within this very year, have laid bare a Roman pavement. Fragments of the London wall of that age are still to be found near Ludgate Hill; and so down: Saxon arches, Norman windows, mediæval towers; Westminster Abbey; palaces of Inigo Jones; St. Paul's Cathedral and fifty-four churches of Christopher Wren; old colleges, immemorial hospitals, immense accommodations which modern commerce has provided for itself, and all the facilities which the wealth of all the monarchs of Europe could not buy, but which are yielded for his small subscription of a few pence or shillings to the private citizen of an old town; facilities that belong to the living on the spot where the great agencies centre and where the ruling men in every kind are found; whence all ships, expresses, roads, and telegraphs radiate for all parts of the world, and where every service you require is rendered by the first masters in that kind.[4] Rothschild or the Barings are your bankers; Stephenson and Brunel your engineers; Pugin and Barry build; Chadwick makes the aqueduct, Wheatstone the telegraph, Reid ventilates; the military arrangements (and, in April last, they were serious,) are made by the Duke of Wellington; the mighty

2. Walter Savage Landor (1775–1864), English romantic poet and prose writer whom Emerson met in England in 1833.

3. Gaius Julius Caesar (100–44 B.C.), Roman general and statesman who invaded Britain in 55 and 54 B.C.; Lud was the legendary king of England who rebuilt the walls of London.

4. Inigo Jones (1573–1652), English architect, designer of the banqueting hall at Whitehall in London; Sir Christopher Wren (1632–1723), English architect, proposed plans for rebuilding London after the Great Fire (1666), including fifty-three churches, the best known of which is St. Paul's Cathedral (1675–1711).

debate in Parliament by Peel, Russell, Cobden, Brougham, and Stanley; Faraday, and Richard Owen, Sedgwick, and Buckland, are the lecturers in science; Herschel, Airy, and Adams, in the observatory; the great heirs of fame are living and talking in society: Turner and Landseer paint; Wordsworth, Landor, Hallam, Tennyson, Dickens, write; and for your entertainment, Rachel plays, and Macready; Lablache, Grisi, and Jenny Lind sing, Taglioni dances, and Soyer cooks.[5]

Happy is the man who lives where the best is cheap! Life is here in extremes; the traveller goes from show to show; he can be pampered to the highest point; he sits in a cloud of pictures; he eats from off porcelain and plate; his rug is the skin of a lion. Science will quiddle for him: if he will, his light is polarised, his water distilled, he sleeps with a puff of chloroform on a water-bed, and all his implements, garments, and trinkets are the work of artists, whose names have been familiar to him for years as the best makers.

But, more than all, the riches of a cultivated population one cannot exaggerate. Every day you may meet a new man who is the centre of a new circle of thought and

5. The Baring Brothers and Company (along with the Rothschilds) was a major banking firm of the day; Robert Stephenson (1803–59), English inventor, constructed the first railway into London, completed in 1838; Sir Marc Isambard Brunel (1769–1849), British engineer and inventor born in France, and his son, Isambard Kingdom Brunel (1806–59), designers of, respectively, the Thames Tunnel and the Great Western Railway; Augustus Welby Northmore Pugin (1812–52), English architect and designer; Sir Charles Barry (1795–1860), English architect, won the competition for the best designs for the Houses of Parliament and built them with Pugin; Sir Edwin Chadwick (1800–1890), English reformer, active in the first sanitary commission of 1839; Sir Charles Wheatstone (1802–75), English physicist and inventor; Sir William Reid (1791–1858), British meteorologist, soldier, and colonial administrator; Arthur Wellesley, first Duke of Wellington (1769–1852), British general and statesman born in Ireland, served in Britain's armies throughout the empire for nearly fifty years; Sir Robert Peel (1788–1850), English politician and prime minister; Richard Cobden (1804–65), English politician and economist, advocate of free trade and peace; Henry Peter Brougham, first Baron Brougham and Vaux (1778–1868), British jurist and statesman born in Scotland, a founder of the *Edinburgh Review*; Edward George Geoffrey Smith Stanley (1799–1869), three-time prime minister of England; Michael Faraday (1791–1867), English chemist and physicist, known for his experiments with electromagnetism; Robert Owen (1771–1858), Welsh social reformer and philanthropist; Adam Sedgwick (1785–1873), English geologist, professor at Cambridge; William Buckland (1784–1856), English clergyman and geologist, professor at Oxford; Sir William Herschel (originally Friedrich Wilhelm) (1738–1822), British astronomer born in Germany, discoverer of the planet Uranus; Sir George Biddell Airy (1801–92), English astronomer, director of the Royal Observatory at Greenwich; John Couch Adams (1819–92), English astronomer, director of the Cambridge Observatory; Joseph Mallord William Turner (1775–1851), English landscape painter known for his experiments with light; Sir Edwin Henry Landseer (1802–73), English painter, popular for animal paintings; William Wordsworth (1770–1850), English poet and, with Samuel Taylor Coleridge, founder of the romantic movement; Henry Hallam (1777–1859), English historian; Alfred, Lord Tennyson (1809–92), English poet, named poet laureate in 1850 after the death of Wordsworth; Charles Dickens (1812–70), popular English novelist; Mlle Rachel (1820–58), stage name of Élisa Félix, French actress; William Charles Macready (1793–1873), English tragedian and theater manager who made several tours of America; Luigi Lablache (1794–1858), Italian singer, most famous bass of his generation; Giulia Grisi (1811–69), Italian opera singer; Jenny Lind (1820–87), singer known as the Swedish Nightingale, brought to America by P. T. Barnum in 1850–52 for a triumphant tour; Marie Taglioni (1804–84), member of a celebrated Italian family of ballet dancers, one of the first women to dance on the points of the toes; Alexis Benoît Soyer (1809–58), English cook.

practice, which, but for what seems an accident, you should never have heard of, in this mob of gifted and educated men. The inequalities of power have their consolation here,—that they are superficial. Everyone can do something. When I see the power that every human being possesses to make himself valued and beloved by making himself useful and necessary to those with whom he finds himself,—I pity him no longer.

Some of the causes of the historical importance of England, I shall enumerate. But I premise with this remark, that the praise of England is not that it has freed itself from the evils under which other countries labor, not that England has found out how to create wealth and power without the creation of poverty and crime,— No, for all have these griefs and England also; but, that England has with this evil produced, in the last five hundred years, a greater number of strong, wise, educated, and humane men,—a greater number of excellent and finished men, than any other nation.

England has the best working climate in the world. It is never hot or cold. There is no hour in the year when one cannot work. Here is no winter, but such days as we have in Massachusetts in November. A climate which makes no exhausting demand on human strength, but allows the fullest development of the form.

Then, England has all the materials of a working country,—all the materials except wood. The constant rain, a rain with every tide in some parts of the island, keeps its multitude of rivers full and swift. It has abundance of water, of stone, of coal, and iron. It is a working country, and everybody works in England. It is computed, that only three or four percent of the whole population are idle.

The only drawback on this advantage that I know is the darkness of its grey sky. The night and day are too nearly of a color. It strains the eyes to read or to write. Add, the smoke of the manufacturing towns, where the *blacks* darken the air, give white sheep precisely the color of black sheep, discolor the human saliva,—and you will know the want of daylight in Leeds and Manchester.

In this climate, (which, however, Ireland also enjoys,) the English appear to possess the advantage of the best blood. Without going into the history,—we may say, the mixture of Britons and Saxons was a good cross. Afterwards, England yielded to the Danes and Northmen in the tenth, and eleventh, and twelfth centuries; and was the receptacle into which all mettle of that strenuous population was poured. It would seem, that, the perpetual supply of the best men in Norway, Sweden, and Denmark to the piratical expeditions of the ninth and tenth centuries, into England, gradually exhausted those countries, like a tree which bears much fruit when young,—and these have been second-rate powers, ever since. Konghelle, the famed town, where the kings of Norway, Sweden, and Denmark, were wont to meet, is now rented to a private English gentleman as a shooting ground.

The English, at the present day, have great vigor of body and endurance. Other countrymen look slight and undersized beside them, and invalids. They are bigger men than the Americans; I suppose, a hundred English, taken at random out of the street, would weigh a fourth more than so many Americans. Yet, I am told, the skeleton is not larger. They are round, ruddy, and handsome; at least, the whole bust is well formed; and there is a tendency to make stout and powerful frames, like castles. This stoutness of shape particularly struck me, on my first landing at Liverpool;—porter, drayman, coachman, guard,—what substantial, respectable, grandfatherly figures, with costume and manners to suit. The American has really arrived at the old mansion-house, and finds himself among his Uncles, Aunts, and Grandmothers. The pictures on the chimney-tiles of his nursery were pictures of these people. Here they are in the identical costumes and air which so took him.

There are two styles of dress here which a traveller in the trains will soon take note of, the tortoise style, and the supple or becoming; the former, wherein the man seems to have obtained by time and pains a sort of house of cloth and buckram built up around him and speaks out of his building, suits English manners well enough.

It is the fault of their forms that they grow stocky, and the women seem to have that defect to their beauty;—few tall, slender persons of flowing shape, but stunted and thickset figures. But they are a very handsome race and always have been. The bronze monuments of Crusaders lying cross-legged in the Temple Church in London and those in Worcester Cathedral which are nine hundred years old are of the same type as the best youthful heads of men now in England, and please by beauty of the same character,—a certain expression, namely, of good nature, refinement, and valor, and mainly with that uncorrupt youth in the face of manhood, which is daily seen in the streets of London. They have a vigorous health and last well into middle and old age. The old men are as red as roses, and still handsome. A clean skin, and a peach-bloom complexion, is found all over the island.

The English head is round, and the animal powers are in perfection. Their veins are full of blood, and the people hearty eaters, attaching great importance to a plentiful and nutricious diet. The cyclops operative of England cannot subsist on food less solid than beef, and his performance is not more amazing to the foreign laborer than his diet is. Good mutton, wheat bread, and malt liquors are universal among the first-class laborers. It is curious that Tacitus found the English beer already in use among the Germans: "*Potui humor ex hordeo aut frumento in quandam simililudi nem vini corruptus.*"[6] Lord Chief Justice Fortescue, in Henry VI's time, says, "the inhabitants drink no water unless at certain times on a religious score and by way of penance."[7] The extremes of poverty and of ascetic temperance never reach cold water in England. Wood, the antiquary, in describing the poverty and

6. "For drink they use the liquid distilled from barley or wheat, after fermentation has given it a certain resemblance to wine," quoted from *Germania*, chap. 23, sec. 1, by Cornelius Tacitus (ca. 56–ca. 120), Roman historian and orator; "simililudi" should be "similitudinem."

7. Sir John Fortescue (ca. 1385–ca. 1479), English jurist, named chief justice of the King's Bench in 1442; Henry VI (1421–71), king of England (1422–61, 1470–71).

maceration of Father Lacey, an English Jesuit, does not deny him beer.[8] He says, "His bed was under a thatching, and the way to it up a ladder: His face was coarse, his drink of a penny a gaun or gallon."

They have more constitutional energy, physical and moral, than any other people, and this is no whit abated, but in full play at this moment. I find the Englishman to be he of all men who stands firmest in his shoes. They have in themselves what they value in their horses: mettle and bottom. A gentleman on the day of my arrival, in describing the Lord Lieutenant of Ireland, said, "Lord Clarendon has pluck like a cock and will fight till he dies;" and what I heard first, I heard last, and the one thing the English value is pluck. The cabmen have it; the merchants have it; the bishops have it; the women have it; the journals have it; the *Times* newspaper, they say, is the pluckiest thing in England; and little Lord John Russell, the minister, would take the command of the Channel Fleet tomorrow.[9]

It requires, men say, a good constitution to travel in Spain. I say as much of England, simply on account of the vigor and brawn of the people. I know nothing but the most serious business that could give me any counter-weight to these Baresarks, though they were only to order eggs and muffins for their breakfast.[10] The Englishman speaks with all his body; his elocution is stomachic as the American's is labial. The Englishman is very petulant and precise about his accommodation at inns and on the roads; a quiddle about his toast and his chop, and every species of convenience; and loud and pungent in his expressions of impatience at any neglect. He has that *aplomb* which results only from a good adjustment of the moral and physical nature, and the obedience of all the powers to the will. The axes of his eyes are united to his backbone, and only move with the trunk.

When I landed, the times were disastrous, and the commercial and political sky full of gloom.[11] But it was evident, that, let who will fail, England will not. It is plain, from the security of their manners, that these people have sat here a thousand years, and here will continue to sit. They will not break up, or arrive at any strange, desperate revolution like their neighbors, for they have as much energy and as much continence of character as they ever had. The immense power and possession which surround them is their own creation, and they exert the same commanding industry at this moment.

In America, we fancy that we live in a new and forming country, but that En-

8. Anthony à Wood (1632–95), English antiquary and historian.

9. George William Frederick Villiers, fourth Earl of Clarendon (1800–1870), English statesman, lord lieutenant of Ireland (1847–52). John Russell, first Earl Russell of Kingston Russell (1792–1878), British politician and prime minister.

10. Baresarks, from berserkers, Norse warriors who were reputed to have enormous strength, be invulnerable, and fight with a wild frenzy in battle, generally means a person who is headstrong and defiant.

11. Emerson had arrived in England in October 1847 during a period of revolutionary fervor on the Continent; the overthrow of the monarchy in Paris occurred the next year.

gland was finished long ago. But we find London and England in full growth. The towns are growing, some of them almost at the rate of American towns. Birkenhead, opposite Liverpool, was growing as fast as South Boston. The towns in Lancashire will by and by meet, and make a city, as big as, and bigger than, London. London itself is enlarging at a frightful rate, even to the filling up of Middlesex, and the decoration and repairs in every part of the old city go on day by day. Trafalgar Square was only new finished in April 1848. The British Museum is in full course of growth and activity and projected arrangement; the Vernon Gallery is just added to the National. The London University opens like our mushroom colleges at the West, and the Houses of Parliament are just sending up their proud Victoria tower, four hundred feet into the air. Everything in England bespeaks an immense and energetic population. The buildings are on a scale of size and wealth far beyond ours. The colossal masonry of the docks and of all public buildings attests the multitudes who are to be accommodated by them and who are to pay for them. England could not now build her old castles and abbeys, but what the nineteenth century wants,— club houses, vaults, docks, mills, canals, railways,—she builds fast and well.

A manly ability, a general sufficiency, is the genius of the English. The land and climate are favorable to the breeding of good men; and it was an odd proof of it, that, in my lectures, I hesitated to read many a disparaging phrase which I have been accustomed to throw into my writing, about poor, thin, unable, unsatisfying bipeds,—so much had the fine physique and the personal vigor of this robust race worked on my imagination. This abundant life and vigor betrays itself, at all points, in their manners, in the respiration, and the inarticulate noises they make in clearing the throat, all significant of burly strength. They have stamina; they can take the initiative on all emergences. And the one rule for the traveller in England, is,—This is no country for fainthearted people. Do not creep about diffidently. Make up your mind, take your course, and you shall find respect and furtherance.

This vigour appears in the manners of the people in the complete incuriosity and stony neglect of each to every other. Each man walks, eats, drinks, shaves, dresses, gesticulates, and, in every manner, is, acts, suffers, without reference to the bystanders, and in his own fashion, only careful not to interfere with them, or annoy them. It is not that he is trained to neglect the eyes of his neighbors; he is really occupied with his own affair, and does not think of them. In the first-class carriage, a clergyman takes his stout shoes out of his carpet bag, and puts them on, instead of thin ones, on approaching the station. Every man in this polished country consults only his convenience, as much as a solitary pioneer in Wisconsin. I know not where any personal eccentricity is so freely allowed, and no man gives himself any concern with it. An Englishman walks in a pouring rain swinging his closed umbrella, like a walking stick; wears a wig, or a shawl, or a saddle; or stands on his head; and no remark is made. And, as he has been doing this for several generations, it is now in the blood.

In short, every one of these islanders is an island himself,—safe, tranquil, incommunicable. In a company of strangers, you would think him deaf; his eyes never wander from his own table and newspaper; he is never betrayed into any curiosity or unbecoming emotion. They seem all to have been trained in one severe school of manners, and never to put off this iron harness. He does not give his hand. He does not let you meet his eye. It is almost an affront to look a man in the face, before being introduced. In mixed, or in select companies, they do not introduce persons, so that a presentation is a circumstance as valid as a contract. Introductions are sacraments. He withholds his name. At the hotel, if they ask his name at the book office, he stoops, and gives it in a low voice. If he give you his private address on a card, it is like an avowal of friendship; and his bearing, on being introduced, is studiously cold, even though he is seeking your acquaintance, and is studying how he shall serve you.

'Tis no wonder that this rigor astonishes their lively neighbors across the Channel, so strongly contrasted with the social genius of the French, and is the standing theme of French raillery. "The islanders of Albion," says a brilliant French writer,

carry with them a peculiar fluid, which I shall call the *Britannic fluid*, and, in the midst of which, they travel, as little accessible to the atmosphere of the regions which they traverse, as the mouse at the centre of the exhausted receiver. It is not only to the thousand precautions with which they go surrounded that they owe their eternal impassivity; it is not because they wear three pair of breeches one over the other that they arrive perfectly dry and clean in spite of rain and mud; it is not because they have woolen wigs that their stiff and wiry frisure defies moisture; it is not because they go loaded each with as much pommade, brushes, and soap as would serve to adonize a whole regiment of Bas Breton conscripts that they have always the beard smooth and the nails irreproachable. It is because the external air does not touch them; it is because they walk, drink, eat, and sleep, *in their fluid*, as in a glass bell of twenty feet diameter, and, across which they behold with pity the cavaliers whose hair the wind discomposes, and the foot passenger whose shoes the snow soils.[12]

'Tis very certain that the Englishman has a confidence in the power and performance of his nation, which makes him provokingly incurious about other nations. It is a very old remark,—some centuries old,—that he dislikes foreigners. Swedenborg, who visited England many times in the last century, remarks: "There is a similitude of minds among them, in consequence of which, they contract a familiarity with friends who are from their nation, and seldom with others. They are lovers of their country, and zealous for its glory, and they regard foreigners

---

12. Attributed to George Sand, pen name of Amandine-Aurore-Lucile Dudevant (1804–76), French novelist whose personal life scandalized Paris, in Emerson's note in the manuscript.

as one looking through a telescope from the top of his palace regards those who dwell or wander about out of the city."[13] But in a much older traveller, the *Relation of England* by a Venetian in 1500, three hundred and fifty years ago, I find a similar testimony: "The English are great lovers of themselves, and of everything belonging to them. They think that there are no other men than themselves, and no other world but England; and whenever they see a handsome foreigner, they say that he looks like an Englishman, and it is a great pity he should not be an Englishman: and when they partake of any delicacy with a foreigner, they ask him whether such a thing is made in *his* country."[14]

It is very certain that this arrogance is really in the true-born Englishman, and all the goodness of heart and studious courtesy that belong to him fail to conceal it. When he accumulates epithets of praise, his climax of commendation is, "*So English,*" and when he wishes to pay you the highest compliment, he says, "I should not know you from an Englishman."

At the same time, I know no national pride that is so easily forgiven and so much respected as his, and for the reason that it is so well-founded. The Englishman is proud,—Yes, but he is admirable; he knows all things, has all things, and can do all things. How can he not be proud? There is a certain general culture wherein he surpasses other nations. There is no man so equally and harmoniously developed, and hence his easy pride when he finds every other countryman inferior to him as a social man. His wide outlook, his birth and breeding in the commercial and political centre of the world, have accustomed his eye and mind to whatever is best in the planet and made him instantly perceptive of any meanness or fault. A certain liberality and catholicism, an air of having seen much and seen the best, appears in all men. They are bored by anything provincial and detect the smutch of native clay sticking to the clothes of a villager. They notice in the American speech a certain purism, the accent of a man who knows how the word is spelled, rather than the unrestrained expression of a man who is only eager to say what he means.

Besides, it is quite inevitable that this spoiled child of nature and fortune should have the fastidiousness which the habit generates. He talks of his politics and institutions, but the real thing which he values is his home and that which belongs to it,—that general culture and high polish, which, in his experience, no man but the Englishman possesses, and which, he naturally believes, have some essential connexion with his throne and laws.

In all culture, so much depends on sympathy, on a great number who keep each other up to a high point, that, 'tis a pleasure to the traveller in England to know that there is all around him an infinite number of educated and thoughtful people, all quietly and calmly carrying forward every variety of profound and elegant study,

13. Emanuel Swedenborg (1688–1772), Swedish scientist, theologian, and mystic.
14. Quoted from *A Relation, or Rather a True Account, of the Island of England . . . about the Year 1500* (1847), trans. Charlotte Augusta Sneyd (*JMN*, 10:198).

with the best aids and materials, though rarely communicating, and, for the most part, each wholly independent and unacquainted with the rest.

And here comes in an element of decisive importance, the existence of a superior or model class, legalised by statute and usage, fostered and privileged from the beginning of the national history, with all the institutions of the country to secure them in their hereditary wealth, owners of all the soil, with the best education to develop and stamp these advantages, and placed in every manner on such high ground, that, whatever benefit the nation reaps with its million arms outstretched from pole to pole,—they more. The finest race of men in the friendliest climate, possessing every natural and accidental advantage and secured in the possession of these by the loyal affection of the people, they easily came to produce sound minds in sound bodies and exhibit more finished men than any other nation.

The favoured class seem to gain as much as they lose by their position. They survey all society as from the top of St. Paul's, and, if they never hear plain truth from men, as the poor do, they see the best of everything in every kind, and they see things so grouped and amassed, as to infer easily the sum and genius, instead of tedious particularities. Their good behaviour deserves all its fame; and they have, in the highest degree, that simplicity and that air of repose which are such chief ornaments of greatness.

It was inevitable that these people should have a controlling influence on the manners of the people. They naturally furnish the best models of manly behaviour to their country and the world. Moreover, it has come to be the ambition of the English system of education,—of their schools and of the universities,—to turn out gentlemen, rather than scholars or skilful masters in any art; and the like feeling runs into the middle and lower classes.

It is not to be disguised, however, that there is much in this English culture, so much prized at home, so much admired abroad, that will not bear analysis,—is by no means the best thing in the English state; is material; is built on wealth, built on trifles, and certainly has another less reputable face and name as the height of cockneyism. For, it rests on land and money, on birth, on diet, on excellence in horsemanship, on hunting, on dogs, on boxing, on boating, and on betting. The self-command and continuity of will are exerted in affairs,—the bribes of speculation, the panics of trade, the game of party, all powerless,—foiled by an insight which commands the law of the game better than any other player,—it is the guarantee of victory.

They have carried inoffensiveness to a very high point. They have applied their strong understanding and their love of animal comfort to a perfect organization of the details of a domestic day, studiously excluding everything annoying or discordant, and have become superstitiously neat and proper, and orderly, and respectable. Their hat, and shoes, and linen, their horse and gun, their egg, and toast, and soda water, and wine, and politics, and visiting-set, are irreproachable. It is a world of trifles, and seems to argue a mediocrity of intellect in the nation which allows it so much importance. Whilst we pay homage to the indisputable merits of the English people, we must not confound their immense regard to trifles, with their virtues.

Their good form and habit are much indebted to the manly exercises to which they are trained from earliest youth. They begin with cricket, archery, and skittles,—in each of which games they acquire some skill at school and at college. They learn the use of oars at Eton and Westminster schools: at Oxford and Cambridge, the boat clubs are in daily practice; and yachting and regattas are favorite amusements of gentlemen in every part of the island where there is water.

Still more universal is their attachment to horses, and to hounds, and to every form of hunting. They are always on horseback, centaurs. Every inn-room is lined with pictures of racers. And expresses bring, every hour, news to London, from Newmarket and Ascot.

The universal practice of betting, too, is not without its uses as it makes the knowledge of all men whom you meet singularly accurate in regard to all common facts. Every distance has been measured in miles, rods, and inches. They know the distance of their towns, the length of their boats, the speed of their horses, the numbers of their partisans, and complain of looseness in the information of other countrymen on these points.

But what I think is the secret of English success, is, a certain balance of qualities in their nature, corresponding to what we call temper in steel. The geographical position of England is excellent; but there are many countries with good seacoasts besides England,—many countries with good climate, which make no pretension to British influence. But here is the best average brain. Men found that this people had a faculty of doing, which others had not. There is an incompatibility in the Italians, in the Spaniards, in the Turks, of dealing with other nations,—of treating with them. But the English brain is of the right temper. Neither too cold, nor too hot; neither too swift, nor too slow.—Calm, energetic, tenacious, just, and wise.

The English metal is not brittle, is not soft, not explosive, but tenacious, incorruptible, and admitting a good working edge: That happy adaptedness to things which makes the ordinary Englishman a skilful and thorough workman, and the higher classes good heads for the combining and arranging of labour. The fabulous St. George has never seemed to me the patron saint of England; but the scholar, monk, soldier, engineer, lawgiver, Alfred,—working-king; often defeated, never discouraged; patient of defeat, of affront, of labor, and victorious by fortitude and wisdom,—he is the model Englishman.[15] They have many such in their

---

15. Saint George (probably third century A.D.), usually depicted slaying a dragon, became the patron saint of England in the fourteenth century; Alfred the Great (849–99), sovereign of all England not under Danish rule from 886 to his death.

annals. Cromwell is one.[16] One is William of Wykeham,—Bishop of Winchester in the reign of Edward II, Edward III, and Richard II,—a poor boy of obscure parentage, who by study, and practical talent, and sound judgment, and a certain humble magnanimity, conceived and carried out great plans; built roads and causeys; built Windsor Castle; built the sublime Winchester Cathedral; and, observing the gross ignorance of the priesthood, in his times, and, attributing many public evils to that cause,—established a school at Winchester, and livings for seventy boys, to be there trained for the university, at his expense, forever; and then established at Oxford Winchester or New College, with livings for seventy fellows, at his expense forever.[17] In May (1848) I visited Oxford, and Dr. Williams, the polite head of the College, showed me the halls, chapel, library, and common rooms and gardens,— over every gate of which was written in stone William of Wykeham's motto, "Manners maketh man",—and assured me that now, after five hundred years, the seventy boys at Winchester school and the seventy fellows at Winchester College, are still maintained on the bounty of the founder.[18]

One of the merits of Wykeham was the stern investigation which he instituted into the embezzlement and perversion of the religious and charitable foundations in his time; especially, the account which he demanded of the revenues of the "Hospital of Saint Cross," where, long before him, Henry of Blois, brother of King Stephen, had founded a charity for the support of a hundred poor, and, with a provision, that a measure of beer and a piece of bread should be given forever to every son of man who should ask for it.[19] As I passed the Hospital of Saint-Cross, on my way from Stonehenge, in July, I knocked at the door, to see if William-of-Wykeham's word was sterling yet in England, and received my horn of beer and my piece of bread, gratuitously, from the charity of a founder who has been dead seven centuries. I hardly think it less honorable that the man whom the English of this age put forward as the type of their race is a man so proverbial for his veracity, perseverance, and moderation as the Duke of Wellington.

I fear, that, in many points, the English tenacity is in strong contrast to American facility. The facile American sheds his Puritanism, when he leaves Cape Cod, runs into all English and French vices, with great zest, and is neither Unitarian, nor Calvinist, nor Catholic, nor Quaker, nor stands for any thought or thing; all which is very distasteful to English honor.

16. Oliver Cromwell (1599–1658), English soldier and statesman, revolutionary who became Lord Protector of the Realm.

17. William of Wykeham (1324–1404), English prelate and politician, bishop of Winchester from 1367 to his death; Edward II of Caernarvon (1284–1327), king of England (1307–27); Edward III of Windsor (1312–77), king of England (1327–77); Richard II (1367–1400), king of England (1377–99).

18. Emerson had been shown the grounds of Oxford by David Williams, warder of New College, when he had visited there in May 1848 (*Letters*, 4:48).

19. Henry of Blois (ca. 1099–1171), English prelate and younger brother of Stephen (ca. 1097–1154, king of England, 1135–54), abbot of Glastonbury and then bishop of Winchester.

I do not think the English quite capable of doing justice to our countrymen. He is annoyed by the free and easy pretension, the careless manners, and the neglect of certain points of decorum and respect, to which he is accustomed to attach importance; and he does not see, that, this is his own self-reliance transferred to a new theatre, where there is no such division of labor as exists in England, and where every man must help himself in every manner, like an Indian, and remember much which the European more gracefully abandons to his valet.

But the main advantage which the American possesses, is a certain versatility, and, as far as I know, a greater apprehensiveness of mind. He more readily and genially entertains new thoughts, new modes, new books, is more speculative, more contemplative, and is really related to the future, whilst the Englishman seems mortgaged to the past. Each countryman is qualified for the part assigned him in history to play.

In drawing these sketches, I am well aware there is a dark side of England, which, I have not wished to expose. The first effect of the extraordinary determination of the national mind for so many centuries on wealth has been, in developing colossal wealth, to develop hideous pauperism. These fair, ruddy, muscular, well-educated bodies go attended by poor, dwarfed, starved, short-lived skeletons. There are two Englands;—rich, Norman-Saxon, learned, social England,—seated in castles, halls, universities, and middle class houses of admirable completeness and comfort, and poor, Celtic, peasant, drudging, Chartist England, in hovels and workhouses, cowed and hopeless.[20] I only recognize this fact, in passing. It is important that it be stated. It will not help us now to dwell on it.

England is the country of the rich. The great poor man does not yet appear. Whenever he comes, England will fall like France. It would seem, that an organizing talent applied directly to the social problem,—to bring, for example, labor to market; to bring want and supply face to face; would not be so rare. A man like Hudson, like Trevylian, like Cobden, should know something about it.[21] The Reform Bill took in new partners, and Chartism again takes in more.[22]

They are "strange, neat-handed Titans, and, if wanting fire from heaven, make, at least, the cheapest and most polished patent lamps for receiving it, when it shall come." They have propriety and parliamentariness, propriety felt both in what they do not say, and in what they say. The schools and universities cling to them, and give a certain mechanical integrity to their manners and culture and make it impossible to them to make a mistake. In the educated English, one feels the advantage of

20. Chartists were English reformers who promoted better conditions for the working classes during the early to mid-nineteenth century.

21. Henry Hudson (d. 1611), English navigator and explorer after whom Hudson Bay and the Hudson River are named; probably Sir Charles Edward Trevelyan (1807–86), British politician much involved with India.

22. The Reform Bill of 1832, sponsored in part by John Russell, first Earl Russell of Kingston Russell, lowered electoral qualifications to allow most members of the middle class to vote.

thorough drill. Eton, and Harrow, and Rugby have done their work; they know prosody, and tread securely through all the humanities.

But the Englishman is the victim of this excellence. The practical and comfortable oppress him with inexorable claims, and the smallest fraction of power remains for heroism and poetry. My own feeling is, that the English have sacrificed their grandeur to their cleverness. They have vaunted their practicalness, until the brain serves the hand, which ought to serve the brain, and until the nobler traits, which, in former times, distinguished the British nation, are disappearing before the indispensable demand of wealth and convenience.

The English boast the grandeur of their national genius; but seem not to observe that a total revolution has taken place in their estimate of mental greatness. The age of their greatness was an ideal and Platonic age: all the great men of the Elizabethan period had that tendency. Now, the intellect of England plumes itself on its limitary and practical turn. Once there was mysticism in the British mind, a deep vein of religion. Once there was Platonism, a profound poetry, and daring sallies into the realm of thought on every side. Now, there is musty, self-conceited decorum,—life made up of fictions hating ideas: but not a breath of Olympian air dilates the collapsing lungs. *Now*, we have clever mediocrity: the paragraph writers, the fashionable-romance writers, the elegant travellers, and dapper diners-out, with anecdote and bons mots,—made up men with made up manners,—varied and exact information; facts,—(facts the Englishman delights in all day long;)— humour too, and all that goes to animate conversation. "Conversational powers," says Campbell, "are so much the rage in London, that no reputation is higher than his, who exhibits them to advantage."[23]

We have plenty of derision and worldliness. The genius of the House of Commons is a sneer. "What delights the House," says Fowell Buxton, "is a mixture of good sense and joking."[24] We have no plain-dealing, no abandonment, but every sentence in good society must have a twist,—something unexpected, something the reverse of the probable, is required. The day's Englishman must have his joke as duly as his bread. Bold is he and absolute in his narrow circle, versed in all his routine, sure and elegant, his stories are good, his sentences firm, and all his statesmen, lawyers, men of letters, and poets, finished and solid as the pavement. But a faith in the laws of the mind like that of Archimedes; belief like that of Euler and Kepler, that experience must follow and not lead the laws of the mind; a devotion to the theory of politics, like that of Hooker, Milton, and Harrington;—the modern English mind repudiates.[25]

---

23. Attributed to Thomas Campbell (1777–1844), British poet and critic born in Scotland (*JMN*, 11:305).

24. Sir Thomas Fowell Buxton (1786–1845), English philanthropist.

25. Archimedes (ca. 287–212 B.C.), Greek mathematician and engineer; Leonhard Euler (1707–83), Swiss mathematician; Johannes Kepler (1571–1630), German mathematician and astronomer; Richard Hooker (ca. 1553–1600), English theologian; John Milton (1608–74), English poet and political writer,

I am forced to say that aristocracy requires an intellectual and moral basis, and that though all the accidents are very well, they indispensably involve real elevation at last. But, in England, one had to humour the society. "It was very well, *considering,*"—as our country people say. Very fine masters, very fine misses, charming saloons,—but where were the great? The Americans who should succeed in it were the well-bred rich, and not those who make America to me. I am wearied and inconvenienced by what are called fine people. The moment I meet a grand person, a man of sense and comprehension, I am emancipated. Such persons I did not find. One would say there was a plentiful sterility of such. One goes through England making believe that this is good society. It is so old, so much has been spent on it, the case is so costly, it has such a history around it,—effigies of a nation of ancestors,—or it has so neatly stepped into the history and place of the real prince, that one easily lets it pass for true, and, nine times out of ten, does not doubt its legitimacy. But such illusion leads to suicide.—If this is the height of life, let me die.

Plutarch tells us, "that Archimedes considered the being busied about mechanics, and, in short, every art which is connected with the common purposes of life, illiberal and ignoble; and those things alone were objects of his ambition, with which the beautiful and the excellent were present, unmingled with the necessary."[26] I have to say that the whole fabric is wonderful, but has cost too much; that the higher faculties have been sacrificed. The English mind is less contemplative, less religious, less open, than it was in former periods. Books of larger scope, as Wordsworth and Coleridge, must come to this country for their fame, before they gain it in England.[27]

My own impression is, the English mind has more breadth and cosmopolitanism, but no ascending scale. He has not the least interest in speculation. No men in England are quite ideal, living in an ideal world, and working in politics and social life, only from that. Her best writer is an earth-son mixed up with politics of the day as a partisan. I suffered myself to be dazzled willingly by the various brilliancy of men of talent. But he who values his days by the number of insights he gets, will as rarely find a good conversation, a solid dealing, man with man, in England, as in any country.

The English are eminently prosaic or unpoetic. All the poetic persons whom I saw, were deviations from the national type. The people have wide range, but no ascending scale in their speculation. An American, like a German, has many

best known for his poem *Paradise Lost* (published in 1667 in ten books); James Harrington (1611–77), English political theorist.

26. Plutarch (ca. 46–ca. 120), Greek historian best known for his series of "lives," or character studies, arranged in pairs in which a Greek and a Roman are compared.

27. Samuel Taylor Coleridge (1772–1834), English poet and philosopher and, with William Wordsworth, founder of the romantic movement.

platforms of thought. But an Englishman requires to be humored, or treated with tenderness, as an invalid, if you wish him to climb.

Herein England has but obeyed the law, which, in the order of the world, assigns one office to one people. Nature does one thing at a time. If she will have a perfect hand, she makes head and feet pay for it. So now that she is making railroad and telegraph ages, she starves the *spirituel*, to stuff the *materiel* and *industriel.*

But with all the deductions from the picture which truth requires, I find the English to have a thorough good nature; they are a true, benign, gentle, benevolent, hospitable, and pious race, fearing God, and loving man. There is respect for truth, and there is milk of kindness in them; and this in all classes, from the Chartist to the Duke. In the shops, the articles you buy are thoroughly made, and you learn to rely on the probity of the tradesman. Probity is the rule. In the large transactions, it is not less. An eminent merchant, by birth American, whose name is known through the world as partner in one of the first houses in London, said to me, "I have been here thirty years, and no man has ever attempted to cheat me."[28] If you stand at the door of the House of Commons, and look at the faces of the members, as they go in, you will say, these are just, kind, and honorable men, who mean to do right. If you go to Englishmen, properly introduced,—which is indispensable in this dense population, with the multitude of strangers, too, from all parts of the earth,—if you go to their houses, I do not think there is in the world such sincerity and thoroughness of hospitality. They see you through. They give you real service: they give you their time: they introduce you cordially to their friends: until you ask yourself,—'if they do thus to every stranger, how many hours will be left to them in the day and the year?'

They are as gentle and peaceful, as they are brave and magnanimous. At Oxford, I was told, among twelve hundred young men, comprising the most noble and spirited in the aristocracy, a duel never occurs. In Cambridge, among seventeen hundred, the same is true. And there is a sentiment of justice and honor resident in the people, which is always sure to respond aright, when any private or public wrong has been attempted.

I trace the peculiarities of English manners and English fortune, then, to their working climate, their dense population, the presence of an aristocracy or model class for manners and speech, to their diet generous and orderly taken, to their force of constitution, to the tenacity or perseverance of their nature, and to their fine moral quality. And these are some of the reasons why England is England. When to this vivacious stock at home, yielding armies of young men, every year, for her business of commercial conquest, all over the globe, you add the steady policy of planting a clear-headed, generous, and energetic gentleman, at every important

---

28. Attributed to Joshua Bates (1788–1864), a partner in the Baring Brothers banking firm, by Emerson (*JMN*, 10:331).

point, all along their immense colonial territory, in islands and on the main, in the shape of a military, or diplomatic, or, at least, a commercial agent, you have the secret of British history. These Clives, Hastingses, Brookes, Cannings, Ponsonbys, and Hardinges, carry the eye and heart of the best circles of London into the extremities of the earth, and the homes of almost bestial barbarism.[29]

It is common to augur evil of England's future and to forbode her sudden or gradual decline under the load of debt, and pauperism, and the unequal competition with new nations where land is cheap. Certainly, she has enormous burthens to carry and grave difficulties to contend with. And her wisest statesmen incline to call her home from her immense colonial system. But though she may yield to time and change, what a fate is hers! She has planted her banian roots in the ground, they have run under the sea, and the new shoots have sprung in America, in India, in Australia, and she sees the spread of her language and laws over the most part of the world made certain for as distant a future as the science of man can explore.

29. Most of these people were involved in the colonization of India: Robert Clive (1725–74), British soldier and colonist, helped with the original settlement of India; Warren Hastings (1732–1818), English colonial administrator, first governor general of India (1773); Sir James Brooke (1803–68), English soldier born in India, rajah of Sarawak, Malaysia; George Canning (1770–1827), British politician, president of the Board of Control for India (1817–20); and Sir Henry Hardinge (1785–1856), British soldier, governor general of India (1844–48). The line of Ponsonbys, an English family in Ireland, included John (1713–89), speaker of the Irish House of Commons for fifteen years; his son George (1755–1817), lord chancellor of Ireland; and his son Sir Frederick Cavendish (1783–1837), a soldier and governor of Malta.

Address to the Citizens of
Concord on the Fugitive Slave Law

(1851)

Throughout the 1840s and 1850s Emerson lent his voice to the antislavery cause, and, like all supporters of the movement, he was outraged when the Fugitive Slave Act was passed in 1850 supported by none other than Daniel Webster, who had formerly been one of his heroes. (The Fugitive Slave Act imposed penalties on anyone who helped a slave escape. Fugitives could not testify on their own behalf, and they were not allowed a jury trial.) In Massachusetts there were a number of attempts to prevent the implementation of the law, and one of the more famous attempts had occurred on 15 February 1851, when the escaped slave Shadrach Minkins was rescued from custody in Boston. The depth of personal pain accompanying the outrage that Emerson felt at the Fugitive Slave Act is evident as he writes at the opening of this address: "We do not breathe well. There is infamy in the air. I have a new experience. I wake in the morning with a painful sensation, which I carry about all day, and which, when traced home, is the odious remembrance of that ignominy which has fallen on Massachusetts, which robs the landscape of beauty, and takes the sunshine out of every hour." At the same time, Emerson's personal commitment to openly undermine and challenge this legislation is evident in his journals, where he wrote, "I will not obey it, by God" (*JMN*, 11:412). After passage of the Fugitive Slave Act Emerson extensively referenced both the legislation and Webster's betrayal of the ideals of freedom in virtually all antislavery addresses he delivered.

Emerson first delivered this powerful address on the Fugitive Slave Act on 3 May 1851 to the citizens of his hometown, Concord. He adapted the address on several occasions during May 1851 as a campaign stump speech in an unsuccessful attempt to have John Gorham Palfrey elected to Congress on the Free Soil ticket. For details on all of Emerson's antislavery addresses and writings from the 1840s through the 1860s see *Emerson's Antislavery Writings*.

Fellow Citizens,

I accepted your invitation to speak to you on the great question of these days, with very little consideration of what I might have to offer: For there seems to be no option. The last year has forced us all into politics, and made it a paramount duty to seek what it is often a duty to shun.

We do not breathe well. There is infamy in the air. I have a new experience. I wake in the morning with a painful sensation, which I carry about all day, and which, when traced home, is the odious remembrance of that ignominy which has fallen on Massachusetts, which robs the landscape of beauty, and takes the sunshine out of every hour. I have lived all my life in this State, and never had any experience of personal inconvenience from the laws, until now. They never came near me to my discomfort before. I find the like sensibility in my neighbors, and in that class who take no interest in the ordinary questions of party politics.

There are men who are as sure indexes of the equity of legislation and of the sane state of public feeling, as the barometer is of the weight of the air; and it is a bad sign when these are discontented. For, though they snuff oppression and dishonor at a distance, it is because they are more impressionable: the whole population will in a short time be as painfully affected.

Every hour brings us from distant quarters of the Union the expression of mortification at the late events in Massachusetts, and at the behavior of Boston. The tameness was indeed shocking. Boston, of whose fame for spirit and character we have all been so proud; Boston, whose citizens, intelligent people in England told me, they could always distinguish by their culture among Americans; the Boston of the American Revolution, which figures so proudly in "John Adams's Diary," which the whole country has been reading; Boston, spoiled by prosperity, must bow its ancient honor in the dust, and make us irretrievably ashamed.[1] In Boston,—we have said with such lofty confidence,—no fugitive slave can be arrested;—and now, we must transfer our vaunt to the country, and say with a little less confidence,— no fugitive man can be arrested here;—at least we can brag thus until tomorrow, when the farmers also may be corrupted.

The tameness is indeed complete. It appears, the only haste in Boston, after the rescue of Shadrach last February, was, who should first put his name on the list of volunteers in aid of the marshal.[2] One is only reminded of the Russian poltroonery,—a nation without character, where, when they cheat you, and you show them that they cheat, they reply, "Why, you did not think we were Germans; we are only Russians;" that is, we all cheat. I met the smoothest of Episcopal clergymen the other day, and allusion being made to Mr. Webster's treachery, he blandly replied, "Why, do you know I think *that* the great action of his life."[3] It looked as if,

1. John Adams (1735–1826), second president of the United States (1797–1801). The ten-volume *Works of John Adams* (1850–56), edited by Charles Francis Adams (1807–86), his grandson, had just begun publication.

2. The escaped slave Shadrach Minkins had been rescued from custody in Boston on 15 February 1851, an early attempt to prevent the implementation of the second Fugitive Slave Act (1850), which provided for the seizure and return of runaway slaves.

3. Daniel Webster (1782–1852), American lawyer, senator from Massachusetts, and secretary of state, supported compromise measures on slavery proposed by Henry Clay (1777–1852), American politician.

in the city, and the suburbs, all were involved in one hot haste of terror,—presidents of colleges and professors, saints and brokers, insurers, lawyers, importers, and manufacturers;—not an unpleasing sentiment, not a liberal recollection, not so much as a snatch of an old song for freedom, dares intrude on their passive obedience. The panic has paralysed the journals, with the fewest exceptions, so that one cannot open a newspaper, without being disgusted by new records of shame. I cannot read longer even the local good news. When I look down the columns at the titles of paragraphs, "Education in Massachusetts," "Board of Trade," "Art Union," "Revival of Religion," what bitter mockeries!

The very convenience of property, the house and land we occupy, have lost their best value, and a man looks gloomily on his children, and thinks 'What have I done, that you should begin life in dishonor?' Every liberal study is discredited: Literature and science appear effeminate, and the hiding of the head. The college, the churches, the schools, the very shops and factories are discredited; real estate, every kind of wealth, every branch of industry, every avenue to power, suffers injury, and the value of life is reduced. Just now a friend came into my house and said, "If this law shall be repealed, I shall be glad that I have lived; if not, I shall be sorry that I was born." What kind of law is that which extorts language like this from the heart of a free and civilized people?

One intellectual benefit we owe to the late disgraces. The crisis had the illuminating power of a sheet of lightning at midnight. It showed truth. It ended a good deal of nonsense we had been wont to hear and to repeat, on the nineteenth of April, the seventeenth of June, and the fourth of July.[4] It showed the slightness and unreliableness of our social fabric; it showed what stuff reputations are made of; what straws we dignify by office and title, and how competent we are to give counsel and help in a day of trial: It showed the shallowness of leaders; the divergence of parties from their alleged grounds; showed that men would not stick to what they had said: that the resolutions of public bodies, or the pledges never so often given and put on record of public men, will not bind them. The fact comes out more plainly, that you cannot rely on any man for the defence of truth, who is not constitutionally, or by blood and temperament, on that side. A man of a greedy and unscrupulous selfishness may maintain morals when they are in fashion: but he will not stick. However close Mr. Wolf's nails have been pared, however neatly he has been shaved, and tailored, and set up on end, and taught to say, "Virtue and Religion," he cannot be relied on at a pinch: he will say, morality means pricking a vein.

The popular assumption that all men loved freedom, and believed in the Christian religion, was found hollow American brag. Only persons who were known and

4. The Battles of Lexington and Concord were fought on 19 April 1775; the Battle of Bunker Hill was waged in Boston on 17 June 1775; the Second Continental Congress adopted the Declaration of Independence on 4 July 1776.

tried benefactors are found standing for freedom: the sentimentalists went down stream. I question the value of our civilization, when I see that the public mind had never less hold of the strongest of all truths. The sense of injustice is blunted,—a sure sign of the shallowness of our intellect. I cannot accept the railroad and tele-graph in exchange for reason and charity. It is not skill in iron locomotives that marks so fine civility as the jealousy of liberty. I cannot think the most judicious tubing a compensation for metaphysical debility. What is the use of admirable law-forms and political forms, if a hurricane of party feeling and a combination of monied interests can beat them to the ground? What is the use of courts, if judges only quote authorities, and no judge exerts original jurisdiction, or recurs to first principles? What is the use of a Federal Bench, if its opinions are the political breath of the hour? And what is the use of constitutions, if all the guaranties provided by the jealousy of ages for the protection of liberty are made of no effect, when a bad act of Congress finds a willing commissioner?

The levity of the public mind has been shown in the past year by the most extravagant actions. Who could have believed it, if foretold, that a hundred guns would be fired in Boston on the passage of the Fugitive Slave bill?[5] Nothing proves the want of all thought, the absence of standard in men's minds, more than the dominion of party. Here are humane people who have tears for misery, an open purse for want, who should have been the defenders of the poor man, but are found his embittered enemies, rejoicing in his rendition,—merely from party ties. I thought none that was not ready to go on all fours, would back this law. And yet here are upright men, *compotes mentis*—husbands, fathers, trustees, and friends, open, generous, and brave—who can see nothing in this claim for bare humanity and the health and honor of their native state, but canting fanaticism, sedition, and "one idea."[6]

Because of this preoccupied mind, the whole wealth and power of Boston,—two hundred thousand souls, and one hundred eighty millions of money,—are thrown into the scale of crime; and the poor black boy, whom the fame of Boston had reached in the recesses of a rice-swamp, or in the alleys of Savannah, on arriving here, finds all this force employed to catch him. The famous town of Boston is his master's hound. The learning of the universities, the culture of elegant society, the acumen of lawyers, the majesty of the Bench, the eloquence of the Christian pulpit, the stoutness of Democracy, the respectability of the Whig party, are all combined to kidnap him.

The crisis is interesting as it shows the self-protecting nature of the world, and of the divine laws. It is the law of the world, as much immorality as there is, so much misery. The greatest prosperity will in vain resist the greatest calamity. You borrow the succour of the devil, and he must have his fee. He was never known to abate a

---

5. One hundred guns were fired on the Boston Common after the passage of the Fugitive Slave Act.
6. Compos mentis, of sound mind and understanding.

penny of his rents. In every nation, all the immorality that exists breeds plagues. Out of the corrupt society that exists, we have never been able to combine any pure prosperity. There is always something in the very advantages of a condition which hurts it. Africa has its malformation; England has its Ireland; Germany, its hatred of classes; France, its love of gunpowder; Italy, its Pope; and America, the most prosperous country in the universe, has the greatest calamity in the universe, negro slavery.

Let me remind you a little in detail how the natural retributions act in reference to the statute which Congress passed a year ago. For these few months have shown very conspicuously its nature and impracticability.

It is contravened,

First. By the sentiment of duty.

An immoral law makes it a man's duty to break it, at every hazard. For Virtue is the very self of every man. It is therefore a principle of law, that an immoral contract is void, and that an immoral statute is void. For, as laws do not make right, but are simply declaratory of a right which already existed, it is not to be presumed that they can so stultify themselves as to command injustice.

It is remarkable how rare in the history of tyrants is an immoral law. Some color, some indirection was always used. If you take up the volumes of the "Universal History," you will find it difficult searching. The precedents are few. It is not easy to parallel the wickedness of this American law. And that is the head and body of this discontent, that the law is immoral. Here is a statute which enacts the crime of kidnapping,—a crime on one footing with arson and murder. A man's right to liberty is as inalienable as his right to life.

Pains seem to have been taken to give us in this statute a wrong pure from any mixture of right. If our resistance to this law is not right, there is no right. This is not meddling with other people's affairs: This is hindering other people from meddling with us. This is not going crusading into Virginia and Georgia after slaves, who, it is alleged, are very comfortable where they are:—that amiable argument falls to the ground: but this is befriending in our own state, on our own farms, a man who has taken the risk of being shot, or burned alive, or cast into the sea, or starved to death, or suffocated in a wooden box, to get away from his driver; and this man who has run the gauntlet of a thousand miles for his freedom, the statute says, you men of Massachusetts shall hunt, and catch, and send back again to the dog-hutch he fled from.

It is contrary to the primal sentiment of duty, and therefore all men that are born are, in proportion to their power of thought and their moral sensibility, found to be the natural enemies of this law. The resistance of all moral beings is secured to it. I had thought, I confess, what must come at last would come at first, a banding of all men against the authority of this statute. I thought it a point on which all sane men were agreed, that the law must respect the public morality. I thought that all men of all conditions had been made sharers of a certain experience, that in certain rare and retired moments they had been made to see how man is man, or what makes the essence of rational beings, namely, that, whilst animals have to do with eating the fruits of the ground, men have to do with rectitude, with benefit, with truth, with something which *is*, independent of appearances: and that this tie makes the substantiality of life, this, and not their ploughing or sailing, their trade or the breeding of families. I thought that every time a man goes back to his own thoughts, these angels receive him, talk with him, and, that, in the best hours, he is uplifted in virtue of this essence, into a peace and into a power which the material world cannot give: that these moments counterbalance the years of drudgery, and that this owning of a law, be it called morals, religion, or godhead, or what you will, constituted the explanation of life, the excuse and indemnity for the errors and calamities which sadden it. In long years consumed in trifles, they remember these moments, and are consoled.

I thought it was this fair mystery, whose foundations are hidden in eternity, which made the basis of human society, and of law; and that to pretend anything else, as, that the acquisition of property was the end of living, was to confound all distinctions, to make the world a greasy hotel, and, instead of noble motives and inspirations, and a heaven of companions and angels around and before us, to leave us in a grimacing menagerie of monkeys and ideots. All arts, customs, societies, books, and laws, are good as they foster and concur with this spiritual element; all men are beloved as they raise us to it; all are hateful as they deny or resist it. The laws especially draw their obligation only from their concurrence with it.

I am surprised that lawyers can be so blind as to suffer the principles of law to be discredited. A few months ago, in my dismay at hearing that the Higher Law was reckoned a good joke in the courts, I took pains to look into a few law-books. I had often heard that the Bible constituted a part of every technical law-library, and that it was a principle in law that immoral laws are void. I found, accordingly, that the great jurists—Cicero, Grotius, Coke, Blackstone, Burlamaqui, Montesquieu, Vattel, Burke, Mackintosh, and Jefferson—do all affirm this.[7]

I have no intention to recite these passages I had marked:—such citation indeed seems to be something cowardly—for no reasonable person needs a quotation

---

7. Marcus Tullius Cicero (106–43 B.C.), Roman philosopher and statesman; Hugo Grotius (originally Huigh de Groot) (1583–1645), Dutch scholar, humanist, and politician; Sir Edward Coke (1552–1634), English lawyer and attorney general; Sir William Blackstone (1723–80), English lawyer and author of *Commentaries on the Laws of England* (1765–69); Jean-Jacques Burlamaqui (1694–1748), Swiss jurist; Charles-Louis de Secondat, baron de La Brède et de Montesquieu (1689–1755), French political philosopher whose chief work, *L'esprit des lois* (1748), influenced political thought in Europe and the United States; Emmerich von Vattel (1714–67), Swiss jurist; Edmund Burke (1729–97), British politician and natural philosopher born in Ireland, wrote on individual liberty; James Mackintosh (1765–1832), Scottish philosopher and lawyer; Thomas Jefferson (1743–1826), member of the committee that drafted the Declaration of Independence, third American president (1801–9), and founder of the University of Virginia.

from Blackstone to convince him that white cannot be legislated to be black—and shall content myself with reading a single passage.

Blackstone admits the sovereignty—"antecedent to any positive precept of the law of nature"—among whose principles are, "that we should live honestly, should hurt nobody, and should render unto every one his due," and so forth. "*No human laws are of any validity, if contrary to this.*" "Nay, if any human law should allow or enjoin us to commit a crime" (his instance is murder) "we are bound to transgress that human law; or else we must offend both the natural and divine." Lord Coke held, that where an act of Parliament is against common right and reason, the common law shall control it, and adjudge it to be void. Chief Justice *Hobart*, Chief Justice *Holt*, and Chief Justice *Mansfield* held the same.[8] Lord Mansfield in the case of the slave Somerset, wherein the *dicta* of Lords Talbot and Hardwicke had been cited to the effect of carrying back the slave to the West Indies, said, "I care not for the supposed *dicta* of judges, however eminent, if they be contrary to all principle."[9] Even the *Canon Law* says, *in malis promissis non expedit servare fidem*: "neither allegiance nor oath can bind to obey that which is wrong."[10]

No engagement (to a sovereign) can oblige or even authorize a man to violate the laws of nature. All authors who have any conscience or modesty, agree, that a person ought not to obey such commands as are evidently contrary to the laws of God. Those governors of places who bravely refused to execute the barbarous orders of Charles IX to the famous St Bartholomew's, have been universally praised; and the court did not dare to punish them, at least, openly. 'Sire,' said the brave Orte, governor of Bayonne, in his letter; 'I have communicated your majesty's command to your faithful inhabitants and warriors in the garrison, and I have found there only good citizens, and brave soldiers; not one hangman: therefore, both they and I most humbly entreat your majesty, to be pleased to employ your arms and lives in things that are possible, however hazardous they may be, and we will exert ourselves to the last drop of our blood.'[11]

The practitioners should guard this dogma well, as the palladium of the profession, as their anchor in the respect of mankind; against a principle like this, all the arguments of Mr. Webster are the spray of a child's squirt against a granite wall.

8. English chief justices Henry Hobart (d. 1625), John Holt (1642–1710), and William Murray, Lord Mansfield (1705–93).

9. The English jurists Charles Talbot (1685–1737) and Philip Yorke, first Earl of Hardwicke (1690–1764), English lord chancellor who helped establish that country's system of equity.

10. Canon law within Roman Catholicism is the body of laws that govern the constitution of the Church, relations between it and other bodies, and internal discipline.

11. In August 1572 Charles IX of France (1550–74, reigned 1560–74), following the Massacre of Saint Bartholomew's Day of up to three thousand Huguenots in Paris, wrote to his provincial governors ordering them to put to death Huguenots who attempted any form of assembly. Several governors refused to obey this edict. There is no hard evidence to confirm the story of Vicomte d'Orthe's response as reported by Vattel, which may be apocryphal, though in fact no massacre took place in Bayonne.

Second. It is contravened by all the sentiments.

How can a law be enforced that fines pity, and imprisons charity? As long as men have bowels, they will disobey. You know that the Act of Congress of September 18, 1850, is a law which every one of you will break on the earliest occasion. There is not a manly whig, or a manly democrat, of whom, if a slave were hidden in one of our houses from the hounds, we should not ask with confidence to lend his wagon in aid of his escape, and he would lend it. The man would be too strong for the partisan.

And here I may say that it is absurd, what I often hear, to accuse the friends of freedom in the north with being the occasion of the new stringency of the southern slave-laws. If you starve or beat the orphan, in my presence, and I accuse your cruelty, can I help it? In the words of Electra, in the Greek tragedy,

> 'Tis you that say it, not I. You do the deeds,
> And your ungodly deeds find me the words.[12]

Will you blame the ball for rebounding from the floor? blame the air for rushing in where a vacuum is made or the boiler for exploding under pressure of steam? These facts are after laws of the world, and so is it law, that, when justice is violated, anger begins. The very defence which the God of Nature has provided for the innocent against cruelty, is the sentiment of indignation and pity in the bosom of the beholder. Mr. Webster tells the President, that, "he has been in the north, and he has found no man whose opinion is of any weight who is opposed to the law."[13] Ah! Mr. President, trust not the information. The gravid old universe goes spawning on; the womb conceives and the breasts give suck to thousands and millions of hairy babes formed not in the image of your statute, but in the image of the universe; too many to be bought off; too many than that they can be rich, and therefore peaceable; and necessitated to express first or last every feeling of the heart. You can keep no secret, for, whatever is true, some of them will unseasonably say. You can commit no crime, for they are created in their sentiments conscious of and hostile to it; and, unless you can suppress the newspaper, pass a law against bookshops, gag the English tongue in America, all short of this is futile. This dreadful English speech is saturated with songs, proverbs, and speeches that flatly contradict and defy every line of Mr. Mason's statute.[14] Nay, unless you can draw a sponge over those seditious Ten Commandments which are the root of our European and

12. Sophocles (ca. 496–406 B.C.), Greek playwright, probably wrote the play *Electra* in about 430 B.C.; see ll. 626–27.

13. Millard Fillmore (1800–1874), thirteenth president of the United States, became president in 1850 after the death in office of Zachary Taylor, supported the Fugitive Slave Act.

14. James Murray Mason (1798–1871), American senator from Virginia, drafted the Fugitive Slave Act of 1850.

American civilization, and over that eleventh commandment, "Do unto others as you would have others do to you," your labor is vain.

Third. It is contravened by the written laws themselves, because the sentiments, of course, write the statutes.

Laws are merely declaratory of the natural sentiments of mankind, and the language of all permanent laws will be in contradiction to any immoral enactment: And thus it happens here: statute fights against statute. By the law of Congress March 2, 1807, it is piracy and murder punishable with death, to enslave a man on the coast of Africa.[15] By law of Congress, September 1850, it is a high crime and misdemeanor punishable with fine and imprisonment to resist the re-enslaving a man on the coast of America. Off soundings, it is piracy and murder to enslave him. On soundings, it is fine and prison not to re-enslave. What kind of legislation is this? What kind of Constitution which covers it? And yet the crime which the second law ordains is greater than the crime which the first law forbids under penalty of the gibbet. For it is a greater crime to re-enslave a man who has shown himself fit for freedom, than to enslave him at first, when it might be pretended to be a mitigation of his lot as a captive in war.

Fourth. It is contravened by the mischiefs it operates.

A wicked law cannot be executed by good men, and must be by bad. Flagitious men must be employed, and every act of theirs is a stab at the public peace.[16] It cannot be executed at such a cost, and so it brings a bribe in its hand. This law comes with infamy in it, and out of it. It offers a bribe in its own clauses for the consummation of the crime. To serve it, low and mean people are found by the groping of the government. No government ever found it hard to pick up tools for base actions. If you cannot find them in the huts of the poor, you shall find them in the palaces of the rich. Vanity can buy some, ambition others, and money others. The first execution of the law, as was inevitable, was a little hesitating; the second was easier; and the glib officials became, in a few weeks, quite practised and handy at stealing men.

But worse, not the officials alone are bribed, but the whole community is solicited. The scowl of the community is attempted to be averted by the mischievous whisper, "Tariff and southern market, if you will be quiet; no tariff and loss of southern market, if you dare to murmur." I wonder that our acute people, who have learned that the cheapest police is dear schools, should not find out that an immoral law costs more than the loss of the custom of a southern city.

The humiliating scandal of great men warping right into wrong was followed up very fast by the cities. New-York advertised in southern markets, that it would go

15. Congress passed a law on 2 March 1807 prohibiting the African slave trade and the importation of slaves into America after 1 January 1808.

16. Flagitious, extremely wicked, guilty of enormous crimes and vices.

for slavery, and posted the names of merchants who would not. Boston, alarmed, entered into the same design. Philadelphia, more fortunate, had no conscience at all, and, in this auction of the rights of mankind, rescinded all its legislation against slavery. And the "Boston Advertiser" and the "Courier," in these weeks, urge the same course on the people of Massachusetts.[17] Nothing remains in this race of roguery, but to coax Connecticut or Maine to out-bid us all by adopting slavery into its constitution.

Great is the mischief of a legal crime. Every person who touches this business is contaminated. There has not been in our lifetime another moment when public men were personally lowered by their political action. But here are gentlemen whose believed probity was the confidence and fortification of multitudes, who, by fear of public opinion, or, through the dangerous ascendancy of southern manners, have been drawn into the support of this foul business. We poor men in the country, who might once have thought it an honor to shake hands with them, or to dine at their boards, would now shrink from their touch, nor could they enter our humblest doors. You have a law which no man can obey, or abet the obeying, without loss of self-respect and forfeiture of the name of a gentleman. What shall we say of the functionary by whom the recent rendition was made? If he has rightly defined his powers, and has no authority to try the case, but only to prove the prisoner's identity, and remand him, what office is this for a reputable citizen to hold? No man of honor can sit on that bench. It is the extension of the planter's whipping-post: and its incumbents must rank with a class from which the turnkey, the hangman, and the informer are taken,—necessary functionaries, it may be, in a state, but to whom the dislike and the ban of society universally attaches.

Fifth. These resistances appear in the history of the statute, in the retributions which speak so loud in every part of this business, that I think a tragic poet will know how to make it a lesson for all ages.

Mr. Webster's measure was, he told us, final. It was a pacification, it was a suppression, a measure of conciliation and adjustment. These were his words at different times; "there was to be no parleying more"; it was "irrepealable." Does it look final now? His final settlement has dislocated the foundations. The state house shakes like a tent. His pacification has brought all the honesty in every house, all scrupulous and good-hearted men, all women, and all children, to accuse the law. It has brought United States' swords into the streets, and chains round the court house.

17. Emerson is referring to such sympathetic editorials as this one entitled "Fugitive Slave Agitation" from the *Boston Daily Advertiser*: "The senseless excitement which was raised at New Bedford on Sunday last, by the active circulation of a false report, shows how ready a portion of the public are to become the dupes of a few designing men. . . . This transaction is a most unfortunate one, from the impression which it must produce abroad of the character of our community and the fidelity of our people to the Constitution" (20 March 1851, 2).

"A measure of pacification and union." What is its effect? To make one sole subject for conversation and painful thought throughout the continent, namely, slavery. There is not a man of thought or of feeling, but is concentrating his mind on it. There is not a clerk, but recites its statistics; not a politician, but is watching its incalculable energy in the elections; not a jurist, but is hunting up precedents; not a moralist, but is prying into its quality; not an economist, but is computing its profit and losses. Mr. Webster can judge whether this sort of solar microscope brought to bear on his law is likely to make opposition less.

The only benefit that has accrued from the law is its service to education. It has been like a university to the entire people. It has turned every dinnertable into a debating club, and made every citizen a student of natural law. When a moral quality comes into politics, when a right is invaded, the discussion draws on deeper sources: general principles are laid bare, which cast light on the whole frame of society. And it is cheering to behold what champions the emergency called to this poor black boy; with what subtlety, what logic, what learning, what exposure of the mischief of the law, and, above all, with what earnestness and dignity the advocates of freedom were inspired. It was one of the best compensations of this calamity.

But the Nemesis works underneath again. It is a power that makes noonday dark, and draws us on to our undoing; and its dismal way is to pillory the offender in the moment of his triumph. The hands that put the chain on the slave are in that moment manacled. Who has seen anything like that which is now done?

The words of John Randolph, wiser than he knew, have been ringing ominously in all echoes for thirty years,—words spoken in the heat of the Missouri debate.[18] "We do not govern the people of the north by our black slaves, but by their own white slaves. We know what we are doing. We have conquered you once, and we can and will conquer you again. Aye, we will drive you to the wall, and when we have you there once more, we will keep you there, and nail you down like base money." These words resounding ever since from California to Oregon, from Cape Florida to Cape Cod, come down now like the cry of Fate, in the moment when they are fulfilled. By white slaves, by a white slave, are we beaten. Who looked for such ghastly fulfilment, or to see what we see? Hills and Hallets, servile editors by the hundred, we could have spared.[19] But him, our best and proudest, the first man of the north in the very moment of mounting the throne, irresistibly taking the bit in his mouth, and the collar on his neck, and harnessing himself to the chariot of the planters?

The fairest American fame ends in this filthy law. Mr. Webster cannot choose but to regret his loss. He must learn that those who make fame accuse him with one voice; that those who have no points to carry, that are not identical with public

18. John Randolph of Roanoke (1773–1833), American senator from Virginia.
19. Probably Isaac Hill (1789–1851), proslavery New Hampshire editor and politician; Benjamin Franklin Hallet (1797–1862), proslavery editor of the *Boston Post*.

morals and generous civilization, that the obscure and private who have no voice and care for none, so long as things go well, but who feel the disgrace of the new legislation creeping like a miasma into their homes, and blotting the daylight,—those to whom his name was once dear and honored, as the manly statesman to whom the choicest gifts of nature had been accorded, disown him: that he who was their pride in the woods and mountains of New England, is now their mortification,— they have torn down his picture from the wall, they have thrust his speeches into the chimney. No roars of New York mobs can drown this voice in Mr. Webster's ear. It will outwhisper all the salvos of the "Union Committee's" cannon. But I have said too much on this painful topic. I will not pursue that bitter history.

But passing from these ethical to the political view, I wish to place this statute, and we must use the introducer and substantial author of the bill as an illustration of the history.

I have as much charity for Mr. Webster, I think, as anyone has. I need not say how much I have enjoyed his fame. Who has not helped to praise him? Simply, he was the one eminent American of our time, whom we could produce as a finished work of nature. We delighted in his form and face, in his voice, in his eloquence, in his power of labor, in his concentration, in his large understanding, in his daylight statement and simple force; the facts lay like strata of a cloud, or like the layers of the crust of the globe. He saw things as they were, and he stated them so. He has been by his clear perception and statement, in all these years, the best head in Congress, and the champion of the interests of the northern sea-board.

But as the activity and growth of slavery began to be offensively felt by his constituents, the senator became less sensitive to these evils. They were not for him to deal with: he was the commercial representative. He indulged occasionally in excellent expression of the known feeling of the New England people: but, when expected and when pledged, he omitted to speak, and he omitted to throw himself into the movement in those critical moments when his leadership would have turned the scale. At last, at a fatal hour, this sluggishness accumulated to downright counteraction, and, very unexpectedly to the whole Union, on the seventh of March, 1850, in opposition to his education and association, and to all his own most explicit language for thirty years, he crossed the line, and became the head of the slavery party in this country.

Mr. Webster perhaps is only following the laws of his blood and constitution. I suppose his pledges were not quite natural to him. Mr. Webster is a man who lives by his memory, a man of the past, not a man of faith or of hope. He obeys his powerful animal nature;—and his finely developed understanding only works truly and with all its force, when it stands for animal good; that is, for property. He believes, in so many words, that government exists for the protection of property. He looks at the Union as an estate, a large farm, and is excellent in the completeness of his defence of it so far. He adheres to the letter. Happily, he was born late,—after the independence had been declared, the Union agreed to, and the Constitution settled. What he finds already written, he will defend. Lucky that so much had got well-written when he came. For he has no faith in the power of self-government; none whatever in extemporising a government. Not the smallest municipal provision, if it were new, would receive his sanction. In Massachusetts, in 1776, he would, beyond all question, have been a refugee. He praises Adams and Jefferson; but it is a past Adams and Jefferson that his mind can entertain. A present Adams and Jefferson he would denounce.

So with the eulogies of liberty in his writings,—they are sentimentalism and youthful rhetoric. He can celebrate it, but it means as much from him as from Metternich or Talleyrand.[20] This is all inevitable from his constitution. All the drops of his blood have eyes that look downward. It is neither praise nor blame to say that he has no moral perception, no moral sentiment, but, in that *region*, to use the phrase of the phrenologists, a hole in the head.[21] The scraps of morality to be gleaned from his speeches are reflections of the minds of others. He says what he hears said, but often makes signal blunders in their use to open the door of the sea and the fields of the earth, to extemporize government in Texas, in California, and in Oregon, and to make provisional law where statute law is not ready.

This liberalism appears in the power of invention, in the freedom of thinking, in the readiness for reforms; eagerness for novelty, even for all the follies of false science, in the antipathy to secret societies; in the predominance of the democratic party in the politics of the Union, and in the allowance of the voice of the public, even when irregular and vicious,—the voice of mobs, the voice of Lynch law, because it is thought to be on the whole the verdict, though badly spoken, of the greatest number.[22] All this forwardness and self-reliance covers self-government; proceeds on the belief, that, as the people have made a government, they can make another; that their union and law are not in their memory, but in their blood and condition. If they unmake a law, they can easily make a new one. In Mr. Webster's imagination, the American Union is a huge Prince Rupert's drop, which, if so much as the smallest end be shivered off, the whole will snap into atoms.[23] Now, the fact is quite different from this. The people are loyal, law-loving, law-abiding. They prefer order, and have no taste for misrule and uproar. The destiny of this country is great and liberal, and is to be greatly administered. It is to be administered according to

20. Prince Klemens von Metternich (1773–1859), Austrian statesman and diplomatist; Charles-Maurice de Talleyrand-Périgord (1754–1838), French politician known for his lack of commitment to established principles.

21. Phrenologists claim to read a person's character through the configuration of his or her skull.

22. William Lynch (d. 1820), American vigilante; a lynch law is the punishment, usually by death, of presumed crimes without due process of law.

23. Prince Rupert's drop is a tadpole-shaped solid glass object formed by dropping a small glob of molten glass into cold water and leaving it to cool. This process results in a tremendous stress between the outside layer, which is cooled by water, and the inside, which is still warm; because of the surface tension, the thick, bulbous end can be struck with a hammer, while even the slightest scratch of the thin tail releases the internal stress so forcefully that the entire piece shatters. These were introduced to England in the 1640s by Prince Rupert of Bavaria (1619–82), nephew of Charles I.

what is, and is to be, and not according to what is dead and gone. The Union of this people is a real thing, an alliance of men of one stock, one language, one religion, one system of manners and ideas. I hold it to be a real and not a statute Union. The people cleave to the union, because they see their advantage in it: the added power of each.

I suppose the Union can be left to take care of itself. As much real Union as there is, the statutes will be sure to express. As much disunion as there is, no statutes can long conceal. Under the Union, I suppose the fact to be that there are really two nations, the north and the south. It is not slavery that severs them, it is climate and temperament. The south does not like the north, slavery or no slavery, and never did. The north likes the south well enough, for it knows its own advantages. I am willing to leave them to the facts. If they continue to have a binding interest, they will be pretty sure to find it out: if not, they will consult their peace in parting.

But one thing appears certain to me, that, as soon as the Constitution ordains an immoral law, it ordains disunion. The law is suicidal, and cannot be obeyed. The Union is at an end as soon as an immoral law is enacted. And he who writes a crime into the statute book, digs under the foundations of the capitol to plant there a powder magazine, and lays a train.

Nothing seems to me more hypocritical than the bluster about the Union. A year ago, we were all lovers of the Union, and valued so dearly what seemed the immense destinies of this country, that we reckoned an impiety any act that compromised them. But in the new attitude in which we find ourselves, the personal dishonor which now rests on every family in Massachusetts, the sentiment is changed. No man can look his neighbor in the face. We sneak about with the infamy of crime, and cowardly allowance of it on our parts, and frankly, once for all, the Union, such an Union, is intolerable. The flag is an insult to ourselves. The Union,—I give you the sentiment of every decent citizen: "The Union! O yes, I prized that, other things being equal; but what is the Union to a man self-condemned, with all sense of self-respect and chance of fair fame cut off, with the names of conscience and religion become bitter ironies, and liberty the ghastly mockery which Mr. Webster means by that word? The worst mischiefs that could follow from secession and new combination of the smallest fragments of the wreck, were slight and medicable to the calamity your Union has brought us."

It did not at first appear, and it was incredible, that the passage of the law would so absolutely defeat its proposed objects: but from the day when it was attempted to be executed in Massachusetts, this result has become certain, that the Union is no longer desireable. Whose deed is that?

I pass to say a few words to the question, What shall we do? First, What in our federal capacity in our relation to the nation? And, second, what as citizens of a state?

I am an unionist as we all are, or nearly all, and I strongly share the hope of mankind in the power, and, therefore, in the duties of the Union; and I conceive it demonstrated,—the necessity of commonsense and justice entering into the laws.

What shall we do? First, abrogate this law; Then, proceed to confine slavery to slave states, and help them effectually to make an end of it. Or shall we, as we are advised on all hands, lie by, and wait the progress of the census? But will slavery lie by? I fear not. She is very industrious, gives herself no holidays. No proclamations will put her down. She got Texas, and now will have Cuba, and means to keep her majority. The experience of the past gives us no encouragement to lie by.

Shall we call a new convention, or will any expert statesman furnish us a plan for the summary or gradual winding up of slavery, so far as the Republic is its patron? Where is the South itself? Since it is agreed by all sane men of all parties—or was yesterday—that slavery is mischievous, why does the South itself never offer the smallest counsel of her own? I have never heard in twenty years any project except Mr. Clay's.[24] Let us hear any project with candor and respect. Is it impossible to speak of it with reason and good nature? It is really the project fit for this country to entertain and accomplish.

Everything invites to emancipation. The grandeur of the design; the vast stake we hold; the national domain; the new importance of Liberia; the manifest interest of the slave states; the religious effort of the free states; the public opinion of the world;—all join to demand it.[25]

It is said, it will cost a thousand millions of dollars to buy the slaves,—which sounds like a fabulous price. But if a price were named in good faith,—with the other elements of a practicable treaty in readiness, and with the convictions of mankind on this mischief once well-awake and conspiring, I do not think any amount that figures could tell, founded on an estimate, would be quite unmanageable. Every man in the world might give a week's work to sweep this mountain of calamities out of the earth.

Nothing is impracticable to this nation, which it shall set itself to do. Were ever men so endowed, so placed, so weaponed? Their power of territory is seconded by a genius equal to every work. By new arts the earth is subdued, roaded, tunneled, telegraphed, and gas-lighted; vast amounts of old labor are disused, the sinews of man being relieved by sinews of steam. We are on the brink of more wonders. The sun paints: presently we shall organize the echo, as now we do the shadow. Chemistry is extorting new aids. The genius of this people, it is found, can do anything

24. Henry Clay was instrumental in preparing the Compromise of 1850 (which included the Fugitive Slave Act), which allowed the residents of new U.S. territories to settle the question of slavery themselves, provided for the enforced return of runaway slaves, and prohibited the slave trade in the District of Columbia.

25. The African nation of Liberia was founded in 1822 by blacks funded by the American Colonization Society and was declared a republic in 1847. A number of reformers suggested black emigration to Liberia as a solution to the slavery crisis.

which can be done by men. These thirty nations are equal to any work, and are every moment stronger. In twenty-five years, they will be fifty millions. Is it not time to do something besides ditching and draining, and making the earth mellow and friable? Let them confront this mountain of poison,—bore, blast, excavate, pulverize, and shovel it once for all, down into the bottomless Pit. A thousand millions were cheap.

But grant that the heart of financiers, accustomed to practical figures, shrinks within them at these colossal amounts, and the embarrassments which complicate the problem. Granting that these contingences are too many to be spanned by any human geometry, and that these evils are to be relieved only by the wisdom of God working in ages,—and by what instruments,—whether Liberia, whether flax-cotton, whether the working out this race by Irish and Germans, none can tell, or by what scourges God has guarded his law; still the question recurs, What must we do?

One thing is plain, we cannot answer for the Union, but we must keep Massachusetts true. It is of unspeakable importance that she play her honest part. She must follow no vicious examples. Massachusetts is a little State. Countries have been great by ideas. Europe is little, compared with Asia and Africa. Yet Asia and Africa are its ox and its ass. Europe, the least of all the continents, has almost monopolized for twenty centuries the genius and power of them all. Greece was the least part of Europe. Attica a little part of that,—one-tenth of the size of Massachusetts. Yet that district still rules the intellect of men. Judaea was a petty country. Yet these two, Greece and Judaea, furnish the mind and the heart by which the rest of the world is sustained. And Massachusetts is little, but, if true to itself, can be the brain which turns about the behemoth.

I say Massachusetts, but I mean Massachusetts in all the quarters of her dispersion; Massachusetts, as she is the mother of all the New England states, and as she sees her progeny scattered over the face of the land, in the farthest south and the uttermost west.

The immense power of rectitude is apt to be forgotten in politics. But they who have brought this great wrong on the country have not forgotten it. They avail themselves of the known probity and honor of Massachusetts, to endorse the statute. The ancient maxim still holds, that never was any injustice effected except by the help of justice. The great game of the government has been to win the sanction of Massachusetts to the crime. Hitherto, they have succeeded only so far as to win Boston to a certain extent. The behaviour of Boston was the reverse of what it should have been: it was supple and officious, and it put itself into the base attitude of pander to the crime. It should have placed obstruction at every step. Let the attitude of the state be firm. Let us respect the Union to all honest ends. But also respect an older and wider union, the law of nature and rectitude. Massachusetts is as strong as the universe, when it does that. We will never intermeddle with your slavery,—but you can in no wise be suffered to bring it to Cape Cod and Berkshire. This law must be made inoperative. It must be abrogated and wiped out of the statute book; but, whilst it stands there, it must be disobeyed.

We must make a small State great, by making every man in it true. It was the praise of Athens, "she could not lead countless armies into the field, but she knew how with a little band to defeat those who could." Every Roman reckoned himself at least a match for a province. Every Dorian did. Every Englishman in Australia, in South Africa, in India, or in whatever barbarous country their forts and factories have been set up,—represents London, represents the art, power, and law of Europe. Every man educated at the northern schools carries the like advantages into the south. For it is confounding distinctions to speak of the geographic sections of this country as of equal civilization.

Every nation and every man bows, in spite of himself, to a higher mental and moral existence; and the sting of the late disgraces is, that this royal position of Massachusetts was foully lost, that the well-known sentiment of her people was not expressed. Let us correct this error. In this one fastness, let truth be spoken, and right done. Here, let there be no confusion in our ideas. Let us not lie, nor steal, nor help to steal; and let us not call stealing by any fine names, such as "union" or "patriotism." Let us know, that not by the public, but by ourselves, our safety must be bought. That is the secret of southern power, that they rest not in meetings, but in private heats and courages. It is very certain from the perfect guaranties in the Constitution, and the high arguments of the defenders of liberty, which the occasion called out, that there is sufficient margin in the statute and the law for the spirit of the magistrate to show itself, and one, two, three occasions have just now occurred and passed, in any of which, if one man had felt the spirit of Coke, or Mansfield, or Parsons, and read the law with the eye of freedom, the dishonor of Massachusetts had been prevented, and a limit set to these encroachments forever.[26]

26. William Parsons (ca. 1570–1650), lord justice of Ireland.

The Anglo-American

(1852–1855)

Emerson first delivered "The Anglo-American" under the title "The Anglo-Saxon" in December 1852 in Cincinnati, Ohio; he continued to use "The Anglo-Saxon" as the title of the lecture when he delivered it between December 1852 and February 1853 in Dayton and Cleveland, Ohio; St. Louis, Missouri; Springfield, Illinois; Philadelphia; and his hometown of Concord, among other places. Emerson undoubtedly used "The Anglo-Saxon" when he lectured on "Traits and Genius of the Anglo-Saxon Race" in November 1852 in Troy, New York.

Early in 1853 Emerson began adding new material to "The Anglo-Saxon" to emphasize its American bias, which, it seemed to him, had been lost on most audiences, and he changed its title to "The Anglo-American" when he delivered it in March 1853 at the Bache Institute in Philadelphia. He repeated the lecture as "The Anglo-American" in December 1853 before the Concord Lyceum in Concord, Massachusetts, in 1854 in Brooklyn and Penn Yan, New York, and in 1855 in Boston. Emerson continued to draw text from "The Anglo-American" until 1865 for lectures he delivered under titles such as "American Character," "Anglo-American Character," and "American Life."

Everything in America is at a rapid rate. The next moment eats the last. Whatever we do, suffer, or propose, is for the immediate entertainment of the company. We have a newspaper published every hour of the day, and our whole existence and performance slides into it. When I went to Ohio, I was asked, When were you here before?—Three years ago.—O, that is just one age in Ohio: Let me introduce you to the new generation.

A gentleman in Cincinnati defended his immoveableness by saying, "Sir, I have held that opinion three weeks." There is no difference between boy and man. As soon as a boy is table high, he contradicts his father.

"American" means speedy in Europe, as if the ingenuity of this country were directed on nothing so much. The impediment on the western rivers is the low water, at certain seasons, so they must have light boats. They once had on the Mississippi a boat called "*Skim*," drawing so little water that they said it would sail in a heavy dew, and when it got aground, the crew jumped out and put their shoulders under the boat, and lifted it over the bar. On the sea, the value of freight is the warrant of quick arrival at the market; and the American builds clipper ships which outrun all other craft so far, that they command a higher freight in foreign ports, and the East India Company send home cargoes in American vessels, in preference to their own![1] The American challenge has not been accepted,—to build and run a freight ship to Canton and home, for a purse of ten thousand pounds to the quickest. Lord DeBlaquiere advertised his yacht to race with all yachts, *not American.*

Everything is sacrificed for speed,—solidity and safety. They would sail in a steamer built of lucifer matches if it would go faster; with spars of the very largest jackstraws.[2] A stability is only to be found in this Country in a few isolated localities as, for example, in Essex, Massachusetts, a little town which builds fishing boats, and where ninety families bear the name of Burnham and all the rest are Cogswells or Choates. Perhaps there is an influence continental, climatic, to modify the race, and free certain forces that lay latent before. The sun of America, and its western wind, as they work on the frame, certainly add vivacity and speed.

This national trait stands in strange contrast with the habit of the land of our forefathers. The English have a Cummerian Conservatism.[3] It is called *the Old Country*, and everything in it is old. Its manufactures reach back beyond the memory of history. Fuller says, "The date of cloth and of civility is one in this island." Sheffield has made knives for five hundred years and more. Staffordshire has made potteries, Cornwall dug its mines, Nottingham woven its laces, for centuries. The Spitalfield weavers still pursue their trade as at the revocation of the Edict of Nantes.[4]

The sun returning to the spring solstice finds each man in England sitting at the same workbench at which he left him on that day twelvemonth. The same tenacity is in families and fames. "The Duke of Buckingham was born," says Wotton, "at Brookely in Leicestershire, where his ancestors had chiefly continued about the space of four hundred years, rather without obscurity, than with any great lustre."[5]

1. England, France, and Holland all had their own East India Companies; Emerson is referring to the English East India Company, formed in 1600 for trade, mostly in spices, with East and Southeast Asia and India. It became the chief agent of British imperialism in India and China during the eighteenth and nineteenth centuries.

2. The fiery and sulfurous burning effect of matches led to their being called "lucifers," after Lucifer, the Latin name for the planet Venus, usually seen as the morning star and the brightest object in the sky after the sun and moon as well as the name of the fallen rebel archangel who is the ruler of Hell in Dante's *Inferno.*

3. Cummer, a Scottish word for a woman or girl, sometimes a midwife or witch.

4. Quote attributed to Thomas Fuller (1608–61), English cleric, poet, and historian, known for his posthumously published *History of the Worthies of England* (1662), by Emerson (*JMN*, 13:93). The Edict of Nantes was a law promulgated by Henry IV of France, a Catholic country, on 13 April 1598, giving religious freedom to the Protestant Huguenots. The Catholic clergy resented the edict, and it was revoked by Louis XIV in 1685. Spitalfields, in the East End of London, became the home of many Huguenots who fled from France after the revocation of the Edict of Nantes, bringing their skills in silk weaving with them.

5. Sir Henry Wotton (1568–1639), English diplomat and author.

The air and aspect of England are loaded with stability and reverence. Take a map, and read the names. In England, it has taken Cambridge between seven and eight hundred years since the monks of Croyland taught in a farm and in a barn to reach the present wealth of its University. Oxford goes back one thousand years to King Alfred for its charter, and much longer, if, as is pretended, the Druids had a school on the same spot.[6] In Merton College Library I found books still chained to the shelves to which they were locked centuries ago when books were precious as gold.

But we have changed all that, and, in our new states, we extemporize an University like a picnic. In 1851, I chanced to witness this rapid crystallization at Rochester, New York. There had been some negociation about removing into the city a college which was situated twenty miles off. But the negociations dragged; no satisfactory result was likely to come: So an enterprising citizen (Mr. Wilder) bought a cheap hotel, (once a railroad terminus-station,) turned the dining-room into a chapel, by putting up a pulpit on one side; made the barroom into a Pythologian society's hall; the drawing-room into a library; the chambers, into recitation rooms and professors' apartments; all for seven hundred dollars a year.[7] He called in a painter, sent him up a ladder to paint "University of Rochester," on the wall; sent an omnibus up to Madison, and brought the whole faculty of professors bodily down,—bag and baggage, Greek, Hebrew, Chaldee, Latin, *Belles Lettres*, Mathematics, and all sciences; sent runners out on all roads to catch students: One lad, they said, came in yesterday; another, this morning; "thought they should like it first-rate." Already, the guardians of the institution evidently thought themselves ill used, if they did not add a new student every day, and were confident of graduating a class of ten, by the time green peas were ripe. Well, the next year they graduated fifteen Bachelors of Arts; the Greek professor published a Greek grammar of good pretention. Last year, Neander's Library was offered for sale, at Berlin, in Prussia.[8] Various colleges and private collectors were in treaty for the purchase; but the wide-awake little University said to itself, in the phrase of the country, "the longest pole takes the persimmon,"—had a man on the spot, with his money in his pocket,—bought the library,—and it is now triumphantly mounted on the shelves at Rochester, to be explored, at leisure, as soon as they have learned enough to read it.

In every part of the country this vigorous people have struck out some bold and effectual resource. In the north, the summers were short, the soil sterile, and the crop uncertain. Near the foggy island of Newfoundland is stretched a sandbank six

6. Alfred the Great (849–99), sovereign of all England not under Danish rule from 886 to his death; druids were ancient Celtic priests.

7. John Nichols Wilder (1814–58), first chair of the board of trustees of the University of Rochester, New York; Pythologian clubs and societies, devoted to the study and discussion of literature, were popular on college campuses during the nineteenth century (Emerson was a member of one such club at Harvard during his student years there).

8. Johann August Wilhelm Neander (originally David Mendel) (1789–1850), German historian and Christian theologian of Jewish parentage.

hundred miles long, and the sea flowing over this vast submarine mountain contains an amount of human food which the nations of Europe and America have for several centuries labored indefatigably to collect with nets, lines, and every process that could be contrived or imagined, and yet not the smallest diminution of fruitfulness has ever been observed. Thither he went, and if one should go to the capes of Massachusetts, to Gloucester, to Plymouth, Barnstable, Provincetown, he would find, that poor men, without other capital than their arms, built a boat of sixty or seventy tons,—all the owners went in her,—every man carrying his own little bag of provisions,—(a little salt, molasses, and meal, and pork;—) every man fished for himself; and hence the phrase *on his own hook.* This fishing led to the hunting of the whale by some bold Quakers who lived in Nantucket, and who planted their little shipyards at New Bedford, and built up that gigantic trade.[9]

East of the Penobscot River, the climate changes, and the earth will no longer produce wheat, or corn, or apples. Even the potato now is cut off. The agricultural societies resolved, that the hackmetach root was their best esculent, and the shingle-mill their best orchard.[10] At Bangor, where the summer is only a two months' thaw, they fill the forests of Maine with lumberers; buy and sell townships and all the timber on the St. John's River; keep up a brisk game of saw- and slitting-mills. They drag a pine log to mill, turn a crank, and it comes out chairs, and tables, and pianos.

An American in this ardent climate gets up early some morning, buys a river, advertises for twelve or fifteen hundred Irishmen, digs a new channel for it, brings it to his mills, and has a head of twenty-five feet of water: to give him an appetite for his breakfast, he raises a house; then carves out, within-doors, a quarter township into streets and building lots, tavern, school, and Methodist meetinghouse; sends up an engineer into New Hampshire to see where his water comes from, and, after advising with him, sends a trusty man of business to buy of all the farmers such mill privileges as will serve him among their waste hill and pasture lots, and comes home with glee, announcing that he is now owner of the great Lake Winnepesaukee, as reservoir for his Lowell mills at midsummer.[11] The Lowell people gave $200,000 for one hundred square miles of water. Now, they put up their flashboards when there is too much water; and let them down, when there is too little; and have a just supply all summer.

Plenty of ability for this taming and subduing the land, and for expediting internal intercourse. There is many a man who has built his city with all needful aids of engineering, ship and boat building, surveying, and machine shops at their disposal. Go into each great capital; Go into Wall Street. See how well the city of New

9. Quakers (Society of Friends), English sect founded in the seventeenth century known for its pacifism and belief in an inner spiritual voice.

10. Hackmatack is a term for several species of coniferous trees; esculent means edible.

11. Lake Winnepesaukee is the largest lake in New Hampshire. Lowell, Massachusetts, was famous for its textile mills, which were water driven.

York is officered for its wants. What large brains, what forcible and persevering gentlemen: six or eight citizens have pioneered the short way to California, and the short way to Liverpool, and the short railway to the Pacific.

The English slow, sure finish has changed into the irresistibility of the American. The climate itself is in extremes. We get, in summer, the splendor of the equator and a touch of Syria, with enormous productiveness. Nature in this climate, ardent, rushing up, after a shower, into a mat of vegetation. Nature goes into the genius, as well as into the cucumbers, whilst the poor polar man only gets the last of it. The man's irresistibility is like nature's. Like nature, he has no conscience. His motto, like her's, is, Our country right or wrong. He builds shingle palaces, shingle cities, picnic universities; extemporizes a state in California; in an altered mood, I suppose, he will build stone cities, with equal celerity. Tall, restless Kentucky strength: good stock;—but, though an admirable fruit, you shall not find one good sound, well-developed apple on the tree. Nature herself was in a hurry with these racers, and never finished one.

If you travel in New England, you will find in each town some manufacture rooted, for which the place offered no special facilities. In one town, there is a whip factory; in another, jewelry; in a third, church-organs; in a fourth, accordions; in a fifth, shoepegs; in a sixth, planes and case knives; in a seventh, fountain pens, and when you inquire what caused this thriving work which feeds hundreds and thousands, to grow up here, Why, Mr. Driver moved into the place, and set up his lathe, and, after a time, one of his men set up another, and so on. It was not that the leather grew here, or the ivory, or the iron; It was not nearer to the market; It was not the water power; It was only that here grew Mr. Driver's brain.

All is hasty, and with the penalty that speed must pay. Time respects nothing but what himself has made. All is hasty, incomplete, cheap, much of it counterfeit. There is superficial finish, and want of solidity. His leather is not tanned; his white lead is whiting; his sulphuric acid has half-strength; in architecture, his pillars are drums; his stone is well-sanded pumpkin-pine; his mahogany is veneered; and, I am sorry to say, in Philadelphia itself, he has learned to build marble houses with veneers instead of blocks.

Our newspapers name it as a merit, that the steam engine of our sea steamers was first put together in the ship. That circumstance will not recommend the boat to the Englishman who knows that his countrymen do not venture to put the machine into the ship until it first it has been kept a'going for months in the works. Instead of the grand old knees of oak which nature has been employed for seven centuries in the forest to knot and gnarl into rocky strength,—we have found out, by more dexterous fashion of our saws, to saw, out of refuse sapling stuff, knees of any shape; if they will hold together till they are nailed, they will hold till they are screwed, and then covered up with boards and veneered with bird's-eye maple, and varnished with copal; Who will ever know the difference! Ah, nobody—Nobody but the ugly Ocean, and the rending and bursting of the Southwestern Gale, and the drowning passengers.

Rashness of adventure marks all their acts and professions. Their steam-marine outnumbers every other nation's, but it is frail, and recklessly hazarded, burned, snagged, run into, and raced to ruin, and proverbially unsafe. The safety-valve is fastened down with a billet of wood. No eastern man travels on the western rivers, without a life-preserver. And I found, that whilst, on the Mississippi, my companions, who were western merchants, did not take off their clothes or their boots,— until they entered the Ohio; then they undressed, and went to sleep. Forty-seven steamboats were burned at St. Louis in the year 1849–1850.

Another form in which this levity shows itself is a social and public action, in which, the individuals composing the assembly do not feel themselves committed. They are fond of excitement, and like crowds; and will lend their hand and voice to swell the clapping and huzzas that applaud some person or sentiment, on whose merits they have by no means made up their minds. They have a superficial heat, a two-inch enthusiasm, a passing flush and are willing to cry for anything with a million. It is a sort of rose-influenza, epidemic for a day or two, far and wide, and then forgotten. And if some foreign celebrity passes by, as Lafayette, or Kossuth, or Dickens, or Lord Morpeth, or Meagher, or Gavazzi, or Thackeray, the shout of welcome, first from a few voices, is echoed about and caught from city to city, East, West, North, South, until it swells into an oriental superlative of adulation, and deceives the object of it into some belief that he is the man they all were waiting for.[12] And they are only humbugging each other. If Kossuth had received on his landing in England, such a welcome as he found at the city of New York, it might have been relied on, whereas the very actors in the New York scene knew it meant nothing.

"Haste," said Mahomet, "is of the devil; Delay is of the All-giving."[13] The like incompleteness runs into education, into the schools, and the trades and professions: The like into manners and plans of life. Fine manners, fine intercourse, require time, and abhor hurry.

The climate adds vivacity, but exhausts. In this close competition, every man is tasked beyond his strength, and grows early old. Life is a lottery, in which everyone may draw a fortune, or a blank. In California, insanity abounds. It frequently happens, that one man is getting out of his digging twenty dollars a day; another, in the

12. Marie-Joseph-Paul-Yves-Roch-Gilbert du Motier, the marquis de Lafayette (1757–1834), French military leader and a hero of the American Revolution; Lajos Kossuth (1802–94), Hungarian patriot and statesman, leader of the Hungarian revolution of 1848–49; Charles Dickens (1812–70), English novelist; George William Frederick Howard, Viscount Morpeth (1802–64), English statesman and viceroy of Ireland; Thomas Francis Meagher (1823–67), American politician and soldier born in Ireland; Alessandro Gavazzi (1809–89), Italian patriot and religious reformer; William Makepeace Thackeray (1811–63), English novelist.
13. Muhammad (ca. 570–632), founder of Islam, born in Mecca.

very next beside him, is getting out a thousand dollars a day. Of course, 'tis vain to say, "Gentlemen, in Digging number one, Keep cool! There's plenty of time." No: They work like dogs, because they are expecting every hour that they will strike on the same shelf. How can brains or bodies stand such excitement? Yet what happens in the mines, happens throughout the Union.

The leading features of national character are less glaring in our large and old cities, which have kept much of the European spirit. In the new-planted territory of the West, it found free play, and is seen without disguise. It is said, if you would see the American, you must cross the Alleghanies.

There is a levity of social and public action. I think there is a reaction on the people from the extraordinary advantages and invitations of their condition. In proportion to the personal ability of each man, he feels the invitation and career which the country opens to him. He is easily fed with wheat and game, with Ohio wine; but his brain is also pampered by finer draughts, by political power and by the power in the railroad board, or the mills, or the banks. This elevates his spirits and gives, of course, an easy self-reliance that makes him self-willed and unscrupulous.

I think, when we are most disturbed by their rash and immoral voting, it is not malignity, but recklessness. The people are better than their votes. They are careless of politics, because they do not ever feel seriously threatened; they feel strong and irresistible; they can do and undo; what they have enacted, they can repeal; and they do not entertain the possibility of being seriously caught and endangered in their own legislation. They stay away from the polls, saying, that *one vote can do no good*; and then they take another step, and say, *one vote can do no harm*, and vote for something which they do not approve, because their party or set, votes for it not from malice, but from levity. Of course, this levity puts them in the power of any party which has a steady interest to promote, which does not conflict manifestly with the pecuniary interest of the voters. New England, it is said, on each new political event, resolves itself into a debating society, and is the Germany of the United States.

The men also are uncertain. It is agreed by those who have lived there, that you can form no conclusion to depend upon, from what a man on the prairie says, he will do. He says, he will come on Monday. He will not come on Monday. He may arrive some days later. He says, he will bring twenty hands. Perhaps he will bring three. Entire want of punctuality and business-habit—a principal cause of which is the uncertainty of health. The miasma takes the labourers.

Go to the states on the Mississippi. Your western romance fades into reality of some grimness. Everything wears a raw and ordinary aspect. You find much coarseness in manners; much meanness in politics; much swagger, and vaporing, and low filibusterism; the men have not shed their canine teeth. Well; don't be disgusted: 'tis the work of this river,—this Mississippi River,—that warps the men, warps the nations, and dinges them all with its own mud.

I found a good many burly fellows, with dangerous eyes, on the banks, everyone with his cigar.—What is that man doing? What is that other man's work? And what of this? And this?—"O, they are river-hands; They follow the river." Never was a truer word. I found it every day more deeply exact, and of thousands and millions. *They follow the river.* They must chop down its woods; kill the alligator; eat the deer; shoot the wolf; mind the boat; plant the Missouri corn; cure, save, and send down stream the wild foison harvest, tilth, and wealth of this huge mud-trough of the two thousand miles or ten thousand miles of river.[14] How can they have a day's leisure for anything but the work of the river? Everyone has the mud up to his knees, and the coal of the country dinges his shirt. How can he know letters, or arts, or sciences?

Centre of all the Valley, and Gate of California, is St. Louis, a little French town when it came into American possession fifty years ago.[15] And I have seen various persons who remember it, when there was only one brick house in it. It has now nearly 100,000 inhabitants, and is a well-built city, with spacious squares, and ample room to grow. The people are fully aware of their advantages: they have long smelled the Pacific Ocean. Cincinnati is a *bagatelle*, and they do not speak with due respect of New York. A certain largeness appears in the designs and enterprise of the people and a generosity. They talk St. Louis in all companies, all day, and great fortunes have been made by such as were wise or lucky enough to hold on to their lands. Governor Edwards, an old pioneer, told me that he remembered when St. Louis consisted of nothing but old tumbledown French houses with their little piazzas, whose columns, rotted away at bottom, and suspended from the top, were swinging in the wind: and that nobody who came here then, would think of buying land, in such a dilapidated place.[16] But a few men had the wisdom to look rather on the map, than in the streets; and they discovered that the two enormous river axes of the Continent, the Mississippi running North and South, and the Ohio and Missouri running East and West, had their practical intersection at St. Louis, and that sixty thousand miles of navigable river were tributary to this town; that this town must come to be "the greatest cross-roads the world ever saw."

I stood at St. Louis and saw the Father of Waters rolling his steady flotilla of cakes and islands of ice, four miles an hour; and, day by day, the stream grew more impressive as one grew better acquainted with it.[17] 'Tis the only divinity that is worshipped on its banks. It is a power not to be trifled with. Here the river is only half a mile wide; But in freshets, it extends from bluff to bluff, or here ten to fifteen

14. Foison is an archaic term for rich harvest or abundance; in Scotland it refers to nourishment or physical strength.

15. St. Louis had been ceded to America by the French in 1804.

16. Emerson confuses Ninian Wirt Edwards (1809–89), first superintendent of instruction in Illinois and friend of Abraham Lincoln, with his father, Ninian Edwards (1775–1833), governor of the Illinois Territory (1809–18) and the state of Illinois, as he had earlier (*JMN*, 11:527).

17. "Father of Waters," loose translation of the Algonquin name for the Mississippi River.

miles, and is crossed in steamboats so far. The engineers think the river here uncon-
querable and that they must follow, not dictate to it. They who know it best, fear
it most. If you drive piles into it, to build a dam or pier, you only stir the bottom,
which dissolves like sugar, and is all gone. Very laborious and costly constructions
have been carried off. Real estate on the shores of Missouri is very floating capital.

Go into the states which make its valley, to know the powers of the river, the in-
satiate craving for nations of men to reap and cure its harvests, and the conditions
it imposes, for it yields to no engineering. The prairie exists to yield the greatest
quantity of tallow. For corn makes swine; swine is the export of all the land; and
St. Louis, furiously, like some Eblis, vociferates, "Men! Men! more men, for I have
more pork to pack."[18]

Cotton has done its office in the South,—cotton and sugar,—but now pig plays
his unctuous part, draws his larded sides, like modest Prosperity, through the
streets of all cities; grunts softly to nations; grunts melodiously to all who are not
preoccupied by the new glitter of California, and seems to say, "My dear men,
henceforth owe your aristocracy and civility to me!"

'Tis ever so. What earldoms of Guienne, Champagne, and Bourgogne lay sleep-
ing in the first grape-store that was carried by travelling man or flying bird into
the country of the Rhine? What civilization and power in the first grain of wheat
on the Nile; in the first orange of Spain; in the tea plant of China; in the coal of
England; in the peach-store of New Jersey; in the sugar cane for the shores of the
Gulf of Mexico? Thrones, constitutions, cities, states, laws, learning, arts, all dependent on some one plant which they ripen and sell: and not less, in all this prairie,
on this modest quadruped. For, though it cannot be disputed that telegraphs are
beautiful triumphs of science and art, if you hold your ear close to the poetic wires,
the lightning is whispering to the packers, "A penny more on lard! An eighth on
candles!"

Such as the people, such is the hero. I asked, "Who was the great man of the
prairie?", and was shown a field of corn containing within one fence one thousand
acres. The owner of this was the hero: one of themselves, a man who owned forty
thousand acres, a cattle dealer who raises three or four thousand head of cattle,
who delights to stand in the gap when great droves of cattle are to be separated,—
these for the market, and those to pasture. The man who stands in the gap is to
choose, on the instant, by their looks, as they come up, which to let through the
gate, and which to keep off the other way, and he must be of such a size and look
that a buffalo would not run over him. He delights in fat steers. He hardly knows
what a bed is, sleeps behind a door, while his horse is baited; lives in the saddle;
never knows leisure; eats his mush and milk with two spoons; he laughs at politics,

18. In Islamic mythology Eblis is the prince of the evil spirits. He was condemned by God to haunt
ruins and eat unblessed food.

as long as he is absolute in the market towns and cattle yards, and nobody can make money out of him.

I tell this story, because I passed a field alleged to be of these dimensions; though it seems, it is something incredible on the Atlantic states. For Mr. Greene of Cincinnati told me he knew of a simple field on the Big Miami River, which contains one thousand acres, and yielded one hundred bushels of corn to the acre.[19] Yet, he says: When he told this story in New England, Gentlemen would always take wine with him.

Narrow views, the narrow trade enforces, and yet the poverty and the habits of the swineherds and cattle dealers are wholesome for liberty. A stern equality is guarded and enjoyed. These men are fierce. Most of them live in loghouses,—the whole family in one room; eat ham and corn cakes; are all day in the open air, and accustomed to serve themselves; their dress is plain, and they pay no regard to a fine coat. Every man alternates the most daring and vigorous exertion, with listless repose.

They are all alike, all in working clothes. The Governor of the state works with his hands, and all the dignitaries must harness their own teams. I called on the Governor of the state at the statehouse, and, whilst I was paying my respects, the Secretary of State came into the room. "Governor," said the Secretary, "Did you take my screwdriver out of my room?" The executive acknowledged the act. It stood confessed, that he had borrowed it for his own uses. Need enough there was to use it: the statehouse was all cracking to pieces. They are all poor country people and live hard. But the sense of freedom and equality is never interrupted. New England men and women said, "We never knew what it was to be free, till we came to Missouri." They affirm, that, after people have been out west, ten years, nothing would draw them back to the old states. An alumnus of Yale, whom I discovered in grey working dress, told me, that, though his eyes ached for the hills when he went back to Connecticut, he could not breathe there;—a man was nothing there,—could not make his mark.

The people are all kings,—if the sceptre is a cattledealer's driving-whip. I noticed an extraordinary firmness, even to ferocity, in the face of many a drover, an air of independence, and lips which expressed more pluck, and perseverance, and wo to all opponents, than could be crowded into a coat of arms.

The condition of the Western states is today what was the condition of all the states fifty or a hundred years ago. It is the country of poor men. Here is practical democracy;—not the old experiment, out of a prostrate humanity, as out of a bank or magazine, to draw materials of culture to a class, and to avenge the injured many by wonderful success in a few; but here is the human race poured out over the continent to do itself justice; all mankind in its shirt-sleeves; not grimacing, like poor

19. William Greene (1797–1881), American lawyer in Cincinnati.

rich men in cities, pretending to be rich, but unmistakably taking off its coat, as in California, to hard work, when labor is sure to pay. This through all the country. For, really, though you see wealth in the capitals, it is only a sprinkling of rich men in the cities and at sparse points: the bulk of the population is poor. In Maine, every man is a lumberer. In Massachusetts, every twelfth man is a shoemaker and the rest millers, farmers, sailors, or fishermen.

Well, the result is, instead of the doleful experience of the European economist who tells us, "In almost all countries the condition of the great body of the people is poor and miserable," here that same great body has arrived at a sloven plenty;— ham and corn cakes, tight roof and coals enough have been attained; an unbut- toned comfort—not clean, not thoughtful, far from polished, without dignity in his repose; the man awkward and restless if he have not something to do; but honest and kind, for the most part; understanding his own rights, and stiff to maintain them; and disposed to give his children a better education than he received.[20]

The Anglo-Saxon race are characterised by their universal interest in politics. The people of England are educated by political discussion. In America, the public topic is not less absorbing; it is the one topic which neither age, nor sex, nor profes- sion can long keep out of any conversation. But in this country a prodigious stride has been taken in practice, through universal suffrage. The fact that everybody elects and everybody is eligible, exasperates the discussion. In England, politics is a monopoly of a few; it is with the people a very distant affair. It is a choice of somebody far above them, and few of them are the choosers. The people whom I saw, eminent people, some of them, had never voted in their lives. But here, it is *you*, and *me*, and *him*, that are immediately concerned.

It were fatal to the happiness of a young man to set out with ultra-conservative notions in this country. He must settle it in his mind that the human race have got possession, and, though they will make many blunders, and do some great wrongs, yet, on the whole, they will consult the interest of the whole.

Practically, the tendency among us, is, to elect middle class men, and, by no means, first class men.

It is certainly desireable that men of capacity and virtue, that the best and wisest, should be entrusted with the helm of power, and the tendency to promote to this charge young men of very imperfect training, is, I know, regretted, and is, on many accounts, a bad feature. But there are certain benefits which mitigate the folly. I said, the people were educated by politics. Well, after a young man of the humblest class has passed through the village school, if he has vivacity and a social talent, and interests himself on the street, and at the railroad station, in talking politics, he is chosen to the Legislature. There, to his great surprise, he finds himself, for a whole

20. Attributed to John Stuart Mill (1806–73), English philosopher and economist, by Emerson (*JMN*, 13:82).

winter, in far better company than he ever kept before; subject to social attentions and opportunities such as he never knew; listening (every day) to debates, to which he must listen, because he is to vote, and to give a reason for his vote, at home; and entertaining in his mind, daily, a class of questions wholly new to him, and quite above his habit. If he have capacity, this ordeal cannot fail to work on him, and I have known (it is notorious) an ordinary tavern brawler lose all his profanity and a large part of his other nonsense, and come back at the end of a single winter at the legislature, at least as much improved, as his young townsman from two years at the University.

There was in the Illinois Legislature a member, to whom plainly all parties looked with interest as a man likely to take a leading part. A gentleman who followed him in debate, took occasion to commend his speech, and to congratulate the legislature that this self-made man, so lately retired from a mechanical trade, had forsaken an honorable toil to lend his powerful service to the state. The new member made haste to correct his colleague (who described him as formerly a working man,) by saying, that he was still a mason, had by no means relinquished his trowel, had laid twenty thousand feet of plaster this fall and valued his work as a mason more than his skill in politics.

The American, in view of these great powers, appears passively to yield to this superincumbent Fate. His task is, to educe the capabilities of the Continent,—to make the most of it.

It is the American discovery, that, it is as easy to occupy large space, and do much work, as, to occupy a small space, and do little. And his task is the easier for the wonderful tools he uses. Mr. Webster had a good head, and loved Union; but the telegraph and railroad are better unionists than ten thousand Websters. He has a finer invention. In this age of tools, one of the skilfullest of all machines is this governing machine, rude as it is yet, which the Americans have so far perfected;—the distributing of political electricity over a vast area to avoid explosion. Last November, we had an election day,—and a revolution,—for every election is a revolution,—went off with the quietness of a pic-nic, or a sermon.

Thanks to his telegraph, his Election day, and his newspaper, he looks with a public eye, he works in a public spirit. The young American must know the geography of his continent, as exactly as his father did the streets of his town; such proximity have steam, rails, and telegraphs wrought.

Indeed, he has a wilderness of capabilities. He is versatile; (πολυτροποσ Οδυσσευσ;) has a many-turning Ulyssean culture.[21] He is confident as Jove in his powers and triumph; has a prospering look. He is a good combiner. The stock companies, the mills of the North, owe everything to the good concert of skilful men. His eyes run up and down, here and out there, and nothing escapes them.

---

21. Possibly a reference to the many voyages of Ulysses in *The Odyssey*.

He thinks of Cuba, he thinks of Japan, he thinks of annexing South America, in due course. Nothing is impossible. He is accustomed to see things mind him. He believes, if he should attach his clamps to a granite mountain, and let on the steam, it would follow him like a spaniel round the globe.

The English are stiff to their own ways. As I showed you, the towns are stiff to their old crafts for five centuries. It is the remark of our people employing English workmen, that they show great reluctance to deviate from their own methods, or proper work; whilst an American will turn his hand to anything. The very existence of our manufactures is a proof of aptitude: The stone cutters become sculptors. The house painters take to landscape and portraits. We can make everything but music and poetry. But also he has chambers opened in his mind which the English have not. He is intellectual and speculative, an abstractionist. He has solitude of mind and fruitful dreams. See what good readers of dreamy Germans we are— books which the English cannot bear. Many and many a good thought of some inspired man floats about for a time among studious men, and, not long after, I have noticed it caught up by some of the gladiators at Washington; and, endorsed or, rather, usurped by them, it passes into the newspapers, and, becomes, under these base colours, the property of the million.

This Fate, this natural growth, is really the ground on which the shrewd men of the world fall back, as their remedy for all evils. Such men do not believe much in any special policy, as free trade, nor put much faith in any statute in our capricious and fluctuating legislation; nor are they wont to trust the honesty of people, or to lift their eyes to considerations so large as the self-avenging power that mixes in human affairs, under the name of morals. But analyse what they say, and they do believe in the natural growth of the Republic; and this Fate really involves, in their mind, melioration, or, the self-avenging moral power. Name any benefit; One way or another, they believe the nation arrives at the same thing, which this ingenious person would compass with his law. Thus a strong party is for free trade; and all the reason and humanity is on their side; all the conclusions of history. But the old man shakes his head, and says, Look, You have got free trade in substance, though not in form; free trade with thirty-one nations, reaching through all climates, some of them manufacturing nations; some agricultural; some seafaring; some mining; and some hunting and fishing; all varieties of production, and not a customhouse.[22] You wanted tariff to protect your iron. Well, you did not get it; but, instead of twenty thousand tons, a year ago you manufactured 800,000.

Peace you want. But Mr. Cobden and Mr. Burritt, however respectable, do not seem to him to say much to the purpose.[23] But trade can't afford to make war, or

22. The "old man" is identified by Edward Waldo Emerson as Thomas Wren Ward (1786–1858), Boston merchant (*JMN*, 11:408n).

23. Richard Cobden (1804–65), English politician and economist, advocate of free trade and peace; Elihu Burritt, called the Learned Blacksmith (1810–79), American linguist and social reformer.

to suffer war to be made, and every man who has land, or money, or goods is by them bound ever to keep the peace. You talk of annexing new territory. It only adds to your burdens. By reciprocity, or free trade with England, you annex England, without the taxation of England.

Here, gentlemen, is a grave interest, the future of a quarter of the world, and of a race as energetic and as able as any in it: and one cannot help asking, What is to come of it?

Everybody working all day and half the night, and no man in this country knows whither we are driving, or can chant the destiny of the Anglo-American. The solar system, astronomers say, is moving toward a star in the arm of the Constellation Hercules: but whither we are drifting, who can tell.

When a new question is before Congress, or in the Courts, the presumption in all men's minds is that it will not be decided as the man within the breast would decide it, and a verdict on grounds of natural equity gives all men the joy of surprise. On Education; on Temperance; on Copyright; on claims of injured parties, whether states or private citizens; the Anglo-American usually gives a selfish and electioneering verdict. What can be worse than our legislation on Slavery? If there be any worse, be sure we shall find it out, and make that law.

But is this the action of legislatures only? It is also the public opinion as expressed in what are called the respectable journals. The tone of the press is not lower on Slavery than on everything else. Criminal on that point, ready to be criminal on every other. It has no great men. Its able men are not patriots, but simply attorneys of gross sectional interests. Its politics are the politics of trade. It goes for wars, if they be profitable wars. Its argument at the elections, is, "Roast Beef and two dollars a day;" and our people will not go for liberty of other people, no, nor for their own, but for annexation of territory, or a tariff, or whatever promises new chances for young men, more money to men of business.

The gain of the means of living absorbs them to the exclusion of the ends. Nothing but the brandy of politics will wake them from brute life. No song of any muse will they hear.

I know we must speak very modestly of the political good sense of the country and of its virtue. Any action of the well-disposed and intelligent class in its affairs is uniformly reckoned an impertinence, and they are presently whipped back into their libraries and churches and Sunday schools. But drive out nature with a fork, and she presently comes back again. The moral sense is still renewed, and every child that is born is of nature's party.

We lack repose. As soon as we stop working, or active thinking, we mope. There is no self-respect, no grand sense of sharing the Divine preference. We are restless, run out and back, talk past, and overdo. When that civilization of their Universities and men of science and thought enters into their politics, I shall think they have made a real advance.

But this perhaps is partial and ungenerous, when we remember the sturdy minority, often for an age the majority, that, in England itself, has striven for the right, and the largest justice, and won so many charters, and still strives there with the lovers of liberty here. Rather, it is right to esteem without regard to geography this industrious liberty-loving Saxon wherever he works,—the Saxon, the colossus who bestrides the narrow Atlantic,—with one foot on England, and one on America,—at home on all land,—at home on all seas, asking no leave to be of any other,—formidable, conquering and to conquer, with his nervous and sufficient civilization weaponed already far beyond his present performing. At least I infer that the decided preference of the Saxon on the whole for civil liberty is the security of the modern world. He is healthy;—nature's democrat, nature's worker;—his instincts and tendencies, sound and right. Only let high and sound counsels be given to these twin nations, admonishing, and holding them up to their highest aim. At present, one hears only the tinkle of preparation. At present, their commerce is but costly trifling belting the world for raisins, oranges, oil, wine, tobacco, gums and drugs, hides and silk. But what for thought? What for humanity? What for the interests of the human soul? Is science, is the head, is the heart, always to be postponed, and only endured or tolerated? And our politics are no better than our trade. Are legislatures convened, with upheaval of the peace of nations in the fury of elections, to any noble, humane purpose? No; but to the most selfish and paltry.

It is impossible that a race so gifted and historied as this, should not presently make good the wonderful education of so many centuries. It is not indiscriminate masses of Europe that are shipped hitherward,—but the Atlantic is a sieve, through which only, or chiefly, the liberal, bold, *America-loving* part of each city, clan, or family, pass. It is mainly the light complexion, the blue eyes of Europe, that come; the black eyes, (the black drop,) the Europe of Europe is left. Still, a portion of both races come, and the old contest of feudalism and of democracy renews itself here on a new battlefield.

That makes sometimes, and, at this moment, the vast interest of American history. Which principle, which branch of this compound English race is here (and now) to triumph? The liberty-loving, the thought-loving, the godly and grand British race, that have fought so many battles, and made so many songs, and created so many reverend laws and charters, and exhibited so much moral grandeur in private and poor men;—or, the England of Kings and Lords; castles and primogeniture; enormous wealth and fierce exclusion? Which is to be planted here? It is wonderful with how much rancour and premeditation at this moment the fight is prepared. Of late years, as I said, England has been materialized by its wealth, and the noble air of other times is gone.

Again, mark the differences more marked in every generation between the English and the Americans. The great majority of the Americans are of pure English descent. In some parts of America, their pedigrees have been well kept in family

Bibles and in the town-clerk's office: Yet differences appear in stature, weight, complexion, feature, voice, widening too, in national character. These spring from new conditions, from climate, from the occupancy of wide territory, inducing solitary labor and sloven cultivation; from new staples of tillage and trade, new laws, new enemies. Climate draws the teeth, emaciates the body, spends the constitution, unbuilds and recomposes the bulky compact Briton into the loose-jointed, spare, swaggering Kentuckian. The Englishman, well-made, and even fatted by his climate of clouded sunshine, walks and sits erect, and his chair rests squarely on its legs. The American lolls and leans, tips his chair, adds rockers to it to keep it tipped, but is capable of equal energy in action and the mental powers are not impaired. The difference of manners is marked. The American is demonstrative; the English, shy and reserved.

When Rome has arrived at Cicero and Caesar, it has no more that it can do, and retreats.[24] When Italy has got out Dante and Raffael, all the rest will be rubbish.[25] So that we ought to be thankful that our hero or poet does not hasten to be born in America, but still allows us others to live a little, and warm ourselves at the fire of the sun; for, when he comes, we others must pack our petty trunks and be gone.

'Tis said, that when the Sphinx's riddle is solved, the Sphinx rolls herself off the precipice and falls into the sea.[26] 'Tis said, every race or age ends with the successful man who knots up into himself the genius or idea of his nation, and, that, when the Jews have flowered into their prophet, or cluster of prophets, there is the practical end of the nation. When Greece is complete in Plato, Phidias, Pericles, the race is spent, and rapidly takes itself away.[27]

The Anglo-American is a pushing, versatile, victorious race. Then it has wonderful powers of absorption and appropriating. The Mississippi swallows the Illinois, the Missouri, Ohio, and Red rivers, and does not widen: And this Anglo-American race absorbs into itself thousands and millions of Germans, French, Irish, Norwegians, and Swedes, and remains unchanged.

Our young men went to the Rhine to find the German genius which had charmed them and it was not there. Lessing, Herder, Schiller, Goethe, Wieland were all dead.[28] They hunted for it in Heidelberg, in Gottingen, in Halle, in Berlin:

24. Marcus Tullius Cicero (106–43 B.C.), Roman philosopher and statesman; Gaius Julius Caesar (100–44 B.C.), Roman general and statesman.

25. Dante Alighieri (1265–1321), Italian poet, author of the *Divina commedia* (completed in 1321), which recounts the poet's journey through Hell, Purgatory, and Paradise; Raphael (1483–1520), Italian painter whose works adorn the Vatican, also called "Raphaelle" or "Raphaello" by Emerson.

26. Numerous writers have dealt with the story of travelers being asked a riddle about existence by the Sphinx; for Emerson's attempt see his poem "The Sphinx" (1841, W, 9:20–25), which concludes with the Sphinx saying, " 'Who telleth one of my meanings / Is master of all I am.' "

27. Plato (ca. 428–348 B.C.), the most famous of the Greek philosophers; Phidias (ca. 500–ca. 430 B.C.), greatest of the ancient Greek sculptors; Pericles (ca. 495–429 B.C.), Athenian statesman and orator.

28. During Emerson's youth many prominent Americans traveled to Germany to seek out the scenes of German literature and the country's major writers and theologians; one of them was Emerson's

no one knew where it was. From Vienna to the frontier, it was not found; and they slowly and mournfully learned, that really America possessed more of that expansive inquisitive spirit, and they must return and look for it in Boston and New York.

The convictions of multitudes are sometimes as well expressed by braggart lips or in jeers that sound blasphemous,—and that word "manifest destiny," often profanely used, yet signifies the sense all men have of the prodigious energy and opportunity lying dormant here. The poor Prussian, or Austrian, or Italian escaping hither discovers that he has been handcuffed, fettered all his early lifetime, with monopolies and duties at every tollgate on his little cart of corn, or wine, or wood, or straw, or on his cow or ox or donkey, and his own lips and mind padlocked. No country, no education, no vote,—but passports, police, monks, and foreign soldiers instead.

The wild, exuberant tone of society in California is only an exaggeration of the uniform present condition of America in the excessive attraction of the extraordinary natural wealth. 'Tis doubtful whether London, whether Paris, whether Berlin can answer the questions which now rise in the American mind. American geography and vast population must be considered in all arrangements of commerce and politics, and we are forced, therefore, to make our own precedents. The radiation of character and manners here, the boundless America, gives opportunity as wide as the morning; and the effect is to dig away the peak of the mountain, to change the peak into a vast table-land, where millions can share the privilege of a handful of patricians.

---

brother William. The German authors mentioned here are Gotthold Ephraim Lessing (1729–81), critic and dramatist; Johann Gottfried von Herder (1744–1803), philosopher, theologian, critic, and poet; Johann Christoph Friedrich von Schiller (1759–1805), poet, playwright, and critic; Johann Wolfgang von Goethe (1749–1832), Germany's most famous writer; and Christoph Martin Wieland (1733–1813), poet and novelist.

Poetry and English Poetry

(1854)

Emerson delivered "Poetry and English Poetry" only once: on 10 January 1854 as the third in a series of six private lectures entitled *Topics of Modern Times* in Philadelphia. In 1865 he merged "Poetry and English Poetry" with some form of his many lectures entitled "Genius" to create a version called "Culture," which he delivered in a series of lectures, *American Life*, before the Literary Societies of Williams College in Williamstown, Massachusetts.

Poetry was, of course, one of Emerson's favorite topics, as his lecture "The Poet," printed in this edition, his essay on "The Poet" published in *Essays: Second Series* in 1844 (*CW*, 3:1–24), and his voluminous correspondence, early lectures on literature, and journals and notebooks devoted primarily to poetry suggest (see, e.g., Notebooks "Orientalist," "PY" ["Theory of Poetry"], and "ZO" in *TN* 2:39–141, 258–329, and 3:179–237, respectively). Among his lectures, "Poetry and English Poetry" stands approximately midway between Emerson's early speculations and pronouncements on poetry and his last. Beginning with his lecture "The Poet" in 1841, Emerson developed his ideas on poetic theory and practice in lectures such as "Poetry and Eloquence" in 1848, "Poetry and Criticism in England and America" in 1861, and "Poetry and Criticism" in 1868 and 1869. Only Emerson's lectures "The Poet" and "Poetry and English Poetry," both of which are printed in this volume, survive in complete manuscript form. Except for these two lectures, Emerson successively mined all lecture manuscripts on poetry in order to create new lectures on poetry and, eventually, to create the text of what became "Poetry and Imagination," which Emerson and James Elliot Cabot with the assistance of Ellen Emerson arranged in its final form for publication in *Letters and Social Aims* in 1876 (*W*, 8:1–75).

When Sir Isaac Newton saw in his garden the apple fall from the tree, he said, 'I see it at last; the moon is only a larger apple falling to the earth; the earth a still larger one falling to the sun. I see the law of all nature. Every particle in the Universe gravitates to every other.'[1] But there was a little boy bestriding the garden-fence who had watched the same apple ripening for some days, and now, when it fell, he ran and picked it up, and before the philosopher had

---

1. Sir Isaac Newton (1642–1727), English natural philosopher and mathematician.

finished his reflection, the boy ate the pippin. Of course, if the boy had overheard Sir Isaac's soliloquy, he would have thought it mighty silly. "You are welcome," he would say, "to all that about the moon, and so forth, as long as I've got the apple." And Newton, on his part, was contented that the boy should have orchards of apples, as long as he had the meaning of it.

Well, society has been divided ever since on the question, Who had the apple? Newton? or the Boy? the majority believing that the boy had the substantial apple, and Newton the shadow, whilst a minority believe that Newton had all the reality of the fruit, and the boy merely the form.

But whilst Newton sees in the fall of apple and moon a law of matter,—sees the immense extent, nay, the universality of a law, that perception is only *one* use of the apple, far higher than the boy's use of the apple, namely, for food,—another mind sees in it its analogies, to human life, its growth, its beauty, its odor, its fruit and its decay, and its resurrection in its progeny, and these so various and so perpetually suggested, as to make its habits and forms a kind of language to convey the accidents of man in a more pleasing manner. What is true of the tree is in like manner true of the animals.—In fact, bird, or beast,—do in their forms, habits, and instincts continually suggest parallels to man, though on a lower scale, and make possible the fables of Æsop, where the beasts are used purely to a human purpose.[2]

Now this secondary use by the intellect belongs to all natural facts, nay, to the whole being and behavior of the material universe. And every thought, every experience of man can be represented or languaged by an analogy from brute nature.

Thus, whilst commonsense looks at things, or visible nature,—the ground, the sky, the house, the men and women, and so forth as real and final facts,—Poetry, or the imagination, which dictates it, is a second sight, which looks *through* these, and uses them as types or words for thoughts which they signify. Nor is this a metaphysical whim of modern times, and quite too refined. It is as old as the human mind. Our best definition of poetry is one of the oldest sentences, and claims to come down to us from the Chaldaean Zoroaster, who wrote it thus; "Poets are standing transporters, whose employment consists in speaking to the Father and to Matter; in producing apparent imitations of unapparent Natures, and inscribing things unapparent in the apparent fabrication of the world."[3] In other words,— the world exists for thought. It is to make appear things which hide. Mountains, crystals, plants, animals are seen; that which makes them is jest with us, but is in earnest,—is the house of health and life. In spite of all the joys of poets, and the joys of saints, the most imaginative and abstracted person never makes with impunity

2. Aesop, legendary Greek fabulist of the sixth century B.C.

3. Attributed to Zoroaster (also known as Zarathushtra) (ca. 628–ca. 551 B.C.), Persian religious reformer and founder of Zoroastrianism, in Thomas Taylor, "Collection of the Chaldaean Oracles," *Monthly Magazine and British Register* (1797).

the least mistake in this particular, never tries to kindle his oven with water, or seizes his wild charger by the tail. We should not pardon it in another, nor should we endure it in ourselves.

But whilst we deal with this as finality, early hints are given, that we are not to stay here; that we must be making ready to go;—a warning that this magnificent hotel and conveniency we call Nature, is not final. First, inuendoes; then, broad hints, then smart taps are given, suggesting that nothing stands still in nature but Death; that the creation is on wheels, in transit, always passing into something else, streaming into something higher, that matter is not what it appears; that chemistry can blow it all into gas. Faraday, the most exact of natural philosophers, taught, that when we should arrive at the monads or primordial elements, the supposed little cubes or prisms of which all matter was built up, we should not find cubes, or prisms, or atoms at all, but spherules of force.[4] It was whispered that the globes of the universe were precipitates of something more subtle; nay, somewhat was murmured in our ear that dwindled astronomy into a toy;—*that*, too, was no finality, only provisional, a makeshift;—under chemistry was power and purpose: Power and purpose ride on matter to the last atom. It was steeped in thought, did everywhere express thought; that, as great conquerors have burned their ships when once they were landed on the wished-for shore, so the noble house of nature we inhabit, has temporary uses, and we can afford to leave it one day. The ends of all are moral, and therefore the beginnings are such.

Thin or solid, everything is in flight. I believe, this conviction makes the charm of chemistry, that we have the same *avoirdupois* matter in an alembic, without a vestige of the old form; and, in animal transformation, not less, as, in grub and fly, in egg and bird, in embryo and man; Everything undressing and stealing away from its form, streaming into something else, and nothing fast but those invisible cords which we call laws, on which all is strung. Then we see that things wear different names and faces, but belong to one family; that these secret cords or laws show their well-known virtue through every variety,—is it animal, is it plant, is it planet,— and the interest is gradually transferred from the forms, to this lurking method. The man finds his own sense written in the drollest variety of disguises all over nature.

This hint, however conveyed, upsets our commonsense systems, upsets our politics, our trade, our customs, our marriages, nay, the commonsense side of religion and of literature, which are all founded on low nature, on the cleanest and most economical mode of administering the material world, considered as final. The admission, never so covertly, that this is a makeshift, sets the dullest brain in ferment. Our little sir, from his first tottering steps, as soon as he can crow, does not

---

4. Michael Faraday (1791–1867), English chemist and physicist, known for his experiments with electromagnetism.

like to be practised upon, suspects that someone is "*doing*" him; and at this hint, everything is compromised; gunpowder is laid under every man's breakfast table.

It is curious that the secret of the march of Science in these days, is, the poetic perception of metamorphosis that is the key to Botany; that the same vegetable point or eye which is the unit of the plant can be transformed at pleasure into every part, as leaf, petal, stamen, pistil, bract, or seed. So in animals; that there is one animal, which new conditions infinitely vary and perfect. What an emotion of the sublime was felt in seeing a bough of a fossil tree in the possession of Playfair which was perfect wood at one end and perfect mineral coal at the other.[5]

The poet is he who, knowing that there is a second sense, looking at the same things with other men, presently sees the meaning that gleams through and instantly feels that this is all their value.

Suppose there were in the ocean certain strong currents which drove a ship caught in them, with such force, that no skill with the best wind, and no strength of oars, or sails, or steam, could make any head against them,—any more than against the current of Niagara. Such currents,—so tyrannical,—exist in thoughts, those finest and subtilest of all waters, that, once thought begins, it refuses to remember whose brain it belongs to,—what country, tradition, or religion,—and goes whirling off,—swim we merrily,—in a direction self-chosen, by law of thought, and not by law of kitchen-clock, or county committee. It has its own polarity. One of these vortices, or self-directions of thought, is the impulse to search resemblance, affinity, identity, in all its objects.

Suppose an anatomist should take a particle of gelatine on the end of a glass rod, and, dipping it in water, it should become a fish. Putting it on the top of a mountain, it should become a chamois; on a prairie, it should be a horse; in the forest, a lion; in the mud, a turtle; on the rock, a lizard; in the air, a bird; on a flower, a bee; underground, a worm; or, suppose, that the same particle, under new conditions of food, and sunshine, and freedom, became a Saxon man; And you have the theory of modern anatomy, namely, that there is one animal, which can be improved or retrograded into any other given animal.

Or, if a botanist on the blade of his pen-knife should take a little pollen, and, laying it on a stem, it should become a leaf; laying it at the bottom of the stem, in the ground, it should become root; at the top of the stem, it should become petals pink or purple; laying it on the top of the flower, it should become fruit,—the same imperceptible atom taking these different forms, at pleasure, to serve the end of the plant; and you have the idea of modern Botany.

Camper, the physiologist, was wont to draw on his blackboard the skeleton of man, and by a few strokes transform him into a horse, then into an ox, into a bird, into a fish.[6] We have or had in the Athenæum a series of fifteen or twenty

---

5. John Playfair (1748–1819), Scottish natural philosopher and geologist.
6. Pieter Camper (1722–89), Dutch physician and comparative anatomist.

drawings beginning with a toad, and by successive, slight modifications the figure was enlarged and harmonized into the Belvedere Apollo.[7]

"What he would write, he was before he writ."[8]

But I do not wish to find that my poet is not partaker, or that he amuses me with that which does not amuse him. He must believe in his poetry, or I shall soon be cured of my belief in it. Homer, Milton, Hafiz, Herbert, and Wordsworth, are heartily enamored of their sweet thoughts.[9]

The world is thoroughly anthropomorphized, as if it had passed through the body and mind of man, and taken his mould and form. He is advertised, that there is nothing to which he is not related, that every thing is convertible into every other. This is like that. The staff in my hand is the *radius vector* of the sun.[10] The chemistry of this is the chemistry of that. Whatever one thing we do, whatever one thing we learn, we are doing and learning all things;—marching in the direction of universal power. Every man's mind is a true Alexander, or Sesostris, building an universal monarchy.[11]

To this belongs the interest of all fables, and that never-dying fable in all conversation, the humour of calling a man a donkey;—the joke of all mankind, that never wears out, the wit of those who have not any other,—to intimate to your companion, never so slily, that he can bray, or that his ears are long. This ticklishness, (if you will pardon me the word), on the subject, can only be explained on the belief, that there is transformation, that this unadmired quadruped is a poor relation of ours. In the same manner, the interest inspired by the qualities imputed to the lion, is inflamed by the belief that his face is an exaggerated man's face; and, the Arabs say, that the roar of the lion almost articulates the syllables, *Ahna ou el ben mera*, "I, and the son, of the woman," as if he believed only in man and himself.

7. The Belvedere Torso, signed by the Greek sculptor Apollonius, dating from the first century B.C., and currently housed in the Vatican Museum, had a profound effect on Renaissance artists, including Michelangelo.

8. The line is from "Upon the Report of the Printing of the Dramatical Poems of Master John Fletcher, Never Collected Before, and now Set Forth in one Volume," a "Commendatory Poem" by William Cartwright (1611–43), English dramatist, at the beginning of *Comedies and Tragedies* (1647) by Francis Beaumont and John Fletcher.

9. Homer (ninth–eighth century B.C.), Greek poet, presumed single author of the *Iliad* and the *Odyssey*; John Milton (1608–74), English poet and political writer, best known for his poem *Paradise Lost* (published in 1667 in ten books); Hāfez (ca. 1325–90), Persian philosopher and lyric poet and a great favorite of Emerson; George Herbert (1593–1633), English metaphysical poet; William Wordsworth (1770–1850), English poet and, with Samuel Taylor Coleridge, founder of the romantic movement.

10. The radius vector is a straight line that joins the center of the sun with the center of a planet in orbit around it.

11. Alexander the Great (356–323 B.C.), ruled as Alexander III of Macedonia (336–323), conqueror of the known civilized world; Sesostris, the Greek corruption of the Egyptian Senusret, is the name of three kings of the twelfth (Theban) dynasty: Sesostris I (reigned ca. 1971–1928 B.C.), second king of the dynasty; Sesostris II (reigned ca. 1897–1878 B.C.), fourth king of the dynasty; and Sesostris III (reigned ca. 1878–1843 B.C.), fifth king of the dynasty.

Chemistry discloses the same self-direction. In the alembic, not only the same atom takes every form,—stone, earth, metal, liquid, and gas,—but, ever since the first experiments, they have been torturing every substance to resolve itself into simpler forms, and they have toiled to change one metal into another, one gas into another, until, at last, they shall find only one, which can at pleasure be transmuted into any other. This is the philosopher's stone.

What is Art, but the translation of one and the same thought into the several languages—of drawing, of sculpture, of architecture, of music, of poetry? Or; analyse the inventions of man, and you find him still brooding on this secret of unity.

Thus, money was an ideal invention. He was poor with all the wheat of Egypt, with all the cedars of Lebanon, with all the land of Asia, marble of Greece, and imagined Aladdin's lamp or Fortunatus' cap, that would bring him, instead of a glut of one thing, the little he wanted of everything.[12] The refined invention of money was Plutus, or Power, to hold all values, all forms, in one value, one form, and convert it at pleasure.[13]

There is one animal, one plant, one chemic matter. Well, the laws of light and of heat translate each other; and so do the laws of sound and of color; and so galvanism, electricity, and magnetism are varied forms of one energy. While he is pondering this strange unity, he observes that all the things in nature, the animals, the mountain, the river, the seasons, wood, iron, stone, vapor,—all have a relation to his thoughts and his life; that all their growths, decays, process, quality, and use so curiously resemble himself, in parts and in wholes, that he is compelled to speak by means of them. All his words and his thoughts are framed by their help. Every word is an image. Nature gives him sometimes in a flattered likeness, sometimes in caricature, a copy of every humor and shade in his character and mind. The world is an immense picture book of every passage in human life.

A central unity inundates nature with itself. Every object he beholds is the mask of a man.

> The privates of man's heart
> They speken and sound in his ear
> As though they loud winds were,

for all the Universe is full of echoes of them.[14]

But to grasp and to articulate these identities of which all are obscurely aware, is

---

12. Aladdin and his lamp, which houses two genii, appear in the collection of ancient Persian-Indian-Arabian traditional tales called *The Arabian Nights' Entertainments* or *A Thousand and One Nights* (1450), originally in Arabic; Fortunatus, in the Spanish nursery tale, possessed both a bottomless purse and a wishing cap.

13. Plutus is the Greek god of riches, which originally referred to the fertility of the earth. Zeus blinded him so that his riches would be equally distributed and go only to people who deserved them.

14. John Gower (1330–1408), English poet and friend of Chaucer, from his *Confessio amantis* 1.2806–8.

rare and divine. 'Tis wonderful the difficulty of taking this step. Hundreds, thousands, read Wordsworth or Tennyson with a perfect sympathy.[15] While they read, they think they might write it, but in millions, there is not one who can. A new verse comes once in one hundred years, and, therefore, Pindar, Hafiz, and Herrick speak so proudly of what seems to you cheap tune enough.[16]

Poetry seems to begin in the slightest change of name, or, in detecting identity under variety of surface. Boys please themselves with crying to the coachman, "Put on the string"; with calling a fire-engine, a tub; and the firemen, tigers. A boy's game of ball is called "Four Cats." When he is older, he calls money tin; his hat a tile. He likes to say, that boiled potatoes open their jackets. In a shipwreck, the novelist finds cordilleras of water.[17] They call a losing gamester, a lame duck; a cheated one, plucked. A lady's tippet is a boa, or python; a camel, is a ship of the desart; sand, is the snow of the desert. Martial calls snow the thick fleece of silent waters, *densum tacitarum vellus aquarum*.[18] This metonomy makes the vivacity of all discourse when each speaker hits off the character of the person or thing in question by some symbol which unexpectedly magnifies the trait with more force.

Swedenborg affirms that, "Names, countries, nations, and the like are not at all known to those who are in heaven; they have no idea of such things, but of the realities signified thereby." "When they saw terrestrial objects, they did not think at all about them, but only about those which they signified and represented, which to them were most delightful."[19]

Now, this metonomy, or seeing the same sense in divers things, gives a pure pleasure. Every one of a million times we take pleasure in the metamorphosis. It makes us dance and sing. It delights all. All men are poets. 'Tis idle to tell me they do not like poetry; For they do.

When people tell me they do not like poetry, and bring me Shelley, or Aikin's *Poets*, or I know not what volumes of rhymed English, to show that it is not likeable, I am quite of their mind.[20] But this dislike only proves their liking of poetry. For they relish Æsop, and cannot forget him or not use him; bring them the *Iliad*, and they like that; and the *Cid*, and that goes well;—and read to them from Chaucer, and they reckon him an honest fellow.[21] *Lear*, and *Macbeth*, and *Richard III* they

15. Alfred, Lord Tennyson (1809–92), English poet, named poet laureate in 1850 after the death of Wordsworth.

16. Pindar (ca. 522–ca. 438 B.C.), the greatest of the Greek lyric poets; Robert Herrick (1591–1674), English lyric poet.

17. A cordillera is a system of mountain ranges often in parallel chains.

18. Martial (ca. 40–ca. 103), Roman poet born in Spain.

19. Emanuel Swedenborg (1688–1772), Swedish scientist, theologian, and mystic.

20. Percy Bysshe Shelley (1792–1822), English romantic poet; *Select Works of the British Poets* (1820) by John Aiken (1747–1822).

21. Rodrigo Díaz de Vivar, known as El Cid (ca. 1034–99), Spanish military leader and national hero of Castile; Geoffrey Chaucer (ca. 1342–1400), English poet, author of *Troilus and Criseyde* and *The Canterbury Tales*.

know pretty well without a guide. Give them Robin Hood's ballads, or "Lady Jane," or "Fair Annie," or "Hardiknute," or "Chevy Chase," or "the Cronachs' cried on Bennachie," or Robert Burns, or Beranger, and they like these well enough.[22] Marie Antoinette said, that, when she read Florian, she thought she ate milk porridge.[23] And the London costermongers say, we like to pay our pennies for something that's worth hearing. They like statues; they like to name the stars; they like to talk and hear of Jove, Apollo, Minerva, Venus, and the Nine.[24] See how tenacious we are of the old names; and our walls are hung with pictures that recall the name of Greece. They like yet better the stars themselves; they like the landscape, the wells of water, the mountain, the plain, sunshine and night; for in these, they obscurely feel the flowings also of their thought.

But the doctrine of poetry reverses the common sense, for it is the doctrine that the soul generates matter. It is the doctrine of the sovereignty of the soul and implies, therefore, all the grandeurs of faith, of love, of duty. Poetry is the speech of man after the ideal. It is the expression of a sound mind speaking after the ideal, and not after the apparent. All becomes poetry when we look from within, and are using all as if the mind made it. All becomes prosaic, when seen from the point of common sense, as if the world existed for material good, or as if matter were a finality.

For events are, not as the brute circumstance that falls, but as the life which they fall upon. The atoms of matter are plastic enough, for they are of us and we of them, and carbon and azote, mountain and planet, play one tune with man and mind.[25] Why we can reach so far to the planets and sun with our short arms, is because we have a pocket edition of the whole. Your brain is timed with the sea-tide, has agreements with the sun.

All this, because Poetry is science, is the breath of the same Spirit by which nature lives, and the Poet is a better logician than the analyzer. His sayings are wise, and to the purpose, and not those of unpoetic men. He sees each fact as an

---

22. Robin Hood, legendary twelfth-century English outlaw and popular hero whose fight against injustice and for the poor gave rise to a series of ballads extolling his virtues; "Lady Jane," "Fair Annie," and "Chevy Chase" were all popular ballads; "Hardiknute" is by Lady Elizabeth Wardlaw (1677–1727), Scottish poet; "Cronach" by Sir Walter Scott (1771–1832), prolific Scottish novelist, is in *Parnassus* (1874); "Bennachie" is probably "Benachie," the highest class of ancient Celtic noblemen; Robert Burns (1759–96), Scotland's most famous poet; Pierre-Jean de Béranger (1780–1857), French poet and songwriter regarded during his lifetime as France's national bard.

23. Marie-Antoinette (1755–93), queen of Louis XVI of France from 1774 to her death by the guillotine; Jean-Pierre Claris de Florian (1755–94), French romancer, dramatist, and writer of fables.

24. Jove or Jupiter, the equivalent of the Greek Zeus, was the central deity of the Roman religious world; Apollo was the Greek god of prophecy who, as the leader of the Muses, was the patron of poetry and music; Minerva, the Roman goddess of wisdom corresponding to Athena, the Greek goddess of war and wisdom; Venus, Roman goddess of love, corresponding to the Greek Aphrodite; the Nine Muses are the Greek goddesses who presided over the arts and sciences.

25. Azote, a type of gas that is fatal when breathed, is another name for nitrogen.

inevitable step in the path of the Creator. He is the right classifier, seeing things grouped, and following the grand way of nature. And never did any science originate, but by a Poetic Perception. "A great natural philosopher without this gift is impossible."[26] The schoolmen think they are logical, and the poet to be whimsical, illogical. Do they think there is any chance or choice in what he sees and says? He knows that he did not make his thought; No, his thought made him, and made the sun and stars also. And it is because his memory is not too strong for him, does not hold him to routine and lists of words, that he is still capable of seeing. For a wise surrender to the currents of nature, a noble passion which will not let us halt, but hurries us into the stream of things, makes us truly know. Passion is logical, and I note that the vine, symbol of the Bacchus which intoxicates the world, is the most geometrical of all plants.[27] And was not this the meaning of Socrates who preferred artists, because they truly knew, and of the tragedians: Horace, and Persius, and Lucretius in the Latin?[28] Dante was faithful, when not carried away by his fierce hatreds.[29]

But if I should count the English poets who have contributed to the bible of existing England and America, sentences of guidance or consolation, which are still glowing and effective,—how few! Milton, Shakspeare, Spenser, Herbert, Jonson, Donne, Dryden, Pope, Young, Cowper, Burns, Wordsworth: What disparity in the names! but these are the authors.[30]

But how shall I find my heavenly bread in the reigning poets? Where is great design in modern English poetry? Where, with the exception of Wordsworth? Tennyson is richly endowed precisely in points where Wordsworth wanted. Since Milton, there was no finer ear, nor more command of the keys of language. But, he wants a subject. He has climbed no mount of vision, and brought its secrets down.

The Poet adopts in every action the method of nature, the most direct; believing, that, in the nature of everything, its own check will appear, and save the absurdity of artificial checks. Liberty is the doctrine of Poets: Liberty of opinion;

26. Attributed to Johann Wolfgang von Goethe (1749–1832), Germany's most famous writer, by Emerson (*TN*, 3:192).

27. Bacchus is the Roman name for Dionysus, the Greek god of nature and the divine ecstasy achieved by communing with the great life forces; wine is his most common symbol.

28. Socrates (ca. 470–399 B.C.), one of the most famous of the Greek philosophers, whose dialogic method of teaching gained many adherents; Horace (65–8 B.C.), Roman poet also known for his writings about poetry; Persius (34–62), Roman satirist; Lucretius (ca. 100–55 B.C.), Roman poet.

29. Dante Alighieri (1265–1321), Italian poet, author of the *Divina commedia* (completed in 1321), which recounts the poet's journey through Hell, Purgatory, and Paradise.

30. The English writers are Edmund Spenser (ca. 1552–99), poet best known for *The Faerie Queene* (1590, 1596); Ben Jonson (1572–1637), poet and dramatist; John Donne (1572–1631), metaphysical poet; John Dryden (1631–1700), metaphysical poet and dramatist; Alexander Pope (1688–1744), poet who championed the heroic couplet; Edward Young (1683–1765), poet, dramatist, and literary critic best known for *The Complaint; or, Night Thoughts on Life, Death and Immortality* (1742–45); and William Cowper (1731–1800), poet and satirist who opposed the artificiality of Pope's classical style.

Liberty of worship; Liberty of Vote, political, universal suffrage, nonjuring; Liberty of trade, banking; Liberty of printing, no censure, and no copyright; even Liberty of Divorce.

Education is better than politics; Race, or native knowledge, than Education. Architecture follows Nature's exact veracity in building for use, and beauty follows. The Poet, thus beholding laws, is believer and lover. The world to him is virgin soil. And the men mean well: it is never too late to do right. He affirms the applicability of the ideal law to this moment, and to the present knot of affairs. But parties, lawyers, and men of the world, invariably dispute such an application, as romantic and dangerous. They admit the general truth; but they and their affair always constitute an exceptional case. Free trade may be very well as a principle, but it is never quite time for its adoption without prejudicing actual interests. Chastity, Temperance, are very well,—Ethical laws are very well, which admit no violation;—but so extreme were the times and manners, that you must admit the miracles of Moses, for the times constituted a case. It is true what you say, that legends are found in all tribes,—but this legend is different and so throughout. Poetry affirms eternal laws; prose busies itself with exceptions, with the local and individual.

The question is often asked, Why no poet appears in America? Other nations in their early, expanding periods, in their war for existence, have shot forth the flowers of verse, and created a mythology which continued to charm the imagination of after-men. But we have all manner of ability, except this: we are brave, victorious; we legislate, trade, plant, build, sail, and combine as well as any others, but we have no imagination, no constructive mind, no affirmative books. We have plenty of criticism; elegant history; all the forms of respectable imitation; but no poet, no affirmer, no grand guiding mind, who intoxicates his countrymen with happy hopes,—makes them self-respecting, with faith that rests in their own minds, and is not imported from abroad.—And,—fruit of all—our lives are impoverished and unpoetic, that is, inhuman.

The answer is, for the time, to be found in the preoccupation of all men. The work of half the world to be done: and it is a hard condition of Nature, that, where one faculty is excessive, it lames all the rest. We are the men of practice, the men of our hands, and, for the time, the brain loses in range what it gains in special skill.

The genius of civilization, except while it is new, is antagonistic to sentiment, utilitarian, and expensive. Taught by England, nay begotten by England, the American mind has learned to call great small, and small things great: Tasteless expense, arts of comfort, and the putting as many impediments as we can between the man and his objects, we have learned; and our arts, and our books, and our characters betray the taming of the Imagination. He does not astonish or intoxicate us much or often. Yet, there is an elasticity in the American mind which may redeem us, and the effect of popular institutions in continually sending back the enervated families into the realities of nature and of toil, may serve the highest medical benefit.

Whilst commonsense draws water, bakes bread, builds houses, keeps shop, and always on the assumption that everything else is a blunder,—in the performing these very works, men are compelled by a certain tyranny which springs up in their own thoughts, to believe in something else. For, their thoughts have an order, and method, and beliefs of their own, very different from the order which this commonsense uses.

Commonsense says, One thing at a time; stick to your fact; keep your cake from burning!—And, meantime, the cake is burning to cinder, whilst the boy's thoughts, to be sure, are running on war and kingdoms, on poetry, on beauty, and the divine life.

As soon as an active mind is born, it is continually comparing its facts, hunting resemblances in them; it is seeking to make things all out of one kind, and it finds them of one kind.

Furthermore, as it is, first, the doctrine of the sovereignty of mind, that Mind makes matter; so second, it is the doctrine of Unity, there are not two things, but one thing. Mind exists; matter has no real existence. Matter is only a rude or temporary form of mind.

Now the doctrine we maintain, is, that the Poet is the healthy, the wise, the fundamental, the only man, the seer of the secret, who sees things after a true scale, sees them as God sees them; in order and beauty. That men who are not yet poets, lack their true humanity. That the children are poets, and the men should be; that politicians, and savans, and critics, and men of business are such in default of real power, that is, because they are out of true relation,—because they fail of being poets,—and these dignities and offices are their poor amends. The flashes of rhetoric and imagination in great orators, Chatham, Burke, Canning, Patrick Henry,—which make them and the nations happy, are the fragments of reason and health which they still retain, and are the last clew, by which, were they logical, they would yet be guided back to the rectitude they have forfeited.[31]

31. William Pitt, first Earl of Chatham (1708–78), English statesman and orator, twice virtual prime minister; Edmund Burke (1729–97), British politician and natural philosopher born in Ireland, wrote on individual liberty; George Canning (1770–1827), British politician, president of the Board of Control for India (1817–20); Patrick Henry (1736–99), American patriot and statesman.

Address at the Woman's Rights Convention

(1855)

Emerson delivered this address, which was originally untitled, on 20 September 1855 before the Woman's Rights Convention at the Meionaon Hall in Boston. He repeated it in December 1860 before the Twenty-eighth Congregational Society in Boston, and he later recast part of this lecture for presentation in May 1869 at the New England Woman's Suffrage Association anniversary at the Tremont Temple in Boston, at which time he was also elected a vice president of the association.

After his death Emerson's 1855 address was published by James Elliot Cabot as "Woman" in *Miscellanies* in 1884 (*W*, 11:403–26). There is also evidence that Emerson was approached to publish this lecture (or an essay on its topic) during his lifetime, and he may have prepared the manuscript entitled "Discours Manqué. Woman" for that purpose. Drawn from his 1855 address, "Discours Manqué. Woman" is printed in full in Emerson's *Later Lectures* (2:16–18).

Woman is the power of civilization. Man is a bear in colleges, in mines, in ships, because there are no women. Let good women sail in the ship, the manners at once are altered and mended; in a college, in California, the same remedy serves. Well, now in this country we are getting a little rough and reckless in voting. Here, at the right moment, when the land is full of committees examining election frauds and misdeeds, woman asks for her vote. It is the remedy at the moment of need. She is to civilize the voting as she has the sailors, the collegians, the miners. For now you must build noble houses proper to the State.

I suppose women feel in relation to men as geniuses feel among energetic workers, that though overlooked and thrust aside in the press, they outsee all these noisy masters. And we feel overlooked,—judged,—and sentenced. In that race, which is now predominant over all the other races of men, it was a cherished belief, that women had an oracular nature. They are more delicate than men, and, as thus more impressionable, they are the best index of the coming hour. I share this belief. I think their words are to be weighed,—but 'tis their inconsiderate words, according to the rule,—"Take their first advice, not their second." As Coleridge was wont to apply to a lady for her judgment in question of taste, and accept it, but, when she added, "I think so, because"—"Pardon me, madam," he said, "leave me to find out the reasons for myself."[1] In this sense, then, as more delicate mercuries of the imponderable and immaterial influences, what they say and think are the shadows of coming events. Their very dolls are indicative. Frigg was the Norse goddess of women: "Weirdes all Frigg knoweth, though she telleth them never," said the *Edda*; that is to say, "All wisdoms woman knoweth, though she takes them for granted, and does not explain them as discoveries, like the understanding of man."[2] Men remark always the figure, they catch always the expression. They inspire by a look, and pass with us not so much by what they say or do, as by their presence. They learn so fast, and convey the result so fast, as to outrun the logic of their slow brother, and make his acquisitions poor. A woman of genius said, "I will forgive you that you do so much, and you me that I do nothing."[3] 'Tis their mood or tone that is important. Does their mind misgive them? or are they firm and cheerful? 'Tis a true report that things are going ill or well. And any remarkable opinion or movement shared by women will be the first sign of revolution.

Her strength is of her own kind. Plato said, "Women are the same as men in faculty, only less in degree."[4] But the general voice of mankind has agreed that they have their own strength; that women are strong by sentiment; that the same mental height which their husbands attained by toil, they attain by sympathy with their husbands.

Man is the will, and woman the sentiment. In this ship of humanity, will is the rudder, and sentiment the sail. When woman affects to steer, the rudder is only a masked sail. When women engage in any art or trade, 'tis usually as a resource, not a primary object. So with their schools and education of others' children. The life of the affections is primary to them, so that there is usually no employment or career which they will not, with their own applause and that of society, quit for a suitable marriage. And they give entirely to their affections; set their whole fortune on the die; lose themselves eagerly in the glory of their husbands and children. Man stands astonished at a magnanimity that he cannot pretend to.

Mrs. Lucy Hutchinson, one of the heroines of the English Commonwealth, who wrote the life of her husband, the governor of Nottingham, says, "If he esteemed her at a higher rate than she in herself could have deserved, he was the author of that virtue he doted on, whilst she only reflected his own glories upon him. All

---

1. Samuel Taylor Coleridge (1772–1834), English poet and philosopher and, with William Wordsworth (1770–1850), founder of the romantic movement.

2. Frigg in Norse mythology is the wife of Odin and principal goddess; the *Prose Edda*, written in the early thirteenth century by Snorri Sturluson, is an Icelandic collection of early Scandinavian mythology.

3. Attributed to Caroline Sturgis Tappan (1819–88), longtime friend of Emerson and Margaret Fuller, by Emerson (*JMN*, 11:428).

4. Plato (ca. 428–348 B.C.), the most famous of the Greek philosophers.

that she was, was *him*, while he was here, and all that she is now, at best, but his pale shade."[5]

For Plato's opinion that "they are the same as men in faculty, only in less degree": it is perhaps true that in no art or science, not in painting, poetry, or music, have women produced a masterpiece. But there is an art which is better than poetry, painting, or music, or architecture, better than botany, geology, or any science, namely, conversation: wise, cultivated, genial conversation. Conversation is the last flower of civility, and the best result which life has to offer us; a cup for gods, which has no repentance. It is our account of ourselves. All we have, all we can do, all we know, is brought into play, and is the reproduction in finer form of all our havings.

The part which women play in education, in the care of young, and the tuition of older children, is their organic office in the world. So much sympathy as they have makes them inestimable as mediators between those who have knowledge, and those who want it. Besides, their fine organization, their taste and love of details, makes the knowledge better in their hands.

Coleridge esteems cultivated women to be the depositories and guardians of English undefiled: and Luther commends that accomplishment of pure German speech in his wife.[6] Women are the civilizers. 'Tis difficult to define. What is civilization? I call it the power of good women. It was Burns's remark, "when he first came to Edinburgh, that between the men of rustic life, and the polite world, he observed little difference; that, in the former, though unpolished by fashion, and unenlightened by science, he had found much observation, and much intelligence; but a refined and accomplished woman was a being almost new to him, and of which he had formed a very inadequate idea."[7]

Lucy Percy, Countess of Carlisle, the friend of Strafford and Pym, is thus described by Sir Toby Matthew.[8]

> She is of too high a mind and dignity not only to seek, but almost to wish the friendship of any creature; they whom she is pleased to choose, are such as are of the most eminent condition, both for power and employment; not with any design towards her own particular, but her nature values fortunate persons. She prefers the conversation of men to that of women; not but she can talk on the fashions with her female friends, but she is too soon sensible that she can set them as she wills: that preeminence shortens all equality. She converses with those who are most distinguished for

5. Lucy Hutchinson (1620–ca. 1680), English Puritan, quoted from *Memoirs of the Life of Colonel Hutchinson, . . . written by his widow Lucy* (1664–70), her biography of John Hutchinson (1615–54), English Puritan soldier who signed the death warrant of Charles I, and critique of the Restoration.

6. Martin Luther (1483–1546), German religious reformer, founder of Protestantism.

7. Attributed to *Reliques of Burns* (1808) by Robert Hartley Cromek (1770–1812), English engraver, in Emerson's note in the manuscript. Robert Burns (1759–96) is Scotland's most famous poet.

8. English politicians or activists Lucy Hay, Countess of Carlisle (1599–1660), Thomas Wentworth, Earl of Strafford (1593–1641), John Pym (1584–1643), and Sir Toby Matthew (1577–1655).

their conversational powers. Of love freely will she discourse, listen to all its faults, and mark all its power, . . . and will take a deep interest for persons of condition and celebrity.

"I like women, they are so finished," said a man of the world.[9] They finish society, manners, language. Form and ceremony are their realm. They embellish trifles; and these ceremonies that hedge our life around are not to be despised, and, when we have become habituated to them, cannot be dispensed with. Certainly, no woman can despise them with impunity. Then, genius delights, in ceremonies, in forms, in decorating life with manners, with proprieties, with order and grace. They are in their nature more relative. The circumstance must always be fit. Out of place they are disfranchised.

"Position," Sir Christopher Wren said, "is essential to the perfecting of beauty."[10] A fine building is lost in a dark lane, and statues should stand in the air. So we commonly say, that easy circumstances seem necessary to the finish of the female character. But they make these with all their might.

The spiritual force of man is as much shown in taste, in his fancy and imagination attaching deep meanings to things and to arbitrary inventions of no real value, as in his perception of truth. He is as much raised above the beast by this creative faculty, as by any other. The horse or ox use no delays: they run to the river, when thirsty, to the corn, when hungry, and say, no thanks, and fight down whatever opposes their appetite. But man invents and adorns all he does with delays and degrees; paints it all over with forms, to please himself better; he invented majesty, and the etiquette of courts, and of drawing rooms; invented architecture, curtains, dress, and the elegance of privacy, to increase the joy of society; invented marriage, and surrounded by religion and comeliness, by all manner of dignities and renunciations, the union of the sexes.

And how should we better measure the gulf between the best intercourse of men in old Athens, in London, or in our American capitals,—between this, and the hedgehog existence of diggers of worms and the eaters of clay and offal, than by signalizing just this department of Taste or Comeliness? Yet herein woman is the prime genius and ordainer. There is no grace that is taught by the dancing master, no style adopted into the etiquette of courts, but was first the whim and action of some brilliant woman, who charmed beholders by this new expression, and made it remembered and copied.

They should be found in fit surroundings, with fair approaches, with agree-

9. Attributed to Samuel Gray Ward (1817–1907), poet, banker, and friend of Emerson, by Emerson (*JMN*, 7:465).

10. Sir Christopher Wren (1632–1723), English architect, proposed plans for rebuilding London after the Great Fire (1666), including fifty-three churches, the best known of which is St. Paul's Cathedral (1675–1711).

able architecture. This convention should be holden in the sculpture gallery. And I think they should magnify their ritual of manners. Society, conversation, decorum, music, flowers, dances, colours, forms, are her homes and attendants.

> The farfetched diamond finds its home
> Flashing and smouldering in her hair.
> For her, the seas their pearls reveal,
> Art and strange lands her pomp supply,
> With purple, chrome, and cochineal,
> Ochre, and lapis lazuli.
> The worm its golden woof presents,
> Whatever runs, flies, dives, or delves,
> All doff for her their ornaments
> Which suit her better than themselves.[11]

There is no gift of nature without some drawback; if we are here, we cannot be there; if we have day, we must forego night. And every extraordinary strength or possession that is added, usually lames the receiver on some part. So to woman this exquisite structure could not exist, without its own penalty: More vulnerable, more infirm, more mortal than men.

They could not be such excellent artists in this element of fancy, if they did not lend and give themselves to it. They are poets who believe their own poetry. They dwell more than men in the element and kingdom of illusion. They see only through Claude Lorraine glass.[12] They emit from all their pores a coloured atmosphere, one would say, wave upon wave of coloured light, in which they walk evermore, and see all objects through this warm tinted mist which envelopes them. And how dare any,—I dare not,—pluck away the coulisses, the roses, the stage effects,—shall I call them?—and routine, ceremonies, with which nature taught them to adorn and to console their life. "Yet fear not," says Mignon, "I shall dance blindfold the egg-dance, and shall not break an egg."[13]

But the starry crown of woman is in the power of her affection and sentiment, and the infinite enlargements to which they lead. Beautiful is the passion of love, painter and adorner of youth and early life; but none suspects in its blushes and tremors what tragedies and immortalities are beyond it. The passion with all its

---

11. *The Angel in the House* (1854–63), pt. 2, *The Espousals*, ll. 7–16, by the English poet Coventry Patmore (1823–96).

12. Claude Gellée, known as Claude Lorrain (1600–1682), French landscape painter. A Claude Lorraine (the earlier English spelling of Lorrain) glass or Claude glass is a convex hand mirror of dark or colored glass that reflects an image of diminished size and subdued color, probably named so after its similarity to the effect Claude Lorrain created in his paintings.

13. Mignon, a young Italian dancing girl, is a character in *Wilhelm Meisters Lehrjahre* (*Wilhelm Meister's Apprenticeship*) (1795–96) by Johann Wolfgang von Goethe (1749–1832), Germany's most famous writer.

grace and poetry is profane to that which follows it. A few years have changed the coy, haughty maiden into a matron existing for her children, a pelican feeding her young with her life. And these affections are only introductory to that which is sublime.

We men have no right to say it, 'tis very ungracious in man, but the omnipotence of Eve is in humility. The instincts of mankind have drawn the Virgin Mother,

> Created beings all in lowliness
> Surpassing as in height above them.[14]

This is the divine person whom Dante and Milton saw in vision: this the victory of Griselda: And it is when love has reached this height, that all our pretty rhetoric begins to have meaning, when we say, that it adds to the soul a new soul: it is honey in the mouth, music in the ear, and balsam in the heart.[15]

> Far have I clambered in my mind
> But nought so great as Love.
> 'What is thy tent? where dost thou dwell?'
> 'My mansion is Humility,
> Heaven's vastest capability;
> The further it doth downward tend,
> The higher up it doth ascend.'[16]

The first thing men think of, when they love, is, to exhibit their usefulness and advantages. Women make light of these, asking only love. They wish it to be an exchange of nobleness. There is much in their nature, much in their social position, which gives them a divining power. Women know at first sight the characters of those with whom they converse. There is much that tends to give them a religious height which men do not attain. Their sequestration from affairs, and from the injury to the moral sense which affairs often inflict, aids them.

"I use the Lord of the Kaaba, what is the Kaaba to me?" said Rabia. "I am so near to God, that, his word, 'whoso nears me by a span, to him come I a mile,' is true for me."

Hassan Basso, a famed Mahametan theologian, asked, "how she had lifted herself to this degree of the love of God?"

She replied, "Hereby, that all things which I had found, I have lost in him."

The other said, "In what way or method hast thou known him?"

---

14. *Paradiso* 33.1–3 by Dante Alighieri (1265–1321), Italian poet, part of the *Divina commedia* (completed in 1321), which recounts the poet's journey through Hell, Purgatory, and Paradise.

15. John Milton (1608–74), English poet and political writer, best known for his poem *Paradise Lost* (published in 1667 in ten books); Griselda is a character in the *Decameron* by Giovanni Boccaccio (1313–75) who typifies patience as a wife and mother subjected to many trials by her husband.

16. "Love and Humility," ll. 1–2, 7–11, by Henry More (1614–87), English philosopher and poet.

She answered, "O Hassan! Thou knowest after a certain art and way, but I without art and way."

When once she was sick, three famed theologians came to her, Hassan Vasri, Malek, and Balchi. Hassan said, "He is not upright in his prayer who does not endure the blows of his Lord." Balchi said, "He is not upright in his prayer, who does not rejoice in the blows of his Lord." But Rabia, who, in these words, detected some trace of egoism, said, "He is not upright in his prayer, who, when he beholds his Lord, forgets not that he is stricken."[17]

I have known one bred in poverty and solitude, who realized to our experience the life of the saints of the convent, and religious houses. She was no statute book of practical rules, nor orderly digest of any system of philosophy divine or human, but a Bible, miscellaneous in its parts, but one in Spirit, wherein are sentences of condemnation, chapters of prophecy, promises, and covenants of love, that make foolish the wisdom of the world with the power of God.[18]

"When a daughter is born," said the Sheking, "she sleeps on the ground; she is clothed with a wrapper; she plays with a tile; she is incapable of evil or of good."[19] With the advancements of society, the position and fortunes of women have changed, of course, as events brought her strength or her faults into light. In modern times, three or four conspicuous instrumentalities may be marked. After the deification of woman in the Catholic Church, the religious ages came again in the sixteenth and seventeenth centuries, when her religious nature gave her, of course, new importance. The *Quakers* have the honor of first having established in their discipline an equality in the sexes. It is even more perfect in the later sect of *Shakers*.[20] An epoch for Woman was in France the building of the Hotel Rambouillet.[21] I think another step was made by the doctrine of Swedenborg; a sublime genius who gave a scientific exposition of the part played severally by man, and by woman, in the world; and showed the difference of sex to run through nature and through thought.[22] Of all Christian sects, this is, at this moment, the most vital and aggressive.

17. Rābiah of Basra, Arab mystic and poetess, described as a "Mahometan saint" by Emerson (*JMN*, 15:42).

18. An allusion to Emerson's aunt Mary Moody Emerson (1774–1863) from an 1835 letter by Charles Chauncy Emerson (1808–36), Emerson's brother (*JMN*, 5:158).

19. Quoted from *Shi King* (*Shih Ching*), a collection of poems attributed to Confucius (Latin name for K'ung Ch'iu) (551–479 B.C.), Chinese philosopher.

20. Quakers (Society of Friends), an English sect founded in the seventeenth century known for its pacifism and belief in an inner spiritual voice. The Shakers are a celibate sect that seceded from the Quakers and came from England to America in 1774. Their name stems from the movements they make during their religious dances.

21. Catherine d'Angennes, marquise de Rambouillet (1588–1665), French hostess, established at her Paris townhouse, the Hôtel de Rambouillet, a salon that influenced the development of French literature.

22. Emanuel Swedenborg (1688–1772), Swedish scientist, theologian, and mystic.

Another step was the effect of the action of the age on the antagonism to slavery. It was easy to enlist woman in this; it was impossible not to enlist her. But that cause turned out, as you know, to be a great scholar: he was a terrible metaphysician; he was a jurist, a poet, a divine. Was never a University of Oxford or Göttingen that made such students. It took a man from the plough, and made him acute, and eloquent, and wise to the silencing of the doctors. There was nothing it did not pry into, no right it did not explore, no wrong it did not expose, and it has, among its other effects, given woman a feeling of public duty, and an added self-respect.

One truth leads in another by the hand; one right is an accession of strength to take more. And the times are marked by the new attitude of woman urging, by argument and by association, her rights of all kinds, in short, to one half of the world: the right to education; to avenues of employment; to equal rights of property; to equal rights in marriage; to the exercise of the professions; to suffrage.

Of course, this conspicuousness had its inconveniences. 'Tis very cheap wit that has been spent on the subject, from Aristophanes, in whose comedies I confess my dulness to find good joke, to Rabelais in whom it is monstrous exaggeration of temperament and not borne out by anything in nature, down to the English comedy, and, in our day, Tennyson, and the American newspapers.[23] The body of the joke is all one, to charge them with temperament—victims of temperament—and is identical with Mahomet's opinion, that they have not a sufficient moral or intellectual force to control the perturbations of their physical structure.[24] These were all drawings of morbid anatomy and such satire as might be written on the tenants of a hospital or an asylum for idiots.

Of course, it would be easy for women to retaliate in kind, by painting men from the dogs and orangs that have worn our shape: and the fact that they have not, is an eulogy on the taste and self-respect of women.

The good, easy world took the joke which it liked. There is always want of thought, always credulity. There are plenty of people who believe women to be incapable of anything but to cook; incapable of interest in affairs. There are plenty of people who believe that the world is only governed by men of dark complexion; that affairs are only directed by such; and do not see the use of contemplative men or how ignoble is the world that wanted them, and so without the affection of woman.

But for the general charge: No doubt the charge is well-founded. They are victims of their finer temperament. They have tears, and gaieties, and faintings, and glooms, and devotion to trifles. Nature's end of maternity,—maternity for twenty

23. Aristophanes (ca. 450–ca. 380 B.C.), Athenian writer of comedies; François Rabelais (ca. 1483–1553), French satirist and writer; Alfred, Lord Tennyson (1809–92), English poet, named poet laureate in 1850 after the death of William Wordsworth.

24. Muhammad (ca. 570–632), founder of Islam, born in Mecca.

years,—was of so supreme importance, that it was to be secured at all events, even to the sacrifice of the highest beauty. They are more personal. Men taunt them, that, whatever they do, say, read, or write, they are thinking of themselves and their set. Men are not to the same degree temperamented, for there are multitudes of men who live to objects quite out of them, as, to politics, to trade, to letters, or an art, unhindered by any influence of constitution.

The answer that, silent or spoken, lies in the mind of well meaning persons, to the new claims, is this: that, though their mathematical justice is not to be denied, yet the best women do not wish these things. These are asked for by people who intellectually seek them, but have not the support or sympathy of the truest women: and that if the laws and customs were modified in the manner proposed, it would embarrass and pain gentle and lovely persons, with duties which they would find irksome and distasteful.

Very likely. Providence is always surprising us with new and unlikely instruments. But perhaps it is because these persons have been deprived of education, fine companions, opportunities, such as they wished; because they feel the same rudeness and disadvantage which offends you,—that they have been stung to say, It is too late for us to be polished and fashioned into beauty; but at least we will see that the whole race of women shall not suffer as we have suffered.

Our marriages are bad enough, but that falls from the defects of the partners; but marriage, as it exists in America, England, and Germany, is the best solution that has been offered of the woman's problem. Orientalism, or Fourierism, or Mormonism, or the New York Socialism, are not solutions that any high woman will accept as even approximate to her ideas of well-being.[25] They have an unquestionable right to their own property. And, if the woman demand votes, offices, and political equality with men, as, among the Shakers, an Elder and Eldress are of equal power, and among the Quakers, it must not be refused.

'Tis very cheap wit that finds it so droll that a woman should vote. Educate and refine society to the highest point; bring together cultivated society of both sexes, in a drawing room, to consult and decide by voices on a question of taste, or a question of right,—and is there any absurdity, or any practical difficulty in obtaining their authentic opinions? If not, then there need be none in a hundred companies, if you educate them and accustom them to judge. And for the effect of it, I can say for one, that certainly all my points would be sooner carried in the state, if women voted.

On the questions that are important: Whether the government shall be in one

25. The New York Socialists, led by Horace Greeley (1811–72), American political leader and editor of the *New York Tribune*, and Parke Godwin (1816–1904), an editor of the *New York Evening Post*, generally followed the doctrines of François-Marie-Charles Fourier (1772–1837), French social thinker whose doctrines guided the later period of the Brook Farm community, a utopian venture at West Roxbury, Massachusetts (1841–47).

person, or whether representative, or whether democratic; whether men shall be holden in bondage, or shall be roasted alive and eaten as in *Typee*, or hunted with bloodhounds as in this country; whether men shall be hanged for stealing, or hanged at all; whether the unlimited sale of cheap liquors shall be allowed; they would give, I suppose, as intelligent a vote as the five thousand Irish voters of Boston or New York.[26]

Why need you vote? If new power is here, if a character which solves old tough questions, which puts me and all the rest in the wrong, tries and condemns our religion, customs, laws, and opens new career to young receptive men and women, you can well leave voting to the old dead people. Those whom you teach, and those whom you half-teach, will fast enough make themselves considered and strong with their new insight, and votes will follow from all the drill.

The objection to their voting is the same that is urged in the lobbies of legislatures against clergymen who take an active part in politics, that, if they are good clergymen, they are unacquainted with the expediences of politics, and if they become good politicians, they are the worse clergymen: so of women, that they cannot enter this arena without being contaminated and unsexed.

Here are two or three other objections to their voting: first, a want of practical wisdom; second, a too purely ideal view; and third, a danger of contamination.

For their want of intimate knowledge of affairs, I do not think this should disqualify them from voting at any town meeting which I ever attended. I could heartily wish the objection were sound. But if any man will take the trouble to see how our people vote—how many gentlemen are willing to take on themselves the trouble of thinking and determining for you, and, standing at the doors of the polls, give every innocent citizen his ticket as he comes in, informing him, that this is the vote of his party; and the innocent citizen, without further demur, carries it to the ballot box; I cannot but think that most women might vote as wisely.

For the other point, of their not knowing the world, and aiming at abstract right, without allowance for circumstances;—that is not a disqualification, but a qualification. Human society is made up of partialities. Each citizen has an interest and a view of his own, which, if followed out to the extreme, would leave no room for any other citizen. One man is timid, and another rash; one would change nothing, and the other is pleased with nothing; one wishes, schools another armies; one gunboats, another public gardens.

Bring all these biases together, and something is done in favor of them all. Every one is a half vote; but the next elector behind him brings the other or corresponding half in his hand. A reasonable result is had. Now there is no lack, I am sure, of the expediency, or of the interest of trade, or of imperative class interests being neglected. There is no lack of votes representing the physical wants; and if, in your

26. *Typee: A Peep at Polynesian Life* (1846) by Herman Melville (1819–91), American writer.

city, the uneducated emigrant vote by the thousands representing a brutal ignorance and mere animal wants, it is to be corrected by an educated and religious
vote representing the desires of honest and refined persons.

If the wants, the passions, the vices are allowed a full vote, through the hands
of a half-brutal, intemperate population, I think it but fair that the virtues, the
aspirations, should be allowed a full vote as an offset, through the purest part of
the people. As for the unsexing and contamination, that only accuses our existing
politics, shows how barbarous we are, that our policies are so crooked, made up
of things not to be spoken, to be understood only by wink and nudge, this man is
to be coaxed, and that man to be bought, and that other to be duped. 'Tis easy to
see there is contamination enough, but it rots the men now and fills the air with
stench come out of that. 'Tis like a dance-cellar. The fairest names in this country
in literature, in law, have gone into Congress and come out dishonored.

'Tis easy to see that many steps must be taken; an education of society; a purging
of bullies out of the state; and a purging of the elegant cowards who have politely
and elegantly betrayed us to them. And when I read the list of men of intellect, of
refined pursuits, giants in law, or eminent scholars, or of social distinction, leading
men of wealth and enterprise in the commercial community, and see what they
voted for, or suffered to be voted for, I think no community was ever so politely
and elegantly betrayed.

I do not think it yet appears that women wish this equal share in public affairs.
But it is they, and not we, that are to determine it. Let the laws be purged of every
barbarous remainder, every barbarous impediment to women. Let the public do-
nation for education be equally shared by them. Let them enter a school, as freely
as a church. Let them have, and hold, and give their property, as men do theirs.
And, in a few years, it will easily appear whether they wish a voice in making the
laws that are to govern them. If you do refuse them a vote, you will also refuse to
tax them according to our Teutonic principle: no representation, no tax.

'Tis idle to refuse them a vote on the ground of incompetency. I wish our masculine voting were so good that we had any right to doubt their equal discretion.
They could not give worse vote, I think, than we do. Besides, it certainly is no new
thing to see women interest themselves in politics. In English, French, German,
Italian, and Russian history, you shall often find some Duchess of Marlborough or
de Longueville or Madame Roland the centre of political power and intrigue.[27] See
the experience of our Quakers, and of the Shakers, and of the Antislavery Society,
in taking women as men into the council and government, and the women often
possess superior administrative capacity.

27. Sarah, Duchess of Marlborough (1660–1744), English noblewoman and member of Queen
Anne's inner circle; Duchess Anne-Geneviève de Longueville (1619–79), French noblewoman active
in French politics; Jeanne-Marie Roland de La Platière, known as Mme Roland (1754–93), French revolutionary who fell to the guillotine.

All events of history are to be regarded as growths and off-shoots of the expanding mind of the race: and this appearance of new opinions, and their currency and force in many minds, is itself the wonderful fact. Whatever is popular, is important, and shows the spontaneous sense of the hour. The aspiration of this century will be the code of the next. It holds of high and distant causes, of the same influences that make the sun and moon. When new opinions appear, they will be entertained and respected by every fair mind according to their reasonableness, and not according to their convenience, or their fitness to shock our customs.

But let us deal with them greatly: let them make their way by the upper road, not by the way of manufacturing public opinion, which lapses continually into expediency, and makes charlatans. All that is spontaneous is irresistible: and forever it is individual force that interests. I need not repeat to you,—your own solitude will suggest it,—that a masculine woman is not strong, but a lady is. The loneliest thought, the purest prayer, is rushing to be the history of a thousand years. Let us have the true woman, the adorner, the hospitable, the religious heart, and no lawyer need be called in to write stipulations, the cunning clauses of provision, the strong investments; for woman moulds the lawgiver, and writes the law.

But I ought to say, I think it impossible to separate the education and interests of the sexes. Improve and refine the men, and you do the same by the women, whether you will or no. Every woman, being the wife, daughter, sister, or mother of a man, she can never be very far from his ear, never not of his counsel, if she has something to urge that is good in itself and agreeable to nature. The slavery of women happened when the men were slaves of kings. The melioration of manners has brought their melioration, of course. It could not otherwise, and hence this new desire of better laws. For there are always a certain number of passionately loving fathers, brothers, husbands, and sons who put their might into the endeavor to make a daughter, a wife, or a mother happy in the way that suits best.

Woman should find in man her guardian. Silently she looks for that; and when she finds, as she instantly will, if he is not, she betakes her to her own defences, and does the best she can. But when he is her guardian,—fulfilled with all nobleness,— knows and accepts his duties as her brother, all goes well for both. The new movement is only a tide shared by the spirits of man and woman, and you may proceed in a faith, that, whatever the woman's heart is prompted to desire, the man's mind is simultaneously prompted to accomplish.

Country Life—Concord

(1857)

Emerson delivered his lecture "Country Life—Concord," which was originally untitled, only once: on 2 December 1857 before the Concord Lyceum in Concord, Massachusetts. Concord was the Emerson family's ancestral home, and from the time he settled there permanently in 1835 Emerson was completely taken with the quaint historic village and its surroundings, and the townspeople embraced him and his growing family as their own. Emerson's correspondence abounds in details and anecdotes of his life in Concord, and his journals and notebooks are filled with reports of his walks in Concord's woods and to nearby ponds and rivers with Henry David Thoreau (his ideal naturalist on such excursions) and the poet Ellery Channing (his ideal artist). Emerson walked with Thoreau throughout the spring and summer of 1857; the inspiration for "Country Life—Concord" appears to have come on 1 May 1857, when he and Thoreau walked to Goose Pond just outside of Concord Center and made an inventory of all the plants they saw along the way:

> Walk yesterday . . . with Henry T. to Goose Pond. . . . Found sedge flowering, & *salix humilis*[;] . . . found Lycopodium dendroides & lucidulum; found *Chimaphila maculata* the only patch of it in town. Found *Senecio* & even *solidago* in the water already forward, & the Sawmill-brook much adorned with hellebore *veratrum viride*. . . . Saw a stump of a conoe-birch-tree newly cut down, which had bled a barrel. From a white birch, H. cut a strip of bark to show how a naturalist would make the best box to carry a plant. . . . & though the woodman would make a better hat of birch-bark than of felt, yes, & pantaloons too,—hat, with cockade of lichens, thrown in. . . .
> We will make a book on walking, 'tis certain, & have easy lessons for beginners. (*JMN*, 14:136–37)

When I bought my farm, I did not know what a bargain I had in the bluebirds, bobolinks, and thrushes, which were not charged in the bill: as little did I guess what sublime mornings and sunsets I was buying,— what reaches of landscape, and what fields and lanes for a tramp. Neither did I fully consider what an indescribable luxury is our Indian river, the Musketaquid, which runs parallel with the village street, and to which every house on that long street has a back-door, which leads down through the garden to the river bank, where a skiff or a dory gives you, all summer, access to enchantments, new every day, and, all winter, to miles of ice for the skater. And because our river is no Hudson or Mississippi, I have a problem long waiting for an engineer,—this,—To what height I must build a tower in my garden, that shall show me the ocean twenty miles away.

Still less did I know what good and true neighbors I was buying, men of thought and virtue, some of them now known the country through, for their learning, or subtlety, or active, or patriotic power, but whom I had the pleasure of knowing long before the country did; and of other men, not known widely, but known at home,—farmers,—not doctors of laws, but doctors of land, skilled in turning a swamp or a sand-bank into a fruitful field, and, where witch-grass and nettles grew, causing a forest of apple trees, or miles of corn and rye to thrive. I did not know what groups of interesting school-boys and fair school-girls were to greet me in the highway, and to take hold of one's heart at the school exhibitions.

"Little joy has he who has no garden," said Saadi.[1] Montaigne took much pains to be made a citizen of Rome; and our people are vain, when abroad, of having the freedom of foreign cities presented to them in a gold box.[2] I much prefer to have the freedom of a garden presented me. When I go into a good garden, I think, if it were mine, I should never go out of it. It requires some geometry in the head, to lay it out rightly, and there are many who can enjoy, to one that can create it. Linnaeus, who was professor of the Royal Garden at Upsala, took the occasion of a public ceremony to say,

> I thank God who has ordered my fate, that I live in this time, and so ordered it, that I live happier than the King of the Persians. You know, fathers and citizens! that I live entirely in the Academy Garden; here is my Vale of Tempe, say rather my Elysium. I possess here all that I desire of the spoils of the East and the West, and, unless I am very much mistaken, what is far more beautiful than Babylonian robes, or vases of the Chinese. Here I learn what I teach. Here I admire the wisdom of the Supreme Artist, dis-closing Himself by proofs of every kind, and show them to others.[3]

Our people are learning that lesson year by year. As you know, nothing in Europe is more elaborately luxurious than the costly gardens,—as the Boboli at

---

1. The Persian poet Mosharref od-Dīn ibn Moṣleḥ od-Dīn Sādī (ca. 1213–92), popularly known in America as Saadi and a longtime favorite of Emerson, who wrote a preface to an 1865 edition of the *Gulistān* (1258, *The Rose Garden*), a collection of stories and personal anecdotes.

2. Michel Eyquem de Montaigne (1533–92), French essayist and philosopher, usually identified with skepticism.

3. Carolus Linnaeus (1707–78), Swedish botanist, is considered one of the founders of modern systematic botany; the Vale of Tempe lies between Mount Olympus and Mount Ossa in northeastern Greece; Elysium is the abode of the blessed in Greek mythology.

Florence, the Borghese, the Orsini, at Rome, the Villa d'Este, at Tivoli, with their greenhouses, conservatories, palm houses, fish ponds, sculptured summer houses, and grottoes. But without going into the proud niceties of an European garden,— there is happiness all the year round, to be had from the square fruit gardens which we plant in the front or rear of every farm house. In the orchard, we build monuments to Van Mons annually.[4]

The place where a thoughtful man in the country feels the joy of eminent domain is in his wood-lot. If he suffer from accident or low spirits, his spirits rise when he enters it. He can spend the entire day therein, with hatchet or pruning-shears, making paths, without remorse of wasting time. He can fancy that the birds know him and trust him, and even the trees make little speeches or hint them. Then he remembers that Allah, in his allotment of life, "does not count the time which the Arab spends in the chase."

If you can add to the garden a noble luxury, let it be an arboretum. In the arboretum, you should have things which are of a solitary excellence, and which people who read of them, are hungry to see. Thus, plant the *Sequoia Gigantea*, give it room, and set it on its way of ten or fifteen centuries. Bayard Taylor planted two; one died, but I saw the other looking well.[5] Plant the banian, the sandal-tree, the lotus, the upas, ebony, century-aloes, the *Soma* of the Vedas, *Asclepias Viminalis*, the mandrake, and papyrus, dittany, asphodel, nepenthe, haemony, moly, spikenard, amomum; trees in clumps, a bath by the brook; on a holiday, Fourth of July or Bunker Hill Day, and so forth, fireworks over water; colored pebbles at the bottom of the pool; plant the flox for its white shoulders in September.[6]

Make a calendar,—your own,—of the year, that you may never miss your favorites in their month. As Linnaeus made a dial of plants, so shall you of all the objects that guide your walks. Learn to know the conspicuous planets in the heavens, and the chief constellations. Thus, do not forget the 14th November, when the meteors come, and, on some years, drop into your house-yard like sky rockets.

And 'tis worth remarking, what a man may go through life without knowing, that a common spy-glass, which you carry in your pocket, will show the satellites of Jupiter, and turned on the *Pleiades*, will show many more. How many poems have been written, or, at least attempted, on the *lost Pleiad*; for, though that pretty constellation is called for thousands of years "the Seven Stars," most eyes can only count six. A telescope in an observatory will show two hundred.

Horses and carriages are costly toys, but the word "park" always charms me. I could not find it in my heart to chide the citizen who should ruin himself to buy a patch of heavy oak timber. I admire the taste which makes the avenue to

4. Jean-Baptiste Van Mons (1765–1842), Belgian horticulturalist.
5. Bayard Taylor (1825–78), American world traveler and writer.
6. The Vedas are the four most sacred books of Hinduism.

the house,—were the house never so small,—through a wood;—as it disposes the mind of the inhabitant and of his guest, to the deference due to each.

There are two companions with one or other of whom 'tis desireable to go out on a tramp. One is an artist, that is, one who has an eye for beauty. If you use a good and skilful companion, you shall see through his eyes; and, if they be of great discernment, you will learn wonderful secrets. In walking with Allston, you shall see what was never before shown to the eye of man.[7] And, as the perception of beauty always exhilarates,—if one is so happy as to find the company of a true artist, he is a perpetual holiday and benefactor.

It is so much easier to learn the elements of botany, geology, and chemistry, by conversation with an expert, than by book, that everyone would willingly have his introduction to science so. That is my ideal of the powers of wealth. Find out what lake or sea Agassiz wishes to explore, and offer to carry him there, and he will make you acquainted with all its fishes: or what district Dr. Gray has not found the plants of, carry him; or where Dr. Wyman wishes to find new anatomic structures or fossil remains; or where Dr. Charles Jackson or Mr. Hall would study chemistry or mines; and you secure the best company and the best teaching with every advantage.[8]

But the country man, as I said, has more than he paid for: the landscape is his. Dr. Johnson said, "Few men know how to take a walk," and 'tis certain that Dr. Johnson was not one of those few.[9] I am sorry to say, the farmers seldom walk for pleasure. It is a fine art. There are degrees of proficiency, and we distinguish the professors of that science from the apprentices. But there is a manifest increase in the taste for it. 'Tis the consolation of mortal men. It is an old saying, that physicians or naturalists are the only professional men who continue their tasks out of study hours. And the naturalist has no barren places, no winter and no night, pursuing his researches in the sea; in the ground; in barren moors; in the night, even, because the woods exhibit a whole new world of nocturnal animals; in winter, because, remove the snow a little, a multitude of plants live and grow, and there is a perpetual push of buds, so that it is impossible to say when vegetation begins.— I think no pursuit has more breath of immortality in it.

7. "Allston" is William Ellery Channing the Younger (1818–1901), American poet, occasional Concord resident, and brother-in-law of Margaret Fuller, usually called "Ellery."

8. Louis Agassiz (1807–73), Swiss-born American naturalist and zoological explorer, began in 1859 the collections now at the Harvard Museum of Comparative Zoology; Asa Gray (1810–88), American botanist and professor of natural history at Harvard; Jeffries Wyman (1814–74), American comparative anatomist and professor at Harvard; Emerson's brother-in-law Charles Thomas Jackson (1805–80), American doctor who abandoned medicine for chemistry and mineralogy, generally credited with the first use of ether; James Hall (1811–98), American geologist and paleontologist.

9. Samuel Johnson, known as Dr. Johnson (1709–84), English lexicographer, editor, critic, and conversationalist.

I admire in trees the creation of property so clean of tears, or crime, or even care. No lesson of chemistry is more impressive to me than this chemical fact,—that, "Nineteen-twentieths of the timber are drawn from the atmosphere." We knew the root was sucking juices from the ground: But the top of the tree is also a tap-root thrust into the public pocket of the atmosphere. This is a highwayman, to be sure. And I am always glad to remember that, in proportion to the foliation, is the addition of wood. There they grow, when you wake, and when you sleep, at nobody's cost, and for everybody's comfort. Lord Abercorn, when some one praised the rapid growth of his trees, replied, "Sir, they have nothing else to do."[10]

Who does not see the farmer with pleasure and respect, knowing what powers and utilities are so meekly worn? They know every secret of work; they change the face of landscape, and put it in a new planet; yet there is no arrogance in their bearing, but a perfect gentleness. The farmer stands well on the world, as Adam did, as an Indian does, or as Homer's heroes.[11] He is a person whom a poet of any clime, Milton, or Firdousi, would appreciate, as being really a piece of the old nature, comparable to sun and moon, rainbow and flood, because he is, as all natural persons are, representative of nature as much as these.[12]

The Hindoos called Fire born in the woods, the bearer of oblations, the smoke-bannered and lord of red coursers, light-shedding, the guest of man, the sacrificer visible to all, protector of people in villages, thousand-eyed, all-beholding, of graceful form, and whose countenance is turned on all sides. The conveying traversers of places difficult of access, stable is their birthplace, *Maruts*, the winds, because they drive the clouds, have harnessed the spotted deer to their chariot; coming with weapons, war cries, and decorations, I hear the cracking of the whips in their hands, I praise their sportive, resistless strength, generators of speech. They drive before them in their course the long, vast, uninsurable, rain-retaining cloud.[13]

The man finds himself expressed in nature. Yet when he sees this annual reappearance of beautiful forms, the lovely carpet, the lovely tapestry of June, he may well ask himself the special meaning of the hieroglyphic, as well as the sense and scope of the whole. And there is a general sense which the best knowledge of the particular alphabet leaves unexplained.

That uncorrupted behavior which we admire in the animals, and in young children, belongs also to the farmer, the hunter, the sailor, the man who lives in the

10. Attributed to James Hamilton, first Duke of Abercorn (1811–85), English politician, by Emerson (*TN*, 1:261).

11. Homer (ninth–eighth century B.C.), Greek poet, presumed single author of the *Iliad* and the *Odyssey*.

12. John Milton (1608–74), English poet and political writer, best known for his poem *Paradise Lost* (published in 1667 in ten books); Firdawsī or Ferdowsī (ca. 935–ca. 1020), Persian poet.

13. Paraphrased from *Rig-veda-sanhitá. A Collection of Ancient Hindu Hymns* (1850–66), translated by H. H. Wilson.

presence of nature. Cities force the growth, and make him talkative and entertaining, but they make him artificial. What alone possesses interest for us, is, the *naturel*
of each, that which is constitutional to him only. This is forever a surprise, and engaging, and lovely; We can't be satiated with knowing it, and about it. And this is
that which the conversation with nature goes to cherish and to guard.

Powers of the Mind

(1858)

Emerson first delivered "Powers of the Mind" in March 1858 in Boston as the third in a series of six lectures entitled *Natural Method of Mental Philosophy*. He delivered the full series of six lectures this one time only. He opened with a lecture entitled "Country Life" (not to be confused with "Country Life—Concord," which also appears in this volume) and "Works and Days," two lectures designed for the general public, and then gave these four lectures on philosophy or, as he then called it, "intellectual science": "Powers of the Mind," "The Natural Method of Mental Philosophy," "Memory," and "Self-Possession." (The lecture manuscript of "Works and Days" does not survive; for the remaining lectures, see *Later Lectures*, 2:49–67, 84–98, 99–116, and 117–29, respectively.) Emerson's intention for these four lectures was, as he wrote to Horatio Woodman on 1 March 1858, "to win the attention of good heads to the attractive side of intellectual science whose very name now repels, and mainly as I think, because the professors pretend & attempt much more than they ought, whilst if they simply gave their own experiences, & stopped when these were out, they would interest everybody" (*Letters*, 8:555). Emerson delivered "Powers of the Mind" one more time: in November 1858 in Salem, Massachusetts, he used this lecture to open a series of five lectures partly drawn from the *Natural Method of Mental Philosophy* series.

Emerson's *Natural Method of Mental Philosophy* series occupies a central place in his continuing work toward a natural history of the intellect. The four lectures on intellectual science that Emerson delivered in his *Natural Method of Mental Philosophy* series in Boston emerge directly from three philosophy lectures he delivered in his *Mind and Manners of the Nineteenth Century* series in England, Boston, and Worcester in 1848 and 1849 and, in part, in various other series in New York City, Philadelphia, and Cincinnati in 1850. Those lectures were "The Powers and Laws of Thought," "The Relation of Intellect to Natural Science," and "The Tendencies and Duties of Men of Thought," the last of which is printed in this edition. Between 1850 and the opening of his *Natural Method of Mental Philosophy* series in 1858 Emerson steadily worked on refining his intellectual science as an analogic system to answer the analytical systems of most metaphysicians. More a poetic than a philosophical or scientific construction in the strict sense, Emerson's intellectual science took shape in several of the journals and notebooks he kept during the 1850s, and it reached its fullest expression in Notebook IT, which Emerson subtitled "Natural History of Intellect." There he named his system "New Metaphysics," and he declared that new metaphysicians "are to write a collection of Accepted Ideas, a Table of Constants," a "Farmers Almanac of Mental moods" (*TN*, 1:134).

After delivering "Powers of the Mind" twice in 1858, Emerson continued to work on it and the other philosophical lectures he delivered with it for the remainder of his active career. Of the four lectures he delivered in 1858, only "Memory" seemed to him able to stand alone, and he delivered it many times through 1871. But all four lectures from this *Natural Method of Mental Philosophy* series are important as precursors of Emerson's further refinement of his "New Metaphysics" in a *Philosophy for the People* series that he delivered in Boston in 1866 and in lectures in his *Natural History of the Intellect* courses at Harvard in 1870 and 1871. The fact that the manuscripts from which Emerson lectured in 1866 and in 1870 and 1871 survive only as fragments adds importance to "Powers of the Mind" and the three additional lectures on intellectual science that survive from his *Natural Method of Mental Philosophy* series of 1858.

Emerson's literary executors, James Elliot Cabot and Edward Waldo Emerson, made extensive use of his lecture manuscripts on philosophy. Cabot mined them for the essay "Natural History of Intellect" that he arranged from the manuscripts and published in his *Natural History of Intellect* volume in 1893, while Edward used Cabot's version of "Natural History of Intellect" as the first section of a three-part essay on thought, instinct and inspiration, and memory that he arranged under the title "Natural History of Intellect" for publication in the Centenary Edition of his father's works in 1903–4 (*W*, 12:3–110). Edward further mined all of his father's later philosophy lecture manuscripts for explanatory notes throughout the twelve volumes of the *Works* (for additional details see Emerson's *University Lectures*).

E ven if our theory be wrong, thoughts are things that require no system to make them pertinent, but they make everything else impertinent. For I hold with Montaigne that "good sentences are never irrelevant, however placed."[1] A single thought has no limit to its value,—a thought, properly speaking; that is, a truth held not from any man's saying so, or any accidental benefit or recommendation it has in our trade or circumstance, but because we have perceived it is a fact in the nature of things, and in all times and places will and must be the same thing,—is of an inestimable value: for instance, a man's perception that he ought to respect himself, and should not profane himself by doing aught that injures him in his own eyes,—no matter what others think of him,—he must not do what will degrade him before himself;—this one truth,—who can set limits to its value? And Plato discovered, that no man could ever be lost, as long as he held fast to the possession of one single truth.[2] "It is the law of Adrastia, that, whoso has perceived one truth shall be preserved from harm until another period."[3]

It is really to the people, it is really to the religious perception of men, and not

---

1. Michel Eyquem de Montaigne (1533–92), French essayist and philosopher, usually identified with skepticism.
2. Plato (ca. 428–348 B.C.), the most famous of the Greek philosophers.
3. Quoted from *Six Books of Proclus . . . on the Theology of Plato* (1816), edited by Thomas Taylor.

to the busy artist faculty, that the best appeal is ever made. And, in the writers and philosophers, it is not propositions that are of the first need, but to watch and tenderly cherish the intellectual and moral sensibilities,—those fountains of right thoughts, and woo them to stay and make their home with us. Whilst they abide with us, we shall not write or think amiss.

I write *mémoires pour servir*. I began by attempting to write the laws of the mind; but, observing that this was indeed the tendency of every man, to conquer the whole world to himself, rewrite literature, reconstruct science and art, and that it was excellent and inevitable, and showed him to be *adamas ex veteri rupe*, a chip of Jove, yet for practical purposes required a longevity which is denied him; yes, arms of Briareus to hold up his books, to eyes of Argus to read them, and to rapider thought, I thought I would take a modester stand—under protest, however—and would content myself with reporting my emphatic experiences.[4] Besides, I did not wish to violate my *naturel*, which promises to draw students from Stockholm and Japan if you stick by it.

And I assay to report such experiences as have been impressive and emphatic to me, some of them older, some newer, for they are a very durable ware, and sometimes two observations that are strictly related appear separately at the distance of long years, like Audubon's great Eagle, which he affirms to have seen first at a vast height in the atmosphere over Lake Superior, and never again until nine years later, when he caught sight of the bird three thousand miles away in South America.—[5] So these detached observations we pretend to report; and no wise to reconstruct a theory or globe of "our glassy essence."[6]

It is incidental experiences that belong to us, not serial or systematic. For we win them casually, here and there, now and then. We are confined in this vertebrate body, convenient but ridiculously provincial, which steps a little way here, a little out there, now opens its eyes wide, then shuts them fast, and, when it opens them again, is prone to give their color to the things it sees. Our experience is irregular, spotty, in veins, very knowing on specialties, profoundly ignorant of the connection of things. There is affectation in assuming to give our chart or orrery of the interior universe; and Nature flouts those who do, trips up their heels, throws them on their back. But so long as each sticks to his private experiences, he may be interesting and irrefutable; and each man has some good ones.

Every man has the whole capital in him, if he does not know how to coin it. Every man knows all that Plato or Kant can teach him.[7] When they have got out

4. *Adamas ex veteri rupe*, figuratively, a chip off the old block; Jove or Jupiter, the equivalent of the Greek Zeus, was the central deity of the Roman religious world; Briareus, in Greek mythology, was a giant with one hundred arms; Argus, in Greek mythology, was a giant with one hundred eyes.

5. John James Audubon (1785–1851), American ornithologist and artist born in Haiti whose elephant folio edition of *The Birds of America* was published in England between 1827 and 1838.

6. William Shakespeare, *Measure for Measure*, 2.2.120.

7. Immanuel Kant (1724–1804), German philosopher.

the proposition at last, 'tis something which he recognizes, and to which he feels himself entirely competent. He was already that which they say; and was that more profoundly than they can say it. "No author ever wrote, no speaker ever said anything to compare with what the most ordinary man can feel."[8] "To construct a philosophy is nothing more than to give the best attention to the operations of one's own mind."[9]

I trust a good deal to commonsense, as we all must. If a man has good corn, or cider, or boards, or cows to sell, or can make better chairs, or knives, or crucibles, or church-organs, than anybody else, you will find a broad, hard-beaten road to his house, though it be in the woods. And if a man knows the law, people find it out, though he live in a pine shanty. And if a man can pipe or sing well, or can paint better than Allston, or can, like Burns or Béranger, intoxicate all who hear him with delicious songs and verses, 'tis certain that the secret cannot be kept; the first witness tells it to a second, and men go to him by fives, and tens, and fifties.[10] Well, it is still so with a thinker.

If he proposes to show me a high human secret, if he profess to have found the hidden pass that leads from Fate to Freedom, all good heads, and all mankind, religiously wish to know it. And, though it sorely taxes their poor brain, they will venture into the dark mountains with him, and they find out, at last, whether they have made the transit, or no. If they have, they will know it, and his fame will surely be bruited abroad. If they come away unsatisfied, though it be easy to impute it,—even in their belief,—to their own dulness, in not being able to keep step with his snow-shoes on the icy mountain-paths,—I suspect, it is because the transit has not been made. 'Tis like that crooked hollow log through which the farmer's pig found access to the field. The farmer moved the log, so that the pig, in returning to the hole, and, passing through, found himself, to his astonishment, still on the outside of the field: he tried it once more, and was still outside: then he fled away with all his might, and would never go near it again.

Whatever transcendent abilities Fichte, Kant, Schelling, and Hegel have shown, I think they lack the confirmation of having given piggy a transit to the field.[11] The log is very crooked, but still leaves Grumphy on the same side of the wall he was before. If they had made the transit, common fame would have found it out.

If a true metaphysician should come, he would accompany you through your

8. Attributed to a J. C. Thompson by Emerson (*JMN*, 14:250).

9. Attributed to Emanuel Swedenborg (1688–1772), Swedish scientist, theologian, and mystic, by Emerson (*JMN*, 15:20).

10. Washington Allston (1779–1843), American historical painter and novelist; Robert Burns (1759–96), Scotland's most famous poet; Pierre-Jean de Béranger (1780–1857), French poet and songwriter regarded during his lifetime as France's national bard.

11. Johann Gottlieb Fichte (1762–1814), German metaphysician; Friedrich Wilhelm Joseph von Schelling (1775–1854), German philosopher; Georg Wilhelm Friedrich Hegel (1770–1831), German philosopher.

mind, pointing at this treasure-crypt, and at that, indicating the wealth lying here and there, which the student would joyfully perceive, and pass on from hall to hall, from recess to recess, ever to more interior and causal forces, being minded to come over again on the same tracks by himself, at future leisure, and explore more nearly the treasures now only verified. But such as we now call metaphysicians, the Lockes, and Reids, and Stewarts, are no more than *valets de place* and *custodi*, who lead travellers through the curiosities of Rome and Verona, and say over by rote the legends that have been repeated from father to son, "Motto Antico, Signore," "un tempio," "C'era battaglia," and so forth.[12] But you must be born for it. In the Tyrol, the old guide knows the passes from mountain to mountain, the bridges over gorge and torrent;—and the salvation of numberless lives is in his oaken staff. And my guide, the guide whom I require, must know not less the difficult roads of thought, the infinitely cunning transitions from law to law in metaphysics; in the most hopeless mazes, he could find a cheerful road leading upward, and lighted as by the midday sun.

Invincible repugnance to introversion, to study of the eyes, instead of that which the eyes see; and, in like manner, to employing the mind to analyse itself, instead of the world; and the belief of men is, that the attempt is unnatural, and is punished by loss of faculty. I share the belief that the natural direction of the intellectual powers is from within outward; and, that, just in proportion to the activity of the thoughts on the study of an outward object, as architecture, or farming, or natural history, ships, animals, chemistry, in that proportion the faculties of the mind had a healthy growth; but a study in the opposite direction, had a damaging effect on the mind. And the gross instances quoted in proof are the ancient or the Mediæval schoolmen running into dialectics; or the destructive meditation of the Hindoos, or in our own times, that, while the Germans have pushed this study farthest, and claimed in it a wonderful success, the human race have in some sort exhibited a certain disgust, and had made the German professors a proverb for verbal sub-tleties. Goethe turned away his encyclopaedical eyes from such pursuit—frankly recognizing the labors of Kant and Hegel.[13] He says, "Kant's *Critik of Pure Reason* had already appeared, but it lay quite out of my circle. I listened to much conversation about it,—and could mark that the old grand questions returned: How much ourselves, and how much the external world, contributed to our spiritual being. I had never separated the two, and if I, in my own way, philosophized over objects, I did it with unconscious naïveté, and believed really that I saw my opinions before my eyes. But when that dispute arose, I gladly leaned to the side of those, who did man the most honor," that is, of Kant.

He thinks he had always held these opinions practically, but now they smiled

12. John Locke (1632–1704), English philosopher, known as the founder of English empiricism; Thomas Reid (1710–96) and Dugald Stewart (1753–1828), Scottish "common sense" philosophers.

13. Johann Wolfgang von Goethe (1749–1832), Germany's most famous writer.

on him in a Theory. "The entrance it was that pleased me; in the labyrinth I dared not trust myself. Sometimes my poetic tendencies hindered me, sometimes my common-sense; and I had never felt myself instructed."

I share the doubt and the repugnance, and, with any confinement to the thoughts, it would be so punished with a paralysis. But the objection really lies against the manner of the study, and not the knowledge itself. It is one of those many things which require alternating with its proper counterparts. Metaphysics is dangerous as a single pursuit. We should feel some more confidence in the same results from the mouth of a man of the world. The inward analysis must be corrected by rough experience. Life itself is mixed. Neither can oxygen be breathed pure; yet without oxygen we could not live. We must alternate waking with sleep: But that is no objection to waking. Solitude is pernicious if continued; but solitude is not a less peremptory condition of sanity. And so metaphysics must be perpetually reinforced by life; must be the observation of a working-man on working-men, must be biography, a record of some law whose working was surprised by the observer in natural action.

I hate dialectics and logomachies; but if one considers how weighty and attractive among his experiences are those few where he has come upon a metaphysical secret,—how deep and far the lines run, as if it were the cropping-out in his mind of a mountain in the Kingdom of Heaven,—the man that has made a discovery in the magical machinery that plies there has gone to Sais; has been admitted to the cave at Delphi.[14] Jove has come to his house. He has learned somewhat which he cannot forget. It realises for us the primeval traditions of men that the Gods came down to them, entered their houses, broke bread at their table, by whatever name adored, whether Johovah, or Jove, or Apollo, or Brahma, or Seeva Vishnu, or Odin.[15]

A day comes when each man detects that there is somewhat in him that knows more than he does. Then he puts the question, Who's who? Which of these two is really me? The one that knows more, or the one that knows less? The little fellow, or the big fellow? And this opinion that the sympathy of mankind and the health of the observer goes with this just combining of the intellectual inquiry with practical life, is confirmed by the fact, that, in general, the science of the mind owes little to professed metaphysicians, but much to the incidental remarks of deep men everywhere. It is Montaigne, Pascal, Montesquieu, even Molière, who make each a contribution to mental philosophy, and not D'Alembert, Condillac, or Jouffroi;

---

14. Saïs was an important ancient Egyptian city in the Nile Delta; in ancient Greece the city of Delphi, which was dedicated to Apollo and Dionysus, had a famous oracle who could predict the future.

15. Apollo was the Greek god of prophecy who, as the leader of the Muses, was the patron of poetry and music; Brahmā the creator of the universe, Vishnu the preserver, and Shiva the destroyer are the three members of the Hindu Trimurti, or trinity; Odin is the supreme deity of Norse mythology.

Shakspeare, Goethe, and Wordsworth, not Hobbes, or Hartley, or Spinosa.[16] The analytic mind never carries us on. Taking to pieces is the trade of those who cannot construct.

We do not own the worship of the intellect as one of our duties. One day we shall own the Creator. See to what base uses we set these miraculous powers: to reading all day in the newspaper railroad accidents, the latest murder, the police record, or the brokers' price current, or our filthy politics; to playing billiards, and to standing at the doors of hotels. It were better and healthier to set them to scrub floors and polish boots.

'Tis the highest compliment we can pay a man, to deal with him as an intellect; to expose to him the grand and cheerful secrets which we never open to our daily companions; to disport ourselves in the sphere of freedom, in the simplicity of truth; to see the men of talents take their place, too, as children of Fate.

Let me have your attention to this dangerous subject in which we will cautiously approach on different points the margin of this dim and perilous lake, so attractive, so delusive. We have had so many guides and so many failures. And now the world is still uncertain whether the pool has been sounded or no.

For my thoughts, I seem to stand on the bank of a river, and watch the endless flow of the stream before me floating objects of all shapes, colors, and natures, nor can I much detain them as they pass, except by running beside them a little way along the bank. But whence they come, or whither they go, is not told me. Only I have a suspicion that, as geologists say, "Every river makes its own valley"; so does this mystic stream; it makes its valley, makes its banks, and makes perhaps the observer too.[17]

What baulks all language is the broad, radiating, immensely distributive action of nature and of mind. If it were linear, if it were successive, step by step, jet by jet, like a small human agency, we could follow with language, but it mocks us by its ubiquity and omnipotence.

We have reformed our botany, our chemistry, our geology, our anatomy, through the appearance of a several genius; but our metaphysics still awaits its author. A high analogic mind, a mind which with one *aperçu* penetrates many

16. Blaise Pascal (1623–62), French scientist, philosopher, and mathematician; Charles-Louis de Secondat, baron de La Brède et de Montesquieu (1689–1755), French political philosopher whose chief work, *L'esprit des lois* (1748), influenced political thought in Europe and the United States; Molière (1622–73), French dramatist and actor most famous for his comedies; Jean Le Rond d'Alembert (1717–83), French mathematician; Étienne Bonnot de Condillac (1715–80), French philosopher, author of works on logic, language, economics, and philosophy and follower of Locke; Théodore-Simon Jouffroy (1796–1842), French philosopher, translated works of Thomas Reid; William Wordsworth (1770–1850), English poet and, with Samuel Taylor Coleridge, founder of the romantic movement; Thomas Hobbes (1588–1679), English materialist philosopher; David Hartley (1705–57), English psychologist and philosopher; Baruch Spinoza (1632–77), Dutch philosopher and rational pantheist of Portuguese-Jewish parentage.

17. Emerson quotes himself; see *JMN*, 13:453.

successive crafts, and strings them as beads on its thread of light, will charm us with disclosing mental structure, as the naturalist with his architectures. Now, our metaphysics is like Kett and Blair.[18]

Now, we have to say that all men are conscious of a steep contrast between the ideal and the actual; that our churches do not represent the absolute holy; nor our filthy government the absolute right; nor our colleges the pure truth; that when two reasonable men meet, a new order takes place in their mind; that it is seen to be possible to work on quite different principles from these in vogue. Are we to live always by our memories; to use Grecian art, and Gothic churches, and Jewish religion, and English law? I don't know why we need have been created at all. We are the most historical people that ever lived. If you complain of some outrage,— instead of righting the wrong, the aggressor shows you blandly, that all the forms have been scrupulously observed; or that the crime is by no means new, but is actually an usage; and you take that as some answer, and proceed to argue the history with him. A belief in its thoughts, 'tis this which the age lacks. What carnage would not the use of simple perceptions make with the public business, and the public servants! I dreamed that I stood in a city of beheaded men, where the decapitated trunks continued to walk.

But if one remembers what happens to him in a conversation of contemplative men, we are apprised that we belong to better society than we have yet beheld; that a mental power is awaiting us more excellent than anything that is now called philosophy; perceptions of immense power native to the soul. We came down to the shore of the sea and dipped our hands in its miraculous waves. We are assured of eternity and can spare all omens, and prophecies, and religions, for we see and know that which these obscurely announce.

And this being so, I affirm that a revolution impends more radical than any whereof we have experience. For does anyone doubt between the strength of a thought and that of any institution? A perception came into my mind, by no chance, by no illusion: it is there by a fate, the same or much older than that in geology or gravitation.

The first fact is the fate in every mental perception: (I use the word Fate in a high sense;) that, my seeing this or that, and that I see it so or so, is as much a fact in the natural history of the world, as is the freezing of water at thirty-two degrees of Fahrenheit. My percipiency affirms the presence and perfection of law, as much as all the martyrs. A perception,—it is of a necessity older than the sun and moon, and the Father of the Gods. It is there with all its destinies. It is its nature to rush to expression,—to rush to embody itself. It is impatient to put on its sandals, and be gone on its errand, which is to lead to a larger perception and, so, to new

18. Henry Kett (1761–1825), English philosopher; Hugh Blair (1718–1800), Scottish Presbyterian clergyman, author, and rhetorician.

action: for thought exists to be expressed. That which cannot externize itself is not thought.

Our culture is so rude and incipient,—we are, at the best, with all our brag, such raw savages, that a metaphysician in a carpenter's shop or an attorney's office, is, however civilly, treated as a trifler. But Archimedes and Kant are as much realists, as blacksmiths and stone masons, and deal with intellections as rigorously, as they with iron bolts and slabs.[19]

The fundamental fact is the correspondence of the human being to the world,—his correspondence and impressionability,—so that every change in that writes a record on the mind. The mind yields sympathetically to the tendencies or laws which stream through things, and make the order of nature. But this obedience is a vital obedience or sympathy, as sharing the same blood and destiny. What we require in a good mind is sensibility to truth. And in the perfection of this correspondence or expressiveness, the health and force of man consist.

I hardly dare to speak of this element in its pure essence—it is too rare for the wings of words. And we must not speak of the mount, except in the mount. I only advert with reverence to the fact, that Intellect is a science of degrees, and, that, as man is conscious of the law of vegetable and animal nature, so he is aware of an Intellect which overhangs his intellectual actions like a sky, of degree above degree, and heaven within heaven.

In its high sense, it is the supreme fact we know, being the soul of matter, and the life and order by which it exists. It was described by the ancient as χιυητιχον, that which is moved by itself. There is nothing else which moves itself except Soul. And thus is it the antagonist of Fate.

All the senses minister to a mind which they do not know. The eye does not see it, the ear does not hear it, the nose does not smell it; the tongue does not taste it; nor the hand touch it; but the mind residing in the body, and giving it all its force, is a force hidden to everything below it. These senses that feed it know no more of it than the granite mountain or the heaving sea do.

All things are full of Jove. You cannot exaggerate the powers of the mind. All that the world admires comes from within: in other words, our whole existence is subjective. What we are, that we see, love, hate. A man externizes himself in his friends, in his enemies, in his parasites, in his aims, in his actions, in his fortunes, and in his religion.

'Tis the fulness of man that runs over into objects, and makes his bibles, and Shakspeares, and Homers so great.[20] The joyful reader borrows of his own ideas to fill their faulty outline, and knows not that he borrows and gives.

19. Archimedes (ca. 287–212 B.C.), Greek mathematician and engineer.

20. Homer (ninth–eighth century B.C.), Greek poet, presumed single author of the *Iliad* and the *Odyssey*.

Whenever we are wise, every book streams with universal light. 'Tis the reader that makes the book. A good head cannot read amiss. In every book, he finds passages which seem confidences or asides hidden from all else, and unmistakably meant for his ear. Only that book can I read which recites to me something that is already in my mind; as I only go to people who can answer my questions. Why then overestimate a book? You are yourself the book's book. Its worth is your worth. Read yourself, and there find the libraries.

In the hour of thought, the world becomes of glass. Whence does the light come that shines on things? From the soul of the observer. When Minerva leads, Telemachus sees the whole house illuminated. "O father! the walls of the house, the spaces between the rafters, the fir beams and columns appear as of fire. Certainly some one of the gods is present." But Ulysses answered, "Be silent, and restrain your thought, for this is the custom of the Gods who dwell in Olympus."[21]

The light by which we see in this world, comes out from the soul of the observer. Wherever any noble sentiment dwelt, it made the faces and houses around to shine. When we are wise, every book streams with universal light. Joy and sorrow are radiations from us. Nay, the powers of this busy shop of the brain are miraculous and illimitable. There are the rules and formulas by which the whole empire of matter is worked. There's no prosperity, trade, art, city, or great material wealth of any kind but, if you trace it home, you will find it rooted in a thought, in the metaphysical energy of some individual man. It feels the antipodes and the poles as much as its limbs; nay, the powers of the instrument reach to the neighboring heavens, and the spheres of astronomy preëxist in the spheres of the mind.

But higher than all feats of talent is the intellect itself: intellections are external to intellect. At certain happy hours, each man is conscious of a secret heaven within him, a realm of undiscovered sciences, of slumbering powers; a heaven, of which these feats of talent, are no measure; it arches like a sky, over all that it has done, or that has been done, and suggests unfathomable power.

All that is urged by the saint, for the superiority of faith over works, is as truly urged for the highest state of intellectual perception or beholding, over any intellectual performance, as the creation of algebra, or of the *Iliad*. Sometimes under the spell of poetry, sometimes in solitude, sometimes in deep conversation on moral problems, we come out of our egg-shell existence into the great Dome, and see the Zenith over us, and the Nadir under us.

Of all the foibles and frenzies of men, was there ever any like this, of valuing practical life, and holding thought cheap? Thought! It is the thread on which the system of nature and the heaven of heavens are strung. All that we see, or touch,

21. Minerva, the Roman goddess of wisdom corresponding to Athena, the Greek goddess of war and wisdom; Telemachus, son of Odysseus (Ulysses) and Penelope who goes in search of his father after he left for Troy and did not return in twenty years.

or experience, came from it, as leaves from a tree. The world, the galaxy, is but a scrap before the metaphysical power.

But after we have recognized this awful essence of Intellect Pure, the first stair down is a steep one, to thoughts or intellections. As the sun in our system is conceived to have made our system by hurling out from himself from time to time the outer rings of diffuse ether, which, slowly, have condensed into earths and moons;—by a higher force of the same law, the mind detaches minds, and a mind detaches thoughts or intellections. These, again, all mimic in their sphericity the first mind and share its discovery. But repeated experiments and affirmations make it visible soon to others. The point of interest is here that these gates, once opened, never swing back. The observers may come at their leisure, and do, at last, satisfy themselves of the fact. The thought, the doctrine, the right, hitherto not affirmed, is published in set propositions, in conversation of scholars, and philosophers, of men of the world, and, at last, in the very choruses of songs. Men over forty years still contradicting. The young hear it, and, as they have never fought it, never known it otherwise, they accept it, vote for it at the polls, embody it in the laws. And this perception, thus satisfied, re-acts on the senses to clarify them, so that it becomes more indisputable. Thus, it does not matter what the opposition may be of presidents, kings, or majorities, but what the truth is as seen by one mind.

And what are thoughts? They are only perceptions of single relations, of the great laws of nature. It is the nature of the human mind to see in succession the facts or laws of nature as the eye looks at one or another object. 'Tis the necessity of man that he cannot look at any object without looking from all other objects in the universe.

What shall we say of these potentates we call Thoughts, so familiar yet so unknown? This endless, silent procession of the makers of the world—There is no herald announcing the advent of a truth that is to alter the condition of mankind. Wonderful is their way and their sequence. To a healthy mind, there is always one waiting at the door when he wakes.[22] Not one of them is solitary. Each leads in another by the hand. They have a life of their own, and a motion proper to themselves. They rank themselves. Every thought, like every man, wears at its first emergence from the creative night its rank stamped upon it,—this is a witticism, and this is a power. And, then again, in Memory, they rank themselves with more precision, as one thought, which at first softly and obscurely presented itself, is found to be indelible, and towers up like a Pharos amid the flowing years.[23]

22. In his unpublished "Notebook TO" (bMS Am 1280 H87, in the Houghton Library of Harvard University) Emerson quotes Henry David Thoreau (1817–62), American writer, as saying that "when he wakes . . . he finds a thought already in his mind, waiting for him. The ground is preoccupied" (51–52, 229, 238; quoted in Emerson's *University Lectures*, 51 n. 303).

23. Paraphrased from "Ode to Memory," ll. 41–42, by Alfred, Lord Tennyson (1809–92), English poet, named poet laureate in 1850 after the death of William Wordsworth. Pharos, a lighthouse in ancient Alexandria, Egypt.

Wonderful, again, is their working and relation each to each. We hold them as lanthorns to light each other, and our present design. Every new thought modifies, interprets old problems. What is written in invisible ink, the fire of thought will bring out and explain. The retrospective value of each new thought is immense. 'Tis like a torch applied to a long train of powder.

Thought constitutes personality. 'Tis that by which a man is a man. For the first difference in nature, the foundation of aristocracy, the source of honor, of nobility, is the difference between *Him* and *It.* The plebeian is *It.* The patrician is *He.* For, let the outward form be never so rude and base, a lump of flesh, if it have reason, we could not choose but say *him*; acknowledge him one of us. We tax a man first for his poll, faculty, or brain; then, for the possessions it has brought him. There is no limit to its elevations: Who has found the boundaries of human intelligence? It has infinite degrees and series of platforms. From the borders of the brute kingdom, the openings of instinct, up to Plato; from the yelps of dogs, up to despotic eloquence; from the diggers that eat worms or cannibals that eat men, up to the lawgivers of arts and science, power is as is the closeness and comprehensiveness of the perception: it never makes a new fact, but sees a fact which always existed, but was never before seen. One man differs from another as he sees things more truly and more deeply.

The Egyptian could not measure his pyramid. Thales stuck his staff into the ground, and said, "As is the shadow of my staff to the staff, so is the shadow of the pyramid to the height of the pyramid."[24] It was easy to measure the three first, and so the last was made known.

And so Tartaglia *invented,* as we say, the rules of algebra, and, as his contemporaries said, made men in love with the mind of man, which could see so admirably.[25] And Kepler, and Newton, and Dalton, those great spiritual lords, saw the ground-plan of the universe.—[26] And always a new perception makes the great man. A man with a new thought is a benefactor of the race. And Davy said, "My greatest discovery was Michael Faraday."[27]

They who have thoughts make room for themselves. What can resist them? Who can do without them? They live in perpetual victory. Ever according to the closeness and truth of their perception is the effect;—for, let me tell you in whisper the secret of human power: a thing intellectually seen,—no matter how great or

24. Thales of Miletus (ca. 625–ca. 546 B.C.), Greek astronomer and geometrician, considered by Aristotle to be the father of Greek philosophy.

25. Niccolò Tartaglia (1499–1557), Italian mathematician who solved the cubic equation.

26. Johannes Kepler (1571–1630), German mathematician and astronomer; Sir Isaac Newton (1642–1727), English natural philosopher and mathematician; John Dalton (1766–1844), English chemist and physicist.

27. Sir Humphry Davy (1778–1829), English chemist who advanced an electrical theory of chemical affinity; Michael Faraday (1791–1867), English chemist and physicist, known for his experiments with electromagnetism.

complicated,—is by that sight already mentally accomplished; since it is easy for the mind so seeing to embody the thing externally in facts and institutions.

The thoughts themselves,—they come so quietly,—no cymbal clashed, no clarion rang, at the advent of ideas. Yet they breathe the breath of life into the millions of men, and fashion history, so as it is, and not otherwise.

On very low platforms the supremacy of metaphysics is indisputable; for what is all this weary talk about public opinion? Simply, that men will do after their belief; this is the helm that guides the ship; if instead of believing that prosperity is in silver and gold, they believe that it is in jumping into the sea, or killing their brothers, or their children, they will do that. Empires rest on the same foundations, namely, on thoughts that drift through one ambitious brain, and on beliefs in the rest that this particular man represents them. The power is shown as much in its errors as in its legitimate activity. Cardinal de Retz says, "Great affairs depend still more upon imagination than small ones. The people's imagination alone is sometimes the cause of a civil war. The influence of the court, the prestige of the royal name, when the court is really in troops, money, and men—the weakest party, is a continual proof."[28]

But high over the men, are the thoughts themselves, and, in every degree, like the angels; Thrones, dominations, princedoms virtues, powers. The whole future of the universe is in them; Fate is in every perception of ours. But higher still are thoughts; in that world is no crime and no sorrow.

And so, those are great who do not wish to use their thoughts for the popular aims, to put them in a shop-order, but who watch and worship the order of thought. 'Tis the difference of the mystic and the lawyer.

See how superior to himself is this which every man calls his ideal. He stands penitent and confounded before its revelations. Our thoughts disdain us, if we do not put them into practice,—disdain us, and forsake us.

And here I have to say that those may well be valued and astonishing, for life is low, its wheels heavy; the calamity of this intellectual creature, is, that he has not thoughts; that his access to the fountain of life is rare and mediate, that he reads the books, uses the arts, worships with the religion of others. A stern enumeration will find few thoughts. All that is known of love or memory is soon told, and hardly Bacon, Goethe, or Coleridge will have added more than one observation apiece.[29]

One sometimes despairs of humanity: Creatures of custom, low instinct, and party names. Thought has its own proper motion, and wonders if the day of original perceptions is gone. A thought would destroy most persons whom we know. Bring a thought into a chamber full of company, it would extinguish most of them.

28. Jean-François-Paul de Gondi, cardinal de Retz (1613–79), French prelate and politician.

29. Francis Bacon (1561–1626), English essayist, statesman, and philosopher; Samuel Taylor Coleridge (1772–1834), English poet and philosopher and, with William Wordsworth, founder of the romantic movement.

They are exposed as counterfeits and charlatans, as rats and mice, they who strutted, a moment ago, as the princes of this world.

We used to be told that, though the stars appear so profusely scattered over the night heaven, yet if the traveller should set out to count them, he would not be able to reckon in a clear night over a few hundreds. Well, the same fact holds in the mind. Young people talk of moments when their brain seemed bursting with the multitude of thoughts. It was a false alarm. It was an illusion of sentiment which acts like a multiplying-glass and a Claude mirror at the same time.[30] There are few thoughts. A rich mind has not many. We commonly say a man can write one book,—has a very small quiver of stories, and of jokes, and of opinions.

Not only so, but the thoughts emerging in a period among all the wits, and poets, and savans, and good heads generally, are not very many. A well informed man could soon give you the pith of all the ideas which the age has contributed in all departments,—Count the books, and you would think there was immense wealth; but any expert knows, that there are few thoughts, which have emerged in his time. Shut him up in a closet, and he could soon tell them all. They are quoted, contradicted, modified, but the amount remains computably small.

And as the theories are few, so the intellectual moods, or, favorable state of the perceptive faculty, are rare. In the Cambridge observatory, the professor will tell you that what we popularly call fine weather, and a clear night, is often no good night for the telescope; that the sky is not clear for astronomical observations perhaps more than one night in a month. And I observe that the old Herschel in England reckoned that there were not above a hundred hours in a year, during which the heavens can be advantageously observed with his telescope of forty feet.[31] I find the days and hours for mental observation and record as few. Not every undisturbed day is good for the Muse.

The intellect gives a new and better property. Until we have intellectual property in anything, we have no right property in it. Only he has a thing who can use it. Who would be my best benefactor,—he who gave me a loadstone? or he who showed me that it would turn to the north? Does the Indian who roams over fifty miles to kill his game, or the chemist who draws food, clothing, iron, coal, electricity, and all means of art, for ten, or twenty, or fifty men out of one acre, possess land?

The present basis of society is brutish; each feeds on the other, after the law of the animal and vegetable, and, what is given to one is taken from all; but the basis

30. Claude Gellée, known as Claude Lorrain (1600–1682), French landscape painter. A Claude Lorraine (the earlier English spelling of Lorrain) glass or Claude glass is a convex hand mirror of dark or colored glass that reflects an image of diminished size and subdued color, probably named so after its similarity to the effect Claude Lorrain created in his paintings.

31. Sir William Herschel (originally Friedrich Wilhelm) (1738–1822), British astronomer born in Germany, discoverer of the planet Uranus.

of intellect and morals, the right and final foundation, is ever a living spring, and so is a new genius in every man, and the power and welfare of society gain with its numbers, and dignify us again, and restore price to life.

The intellectual man is stronger than the robust animal man, for he husbands his strength and endures. Franklin and Richardson of Arctic expeditions outlived their robuster comrades, and Frémont his soldiers, by more intellect.[32] Everybody was worn down in Napoleon's army but he; he grew fat on exposure and toil.[33] This is the tough tannin that cures the fibre, when Irish and Dutch are killed by fever and toil. "An apt breakfast," says Lord Bacon, "and heroic desires." In these cases, the activity of mind is salubrious. But a true philosophy requires a deeper cure, a more universal *hygeia*, than we have yet seen.

The intellect is Aesculapian.[34] Plutarch finds eloquence to use and strengthen the nobler powers of the frame.[35] And intellect is curative, and long-lived, has much resistance. The poets, the philosophers, the geometers, have lived to full age. All kinds of power develop simultaneously, and I shall wager on the thinker and not on the gymnast.

Nay, if we look further into it, we shall find that the mind is not only Aesculapian or medicinal, and resists disease, but can absolutely subdue all physical pain.

I do not wish to disparage Dr. Jackson's discovery of the anaesthetic power of sulphuric ether; but the first and best anaesthetic was the power in the mind to withdraw from pain.[36] There are plenty of martyrs in the history of religion, who, as soon as they are born, take a bee line to the axe of the inquisitor; who throw themselves into any forlorn hope of persecution, any Kansas or Crete, where tyranny is to be fought down. Men have been burned, and not apprehended it; been transfixed with spits, and do not perceive it; their shoulders cloven with axes, or their sides laid open with knives, and are not conscious of what is done to them.

There are times when the intellect is so active, that everything seems to run to meet it. Its supplies are found without much thought as to studies. Knowledge runs to the man, and the man runs to knowledge. In spring, when the snow melts, the maple trees flow with sugar, and you cannot get tubs fast enough, but it is only for a few days. The hunter on the prairie, at the right season, has no need of choosing

32. Sir John Franklin (1786–1847), English Arctic explorer; Sir John Richardson (1787–1865), Scottish naturalist and explorer, naturalist to Franklin's polar expeditions; John Charles Frémont (1813–90), American soldier, explorer, and presidential candidate.

33. Napoléon Bonaparte (1769–1821), born in Corsica, general and later emperor of the French as Napoléon I.

34. Aesculapius, legendary Greek physician who later became god of the healing arts. He learned to bring the dead back to life, so Zeus destroyed him so that men would not be able to avoid death.

35. Plutarch (ca. 46–ca. 120), Greek historian best known for his series of "lives," or character studies, arranged in pairs in which a Greek and a Roman are compared.

36. Emerson's brother-in-law Charles Thomas Jackson (1805–80), American doctor who abandoned medicine for chemistry and mineralogy, generally credited with the first use of ether.

his ground;—East, west, by the river, by the timber, near the farm, he is everywhere by his game.

The thought of each is the key to his history. Men ride on a thought, as if each bestrode an invisible horse, which, if it became visible, all their seemingly mad plunging motions would be explained. When Swedenborg described the roads leading up into heaven as not visible at first to any spirit, but, after a time, visible to such as are good,—he reports a familiar truth in the history of thought. The gates of thought, how slow and late they discover themselves! Yet, when they appear, we see they were always there, and always open.

You have been pleased with stories of gods in Homer, Ovid, and the *Edda*.[37] I invite you to the beholding and knowing of real gods, who work and rule forever and ever,—Memory and Vision; the Power of Imagination, the Poet Apollo; the Zodiackal Chain of Cause and Effect; Illusion, the Veil; and Transition, the Energy. Wisdom with his solar eye, his look is classification, and distributes natures. And high over all its perceptions and its powers, the Intellect Pure, which we cannot discriminate from the Cause of Causes.

'Tis a grave question that is continually agitated, What is originality? A frank man will say, Whoever is original, I am not. What have I, that I have not received? Let every creditor take his own, and what would be left? 'Tis the old riddle of King Amasis of the Sea, which, he said, if you would only stop all the rivers flowing into it, he would soon drink up.[38]

Yet this is true and not true. Every man brings a certain difference of angle to the old identical picture—which makes all new. But this constitutes originality that the beholder of this particular knot of things or thoughts has the habit of recurrence to universal views. The boy sits in the school, or in his father's house, adorned with all the color, health, and power, which the day spent out of doors has lent him. The man interests in the same way, not for what he does in our presence, at table, or in his chair, but for the authentic tokens he gives us of powers over the landscape, over fields, ships, railroads, cities, senates, or other out-door organizations. The girl charms us with the distant contributions which she reconciles. She has inherited the feature which manly joy and energy formed long ago, softened and masked under this present beauty, and she brings the hint of the romance of fields, and forest, and forest-brooks, of sunsets, and music, and all-various figures that deck it. A white invalid that sits in the corner is good for nothing. To be isolated is to be sick, and, in so far, dead. The life of the All must stream through us, to make the man and the moment great. So in thought, the mind has gone out of its little

37. Ovid (43 B.C.–A.D. 17), Roman poet whose chief work, *Metamorphoses* (1–8), is a narrative poem that recounts legends of miraculous transformations of form; the *Prose Edda*, written in the early thirteenth century by Snorri Sturluson, is an Icelandic collection of early Scandinavian mythology.

38. There were two Egyptian kings of this name: Amasis (or Ahmose) I (d. ca. 1557 B.C.) and Amasis II (fl. ca. 569–525 B.C.).

proposition into the great sky of universal truths, and has not come back poor, but enriched, and with the necessity of repairing habitually to the same firmament, and importing its generosities into all its particular thoughts.

He who compares all his traditions with this eternal standard, he who cannot be astonished by any vanities or fireworks because the immensities and eternities from which he newly came, to which he familiarly returns, have once for all put it out of his power to be surprised by trifles: that man conveys somewhat of the ecstasy in which he lives, into every word he speaks. It is in his manners, and feeds the root of his life. It is the magic of nature, that the whole life of the universe concentrates itself on its every point.

Morals

(1859)

Emerson first delivered "Morals" in April 1859 in a series of six private lectures in Boston, and he drew some passages from the lecture for "Morals and Religion," which he delivered in May 1872 in a series of six private "conversations" in Boston. However, his most important use of the lecture occurred on 4 December 1859, when he delivered it before the Twenty-eighth Congregational Society in Boston during memorial services conducted for John Brown, the radical abolitionist who had been hanged for leading the famous raid on Harpers Ferry, Virginia, in 1859, intended to spur a slave revolt. Parts of "Morals" were used in "Character," published by Emerson in the *North American Review* 102 (April 1866): 356–73, and collected by James Elliot Cabot in *Lectures and Biographical Sketches* in 1884 (*W*, 10:89–122), and in "The Sovereignty of Ethics," assembled by Cabot for publication in the *North American Review* 126 (May–June 1878): 404–20, and also collected in *Lectures and Biographical Sketches* (*W*, 10:181–214).

I am happy to meet the friends who are met in a spirit of humility, but of freedom to seek the truth, for the conduct of life. I lament the absence, and the cause of the absence, of your Pastor.[1]

It is an objection necessary to every affirming of truth that it stands in a hostile attitude to existing belief, and so begins with much denial. Contradiction arises, and the truth-speaker finds it easier to show the faults of the old, than the values of the new. Hence, a certain tendency in reformers to skepticism.

'Tis a sort of proverbial dying speech of scholars, at least, 'tis attributed to many, that which Anthony à Wood reports of Nathaniel Carpenter, an Oxford fellow; "It did repent him," he said, "that he had formerly so much courted the maid instead of the mistress;" meaning philosophy and mathematics, to the neglect of *divinity*.[2] This, in the language of our time, would be *Ethics*.

Morals respects what men call goodness, that which all men agree to honor, as, justice, truth-speaking, good will, and good works. Morals respects the source or

---

1. Theodore Parker (1810–60), American reform minister and friend of Emerson, had traveled abroad for health reasons.
2. Anthony à Wood (1632–95), English antiquary and historian.

motive of this action. It is the science of substances, and not of shows. It is the what, and not the how. It is that which all men profess to regard, and by their real respect for which recommend themselves to each other. Men may well come together to confirm their confidence in goodness. 'Tis that which all speech aims to say, and all action to evolve. Literature with its libraries is only apology, interlude, pastime, in the absence of that. "The deepest speculations are but difficult trifles, if they are not employed to guide men's actions in the path of virtue."[3]

Morals differ from intellectuals in being instantly intelligible to all. We are easily great with the loved and honoured associate. Then, the sentiments appear as new and astonishing as lightning out of the sky and disappear as suddenly without any sequel. The best is accessible, is cheap. Every man cannot have land or jewels, but every man can get what land, and money, and rank are valued for: namely, substantial manhood, thoughts—self-realizing and prophetic of the farthest future—thoughts, of which poetry and music are the necessary expression. "The true coin, for which all else ought to be changeable, is a right understanding of what is good," says Plato in *Phaedrus*.[4]

Theophrastus said, "that the most illiterate were able to speak in the presence of the most elegant persons while they spake nothing but truth and reason."[5] The moral equalizes all,—enriches, empowers all. It is the coin which buys all, and which all find in their pocket. Under the whip of the driver, the slave shall feel his equality with saints and heroes. In the greatest destitution and calamity, it surprises man with a feeling of elasticity which makes nothing of its loss.

If I should go now to say *how* it helps us, I should say, it is not after the way of other benefits, not by adding anything, which is a deceptive benefit. The way of benefit in the world is to give something; but everything given has an evil as broad as its good, so that we are not really better than before. I mean, that we pay a full equivalent for everything we acquire. Every new possession brings care. Every new possession is bought by the loss of some old possession. We have employment, but have lost our freedom. We have a new friend, but have lost the old one. We have experience, but have lost youth.

So, with our intellectual gains, we are not really enriched; every new fact crowds out some other. See a man after many years; he has a different circle of sensations, and objects of thought, and affection, but he is not really worth more (measured by an absolute standard) than he was years ago. As a magnet will carry a certain weight of iron suspended from its poles, a little more or less, but you quickly reach

3. Attributed to Sir Kenelm Digby (1603–65), English courtier, naval commander, diplomat, and religious writer, in Emerson's note in the manuscript.

4. Plato (ca. 428–348 B.C.), the most famous of the Greek philosophers. *Phaedrus* is a dialogue in which Socrates and his friend Phaedrus discuss the differences between conventional rhetoric and true rhetoric, using love as a subject.

5. Theophrastus (ca. 372–287 B.C.), Greek philosopher and disciple of Aristotle.

its limit, and you may change the bars or balls with which it is loaded as often as you will, it will not carry any more, so it seems as if every human being had a certain amount of vital power, which he was at liberty to expend in what manner he will, but which is never increased.

Not by adding, then, does the moral sentiment help us; no, but in quite another manner. It puts us in place. It centres, it concentrates us. It puts us at the heart of nature, where we belong; in the cabinet of Science and of Causes; there, where all the wires terminate which hold the world in magnetic communication, and so converts us into universal beings.

Placed rightly, centred, all goes well. All work for him, the man in the street, all men in all streets, in all fields, on the seas, the flower in the field, the coal in the mine, the sun in heaven. He who is in the circle of the divine communications serves all, and is served by all.

Strength enters as much as the moral element prevails. The strength of the animal to eat, and be luxurious, and to usurp, is rudeness and imbecility. All that repels and is dreary is not power, but the absence of power.

The moral element is a perpetual ennobling of man. It invites him to great enlargements, to find his satisfaction not in particulars or events, but in the purpose and tendency; not in bread, but in his right to his bread; not in much corn or wool, but in its communication.

No one is accomplished, whilst any one is incomplete. Weal does not exist for one with the wo of any other. I value morals because it gives me what to do today. It lights every place, enhances every property, endears every companion. The foreign which so captivates in idle moments has lost its charm. The beauty of youth has come back to our latest hour.

There is this eternal advantage to morals, that in the question between truth and goodness, the moral cause of the world lies behind all else in the mind. It was for good,—it is to good, that all works.— Surely, it is not to prove or show the truth of things: that sounds a little cold and scholastic; no, it is for benefit, that all subsists.

As we say in our modern politics, catching at last the language of morals, that the object of the state, is, the greatest good of the greatest number; so, the reason we must give for the existence of the world, is, that it is for the benefit of all being. The animal who is wholly kept down in nature has no anxieties. By yielding, as he must do, to it, he is enlarged, and reaches his highest point. The poor grub in the hole of a tree, by yielding itself to nature, goes blameless through its low part, and is rewarded at last; casts its filthy hull, expands into a beautiful form with rainbow wings, and makes a part of the summer day. The Greeks called it *psyche*, a manifest emblem of the soul.

Reality rules Destiny. They may well fear fate who have any infirmity of habit and aim. But he who rests on what he is, has a destiny above destiny, and can make mouths at fortune.

We have the strict analogy of the moral force in our use of universal material force. When a man chops a stick, or digs, or rides, or runs, or walks, or builds, he does it not by muscular force, but borrows the strength of the globe. We lift the axe with a feeble muscular force, but it is the gravity of the globe that brings it down with a strong one. We put forward the foot in walking, we bend the body in running, and fall forward through gravity. 'Tis the weight of the globe which holds the rider down to his horse, that holds every stone of the house firmly in place, and permits us to build up into the air.

Will is man, and the right direction of the will—that is morals. A man is made, at one point, coincident with the axis of things. There is somewhat constitutional to him to do, somewhat which he does with joy, and with the consent of all men and things, and which nature backs him in doing. The sun shines to light him to this task; the sea calls to him with tides and waves; the fragrant air inflates his lungs, and makes his words musical; the harvest feeds him for this; and all other creatures treat him as a benefactor. And in doing this, he has more than his own strength— the countenance and aid of all. Men fall from him when he withholds to do this. He is conscious of all this invitation, and of all this support, and is cheered by it to contemn the petty harm which his sleep, or his digestion, or his tired limbs suffer.

Spiritual is groped after by our definitions in making it invisible. The true meaning of spiritual is *real*; that law which executes itself; that which works without means; that which cannot be conceived as not existing.

Low degrees of this action according to nature make all the valued distinctions. If into any company a generous patriot, if Burke, or Washington, or Franklin came, what a caution would creep over all the assembly![6] So many charlatans and strutting triflers are exposed. It was this action of the presence of the good, that Plato signified, when he said, "A wise man is a perpetual magistrate." Lord Wellington said, "when our Journal appears, many statues must come down."[7]

Lowest degrees of this life according to nature instantly raise the person. You set the house maid to polish brasses, and the maid applies herself to the task, not saving her strength, nor with thoughts on somewhat else, but according to the law of brasses and of rubbing cloths, and your respect is commanded; and if the artist is more occupied in making the work true, than in pleasing you, or in selling it, your respect is commanded; and, in both cases, you say this is reality, and not a lie. I choose to will with reason, the right of all souls, and not for the pleasure of me.

So deep is our sense of the necessity of resting on nature and of universal motives, that, we call such, real men;—whilst men acting for by-ends, or not from

6. Edmund Burke (1729–97), British politician and natural philosopher born in Ireland, wrote on individual liberty; Benjamin Franklin (1706–90), American statesman, author, printer, editor, and inventor.

7. Arthur Wellesley, first Duke of Wellington (1769–1852), British general and statesman born in Ireland, served in Britain's armies throughout the empire for nearly fifty years.

central and constitutional reason, false and superficial. This acting after your constitution and for that which is always the same, as, justice, goodness, human freedom, and benefit,—we call reality.

Lucifer's wager was, there's no great, that is, steadfast man on earth.[8] 'Tis very rare. A man is already of consequence in the world when it is known we can implicitly rely on him.[9]

Great men serve us, as insurrections do, in tyrannical governments. The world would run into endless routine, and forms incrust forms, till the life was gone. But the perpetual supply of new genius shocks us with thrills of life. It happens now and then in the ages, that a soul is born which has no weakness of self; which offers no impediment to the divine spirit; which comes down into nature as if only for the benefit of souls; and all its thoughts are perceptions of things as they are, without any infirmity of earth. Such souls are as the apparition of Gods among men, and simply, by their presence, pass judgment on them. All are struck when they appear, and shrink, and pay involuntary homage, by hiding or apologizing for their action. One would say of these, they are forever restrained from descending into nature; while others are prevented from ascending out of it; and still a third class see sometimes from nature,—and sometimes are lifted out of it.

Terrible eyes, terror of perception in Napoleon:

> "You are losing confidence in Salicetti. I can imagine no greater misfortune for you than to alienate so valuable a man."
>
> "I see you are no wiser then three-fourths of mankind who do not appreciate the difference which exists between troops. You cannot replace with foreigners such troops as I have given you."

And he was right in saying, "I have three hundred millions in my vaults, and I would give them all for Ney."[10] Here was a man before whom all the walls of our being were laid flat. What to do with a man who converts five censors into five hot advocates for his cause?[11] The wits excluded from the Academy met in clubs, and threw the Academy into shade. Boerhaave said of Newton, "That man comprehends as much as all mankind besides."[12] What to do with Talleyrand, a man of so

8. Lucifer is the name of the fallen rebel archangel; in John Milton's *Paradise Lost* he is called Satan, and in Dante's *Inferno* he is the ruler of Hell.

9. Attributed to Edward George Earle Lytton Bulwer-Lytton, first Baron Lytton of Knebworth (1803–73), English novelist and politician, by Emerson (*JMN*, 14:65, 123).

10. Michel Ney, duc d'Elchingen (1769–1815), French soldier, made a peer by Louis XVIII but rallied to Napoléon during the Hundred Days.

11. The person Emerson associates with this quality is not Napoléon Bonaparte (1769–1821), general and later emperor of the French as Napoléon I, but Pierre-Augustin Caron de Beaumarchais, known as Beaumarchais (1732–99), French dramatist and man of public affairs (*JMN*, 13:408, 14:34; "Clubs," *W*, 7:240). His two most famous comic masterpieces are *The Marriage of Figaro* and *The Barber of Seville*.

12. Hermann Boerhaave (1668–1738), Dutch physician and scientist; Sir Isaac Newton (1642–1727), English natural philosopher and mathematician.

fatal a perception that the dynasty is doomed which has not his support?[13] We had a politician, too, who, when he differed from the country, was able to say to it, "The Whig Party goes in this direction, the Democratic Party in that,—but, Where shall I go?" And such was the individual force, that the nation saw, a new distribution must at once be made to accommodate him. (I wish I had a better example, for this man, preeminently strong as a nature, was a weak and abject character.)[14]

A man is as the angle of his vision. A man cannot utter three or four sentences, without disclosing the angle larger or less at which he looks at things,—more comprehensively or less than ours. The chief event of life is the day in which we have encountered a mind that startled us by its large scope. I am in the habit of thinking,—not I hope out of a partial experience,—but confirmed by what I notice in many lives, that to every serious mind Providence sends from time to time six or seven teachers, who are of the first importance to him in the lessons they have to impart. The highest of these not so much give particular knowledge, as they elevate by sentiment and by their habitual grandeur of view.

The English seem to have had these grand figures, not doctrinaires, but influences, moving now and then among their cultivated crowd, amazing the best men of talents by their eagle perception and great style. The young Cotes, for example, of whom Sir Isaac Newton said, "If he had lived, we had known something."[15] On a lower platform, one is struck with the way in which they cite the names of Frere and Horner, with nothing to show for it, but recognized by all as of transcendent superiority: people who make nothing and do nothing, but, like children, simply express themselves, and by word, and by silence, indicate no vulgar mind.[16]

Character—not feats but forces, not set days, or public occasions, but at all hours, and in repose still formidable, and can't be disposed of. Cato is character, and the Republic cannot perish as long as he lives.[17] I like those who did not choose to defend this or that, but who were appointed by God Almighty, before they came into this world, to stand for that thing.

It is remarkable also that persons of this divine character wonderfully augment the power of those near them, as a horse or a dog, if backed by his master, will accomplish what it could never do alone; so, the spirits and performance of the friends of the prophet are prodigiously increased. Then their imagination is addressed. They see all things in mirage and rainbow. Their affections and enlarged

13. Charles-Maurice de Talleyrand-Périgord (1754–1838), French politician known for his lack of commitment to established principles.

14. The subject of this anecdote is Daniel Webster (1782–1852), American statesman and orator (*JMN*, 14:34).

15. Roger Cotes (1682–1716), English mathematician, astronomer, and philosopher.

16. John Hookham Frere (1769–1846), British diplomat and writer, wrote witty parodies for the *Anti-Jacobin*; Francis Horner (1778–1817), British politician and economist and a founder of the *Edinburgh Review*.

17. Cato the Younger (95–46 B.C.), Roman politician.

thoughts transfigure his form and actions. Therefore, the legend of miracle always attends these divine persons, like Pythagoras, Socrates, Jesus, Menu, Mahomet.[18] How rightly we paint the saint with a halos! He was seen in life so!

We are thrown back on rectitude, forever and ever,—only rectitude,—to mend one;—this is all we can do. But *that*, the zealot stigmatizes as a sterile chimney-corner philosophy. The times change, the men are a multitude, but as soon as we leave the outward fact, and come to that power which they all share and express, we behold somewhat which refuses to be disparted. When I think of Reason, of Truth, of Virtue, I cannot conceive them as lodged in your soul, and lodged in my soul, but that you, and I, and all souls, are lodged in that, and I may easily speak of that adorable nature, there, where only I behold it, in my own heart, in such terms, as shall seem to the frivolous who dare not fathom their own consciousness, as profane. That which is best in nature and life, is, that private access of the heart to the Universal.

How is a man a man? How can he exist, to weave relations of joy and good with his brother, but because he is inviolable, alone, complete? I stand here glad at heart of all the sympathies I can awaken and share, clothing myself with them as with a garment of shelter and beauty, and yet knowing that it is not in the power of all who surround me to take from me the smallest thread I call mine. If all things are taken away, I have still all things in my relation to the Eternal. In the *Tarare* of Beaumarchais, the *Genius of Life* "sings majestically," says the stage direction—

> Mortal, whosoe'er thou art,
> Prince, or priest, or halberdier,
> Hunter, page, or mariner,—
> On the earth wilt thou be great?
> It belongs not to thy state,
> But alone to character.[19]

I talked not long since with a pioneer, a man who had really spent the best part of his life in new countries and hard work, manfully bringing order out of disorder, farms out of forests, towns out of buffalo prairie, and, at last, was forced by our admirable government to fight against the scum of the human race for the protection of freedom, life, and property against brigands. He believed, on his own experience, that one good, believing, strong-minded man is worth a hundred, nay, twenty thousand men, without character, for a settler in a new country; and that

18. Pythagoras (ca. 580–ca. 500 B.C.), Greek philosopher who raised mathematics to a science; Socrates (ca. 470–399 B.C.), one of the most famous of the Greek philosophers, whose dialogic method of teaching gained many adherents; *The Laws of Menu* (or *Manu*), Indian commentaries on religious laws and social obligations compiled between 200 B.C. and A.D. 200; Muhammad (ca. 570–632), founder of Islam, born in Mecca.

19. Beaumarchais wrote the libretto for the opera *Tarare* (1787).

the right men give a permanent direction to the fortunes of a state. He certainly did not share Falstaff's and the popular notion that any man is good enough for a soldier.[20] For the bullying rowdies,—he seemed to think cholera, small pox, and consumption, as valuable recruits.

But it is not only in founding new states, but in maintaining old ones, that we want character. Our politics are full of adventurers, who, having by education and social innocence a good repute in the state, break away from the law of honesty, and think they can afford to join the devil's party. They have heard Rochester's wicked sentence: "If men had a very little more courage, they would be rogues." "Il ne manque à tous les hommes qu'un peu de courage pour être laches."[21] 'Tis odious, these offenders in high life, but you shall meet them when, quite innocent of all ambition, you rally yourself to the support of old charities, and the cause of literature, and so forth. There, to be sure, are these brazen faces, and in this innocence you are puzzled how to meet them, and must shake hands with them under protest. We feel toward them, as the minister about the Cape Cod farm. In the old time, when the minister was still invited, in the spring, to make a prayer for the blessing of a piece of land,—the good divine being brought to the spot,— stopped short. "No; this land does not want prayer; this land wants manure."

> 'Tis virtue which they want, and, wanting it,
> Honor no garment to their backs can fit.[22]

A great deal of learned pains have been taken to prove the existence of God by the design apparent in the material world. And each philosopher accumulates a multitude of examples showing thought, which, of course, we read with pleasure. But this seems wasted labor, when one considers that there is no fact in the universe which the least attention does not bring into the category; nay, that the looking for it, was already the announcement of it, as he who is able to state a question, is already near the solution of it.

No, not in high sun-spots, but at the point in which any serious mind studies the genius of the world is that miraculous, self-executing energy which bends every agent and every fact into the order of the universe; proclaims its agreement or its opposition, neutralizes the opposition, and destroys the opponent; and so pours irresistible unity through worlds of discordant elements. This is the perpetual miracle of omnipotence, this moral purgation, and those examples in the vegetable and animal world seem only a remote and typical working of this power.

It is the privilege of moral power always to confer insight. Wisdom has its root in goodness. In high degrees, it confers a certain divination of states of mind. It

---

20. Sir John Falstaff, boisterous and earthy character in both parts of Shakespeare's *Henry IV* and *The Merry Wives of Windsor*.

21. John Wilmot, second Earl of Rochester (1647–80), English poet and wit, companion of Charles II.

22. Ben Jonson (1572–1637), English poet and dramatist, from his *Cynthia's Revels*, 5.11.117–18.

distributes by a higher and more searching principle than the vague and ignorant eye. It sees those things which are *alike*, however widely they may be separated, as *near*, and what is *unlike* as *far off*. To a well-principled man, there is
always victory,—better say, there is always rest in truth. Defeats are temporary accidents, that is, delays, not crises. He defends himself against failure in his main
design, by making every inch of the road to it pleasant. He can well afford to
wait.

What we are, *that* we see, love, and hate. If I met no gods, it was because I
harboured none. That is musk which betrays itself by the smell, and not what is
so labelled in the box. The fever is my enemy, though it be in my body; and the
febrifuge is my friend, though it grow on the mountains of Asia. The physician
goes on stimulating the diseased patient, but 'tis the fever that is fed on the rich
diet, and not the patient. And so always, moral power flies at the reality, not at
the appearance. Edward Pyot, being entreated to stay by the Quakers in Newport,
answered; "Should we, having no command to stay, but being permitted to pass
from hence, the pure power moving thereto,—should we yet stay; or, should we go,
if the Lord commands us to stay; we should then be wanderers indeed; for, such
are wanderers, who wander out of the will and power of God, abroad at large in
their own wills and earthly minds."[23]

The simplest forms of botany, as the lichens, are alike all over the globe: the
lichens of Sweden, and Brazil, and Massachusetts are the same; whilst in the more
complex classes of the Flora, each zone and country has its own. So is it with the
simple and grand characters among men, they do not hold of any nationality or of
any catechism. So of the grand ideas of religion and morals. Viasa, and Pythagoras,
and Swedenborg see the same thing.[24] The grand simple characters appear in one
race as in another. Even the French, weak in moral traits, have Pascal, Fenelon,
and Guion.[25] A traveller in our Northwest Indian country, came back to assure his
mystic society in New York, of his own discovery with surprise, "that the Indians
also had the Spirit."[26] These affinities destroy nationality, take away its fences. The
moral sentiment domesticates us at once with entire strangers. A brahman shuns
worldly honor as he would shun poison; and seeks disrespect, as he would seek nectar. For, though scorned, he may sleep with pleasure, with pleasure he may awake;
with pleasure pass through life, but the scorner perishes.

    23. Edward Pyot (d. 1670), religious reformer; Quakers (Society of Friends), English sect founded
in the seventeenth century known for its pacifism and belief in an inner spiritual voice.
    24. Vyāsa, fifth century B.C. Indian sage and compiler of the *Mahābhārata*, a collection of leg-
endary and didactic Indian poetry; Emanuel Swedenborg (1688–1772), Swedish scientist, theologian,
and mystic.
    25. Blaise Pascal (1623–62), French scientist, philosopher, and mathematician; François de Salignac
de La Mothe-Fénelon (1651–1715), French prelate and author of an early utopian novel; Jeanne-Marie
de La Motte Guyon, known as Mme Guyon du Chesnoy (1648–1717), French mystic identified with
quietism.
    26. Attributed to a "Mr Green of New York, or his friend" by Emerson (*JMN*, 16:80).

Foreigners, to be sure! I had foreigners enough in my own town, streets full of people who used the same nouns, and verbs, and pronunciation that I do, but Turkish or Feejee in their ideas.

You will see the results of inquiry into the moral nature: it is the same fact existing as sentiment and as will in the mind, which works in nature as irresistible law, exerting influence in nations, intelligent beings, or down in the kingdoms of brute or of chemical nature. The doctrine of inspiration is the presence of the deity thus to the individual; the only key to the existence of nature is here. Bereaved of it, Nature is Chaos. And it remains the consolation, the commandment, the health, the power, and the beatitude of men.

The world was made for benefit. Why is it not just? It was made for melioration. Why does it advance in spiral line? Christianity came to save it. Is the world saved? The progress of the civilization inevitably confirms right. Why does tyranny exist?

The geologic world is chronicled by the growing ripeness of the strata from lower to higher, as it becomes the abode of more highly organized plants and animals. The civil history of men might be traced by the successive meliorations as marked in higher moral generalizations. Virtue, meaning physical courage, then chastity and temperance, then justice and love, the proclamation of years of jubilee reprieves, the bargains of kings with peoples of certain rights to certain classes,— then, of rights to masses,—toleration being vouchsafed. At last came the day when, as the historians rightly tell, the nerves of the world were electrified by the proclamation that all men are born free and equal, and unprepared France was intoxicated with a thought too sublime for its practice.

Let us enjoy the recollection, and yet it is not creditable to us, it is not creditable to mothers who bore us, that after this world was thrilled by this divine word made flesh, a department of this government, speaking for the people of America, should be permitted to say, "The black man has no rights which the white man is required to respect."[27] I never fear the effect of any blasphemy on any but the blasphemer, but the acknowledgement of a court thus disqualified does not honor the moral perceptions of the people.

We are always forbidden any satisfaction in the history of masses. The history of virtue is the history of the private soul. It, only, can be just, wise, obeying, lowly, pure, brave. Nature has made up her mind on one point,—that what can't defend itself, shall not be defended.

We are not safe with our fatal reliance on laws and machinery. Not until the hero has come to the sticking point and says to himself: I will not be taken alive; I am the government for me. Once for all, expect no complicity by speech or by silence,

27. Quoted from the decision made by Chief Justice Roger Brooke Taney (1777–1864) in the Dred Scott case of 1857, which made slavery legal in all territories and essentially stripped blacks of their legal rights in fugitive slave cases.

by act, or by forbearance to act, from me. But I am for freedom: first my own, and then yours, and everybody's the same, on Kant's principle, "the intelligent being is its own proper end, and can never become a simple means for the end of another."[28]

See the events of these very days: how love,—this deep feeling that the wrongs of the poorest fellowmen were his wrongs, and that he owed his life not to the great, and rich, and powerful, but to those who had none to succor them, has lifted an obscure Connecticut farmer into the love and admiration of men, has educated him to great wisdom, has shown him the secrets of religious life, and made all other men appear his inferiors.[29] It would be hard to find in history an example of a greatness so suddenly made known to all good men.

> 'And may not we with sorrow say
> A few strong instincts and a few plain rules
> Among the herdmen of the hills have wrought
> More for mankind in this unhappy day
> Than all the pride of intellect and thought.'

'Tis sad, that, as people rise in social scale, they think more of each other's opinion than of their own. And 'tis almost hopeless to find one who does not measure his business and daily performance from their supposed estimate. And yet his own is the only standard.

Down in the pits of hunger and want, life has a new dignity from this doing the best, instead of the seemly. The sailor on the topmast in a storm, the hunter amidst the northern snowdrifts, the woodman in the depth of savage forests cannot stop to think how he looks, or what London or Paris would say, and, therefore, his garb and behaviour have a certain dignity like the works of nature around him. He would as soon concern himself with what the crows and muskrats think of him.

A righteous edict of the Government works when we sleep, when the Army goes into winter-quarters, when generals are treacherous or imbecile; works at home among the citizens, among the women, among the troops;—works down South among the planters, in the negro cabins, works over sea among candid, virtuous people discussing America in their sitting-rooms; comes thence, in a tone ever growing firmer, up into Cabinets, and compels Parliaments and Privy Councils to hear and obey.

Pose that as a principle,—that what is immoral is inhuman. The very fame which follows the greatest artist withers before one defect in his moral greatness.

What anthropomorphists we are in this, that we cannot let moral distinctions be, but must mould them into human shape. *"Mere morality"* means,—not put

---

28. Immanuel Kant (1724–1804), German philosopher.

29. This is Amos Bronson Alcott (1799–1888), American Transcendentalist, teacher, and writer and Emerson's longtime friend and Concord neighbor.

into a personal master of morals. Mere morality. Religion, some years ago, was defined in Boston to be, whatever Doctor Channing held.[30] Elsewhere, it had been what Jonathan Edwards held; or Bishop Butler; or Jeremy Taylor; or Bossuet; or John Calvin.[31]

The religious sentiment is a domesticating sentiment. I knew a person who came into a family of strangers, and presently remarked, 'Tis strange, but you are so honest, that I feel more at home than among my own relations. A traveller enters a foreign church, and reads on the walls, or hears from the priest a devout sentiment, and is a foreigner no longer. A spiritual woman once said to me, "Some persons use my language, but are foreign to me; and others, who use a style of speaking strange to me, are very near me."

We are to know that we are never without a pilot. When we know not how to steer, and dare not hoist a sail, we can drift. The current knows the way, though we do not. When the stars and sun appear, when we have conversed with other navigators who know the coast, we may begin to put out an oar, and trim a sail. The ship of heaven guides itself, and will not accept a wooden rudder.

Everything connected with our personality fails. Nature never spares the individual. We are always baulked of a complete success. No prosperity is promised to that. We have our indemnity only in the sure success of that to which we belong. *That, that* is immortal, and we only through that.

One polarity is impressed on the Universe and on its particles. As the whole has its law, so the individual has his genius. Obedience to the genius, (to speak a little scholastically) is the particular of faith; perception that the tendency of the whole is to the benefit of the individual, is the universal of faith.

We go to famous books for our examples of character, just as we send to France and Italy for oaks and firs, which grow as well in our own door yards and cow pastures. Life is always rich; and spontaneous graces and forces elevate it in every domestic circle, which are overlooked, whilst we are reading something less excellent in old authors. I think, as I go through the streets, each one of these innumerable houses has its own calendar of saints, its unpublished anecdotes of courage and patience, of wit and cheerfulness—and why not of enthusiasm and the heights of piety? For the best I know were in the most private corners.

Everything draws to its kind, and frivolous people will not hear of noble traits: but let any good example of secret virtue come accidentally to air, like Florence

30. William Ellery Channing (1780–1842), American clergyman, known as the "apostle of Unitarianism," widely involved in the social and philanthropic issues of his time.

31. Jonathan Edwards (1703–58), American Congregational clergyman and theological writer; Joseph Butler (1692–1752), English theologian, bishop of Bristol and of Durham; Jeremy Taylor (1613–67), English bishop and theologian; Jacques-Bénigne Bossuet (1627–1704), French historian and theologian who attacked quietism and obtained a condemnation of Fénelon; John Calvin (originally Jean Cauvin) (1509–64), French Protestant reformer and theologian.

Nightingale, and we presently hear of parallels in every direction.[32] From the obscurity and casualty of those whom I know, I infer the obscurity and casualty of the like balm, and consolation, and immortality in a thousand homes which I do not know, all round the world. Let it lie safe in the shade there, from the compliments and praise of foolish society: It is safer so. All it seems to demand, is, that we know it, when we see it. This is no mean reward. If an intelligent and generous witness, passing by, sees our plight, and so much as exchanges a searching glance of sympathy,—"Well done, brave heart!"—it is better than the thunder of theatres, and the world full of foolish newspapers, which only echo each other.

32. Florence Nightingale, known as the Lady with the Lamp (1820–1910), English nurse and health reformer.

Reform

(1860)

Emerson delivered this lecture, which was originally untitled, only once: on 4 November 1860 before the Twenty-eighth Congregational Society in Boston. Reform, broadly construed, was a lifelong concern of Emerson, as his early lectures "Reforms" (1840) and "Man the Reformer" (1841) show. (For "Reforms" see *Early Lectures*, 3:256–70; for "Man the Reformer" see *Dial* 1 [April 1841]: 523–28.) In "Reform" Emerson is primarily interested in advocating a theory of reform, but he was also very concerned with reform in immediate and practical ways, as his "Address to the Citizens of Concord on the Fugitive Slave Law" (1851) and "Address at the Woman's Rights Convention" (1855), in this volume, admirably demonstrate.

Look at the plea which is continually recurring. A serious man comes to you to urge his social project.— 'And what *is* your project?' He explains, that there should be a farm of a hundred acres in excellent condition with good buildings, good orchard and grounds, which admit of being laid out with great beauty, and this should be purchased and given to them, in the first place.

I reply, You ask too much. This is not solving the problem; there are hundreds of innocent young persons, whom, if you will thus establish, and endow, and protect, will find it no hard matter to keep their innocency. And to see their tranquil household, after all this has been done for them, will in no wise instruct or strengthen me. But he will instruct and strengthen me, who, there where he is, unaided, in the midst of poverty, toil, and traffic, extricates himself from the corruptions of the same and builds on his land a house of peace and benefit, good customs, and free thoughts.

But, replies the reformer, how is this to be done, how can I do it who have a wife and family to maintain?

I answer, that he is not the person to do it, or he would not ask the question. When he that shall come is born, he will not only see the thing to be done, but invent the life, invent the ways and means of doing it. The way you would show me, does not commend itself to me as the way of greatness.[1]

Reform is a vital function. It is not an old impulse by which we move, like a stone thrown into the air, but by an incessant impulse like that of gravitation. We are not potted and buried in our bodies, but every body is newly created from day to day, and every moment. Just as much life, so much is the power it exerts,—a strong race, a victorious civilization. What we call preservation of the body is recreation. There is no death in nature, but only passing of life from this to that: decomposition is recomposition; and cholera and palsy are the conversion of old organization into buds and embryos of new.—

To the poet, the world is virgin soil, all new. All is practicable. The men are ready for virtue. It is always time to do right. He is a recommencer and affirms. Reformers are our benefactors, our practical poets, hindering us of absurdity, and self-stultification. The sensible conservative likes the reformers, though they may not know it. If I were not Alexander, I would be Diogenes.[2]

There are more reformers than are down on the list of the Total Abstinence, or Non-Resistance, or Non-Juring, or Antislavery Society.[3] Satire itself has taken this direction, and Dickens has described the institution which aims how not to do it.[4] *Punch* is every week enlisting the boys and the drawing rooms by their love of wit on the side of humanity; and native inspirations of commonsense alike in kitchens, and farms, and palaces, are ever and anon leading the most unlooked for allies to your side.[5] 'Tis said that Leo X was not less a promoter of the Reformation than Luther;—Leo X, who ridiculed in secret the fanaticism of the Church, and whose artists, Michel Angelo, and Raphael, and the poets, were protesting in colors and in *terza rima* against the priests.[6]

---

1. The "reformer" in the exchange reported in this and the preceding three paragraphs is Amos Bronson Alcott (1799–1888), American Transcendentalist, teacher, and writer and Emerson's longtime friend and Concord neighbor (*JMN*, 8:310–11).

2. Alexander the Great (356–323 B.C.), ruled as Alexander III of Macedonia (336–323), conqueror of the known civilized world; Diogenes (ca. 412–323 B.C.), Greek Cynic philosopher, advocated voluntary poverty and self-sufficiency, subject of the legend that he once went through the streets with a lantern, seeking an honest man.

3. The Total Abstinence Society usually avoided alcoholic beverages, the Non-Resistance Society preached passive resistance to authority, and the Non-Juring Society refused to swear allegiances (based on the English group that refused to swear fealty to William and Mary and their successors).

4. Charles Dickens (1812–70), popular English novelist.

5. *Punch*, the illustrated London satirical weekly, was started in 1841.

6. Giovanni de' Medici (1475–1521) became Pope Leo X (1513–21), a scholar and patron of all forms of art; Martin Luther (1483–1546), German religious reformer, founder of Protestantism during the Reformation; Michelangelo (1475–1564), Italian painter, sculptor, and poet; Raphael (1483–1520), Italian painter whose works adorn the Vatican; terza rima is a verse form, usually *aba, bcb, cdc.*

Shakspeare was of us, Milton was for us,
Burns, Shelley, were with us; they watch from their graves.[7]

Do not detach the consideration of diet. Temperance, which is only the sign of intrinsic virtue, is graceful as the bloom on the cheek that betokens health; but temperance that is nothing but temperance, is phlegm or conceit. Temperance that knows itself, is not temperance,—when it peaks and pines, and knows all it renounces.

But in the connexion of this asceticism with the highest prudence,—its connexion with that health and beauty which is now rather the exception than the rule of human nature, and, above all, with that higher instinctive life which will give us to know the properties of plants, and of animals, and the laws of nature, by our coincidence and sympathy with these,—which is now the dream of poets, then, as a key to knowledge, and for its own elegance, it is worth the practice of every pure and refined person. Cannot this blood, which in all men rolls with such a burden of disease, roll pure? Are there not limits and abstinences which will secure a clearer head, and an unclouded afternoon?

The diet of men in these countries is not agreeable to the imagination. Other creatures eat without shame. We paint the bird pecking at fruit, the browsing ox, the lion leaping on his prey: but no painter ever ventured to draw a man eating. The subject is burlesque. Partly the difference seems to consist in the presence or absence of the world at the feast. The caterpillar, robin, and squirrel, mix the sun and blue sky with their diet. We hide our bread in cellars, in caves, and in houses, and there it is sodden and eaten. It matters not how plain is the fare, which is spiced by the sun and moon. This gives dignity to the hunter and the Indian. If you have eaten your bread on the top of a mountain, or drunk water,—if you camp out with lumbermen, or travellers on the prairie,—did not the sky and the wilderness give your food a certain mundane savor and comeliness? Our sequestration from nature, and our artificial elaboration of food from so many climates, and mills, and stills, and laborers, add to the evil, by making food an end, and not a means, and the dinner the event of the day.

What we have to say of the Reforms mainly, is, that they are superficial, and no wise entitled to that serious approbation we give them. We should not think of praising very highly one who, in India, abstained from throwing children into the Ganges, or committing suicide under the idol's car. Or, in Typee, one who abstained from eating the body of his enemy; or, those who, among the offscouring of mankind, abstain from beastly vices.[8] Yet these evils, against which with such

7. "The Lost Leader" (1845), ll. 13–14, by Robert Browning (1812–89), English poet; John Milton (1608–74), English poet and political writer, best known for his poem *Paradise Lost* (published in 1667 in ten books); Robert Burns (1759–96), Scotland's most famous poet; Percy Bysshe Shelley (1792–1822), English romantic poet.

8. *Typee: A Peep at Polynesian Life* (1846) by Herman Melville (1819–91), American writer.

laudation, our popular reforms are aimed, are just so gross and savage, and it implies no discernment to see their criminality.

But the whole society lies in darkness. The very emphasis laid on these crimes shows how drowsy and atheistic men are, and a few more or less crimes don't signify in a society in which faith does not exist. The existence of the spiritual world is not known: the words are repeated, but the sight, and hearing, and handling of it are not used by the mind. The believed realities are the senses and their pleasures—money, favor, health, and material power, whether political or commercial—and other goods are reckoned delusions. And what is called philosophy, and what is called genius, does not report of any more interior world. Genius itself is valued only for its popularity.

The realities which are the basis of all we see and hear, the spiritual facts and powers which made and make this world of eye and ear, are ignored by America and by Europe; they are the lonely vision of some sad, solitary man or woman, in the woods or in a chamber, who is heard with curiosity and pleasure as long as he tells his vision as a legend to amuse, but when he insists that duty and sanity are in it, the doors of rich and poor are closed to him.

Honor among thieves, let there be truth among skeptics. Are any or all the institutions so valuable as to be lied for? Learn to esteem all things symptomatic, no more. Believe in the great and unweariable power of Destiny.

But faith,—has it not its victories also? Behold these sacred persons, repulsive perhaps to you, but undeniably born of the old simple blood, to whom rectitude is native; see them here, white silver amid the bronze population; one, two, three, four, five, six, and I know not how many more, conspicuous as fire in the night. Each of them can do some deed of the impossible. Do you say our Republic can never be? But let citizens be born for it, and it can.

The moment in which a man sees that the evil institution in which he has always lived has no root in the world; sees it detach itself in his mind from society, and yet society remains unharmed; sees that he can do without it;—that moment its doom is sealed: from that moment it begins to die; and, however long the struggle, it must end. When two men talk together, in the moment when he is not convinced, in that moment he begins to convince.

'Tis of small importance your activity more or less in these directions, by what arguments, by what methods, or the degree of ability or of success. That shall be as your condition, your character, and your genius are. But what is imperative, is, that you be on the right side, on the side of man, and the Divine justice, of largest liberty, of general humanity, not with the vulgar cavilling at the Reformers, but man-like to say, Here is the part for youth, for innocence, for genius, and for manhood to stand.

'Tis wonderful how rare is an open and a candid soul. In the educated class, hardly to be found. We are timorous and attached to routine. We educate our boys and girls, drill every faculty, appeal to every sensibility in them—to their love of truth, of beauty, of goodness; they shall be geometers, poets, painters, pianists, harpists, botanists, zoologists, geologists, astronomers—nothing comes amiss. But when this training has been carried far, do we show the same courage logically to the end? When the boy comes to think, as a young man, how he shall employ his time, and will be a naturalist, chemist, artist, or philosopher, and shows no disposition to go into trade or the mechanic arts, or into either of the four or five liberal professions,—law, medicine, divinity, civil engineering, nor so much as to be sailor or soldier,—the parents grow nervous, and on his talk of going as an explorer to the Yellowstone River, or of going to live in some untried way in the prairie, or the mountains,—they look grave, and think he will outgrow these whimsies soon, and are only relieved, at last, when want of encouragement from all, and pointed resistance from the nearest, drive him to postpone his ambition for the present, and to disappoint all his and their once grand hopes of his future, by sliding into one or other of the old ruts, which leave nothing to be hoped from him but a reputable drudge, like all those about him.

Abuse is a proof you are felt. If they praise you, you will work no revolution. It does not signify so much about the practice, if the theory is right. I am struck with nothing more than the disproportionate power of certain hours: with the fact that years cannot compare with the force of moments. Newton's discovery of gravity—Kepler's laws—Adam Smith's free trade.[9] Christianity was once a schism and the opinion of a private person. A time of thought arrives, that is the Judgment Day of months and years; a moment which counts stock; sums up long accounts; casts the balance; reverses old opinions; detects some half-forgotten, lurking experience,—drags it into day, sets it on the Judgment-seat, and tries all the pompous usages, properties, and people; finds them false and rotten; finds that valor, commonsense, and happiness are not in the things we prize, but in quite other things, of which we had little thought. This dangerous little minute revolutionizes a long life of plausibilities; and these dangerous moments cannot be guarded against. 'Tis like the secret fire which gave us a hint of its presence, the other day, under our cities, under our Alleganies, and shook New England and Canada, for fifteen seconds, gently enough, but in a manner to show that the weight of the continent of America could not keep it down, and, perhaps, another time, it would rock the overlying land half a minute longer, and not quite so gently, and let the fire out, or let the sea in.[10]

Church and state are in danger, and you must set your shoulders to uphold these masses, now in your tender youth, when all the muses and demigods are sporting in the fields, and long 'ere yet you have measured what you call church

9. Sir Isaac Newton (1642–1727), English natural philosopher and mathematician; Johannes Kepler (1571–1630), German mathematician and astronomer; Adam Smith (1723–90), Scottish political economist and moral philosopher.

10. An earthquake had struck Charleston, South Carolina, on 19 January 1860.

and state, by the golden Scale of Justice. God forgive this rapid conservatism! His world, you think, needs many a patch and cleet to make it hold together. 'Tis pity, when church and state ask the sacrifice of a fine genius. Could they not manage to do with less costly materials? He is a church and a state himself, and should not desert the priesthood of ideas. Nature is rich, but to a defender of the establishment, to a fixture, to one who has halted and sat down, she gives nothing; only to the marchers, only to the actors, only to the innovators. Which class interests us? The forward class have this good, that everything they do and say, their mere presence, has great significance; gives rise to comic and picturesque situations; suggests thoughts; and is worthy of record by historian, whilst the life and actions of the wittiest defender of the establishment are tame, and have nothing generative. For the conservative always rests on a fact, whilst the reformer always rests on a thought.

Those who defend the establishment are always less than it. Those who speak from a thought must always be greater than any actual fact. I see behind the conservative no mighty matter. Through his eyes sparkles nothing better than the small and well-known fact of that good order and convenience of living we know. But through the eyes of the theorist, stares at me a formidable, gigantic spirit, who will not down, if I bid him, who has much more to say than he has yet told, and who can do great things with the same facility as little.

Is it for us who, at the present day, find ourselves not expressed in the science, politics, and religion of our fathers, to be ashamed of that fact? If we have thoughts of deeper origin, hopes of bolder living, shall we deny them? The inevitableness of the new spirit is the grand fact, and *that* no man lays to heart, or sees how the hope and palladium of mankind is there. But one blushes, and timidly insinuates palliating circumstances for a new thought, and one ridicules the foible or absurdity of some of its advocates. But on comes the God, to confirm and to destroy; to work through us, if we be willing, to crush us, if we resist.

The hater of property and government takes care to have his warranty-deed recorded; and the book written against fame and learning has the author's name on the title-page.

'Tis true that some men only feel themselves in antagonism, are critics and contradictors. Others love excitement, and the threat of revolution. 'Tis as good as going to a theatre. 'Tis possible, men may have griefs and grudges to feed. And, on the whole, the Reformer is to be tried at last by the question, Has he grown? Does he interest me still? Is he become somewhat which can't be disposed of, but is crescent propagandist and threatens and will overpower the institutions, repeal the laws, and write the new?

It is not Reform: It is form, and substance. It is primary truth, the clearing away all the delusions, so that you live to honor, justice, and use; everything perishes, but these abide. Be an intellectual power, and, seeing yourself, make others see. You live a spirit among spirits. The intellectual and heavenly world is all around you, whilst your body is among bodies, to give to these moments of perception a controlling influence over the habits. The intellectual world should meet us everywhere, and the presence of a true man will bring Hope and Gladness where he goes, and the assurance of the majestic laws that uphold the universe.

Then, 'tis wonderful how much anger sharpens our wit. We complain of the dulness of the conservative class. But they show unexpected acuteness in their objections to the Reformer.

Every man is entitled to the best interpretation that can be put on his action. Let us not lower ourselves by suspecting him. They have the same regard for comfort and seemliness as you, and it is out of probity, not out of treachery, that they have resisted the custom. 'Tis because they have a greater regard to truth than to their day's wages, that they speak so downright. Are any or all the institutions so valuable as to be lied for? Would you have them make believe, think, and feel a respect for customs and traditions which have lost them respect?

Well, entertain them all. Why should you not? You need not go into them farther than your genius will. Don't exchange the yoke of abuse for the yoke of Reform; No, but only see their value: Give your voice on the right side.

Applaud rightly. Tell the civilization of it. See the advantage of this enlightened criticism on the dead ages, the deaf and dumb ages; the stealing and kidnapping ages; the ages when half mankind stood saddled and bridled for the few to ride in boots and spurs.

Now, see the eternal advantage of the reformer. Honor his manliness. He stands at his peril for a truth. He stands for something more, and what if now society don't like the Reformer? Property don't—Inertia don't—Comfort don't—Taste don't like him. And they have some reason not to. See what an incendiary is pulling my house about my ears.

Abolitionists are not better men for their zeal. They have neither abolished slavery in Carolina, nor in me. If they cannot break one fetter of mine, I cannot hope they will of any negro. I flee from bitter, sterile people to the unpretentious whom they disparage. I see them to be logically right, but to great human purposes insolvent, like the rest. Fate rides them all.

To be sure, the reformer's a poor creature, as bad as you or I:—egotist, tyrant, compounding for some sin here, because he has been so brave and generous there. What of that? What have you to do with his nonsense? only with his sense. He is not to have any ray of light, any pulse of goodness, that I do not make my own. See, too, that he is nobody. 'Tis the greatness behind that I see through his flimsy self. See the difference between Conserver and Reformer.

Many of these reforms, like that of temperance, only address the private conscience; but many of them, like those touching trade, and property, and political law, put the reformer into a war-like attitude, and require courage of a high degree. Then, the questions of ecclesiastical and of civil right, of Man's Rights, and Woman's Rights, of the consent to wrongs, of the majority and recognising the state by voting; the tenet of non-resistance and universal peace; the resistance to slavery; the political questions of tariff and trade and of banking; of the right of the people to instruct their representative; of the treatment of Indians, of the Boundary Wars, of the Congress of Nations, are all pregnant with ethical conclusions.

What spark of honest meaning as yet undiscovered sleeps in Mormonism—in the ecclesiastical reforms of which the last, imposing by numbers, is the organization of the so called Spiritualists; in the relation of labor to capital as presented by Owen and Fourier; in the project of universal education, the universal free and secret suffrage, the medical reforms of Hahnemann and Priessnitz, and the gymnasium?[11]

Let us entertain these projects. The part of man is to advance, to stand always for the Better, not himself, his property, his grandmother's spoons, his corner lot, and shop-till, and the petty tricks that he and his have done over and over again, till the patience of Nature is exhausted; but to stand for his neighbors, and mankind; for the making others as good as he is; for largest liberty; for enriching, enlightening, and enkindling others, and making life great and happy to nations.

Oppression is felt, when it is not seen. The public interest demands the abatement of all these injuries which are breeding bad blood long before the injured know who it is that injures them. Wherever there is a wrong, the response is pain. The rowdy eyes that glare on you from the mob say plainly, that they feel that you are doing them to death; you have got the chain somehow round their limbs, and, though they know not how, war to the knife is between us and you. Your six percent is as deadly a weapon as the gun and tomahawk. And the result is the accumulation of abuses, of wrongs, to classes by classes; of tyranny, jealousy, fraud, and pampered sense, and smothered reason, which make the evil of life.

The whole difference between men is whether the foot is advancing or receding. Men interest us only as long as they advance. Man is in transition; that is the attitude of power. Wisdom consists in keeping the soul liquid, or resisting the tendency to too rapid petrifaction. The habit of saliency, of not pausing, but going on, is a sort of importation and domestication of the Divine Effort into a man.

New is made out of old, and the publication of the Bible was the burning of old bibles, which, in their turn, had burned the bibles before them.

But 'tis the order of Nature that each age shall make its own world, with little

---

11. Robert Owen (1771–1858), Welsh social reformer and philanthropist; François-Marie-Charles Fourier (1772–1837), French social thinker whose doctrines guided the later period of the Brook Farm community, a utopian venture at West Roxbury, Massachusetts (1841–47); Christian Friedrich Samuel Hahnemann (1755–1843), German physician and founder of homeopathy; Vincenz Priessnitz (1799–1851), Silesian farmer and founder of hydrotherapy, the system of treating ailments with cold water; a gymnasium is a European secondary school that prepares students for university.

assistance from its fathers. The old man dies, with accumulated wisdom and virtue. His son, a passionate, ignorant person, quite without his father's genius or rectitude, lives in his house. And so the world is at every moment really in the hands of a majority of rash young barbarians. One of our illusions is the tenacious belief that we know more than the earlier generations. Sometimes the illusion works the other way, and we have an immense respect for our fathers and think their institutions sacred. But whenever we speak of knowledge, we think we stand on their shoulders and see further.

Nature's endurance is by perpetual creation. She does not make two leaves alike. She does not hoard her old leaves, and hang them on the boughs again, but makes new; nor prolong her old animals into immortality, but supplies their decays by generation. Incessant flux, as of a river, as of fire, as of time, marks all her works. Life is a perpetual consumption of this fuel of matter. The eye of science sees everything evaporating, exhaling, radiating off into space, like a flame; the most solid substance—the rock and mountain—like dewdrops and petals of the flower. Always new individuals, nor does the new individual repeat the old one, but ever with a difference. Nor does the new race repeat the fossil race, but always with new adaptation to the now state of the world. The men themselves were made up of elder men; the air we breathe passed yesterday out of organized forms of men and plants, and is now entering already again into new plants and animals.

The thinking of the mind is a perpetual arrival at new generalizations which open into others and larger, which supersede them. Every truth leads in a new truth by the hand. And every man may well die when his son can supply his place.

As the bird alights on the bough, then plunges into the air again, so the thoughts of God pause but for a moment in any form: Piracy meliorates into commerce. Slavery, which is robbing men in your yard, is found as bad economy as robbing on the highway, and passes into honest payment of wages. Monopoly surrenders to equal rights. Despotism, to representative government. Privilege, patronage, and nepotism, to the highest bidder. Bounties, to emulation. Embargo and prohibition, to free trade. Arbitriment of war, to International Congress. Duel, to course of law. Paper money, to specie basis. Quackery and conjuring, to science. Tattoo and painting, to natural beauty. Gluttony and drunkenness, on one side, and abstinence, on the other, to Temperance. Drudgery, to educated labor. Gambling, to healthy accumulation of small savings. Hierarchy and the rack, into free discussion. Censorship, into free press.

Yes, incessant change and organic action, but with different velocities. We have a strange society of faculties held together in this mortal body, and with great difference of high and low. All must have motion, but at such different rates of speed. Some of them need sleep, which is movement also, but very slow. Then, there is great difference of rank, and of opinion, among these. Some of them wish what is not wholesome for the rest, and if they could be gratified, would quickly decompose and explode the machine.

You know the story of the Belly and the Members.[12] Well, what happens in the body and soul of one man, happens at large in the great society of men. They do what is easy; they work for the senses, they work for parts, against the interest of the whole; they work for pleasure, they work for the body, and not for the mind. Then, every opinion and system gathers property about it. The wrong done is for the sake of property: The property is always timorous and abhors new ideas.

But nature is no democrat, but an inexorable enforcer of her perfect gradation. The law of our members, she makes forever subject to the law in our mind. And the effort that lasts as long as life in every healthy soul, is, to fight down this rebel pretension of the passions to rule the reason, and to sit on the throne of this world. The circulation of the waters, the circulation of sap, the circulation of the blood, the immortality of an animal species through the death of all the individuals, the balance and period of planetary motion—these are works of art, quick and eternal.

Each man is a new power in nature; has an aptitude which none else has; is a new method, and distributes things anew. If he could attain full size, he would take up first or last, atom by atom, all the world into a new form.

The communities will never have men in them, but only halves and quarters. They require a sacrifice of what cannot be sacrificed without detriment. The community must always be ideal,—the individual unbound. "A stubborn retention of customs is a turbulent thing, not less than the introduction of new," said Bacon.[13]

12. According to Aesop, a legendary Greek fabulist of the sixth century B.C., the Members of the Body rebelled against the Belly because they felt they were working while the lazy Belly did nothing. The Members carried out their plan to refuse their assistance to the Belly. The whole Body quickly became debilitated, and the Members repented of their folly too late.

13. Francis Bacon (1561–1626), English essayist, statesman, and philosopher.

Essential Principles of Religion

(1862)

Emerson delivered "Essential Principles of Religion" only once, on 16 March 1862 before the Twenty-eighth Congregational Society in Boston. Parts of this lecture were used in "Character," published by Emerson in the *North American Review* 102 (April 1866): 356–73, and collected by Emerson's literary executor, James Elliot Cabot, in *Lectures and Biographical Sketches* in 1884 (*W*, 10:89–122) and in "The Sovereignty of Ethics," assembled by Cabot for publication in the *North American Review* 126 (May–June 1878): 404–20. It was also included in *Lectures and Biographical Sketches* (*W*, 10:181–214).

The chemist counts sixty-six elements that make up all the vast variety of things solid, liquid, and gaseous. But the philosophy of chemistry finds these too many, and every new genius that appears in that science is on the stretch to make them less, to decompose these reputed elements and find five, or four, or three, or two. The great physicists, Newton, Boscovich, Davy, and Faraday, have signified their belief, that our analysis will reach at last a sublime simplicity, and find two elements, as oxygen and hydrogen; or one element, hydrogen, with two polarities, at the base of things,—the one stuff out of which the million textures of nature are woven.[1] This perpetual craving to simplicity is a structural instinct of the mind, and is hinted by every experience.

'Tis one of our first illusions, this belief in multitude, and it takes a long experience to disabuse us. We believe we see countless hosts of stars in the midnight firmament, but when counted, one by one, we do not make ten hundred. We talk of the multiplicity of our affairs, of the loss of acquaintances, of volumes of letters, of libraries of books, but we spend the most of our life in the company of a few persons; a principle of order reduces our affairs to an easy routine. We write more letters than we need and could easily write more. And so with all life; there is much

---

1. Sir Isaac Newton (1642–1727), English natural philosopher and mathematician; Ruggiero Giuseppe Boscovich (originally Rudjer Josip Bošković) (1711–87), Croatian mathematician and physicist active in Italy; Sir Humphry Davy (1778–1829), English chemist who advanced an electrical theory of chemical affinity; Michael Faraday (1791–1867), English chemist and physicist, known for his experiments with electromagnetism.

noise, confusion, and chatter, but the net result of each day is a quite moderate amount.

We talk of the variety of influences, of the variety of characters, of the conflict of principles, of the education of all the virtues, and life looks large, duty manifold, the future confused. Is it that there is some conspiracy to disconcert and embarrass us, and hide the simplicity of life? For really, as we grow older, we are struck with the steady return of a few principles. We are always finding new applications of the maxims and proverbs of the nursery: One old Bible is still enough to enunciate all the commandments for the most complex life in this giddy and arrogant century. Nay, a very small part of the book—a few chosen pages, a few golden rules—suffice for the guidance and comfort of the most advanced and advancing genius.

The Stoic said, *Ne te quae siveris extra. Seek nothing outside of yourself.*[2] Christianity, Blessed are the poor and lowly; Hunger and thirst after righteousness. The lapse of ages makes little difference. The man in Boston feels the same motive and spiritual government pressing on him today, as did the man in Egyptian Memphis, thirty-four centuries before Christ.

The Hindoo said, You are enveloped in the deceptions of matter. You call "*me*" that which is not yourself, and you call "*mine*" that which is flowing away from you. These illusions are the two branches of the tree of ignorance.

The Quakers or Friends in the seventeenth century gave their memorable testimony to the doctrine of universal and perpetual inspiration, to the worthlessness of forms. The world was not wound up and left to go by itself, but was a new creation, and George Fox was not afraid to say, that he saw by the same light as prophet and apostle, and was made a judge, whether that which purported to come from God really came from him.[3]

Swedenborg said, The Lord floweth into all spirits and natures, and so they live.[4] The soul makes its own place and associates with such companions as fit its state; the good with good, the bad with Satans, surrounds itself with such things as it loves and everywhere makes a heaven for itself. And that a man's life is original, after his nature, and that what he does is constitutional to him. There is no such waste in the history of men, as the misapplication of genius, and it is very late in life, often too late, that a man finds he has been out of his proper work all this time.

A man self-poised, and who will not be a mockingbird, is a benefactor. All that he does is memorable, and has its own flavor. His kindness is felt as a costly compliment, because it is not facility, but a choice. We are very clumsy about giving, and unless a fine sentiment enters into the act, it is much better omitted.

2. Quoted from *Satires* 1.7 by Aulus Persius Flaccus (34–62), Roman satirist (*JMN*, 15:7).

3. Quakers (Society of Friends), English sect founded in the seventeenth century known for its pacifism and belief in an inner spiritual voice; founder George Fox (1624–91) preached the superiority of God-given inspiration, or inward light, over the authority of Scripture.

4. Emanuel Swedenborg (1688–1772), Swedish scientist, theologian, and mystic.

A young friend of mine came one day to my house, some fifteen years ago, and pleased himself with putting up on my barn a blue bird's box, and there it is still, with, every summer, a melodious family in it, adorning the place, and singing his praise.[5] There's a gift for you, which cost the giver no money, but nothing he could have bought would be so good.

When I bought a house in the country, it was on low land, under a hill: the wind swept rather freely over us in winter, and the sand of the hillside gave us a burning reflection of the sun in summer. Ten miles off from me lives a friend, who sometimes passed my house, and one day sent me a load of young shade trees, directing his man to plant them. I was surprised, and took the hint, and followed up his planting with my own, and have been happy in the shade and shelter of my pines for many years.

As with gifts, so with manners whose best charm is their originality: they cannot be dissevered from the person. So with the rule of dress: it is not this stuff, or that stuff, or pattern, but its fitness to you, and the less it obtrudes, or makes us think of it instead of you, the better. Herbert's rule is,

"This with my discretion shall be brave."[6]

The mother of Taliessin, wishing to secure the gift of foresight for her son, and being herself skilled in magic arts, having prepared a pottage of virtuous herbs which were to boil for a whole moon, employed a herdsman to keep the fire supplied with fuel and to stir the brewage.[7] But a raven on an oak branch that hung over it, dropped a twig into the cauldron, and the eyes of the herdsman were spattered with three drops from the pot, and he saw the future as today, and knew his danger from the witch who set him to watch the pot and designed to kill him when the labor is ended, and he instantly took flight, and hid in the forest.

The story admits of a good interpretation; but suppose the three drops should spatter the crowd in Washington Street at noon-day, how many passengers would go on to do the errand they were at the moment running after?

And this is my belief: that there would be for the most part an abrupt and absolute stop put to present proceedings, but that a few happy children would quietly follow the same leading as before, namely, such as were pursuing their organic employments.

And that is a primal difference between men. The question which each event and crisis puts, is, Who are you? What is dear to you? What do you stand for?

5. Identified by Emerson as John Thoreau Jr., brother of Henry David Thoreau (1817–62), American writer (*JMN*, 15:165).

6. George Herbert (1593–1633), English metaphysical poet.

7. Taliesin, sixth-century Welsh bard. Emerson's source for this story is *The Mabinogion*, the title of the English translation of old Welsh tales made in 1838–49 by Lady Charlotte Guest (1812–95) (*JMN*, 15:155).

History is nothing but a string of biographies. It is all dated by the appearance of individuals, who came armed each with some new service, timed and offset against each other.

Each man has an aptitude, and can do easily some feat impossible to any other. Each is a new method, and distributes things anew. If he could attain full size, he would take up, first or last, all the world into a new form.

A good determination is next best to genius. Determination of blood is all one with intrinsic value. If a man is set on collecting coins, or diamonds, or Arabian horses, or an arboretum, or obtaining a particular piece of land, or a telescope, his heat makes the value. "A man is already of consequence in the world, when, it is known we can implicitly rely on him."[8] 'Tis hardly of importance what party, what aim, what interest he drives, only let it be in his bones, in his structure, and we know where to find him. We must have vitriol and mercury as well as wheat and salt.

Self-truth and self-trust cannot be excessive; and why? because this self in the high sense in which we speak, this self of self, is our door to the Supreme Reason. This is whence our intelligence comes. Man is not as the world is, but the world is as the man is.

Do you not see that the circumstance is nothing, that the man is everything? The largest army and the best appointed with all means—artillery, cavalry, riflemen—if ill-commanded, is only a richer spoil to the enemy. Its successes, if the leader does not comprehend them, are none. Suppose they have thrown their strength on an important ground. When the troops wake up the next morning, they look out on their conquest with new eyes. If their commander knows what to do with it, the feeling of victory continues—if not, they already are the timorous, apprehensive party, and must take their direction from the enemy, instead of forcing the enemy to follow theirs.

In the midst of stupendous difficulties, Napoleon was cheerful and fat, because he saw clearly what to do, and had it to do.[9] To a stout heart there is no danger. To a good head, no problem is inscrutable. To a good foot, no place is slippery. To a good sailor, every wind has something of his course in it. To good hands, nothing is impossible.

The sculptor works at his statue with a lamp in his cap. But the real illumination is more strictly his own. The light by which we see in this world comes out of the soul of the observer: Wherever any noble sentiment dwelt, it made the faces and houses around to shine.

When I talked with an ardent missionary, and pointed out to him that his creed

---

8. Attributed to Edward George Earle Lytton Bulwer-Lytton, first Baron Lytton of Knebworth (1803–73), English novelist and politician (*JMN*, 14:65, 123).

9. Quoted from *The Confidential Correspondence of Napoleon Bonaparte with his Brother Joseph, sometime King of Spain* (1856) (*JMN*, 14:49); Napoléon Bonaparte (1769–1821), born in Corsica, general and later emperor of the French as Napoléon I.

found no support in my experience, he replied, "It is not so in your experience but is so in the other world." I answer,—Other world! there is no other world. God is one and omnipresent: here or nowhere is the whole fact. All the universe over, there is but one thing,—one Creator, one mind, one right.

Now, that which men need in their moral and religious thought is a stern realism, such as they use in mathematics and in physics.

> We receive but what we give
> And in our life alone does Nature live.[10]

Not what you see imports, but with what idea.

What is a day? To a stone, it is duration; to an ox, it is hay, grass, and water; to a rational man, it is a splendor of beauty and opportunity. 'Tis heavy to an idle, empty man, for it will defeat him. If the physician apply blister or irritation to the skin, he gives a drop or pill internally as counteraction. A day is an inflammation of nature, which requires an idea or purpose in the man to counteract. The morning sun, the sparkling world, the great spectacle of human works around him, his wife, his child, his fellows, are all promises of defeat to a man empty of knowledge and of purposes. In him is the source of all the romance, the lustre and dignity which fascinated him. For truth, honor, learning, perseverance, are the Jove and Apollo who bewitched him.[11]

'Tis wonderful the enlargement which belongs to natural characters who, by happy seclusion, and by blessed poverty, and being of no social importance, have been left to draw their opinions purely from things, without any second-thought of self. They make the same impression of largeness and of health as the mountains, the sea, and the objects of nature, instead of this chattering and aimless nobody, that too much society makes: and their opinion weighs.

When I fancy that all my neighbors in the country are despairing in the drought, I meet an old farmer, and find him fresh, serene, and making slight account of the circumstance.[12] In the cars we all read the same fool bulletin, and smile or scowl all as one man; and they who come to ask your opinion, find you only one flat looking-glass more, when you ought to have stayed at home in your own mind, and to have afforded them the quite inestimable element of a new native opinion or feeling—of a new quality.

You look with pride at majorities. Your party has a great many voters. Hundreds,

---

10. "Dejection: An Ode," ll. 47–48, by Samuel Taylor Coleridge (1772–1834), English poet and philosopher and, with William Wordsworth, founder of the romantic movement; incorrectly attributed by Emerson to lines contributed by John Leyden (1775–1811), Scottish poet and Orientalist, to *Minstrelsy of the Scottish Border* (1802–3) by Sir Walter Scott (1771–1832), prolific Scottish novelist (*JMN*, 11:121).

11. Jove or Jupiter, the equivalent of the Greek Zeus, was the central deity of the Roman religious world; Apollo was the Greek god of prophecy who, as the leader of the Muses, was the patron of poetry and music.

12. The "old farmer" is Edmund Hosmer (*JMN*, 15:159).

thousands, did you say? But are you quite sure there is *one*? Let us have as much sympathy as you will, but remain yourself; as much sympathy as you will, but no surrender.

Cannot we let people be themselves, and enjoy life in their own way? You are trying to make that man another *You*. One's enough.

Talent without character is friskiness. We allow the largest charter to the man of self-poise,—what whims, what holidays, almost what sins he will, if only we are sure of his return, that he exists for one aim. Montaigne must be the *seigneur* and not a writer for booksellers.[13] Make your work excellent, and the circumstance, and the company, and the reputation are indifferent. Only make your work excellent, and you may do it for love or money, in good or in bad company, in disgraceful places; call yourself tinker, saloon-keeper, senator, president, priest, or pedlar, only make the work excellent, and all is well.

It is not enough that we have the truth; it needs also that it be made to prevail.

Everything yields. The very glaciers are viscous, or regelate into conformity; and the stiffest patriots falter and compromise; so that will cannot be depended on to save us. Parties keep the old names, but exhibit a surprising fugacity in creeping out of one snake-skin into another of equal ignominy and lubricity; and the grasshopper on the turret of Faneuil Hall gives a proper hint of the men below.[14]

A man must have his roots in nature, and draw his strength there from; his desires and needs are great: he has immense suction; pumps up the Atlantic Ocean into him,—the atmosphere,—the electricity of the world. But the efflux must be equal; and his health is as the perfectness of the influx and efflux. Any obstruction, any appropriation,—if the circulation is interrupted,—if any organ detains the flowing blood, it is disease, tumor, dropsy, and death.

"Take this flowerpot: What is this hole in the bottom for? To re-new the water. And why to renew the water? Because it gives life or death: life, when it only passes through the shell of soil, for it gives the plant the fertilizing atoms which it carries along with it, and it dissolves the food necessary to nourish the plant: death, on the contrary, when it stays in the pot, for it does not cease to corrupt, and to rot the roots, and it prevents the fresh water from penetrating them."

Everything good is the result of antagonisms, and the height of civilization is absolute self-help combined with most generous social relation. A man must have his root in nature, draw his power directly from it, as the farmer, miller, smith, shepherd, and sailor do—as do Bonaparte or Brunel.[15] He must be such, that, set

---

13. Michel Eyquem de Montaigne (1533–92), French essayist and philosopher, usually identified with skepticism.

14. Emerson is alluding to the weather vane in the shape of a grasshopper on the top of Faneuil Hall in Boston.

15. Sir Marc Isambard Brunel (1769–1849), British engineer and inventor born in France, designer of the Thames Tunnel.

him down where you will, he shall find himself at home, shall see how he can weave his useful lines here as there, and make himself necessary to society by the method of his brain. This is self-help, and this is common. But the opposite element makes him, while he draws all values to him, feel an equal necessity to radiate or communicate all, and combine largest accumulation with bounteous imparting, and raise the useful to the heroic.

These arts are superficial effects, but the credence of men it is that moulds them, and creates at will one or another surface. The Mind, as it opens, transfers very fast its choice from the circumstance to the cause, from courtesy to love, from inventions to science, from London or Washington law or public opinion, to the self-revealing idea; from all that talent executes, to the sentiment that fills the heart and dictates the future of nations. A purer moral sentiment civilizes civilization, casts backward all that we held sacred into the profane, as the flame of oil casts a shadow when shined upon by the flame of the Bude light.[16]

Be assured, men have no predilection for absurdity. So neither have they for malignity, nor selfishness, nor gluttony. There was in the old Saturnalia of Bacchus; there is, in modern India, lascivious dancing.[17] But the Catholic Church has no such pictures or rites.

As men refine, they require manners indicating the highest style of man, and as soon as they have seen this magnanimity, they exalt the saint—as Saint Louis, or Carlo Borromeo, or the Cid, or Sir Philip Sidney, or Bayard—over all the degrees in the Golden Book, and the church with its martyrs and self-sacrificers becomes adorable in their eyes.[18] Just in proportion as this healthy light comes upon the mind, it condemns the selfishness which hoards, and does not impart, and the ruder and grosser drone who does not even accumulate, but robs those who do. Hence, the sterility of thought, the want of generalization, and the curious fact, that, with a general ability that impresses all the world, there is not one general remark, not an observation on life and manners, not a valuable aphorism, that can pass into literature from all *his* writings.[19]

16. Sir Goldsworthy Gurney (1793–1875), English inventor, developed a light in which a jet of oxygen is introduced into the center of a flame fed with coal gas or oil. It was named the Bude (after the city in Cornwall where he lived) or Gurney Light.

17. Bacchus is the Roman name for Dionysus, the Greek god of nature and the divine ecstasy achieved by communing with the great life forces; wine is his most common symbol. A saturnalia is an unrestrained celebration.

18. Louis IX, known as Saint Louis (1214–70), king of France (1226–70), maintained the country against invaders; Saint Carlo Borromeo (1538–84), Italian cardinal; Rodrigo Díaz de Vivar, known as El Cid (ca. 1034–99), Spanish military leader and national hero of Castile; Sir Philip Sidney (1554–86), English soldier, politician, and poet; Pierre Terrail Bayard, Seigneur de Bayard (ca. 1473–1524), French military man and a national hero renowned for his knightly character, known as "Chevalier sans peur et sans reproche."

19. The subject of this passage is Daniel Webster (1782–1852), American statesman and orator (*Emerson's Antislavery Writings*, 77).

But not by such as he have the benefits for mankind been won, but by men of elastic, men of moral mind, who could live in the moment and take a step forward. Columbus was no backward-creeping crab, nor was Martin Luther, nor John Adams, nor Patrick Henry, nor Thomas Jefferson.[20] And the Genius or Destiny of America is no log or sluggard, but a man incessantly advancing, as the shadow of the dial's face, or of the heavenly body by whose light it is marked. The office of America is to liberate, to abolish king-craft, priest-craft, caste, monopoly, to pull down the gallows, to burn up the bloody statute book, to take in the immigrant.

The peculiarity of divine souls is shown by Parmenides, to consist in their being younger, and at the same time older both than themselves, and other things.[21] Every man has had one or two moments of extraordinary experience, has met his soul, has thought of something which he never afterwards forgot and which revised all his speech and moulded all his forms of thought. A perfect resignation was with every want and every loss. None was so ardent in loving and admiring Genius. He could feel its influence on each hour of his life. He knows he does not exist so largely as these benefactors, but his own few prized thoughts were never sacrileged by soliciting for them the sympathy of crowds. Besides, it is the purpose of the great ordainer, whom he adores, who could endow him as highly as those he admires, were it best.

"What matters it," said Marcus Antoninus, "by whom Good is done?"[22] Men must act out themselves: the good, their goodness; the bad, their evil. And for force, there must be no half-way action, no divided counsels. The good aspiration in an evil man weakens his practical power as he neither strikes nor benefits. And Swedenborg held that full expression of the real state of any nature, whether good or evil, was best. And that is the meaning of the common remark, What force for evil is gained by the abdication once for all of conscience?

I believe in the perseverance of the saints, I believe in effectual calling, I believe in the Life Everlasting. I am here to represent humanity: it is by no means necessary that I should live, but it is by all means necessary that I should act rightly. If there is danger, I must face it. I tremble; What of that? So did he who said, "my body trembles, knowing into what dangers my spirit will carry it."

How many people are there in Boston? Two hundred thousand. Then there are so many sects. I go for Churches of one. Break no springs; make no cripples. A fatal disservice does this Swedenborg, or other lawyer, who offers to do my thinking for me. Nature, when she sends a new mind into the world, fills it beforehand

20. Martin Luther (1483–1546), German religious reformer, founder of Protestantism; John Adams (1735–1826), second president of the United States (1797–1801); Patrick Henry (1736–99), American patriot and statesman; Thomas Jefferson (1743–1826), member of the committee that drafted the Declaration of Independence, third American president (1801–9), and founder of the University of Virginia.
21. Parmenides (b. ca. 515 B.C.), Greek philosopher who stressed the unity of all things.
22. Marcus Aurelius Antoninus (188–217), Roman emperor (211–17).

with a desire for that which she wishes it to know and do. The charm of life is this *variety* of genius, these contrasts and flavors by which Heaven has modulated the identity of truth. And there is a perpetual hankering among people to violate this individuality,—to warp his ways of thinking and behaviour to resemble or reflect their thinking and behavior. And I suffer whenever I see that common sight of a parent or senior imposing his opinion and way of thinking and being on a young soul to which it is totally unfit.

Can any one doubt that if the noblest saint among the Buddhists, the best Mahometan, the highest Stoic of Athens, the purest and wisest Christian,—Buddha and Menu in India, Confucius in China, Spinoza in Holland, could somewhere meet and converse,—they would all find themselves of one religion,—would find themselves denounced by their own sects, and sustained by these believed adversaries of their sects.[23] Could these converse intimately, two and two, how childish their traditions would appear! We have to say that all minds feel the mystery of this two-fold genius at the head of Creation, and they only solve it by asserting, when they have attempted the soaring to the Divine Nature, And above this is somewhat higher.

---

23. Mahometan, a follower of Islam, founded by Muhammad (also spelled Mahomet); Zeno of Citium (ca. 362–264 B.C.), Greek philosopher who around 308 B.C. founded Stoicism, a school of thought that included an emphasis on austerity and freedom from desire; Buddha (Sanskrit for "the enlightened one") is the title given to Siddhārtha Gautama (563–483 B.C.), the founder of Buddhism, the earliest doctrines of which were based on the Four Noble Truths, the first of which is that life is suffering; *The Laws of Menu* (or *Manu*), Indian commentaries on religious laws and social obligations compiled between 200 B.C. and A.D. 200; Confucius (Latin name for K'ung Ch'iu) (551–479 B.C.), Chinese philosopher; Baruch Spinoza (1632–77), Dutch philosopher and rational pantheist.

Perpetual Forces

(1862–1863)

Emerson first delivered "Perpetual Forces" on 18 November 1862 before the Parker Fraternity in Boston; he repeated the lecture another twelve times between his first delivery and 11 February 1863 throughout Massachusetts and once each in Albany, New York, and Chicago. In his notes on the essay "Perpetual Forces" Edward Waldo Emerson comments that this topic had occupied his father's mind throughout 1862, and he suggests that the lecture "Perpetual Forces" may have been inspired by his father's delivery of "Moral Forces" on 13 April 1862, a national day of fasting and prayer declared by Abraham Lincoln (*W*, 10:526–27; Emerson's lecture "Moral Forces" is printed in *Later Lectures*, 2:289–301). Indeed, toward the end, the lecture "Perpetual Forces" dramatically shifts into a Civil War discourse, with Emerson's theory of the spiritual content of "forces" (broadly construed) moderating the negative effects of the war and challenging the North to apply moral rules to reconstruction, at least as he anticipated it. These features were not lost on the lecture's initial audience. In a report of his first delivery of "Perpetual Forces" that appeared in the *Boston Daily Evening Transcript* Emerson's delivery was called "brilliant," and his theme was soundly endorsed by Charles Sumner, who was in the audience and responded to Emerson's words this way:

> In coming forward now, after listening to the admirable address which has just been concluded, and whose success has been so deserved, it appears as if there was nothing which I can now add to what has already been said. "Permanent Forces." There is something good in that phrase. It is instructive and cheering both to know that there are forces that are permanent, and that they are always on the side of right. That I take to be the moral of the lecture. I accept it gladly and apply it to the hour. There are forces working for us which cannot be resisted. The God of Battles is on our side and will prevail. Men may be weak, but our cause is mighty. Men may become weary, but the great principles of justice never tire, and all these principles are fighting on our side. ("Lecture by Mr. Emerson," 19 November, 4)

With Ellen Emerson's assistance, James Elliot Cabot arranged the essay "Perpetual Forces" from this lecture manuscript and others for publication in the *North American Review* 125 (September 1877): 271–82, and he collected the essay in *Lectures and Biographical Sketches* in 1884 (*W*, 10:67–88).

We cannot afford to miss any advantage. Never was any man too strong for his proper work. Art is long, and life short, and we must supply this disproportion, by borrowing and applying to our task the energies of Nature.

Reinforce his self-respect. Show him his means, his arsenal of forces, physical, metaphysical, immortal. More servants wait on man than he'll take notice of. Show him the riches of the poor. Show him what mighty allies and helpers he has. The world is nothing but a fagot of forces. Heat, light, gravity, affinity, repulsion are forms of force. So are, on a higher platform, Temperament, Thought, and Will,— and Sensibility and Time are conditions of force.

A rush of thoughts is the only conceivable prosperity that can come to us. Fine clothes, equipages, villas, parks, and social consideration may amuse younger people for a time, but cannot cover up real poverty and insignificance from older eyes. And though King David had no good from making his census out of vain glory, yet I find it wholesome and invigorating in this gloom of events and opinions to enumerate the resources we can command, to look a little into this arsenal,— how many rounds of ammunition, and what muskets, and what arms better than Springfield muskets, we can bring to bear.[1] Like the hero in our nursery tale, who has one servant who eats slices of granite rocks, and another who can hear the grass grow, and a third who can run to Babylon in half an hour, so man in Nature is surrounded by a gang of friendly giants who can do harder stints than these.[2]

Our Copernican globe is a great factory or shop of power, with its rotating constellations, times, and tides, bringing now the day of planting, then of reaping, then of curing and storing; bringing now water-force, then wind, then caloric, and such magazine of chemicals in its laboratory.[3] The machine is of colossal size; the diameter of the waterwheel, the arms of the levers, and the volley of the battery, are out of all mechanic measure, and it takes long to understand its parts, and its working. This pump never sucks; These screws are never loose. This machine is never out of gear; the vat, and piston, and wheels, and tires, never wear out, but are self-repairing.

These friendly giants help man in every kind. There is no porter like gravitation, who will bring down any weight which you cannot carry, and, if he wants aid, knows where to find his fellow laborers. Water works in masses, and sets his irresistible shoulder to your mills, or to your ships, or transports vast boulders of rock nicely packed in his iceberg atmosphere a thousand miles. The water, that

1. David (d. 962 B.C.), second king of Judah and Israel (ca. 1000–960 B.C.).

2. Emerson is probably referring to the prince and three of the servants in "The Six Servants" by Jacob Ludwig Carl Grimm (1785–1863) and Wilhelm Carl Grimm (1786–1859), German scholars and the founders of German philology. Their most famous work is *Kinder- und Hausmärchen* (Children's and Household Tales), usually referred to in English as *Grimms' Fairy Tales*.

3. Nicolaus Copernicus (or Mikołaj Kopernik) (1473–1543), Polish astronomer credited with founding the science of modern astronomy, believed that the planets revolved around the sun.

daily miracle, a substance as explosive as gunpowder; the electric force contained in a drop of water being equal in amount to that which is discharged from a thunder cloud. But its far greater power depends on its talent of becoming little; and entering the smallest holes and pores. By this agency, the vegetable world exists, carrying in solution elements needful to every point.

You admire the lake;—now look at that cloud-rack that overspreads it in the morning. That is the same lake in the air. Now a picture, a bed for angels, hangings of adornment for the stars of God; But tonight there is a chill in the air, and tomorrow it will be a lake, a river flowing calmly in an old bed, bounded by firm shores, edged by forests, and itself gliding down to the sea, there tossing in tempests against the rocky coast, to come back again shortly to be a cloud over the lake.

Who are the farmer's servants? Who but geology, chemistry, the quarry of the air, the water of the brook, the lightning of the cloud, the plough of the frost? Before he was born into the field, the sun of ages soaked it with light and heat, mellowed his land, decomposed the rocks, covered it with vegetable film, then with forests, and accumulated cubic acres of sphagnum, whose decays make the peat of his meadow. The rocks crack like glass by inequality of contraction in heat and cold, and flakes fall constantly into the soil.

We have the strict analogy of the moral force in our use of the elemental material force. When a man chops a stick, or digs, or rides, or walks, or builds, he borrows the strength of the globe. We lift the axe with a feeble muscular force; but it is the gravity of the globe that brings it down. We put forward the foot in walking, we bend the body in running, and fall forward through gravity. 'Tis the weight of the globe which holds the rider down to his horse; that holds every stone of the house firmly in place, and permits us to build into the air. The ripe fruit is dropped at last without violence, but the lightning fell, and the storm raged, and strata were deposited, and uptorn, and bent back, and chaos moved from beneath to create and flavor the fruit on your table today.

Every plant, is a manufacturer of soil. In the stomach of the plant, development begins. The tree can draw on the whole air, the whole earth, on all the rolling main. The plant, the tree, is all suction-pipe, imbibing from the ground by its roots, from the air by its twigs, with all its might.

Nature sticks by her laws. You can't write up what gravitates down. Art does not consist in trying to give prominence to the obscure, but in showing the real eminence that has been hidden.

> If this great world of joy and pain
> Revolve in one sure track,
> If freedom, set, will rise again,
> And virtue flown come back;
> Wo to the purblind crew who fill

The heart with each day's care,
Nor gain from past or future skill,
To bear or to forbear.[4]

Take up a spade-full or a buck-load of loam,—who can guess what it holds? But a gardener knows that it is full of peaches, full of oranges, and he drops in it a few seeds by way of keys to unlock and combine its virtues, and lets it lie in sun and rain, and, by and by, it has lifted into the air its full weight in golden fruit.

Nature, like a cautious testator, ties up her estate so as not to bestow it all on one generation, but has a fore-looking tenderness and equal regard to the next, and the next, and the fourth and the fortieth. Her wheels never break, her machinery is never out of gear. The winds and the rains come back a thousand and a thousand times. The coal on your grate gives out in decomposing today, exactly the same amount of light and heat which was taken from the sunshine in its formation in the leaves and boughs of the antediluvian tree.

What agencies of electricity, gravity, light, affinity, combine to make every plant what it is, and in a manner so quiet, that the presence of these tremendous powers is not ordinarily suspected. The air is an immense distillery, a sharp solvent, and drinks the oxygen from plants, carbon from animals, drinks the essence and spirit of every solid on the globe. It is a menstruum which melts the mountains into it. All the earths are burnt metals. Air is matter subdued by heat. As the sea is the receptacle of all rivers, so the air is the receptacle from which all things spring, and into which they all return. The invisible and creeping air takes form and solid mass. Our senses are skeptics, and do not believe what they cannot follow; do not believe that these vast mountain-chains are made up of gases and rushing wind. Yet they are. One half of the *avoirdupois* of the rocks which compose the solid crust of the globe consists of oxygen.

But nature is as subtle as she is strong. The adamant is always passing into smoke. She turns her capital day by day. All things are flowing, even those that seem immoveable.

The earth burns; the mountains burn and decompose slower, but as incessantly as wood in the fire. The marble column, the brazen statue, burn under the daylight, and would soon decompose, if their molecular structure, disturbed by the raging sunlight, were not restored by the darkness of night.

Plants consume the materials they want from the air and the ground. They burn or perpetually exhale and decompose their own bodies into the air and earth again. The animal burns, or undergoes this perpetual consumption.

Whilst all thus burns,—the Universe in a blaze,—kindled from the torch of the sun, it needs a perpetual tempering, a phlegm, a sleep, atmospheres of azote,

---

4. "If This Great World of Joy and Pain" (1833), ll. 1–8, by William Wordsworth (1770–1850), English poet and, with Samuel Taylor Coleridge, founder of the romantic movement.

deluges of water, to check the fury of the conflagration, a hoarding to check the spending, a centripetence to the centrifugence.[5] And this is uniformly supplied.

Go out of doors and get the air. Ah, if you knew what was in the air! See what your robust neighbor, who never feared to live in it, has got from it;—strength, cheerfulness, talent, power to convince, heartiness, and equality to each event. It is imputed to some climates that the people who breathe their air think well and construct well. I should say, let us spend six months there, rather than sixty years elsewhere.

The earliest hymns of the world were hymns to these natural forces. The *Vedas* of India, which have a date older than Homer, are hymns to the winds, to the clouds, and to fire.[6] These forces have certain properties which adhere to them all, such as conservation and persisting to be themselves—the impossibility of being warped.

The sun has lost no beams, the earth no virtues; gravity is as adhesive, electricity as swift, heat as expansive, light as joyful, air as virtuous, water as medicinal as on the first day.

There is no loss, only transference: when the heat is less here, it is not lost, but more heat is there. When the rain exceeds on the coast, there is drought on the prairie. When the continent sinks, the opposite continent,—that is to say, the opposite shore of the ocean, rises. Arago says, "Every change in nature is effected by a minimum of force."[7]

Arago says, "It must not be imagined that any force or fraction of a force can be ever annihilated. All that which is not to be found in the useful effect produced by the motive power, nor in the amount of force which it retains after having acted, must have gone towards the shaking and destroying of the machine." These forces are in an ascending series, but seem to leave no room for the individual man or atom; he only shares them: he sails the way these irresistible winds blow. But when we arrive at man, we come to a new style and series,—the Spiritual; Intellect and Morals appear only the material forces on a higher plane.

But the laws of force apply to every form of it. The husbandry of force learned in the economy of heat, or light, or steam, or muscular fibre, applies precisely to the use of wit.

The man must bend to the law,—never the law to him.[8] What I have said of the inexorable persistence to remain itself in every elemental force, the impossibility of tampering with it, or warping it,—it must be used in its own channel, following its own polarity, or it cannot be used at all,—the same rule applies again strictly to this force of Intellect, that it is perception—a seeing, not making thoughts, but

5. Azote, a type of gas that is fatal when breathed, is another name for nitrogen.

6. The Vedas are the four most sacred books of Hinduism; Homer (ninth–eighth century B.C.), Greek poet, presumed single author of the *Iliad* and the *Odyssey*.

7. François Arago (1786–1853), French astronomer and physicist.

8. Attributed to Michael Faraday (1791–1867), English chemist and physicist known for his experiments with electromagnetism, in Emerson's note in the manuscript.

seeing thoughts which pass through him. Certain truths rush into his mind; they take possession of him, he becomes their servant and reporter. He is most careful to watch them, and learn them by heart.

The brain of man has methods and arrangements corresponding to these material powers, by which he can use them. See how trivial is the use of the world by any other of its creatures. Whilst these forces act on us from the outside, and we are not in their counsel, we call them Fate. The animal instincts guide the animal, as gravity governs the stone; and in man that bias or direction of his constitution is often as tyrannical as gravity. We call it temperament, and it seems to be the remains of wolf, ape, and rattlesnake in him.

While the Reason is yet dormant, this rules. As the reflective faculties open, this subsides. We come to reason and knowledge: we see the causes of evils, and learn to parry them, and use them as instruments,—by knowledge being inside of them, and dealing with them as the Creator does.

But there always remain a vast amount of facts unconquered by us, not brought into our knowledge, and so they remain outside of us. It were bold to say that any of us knew what we are doing, or whither we are going, than when we think we know best. Every Jersey wagon that goes by my gate moves from a motive as little comprehended by the driver as by his horse.

Now it is curious to see how a creature so feeble and vulnerable as a man, who, unarmed, is no match for the wild beasts, crocodile or tiger—none for the frost, none for the sea, none for the fire, none for a fog, or a damp air, or the feeble fork of a poor worm,—each of a thousand petty accidents put him to death every day,—and yet this delicate frame is able to subdue to his will these terrific forces, and more than these.

His whole frame is responsive to the world, part for part, every sense, every pore, to a new element, so that he seems to have as many talents as there are qualities in nature. Man in Nature is a suction pipe through which the world flows. No force, but is his force. He does not possess them: he is a pipe through which their currents flow. If a straw be held still in the direction of the ocean current, the sea will pour through it as through Gibraltar. But the whole ocean can't sink a cork. If he should measure strength with them, if he should fight the sea, and the whirlwind, with his ship, he would snap his spars, tear his sails, and swamp his bark, but by cunningly dividing the force, and tapping the tempest for a little side wind, he uses the monsters, and they carry him where he would go.

Look at him: You can give no guess at what power is in him. It never appears directly,—but follow him and see his effects,—see his productions; he is a planter, a miner, a ship builder, a machinist, a musician, a steam-engine, a persuader of men, a builder of towns, a lawgiver, a geometer, an astronomer, and each of these by dint of a wonderful method or series that resides in him, and enables him to work on the material elements.

These thoughts no man ever saw;—look at the man, you have no clew to them,—but they stream through him incessantly, and, if you follow him, you shall see that disorder becomes order where he goes; weakness becomes power; surprising and admirable effects follow him like a creator.

All forces are his. As the wise merchant by truth in his dealings finds his credit unlimited;—he can use in turn, as he wants it, all the property in the world,—and, first or last, vast amounts pass through his hands; so a man draws on all the air, for his occasions, as if there were no other breather, on all the water, as if no other sailor; he is warmed by the sun, and so of every element he walks and works by the aid of gravitation. He draws on all knowledge, as his province; on all beauty, for his innocent delight; and, first or last, he exhausts by his use all the harvests, all the elements of the world.[9]

We are surrounded by human thought and labor. Where are the farmer's days gone? See, they are hid in that stone wall, in that excavated trench, in the harvest grown on what was shingle and pine barren. He put his days into carting from the distant swamp the mountain of muck, which has been trundled about until it now makes the cover of fruitful soil.

Labor hides itself in every mode and form. It is massed and blocked away in a stone house for five hundred years:—It is twisted and screwed into fragrant hay which fills the barn;—it surprises in the perfect form and condition of trees, clean of caterpillars and borers, rightly pruned, and loaded with grafted fruit. It is under the house, in the well; it is over the house, in slates, and copper, and water spout; it grows in the corn; it delights us in the flower bed; it keeps the cow out of the garden, the rain out of the library, the miasma out of the town. It is in dress, in pictures, in ships, in cannon, in every spectacle, in odours, in flavors, in sweet sounds, and in works of safety, of delight, of wrath, of science.

"Our stock in life, our real estate, is that amount of thought which we have had," and which we have applied, and so domesticated.[10] The ground we have thus created is forever a fund for new thoughts. If we were truly to take account of stock before the last court of appeals, that were an inventory. What are my resources?

A few moral maxims confirmed by much experience would stand high on the list constituting a supreme prudence. Then, the knowledge unutterable of our private strength, of where it lies, of its accesses and facilitations, and of its obstructions, my conviction of principles,—that is the great part of my possession. Having them, it is easy to devise or use means of illustrating them. I need not take thought for that. Certain thoughts, certain observations, long familiar to me in nightwatches and daylights, would be my capital, if I remove to Spain or China, or,—by stranger translation,—to the planet Jupiter, or Mars, or to new spiritual

9. Attributed to Francis Bacon (1561–1626), English essayist, statesman, and philosopher, by Emerson (*TN*, 2:220).

10. Attributed to Henry David Thoreau (1817–62), American writer, by Emerson (*JMN*, 15:282).

societies. To work by your strength,—never to speak, or act, or behave, but on the broad basis of your constitution.

For man, the receiver of all and depository of these volumes of power, I am to say, that his ability and performance are according to his reception of these various streams of force. We define Genius to be,—a sensibility to all the impressions of the outer world,—a sensibility so equal that it receives accurately all impressions, so that it can truly report them, without excess or loss, as it received. It must not only receive all, but it must render all. And the health of man is an equality of inlet and outlet, gathering and giving. Any hoarding is tumor and disease.

It would be easy to awake wonder by sketching the performance of each of these Mental Forces; as of the diving-bell of the *Memory*, which descends into the deeps of our past and oldest experience, and brings up every lost jewel;—or, of the Fancy, which sends up its gay balloon aloft into the sky to catch every tint and gleam of romance;—of the Imagination, which turns every dull fact into pictures and po-etry, by making it an emblem of a thought. What a power: when combined with the analysing understanding, Imagination makes Eloquence,—the art of compelling belief, the art of making peoples' hearts dance to his pipe, and carrying war and peace in either hand.

Every valuable person who joins in any enterprise,—is it a piece of industry, or the founding of a colony, or of a college, the reform of some public abuse, or in some effort of patriotism,—what he chiefly brings, is, not his land, or his money, or bodily strength, but his thoughts, his ways of classifying and seeing things, his method. And thus with every one, a new power.

In proportion to the depth of the insight, is the power and reach of the kingdom he controls. I knew a stupid young farmer, churlish, living only for his gains, and with whom the only intercourse you could have was to buy what he had to sell. One day I found his boy of four years dragging about the prettiest little wooden cart, so neatly built, and with decorations too, and learned that Papa had made it; that, hidden deep back in that thick skull was this gentle art and taste which the little fingers and caresses of his son had the power to draw out into day. He was no peasant after all; so near to us is the flowering of fine art, in the rudest population.

See, in a circle of school girls, one with no beauty, no special vivacity, but she can so recite her adventure, that she is never alone, but, at night or at morning, wherever she sits, the inevitable circle gathers round her, willing prisoners of that wonderful memory, and fancy, and spirit of life. Would you know where to find her? Listen for the laughter, follow the cheerful hum, see where is the rapt attention, and a pretty crowd all bright with one electricity;—there, in the centre of fellowship and joy, is Scheherazade again.[11]

---

11. Scheherazade, teller of the tales in the collection of ancient Persian-Indian-Arabian traditional tales called *The Arabian Nights' Entertainments* or *A Thousand and One Nights* (1450), originally in

You have read the pathetic tale, not long ago in the magazine, of "Blind Tom," the negro idiot, with a surpassing musical memory and musical touch, reproducing on the piano, long compositions after one hearing, without fault.[12] And it is only a parallel of a historical case they had in the Southern country, some years ago, of an idiotic slave, who could do feats of mathematical computation in his head, without fault, rivalling the achievements of Zerah Colburn, and of a well-known mathematician of Cambridge in his boyhood.[13]

Or see the feat of eloquence in senates and in popular assemblies; Chatham carrying in his hand joy and rage, and letting the one or the other loose at his pleasure.[14] There was a story in the journals of a poor prisoner in a western police court, who was told he might be released, if he would pay his fine. He had no money, he had no friend, but took his flute out of his pocket, and began to play to the surprise, and, as it proved, to the delight of all the company: the jurors waked up; the Sheriff forgot his duty, the Judge himself beat time,—and the prisoner was, by general consent of court and officers, allowed to go his way, without any money. And, I suppose, if he could have played loud enough, we here should have beat time, and the whole population of the globe would beat time, and consent that he should go without his fine.

Bonaparte, with his celerity of combinations,—mute, unfathomable, reading the geography of Europe as if his eyes were telescopes,—his will seemed to be an immense battery discharging irresistible volleys of power always at the right point in the right time.[15]

The geometer, shows us the true order in figures and quantities; the painter, shows it in laws of color; the dancer, in grace; the botanist, in plants; the physician, in animal economy; the musician, in sweet sounds; the novelist, in sketching ideal society; Each of these artists is a perception of an order and series in that department he deals with, of an order and series which preexisted in nature, and which this mind sees and conforms to. He does not create it;—No, it is the law of nature which he sees and declares by word or act; and men easily see it, when it is shown.

The sensibility is all. Everyone knows what are the effects of music to put people in gay or mournful or martial mood. But these are effects on dull subjects, and only the hint of its power on a keener sense. It is a stroke on a loose or a tense cord. The

---

Arabic, told the sultan, her husband, part of a story each night, thereby keeping his interest and postponing her execution.

12. Blind Tom Bethune (1849–1908), born a slave, became a pianist and composer who toured widely in England and America.

13. Zerah Colburn (1804–39), American minister in Vermont, considered a mathematical prodigy as a youth; the other reference is to Truman Henry Safford (1836–1901), American mathematician, astronomer, and child mathematics prodigy.

14. William Pitt, first Earl of Chatham (1708–78), English statesman and orator, twice virtual prime minister.

15. Napoléon Bonaparte (1769–1821), born in Corsica, general and later emperor of the French as Napoléon I.

story of Orpheus, of Arion, of the Arabian Minstrel, are not fables, but experiments on the same iron at white heat.[16]

See how rich life is, rich in private talents, each of which charms us in turn, and seems the best. If we hear music, we give up all to that; if we fall in with a cricket-club, and see the game masterly played, the best player is the first of men. If we go to the regatta, we forget the bowler, for the stroke oar. And when the soldier comes home from the fight, he fills all eyes. But the soldier has the same admiration of the great parliamentary debater. And poetry and literature are disdainful of all these claims, beside their own.

And it seems as if the child's story were gospel truth,—of the boy who thought in turn each of the four seasons best; or, better, each of the three hundred and sixty-five days of the year was the crowner. By this wondrous sensibility to all the impressions of Nature, he finds himself the receptacle of celestial thoughts, of happy relations to all men. The *Imagination* enriches him, as if there were no other; the *Memory* opens all her cabinets and archives; *Science* in her length and breadth; *Poetry* in her splendor and joy; and the august circles of eternal Law. And all these are means and stairs for new ascensions of the mind. But all these are no wise impoverished for any other mind,—not tarnished,—not breathed upon—for the mighty Intellect did not stoop to him and become property, but the student rose to it, and followed its circuits. "It is ours while we use it; it is not ours when we do not use it."[17]

And so, one step higher, when he comes into the realm of Sentiment and Will,—he sees the grandeur of Justice, the victory of Love, the eternity that belongs to all Moral Nature,—he does not then invent his sentiment, or his act, but obeys a pre-existing right which he sees.

We arrive at virtue only by taking its direction, instead of imposing ours. And the last revelation of intellect and of sentiment,—namely, that of, in a manner, severing the man from all other men, and making known to him that the spiritual powers are sufficient to him, if no other being existed;—that he is to deal absolutely in the world, as if he alone were a system and a state, and, though all should perish, can make all anew,—that no numbers and no masses are any reason for sacrificing a right. 'Tis like the village operator who taps the telegraph wire, and surprises the secrets of empires as they pass to the capital. So is this child of the dust throwing himself by obedience into the circuits of the heavenly wisdom, and sharing the secret of God.

The forces are infinite. Every one has the might of all; for that is the secret of the world,—that its energies are *solidaires*; that they work together on a system of

16. Orpheus, in the Greek myth, was given a lyre by Apollo; Arion is either the Greek musician who appears in the constellations as a lyre and dolphin or the horse possessing fabulous gifts; the Arabian Minstrel, a reference to *The Arabian Nights' Entertainments.*

17. Attributed to Plotinus (205–70), Roman Neoplatonic philosopher, by Emerson (*JMN*, 13:296).

mutual aid, *all for each, and each for all*; that the strain made on one point bears on every arch and foundation of the structure; that is to say, every atom is a little world, representing all the forces. But if you wish to avail yourself of their might, and, in like manner, if you wish the force of the intellect, and the force of the will, you must take their divine direction, not they yours. Obedience alone gives the right to command.

The effort of men is to use these purely for private ends. They wish to pocket land, and water, and fire, and air, and all fruits of these for property, and would like to have Aladdin's lamp to compel darkness, and iron-barred doors, and hostile armies, and lions, and serpents, to serve them like footmen.[18]

And they wish the same service from the spiritual faculties. A man has a rare mathematical talent inviting him to the beautiful secrets of geometry and wishes to clap a patent on it; or, has a fancy and invention of a poet, and says, I will write a play that shall be repeated in London a hundred nights; or a military genius, and instead of using that to defend his country, he says, I will fight the battle so as to give me place and political consideration; or Canning or Thurlow has a genius of debate, and says, I will know how with this weapon to defend the cause that will pay best, and make me Chancellor or Foreign Secretary.[19] But this perversion is punished with instant loss of true wisdom and real power.

"All that the world admires comes from within."[20] I say, that all superiority is this, or related to this. Power of thought makes us men, ranks us, distributes society, distributes the work of the world, is the prolific source of all arts, of all wealth, of all delight, of all grandeur.

Men are as they believe. Men are as they think. A certain quantity of power belongs to a certain quantity of truth. And the man who knows any truth not yet discerned by other men, is master of all other men, so far as that truth, and its wide relations, are concerned.

Intellect measures itself by its counteraction to any accumulation of material force. There is no mass it cannot surmount and dispose. Does anyone doubt between the strength of a thought, and that of an institution? Does anyone doubt that a good general is better than a park of artillery? A larger angle of vision commands centuries of facts and millions of thoughtless people.

Thus is the world delivered into your hand, but on peremptory conditions,— not for property, but for use,—use according to the noble nature of the gifts, and not for toys, not for self-indulgence. Things work to their ends, not to yours, and will certainly defeat any adventurer who fights against this ordination.

18. Aladdin and his lamp, which houses two genii, appear in *The Arabian Nights' Entertainments*.

19. George Canning (1770–1827), British politician, president of the Board of Control for India (1817–20); Edward Thurlow, first Baron Thurlow (1731–1806), English jurist and statesman.

20. "An Inquisition upon Fame and Honor" (1633), l. 503, by Fulke Greville, first Baron Brooke (1554–1628), English poet and statesman, favorite of Queen Elizabeth.

I find the survey of these cosmical powers a doctrine of consolation in the dark hours of private or public fortune. It shows us the world alive, guided, incorruptible; that its cannon cannot be stolen, nor its virtues misapplied. It shows us the long Providence, the safeguards of rectitude. It animates exertion. It warns us out of that despair into which Saxon men are prone to fall,—of an idolatry of forms, instead of working to simple ends in the belief that Heaven always succors us in working for these. Our people better endure tyranny according to law a thousand years, than irregular and unconstitutional happiness for a day. Of course, they had rather die in the hands of a physician, than be cured by a quack. But that is not the law of forces. This world belongs to the energetical. And a true analysis of the laws of force showing how immortal and how self-protecting they are would be a wholesome lesson for every time, and this time.

All our political disasters grow as logically out of our attempts in the past to do without justice, as the sinking of some part of your house comes of defect in the foundation. One thing is plain: A certain personal virtue is essential to freedom; and it begins to be doubtful whether our corruption in this country has not gone a little over the mark of safety, and now, when canvassed, we shall be found to be made up of a majority of reckless self-seekers: the divine knowledge has ebbed out of us, and we do not know enough to be free.

I hope better of the state. Half a man's wisdom goes with his courage. A boy who knows that a bully lives round the corner which he must pass on his daily way to school, is apt to take sinister views of streets and of school-education: And a sensitive politician suffers his ideas of the part New York, and Pennsylvania, and Ohio are to play in the future of the Union, to be fashioned by the election of rogues in some counties. But we must not gratify the rogues so deeply. There is a speedy limit to profligate politics.

Fear disenchants life and the world. If I have not my own respect, I am an imposter, not entitled to other men's, and had better creep into my grave. And I admire the sentiment of Thoreau who said, "Nothing is so much to be feared as fear; God himself likes atheism better."[21] For the world is a battle ground; Every principle is a war-note, and the most quiet and protected life is at any moment exposed to incidents which test your firmness.

How then to reconstruct? I say, this time go down to the pan. See that your wheels turn on a jewel. Do not lay your cornerstone on a shaking morass: that will let down the superstructure into a bottomless pit, again.

Leave slavery out. Since nothing satisfies men but justice, let us have that, and let us stifle our prejudices against commonsense and humanity, and agree that every man shall have what he honestly earns, and, if he is a sane and innocent man, have an equal vote in the state, and a fair chance in society. Ernest Renan, the first living

21. Emerson quotes Henry David Thoreau (*JMN*, 15:29).

writer in France, speaking of the Jews, says, that "they everywhere in the world at this day form a society apart, except only in France, which has exhibited in the world the principle of a civilization purely ideal, ignoring all thought of difference of races."[22] Well, the day will come here of an equal glory.

And speaking in the interest of no man and no party, but as a geometer of his forces, I say, that the smallest beginning, so that it is just, is better and stronger than the largest that is not quite just. This time no compromises, no concealments, no crimes.

The illusion that strikes me as the masterpiece, in that ring of illusions which our life is, is the timidity with which we assert our moral sentiment. We are made of it, the world is built by it, things endure as they share it; all beauty, all health, all intelligence, exist by it; yet we shrink to speak it, or to range ourselves on its side. Nay, we presume strength of him or them who deny it. Cities go against it, the college goes against it, the courts snatch at any precedent, at any vicious form of law, to rule it out; legislatures listen with appetite to declamations against it, and vote it down. Every new assertor of the right surprises us, like a man joining the church, and we hardly dare believe he is in earnest.

Besides, what we do and suffer is in moments, but the cause of right for which we labor, never dies, works in long periods, can afford many checks, gains by our defeats, and will know how to compensate our extremest sacrifice. Wrath and petulance may have their short success, but they quickly reach their brief date, and decompose, whilst the massive might of ideas is irresistible at last. Whence does this knowledge come? Where is the source of power? The soul of God is poured into the world through the thoughts of men. As cloud on cloud, as snow on snow, as the bird on the air, and the planet rests on space in its flight, so do nations of men and their institutions rest on thoughts.

My point is, that the movement of the whole machine, the motive force of life, and of every particular life, is moral. The world stands on our thoughts, and not on iron or cotton; and the iron of iron, the fire of fire, the ether and source of all the elements, is moral force. It is a fagot of laws, and that band which ties them together is Unity, is Universal Good, saturating all the laws with one being and aim, so that each law translates the other; is only the same Spirit applied to new departments that, if we should really come down to atoms, of which men believed that the universe is composed, we should not find little cubes or atoms at all, but only spherules of force, a fagot of forces, a series of currents in which all things are forced to run;—a series of threads, on which men, and animals, and plants, and brute matter are strung as beads;—those forces only exist.

22. Joseph-Ernest Renan (1823–92), French philosopher, philologist, and historian, leader of the school of critical philosophy.

The Scholar

(1863)

Emerson delivered this discourse, which was originally untitled, on 22 July 1863 before the
United Literary Societies of Dartmouth College in Hanover, New Hampshire, substantially
repeating it on 11 August before the Erosophian Society of Waterville (now Colby) College in
Waterville, Maine. Invitations to speak at college exercises were familiar to Emerson between
the 1830s and 1860s, as his "Discourse" read before the Philomathesian Society of Middlebury College and the Philorhetorian and Peithologian Societies of Wesleyan College in 1845,
"Address" to the Adelphic Union of Williamstown College in 1854 and the Social Union of
Amherst College in 1855, and "Celebration of Intellect," an address at Tufts College in 1861,
show. (For these addresses see *Later Lectures*, 1:81–100, 348–66, and 2:240–52, respectively.)

James Elliot Cabot, Emerson's literary executor, eventually drew an additional lecture
and two essays from the body of "The Scholar" as Emerson had delivered it in 1863 and from
sections of his earlier academic addresses. With Ellen Emerson's assistance Cabot composed
"Oration Addressed to the Senior Class of the University of Virginia," which Emerson delivered on 28 June 1876, and the two essays, "The Man of Letters: An Address Delivered before
the Literary Societies of Dartmouth and Waterville Colleges, 1863" and "The Scholar: An
Address before the Washington and Jefferson Societies at the University of Virginia, 28 June,
1876," both of which he published in *Lectures and Biographical Sketches* in 1884 (*W*, 10:239–
58, 259–89). The version of "The Scholar" that follows is from the complete manuscript in
Emerson's hand from which he read in 1863.

Gentlemen of the Literary Societies,
The anniversaries of the College never lose their interest. You have wisely
united your anniversary to the academical holiday, so to add your tribute
to the literary excitement of the season, and to borrow from the interest which a
graduating class is sure to awaken, a share for all the College. Some of you are today
saying your farewells to each other, and tomorrow will receive the parting honors
of the College. You go to be teachers, to become physicians, lawyers, divines; in due
course, statesmen, naturalists, philanthropists; I hope, some of you, to be the men
of letters, critics and philosophers; perhaps the rare gift of poetry already sparkles,
and may yet burn. At all events, before the shadows of these times darken over your

youthful sensibility and candor, let me use the occasion which your kind request gives me, to offer you some counsels which an old scholar may without pretension bring to youth in regard to the career of letters, the power and joy that belong to it, and its high office in evil times.

They are the minority to stand fast for eternal truth, and say, cannons and bayonets for such as already know nothing stronger. But we are here for immortal resistance to wrong. We are they who make the essence and stability of society.

I offer perpetual congratulation to the scholar—he has drawn the white lot in life. The very disadvantages of his condition point at superiorities. He is too good for the world, is in advance of his race, his function is prophetic. He belongs to a superior society and is born one or two centuries too early for the rough and sensual population into which he is thrown. But the Heaven which sent him hither knew that well enough, and sent him as a leader to lead.

Are men perplexed with evil times? The inviolate soul is in perpetual telegraphic communication with the source of events. He has earlier information, a private dispatch which relieves him of the terror which presses on the rest of the community. He is a learner of the laws of nature and the experiences of history; an ear to hear; an organ to receive and impart; a prophet surrendered with self-abandoning sincerity to the Heaven which pours through him its will to mankind.

This is the theory. But you know how far this is from the fact:—that nothing has been able to resist the tide with which the material prosperity of America in years past has beat down the hope of youth, the piety of learning.

The country was full of activity, with its land, wheat, coal, iron, cotton;—the wealth of the globe was here,—too much work, and not men enough to do it. Britain, France, Germany, Scandinavia, sent millions of laborers;—still the need was more. Every kind of skill was in demand, and the bribe came to men of intellectual culture; Come, drudge in our mill, and you shall have wealth soon to go back to your own libraries again.

America at large exhibited such a confusion as California showed in 1849, when the cry of gold was first raised. All the distinctions of profession and habit ended at the mines. All the world took off their coats, and worked in shirt-sleeves. Lawyers went and came with pick and wheelbarrow; doctors of medicine turned teamsters; stray clergymen kept the bar in saloons; professors of colleges sold mince pies, matches, cigars, and so on.

It is the perpetual tendency of wealth to draw on the spiritual class, not in this coarse way, but in a plausible and covert way. Here is ease, here is refinement, here is elegance of living. Do not denounce me. Don't be such a cynic. The bribe to many proves irresistible. "We are men of like passions with you," and the sequel might be told in the old story of the preacher on the seacoast, when a wreck was seen from the church windows: "Stop, brethren, till I come down from the pulpit, and let us start fair."

Now this, as medicine to a sick scholar, or as necessity to a starved one, might be a manly part;—but, in any other plight, it was profanation. It was not for this that this costly culture was given. The provision of Nature is to keep the balance of matter by the infusion of mind. As certainly as water falls in rain on the tops of mountains, and runs down into valleys, plains, and pits,—so does thought fall first on the best minds, and run down, from class to class, until it reaches the masses, and works revolutions.

It is charged that all vigorous nations except ourselves have balanced their labor by mental activity, and especially by the Imagination, the cardinal human power, the Angel of earnest and believing ages. The subtle Hindoo, who carried religion to ecstasy, and philosophy to idealism, produced the wonderful *Epic of the Mahabarat*, of which in the present century the translations have added new regions to thought.[1] The Egyptian built Thebes and Karnak on a scale which dwarfs our art, and by the paintings on the interior walls of the pyramids, invited us into the secret of the religious belief whence he drew such power. The Hebrew nation compensated the insignificance of its numbers and territory by its religious genius, its tenacious belief; and its poems and histories cling to the soil of this globe like the primitive rocks. The Greek was so perfect in action and in imagination, his poems, from Homer to Euripides, so charming in form, and so true to the human mind, that we cannot forget or outgrow their mythology.[2] On the south and east shore of the Mediterranean, Mahomet impressed his fierce genius how deeply into the manners, language, and poetry of Arabia and Persia.[3]

See the activity of the imagination in the Crusades.[4] The front of morn was full of fiery shapes; the chasm was bridged over; heaven walked on earth, and earth could see with eyes the *Paradiso* and the *Inferno*.[5] Dramatic "Mysteries" were the entertainment of the people.[6] Parliaments of love and poesy served them, instead of the House of Commons, Congress, and the newspaper. In Puritanism, how the whole Jewish history became flesh and blood in those men,—let Bunyan show.[7]

1. A reference to the *Mahābhārata*, a collection of legendary and didactic Indian poetry.

2. Homer (ninth–eighth century B.C.), Greek poet, presumed single author of the *Iliad* and the *Odyssey*; Euripides (ca. 484–406 B.C.), Greek playwright and one of the great tragic poets.

3. Muhammad (ca. 570–632), founder of Islam, born in Mecca.

4. The Crusades (the name comes from the Latin word for cross) were a series of eight military campaigns between 1095 and 1291 led by European Christians against Muslims in an attempt to gain control of Jerusalem.

5. Dante Alighieri (1265–1321), Italian poet, author of the *Divina commedia* (completed in 1321), which recounts the poet's journey through Hell (*Inferno*), Purgatory (*Purgatorio*), and Paradise (*Paradiso*).

6. During the Middle Ages mystery plays, sometimes known as morality plays, represented biblical subjects and were often performed from the backs of wagons. They included scenery that represented heaven, earth, and hell and sometimes featured flying angels and fire-spouting devils.

7. John Bunyan (1628–88), English cleric and author of *The Pilgrim's Progress from This World to That Which Is to Come* (1678), an allegory in which Christian, the main character, leaves his home and family to journey to the Celestial City.

Now it is agreed that we are utilitarian, that we are skeptical, frivolous; that with universal, cheap education, we have stringent theology, comparable in power to the severe doctrine of the monastic orders, Franciscan, Dominican, and Jesuit, but religion is low. There is much criticism, not on deep grounds; but an affirmative philosophy is wanting.

Our profoundest philosophy, (if it were not contradiction in terms,) is Skepticism. The great poem of the age is the disagreeable poem of *Faust*, of which the "Festus" of Bailey and the "Paracelcus" of Browning are English variations.[8] We have superficial sciences: restless, gossiping, aimless activity. We run to Paris, to London, to Rome, to mesmeric spiritualism, to Pusey, to the Catholic Church, as if for the want of thought.[9] And those who would check and guide them have a dreary feeling that in the change and decay of the old creeds and motives, there was no offset to supply their place. Our industrial skill and arts, ministering to convenience and luxury, have made life expensive, and therefore greedy, careful, and anxious, and turned the eyes downward to the earth, not upward to thought.

Ernest Renan finds, that Europe has twice assembled for exhibitions of industry, at the Crystal Palace in London, in 1851, and at Paris in 1855, and not a poem graced the occasion, and nobody remarked the defect.[10] A French prophet of our age, Fourier, predicted, that, one day, instead of by battles and Oecumenical Councils, the rival portions of humanity would dispute to each other excellence in the manufacture of little cakes.[11] So Coleridge of improved breeds in Highlands.

"In my youth," said a Scotch mountaineer, "A highland gentleman measured his importance by the number of men his domain could support. After some time, the question was, to know how many great cattle it would feed. Today we are come to count the number of sheep—I suppose posterity will ask, how many rats and mice it will feed."[12]

Dickens complained in America that, as soon as he arrived in the western towns, the committees waited on him, and invited him to deliver a Temperance Lecture.[13] Bowditch translated Laplace, and, when he removed to Boston, the Hospital Life

8. *Faust, der Tragödie erster Teil* (*Faust, the First Part of the Tragedy*, 1808), a play by Johann Wolfgang von Goethe (1749–1832), Germany's most famous writer, is the story of an old scholar, Faust, who promises his soul to Mephistopheles in return for all knowledge and experience; *Festus* (1839) by Philip James Bailey (1816–1902), English poet; *Paracelsus* (1835) by Robert Browning (1812–89), English poet.

9. Edward Bouverie Pusey (1800–1882), English theologian who tried to reunite the Catholic Church and the Church of England.

10. Joseph-Ernest Renan (1823–92), French philosopher, philologist, and historian, leader of the school of critical philosophy.

11. François-Marie-Charles Fourier (1772–1837), French social thinker whose doctrines guided the later period of the Brook Farm community, a utopian venture at West Roxbury, Massachusetts (1841–47).

12. Possibly Samuel Taylor Coleridge (1772–1834), English poet and philosopher and, with William Wordsworth (1770–1850), founder of the romantic movement, as attributed by Emerson (*JMN*, 15:334–35; *TN*, 3:277).

13. Charles Dickens (1812–70), popular English novelist.

Assurance Company insisted that he should make their tables of annuities.[14] Napoleon knows the art of war, but should not be put on picket duty.[15] Linnaeus or Robert Brown must not be set to raise gooseberries and cucumbers, though they be excellent botanists.[16] A shrewd broker out of State Street visited a quiet countryman possessed of all the virtues, and in his glib talk said, "With your character, now, I could raise all this money at once, and make an excellent thing of it."[17]

There is an oracle current in the world that nations die by suicide: And the sign of it is the decay of thought. Niebuhr has given striking examples of that fatal portent, as in the loss of power of thought that followed the disasters of the Athenians in Sicily.[18] The country complains loudly of the inefficiency of the army. It was badly led. But before this, it was not the army alone,—it was the population that was badly led. The clerisy, the spiritual guides, the scholars, the seers, have been false to their trust.

My point is, that the movement of the whole machine, the motive force of life, and of every particular life, is moral. The world stands on thoughts, and not on iron nor on cotton: And, the iron of iron, the fire of fire, the ether and source of all the elements, is, moral forces.

I cannot forgive a homeless scholar his despondency. The worst times only show him how independent he is of times,—only relieve and bring out the splendor of his privilege. Disease alarms the family,—but the physician sees in it a temporary mischief, which he can check and expel.

The fears and agitations of men who watch the markets, the crops, the plenty or scarcity of money, or other superficial events are not for him even more serious disasters. He knows that the world is always equal to itself; that the forces which uphold and pervade it are eternal. Air, water, fire, iron, gold, wheat, electricity, animal fibre have not lost any particle of power, and no decay has crept on the spiritual force which gives bias and period to boundless nature.

Bad times! What are bad times?

The world is always equal to itself. Nature is rich, exuberant, and mocks at the puny forces of destruction: Man makes no more impression on her wealth, than the caterpillar or the cankerworm, whose petty ravage, though noticed in an orchard or a village, is insignificant in the vast exuberance of the summer. The world shines with works of men: towns, railroads, forts, and fleets. War comes, and

14. Nathaniel Bowditch (1773–1838), American mathematician and astronomer, was employed as an actuary by the Massachusetts Hospital Life Assurance Company beginning in 1823; from 1829 to 1839 he translated, with commentary, the first four volumes of *Mécanique céleste* (*Celestial Mechanics*) by Pierre-Simon de Laplace (1749–1827), French astronomer and mathematician.

15. Napoléon Bonaparte (1769–1821), born in Corsica, general and later emperor of the French as Napoléon I.

16. Carolus Linnaeus (1707–78), Swedish botanist, is considered one of the founders of modern systematic botany; Robert Brown (1773–1858), Scottish botanist and physicist.

17. State Street, the main commercial center of Boston.

18. Barthold Georg Niebuhr (1776–1831), German historian and critic.

they are annihilated;—gone like the last year's snow—and caring Nature cannot pause. Weeks, months, pass,—a new harvest;—trade springs up, and there stand new cities, new homes, all rebuilt, and sleepy with permanence. Italy, France: a hundred times the soils of those countries have been trampled with armies, and burned over: a few summers, and they smile with plenty, and yield new men and new revenues to the state.

Great is Nature, who cunningly hides every wrinkle of her inconceivable antiquity under roses, and violets, and morning dew. Every inch of the mountain is scarred by horrible convulsions, yet the new day is purple with the bloom of youth and love. Look out into this August night, and see the broad silver flame which flashes up the half of heaven fresh and delicate as the bonfires of the meadow flies. Yet the powers of numbers cannot compute its enormous age,—embosomed in Time and Space. What are they? Our first problems, which we ponder all our lives through, and leave where we found them; whose outrunning immensity, the ancients believed, astonished the gods themselves; on whose dizzy vastitudes all the worlds of God are a mere dot on the margin, impossible to deny, impossible to believe.

Stand by your order, but the first lesson and the first power of the scholar is that he is not stubborn, but docile. He does not begin with brag, but sets himself accurately, acquaints himself with his duties. Nature is rich and strong. We brag our arts; that is, we have learned two or three of her secrets; but our knowledge is a drop of the sea. Roger Bacon, and Monk Schwartz, invented gunpowder: and today the whole art of war, all fortifications by land and sea, all our drill and military education,—all our arms, are founded on that,—one chemic compound.[19] All are an extension of a gunbarrel, as if the gases, the earth, water, lightning, and caloric, had not a million energies, the discovery of any one of which will change the art of war again, and put an end to war, by the exterminating forces man can apply.

Our modern wealth stands on a few staples. And the interest nations take in our war is exasperated by the importance of cotton trade. And, what is cotton? One plant in 200,000 plants known to the botanist, vastly the largest part of which are reckoned weeds; that is to say, because their virtues are not yet discovered; and every one of them probably yet to be of utility in the arts. As Bacchus was of the vine, as Arkwright and Whitney were the gods of cotton,—so, prolific Time will yet bring an inventor to every plant.[20] There is not a property in Nature but a mind is born to accost it.

There is no unemployed force in nature: All decomposition is recomposition.

19. Roger Bacon (ca. 1220–92), English philosopher and scientist, and Berthold Schwarz (fourteenth century), German monk and alchemist, were both reputed inventors of gunpowder.

20. Bacchus is the Roman name for Dionysus, the Greek god of nature and the divine ecstasy achieved by communing with the great life forces (wine is his most common symbol); Sir Richard Arkwright (1732–92), English inventor of the spinning frame for producing cotton warp thread; Eli Whitney (1765–1825), American inventor of the cotton gin, which separated the fiber from the seed.

War disorganizes, but it is to reorganize. If churches are effete, it is because the new heaven forms. If men are sensible of the decay, it must be that the new birth is far on its way. For a new population is incessantly arriving, to whom the utmost stability and supreme benefit of natural and social order is due, and by them will be claimed.

You are here as the carriers of the power of Nature, as Roger Bacon with his secret of gunpowder, with his secret of the balloon, and of steam. As Copernicus with his secret of the true astronomy, as Columbus with America in his log-book.[21] As Newton with his gravity; Harvey with his circulation; Smith with his law of trade.[22] Franklin with lightning; Adams with independence; Kant with pure reason; Swedenborg with his spiritual world.[23] You are the carrier of ideas which are to fashion the mind and so the history of this breathing world, so as they shall be and not otherwise. Steward of Power, Doctor of Laws, interpreter of secrets, Poet, Master,—Every man is a scholar potentially, and does not need any one good so much as this of right thought.

> Calm pleasures here abide, majestic pains.[24]

Coleridge traces "three silent revolutions," and the first occurred "when the clerisy fell from the church."[25] A scholar was once a priest. But the church clung to ritual, and the scholar clung to joy, low as well as high, and thus the separation was a mutual fault. But I think it a schism which must be healed. The true Scholar is the Church. Only the duties of Intellect must be owned.

Down with these dapper trimmers and sycophants! and let us have masculine and divine men, formidable lawgivers, Pythagoras, Plato, Aristotle, who warp the churches of the world from their traditions, and penetrate them through and through with original perception.[26] Intellectual man lives in perpetual victory. So let his habits be formed, and all his economies heroic; no spoiled child, no drone, no epicure, but a stoic, formidable and athletic, knowing how to be poor, loving

---

21. Nicolaus Copernicus (or Mikołaj Kopernik) (1473–1543), Polish astronomer credited with founding the science of modern astronomy, believed that the planets revolved around the sun.

22. Sir Isaac Newton (1642–1727), English natural philosopher and mathematician; William Harvey (1578–1657), English anatomist and physiologist known for his work detailing how the blood circulates; Adam Smith (1723–90), Scottish political economist and moral philosopher.

23. Benjamin Franklin (1706–90), American statesman, author, printer, editor, and inventor; John Adams (1735–1826), second president of the United States (1797–1801); Immanuel Kant (1724–1804), German philosopher whose most famous work is entitled *Kritik der reinen Vernunft* (*Critique of Pure Reason*, 1781); Emanuel Swedenborg (1688–1772), Swedish scientist, theologian, and mystic.

24. "Laodamia" (1815), l. 72, by William Wordsworth.

25. Quoted from *Specimens of the Table-Talk of the Late Samuel Taylor Coleridge* (1835) (*JMN*, 5:52; *TN*, 3:120).

26. Pythagoras (ca. 580–ca. 500 B.C.), Greek philosopher who raised mathematics to a science; Plato (ca. 428–348 B.C.), the most famous of the Greek philosophers; Aristotle (384–322 B.C.), Greek philosopher and scientist.

labor, and not flogging his youthful wit with tobacco and wine;—treasuring his youth.—

The ambassador is held to maintain the dignity of the Republic which he represents. But what does the scholar represent? The organ of ideas, the subtle force which creates nature, and men, and states,—consoler, upholder, imparting pulses of light, and shocks of electricity,—guidance and courage. Let his manners and breeding accord. I wish the youth to be an armed and complete man; no helpless angel to be slapped in the face, but a man dipped in the river Styx of human experience, and knowing good and evil, and made invulnerable so; and self-helping.[27]

A redeeming trait of the Sophists of Athens, Hippias and Gorgias, is that they made their own clothes and shoes.[28] Learn to harness a horse, to row a boat, to camp down in the woods, to cook your supper. I chanced lately to be at West Point, and after hearing examination in scientific classes, I went into the barracks. The chamber was in perfect order, the mattress on the iron campbed rolled up, as if ready for removal. I asked the first cadet, Who makes your bed? "I do." Who fetches your water? "I do." Who blacks your shoes? "I do." It was so in every room.[29]

These are first steps to power. Learn of Samuel Johnson that it is a primary duty of the man of letters to secure his independence.[30] These times of ours are serious—full of calamity. But all times are essentially alike. As soon as there is life, there is danger. Aplomb rules,—he whose word or deed you cannot predict, who answers you without any supplication in his eye, who draws his determination from within and instantly—that man rules.

It will always be so. Every principle is a war-note. Whoever attempts to carry out the rule of right, and love, and freedom, must take his life in his hand. Stand by your order. 'Tis some thirty years since the days of the Reform Bill in England, when on the walls in London you read everywhere placards, "Down with the Lords."—At that time, Earl Grey, who was a leader of Reform, was asked in the Parliament his policy on the measures of the radicals; he replied, "I shall stand by my order."[31]

What I would say to you is: Where there is no vision, the people perish. The

27. The Styx is the mythical river that the dead crossed into Hades.

28. Hippias of Elis (fifth century b.c.), Greek Sophist; Gorgias of Leontini (ca. 483–376 b.c.), Greek Sophist and rhetorician.

29. On 6 May 1863 Edward McMasters Stanton (1814–69), U.S. secretary of war (1862–68), appointed Emerson a member of a visiting board of eighteen citizens charged to conduct examinations of all the classes of West Point cadets in June 1863. While Emerson probably had little to do with the final report of the board, he may have been instrumental in having the study of ethics explicitly recommended in any revised curriculum (*Letters*, 5:328n).

30. Samuel Johnson, known as Dr. Johnson (1709–84), English lexicographer, editor, critic, and conversationalist.

31. The Reform Bill of 1832 is a British parliamentary act that redistributed seats in the House of Commons and lowered electoral qualifications to allow most members of the middle class to vote. Charles Grey, second Earl Grey (1764–1845), English statesman, conceived the bill while he was prime minister. It passed the House of Commons three times but each time was then blocked by the House

fault lies with the educated class, the men of study and thought. There is a very low feeling of duty; the merchant is true to the merchant; the noble in England and Europe stands by his order; the politician believes in his arts and combinations, but the scholar does not stand by his order, but defers to the men of this world.

Pythias of Aegina was victor in the Pancratium of the boys, in the Isthmian games. He came to the poet Pindar and wished him to write an ode in his praise, and inquired what was the price of a poem. Pindar replied that he should give him one talent, about a thousand dollars of our money. "A talent!" cried Pythias, "Why for so much money I can erect a statue of bronze in the Temple." "Very likely." On second thought, he returned and paid for the poem. And now not only all the statues of bronze or marble in the temples of Aegina are destroyed, but the temples themselves and the very walls of the city are utterly gone, whilst the Ode of Pindar in praise of Pythias remains entire.[32]

Education itself is on trial. And war seems at first to make it an impertinence, and shoulders it aside, as rich men and kings have done before. Stand by your order, and show these upstarts their place.

There is a proverb that Napoleon, when the Mameluke Cavalry approached the French lines, ordered the grenadiers to the front, the asses and the savans to fall into the hollow square.[33] It made a good story, and circulated in that day. But how stands it now? The military expedition was a failure, Bonaparte deserted himself, and the army got home as it could,—all fruitless,—not a trace of it remains. All that is left of it, is, the researches of those savans on the antiquities of Egypt, including the great work of Denon, which led the way to all the subsequent studies of Wilkinson and the English and German scholars, who, on that foundation, France, least of all, should disparage the intellect.[34] It is her sons who have made war a science. Napoleon came to know, or, I may say, never did not know his debt to it. Carnot was his geometer, who, by his warlike mathematics, organized victory.[35] Bonaparte was accustomed to say that, "the Ecole Polytechnique was the hen that laid him all the golden eggs." And as compared with France in the distinction given to intellect in the state and in society, England is Chinese in her servility to wealth and old wealth.[36]

Gentlemen, I am here to commend your art and profession as thinkers to you.

---

of Lords. Grey threatened to create fifty new peers, enough to carry the bill, and the House of Lords finally passed it.

32. Nemean Ode 5 by Pindar (ca. 522–ca. 438 B.C.), the greatest of the Greek lyric poets.

33. Savans is another word for savants, men of learning or scholars.

34. Baron Dominique-Vivant Denon (1747–1825), French illustrator and government official who published a book about Egypt; Sir John Gardner Wilkinson (1797–1875), English traveler and Egyptologist, author of many books on the subject.

35. Lazare-Nicolas-Marguerite Carnot, called le Grand Carnot and l'Organisateur de la Victoire (1753–1823), French soldier and administrator.

36. Attributed to Francis Lieber (1800–1872), American historian, political economist, and professor at South Carolina College, in Emerson's note in the manuscript.

It is real. It is the secret of power. It is the art of command. Greek gods, Norse Gods, and Yankee Gods are well agreed in this matter. All superiority is this, or related to this; for I conceive morals and mind to be in eternal solidarity.

"All that the world admires comes from within."[37] Thought makes us men; ranks us; distributes society; distributes the work of the world; is the prolific source of all arts, of all wealth, of all delight, of all grandeur. Men are as they believe. Men are as they think. A certain quantity of power belongs to a certain quantity of truth, and the man who knows any truth not yet discerned by other men is master of all other men so far as that truth and its wide relations are concerned.

Stand by his order. He represents intellectual or spiritual force. I wish him to rely on the spiritual arm; to live by his strength, not by his weakness. Swedenborg and Behmen were great men because they knew that a spiritual force was greater than any material force.[38] Swedenborg knew that a text of Scripture would make men black in the face,—drive them out of their houses,—pull down towns and states;—or, build up new, on despised or unthought of foundations.

Intellect measures itself by its counteraction to any accumulation of material force. There is no mass which it cannot surmount and dispose. The exertions of this force are the eminent experiences—out of a long life all that is worth remembering. These are the moments that balance years. Does anyone doubt between the strength of a thought and that of an institution? Does anyone doubt that a good general is better than a park of artillery? See a political revolution dogging a book. See armies, institutions, literatures, appearing in the train of some wild Arabian's dream. See the ponderous instrumentalities which follow a speech in parliament, or a vote in congress.

Scholars are idealists, and should stand for freedom, justice, and public good. They are bound to stand for all the virtues, and all the liberties,—liberty of trade, liberty of press, liberty of religion, and they should open all the prizes of success, and all the roads of Nature to free competition. Scholars are they who make the essence and stability of society. We stand for truth and immortal resistance to wrong.

Gird up the loins of your mind. Every principle is a war-note. See on which side you are. A scholar defending the cause of slavery, of arbitrary government, of monopoly, of the oppressor, is a traitor to his profession. He has ceased to be a scholar. He is not company for clean people.

We have many revivals of religion. We have had once what was called the revival of letters. I wish to see a revival of the human mind; to see men's sense of duty extend to the cherishing and use of their intellectual powers; their religion should

37. "An Inquisition upon Fame and Honor" (1633), l. 512, by Fulke Greville, first Baron Brooke (1554–1628), English poet, statesman, and favorite of Queen Elizabeth.

38. Jacob Behmen (or Jakob Böhme) (1575–1624), German mystic, influenced romanticism and the Quakers.

go with their thought and hallow it. Is thought to be confined to a class? No more than goodness. The immortality is as truly preached from the mind as from morals.

All that is urged by the saint for the superiority of faith over works, is as truly urged for the higher state of intellectual perception or beholding over any intellectual performance, such as the creation of algebra, or of the *Iliad*. The conscience of the coming age will put its surveillance on the intellect. We accuse ourselves that we have been useless; we ought to accuse ourselves that we have been thoughtless. It is the Law of Adrastia, that whatever soul has perceived any truth shall be safe from harm.[39]

The English nation have the common credit of being more individual, more outspoken, and downright, than we are. Each man of them is, very likely, narrow and committed to opinions of no great liberality or dignity, but, such as they are, he heartily stands for them; silent or loud, he is content to be known to all the world as their champion; they grow to him; he is enraged, he curses and swears for them. In the House of Lords, the patrician states his opinion, very clumsily and drearily perhaps, but at least not looking for your ballot and approbation, rather with an air that says, such is my opinion, and who the devil are you?

Our people have this levity and complaisance, fear to offend, do not wish to be misunderstood, do not wish of all things to be in the minority.

God and nature are altogether sincere, and art should be as sincere. It is not enough that the work should show a skilful hand, ingenious contrivance, and admirable polish and finish: it should have a commanding motive in the time and condition in which it was made. We should see in it the great belief of the artist which caused him to make it so as he did, and not otherwise; nothing frivolous, nothing that he might do or not do, as he chose, but somewhat that must be done then and there by him; he could not take his neck out of that yoke, and save his soul, and this design must shine through the whole performance.

Never was anything great accomplished but under a religious impulse. The same law holds for the intellect, as for the will. When the will is absolutely surrendered to the moral sentiment,—that is virtue; when the wit is totally surrendered to intellectual truth,—that is genius. Talent for talent's sake is a bauble and a show. Talent working in rapture in the cause of universal truth, lifts the possessor to new power as a benefactor.

Sincerity is, in dangerous times, discovered to be an immeasurable advantage. Bishop Latimer tells us, that his father taught him, when a boy, not to shoot with his arms, but to lay his body to the bow.[40] For sincerity is the test of truth, of talent, of genius. True genius is always moral: "Show me a wicked man who has written

---

39. Paraphrased by Emerson from *Six Books of Proclus . . . on the Theology of Plato* (1816).

40. Hugh Latimer (ca. 1485–1555), English Catholic priest and religious reformer who converted to Reformist doctrine and later became bishop of Worcester.

poetry, and I will show you where his poetry is not poetry; or rather, I will show you in his poetry no poetry at all."—[41]

I distrust all the legends of great accomplishments or performance of unprincipled men. Very little reliance must be put on the common stories that circulate of this great senator's or that great barrister's learning, their Greek, their varied literature. That ice won't bear. Reading! Do you mean that this senator or this lawyer who stood by, and allowed the passage of infamous laws, was a reader of Greek books? That is not the question—but, to what purpose did they read? I allow them the merit of that reading which appears in their opinions, tastes, beliefs, and practice. They read that they might know, did they not? Well, these men did not know. They blundered. They were utterly ignorant of that which every boy or girl of fifteen knows perfectly,—the rights of men and women. And this big-mouthed talker, among his dictionaries and Leipsic editions of Lysias, had lost his knowledge.[42] But the President of the Bank nods to the President of the Insurance Office, and relates, that, at Virginia Springs, this idol of the forum exhausted a trunk full of classic authors.

There is always the previous question, How came you on that side? Your argument is ingenious, your language copious, your illustrations brilliant, but your major proposition palpably absurd. Will you establish a lie? You are a very elegant writer;—but you can't write up what gravitates down.

Stand by your order. Stand by yourself. Stay at home in your mind. Aplomb is power in all companies. Sit silent, and hearkening, and docile, not like the vulgar who say whatever occurs to them, but as the liege of truth. In your study of great books, I should say, read a little proudly; as if one should say to the author, 'tis of no account what your reputation is abroad: You have now to convince *Me*, or I leave you.

Rely on yourself. There is respect due to your teachers exactly in proportion to their faithful labors, but every age is new, and has problems to solve insoluble by the last age. Men over forty are no judges of a book written in a new spirit. Neither your teachers, nor the universal teachers, the laws, the customs or dogmas of nations, neither saint nor sage, can compare with that counsel which is open to you. "No angel in his heart acknowledges anyone superior to himself, but the Lord alone."[43]

But I shall be told it is of no use for one to resist a thousand, for a solitary scholar to waste his breath in protesting against tendencies of the continent. Not literary history alone, but all history, is a record of the power of minorities—and of

---

41. Quoted from *Counterparts* (1854) by Elizabeth Sara Sheppard (ca. 1830–62), English novelist (*TN*, 2:207).

42. Lysias (ca. 445–ca. 380 B.C.), Athenian orator.

43. Attributed to Emanuel Swedenborg by Emerson (*JMN*, 15:25).

minorities of one. Every book is written with a constant secret reference to the few intelligent persons whom the writer knows or believes to exist in the million. The artist has always the masters in his eye, though he affect to flout them. Michel Angelo is thinking of Da Vinci, and Raffaelle is thinking of Michel Angelo. Tennyson would give his fame for a verdict in his favor from Wordsworth.[44]

In the recovery of the antique marbles in the last century, what were the marbles till Winckelmann could see and pronounce?[45] When the Elgin Marbles came to England, the cry of voices went against them; but Haydon and Fuseli asserted their genuineness to Parliament and people, until the whole world came and saw them through their wiser eyes.[46] Agassiz, and Owen, and Huxley affect to address the American and the English people, but are really writing to each other.[47] Everett dreamed of Webster; McKay, the shipbuilder, thinks of George Steers, and Steers thinks of Pook, the naval constructor.[48] The names of the masters at the head of each department of science, art, or quality, are often little known to the world, but are always known to the adepts; as Robert Brown in Botany, and Gauss in Mathematics.[49] Often, the master is a hidden man, but not to the true student. Invisible to all the rest, but resplendent to him. All his own work and culture forms the eye to see the master.

See in politics the importance of minorities of one, as of Socrates, of Phocion, Cato, Lafayette, Arago.[50] The importance of the one person who has the truth, over

44. Michelangelo (1475–1564), Italian painter, sculptor, and poet; Leonardo da Vinci (1452–1519), Italian painter, sculptor, architect, engineer, and scientist; Raphael (1483–1520), Italian painter whose works adorn the Vatican. Alfred, Lord Tennyson (1809–92), English poet, named poet laureate in 1850 after the death of William Wordsworth.

45. Johann Joachim Winckelmann (1717–68), German antiquities expert.

46. Thomas Bruce (1766–1841), seventh Earl of Elgin, as envoy to the Ottoman sultan brought a collection called the "Elgin marbles," including the Parthenon frieze, from the Acropolis to the British Museum; Benjamin Robert Haydon (1786–1846), English painter of historical and biblical scenes; Henry Fuseli, originally Johann Heinrich Füssli (1741–1825), British painter and art critic born in Switzerland.

47. Louis Agassiz (1807–73), Swiss-born American naturalist and zoological explorer, began in 1859 the collections now at the Harvard Museum of Comparative Zoology; Robert Owen (1771–1858), Welsh social reformer and philanthropist; Thomas Henry Huxley (1825–95), English geologist, strong advocate of Charles Darwin's theory of evolution.

48. Edward Everett (1794–1865), American Unitarian minister, Harvard professor, orator, and politician; Daniel Webster (1782–1852), American statesman and orator; Donald McKay (1810–80), American naval architect and shipbuilder, best known for his fast clipper ships; George Steers (1820–56), American yacht builder; Samuel Hartt Pook (1827–1901), American designer of the first New England clipper ship in 1850.

49. Carl Friedrich Gauss (1777–1855), German mathematician and astronomer.

50. Socrates (ca. 470–399 B.C.), one of the most famous of the Greek philosophers, whose dialogic method of teaching gained many adherents; Phocion (ca. 402–318 B.C.), Athenian general and statesman and student of Plato, after the death of Alexander the Great ruled Athens but was executed on a false charge of treason; Cato the Younger (95–46 B.C.), Roman politician; Marie-Joseph-Paul-Yves-Roch-Gilbert du Motier, the marquis de Lafayette (1757–1834), French military leader and a hero of the American Revolution; François Arago (1786–1853), French astronomer and physicist.

nations who have it not, is because power obeys reality, and not appearance: power is according to quality, and not quantity.

Let me recall your own experience, when I say that every generous youth capable of thought and action,—with however bold a front and stoical demeanor,—dwells in a little heaven of his own with the images of a few men and a few women,— perhaps with two or one. There was a time when Christianity existed in one child. If the child had been killed by Herod, would the element have been lost?[51] God sends his message, if not by one, then quite as well by another, or could have made every heart preach his commandment. When the Master of the Universe has ends to fulfil, he impresses his will on the structure of single minds.

Whoever looks with heed into his thoughts will find our science of the mind has not got far. We divide the mind into faculties of Perception, Conception, Understanding, Imagination, Reason, and Memory, and we attempt some education of these faculties. But who looks with his own eyes will find that there is somebody within him that knows more than he does; (that this education of the Understanding is not always wise: a low and limitary power which works to short ends, to the senses, to daily life in house and street;) a certain dumb life in life; a simple wisdom behind all acquired wisdom; somewhat not educated, or educable, not altered or alterable; a motherwit, which does not learn by experience or by books, but knew it all already; makes no progress,—but was wise in youth as in age.

More or less clouded, it yet resides the same in all, saying *Aye, Aye,* or *No, No,* to every proposition: Yet its grand *Aye* and its grand *No,* are more musical than all eloquence. Nobody has found the limits of its knowledge. Whatever object is brought before it is already well known to it.

It is impossible to extricate oneself from the questions in which our age is involved. I am not insensible to the stern benefits wrought by the War. War always exalts an age, speaks to slumbering virtue, makes of quiet, plain men unexpected heroes; out of a territory which was hitherto vulgar farm and market, makes a country, and of people whom we did not know, and only counted in the census, or, as producers and customers, makes countrymen.

All of us have shared the new enthusiasm of country and of liberty, which swept like whirlwind through all souls at the outbreak of war; and brought, by ennobling us, already an offset for its calamity. I learn with joy and with deep respect, that this College has sent its full quota to the field. I learn with grief, but with honoring pain, that you have had your sufferers in the battle, and the noble youth have returned wounded and maimed.

The War uplifted us into generous sentiments: War ennobles the age. We do not

---

51. Herod I, known as Herod the Great (73–4 B.C.), king of Judea, was given the title "king of the Jews" by the Roman Senate but was never popular with his Jewish subjects. Emerson is referring to Matthew 2, the story of Herod's massacre of the infants of Bethlehem because of his fear of a rival Jewish king.

often have a moment of grandeur in these hurried, slipshod lives. But the behaviour of the young men has taught us much. The solemnity of action of those who had been gay and thoughtless until now. We will not again disparage America, now that we have seen what men it will bear. Battle with his sword has cut many a Gordian knot in twain, which all the wit of East and West, of Northern and Border statesmen, could not untie.[52] We have abandoned ourselves to the current, and the current has known the way. The War floated us into Emancipation, which we dared not enact; into arming the blacks; into treating an enemy as an enemy.

The mind always responds to any just demand. It is the nobility of the mind, its military armament, Nature's Home-Guard,—that danger brings its own concentration and added activity, and, if even to gentle natures, a grim joy which the sense of power always gives, and which many private experiences in the present war, told in army letters, abundantly confirm. Tender youths who have passed from every luxury to every hardship, say, "Do not pity me. I assure you I have never spent a year so happily."

The times are dark, but heroic. The times develop the strength they need. Boys are heroes. Women have shown a tender patriotism and inexhaustible charity: and, on each new threat of faction, the ballot of the people has been unexpectedly right and decisive. But the issues already appearing overpay the cost. The slavery is broken, and, we use our advantage,—irretrievably. For such a gain,—to end once for all that pest of all free institutions, one generation might well be sacrificed— perhaps it will,—that this continent be purged and a new era of equal rights dawn on the universe.

Who would not?—If it could be made certain that the new morning of universal liberty should rise on our race, by the perishing of one generation,—who would not consent to die? The War is a new glass through which to see things. It has undeceived us about European states. They had exhibited a great dislike of America in France and in England on account of our slavery. And we gave England credit for sincerity. She had at least achieved the emancipation of slaves in the West Indies.[53] But deeper than in freedom was her interest in her trade, and naval superiority, and superiority of all kinds, which we threatened. Her joy was great at seeing our nation broken, and her interest in the success of the rebellion undisguised. Money, law, tacit protection, aid of the press; loud advocacy by nobility and Parliament; were freely given to the rebellion. And when challenged on the point of all this protection to slavery, they affected to think that the North was not emancipating, and they talked through their noses. War, seeking for the roots of strength, comes upon the moral aspects at once. In quiet times, custom stifles this discussion as sentimental, and brings in the brazen devil, as by immemorial right.

52. Gordius, king of Phrygia, tied a knot that could only be untied by the future ruler of Asia; Alexander the Great cut it with his sword.

53. Parliament had freed the slaves in British possessions on 1 August 1834.

When the course of events goes amiss, there is always a spiritual cause. Have we Despondency, Luxury, Avarice, Slavery, War?—Why these are as natural as eating. Every man is an animal. It was said of the precocity of Siberian civilization, "Skin a Russian, and you have a Tartar"; and Hobbes said, "Man is to man a wolf."[54] Wolf and tiger tear and slay to eat, and slay a great deal more than they eat; and man in his savage state does the same. But why did he not know and do better? Was there no Bible? Was there no tamer? no Von Amburg among the lions?[55] Manco Capac among the cannibals?[56] No scholar? no college? no clerisy? no missionary? no reason? A Mexico of wild horses, and no Rarey; a Rocky Mountain of grizzly bears, and no Grizzly Bear Adams?[57] An America full of cotton, land, and money, and no literature? Slave-hunters, and slave commissioners, and truckling merchants, and politicians,—and no hero to befriend the friendless, no redeemer with a whip of cord to drive away the profaners of the temple?[58]

Gentlemen, I hold the Scholars, when they are truly such, to be the first-class in the state. I shall treat them so, and speak to their interest as the first. Now the War, which, while it afflicts, ennobles this country, has this inconvenience,—that it absorbs all conversation, and displaces everything but itself. But in the precinct of the College, let us be severely just. Let us indulge ourselves with defying for this day the political and military interest and indulge ourselves with topics proper to the place at the risk of disgusting the popular ear. I please myself with the belief that you, members of this literary association, have kept your ear and heart open to the voice of wise men, to the voice of poets,—still better, to the great hope and lofty counsels of perfect solitude; that you have not been pained when fashion and frivolity did not smile on you, while you had a better ambition, and were seeking selecter companions.

It is an ever ascending profession. You cannot go back to your childish books. Every step you make disqualifies you for the lower plane of thought you leave behind. He who has learned to read Plato, and once tasted the true joy of that book, does not care much for *Sinbad, the Sailor*.[59] Every piece of new knowledge refines you, and you can never be again the savage you were.

54. Thomas Hobbes (1588–1679), English materialist philosopher.

55. Isaac H. Von Amburg (1811–65), German animal trainer who was the first man to put his head in the mouth of a lion.

56. Manco Capac (fl. ca. 1200), traditional founder of the Inca dynasty in Peru.

57. John Solomon Rarey (1827–66), American horse trainer in Ohio; Grizzly Adams (1812–60), frontiersman and hunter.

58. See, for example, Matthew 21:12–13, Mark 11:15–17.

59. "Sinbad the Sailor" is a tale in the collection of ancient Persian-Indian-Arabian traditional tales called *The Arabian Nights' Entertainments* or *A Thousand and One Nights* (1450), originally in Arabic.

Fortune of the Republic

(1863–1864)

Emerson first delivered "Fortune of the Republic," which has come down to us as one of his most important Civil War discourses, on 1 December 1863 before the Parker Fraternity in Boston; he repeated the lecture another thirteen times between its first delivery and 9 February 1864 throughout Massachusetts, twice in Maine, and once each in Brooklyn, New York, and North Bennington, Vermont.

As James Elliot Cabot describes it, in 1878, when his creative powers had declined and after he had ceased original writing, Emerson was "asked to give a summing-up of the position of the country after the war, and its spiritual needs and prospects for the new generation." He spoke on 25 February at the Old South Church from "a paper of the war-time" (i.e., from the original manuscript of "Fortune of the Republic") "with additions from his journals" (Cabot, *A Memoir*, 2:677). Emerson repeated this version of the lecture at least once more (at the home of Cyrus Bartol on 30 March), but when the *Atlantic Monthly* declined to print the lecture, Cabot and Ellen Emerson extensively reworked it for a separate publication as *Fortune of the Republic* (Boston: Houghton, Osgood, 1878). The 1878 version of the lecture was subsequently printed in *Miscellanies* in 1884 (*W*, 11:511–44).

The version of "Fortune of the Republic" that follows is from the complete manuscript in Emerson's hand from which he read in 1863.

It is a rule that holds in economy as well as in hydraulics, that you must have a source higher than your tap. The mills, the shops, the theatre, the caucus, the college, and the church, have all found out this secret. The sailors sail by chronometers that do not lose two or three seconds in a year, ever since Newton explained to Parliament that the way to improve navigation, was, to get good watches, and they must offer public premiums for a better timekeeper than any in use.[1] The manufacturers rely on turbines of hydraulic perfection. The carpet-mill, on mordants and dyes, which exhaust the skill of chemists. The calico-print, on designers of genius, who draw the wages of artists, not of artisans. Wedgewood, in England, bravely took the sculptor Flaxman to counsel, who said, send to Italy, search the

---

1. Sir Isaac Newton (1642–1727), English natural philosopher and mathematician.

museums for the forms of old Etruscan vases, urns, waterpots, and domestic and sacrificial vessels of all kinds.[2] They built great works, and called their manufacturing village, *Etruria*.[3] Flaxman, with his Greek taste, selected and combined the loveliest forms which were executed in English clay; sent boxes of these as gifts, to every court of Europe, and formed the taste of the world. It was a *renaissance* at the breakfast table and china-closet. The brave manufacturers made their fortune. The jewellers imitated the revived models in silver and gold. The theatre avails itself of the best talent of poet, of painter, and of amateur of taste, to make the ensemble of dramatic effect. The marine insurance office has its mathematical counsellor to settle averages. The Life Assurance, its Table of Annuities. The wine-merchant has his analyst and taster,—the more exquisite the better. He has also, I fear, his debts to the chemist, as well as to the vineyard.

Our modern wealth stands on a few staples, and the interest nations take in our war is exasperated by the importance of the cotton-trade. And what is cotton? One plant out of some two hundred thousand plants known to the botanist,—vastly the largest part of which are reckoned weeds. And what is a weed? A plant whose virtues have not yet been discovered, and every one of the two hundred thousand, probably yet to be of utility in the arts. As Bacchus of the vine, Ceres of the wheat,— as Arkwright and Whitney were the demi-gods of cotton, so prolific Time will yet bring an inventor to every plant.[4] There is not a property in nature, but a mind is born to seek and find it.

Our sleepy civilization,—when Roger Bacon and Monk Schwartz had invented gunpowder,—built its whole art of war,—all fortification by land and sea, all drill and military education, on that one compound; all is an extension of a gun barrel;—and is very scornful about bows and arrows, and reckons Greeks, and Romans, and middle ages little better than Indians and bow and arrow times.[5] As if the earth, water, gases, lightning, and caloric, had not a million energies,—the discovery of any one of which could change the art of war again, and put an end to war, by the exterminating forces man can apply.

Now, if this is true in all the useful, and in the fine arts, that the direction must

2. Josiah Wedgwood (1730–95), English potter who developed a cream-colored earthenware known as Queen's ware and was the inventor of jasperware, developed his firm into one of the world's leading producers of ceramics; John Flaxman (1755–1826), English sculptor and draftsman, was the leading Neoclassical artist in England and a designer for Josiah Wedgwood.

3. Etruria was originally the name of an ancient country in central Italy. Its residents, the Etruscans, were renowned for their art.

4. Bacchus is the Roman name for Dionysus, the Greek god of nature and the divine ecstasy achieved by communing with the great life forces (wine is his most common symbol); Ceres is the Roman god of grain and the harvest, corresponding to the Greek goddess Demeter; Sir Richard Arkwright (1732–92), English inventor of the spinning frame for producing cotton warp thread; Eli Whitney (1765–1825), American inventor of the cotton gin, which separated the fiber from the seed.

5. Roger Bacon (ca. 1220–92), English philosopher and scientist, and Berthold Schwarz (fourteenth century), German monk and alchemist, were both the reputed inventors of gunpowder.

be drawn from a superior source, or there will be no good work,—does it hold less in our social and civil life? In our popular politics, you may note that each aspirant who rises above the crowd, however at first making his obedient apprenticeship in party tactics, if he have sagacity, soon learns, that it is by no means by obeying the vulgar weathercock of his party, the resentments, the fears and whims of it, that real power is gained, but that he must often face and resist the party, and abide by his resistance, and put them in fear: that the only title to their permanent respect and to a larger following, is, to see for himself what is the real public interest, and stand for that;—that is a principle,—and all the cheering and hissing of the crowd must by and by accommodate itself to that. Our times easily afford you very good examples.

The law of water and all fluids is true of wit. Prince Metternich said, "Revolutions begin in the best heads, and run steadily down to the populace."[6] It is a very old observation, and not truer because Metternich said it, and not less true. With all the immense sympathy which at first and again has upheld the War, I fear the country does not yet apprehend the salvation that is offered it;—that we may yet be punished to rouse the egotists, the skeptics, the fashionists, and the pursuers of ease and pleasure. Never a country had such a fortune,—as men call fortune,—as this,—in its geography, in its history, in the present attitude of its affairs, and in its majestic possibility. Yet our young soldiers returning on thirty days' furlough from the camps, wonder at the apathy of the cities, and at the more than apathy of multitudes of young men seeking their pleasure in the streets, and even putting on airs of superiority, and wondering, like so many Talleyrands, at their too much zeal and excitement.[7] But we cannot think of what is passing, of what is still at risk, and on what questions the nation may presently rest.

At every moment, some one country more than any other represents the sentiment and the future of mankind. At the present time, none will doubt that America occupies this place in the opinion of nations. Not only is it the illustration of the theories of political economists, it is the topic to which all foreign journalists return as soon as they have told their local politics. Not only Buonaparte affirmed in 1816, that, in twenty-five years, the United States would dictate the politics of Europe,— a prophecy a little premature, but fast being confirmed,—but it is proved by the fact of the vast emigration into this country from all the nations of western and central Europe: and, when the adventurers have planted themselves, and looked about, they send back all the money they can spare to bring their friends.[8] Meantime, they find this country just passing through a great crisis in its history, as

---

6. Prince Klemens von Metternich (1773–1859), Austrian statesman and diplomatist.

7. Charles-Maurice de Talleyrand-Périgord (1754–1838), French politician known for his lack of commitment to established principles.

8. Napoléon Bonaparte (1769–1821), born in Corsica, general and later emperor of the French as Napoléon I.

necessary as lactation, or dentition, or puberty, to the human individual. We are in these days settling for ourselves and our descendants questions, which, as they shall be determined in one way or another, will make the peace and prosperity, or the calamity of the next ages.

The questions of Education, of Society, of Labor, the direction of talent, of character, the nature and habits of the American, may well occupy us: and more, the question of Religion. "The superior man thinks of virtue; the small man thinks of comfort."[9] "There are times," said Niebuhr, "when something better than comfort can be obtained."[10] It is an old oracle, that nations die by suicide, and the sign of it is the decay of thought.

The difficulty with the young men is, not their opinion and its consequences, not that they are copperheads, but that they lack idealism.[11] A man for success must not be *pure* idealist;—then he will practically fail: but he must have ideas, must obey ideas, or he might as well be the horse he rides on. A man does not want to be blind,—sun-dazzled,—sun-blind,—but every man must have glimmer enough to keep him from knocking his head against the walls. And it is in the interest of civilization, and good society, and friendship, that I dread to hear of well-born, gifted, and amiable men, that they have this indifference, this despair, disposing them in the present attitude of the war to short and hasty peace, on any terms.

It is the young men of the land, who must save it: It is they to whom this wonderful hour, after so many weary ages, dawns: the Second Declaration of Independence, the proclaiming of liberty, land, justice, and a career for all men, and honest dealings with other nations. Philip de Comines says, in writing of the wars of Charles of Burgundy with Louis XI of France, "Our Lord does not wish that one kingdom should play the devil with another."[12]

Nations were made to help each other as much as families were; and all advancement is by ideas, and not by brute force, or mechanic force. I call this spirit a remainder of Europe, imported into this soil. To say the truth, England is never out of mind. Nobody says it, but all think and feel it. England is the model in which they find their wishes expressed, not, of course, middle-class England, but rich, powerful, and titled England.

Now, English nationality is babyish, like the self-esteem of villages, like the nationality of Carolina, or of Cheraw, or of Hull, or the conceit and insolence of the shabby little kings on the Gambia River, who strut up to the traveller, "What

9. *Analects*, bk. 4, no. 11, by Confucius (Latin name for K'ung Ch'iu) (551–479 B.C.), Chinese philosopher.

10. Barthold Georg Niebuhr (1776–1831), German historian and critic.

11. The "Copperheads," or Peace Democrats, were Northerners who opposed Lincoln's war policy.

12. Philippe de Commynes (ca. 1447–1511), French politician and historian; Charles the Bold, Duke of Burgundy (1433–77), led a conspiracy of nobles against Louis XI (1423–83), king of France (1461–83), but lost his war and his life.

do they say of me in America?"[13] The English have a certain childishness,—it is at once their virtue and their fault, and every traveller, I am sure, can find in his personal experience comic examples of it. They are insular, and narrow. They have no higher worship than Fate. Excellent sailors, farmers, ironsmiths, weavers, and potters, they retain their Scandinavian strength and skill; but their morals do not reach beyond their frontier. The old passion for plunder: England watches like her old war-wolf for plunder.

Never a lofty sentiment, never a duty to civilization, never a generosity, a moral self-restraint is suffered to stand in the way of a commercial advantage. In sight of a commodity, her religion, her morals are forgotten. Even Carlyle, her ablest living writer, a man who has earned his position by the sharpest insights, is politically a fatalist. In his youth, he announced himself as a "theoretical sansculotte fast threatening to become a practical one." Now, he is practically in the English system, a Venetian aristocracy, with only a private stipulation in favor of men of genius. In the "History of Frederick the Great," the reader is treated as if he were a Prussian adjutant, solely occupied with the army and the campaign.[14] He is ever in the dreary circle of camp and courts. But of the people, you have no glimpse. No hint of their domestic life. Were there no families, no farms, no thoughtful citizens, no beautiful and generous women, no genial youth with beating hearts then alive in all the broad territories of that kingdom?

We are, to be sure, well accustomed to this pedantic way of writing history. We should not bring this criticism on another writer. But from Carlyle, who has taught us to make it, we had a right to expect an account of a nation, and not of a campaign.

But if the leaders of thought take this false direction, what can you expect from those who do not think, but are absorbed in maintaining their class privileges, their luxury, or their trade? As compared with France, in the distinction given to intellect in the state, and in society, England is Chinese in her servility to wealth, and to old wealth. Hence, the discovery of 1848,—that Paris was the capital of Europe, Paris, and not London. All men waited for Paris. If Paris revolted, so would Vienna and Berlin, and in the same way.[15] In the revolt of the German cities, in that year, they imitated the forms and methods of the insurrectionists in the French capital.[16]

13. Cheraw, South Carolina, was captured by Gen. William T. Sherman in 1865; Hull, Massachusetts, was a seaside resort; the Gambia River flows northwest through Senegal and west through Gambia, Africa.

14. *The History of Frederick the Great* was published between 1858 and 1865 by Thomas Carlyle (1795–1881), prolific Scottish essayist and historian who was Emerson's lifelong friend and correspondent.

15. Louis-Phillipe (1773–1850), king of the French (1830–48), a member of the Jacobin Club, was proclaimed "citizen king" and elected by the deputies but never won the allegiance of the industrial classes; he was overthrown and replaced by a democratic republic in 1848.

16. Riots in Berlin in 1848 were followed by the establishment of a new parliament at Frankfurt am Main.

They had the creed that the idea of human freedom was purest in Paris, while the liberty of London was selfish and mixed, a liberty quite too much drenched in respect for privileges, cast-iron aristocracy, and church hierarchy. The socialism of France indicates the more searching character of their aims, full of crude thoughts and wishes, but sincere, and aiming to lift the condition of mankind; to be a new experiment for a higher civilization. The continent waited for the action of Paris; London waited too, showing that Paris was the capital, not of Europe only, but of London also. And London waits still. By the accident of a strong Emperor, and by the energy of the French nation when firmly led, the whole policy of England in the last ten years has waited on France like a spaniel. Silently, Waterloo is avenged by the falling of the court of London into the second place, and expecting the initiative in every question from the French.[17] It was not that France was wise, but that England was weak.

There have been revolutions which were not in the interest of feudalism and barbarism, but in that of society. A series of wars in Europe are read with passionate interest, and never lose their pathos by time. First, the planting of Christianity. Second, the driving of the Moors from Spain, France, and Germany. Third, the rise of towns. Fourth, the Reformation of Luther.[18] Fifth, the decay of the temporal power of the Pope; the breaking of the power of the Jesuits; the breaking of the power of the Inquisition.[19] Sixth, the establishment of free institutions in England, France, and America. Seventh, the revolutions effected in all the arts of life by science. Eighth, the destruction of slavery. And these are distinguished not by the numbers of the combatants, or the numbers of the slain, but by the motive. No interest now attaches to the wars of York and Lancaster, to the wars of England and Scotland, to the wars of German, French, and Spanish emperors, which were only dynastic wars, but to those in which a principle was involved.[20]

When the cannon is aimed by ideas, then gods join in the combat, then poets are born. More gunpowder is burned in this state on the fourth of July in squibs and fireworks, than in battles that have decided the fate of nations. 'Tis when men with religious convictions are behind the cannon, when men die for what they live for, and the mainspring that works daily urges them to hazard all, that the cannon articulates its explosions with the voice of a man. Then, the rifle seconds the cannon, and the fowling-piece, the rifle, and the women make cartridges, and all shoot at one mark, and the better code of laws at last records the victory. Now

17. Napoléon Bonaparte's defeat at the Battle of Waterloo in 1815 marked the end of his public career.

18. Martin Luther (1483–1546), German religious reformer, founder of Protestantism.

19. Emerson may be thinking of either the Inquisition of the Roman Catholic Church against heretics during the thirteenth century in Italy and France or the Spanish Inquisition against Jews and Moors (1478–1835).

20. The Houses of York and Lancaster fought the Wars of the Roses (1455–87) for the throne of England.

the chiefest of these,—culmination of these triumphs of humanity, and which did virtually include the extinction of slavery,—is, the planting of America.

If the general history of Europe is dreary with war and oppression, neither can we pretend that our own record is quite clean. In America, we have had great faults also. Here, there has been torpor of the nobler faculties; here have prevailed vulgar estimates of success. Our foreign policy has not been republican, not in the interests of freedom or humanity. We had no character. In the European crisis, once and again we should have had great weight, if we had character. But Austria, Prussia, France, and Russia, looked at America, and said,—" 'Tis worse than we."

For this reason, there is very little in our history that rises above commonplace, and we are forced to go back to the Revolution in 1775, to find any ground of praise. In the Greek Revolution, Clay and Webster persuaded Congress into some cold declaration of sympathy.[21] Once we tendered Lafayette a national ship, gave him an ovation, and a tract of land.[22] We attempted some testimony of national sympathy to Kossuth and Hungary.[23] We sent corn and money to the Irish Famine.[24] These were spasmodic demonstrations. They were ridiculed as sentimentalism. They were sentimentalism, for it was putting us into a theatrical attitude. We belied our sympathy with Hungary, by greeting her oppressor: our sympathy with French liberty, by striking hands with her usurper: our sympathy with Ireland, by the dimensions of the Know-Nothing party.[25]

Our estimate of America is variable. Yesterday is insignificant; today, all-commanding. Now let me show you some of the points that make the fortune or felicity of this nation.

America was opened after the feudal mischief was spent, and so the people made a good start. We began well. No inquisition here; no kings, no nobles, no dominant church. In every other country, the accusation of heresy brings want and danger to a man's door; here it has lost its terrors. Sadi says, "The subjects are always of their

---

21. Henry Clay (1777–1852), American politician and secretary of state, was instrumental in preparing the legislation that included the Fugitive Slave Act; Daniel Webster (1782–1852), American statesman and orator; for a discussion of their support of Greece in its war against Turkey see Claude Moore Fuess, *Daniel Webster*, 2 vols. (Boston: Little, Brown, 1930), 1:310–14.

22. The marquis de Lafayette (Marie-Joseph-Paul-Yves-Roch-Gilbert du Motier [1757–1834], French military leader and a hero of the American Revolution) had been given use of the ship *Alliance* by Congress for return trips to France in 1781 and 1788, had made an enormously successful tour of the eastern states in 1824, and had been deeded 11,520 acres of land near the Kentucky and Ohio Rivers by Congress for his services to the United States.

23. Lajos Kossuth (1802–94), Hungarian patriot and statesman, leader of the Hungarian revolution of 1848–49.

24. Congress sent three ships full of provisions to famine-stricken Ireland and Scotland in March 1847.

25. The Know-Nothing or American Party in the United States during the 1850s was violently anti-Catholic and anti-immigrant; it declined rapidly after unsuccessfully running Millard Filmore for president in 1856.

master's opinion in religion."[26] We have eight or ten religions in every large town, and the most that comes of it is a degree or two on the thermometer of fashion. A pew in a particular church gives an easier entrance to the subscription ball. We have repealed the old abuses. Greater freedom of circumstance is here. English and Europeans are girt with an iron belt of condition. We have ample domain,—and thence facility of living.

The legislature heard and heeded the voice of the professor of Natural History, when he told them that he trusted to live to see the day when as many scholars would come to his museum from Europe as now go hence to theirs; and that he wished them to put Natural Science on an equal footing with the support of public worship.[27] And if one sees the tendency of our steps—the gifts to learning by private benefactors; the enlarging appropriations of town meetings and of states to the schools; the gift of scholarships and fellowships and recent foundation of agricultural schools,—of military, of naval, of gymnasiums, of the Nautical Almanac, and astronomic observatories—it looks as if vast extension was given to this popular culture, and, as the appetite grows by feeding, the next generation will vote for their children,—not a dame-school, nor a Latin school, but a university: complete training in all the arts of peace and war, letters and science, and all the useful and all the fine arts. And, thus, the voters in the Republic will at last be educated to that public duty.

In America, the government is acquainted with the opinions of all classes, knows the leading men in the middle class, knows the leaders of the humblest class. The President comes near enough to these: if he does not, the caucus does,—the primary ward- and town-meeting,—and, what is important does reach him. Not such,—far enough from such,—is England, France, and Austria: and, indeed, not such was America under previous administrations.

The politics of Europe are feudal. The six demands of chartism, are: first, universal suffrage; second, vote by ballot; third, paid legislation; fourth, annual Parliament; fifth, equality of electoral district; and sixth, no property qualification.[28] In England, they are still postponed. They have all been granted here to begin with.

We are coming,—thanks to the war,—to a nationality. Put down your foot, and say to England, we know your merits. In past time, we have paid them the homage of ignoring your faults. We see them still. But it is time that you should hear the truth,—that you have failed in one of the great hours that put nations to the test.

26. Sādī (ca. 1213–92), popularly known in America as Saadi, Persian poet and playwright who lived in Italy and introduced the Renaissance into Portugal.

27. Identified as Louis Agassiz (1807–73), Swiss-born American naturalist and zoological explorer, began in 1859 the collections now at the Harvard Museum of Comparative Zoology, by Emerson in a note in the manuscript.

28. Chartists, active between 1838 and 1849, were English reformers who promoted better conditions for the working classes during the early to mid-nineteenth century. They found the Reform Bill of 1832 too limited; Emerson lists their proposed changes.

When the occasion of magnanimity arrived, you had none: you forgot your loud professions, you rubbed your hands with indecent joy, and saw only in our extreme danger the chance of humbling a rival and getting away his commerce. When it comes to divide an estate, the politest men will sometimes quarrel. Justice is above your aim. Stand aside. We have seen through you. Henceforth, you have lost the benefit of the old veneration which shut our eyes to the altered facts. We shall not again give you any advantage of honor. We shall be compelled to look at the stern facts. And, we cannot count you great. Your inches are conspicuous, and we cannot count your inches against our miles, and leagues, and parallels of latitude. We are forced to analyse your greatness. We who saw you in a halo of honor which our affection made, now we must measure your means; your true dimensions; your population; we must compare the future of this country with that in a time when every prosperity of ours knocks away the stones from your foundation.

My own interest in the country is not precisely the same as that of my neighbors. I do not compute the annual production, the imports, or the valuation. My interest is perhaps professional. I wish that war, as peace, shall bring out the heart and the genius of the men. In every company, in every town, I seek knowledge and character, and so in every circumstance. War, I know, is a potent alternative, tonic, magnetiser,—reinforces manly power a hundred and a thousand times. I see it come as a frosty October, which shall restore intellectual and moral vigor to these languid and dissipated populations. For it is not the plants or the animals, innumerable as they are, nor the whole magazine of material nature, that can give the sum of power; but the infinite applicability of these things in the hands of thinking man—every new application being equivalent to a new material—is turning the globe into a brain. Over it, and under it, are laid nerves and straps, which throb across seas and territories, and, at each city and town in the course an operator plays on the elemental forces as on the keys of a piano.

A land is covered with settlers' camps; then, presently, with log-cabins; then, soon after, with white wooden towns, which look to the European eye as slight and perishable as the emigrant camps they succeeded: but, almost as quickly, these yield to solid blocks of brick and granite, which, anywhere else would last for centuries, but will give place very soon to marble architecture. Our white wooden towns are like the paper kite which Mr. Ellet, the engineer, flew across the Niagara River, and let it fall on the other side.[29] By means of the kite string, a stronger cord was drawn, and then a rope, and then a cable, and then an iron chain, and then a light bridge, and, in good time, the huge Suspension Bridge. So here the squatters' little town is presently a stone city with two hundred thousand men, like Chicago and San Francisco. It is not the fault of Nature if the healthy man has not bread for himself and his household.

29. Charles Ellet (1810–62), American civil engineer.

These native masters, and only these should have the discretion in every department. Therefore, I read with great pleasure that Mr. Jenckes of Rhode Island has submitted to Congress a bill prescribing an examination for every officer who may be appointed to a civil office under government, and for every promotion, with certain exceptions.[30] Of course, all incompetent persons would at once cease to apply, whilst fit persons, who will not now submit to the degradation of lobbying, begging, and bribing, would offer themselves, when the knowledge and skill were to be tested. Honest members of Congress who have appointments in their gift to the Naval School, or to West Point, have already set the excellent example of advertising a fair competition by examination free to all candidates in their district. In the English government, Lord Macaulay introduced the like innovation to the East-India service.[31] If this become American law, we shall not send ignorant drunkards, who happen to be political favorites, to represent the Republic in foreign nations, whose languages they do not know, and will not learn, and so become ridiculous there.

Our forefathers scraped the rough surface of the earth for clams and acorns, or venison brought down with a flint arrowhead, and a little corn ground between two stones. We, by civilization and ideas. Why need I recall the proud catalogue of your mechanical arts? Every invention carries us forward a century: steam and the telegraph have blotted out the word *distance* from the Dictionary; Hoe's press, and McCormick's reaper, and the sewing machine, and the photograph, and the use of ether—American inventions—have left behind them the witchcraft of Merlin and Cornelius Agrippa.[32]

See how this civil freedom moderates the ferocity incident elsewhere to political changes. We, in the midst of a great revolution, still enacting the sentiment of the Puritans, and the dreams of young people of thirty years ago,—we, passing out of old remainders of barbarism into pure Christianity and humanity, into freedom of thought, of religion, of speech, of the press, of trade, of suffrage or political right, and working through this tremendous ordeal which elsewhere went by beheadings and reign of terror, passed through this like a sleep, calmly reading the newspaper, and drinking our tea the while. This serenity of the northern states: 'Tis like a brick house moved from its foundations, and passing through our streets, whilst all the family are pursuing their domestic work as usual within doors.

Nature says to the American,

30. Thomas Allen Jenckes (1818–75), American politician, congressman from Rhode Island, proposed civil-service reforms that failed to win passage in 1865 and 1868.

31. Thomas Babington Macaulay, first Baron Macaulay (1800–1859), English writer and politician, member of the Supreme Council of India (1834–38).

32. Richard March Hoe (1812–86), American developer of the rotary press; Cyrus Hall McCormick (1809–84), American inventor of a version of the modern grain reaper; Merlin, the magician at Camelot in Arthurian times; Heinrich Cornelius Agrippa, called Agrippa von Nettesheim (1486–1535), German physician, theologian, and philosopher interested in alchemy.

I understand mensuration and numbers. I compute the ellipse of the moon; the ebb and flow of waters; the curve and the errors of planets; the balance of attraction and recoil. I have measured out to you by weight and tally the power you need. I give you the land and sea, the forest and the mine, the elemental forces, nervous energy. When I add difficulty, I add brain. See to it that you hold and administer the continent for mankind. One thing you have rightly done. You have offered a patch of land in the wilderness to every son of Adam who will till it. Other things you have begun to do;—to strike off the chains which snuffling hypocrites have bound on the weaker race. You are to imperil your lives and fortunes for a principle.

Chartism in England asks that intellect and not property, or, at least, intellect as well as property, be represented in Parliament. Humanity asks that government shall not be ashamed to be tender and paternal, but that democratic institutions shall be more thoughtful for the interests of women, for the training of children, for the care of sick and unable persons and the serious care of criminals, than was ever any the best government of the old world.

Mathematicians say, that, "in the end, the cards beat all the players, were they never so skilful." And we say, that revolutions beat all the insurgents, be they never so determined and politic; that the great interests of mankind, being at every moment, through ages, in favor of justice, and the largest liberty,—will always, from time to time, gain on the adversary, and, at last, win the day. The same felicity comes out of our reverses now, as we have owed commanding advantages to our geography, and to the planting of the country by exiles from Europe, who wished to avoid the evils of the old world, and these exiles were the idealists of Europe, aiming at freedom in religion and state.

It will hereafter be found that what immense benefit accrued to this country, and to the society of nations from the American Revolution of 1775, no less benefit accrued from the present calamities. Now, in a plight like this, harsh remedies, crises, and war help us. War shatters porcelain dolls,—breaks up in a nation Chinese conservatism, death in life. War always ennobles an age. What munificence has it not disclosed! How easily a sentiment has unclasped the grip of avarice in the rich, and made those who were not rich prodigally generous, through the painfullest economy!

We used to think that the feeling of patriotism did not exist in this country, or had a feeble pulse. The country was too large. We could not be very hot about the enormous reaches of a continent. It was as if one were to praise the Atlantic as a better ocean than the Pacific or Indian, or take a pride in our globe as a more desireable globe to live on than Saturn or Mars. But the moment an enemy appeared, we woke out of sleep. No country! We had nothing else but a country. Business was thrust aside. Every house hung out the flag. Every street was full of patriotic songs. Almost every able-bodied man put on a uniform.

Our politics were at an extreme pass. Battle cut the knot which no wisdom could untie, and showed you how to destroy slavery, which was harming the white nation more than it was harming the black.[33] As the smoke of the combat begins to lift, the people see their debt successively to passages that gave most alarm when they befel. To enumerate some of these shortly:

First. To South Carolina for taking the initiative, as relieving us from the far greater danger, which, in the last years of the peace, overhung us,—that the South in possession of the government should have forced through Congress an act securing to the planter the right of transit with his slaves, which, it is easy to see, in the old state of parties, would have made slavery familiar in Massachusetts and Illinois, and, with the army and navy in the possession of the South, could only have been resisted by a religious war in the North.[34]

Second. That an eminent benefactor of the Union in this war has been the Vice President of the Confederacy proclaiming the theory and policy of his government,—a manifesto hitherto unrebuked, never disowned,—that "Slavery was the cornerstone of their State." No public act has served us so much at home and abroad, except Emancipation.

Third. A felicity of the Republic has been, what gave great apprehension in the beginning, the extreme caution, not to say timidity and tardiness, of President Lincoln, who has served us as a more determined leader might not.

Fourth. We owe very much to the sympathizers with the rebellion in the North to Governor Seymour, Vallandigham, the Woods, and Pierce, whose mobs, councils, platforms, and the casual disclosure of the correspondence of some of these persons have repelled honest men, and driven them to the support of the country, as entreaties from the Republicans could never have drawn them.[35]

Fifth. Lastly, we owe main thanks to the firmness of the tone of the Rebels, and the rancor of their hatred, now in the extreme of their fortunes.

'Tis vain to say that the war was avoidable by us, or, that both sides are in the wrong. The difference between the parties is eternal,—it is the difference of moral and immoral motive. Your action is to build, and their action is to destroy: yours to protect and establish the rights of men; and theirs to crush them, in favor of a

33. "Battle cut the knot which no wisdom could untie": Emerson is referring to the story of Gordius, king of Phrygia, who tied a knot that could only be untied by the future ruler of Asia; Alexander the Great cut it with his sword.

34. Emerson is referring to the Fugitive Slave Act.

35. Horatio Seymour (1810–86), American politician, governor of New York who sympathized with the South but supported the Union when war broke out; Clement Laird Vallandigham (1820–71), American politician, Ohio congressman, and leader of the Copperheads, arrested for pro-Confederacy speeches during the Civil War and banished to the Confederacy; George Wood (1789–1860), American jurist in New York, argued for preserving the Union at all costs; Fernando Wood (1812–81), American politician, mayor of New York, and congressman who, with Vallandigham, was a strong Southern sympathizer; Franklin Pierce (1804–69), fourteenth president of the United States (1853–57) known for his proslavery sentiments, supported passage of the Kansas-Nebraska Act of 1854.

few owners. Machiavel himself said, " 'Tis not the violence which repairs, but the violence which destroys, that is to blame."[36]

It is difficult to exasperate the Northern people. In this climate, the genius of the people is mild, the mind active, and perpetually diverted to trade, manufactures and railroads, public works, politics, and general knowledge, which hinder men from brooding on any bad blood. We are, therefore, placable, and, through the whole war, there has been danger that, on the first hint of peace from the South, our people would forget and forgive all, and rush inconsiderately into the arms of their returning prodigals, and, in the gladness of the hour, would accept any terms,—the Union as it was,—losing by this social weakness half the fruit of their valor and their sacrifice of life and treasure. If we had conquered in the early part of the War, there was the greatest danger of a reckless generosity on our part. But, better than we could think, our defeats have been our protection from this fatal imprudence. And now, when the rebels seem to be pushed almost to their boundaries, and ready to be driven overboard into the Gulf, they exhibit the same effrontery in their demands as at their best fortunes—the vanquished claiming the terms of victory. This audacity comes timely in to disgust us, and teach, "What one is, why may not millions be?"

The American part is diffusion. We have a longer scale, and can reach the highest and the lowest degrees. And it is possible that here we shall have the happiness of lifting the low. Everybody hates vulgarity. But he that goes to the outcast to save him is defended by his motive from the pollution of that society. The steps already taken to teach the freedman his letters, and the decencies of life, are not worth much if they stop there. They teach the teacher,—open his eyes to new methods. They give him manliness and breadth he had not, and accustom him to a courage and poise: he learns to encounter the vulgarities of common society in town and country. And there is no society,—there is hardly the individual,—that has not his vulgar side, for as people are not altogether wise, but wise locally or topically, so they are locally or in some points graceful and cultivated, and in others strangely obtuse and mean.

Two facts appear:

First. That, in the activity of the people, up to this time, is a certain fatalism: That they have obeyed the materialities the continent offered them, and, being the contemporary of pine, chestnut, oak, granite, ice, waterfall; of wheat, cotton, copper, iron, and coal, they have wrought in them, and have done the best with these means. What could be done with leather, or with calico, or a pine log, that they have not done? This productivity, the admirable tools, finer and coarser, embracing all the armoury of modern Mechanics,—steam, railway, telegraph, up to Represen-

---

36. Niccolò Machiavelli (1469–1527), Italian statesman, historian, and political theorist. His most famous work, *The Prince* (published in 1532), a handbook for rulers, condones ruthless government in order to control self-serving subjects.

tative Government and Common School,—all these, they have conquered for the use of posterity. In short, they have been, in system and detail, the river-hand, and the sea-hand. On the coast, they have followed the sea; in the west, followed the river. We have worked and have eaten. We have got our wages. This was the poor man's paradise;—it has fed him fat. The poor man is getting rich: he is getting nervous, too. His prosperity has fairly alarmed him. What! nothing but putting money in our pockets, and having everything we want! There must come some end to this, or it would go to madness. Meat, and drink, and pampering, at last, pulls the man down. It runs to softening of the brain, to corruption of principles, and to hypocrisy and canting. Already the verdict of mankind is that the race is morally injured, that they have not kept the promise of their founders and early constitutions. They are in search of nothing grand or heroic. They have shown no trait of enlarged policy. A liberal measure has no chance; a just measure, very little chance, if there is no powerful party to extort it.

Crisis and war are often useful, even though the insurgents for liberty may be foiled. They trace the lines, they show what justice they seek, and they see it clearer by the light of the passions and the battle fires. They spot the bad church, or bad priesthood, or bad king, or bad law, and the tradition of these is well kept, and secures a new attempt by larger numbers, in the next age.

Second. Let the passion for America cast out the passion for Europe. Here, let there be what the earth waits for,—exalted manhood. America, the Paradise of the Third Class, of the Middle Interest; home of the poor, of mankind in their shirt-sleeves; the day of the omnibus, of third person plural, of the new man, whom plainly this country must furnish. Freer swing his arms, further pierce his eyes, more forward and forthright his whole build and carriage, goeth, than the Englishman's, who, we see, is much imprisoned in his backbone.

What a change! We are all of English race. But climate and country have told on us, so that John Bull does not know us.[37] That old race is the Jonathanizing of John.[38] They have grown cosmopolitan. Once the most English of English men, hating foreigners, they have grown familiar with the foreigner, and learned to use him according to his gift.

England has long been the cashier of the world. The progress of trade threatens to supplant London by New York, and that England must cross to India, if she keeps it, and to China, by the Pacific Railroad; and the London merchant must lose his privilege of selling in all markets on the Exchange in London, and buy on the Exchange in New York. This hastens, and is only checked by the War, and, though no man in England suffers such a word to pass his lips, it passes through his nose

37. "John Bull" is a character in *The History of John Bull* (1712) by John Arbuthnot (1667–1735), Scottish writer, Queen Anne's court physician, and close friend of Jonathan Swift. The name has come to mean the English nation personified.

38. "Jonathan" is a slang word for an American, especially a New Englander.

in this translation: How dreadful it is to see the Americans slaughter each other! Let us recognize the Southern independence, and we will have a strict alliance with the South, and check the Yankee prosperity, or share it.

In every crisis, people look for the master of the situation, who is usually slow to appear. He does not come when he is called. We have found none in America. But in England, which our politics immensely concern, they have found none. The one foreign interest of England is to assure herself in all times of the alliance of America, as bound by blood, language, religion, trade, and equal civilization. In all the dangers which are likely to threaten her from France, Austria, or Russia, America is sure to sympathize, and what protection would be so noble to bestow and to receive. Then, the more ambitious a state is, the more vulnerable. England, France, have ships, towns, colonies, treasure, and can very ill afford to give every Yankee skipper a chance to hack at these. A mob has nothing to lose, and can afford to steal; but England and France not.

In speaking of England, I lay out of question the truly cultivated class. They exist in England, as in France, in Italy, in Germany, and in America. The inspirations of God, like birds, never stop at frontiers or languages, but come to every nation. This class, like Christians, or poets, or chemists, exists for each other, across all possible nationalities, strangers to their own people,—brothers to you. I lay them out of question. They are sane men, as far removed as we, from the arrogance and mendacity of the English press, and the shop-tone of the cities. They wish to be exactly informed and to speak and act not for us or against us, but for the public good and the truth.

Neither do I think that we are to lay up malice against England, or to make *Punch*'s pictures or the opinions of the House of Lords a *casus belli*.[39] Shall we go to war with England on account of *Punch*'s pictures, or the opinions of a drunken Lord Soft, or the imbecility of Lord Brougham?[40] Having penetrated the people, and known their unworthiness, we can well cease to respect their opinion, even their contempt, and not go to war, at our disadvantage, for the avoiding of this. Who are they that they should despise us? these who cringe before Napoleon and Gortchakov.[41] We remember the wise saying of General Scott, "Resentment is a bad basis for a campaign."[42] When I think who these are that insult us, and pierce to the motive, I am not sure of the wisdom of Burke's saying, "Contempt is not a thing to be despised."[43]

---

39. *Punch*, the illustrated London satirical weekly, was started in 1841. Casus belli, an event that justifies (or allegedly justifies) a war.

40. "Lord Soft" is a generic reference to weak English lords.

41. Prince Mikhail Dmitrievitch Gortchakov (1795–1861), Russian soldier.

42. Gen. Winfield Scott, nicknamed Old Fuss and Feathers (1786–1866), American army officer, commander of the American army during the Mexican War.

43. Edmund Burke (1729–97), British politician and natural philosopher born in Ireland, wrote on individual liberty.

I believe this cannot be accomplished by dunces or idlers, but requires docility, sympathy, and religious receiving from higher principles; for Liberty, like religion, is a short and hasty fruit, and, like all power, subsists only by new rallyings on the source of inspiration. Power *can* be generous. The very grandeur of the means which offer themselves to you should suggest grandeur in the direction of your expenditure. If your mechanic arts are unsurpassed in usefulness, if you have taught the river to make shoes, and nails, and carpets, and the bolt of heaven to write your letters like a Gillot pen,—let these wonders work for honest humanity, for the poor, for justice, genius, and the public good.[44] I wish you to see that this country, the last found, is the great charity of God to the human race.

The times are dark, but heroic. The war uplifts us into generous sentiments. We do not often have a moment of grandeur in these hurried, slipshod lives. The people have met the dreadful issues so frankly. The youth have shown themselves heroes. The women have shown a tender patriotism, and an inexhaustible charity. And in each new threat of faction, the ballot of the people has been beyond expectation right and decisive. We will not again disparage America, now that we have seen what men it will bear. The slavery is broken, and, if we use our advantage, irretrievably. For such a gain,—to end once for all that pest of all free institutions,—one generation might well be sacrificed,—perhaps it will be,—that this continent be purged, and a new era of equal rights dawn on the universe. Who would not, if it could be made certain, that the new morning of universal liberty should rise on our race, by the perishing of one generation,—who would not consent to die?

The revolution is the work of no man, but the eternal effervescence of nature. It never did not work. And not a republican, not a statesman, not an idealist, not an abolitionist, can say without effrontery, I did it. Go push the globe, or scotch the globe, to accelerate or to retard it in its orbit. It is elemental. It is the old gravitation. Beware of the firing and the recoil! Who knows or has computed the periods? A little earlier, and you would have been sacrificed in vain. A little later, and you are unnecessary. "If I had attempted in 1806, what I performed in 1807," said Napoleon, "I had been lost."[45] Frémont was superseded in 1861, for what his superseders are achieving in 1863.[46]

Mazzini and Kossuth,—'tis fine for them to sit in committee in London, and hope to direct revolution in Italy, Hungary, or Poland.[47] Committees don't manage revolutions. A revolution is a volcano, and from under everybody's feet flings its sheet of fire into the sky. The end of all political struggle, is, to establish morality

44. A reference to Claude Gillot (1673–1722), French engraver and painter.

45. Among Napoléon's military accomplishments in 1807 were forcing Russia and Prussia to sue for peace and invading Spain and Portugal.

46. John Charles Frémont (1813–90), American soldier, explorer, and presidential candidate, had been appointed by Lincoln as major general in charge of the West. In that capacity he declared on 30 August 1861 that all slaves in Missouri were emancipated; Lincoln countermanded the order.

47. Giuseppe Mazzini (1805–72), Italian patriot.

as the basis of all legislation. 'Tis not free institutions, 'tis not a republic, 'tis not a democracy, that is the end,—no, but only the means: morality is the object of government. We want a state of things in which crime will not pay, a state of things which allows every man the largest liberty compatible with the liberty of every other man.

The guiding star to the arrangement and use of facts, is in your leading thought. You will have come to the perception that justice satisfies everybody, and justice alone. You will stand there for vast interests; North and South, East and West will be present to your mind, and your vote will be as if they voted. And you well know that your vote secures the foundations of the state, and good will, and liberty, and security of traffic and of production, and mutual increase of good will in the great interests, for no monopoly has been foisted in, no weak party or nationality has been sacrificed, no coward compromise has been conceded to a strong partner. Every one of these is the seed of vice, war, and national disorganization.

In seeing this guidance of events, in seeing this felicity without example, that has rested on the Union thus far,—I find new confidence for the future. I could heartily wish that our will and endeavor were more active parties to the work. But I see in all directions the light breaking; that trade and government will not alone be the favored aims of mankind, but every useful, every elegant art, every exercise of imagination, the height of Reason, the noblest affection, the purest religion will find their house in our institutions, and write our laws for the benefit of men.

Resources

(1864–1871)

Emerson's lecture "Resources" has a very complex genealogy. "Resources" began as one lecture Emerson typically delivered among six in his series *American Life* in 1864 and 1865; however, enlarging the manuscript over repeated deliveries with pages of his lectures "Works and Days" and "Success," among others, from the late 1850s and 1860s, he eventually transformed "Resources" into a popular lecture independent of the *American Life* series. Delivering the lecture regularly and more than thirty times between 1864 and 1872, Emerson read pages from the manuscript of "Resources" during his *Natural History of the Intellect* series at Harvard in 1870 and 1871. He also carried the manuscript of "Resources" with him cross-country for delivery in San Francisco in 1871, and he drew some portion of text from it for delivery in Baltimore in 1872.

In introducing the essay "Resources," which Emerson and James Elliot Cabot with the assistance of Ellen Emerson arranged for publication in *Letters and Social Aims* in 1876 (*W*, 8:135–54), Edward Waldo Emerson explains the popularity of the lecture in its series and independent-lecture formats both during and after the Civil War, and he distinguishes between the lecture and the essay it became. He states that as a lecture, its topic

was one that all the people of the United States had . . . brought home to them in earnest. The long drain which four years of war had made upon their lives, their fortunes, their courage and hopes made Mr. Emerson's word of cheer timely and welcome. But the essay represents only a scant half of what was . . . said [in the lecture]. Many of the sheets used [in the lecture] are marked . . . [to show] that they had done duty in some other cheering address in the anxious and sad days, and many . . . more immediately dealing with the conditions of the day, are omitted [from the essay]. But nearly all of the latter half, the ascension to a loftier plane, such as occurs in all his lectures, was taken for the later lecture on Inspiration, and much of it is found in the essay of that name in this volume. (*W*, 8:390; for the essay "Inspiration" see *W*, 8:267–97)

The version of "Resources" that follows is from the complete manuscript in Emerson's hand from which he read in San Francisco on 29 April 1871.

In a community so exceptional to the whole course of history as your own,—so recent in formation, and so prodigious in growth, combining such unparalleled advantages of climate, of geographic position, of production, in its grains, its vines, its trees, its animals, and its minerals; in its commerce and its plantation, and its rising manufactures, a new observer is apt to believe that the thoughts of men must be more occupied than elsewhere on the laws of progress, and the resources already possessed, and those still offered to mankind. Perhaps they are not; but no thoughtful visiter can come hither without this unexampled speed of growth setting him on reckoning the wealth of human ingenuity and power.[1]

Men are made up of potences. We are magnets in an iron globe. We have keys to all doors. We are all inventors, each sailing out on a voyage of discovery, guided each by a private chart, of which there is no duplicate.

The world is all gates,—all opportunities,—strings of tension waiting to be struck: the earth, sensitive as iodine to light, is the most plastic and impressionable medium, alive to every touch, and, whether rubbed by the plough of Adam, the sword of Caesar, the boat of Columbus, the quill of Shakspeare, the telescope of Galileo, the surveyor's chain of Picard, or the submarine telegraph,—to every one of these experiments, it makes a gracious response.[2]

And I am benefitted by every observation of a victory of man over nature, by seeing that wisdom is better than strength, by seeing that every healthy and resolute man is an organizer; a method coming into a confusion, and drawing order out of it. We are touched and cheered by every such example. We like to see the inexhaustible riches of nature, and the access of every soul to her magazines. These examples wake an infinite hope and call every man to emulation.

A low, hopeless spirit puts out the eyes. Skepticism is slow suicide. A philosophy which sees only the worst, believes neither in virtue nor in genius;—which says, 'tis all of no use—life is eating us up; 'tis only a question, who shall be last devoured;—dis-spirits us; the sky shuts down before us. A Schopenhauer with logic, and learning, and wit teaching pessimism,—teaching that this is the worst of all possible worlds, and inferring that sleep is better than waking, and death than sleep,—All the talent in the world cannot save him from being odious.[3]

But, if instead of these negatives, you give me affirmatives; if you tell me that there is always life for the living; that what man has done, man can do; that this world belongs to the energetic; that there is, always, a way to everything desireable, and every man is provided in the new bias of his faculty with a key to Nature; and

---

1. Emerson added this opening paragraph to the lecture for his delivery in San Francisco in 1871.
2. Gaius Julius Caesar (100–44 B.C.), Roman general and statesman; Galileo Galilei (1564–1642), Italian physicist and astronomer indicted as a heretic by the Catholic Church; Jean Picard (1620–82), French Roman Catholic priest and astronomer who measured the degree of a meridian and then computed the size of the earth.
3. Arthur Schopenhauer (1788–1860), German pessimistic philosopher.

that man only rightly knows himself, as far as he has experimented on things, I am invigorated: put into genial and working temper; the horizon opens, and we are full of good will to men and gratitude to the Cause of Causes.

I like the sentiment of the poor woman, who, coming from a wretched garret in an inland manufacturing town, for the first time to the sea shore, and gazing at the ocean, said, "she was glad for once in her life to see something which there was enough of!" Nothing is great but the inexhaustible wealth of Nature. She shows us only surfaces, but she is million-fathoms deep. What spaces! What durations! dealing with races as merely preparation of somewhat to follow. Or, in humanity, millions of lives of men to collect the first observations on which our astronomy is built; millions of lives to add only sentiments and guesses, which at last, gathered in by an ear of sensibility, make the furniture of the poet. How many generations of men it took only to make the earth's motion round the sun suspected!

See how the children build up a language; how every traveller, every laborer, every impatient boss, who sharply shortens the phrase, or the word, to give his order quicker,—reduces it to the lowest possible terms,—and there it must stay. What power does not Nature owe to her duration, of amassing infinitesimals into cosmical forces.

The marked events in history, as, the emigration of a colony to a new and more delightful coast; the building of a large ship; the discovery of the mariner's compass, which perhaps the Phoenicians made; the arrival among an old, stationary nation of a more instructed race with new arts; each of these events electrifies the tribe to which it befalls, supples the tough, barbarous sinew, and brings it into that state of sensibility, and brings the community into that state of melioration, which make the transition to civilization possible and sure.

By his machines, man can dive, and remain under water like a shark; can fly like a hawk in the air; can see atoms like a gnat and see the system of the universe, like Uriel, the Angel of the Sun; can carry whatever loads a ton of coal can lift; can knock down cities, with his fist of gun-powder; can recover the history of his race by the medals which the Deluge and every creature, civil, or savage, or brute, have involuntarily dropt of its existence; and divine the future possibility of the planet and its inhabitants, by his perception of laws of nature.[4]

Ah! what a plastic little creature he is! So shifty, so adaptive, his body a chest of tools, and he, fitting and making himself comfortable in every climate, in every condition. Perhaps never better shown than in the rapidity with which the Saxon race accommodates itself to exigences in America.

There does not seem any limit to these new applications of the same Spirit that made the elements at first, and now through man works them. Art and power will

---

4. Uriel, "light of God" in Hebrew and one of the four archangels, was, to John Milton (1608–74), English poet and political writer, "Regent of the Sun" and the "sharpest sighted Spirit of all in Heav'n" (*Paradise Lost*, bk. 3, ll. 690–91).

go on as they have done, will make day out of night, time out of space, and space out of time.

Invention breeds invention. No sooner is the electric telegraph devised, than gutta-percha, the very material it requires, is found. The aeronaut is provided with gun-cotton, the very fuel he wants for his balloon. When commerce is vastly enlarged, California and Australia expose the gold it required. When Europe is over-populated, America and Australia crave to be peopled. And so throughout, every chance is timed, as if Nature who made the lock, knew where to find the key.

Another result of our arts is the new intercourse which is surprising us with new solutions of the embarrassing political problems. The intercourse is not new, but the scale is new. Our selfishness would have held slaves; or would have excluded from a quarter of the planet, all that are not born on the soil of that quarter. Our politics are disgusting: but what can they help or hinder, when from time to time the primal instincts of emigration are impressed on masses of mankind, when the nations are in exodus and flux? Nature loves to cross her stocks; and German, Chinese, Turk, Russ, and Kanaka were putting out to sea, and intermarrying race with race, and commerce took the hint, and ships were built capacious enough to carry the people of a country.[5]

Vulgar progress is in extending yourself; claiming and fencing a great deal of land; conquering and counting by continents and by millions. True progress is in making the most of that you have, in disclosing the arsenal of powers that belong to an acre of ground; in unlocking the irresistible faculties that belong to a cultivated man; that control over mankind which belongs to him who controls himself; the knowledge of all men which belongs to self-knowledge; the inevitable radiation of centrality.

This thousand-handed art has introduced a new element into the state. The science of power is forced to remember the power of Science. Civilization mounts and climbs. Malthus, when he stated that the mouths went on multiplying geometrically, and the food only arithmetically, forgot to say, that the human mind was also a factor in political economy, and that the augmenting wants of society would be met by an augmenting power of invention.[6]

Yes, we have a pretty artillery of tools now in our social arrangements; we ride four times as fast as our fathers did; we travel, grind, weave, forge, plant, till, and excavate better. We have new shoes, gloves, glasses, and gimlets. We have calculus; we have the newspaper, which does its best to make every square acre of land and sea give an account of itself to your breakfast-table. We have money, and paper money.

We have language, the finest tool of all, and nearest to the mind. 'Tis singular that our English language, so rich as it is, should have no word to convey the face

5. "Kanaka" is the Hawaiian word for human being; it refers to anyone from the islands of Oceania.
6. Thomas Robert Malthus (1766–1834), English political economist whose most controversial work is *An Essay on the Principle of Population* (1798).

of the world. *Kinde* was the old English, which, however, only filled half the range of our fine Latin word with its delicate future tense, *Natura, about to be born,* or, what German philosophy denotes as a *becoming.* But nothing expresses that power which seems to work for beauty alone. The Greek *KOSMOS* did: and therefore, with great propriety, Humboldt calls his book which recounts the last results of Natural Science, *Kosmos.*[7]

Here in America are all the wealth of soil, of timber, of mines, and of the sea, put into the possession of a people who wield all these wonderful machines, have the secret of steam, of electricity, and have the power and habit of invention in their brain.

There is a story of an old lady who was carried to see a mountain and a cataract, and afterwards shown the steam mill and the new railroads, and, very grateful, and a little confused, she said, "God's works are great, but man's works are greater."

We Americans have got suppled into the state of melioration. Life is always rapid here, but what acceleration to its pulse in ten years,—what in the four years of the war! We have seen the railroad and telegraph subdue our enormous geography; We have seen the snowy desarts on the North West, seats of Esquimaux, become lands of promise; When our population swarming west had reached the boundary of arable land, as if to stimulate our energy in the face of the sterile desarts beyond, the land was suddenly in parts covered with gold and silver, and floored with coal.

It was once thought a fable,—what Guthrie, a traveller in Persia, told us, that in Taurida, "in any piece of ground where springs of naphtha (or petroleum) obtain, by merely sticking an iron tube in the earth, and applying a light to the upper end, the mineral oil will burn till the tube is decomposed, or, for a vast number of years."[8] But we have found the Taurida in Pennsylvania and Ohio.

Resources of America! Why, one thinks of Saint Simon's saying, "The Golden Age is not behind, but here before you."[9] Here is Man in the Garden of Eden. Here the Genesis and the Exodus. What will you say to a landlord, who offers you a farm, and says, Here are five hundred acres for wheat; fifty in timber; underneath is your coal cellar, where is stored fat bitumen that will flame at the touch of a candle; make a shaft here, and you have an oil-well; and nearby are excellent gold washings, not to mention the copper, and the iron. If Pennsylvania and Ohio have not the lamp of Aladdin, they have the Aladdin oil.[10]

We have seen slavery disappear like a painted scene in a theatre; We have seen the old oligarchs tumbled out of their powerful chairs into poverty, exile, and shame. We have seen those who were their victims, occupy their places, and dictate their

7. *Kosmos* (1845–62) by Alexander von Humboldt (1769–1859), German traveler and scientist.

8. *A Tour, Performed in the Years 1795–6, Through the Taurida, or Crimea* (1802) by Maria Guthrie, who had served as directress of the Imperial Convent for the education of the female nobility of Russia.

9. Claude-Henri de Rouvroy, comte de Saint-Simon (1760–1825), French philosopher and socialist.

10. Aladdin and his lamp, which houses two genii, appear in *The Arabian Nights' Entertainments* or *A Thousand and One Nights* (1450), originally in Arabic, a collection of ancient Persian-Indian-Arabian traditional tales.

fate. We have seen the most healthful revolution in the politics of the nation. The Constitution is not only amended, but construed in a new spirit.[11] We have seen China opened to European and American ambassadors and commerce, and the like in Japan.[12] Our arts and productions begin to penetrate both; as the walls of a modern house are perforated with water-pipes, sound-pipes, gas-pipes, heat-pipes, so geography and geology are yielding to man's convenience, and we begin to perforate and mould the old ball, as a carpenter does with wood.—All is ductile and plastic. We are working the new Atlantic telegraph.[13]

American energy is overriding every venerable rule of political economy. America is such a garden of plenty, such a magazine of power, that at her shores all the common rules of political economy utterly fail. Here is bread, and wealth, and power, and education, for every man who has the heart to use his opportunity. The creation of power had never any parallel. It was thought that the immense production of gold would make gold cheap as pewter. But the immense expansion of trade has wanted every ounce of gold, and it has not lost its value.

See how nations of customers are formed. The disgust of California has not been able to drive nor kick out the Chinaman back to his home; and now it turns out, that he has sent home to China American food, and tools, and luxuries, until he has taught his people to use them, and a new market has grown up for our commerce. The emancipation has brought a whole nation of negroes, as customers to buy all the articles which once their few masters bought. And every mill, and manufactory, and producer in the north has an interest in protecting the negro as the consumer of his wares.

It is easy to read that there is no knowledge that is not valuable; that every man is rightly esteemed for what he can do; that we must avoid negative, but seek and treasure affirmative experience.

The rise in value of wheat caused by the famine in Europe enabled us in one year to pay the cost of the Mexican War; and not long since, Mr. Walker affirmed, that the additional value of free labor will in one year equal the whole national debt.[14]

The invalid sits shivering in lamb's wool and furs: the woodman knows how to make warm garments out of cold and wet themselves. The Indian, the sailor, the hunter,—only these know the powers of the hands, the feet, the teeth, the eyes

11. The thirteenth amendment to the Constitution, outlawing slavery, was officially adopted on 18 December 1865.

12. America signed its first treaty with China in July 1844. Emerson's remarks at the reception for the Chinese embassy on 21 August 1868 (*W*, 10:469–74) may help date this passage of the lecture from that period. Trade was opened with Japan in July 1853, when U.S. warships forced the emperor to accept the Americans' credentials; the first Japanese ambassador to America arrived in March 1860.

13. The new Atlantic cable was completed on 27 July 1866.

14. The Mexican War or Mexican-American War (1846–48) stemmed from a border dispute between the United States and Mexico after the United States annexed Texas; Amasa Walker (1799–1875), American political economist and congressman from Massachusetts.

and ears. It is out of the obstacles to be encountered that they make the means of
destroying them. The sailor, by his boat and sail, makes a ford out of deepest waters.
The hunter, the soldier, makes warm garments out of cold and wet; rolls himself in
his blanket, and the falling snow, which he did not have to bring in his knapsack, is
his eiderdown, in which he sleeps warm till the morning. Nature herself gives the
hint and the example, if we have the wit to take it. See how Nature keeps the lakes
warm, by tucking them up under a blanket of ice and the ground under an eider
of snow.

In these very days, our people have been reading one or two remarkable tracts
on the material resources of the country; one, called "Commercial and Financial
Strength of the United States" by Mr. Lorin Blodget, showing, that the balance
of trade with Europe was in our favor still, during the late war; the other, called
"Our Burden and Our Strength," by David A. Wells, of New York, giving some
remarkable details, drawn from the national census.[15] It seems our little state of
Massachusetts employs machinery to do the work of more than a hundred millions
of men;—Massachusetts, with 1,400,000 souls.—

I had, at my own door, or in my walk, corroborative confirmation. There were
not men enough, in my own town in 1864, to till the land, and cut the hay. The hay-
crop, which was abundant, would rot on the ground, but for the timely invention
of our horse-mower and horse-rake. In the shoe-shop, I asked, Why do these boots
cost two or three prices? The manufacturer replied, "It is not so much the stock,
it is the labor. Here," said he, "in the neighboring town of Weymouth, the other
day, one hundred twenty-nine men went to the war. Of these, one hundred were
shoemakers." How, then, can shoes be made? Ten miles from my house, is the town
of Feltmoille, where I went into a house in which I learned that twenty-five hundred
pairs of shoes are made every day, by a few women and boys, assisted by patent
machines, wonderful to see.

A like substitute for hand-labor is found in every art and trade, and hence the
incomparable growth. There are many men in this country who have built cities;
hunters, who have founded states; inventors, who have obliged all mankind.

I delight in the man of resources. I am cheered by the bold and resolved mind.
I like to see that every mind is born with a bias or talent, has a way of his own into
Nature, that Nature has given him a private key. And I notice that not only the
display of grand ability—penetration into the secret of largest laws, and, so, into
their working on nations and times—instructs us, but that every anecdote, where
a sharper observation of nature in some particulars bestows some petty advantage,
gives a fillip to the attention and to our courage.

On the Rhine, Dr. Polidori said to Byron, "After all, what is there you can do

15. *The Commercial and Financial Strength of the United States . . .* (1864) by Lorin Blodget; *Our
Burden and Our Strength: or, A Comprehensive and Popular Examination of the Debt and Resources of
Our Country . . .* (1864) by David Ames Wells.

that I can not?"—"Why, since you force me to say," answered Byron, "I think there are three things I can do, which you cannot." Polidori defied him to name them. "I can," said Byron, "swim across this Rhine; I can snuff out that candle with a pistol-shot at the distance of twenty paces; and I have written a poem, of which fourteen thousand copies were sold in one day."[16]

Evelyn writes from Rome: "Bernini, the Florentine sculptor, architect, painter, and poet, a little before my coming to Rome, gave a public opera, wherein he painted the scenes, cut the statues, invented the engines, composed the music, writ the comedy, and built the theatre."[17]

Sheridan on one and the same day took a leading part in the prosecution of Hastings, speaking for several hours in Westminster Hall; then, in the evening, in the debates of the House of Commons; and then, at night, the two theatres played, one, the "Duenna," and the other, the "School for Scandal."[18]

The whole history of our Civil War is rich in a thousand anecdotes attesting the fertility of resource, the presence of mind, the skilled labor of our people. The *National Intelligencer* said of the Eighth Massachusetts Regiment at Annapolis, "Probably, no other regiment in the Country could do what this regiment did;—put a locomotive together, lay the rails on the broken railroad, bend the sails of a man of war, the frigate *Constitution*, man and work the frigate."[19]

Linnaeus enriched his country and medicine with a great many keen observations: he found what plants poisoned the cattle, and so protected the farmer, and what plants were specifics for certain diseases.[20] The annals of medicine indicate many of these benefactors,—from Hippocrates, who stayed the plague of Athens, to Galen, to van Helmont, to Sydenham, to Dr. Rush of Philadelphia, to Abernathy.[21] And it is hard to think of any hero who serves mankind so decisively, so intelligibly, so acceptably as the natural physician and surgeon who restores sight

16. John William Polidori (1795–1821), English physician, author, and friend of the romantic poets; George Gordon Byron, known as Lord Byron (1788–1824), English romantic poet.

17. John Evelyn (1620–1706), English writer of political and botanical works; Giovanni Lorenzo Bernini (1598–1680), Italian painter, sculptor, and architect of St. Peter's in Rome.

18. Richard Brinsley Sheridan (1751–1816), Irish dramatist and statesman; Warren Hastings (1732–1818), English colonial administrator who was impeached in 1788 for corruption and cruelty in his administration of India. Sheridan was among the prosecuting counsel at Hastings's famous trial, after which he was acquitted. *The Duenna* (1775), a comic opera, and *The School for Scandal* (1777), a comedy of manners, are both by Sheridan.

19. Quoted from the *National Intelligencer and Washington Advertiser* (*JMN*, 15:137).

20. Carolus Linnaeus (1707–78), Swedish botanist, is considered one of the founders of modern systematic botany.

21. Hippocrates (ca. 460–ca. 377 B.C.), Greek physician, traditionally but incorrectly credited with the Hippocratic oath taken by modern doctors; Galen (129–ca. 200), Greek physician and philosopher; Jan Baptista van Helmont (1579–1644), Flemish physician and chemist who studied digestion; Thomas Sydenham (1624–89), English physician, known as the "English Hippocrates"; Benjamin Rush (1745–1813), American physician, educator, and patriot, signer of the Declaration of Independence and professor at the Medical School of Philadelphia; John Abernethy (1764–1831), English surgeon.

to the blind, or rescues a valuable life from the malignant fevers. In his hands, medicine becomes a heroic art. Every discovery he makes, he has presently a signal occasion to apply and verify, to the delight of the patient who comes back to life, and of trembling friends who cannot enough reward and prize him. No place is obscure, no country dreary or ungrateful, to such a talent. Wherever is pain, wherever life is dear, he is greeted as a demi-god. Here we have lately from London a remarkable pamphlet, Dr. Wilkinson's tract on small pox, containing his journal of his experiments on malignant cases, with *Hydrastis* and *Veratrum*, two plants that are common in our woods.[22] If his experience shall be confirmed, it is of high importance.

The old forester is never far from shelter. No matter how remote from camp or city, he carries Bangor with him. A sudden shower cannot wet him, if he cares to be dry: he draws his boat ashore, turns it over in a twinkling against a clump of alders,—with cat-briars, which keep up the lee-side,—crawls under it, with his comrade, and lies there till the shower is over, happy in his stout-roof.

The boat is full of water, and resists all your strength to drag it ashore, and empty it. The fisherman looks about him, puts a round stick of wood underneath, and it rolls on wheels at once.

In the Swedish shipyards, they suffered serious damage from the rot in the timber. The government called in the counsel of Linnaeus. Linnaeus made a study of the insect malefactor, and found, that the cynips deposited its eggs between the tenth and twentieth April, and advised his majesty to submerge all timber in the water in the docks, during ten days in April. This was done and the mischief stopped. We want him very much in Cambridge to furnish a prescription for the cankerworm and the curculio.

Mr. Haggerston has given good advice for the rose slug. A bowl of hot water in the early morning when the rose bug is heavy, is the safety of the grapevine.

Of the minor strokes of practical wisdom, there is happily no end. Every hour of the day is made of emergences which expose your ignorance, and may teach you what sages and inventors you live among, and did not know them. I knew a merchant who would show his friend his big bull-calf thriving at five weeks old, and untied the young beast to frisk on the lawn. But, when he attempted to put it into the barn again, he and his friend struggled in vain to drag or boost the beast the way it should go. The Irish girl came out to the rescue, put her finger into the calf's mouth, and led him in directly.

At Nantucket and the Cape, and all along our river towns, the cranberry swamps are in some years of more value than all the tillage of the fields, since the farmers have learned to export them: but how to export this delicate berry? At the end of

22. *On the Cure, Arrest, and Isolation of Smallpox by a New Method* (1864) by James John Garth Wilkinson (1812–99), English physician and Swedenborgian.

a hundred miles, they would be all spoiled by jolting and rubbing. Shall we wrap every berry in an envelope, as we do oranges and pears. Yes, we must do that. A wily man filled his barrel to the top with berries, then pumped water into the barrel; and every berry had a perfect envelope, and floated in safety across the Atlantic to a market.

Your trellis is loaded with grapes: if the frost would only hold off a fortnight, you will be rich with your harvest. But the air is still and cold, and 'tis too plain that this first night of September will ruin the whole summer's care. Look over into your neighbor's vineyard, and see that he has kindled a little smudge of damp brush to the windward of each trellis or row, and the smoke makes all night a climate of Cuba for his clusters.

Again, in danger, the history of the savage, the history of war, of passion, abound in examples where the wit of man is all in all, where is no outward aid, but all depends on personal qualities and presence of mind.

> When a man is once possessed with fear, and that he loses his judgment, as all men in a fright do, he knows not what he does; and it is the principal thing you are to beg at the hands of Almighty God, to preserve your understanding entire; for what danger soever there may be, there is still one way or other to get off, and perhaps to your honor. But, when fear has once possessed you,—God yᵉ good even!—you think you are flying towards the poop, when you are running towards the prow, and for one enemy think you have ten before your eyes, as drunkards who see a thousand candles at once.[23]

What a new face courage puts on everything! A determined man by his very attitude, and the tone of his voice, puts a stop to defeat, and begins to conquer.

> For they can conquer, who believe they can.[24]

The world belongs to the energetic man. His will gives him new eyes. He sees expedients and means, where we saw none. Everyone hears gladly that cheerful voice. He reveals to us the enormous power of one man over masses of men; that one man whose eye commands the end in view, and the means by which it can be attained, is not only better than ten men, or a hundred men, but victor over all mankind who do not see the issue and the means.

M. Tissenet had learned among the Indians to understand their language, and, coming among a wild party of Illinois, he overheard them say, that they would scalp him.[25] He said to them "Will you scalp me? Here is my scalp," and confounded them

---

23. Attributed to Blaise de Lasseran Massencôme, seigneur de Monluc (ca. 1500–1577), French military man, in Emerson's note in the manuscript.

24. Quoted from the *Aeneid* (30–19 B.C.), the great epic of the founding of Rome by Virgil (or Vergil) (70–19 B.C.), Roman poet (*JMN*, 7:172).

25. A M. du Tissenet explored the areas west of the Mississippi at the order of the governor of Louisiana in 1719.

by tearing off a little periwig he wore. He then explained to them that he was a great medicine man and they did great wrong in wishing to harm him who carried them all in his heart. So, he opened his shirt a little and showed to each of the savages in turn the reflection of his own eye-ball in a small pocket mirror which he had hung next to his skin. He assured them, that, if they should provoke him, he would burn up their rivers and their forests; and, taking from his portmanteau a small phial of white brandy, he poured it into a cup, and, lighting a straw at the fire in the wigwam, he kindled the brandy, which they believed to be water, and burned it up before their eyes. Then taking up a chip of dry pine, he drew a burning-glass from his pocket, and set the chip on fire.

The resources of the savage man sometimes suggest that we have not so many advantages as we claim; as when we found the Esquimaux fat and hearty, living in great comfort, where the best appointed English and American voyagers, with all the inventions of London and New York, could not exist. We had to go to school to them and learn to live on blubber, and dress in skins, to save us alive.

The Indian can talk with a muskrat swimming in the river and make it land on the side where the Indian stands. He can be blindfolded in the lakes, and paddled round and round,—then loose him, and he can go off in straight line to camp or to old town. He can give you a new tea or a new soup every day from herbs and leaves in the woods. He can cut a string from the spruce root.

At length, Colonel Wood, completely harassed, and weary of the pursuit, adopted a very singular expedient to effect his purpose: he wrote a letter to Hyder Ali, stating, that it was disgraceful for a great prince, at the head of a large army, to fly before a detachment of infantry, and a few pieces of cannon, unsupported by cavalry.[26] The nabob's answer to this extraordinary letter, was this.

> I have received your letter, in which you invite me to an action with you. Give me the same sort of troops that you command, and your wishes shall be accomplished. You will in time understand my mode of warfare. Shall I risk my cavalry, which cost a thousand rupees each horse, against your cannonballs, which cost two *pice*? No; I will march your troops, until their legs shall become the size of their bodies. You shall not have a blade of grass, nor a drop of water. I will hear of you every time your drum beats, but you shall not know where I am, once in a month. I will give your army battle, but it must be when I please, and not when you choose.

Against the terrors of the mob which, intoxicated with passion, and once suffered to gain the ascendant, is diabolic, and chaos come again, a determined man has many arts of prevention and of relief: disorganization he confronts with organization, with police, with military force. But in earlier stages of the disorder, he applies milder and nobler remedies. The natural offset of terror is ridicule. And

---

26. In 1768 Col. James Wood, a British division commander, participated in a series of attacks and skirmishes against Hyder Ali (1722–82), maharaja of Mysore who opposed British rule in India.

we have noted examples among our orators who have, on conspicuous occasions, handled and controlled, and, best of all, converted a malignant mob, by superior manhood, and by a wit which disconcerted, and, at last, delighted the ringleaders. What can a poor truck-man who is hired to groan and to hiss do, when the orator shakes him into convulsions of laughter so that he cannot throw his egg? If a good story will not answer, still milder remedies sometimes serve to dispense a mob. Try sending round the contribution box.

Mr. Marshall, the eminent manufacturer at Leeds, England, was to preside at a Free Trade festival in that city; it was threatened that the operatives, who were in bad humor, would break up the meeting by a mob. Mr. Marshall was a man of peace. He had the pipes laid from the waterworks of his mill, and had a stopcock by his chair from which he could discharge a stream that would knock down an ox, and sat down very peacefully to his dinner, which was not disturbed.

We have not a toy or trinket for idle amusement, but somewhere it is the one thing needful for solid instruction, or to save the ship or the army. In the "Mammoth Cave" in Kentucky, the torches which each traveller carries make a dismal funeral procession, and serve no purpose but to see the ground. When now and then the vaulted roof rises high overhead and hides all its possibilities in lofty crypts, 'tis but gloom on gloom. But the guide kindled a Roman candle and held it here and there, shooting its fireball successively into each crypt of the groined roof, disclosing what secrets of its sparry splendor, and showing for the first time what that plaything was good for.

It is certain that our own youth exerts enormous influence through all our life: a most disproportionate part of our happiness comes from the recollection or restoring of its images and feelings. There is no poetry or sentiment, no love of beauty, which does not draw a charm from its reminder of that magazine of good. Genius and virtue seem to be only a preternatural prolongation of that. It is a little sad, that we should always be spending on this patrimony, instead of multiplying a thousandfold our original stock.

These strokes, whether larger or less, and all exploits rest at last on the wonderful structure of the mind. And we learn that our doctrine of resources must be carried into higher application, namely to the intellectual sphere. But every power in energy speedily arrives at its limits, and requires to be husbanded; the law of light which Newton said proceeded by "fits of easy reflection and transmission," the come and go of the pendulum, is the law of mind; alternation of labors is its rest.[27]

See the dexterity of the good aunt in keeping the young people, all the weary holiday, busy and diverted without knowing it;—the story, the pictures, the ballad, the game, the cuckoo-clock, the stereoscope, the rabbits, the mino bird, the pop-corn and christmas hemlock spurting in the fire. The children never suspect how much

27. Sir Isaac Newton (1642<n>1727), English natural philosopher and mathematician.

design goes to it, and that this unfailing fertility has been rehearsed a hundred times. When the necessity came of finding for the little Asmodeus a rope of sand to twist, she relies on the same principle that makes the strength of Newton,—alternation of employment.[28] See how he refreshed himself, resting from the profound researches of the calculus, by astronomy; from astronomy, by optics; from optics, by chronology. 'Tis a law of chemistry, that every gas is a vacuum to every other gas; and, when the mind has exhausted its energies for one employment, it is still fresh and capable of a different task.

I should like to have the statistics of bold experimenting on the husbandry of mental power. In England, men of letters drink wine; in Scotland, whiskey; in France, light wine; in Germany, beer. In England, everybody rides in the saddle. In France, the theatre and the ball occupy the night. In this country, we have not learned how to repair the exhaustions of our climate. Is the seaside necessary in summer? Amusement, fishing, bowling, hunting, gymnastics, dancing—are these needful to him?

Every gas is a vacuum to every other gas. And the mind fatigued with mathematics is fresh for history. So De Quincey relates, that, when great news was daily arriving from France, Wordsworth and he walked out miles from home to meet the mail at night, and Wordsworth, listening for the horn of the newsman, finds his eye preternaturally sensible to the rays of a star.[29] The old device which we call "ride and tie" is founded on the observation that walking is the grateful exercise after a ride in the saddle, and riding after a long walk.

> There was a boy,—Y^e knew him well ye cliffs
> And islands of Winander! Many a time
> At evening, when the earliest stars began
> To move along the edges of the hills
> Rising or setting, would he stand alone
> Beneath the trees or by the glimmering lake
> And there with fingers interwoven, both hands
> Pressed closely, palm to palm, and to his mouth
> Uplifted, he, as through an instrument,
> Blew mimic hootings to the silent owls,
> That they might answer him.
>   And they would shout
> Across the watery veil, and shout again
> Responsive to his call—with quivering peals

28. Asmodeus, the demon of vanity and dress; a rope of sand refers to something that has no stability or that is a feeble union.

29. Thomas De Quincey (1785–1859), English author whose most famous work is the *Confessions of an English Opium Eater* (1821).

And long halloos and screams and echoes loud.
      Redoubled and redoubled; concourse wild
Of mirth and jocund din! And, when it chanced
That pauses of deep silence mocked his skill,
That sometimes, in that silence, while he hung
Listening, a gentle shock of mild surprise
Has carried far into his heart the voice
Of mountain torrents; or the visible scene
Would enter unawares into his mind
With all its solemn imagery, its rocks,
Its woods, and that uncertain heaven, received
Into the bosom of the steady lake.[30]

—Whilst the ear was tense to catch the faintest sound, the eye and brain became suddenly preternaturally receptive of the spectacle of nature around him.

I do not know that the treatise of Brillat-Savarin on the "Physiology of Taste" deserves its fame.[31] I know its repute, and I have heard it called the "France of France." But the subject is so large and exigent, that so few particulars, and those the pleasures of the epicure, cannot satisfy. I know many men of taste whose single opinions and practice would interest much more. It should be extended to gardens and grounds which can ennoble any landscape by matchless taste, and mainly one thing should be illustrated; that good life in the country wants all things on a low tone: wants coarse clothes, old shoes, no fleet horse that a man can't hold, but an old horse that will stand tied in a pasture half a day, without risk, so allowing the picnic party the full freedom of the woods. It is the excellence of beer in England not to be strong, but to be weak, so that much may be drunk in hot weather with impunity.

Napoleon says, the Corsicans at the battle of Golo, not having had time to cut down the bridge which was of stone,—made use of the bodies of their dead to form an entrenchment.[32]

Aubrey tells of Sir Adrian Scope who covered himself with dead bodies to keep himself warm on a battlefield. At Borodino, a French soldier crept into the carcass of a horse to sleep.[33]

Malus, known for his discoveries in the polarization of light, was captain of

30. "There Was a Boy" (1800) by William Wordsworth (1770–1850), English poet and, with Samuel Taylor Coleridge, founder of the romantic movement.
31. *Physiologie du goût* (1825), a literary work on gastronomy by Anthelme Brillat-Savarin (1755–1826), French politician and writer.
32. Napoléon Bonaparte (1769–1821), born in Corsica, general and later emperor of the French as Napoléon I.
33. John Aubrey (1626–97), English antiquary. Borodino story quoted from "The Gates of Death. A Revelation of the Horrors of the Battle-field," *Bentley's Magazine* (1844) by Bayle St. John (1822–59), English traveler and author (*JMN*, 9:158).

a Corps of Engineers in Bonaparte's Egyptian campaign, which was heinously unprovided and exposed.[34] "Wanting a picquet to which to attach my horse," he says, "I tied him to my leg. I slept, and dreamed peaceably of the pleasures of Europe."

An old scholar said to me, very many years ago, when speaking of his own methods, "I build: In the morning, I am athletic, and begin with Hebrew for foundation; after that, I am still good for Greek; later in the day, I can read philosophy and history; in the afternoon, poetry and the journals."[35]

The chapter of pastimes is very long. There are better games than billiards and whist. The first care of a man settling in the country should be to open the face of the earth to himself, by a little knowledge of nature,—or a great deal, if he can,— of birds, plants, rocks, and astronomy, in short, the art of taking a walk. Does he know the fine friendship of the forest and the river? These will take the sting out of frost, dreariness out of November and March, and drowsiness out of August. "To know the trees" is, as Spenser says, "for nothing ill."[36] When his task requires the "wiping out of memory all trivial fond records that youth and observation copied there,"—requires self-communion and insights;—he must leave the house, and the streets, and the club, and go to wooded uplands, to the clearing, and the brook.[37] Well for him, if he can say, with the old minstrel, "I know where to find a new song."[38] I doubt not there are those before me who know these secrets,—who perhaps have

> slighted Minerva's learned tongue
> But heard with joy when on the wind
> The shell of Clio rung.[39]

It is easy to see that there is no limit to the chapter of Resources. I have not, in all these rambling sketches, got beyond the beginning of my list. *Resources of Man*,—it is the inventory of the world, the roll of Arts and Sciences; it is the whole of memory, the whole of invention; it is all the power of passion, the majesty of virtue, and the omnipotence of will.

'Twas a pleasing trait in Goethe's romance, that Makaria retires from society "to astronomy, and her correspondence."[40] Natural history is, in the country, most attractive, at once elegant, immortal, always opening new resorts. Poetry too,

---

34. Étienne-Louis Malus (1775–1812), French physicist and engineer.

35. Nathaniel Langdon Frothingham (1793–1870), American Unitarian clergyman in Boston.

36. Paraphrased from *The Faerie Queene* (1590, 1596), bk. 1, canto 1, stanza 9, by Edmund Spenser (ca. 1552–99), English poet.

37. Shakespeare, *Hamlet*, 1.5.98–99, 101.

38. Identified by Edward Waldo Emerson as "one of the songs of the Welsh Bards" (*W*, 8:394n).

39. Emerson, "Fragments on the Poet and the Poetic Gift" (*W*, 9:334).

40. Mikaria, a character in *Wilhelm Meisters Wanderjahre, oder die Entsagenden* (*Wilhelm Meister's Travels, or the Renunciants*, 1829) by Johann Wolfgang von Goethe (1749–1832), Germany's most famous writer.

Try the might the muse affords,
And the balm of thoughtful words.[41]

If I go into the fields in winter, and am shown the thirteen or fourteen species of willows that grow in Massachusetts, I learn, presently, that they quietly expand in the warmer days, or when nobody is looking at them, and, though insignificant enough in the general bareness of the forest, yet a great change takes place in them between fall and spring, and, in the first relentings of March, they hasten, and, long before anything else is ready, these osiers hang out their joyful flowers in contrast to all the woods. It seems you cannot tell when they do bud and blossom, these vivacious trees, so ancient,—for they are almost the oldest of all: Among fossil remains, the willow and the pine appear with the ferns. They bend all day to every wind. The cartwheel in the road may crush them; every passenger may strike off a twig with his cane; every boy cuts them for a whistle; the cow, the rabbit, the insect bite the sweet and tender bark. Yet, in spite of accident and enemy, their gentle persistency lives when the oak is shattered by storm, and grows in the night, and snow and cold. When I see in these brave plants, this vigor and immortality in weakness, I find a sudden relief and pleasure in observing the mighty law of vegetation, the beauty and the vigor: and I think it more grateful and health-giving, than any news I am likely to find of man in the journals,—better than Washington politics.

But the one fact that shines through all this plenitude of powers is, that, as is the receiver, so is the gift,—that all these acquisitions are victories of the good brain and brave heart, that the world belongs to the energetic; belongs to the wise. It is in vain to make a paradise but for good men. The tropics are one vast garden; yet man is more miserably fed and conditioned there than in the cold and stingy zones. The healthy, the civil, the industrious, the learned, the moral race,—Nature herself only yields her secret to these. And the resources of America and its future will be immense only to wise and virtuous men.

This insecurity of possession, this ebb and flow of power, as if life were a thunderstorm, wherein you could now see by a flash the horizon, and then cannot see your hand,—tantalizes us. If we knew how to use these divine energies!—If we knew how to draw the electricity!—But where is the Franklin who can safely handle this fire?[42] If we knew, in any torpid hour, where to seek the tonics of the mind!—

I value literary biography for the hints it furnishes from so many scholars in so many countries, of what hygeian, what ascetic, what gymnastic, what social practices, their experience suggested and approved. They are men who needed only

41. Emerson, "Fragments on the Poet and the Poetic Gift," 10.1–2 (*W*, 9:329).
42. Benjamin Franklin (1706–90), American statesman, author, printer, editor, and inventor, known for his experiments with kites drawing down electricity from thunderstorms.

a little wealth.—Large estates, political relations, great hospitalities, would have been impediments to them. Liberty was all they wanted. They are men whom a book could make happy; a new thought, intoxicate, and hold them prisoners for long years perhaps. Aubrey, and Burton, and Wood tell me incidents which I find not insignificant, and Scaliger is mistaken about Montaigne.[43]

I am tempted to go one step deeper into my subject, and say a few words as to our means for repairing the wastes and torpor of the mind. We are all skilful to find the tonics which the body needs, but I sometimes ask, What metaphysician has undertaken to enumerate the excitants and tonics of the torpid mind? Where are the rules for the recovery of inspiration?

Sometimes the electric machine will not work,—no spark will pass; then, presently, the world is all a cat's back,—all sparkle and shock. Sometimes there is no sea-fire,—and, again, the sea is all a-glow. Sometimes the Aeolian harp is dumb all day in the window,—and, again, it is garrulous, and tells all the secrets of the world.[44] In June, the morning is noisy with birds; in August, they are already getting old and silent.

Hence arises the question: Are these moods in any degree within control?

That is least within control which is best in them. But in the experience of meditative men, there is a certain agreement as to the conditions favorable to this reception.

We cannot carry on the inspiration, and make it consecutive. A glimpse, a point of view, that by its very brightness excludes the purview, is granted,—but no panorama. A fuller inspiration should cause the point to flow, and become a line, should bend the line, and complete the circle.

How many sources of inspiration can we count? As many as our affinities. But, in an external and practical way, we are prepared for thought by sleep. *Il n'y a que le matin en toutes choses.* Everything has its morning, and that is its best chance.

'Tis a primal rule to defend the morning, to keep all its dews on, and, with some foresight, to relieve it from any jangle of affairs, even from the question, Which task? I remember a capital prudence of old President Quincy, who told me, that he never went to bed at night, until he had laid out the studies for the next morning.[45]

First. I honor health as the first muse; and sleep, as the condition of health. Sleep benefits mainly by the sound health it restores; incidentally, also, by dreams,

43. John Aubrey (1626–97), English antiquary, is best known for *Lives of Eminent Men* (1813); John Hill Burton (1809–81), Scottish historian, author of *Life of David Hume* (1846); Anthony à Wood (1632–95), English antiquary and historian; Joseph Justus Scaliger (1540–1609), Italian scholar, collected all available writings of classical Greek and Latin; Michel Eyquem de Montaigne (1533–92), French essayist and philosopher, usually identified with skepticism.

44. An aeolian harp is a box-shaped string instrument that produces various tones when the strings are touched by the wind.

45. Josiah Quincy (1772–1864), American politician and educator, president of Harvard (1829–45).

into whose farrago a divine lesson is sometimes slipped. Life is in short cycles or periods. We are quickly spent, but we have rapid rallies. After utter prostration and despondency, a good night's sleep restores us to full power. We are gay with hope, and sure of victory.

> "Sleep is like death, and, after sleep,
> The world seems new begun,
> Its earnestness all clear and deep,
> Its true solution won;
> White thoughts stand luminous and firm,
> Like statues in the sun;
> Refreshed from supersensuous founts,
> The soul to purer vision mounts."[46]

Another consideration,—which, though it will not so much interest young men, will cheer the heart of older scholars. Namely, that as the diurnal, so the secular recoveries,—there is this daily renovation of sensibility,—so it sometimes, if rarely, happens, that, after a season of decay or eclipse, darkening months or years, the faculties revive to their fullest force. One of the best facts I know in metaphysical science, is Niebuhr's joyful record, that, after his genius for interpreting history had failed him for several years, this divination returned to him. So Herbert's.[47]

Second. The second source is solitary converse with Nature; for thence are ejaculated sweet and dreadful words never uttered in libraries. Ah! the spring days, summer dawns, and October woods! Plutarch says, Souls are naturally endowed with prediction flowing from the natural temperature of the air and winds.[48]

Nature,—she is strong, exuberant, omnific, delighting in speedy rallies. A man is spent by his work, starved, prostrate, he will not lift his hand to save his life;—he can never think more. He sinks into deep sleep, and wakes with renewed youth,— with hope, courage, fertile in resources, and keen for daring adventure.

Are you poetical, impatient of trade, tired of labor and affairs? Do you want Helvellyn, Plinlimmon, in your closet? Caerleon, Provence, Ossian, and Cadwallon?[49] Tie a couple of strings across a board, and set it in your window,—and you have a wind harp which no artist's harp can rival. It needs no instructed ear; if you

46. "Sleep," ll. 8–15, by William Allingham (1824–89), Irish poet.

47. Barthold Georg Niebuhr (1776–1831), German historian and critic; George Herbert (1593–1633), English metaphysical poet.

48. Plutarch (ca. 46–ca. 120), Greek historian best known for his series of "lives," or character studies, arranged in pairs in which a Greek and a Roman are compared.

49. Helvellyn, second highest mountain in the English Lake District; Plinlimmon, a mountain group in Wales; Caerleon, town in southeastern Wales that is one of several sites suggested as the real location for King Arthur's court at Camelot; Provence, a section of southeastern France; Ossian, the supposed third-century Gaelic author of the verses "translated" between 1760 and 1763 by James

have sensibility, it admits you to sacred interiors. It has the sadness of nature; yet, at the changes, tones of triumph and festal notes ringing out all measures of loftiness.

But the solitude of nature is not so essential as solitude of habit. I have found my advantage in going,—in summer, to a country inn;—in winter, to a city hotel,—with a task which could not prosper at home. I thus secured a more absolute solitude: for it is almost impossible for a householder, who, in the country, is also a small farmer, and who has guests in the house, to exclude interruptions and even necessary orders, though I bar out by system all I can, and resolutely omit, to my constant loss, all that can be omitted. At home, the day is cut into short strips. In the hotel, I have no hours to keep, no visits to make or receive, and I command an astronomic leisure. I forget rain, wind, cold, and heat. At home, I remember in my library the wants of the farm, and have all too much sympathy. I envy the abstraction of some scholars I have known, who could sit on a curbstone in State Street, put up their back, and solve their problem.[50] Most of us have more womanly eyes. All the conditions must be right for our success, slight as that may be. What untunes is as bad as what cripples or stuns us. I extol the prudence of Carlyle, who, for years, projected a library at the top of his house, high above the orbit of all housemaids, and out of earshot of doorbells. Could that be once secured,—a whole floor, room for books, and a good bolt,—he could hope for ten years of history: And he kept it in view until it was brought to pass, and wrote the *History of Friedrich* under precisely those advantages.[51]

I know there is room for whims here. But in regard to some apparent trifles, there is great agreement as to their annoyance. And the machine with which we are dealing is of an inconceivable delicacy that whims also must be respected. George Sand says, "I have no enthusiasm for nature which the slightest chill will not instantly destroy."[52] Evenus said, "Fire is the best sauce."[53] And I remember, that, Henry Thoreau with his robust will, yet found certain trifles disturbing the delicacy of that health which composition exacted, namely, the slightest irregularity, even to the drinking too much water on the preceding day.[54] I abstain from so much exertion as to go to my cabinet for a heavy dictionary. Even a steel pen is a nuisance to some writers. You have seen, in the English journals, the petition

---

Macpherson (1736–96), Scottish poet, which proved to be a fraud; Cadwallon or Caedwalla (d. 633), Welsh king of Gwynedd.

50. State Street, the main commercial center of Boston.

51. The library room used by Thomas Carlyle (1795–1881), prolific Scottish essayist and historian who was Emerson's lifelong friend and correspondent, on the top floor of his house in Cheyne Row, London, is still there today. His *History of Frederick the Great* was written between 1851 and 1865.

52. George Sand, pen name of Amandine-Aurore-Lucile Dudevant (1804–76), French novelist whose personal life scandalized Paris.

53. Possibly a reference to Evenus, the Greek mythological charioteer.

54. Henry David Thoreau (1817–62), American writer.

signed by Tennyson, Dickens, Browning, Carlyle, and other writers, in London, against the license of the organ grinders, who infest the streets near their houses, to levy on them a tax of blackmail.[55]

Certain localities, as mountain tops, the seaside, the shores of rivers and rapid brooks, natural parks of oak and pine, where the ground is smooth and unencumbered, are excitants of the muse. Every artist knows well some favorite retirement. Ossian tells us that Cathmore dwelt in the wood. And yet the experience of some good artists has taught them to prefer the smallest and plainest chamber with one chair and one table, to these picturesque liberties. William Blake said, "Natural objects always did and do weaken, deaden, and obliterate imagination in me."[56] These are to be used with great prudence. Allston rarely left his studio by day.[57] An old friend drove him one fine afternoon a spacious circuit into the country, and he painted two or three pictures as the fruits of that ride. But he made it a rule not to go to the city on two consecutive days. One was rest, more was lost time.

There must be a fine prudence, which each will learn by studying his own constitution. Sir Gawaine took care to fight in the hours when his strength increased, for from noon to night his strength abated.[58]

Third. New poetry; by which I mean chiefly old poetry that is new to me. One who has a poetic turn will find it sufficient to set himself on writing verses, to read any original poetry. What is best in literature is initiative, prophesying, spermatic words of men-making poets.

Words used in a new sense, and figuratively,—dart a delightful lustre: and *every* word admits a new use, and hints ulterior uses. Almost we then say, it is not even friends, but this power of words that is best. You shall not read newspapers, nor politics, nor novels, nor Montaigne, nor any French book. You may read Plutarch, you may read Plato, or Plotinus; You may read Hindoo mythology, and ethics, and *Mahabarat.*[59] You may read Shakspeare and Milton all the year round, and Milton's prose as poetic as his verse, Chaucer, Ben Jonson, Collins, the Trouveurs, and Hafiz; nay, Welsh and British mythology of Arthur; and, in your car, Ossian and Taliessin.[60] You may read fact-books, which all geniuses prize as raw

55. Alfred, Lord Tennyson (1809–92), English poet, named poet laureate in 1850 after the death of William Wordsworth; Charles Dickens (1812–70), popular English novelist; Robert Browning (1812–89), English poet.

56. William Blake (1757–1827), English printer, engraver, painter, and romantic poet.

57. Washington Allston (1779–1843), American historical painter and novelist.

58. Sir Gawaine, a legendary knight of King Arthur's Round Table.

59. Plato (ca. 428–348 B.C.), the most famous of the Greek philosophers; Plotinus (205–70), Roman Neoplatonic philosopher; the *Mahābhārata* is a collection of legendary and didactic Indian poetry.

60. Geoffrey Chaucer (ca. 1342–1400), English poet, author of *Troilus and Criseyde* and *The Canterbury Tales*; Ben Jonson (1572–1637), English poet and dramatist; William Collins (1721–59), English lyrical poet whose neoclassical odes are considered preromantic; the trouvères were eleventh- to fourteenth-century poets who specialized in narrative works; Ḥāfez (ca. 1325–90), Persian philosopher and lyric poet and a great favorite of Emerson; Taliesin, sixth-century Welsh bard.

material, and as antidote to verbiage and false poetry. Fact-books, if the facts be well and thoroughly told, are much more nearly allied to poetry than many books are that are written in rhyme. Only our newest knowledge works as a source of inspiration and thought, as only the outmost layer of *liber* is well-alive in the tree.

Books of natural science, especially those written by the ancients,—geography, botany, metals, agriculture, explorations of the sea, of meteors, astronomy, especially if written without literary aim or ambition. Every book is good to read which sets the reader in a working mood.—The deep book,—no matter how remote the subject,—alone helps. But here is a wide disparity of tastes. Lord Chatham found Bailey's dictionary good when preparing to speak.[61] Even dictionaries are good for iodized minds and, as the Aeolian harp, are preparations of the poet for his hour.—

Neither are these all the sources; nor can I name all. The receptivity is rare. The occasions or predisposing circumstances I could never tabulate; but now one, now another landscape, forum, color, or companion, or perhaps one kind of sounding word or syllable "strikes the electric chain with which we are darkly bound."[62] And it is impossible to detect and wilfully repeat the fine conditions to which we have owed our happiest frames of mind. The day is good in which we have had the most perceptions. The analysis is the more difficult, because it is certain poppy-leaves are strewn, when a generalization is made; for I can never remember the circumstances to which I owe it, so as to repeat the experiment, or put myself in the conditions.

I suppose every scholar, writer, and speaker has his own aids to intellect, to which he resorts in time of need. When you cannot flog the mind into activity in your library, you go to your family, your friend, or pupil, and unfold your pack to them, as you could not to yourself. Everyone knows where and with whom he breathes freest, comes into a genial mood and finds his thoughts flowing faster. Some men accustomed to speak to public assemblies have found their school and closet *there*, that is to say, are conscious of a larger horizon of thought, and more power of illustration when called upon to address an assembly than they can command at home or in solitude: So that they go to the audience as others go to a closet to find out what their own thoughts are. But I believe that as berries, and wine, and all fine food furnish some elemental wisdom, so does the fire, too, as it burns; for I fancy that my logs which have grown so long in the sun and wind are a kind of Muses. Lord Ravensworth, an enthusiastic agriculturist, used to say, "There was nothing grateful but the earth: You cannot do too much for it; it will continue to pay tenfold the pains and labor bestowed upon it."

---

61. William Pitt, first Earl of Chatham (1708–78), English statesman and orator, twice virtual prime minister; Nathaniel Bailey (d. 1742), English lexicographer, first published in 1721 his *An Universal Etymological English Dictionary*, which not only defined words but contained instructions for pronouncing them as well.

62. *Childe Harold's Pilgrimage* (1812–18), canto 4, stanza 23, by Lord Byron.

The Rule of Life

(1867–1871)

Emerson first delivered "The Rule of Life" in May 1867 in the Radical Course, which was sponsored by the Parker Fraternity, in Boston, and he delivered it again in March 1871 before the Free Religious Association in Boston. He may have delivered the lecture one more time: in 1868 in a series of four lectures before the Liberal Christian Union in Brooklyn, New York.

Emerson copied text from "The Rule of Life" for "The Preacher," a lecture he delivered in September 1867 before the Radical Club in Boston. In April 1879 James Elliot Cabot drew additional material from "The Rule of Life" as he extensively reworked the manuscript of "The Preacher" for an address Emerson delivered under that title on 5 May at the Harvard Divinity School. As reworked by Cabot, "The Preacher" was published in the *Unitarian Review* 13 (January 1880): 1–13, from which it was reprinted as a pamphlet (*The Preacher* [Boston: George H. Ellis, 1880]) and collected in *Lectures and Biographical Sketches* in 1884 (*W*, 10:215–38). Parts of "The Rule of Life" were also used in "The Sovereignty of Ethics," assembled by Cabot for publication in the *North American Review* 126 (May–June 1878): 404–20, and also collected in *Lectures and Biographical Sketches* in 1884 (*W*, 10:181–214).

W e can hardly take up a pamphlet or a journal in these days, which does not announce some new and important discovery in science and practical art,—in astronomy, in chemistry, in navigation, or in mechanics. And these announcements are no longer turned over to adepts, but are examined with avidity by all readers as somewhat which will directly be realized and made useful to the community. Not only so, but we have long ago found that these facts of nature react directly on our opinions of society and life.

Oersted said, that the religion of each nation must rest on the views they entertained of Nature.[1] What a revolution was wrought in theology by the Copernican system.[2] Like every secluded community, we had fancied our ball the type planet; the seat of a chosen race favored by the Creator and, in the dark imagination of the Calvinist Saurin, surrounded by good and evil angels; and here the drama of

1. Hans Christian Ørsted (1777–1851), Danish physicist and chemist who worked with electricity.
2. Nicolaus Copernicus (or Mikołaj Kopernik) (1473–1543), Polish astronomer credited with founding the science of modern astronomy, believed that the planets revolved around the sun.

the Divine Judgment was to be performed for the instruction of the Universe.[3] "The Earth was the scaffold of Divine vengeance, and all created existences were watching in suspense."[4]

But when Copernicus dismissed our little ball to its tiny insignificance in the solar system, and then in the vast ether in which the system revolves, the mortified inhabitant was forced to abate his claim to hold the central city of the God of Nature. The nebular theory spoiled our nursery clock. Then the new measures by geology of the antiquity of the planet, interfered with our sacred chronology; the new doctrine of the correlation of forces, showing that all force was one and that, whether in the form of gravity, or velocity, or heat, or electricity, or muscular force,—suggesting also, that, will was not far off,—each is convertible into the other, showed one all-dissolving unity.

Then chemistry lately came in aid of astronomy to show the substance, the atoms of the sun and stars, to be identical with our own.

Then the doctrine of compensations, the very word *analogy*, the doctrine of correspondences, showed a unity still stupendous.

The study of animals disclosed the same intellect as in man, only initial, only working to humble ends, but, as far as it went, identical in aim with his: full of good sense, baffling him sometimes, by showing a more fertile good sense in the animal, than in the hunter; but everywhere intelligible to us, because like ours.

Science corrects theology line after line, until not one is left. Its irresistible generalizations destroy the importance of persons and anecdotes. As this astronomy dealt with the old legends of Orion, and the Milky Way, and Hercules, and Cassiopeia's Chair, Castor and Pollux, or with a gipsy's or an astrologer's heaven to tell fortunes by, at a shilling a head, so does this make a mean, or national, or personal interpretation impossible: It requires a history up to the style of the works: makes miracles which were the material of the religious history of all barbarous nations impossible, by supplying a truth which defies all prodigy to equal it in wonder.[5]

What if we see these grand laws only in glimpses? The glimpse is final. The smallest inch of the curve of the ecliptic being once positively ascertained, determines the entirety of the enormous round for me, as surely as if I saw it with eyes.

Science has made it impossible to introduce persons, or places, or the schemes of theologians into the mind. The vast generalizations of science destroy such toy-heavens. In this nineteenth century, everything told us of the Creator must be on the scale in which he is known to us in his Works, and not on the fond legends of an ignorant tribe.

3. John Calvin (originally Jean Cauvin) (1509–64), French Protestant reformer and theologian; Jacques Saurin (1677–1730), French Protestant pulpit orator.

4. Attributed to Jacques Saurin by Emerson (*JMN*, 2:225).

5. Orion, Hercules, Cassiopeia, and Castor and Pollux are all constellations named after mythological figures.

Astronomy, chemistry, botany, and zoology, have made the old Calvinism and other once popular creeds impossible to be the food of the new age,—not only these, but what modern Conservatism has borrowed of these, and holds on to every old rag with both hands. The traditions of ransom, of atonement, of expiation, of passover, of song, and of angels, justification, and vicarious sacrifice are only a petrifaction of momentary tropes by too frequent use into articles of a creed.

The immortality of thought: The most disastrous hour is brightened by some new character of beauty and influence though ages have paced over their dust.[6] The unsparing, impersonal, thorough lights have disposed once for all of these dust-corners and cobwebs, and the Middle-Age-Christianity is as dead as Paganism.

I confess our later generation appears ungirt, frivolous, compared with the religions of the last or Calvinistic age. There was, in the last century, a serious acknowledgment and habitual reference to the spiritual world, running through diaries, letters, and conversation, yes and into wills, and legal instruments also,—compared with which our liberation looks a little foppish and dapper. But I hope that the defect of faith with us is only apparent. We shall find freedom has its own guards, and, as soon as in the vulgar it runs to license, sets all reasonable men on exploring those guards.

The Roman Catholic Church again had a power which appears still in its early literature, its alms giving, its monastic orders, and, how wonderfully in its architecture in France and Germany, which the English and the Reformed Church have never reached. St. Augustine, Thomas à Kempis, and the Latin hymns, breathe a religious genius, which is still delightful to solitary meditation.[7]

It does appear to me that we have some defect of manliness, as if we were the sport of gnomes or witches, and had a great talent of losing the substance for the shadow; that we are very polemic, for example, and fight people about the meaning of creeds and texts; that we affect a sympathetic interest in what we do not care for, and tenderly abstain to say, 'I don't know and don't care.' You are really interested in your thought;—you have meditated in silent wonder on your existence in this world; have perceived that the first fact of your conscious life here is a miracle so astounding (such a miracle comprehending all the Universe of miracles to which your intelligent life gives you access,)—as to exhaust wonder, and leave you no need of hunting here or there for any particular exhibition of power.

That fact, that experience, is the whole world for you; is and should be. A man comes by with a text of John V. 7. or a knotty sentence of St. Paul which he considers as the axe at the root of your tree. Cut away, my tree is the tree Igdrasil.[8] You can't bring yourself to care for it. He only interrupts, for the moment, your peaceful

6. Attributed to Mary Moody Emerson in Emerson's note in the manuscript.
7. Saint Augustine of Hippo (354–430), early Christian Church father and philosopher; Thomas à Kempis (ca. 1380–1471), Dutch ecclesiastic and writer.
8. Yggdrasill in Norse mythology is an ash tree that binds earth, hell, and heaven together.

trust in the divine Providence. Rest in that peace. Let him know by your serenity and self-truth, that your conviction, is real and efficient, and, though he be Paul or Apollos, that you also are here, and with your creator.[9] In my early life, I was wont to hear in an almost daily prayer the expression, Teach us to give to every being and thing in the universe its just measure of importance.

The opinions of men on theologic matters differ widely in every nation, and often in every town. Each nation has its own religion, and each religion has its several sects. In the Christianity of this country, what wide difference in the opinions held in regard to Inspiration, to Prophecy, to Miracles, to the future state of the Soul: Every variety of opinion, and of very rapid revolution in opinions, in the last half century.

The word miracle, as it is used, only indicates the ignorance of the devotee, staring with wonder to see water turned into wine, and heedless of the stupendous fact of himself being there present. If the water became wine, became fire, became a chorus of angels, it would not compare with the amazing fact of his own perception. Here he stands, a lonely thought, harmoniously organized into correspondence with the universe of mind and matter. What narrative of wonders coming down from a thousand years ought to charm his attention like this ineffable personal experience of his own, this fact of his existence in harmonious relations to this universe of worlds, which actual science has disclosed to him by means and experiments which he can repeat, if he will?

Meantime, there is a great centrality: a centripetence equal to the centrifugence. If theology shows many opinions and is fast changing, 'tis not so with the convictions of men in regard to conduct. These remain. Thirty years ago, Dr. Spurzheim drew general attention in this country to Phrenology.[10] I suppose no man ever had so many statues raised to him. The land was filled with plaster heads, on which the faculties were marked and numbered. The new science was everywhere discussed and carried out to its results. The adepts undertook to examine the head of a clerk you would take into your counting-room, or of a scholar you were sending to college, and pronounce on the fitness for each employment. Presently, with the progress of the doctrine, it came into the courts, and, when a man was arraigned for theft or arson, his counsel pleaded in defence, malformation: that the skull showed acquisitiveness or destructiveness, large, and conscientiousness small.

But though this opinion, this philosophy made easy, was very widely received, and though I do not know any neology that has left so many marks on the language, it has made no change whatever in practice. The juries convicted the thief,

9. Saint Paul (d. between 62 and 68 A.D.), born a Jew but converted to Christianity after having a vision on the road to Damascus; Apollo was the Greek god of prophecy who, as the leader of the Muses, was the patron of poetry and music.

10. German physician Johann Christoph Spurzheim (1776–1832), cofounder of the pseudoscience of phrenology, a way of reading a person's character through the configuration of his or her skull.

or incendiary,—without taking any account of the protuberances or the depressions in his skull.

The real life of the time is quite independent of accidental systems, and establishes itself on much the same terms under all politics and manners. Well, the like variety in *opinion*, the like stability in the *convictions*, obtains in all nations, in all ages, from the beginning of mankind.

'Tis the necessity of the human mind, that he who looks at one object, looks away from all other objects. A man may throw himself on some sharp statement of one fact, some verbal creed, with such concentration, as to hide the universe from him. But the stars continue to roll above,—the sun still warms him, and a million energies co-operate through him, as if he were not mortified to them all. With patience and fidelity to truth, he will work his way out of this narrowness, which is blindness, if it be only by coming against somebody who believes more fables than he does, and in trying to show him *that* superstition, he opens his own eyes.

It is the sturdiest prejudice in the public mind, that religion is something by itself, a department distinct from all other experience, and to which the tests and judgment men are ready enough to show on other things, do not apply. You may sometimes talk with the gravest and best citizen, and the moment the topic of religion is broached, he loses his wits; he runs into a childish superstition. His face looks infatuated, and his conversation is. If you could make men feel that this also was most properly the domain of reflection; that every one was to act for the benefit of the public, or universal man; that his welfare was sacred; injury to him was injury to the malefactor.

When Mr. Watson Haynes attempted to enlist the clergy in the protest against flogging in the Navy, he was answered, that their duty was "to preach the gospel, and not to interfere with the regulations of the Navy;" and when the clergy prayed our great Massachusetts statesman to sustain the cause of freedom, his reply was, that the part of "Religion was to touch the heart, and not to abolish Slavery."

Well, we must reconcile ourselves to the new order of things. But is it a calamity? The poet Wordsworth greeted even the steam-engine and railroads when they came into his poetic Westmoreland, bisecting every delightful valley, deforming every consecrated grove, yet manned himself to say,

> "In spite of all that beauty may disown
> In your harsh features, Nature doth embrace
> Her lawful offspring in man's Art, and Time,
> Pleased with your triumphs o'er his brother Space,
> Accepts from your bold hands the proffered crown
> Of hope, and smiles on you with cheer sublime."[11]

11. *Poems Composed or Suggested during a Tour in the Summer of 1833*, no. 42, "Steamboats, Viaducts, and Railways" (1835), ll. 9–14, by William Wordsworth (1770–1850), English poet and, with Samuel Tay-

And we can keep the sentiment which is the fountain of our religion, despite of the violent railroads of generalization, whether French or German, that block and intersect our old parish highways.

Do you know how simple a faith has sufficed the Quakers and made the energetic and prevailing piety through which they accomplished great political and social results?[12] They had but one principle,—the Perpetual Presence of the Spirit in the human heart. They called it the seed, the light, the direction, and many names beside; but they preferred to indicate it in a negative way, as making an obstruction when they would do anything wrong. Whatever the plan or purpose they entertain, they let it lie a while quietly in mind. It, perhaps, presently appears that there is an obstruction, a feeling that this should not be done. They wait longer, thinking that perhaps this obstruction will pass off. If it remains, they give up their design. "I cannot tell you," said a devout Quaker to me, "how simple this influence is; it is less than a mustard seed; it can hardly be spoken of, 'tis so little; yet such as it is, it is something which the dissent of all mankind cannot shake, and which the consent of all mankind could not confirm."[13]

The Quaker mother tells her child, "My son, thou wilt often think of doing things that are wrong, and thy father and mother will not know of them, but thou wilt know." And this is the whole religious education they give.

I wish his position and his speech to be simply affirmative. I certainly shall not permit myself to fight with shadows which, to me, have no real existence, however formidable they show to others. Let the dead bury the dead, for me.

History can spare nothing. The virtues of paganism are instructive and tonic to us: the piety of Antigone, the public soul of Demosthenes, the Indian ascetic with his monstrous privations and self-torture; the haircloth and penance of monks.[14] The iron belt of the New England Calvinist yielded a religious rapture and self-abandonment which I must revere and thank, however impossible it is to accept his creed. He thinks the rapture sprang from that: I see that it sprang from the Divine Presence which rushes through all his pragmatic straws.

The emphasis of that blessed doctrine lay on lowliness. The new Saint gloried in infirmities. Who or what was he? His vice and his recovery were vicarious. He has fallen in another: he rises in another. He rejoices that others are truer and kinder: that God has made others wiser. Where were thy own intellect, if wiser had not

---

lor Coleridge, founder of the romantic movement. Westmorland is the former name of a county in northwestern England where the Lake District is located.

12. Quakers (Society of Friends), English sect founded in the seventeenth century known for its pacifism and belief in an inner spiritual voice.

13. Attributed to Mary Rotch (1777–1848), a liberal New Bedford, Massachusetts, Quaker, by Edward Waldo Emerson (*W*, 8:431n).

14. Antigone, in Greek mythology, is the eldest daughter of Oedipus by his mother, Jocasta, and the subject of a play by Sophocles; Demosthenes (384–322 B.C.), Athenian statesman, regarded as the greatest Greek orator.

been? What matter by whom the good is done, by yourself or another? If it is truth, what signifies who said it?

The fiery soul said, "Let me be a blot on this fair world—the obscurest, the loneliest sufferer, with one proviso,—that I know it is *his Agency*,—I will love him, though he sheds frost and darkness on every way of mine." Nay, it came up to the point of saying, "To obey God is joy, though there were no hereafter."[15]

Wonderful the way in which the world is saved by the unfailing supply of the moral element. There are ever being born men, who, as soon as they are born, take a bee-line to the rack of the inquisitor, the axe of the tyrant, like Giordano Bruno, Vanini, Huss, Paul, Jesus, and Socrates.[16] Look at Foxe's *Lives of the Martyrs*, at the Bollandi, who collected the lives of twenty-five thousand martyrs, confessors, ascetics, and self-tormentors, at Sewel's *History* of the Quakers, at the yet ungathered relics of the martyrs assassinated by the slave-holder.[17]

This virtue is never extinct. And we have seen our John Browns and other martyrs set the country on fire with the flames of their spirit.[18] What hecatombs of heroes did the war burn up! and every one with a history full of tears. But this fire never goes out. There is not one of us who has not known in his own circle of family or acquaintance anecdotes of virtue in peace and in private, that keep his heart warm to remember. And 'tis pleasant to think that such things also happen every day, near or far.

From the *Illustrated London News*.

On the night of the thirty-first of January, the packet from Dover to Calais, after experiencing very heavy weather, was unable in consequence of the continued violence of the storm, to enter the port of Calais. Two English travellers on board expressed great anxiety to catch the train for Paris, and insisted on being allowed to land. For this purpose, they got into a small boat with three sailors. The boat had scarcely left the ship's side, when she was capsized by a tremendous sea, and the whole five were precipitated into the water. An English gentleman, who had remained on deck, immediately took off his coat, and sprang into the sea, and, at the imminent hazard of

15. "The fiery soul" is identified as Mary Moody Emerson in Emerson's note in the manuscript; the quotations are identified as from her "diary" by Edward Waldo Emerson (*W*, 10:551n).

16. Lucilio Vanini (1584–1619), Italian mechanistic philosopher; Jan Hus (ca. 1372–1415), Czech religious reformer; Giordano Bruno (1548–1600), Italian pantheistic philosopher. All three were burned at the stake for heresy. Socrates (ca. 470–399 B.C.), one of the most famous of the Greek philosophers, whose dialogic method of teaching gained many adherents.

17. Emerson's references are to *Actes and Monuments of These Latter Perilous Dayes* (1563), popularly known as *The Book of Martyrs* by John Foxe (1516–87), English martyrologist; the "Bollandi" or, more usually, the Bollandists were collaborators and successors of Jean de Bolland (1596–1665), Flemish Jesuit hagiologist; *The History of the Rise, Increase, and Progress of the Christian People Called Quakers*, first published in Dutch in 1717 and in English in 1722 by William Sewel (1654–1720), English Quaker historian.

18. John Brown (1800–1859), American abolitionist who was hanged for leading a raid on Harpers Ferry, Virginia, intended to spur a slave revolt.

his own life, succeeded in reaching two of the unfortunate passengers, and brought them safely to the ship's ladder. He was himself assisted upon deck, little or none the worse,—the wetting excepted. On turning round, he saw the other three persons struggling in the water, or holding on to the sides of the boat. Once more in the coolest manner possible, he leaped into the sea, and succeeded, to the admiration of all on board, in rescuing them. Thus the whole five were saved. The gentleman, with a modesty as rare as it was noble, refused to give his name, insisting that he had merely done his duty. The circumstances were made known at Calais in the morning, and, when the passengers landed, the authorities of the town presented themselves to thank the hero of the adventure, and to demand his passport. The passport, on being produced, bore the name of Lieut. General Sir Stephen Lakeman.[19] The public will remember this gallant soldier in connection with the Kaffir War, for his services in which he received the honor of Knighthood: his connection also with the War on the Danube, and his maintenance of the rights of the Sultan, when he was Governor of Buchan. He holds the title of Lieut. General in the service of the Sultan.

I think we must accept thankfully all the lights and influences of the time.

But that which is adequate and harmonious with astronomy and zoology, is the moral law, as mankind begin to see it in this age: self-equal, self-executing, instantaneous, and self-affirmed: needing no voucher, no prophet, and no miracle beside its own irresistibility. It is impossible that these extraordinary triumphs of the intellect should be without effect on theology. The mind and heart perpetually react and revivify each other.

The earth revolves in the solar system with a certain obliquity of the plane of its equator to the plane of the ecliptic, producing the change of seasons to the climates of the planet. It keeps that obliquity invariably. There are abundant examples in Nature of eccentricity in orbits which are uniformly restored by compensations of opposite eccentricity. The errors are periodic, as the seasons, as night and day, as sleep and waking, in plant and in animal. The eternal equilibrium is restored.

Now, can anything be so great as that inner Copernican system, that inner astronomy, whose equilibrium is as perfect as the other; whose periodicities are as compensatory; which never tilts, and never decays; to which, or from which, nothing can be added or subtracted; which was before the other, and will be after it, and to which that is a shadow and a type; which builds and unbuilds the men and kingdoms of earth, and is the Source and Law of all existence?

What is this intoxicating sentiment, that allies this scrap of dust to the whole of Nature, and the whole of Fate? that makes this doll a dweller in Ages, mocker at Time, able to spurn all outward advantages; peer and master of the elements? I am taught by it, that, what touches any thread in the vast web of being touches me. I am representative of the Whole, and the good of the Whole, or, what I call

19. Sir Stephen Bartlet Lakeman (b. 1823) published *What I Saw in Kaffir-Land* in 1880.

the Right,—makes me invulnerable. Crush me in a mortar, pound me to powder, destroy my name and vestige out of earth, and I rise unhurt: Fire cannot burn, nor seas drown, nor tempests blow away this holy dream.

How came this creation so magically woven, that nothing can do me mischief but myself? that an invisible fence surrounds my being, which screens me from all harm that I will to resist? that we pass for what we are; that we do not live by times, but by qualities; that the evils we suffer are the just measures of those we have done? If I will stand upright, the creation cannot bend me. But if I violate myself, if I commit a crime, the lightning loiters by the speed of retribution, and every act is not hereafter, but instantaneously rewarded according to its quality.

It seemed to me an impiety to be listening to one and another saint, when the pure heaven was pouring itself into each one of us on the simple condition of obedience. To listen to any second-hand Gospel is perdition of the First Gospel,—that is, your own. Jesus was better than others, because he refused to listen to others, and listened at home, and, hence, his munificent power over the affection, and sympathy, and practice of ingenuous men.

For the realist, the common barriers of sect, or nation, or person are not important. Mr. Landor had a picture and said he would give fifty guineas to any man who would swear that Domenichino painted it. But the realist says, If the picture is good, who cares who made it? The public are distressed because Delia Bacon and Judge Holmes are engaged or enraged to show that Shakspeare did not write the plays.[20] But the public is no loser. Somebody wrote them, and we shall still enjoy our fill of wonder and delight, if we must spell the name differently. Confucius says, "A soldier of the Kingdom of Ci has lost his buckler. What then? A soldier of the Kingdom of Ci has found the buckler."[21]

So, in regard to all our mental treasures, we are drenched in personality. Truth is uninjurable which gathers itself spotless, unhurt, and whole, after all our surrenders, and concealments, and partisanship: never hurt by the treachery or ruin of its best defender, were it William Penn, or Luther, or Paul, whose short-comings are told us.[22] We answer, Well, what if he did? It was only Penn, or Luther, or Paul.

We attach ourselves fondly to our teachers, and historical personalities, and think the foundations shaken if any fault is shown in their patron. But how is the

20. Walter Savage Landor (1775–1864), English romantic poet and prose writer whom Emerson met in England in 1833; Domenichino (1581–1641), Bolognese painter of religious subjects and landscapes and, for a time, the Vatican's chief architect; Delia Salter Bacon (1811–59), American writer, in *Philosophy of the Plays of Shakespeare Unfolded* (1857), proposed Francis Bacon and others as the authors of Shakespeare's plays and tried to enlist Emerson in her support; Nathaniel Holmes (1815–1901), American jurist and Harvard professor, defended Bacon in *The Authorship of Shakespeare* (1866).

21. Confucius (Latin name for K'ung Ch'iu) (551–479 B.C.), Chinese philosopher.

22. William Penn (1644–1718), English Quaker who helped found Pennsylvania; Martin Luther (1483–1546), German religious reformer, founder of Protestantism.

truth hurt by their falling from it? The law of gravity is not hurt by our neglect of it, though our legs are broken. No more is the law of justice by our dishonesty.

Certainly, 'tis human to value a general consent; but, as the sentiment purifies and rises, it leaves crowds; it makes churches of two, churches of one. Such must be. Break no springs; make no cripples. A fatal disservice does this Swedenborg or other lawyer who offers to do my thinking for me.[23]

I know there are those to whom the question of what shall be believed is the more interesting because they are to proclaim and teach what they believe. They do not wish to needlessly shock good people who are contented with old interpretations, unless they see clearly how to help them by purer truth. And often, one's proper part for himself and for others is simply to hold firmly what he values, and not obtrude it on those who do not want it. But one thing is plain, not to be content with the literature of virtue, but try the essence of the article. Let us keep ourselves a little in practice.

Many years ago, the American people attempted to carry out the Bill of Political Rights to an almost ideal perfection. They have made great strides in that direction since. They are now proceeding, instructed by their success, and by their many failures, to carry out not the Bill of Rights, but the Bill of Human Duties. And look what revolution that attempt involves. Hitherto, government has been that of the single person, or of the aristocracy. And, in this country, the attempt to resist these elements, it is asserted, must throw us into the government not quite of mobs, but, in practice, of an inferior class of professional politicians, who, by means of newspapers and caucuses, really thrust their unworthy minority into the place of the old aristocracy, on one side, and of the good, industrious, well-taught but unambitious population, on the other, and win the posts of power, and give their direction to affairs. Hence, liberal congresses and legislatures ordain, to the surprise of the people, equivocal, interested, and vicious measures. The men themselves are suspected and charged with lobbying, and being lobbied.

Now, if the spirit which six years ago armed this country against rebellion, and put forth such gigantic energy in the charity of the Sanitary Commission, could be waked to the conserving and creating duty of making the laws just and humane,—it were to place a great constituency of religious, self-respecting, brave, tender, faithful obeyers of duty, and lovers of men, filled with loyalty to each other, and with the simple and sublime purpose of carrying out in private and in public action, the desire and need of mankind. Here is the post where the patriot should plant himself; here, the altar where virtuous young men, where those to whom friendship is the dearest covenant, should bind each other to loyalty; where Genius should kindle its fires, and bring forgotten truth to the eyes of man.

To speak the truth—who does? It requires a rare courage; and a man who shall

23. Emanuel Swedenborg (1688–1772), Swedish scientist, theologian, and mystic.

in all companies speak the truth, the whole truth, and nothing but the truth, will find himself every day in dramatic situations.

Don't be content with the literature of virtue. Try the essence of the article. I like to see the apple woman, who sits so patiently all day on the Common, now and then at dinner time try one of her own peaches. We, who speak much of the power and joy of the intellect and soul, might occasionally, I hope, taste these ineffable sweets, and see if patience and poverty are as good as we say. And, perhaps, it may come in this very necessity of speaking out frankly all that you believe. And then you expose yourself to resistance. Persecution, even in New England, is never very sound asleep. You may be attacked and defeated.

George Fox's father said to his son, "I see, that, if a man stand by his principle, it will, after a time, bear him out."[24] I do not see how a man, whose eye has once apprehended the moral laws which traverse heaven and earth alike in all ages and are the legislation and the executive in all human action, can stoop to consider seriously such monkish studies as the polemics of the sects, or waste time on their too pagan pictures of the Creator.

Defeated! Why, the man that carries the intellect and the moral sentiment, carries the arsenal of the Divine Power in his breast, carries that which is victory forevermore. Can humility, or the thirst for knowledge, be defeated? Impediments are the very stairs on which he climbs: And he alone understands the meaning of the chief who said,

> "And all that cowards have is mine."[25]

Well, I can be poor. A good soul has the art of being poor, does not need fine cloths, nor sweet cake, and spiced food. Almost, in America, there need be no poverty to the wise. America is the glorious charity of God to the poor. If you go out west,—and you need not go very far west, you may find multitudes of men in America who bought last year a piece of land, and a house, and with their own hands raised a crop which paid for their land and buildings. They can defy the cold patron, the official secretaries, and the conservative committees who refused, on account of the knotty text, to give you the employment you preferred.

By wise, I mean firm and exact. The martyrdom which came to others in the form of bloody mobs, or stakes ringed round with blazing faggots, or in rebel regiments, comes to you in the milder form of the Wisconsin or Minnesota farm with its hard work and its risk of chills and fevers now and then.

It does not yet appear what forms the religious feeling will take. It prepares to rise out of all forms an absolute justice and healthy perception. But one would like

24. George Fox (1624–91), English religious leader, founder of the Society of Friends, or Quakers. Fox preached the superiority of God-given inspiration, or inward light, over the authority of Scripture.
25. "The Highland Widow," chap. 2 in *Chronicles of the Canongate: First Series* (1827) by Sir Walter Scott (1771–1832), prolific Scottish novelist.

to see moral changes and reforms. We have seen every other kind. Here is now a new feeling of humanity infused into public action. Here is contribution of money, on a more extended and systematic scale than ever before, to repair public disasters at a distance, as in the case of conflagrations and famine, and for political support to oppressed parties, like the Greeks in Crete.[26] Then there are the new conventions of social science, before which are the questions of the rights of women, the law of free trade, the treatment of crime, and regulation of labor. If these are tokens of the steady currents of thought and will in these directions, one might well anticipate a new nation.

I know how delicate this principle is;—how difficult of management to practical and social arrangements. It cannot be profaned; it cannot be forced; to draw it out of its natural current, is to lose at once all its power. But I think that such experiments as we recall are those in which some sect or dogma made the tie, and that was an artificial element, which chilled and checked the Union. But, is it quite impossible to believe that men are drawn to each other by the simple respect which each man feels for another in whom he discovers absolute honesty; the respect he feels for one who thinks life is quite too coarse and frivolous, and he should like to lift it a little; he should like to be the friend of some man's virtue; for another, who, underneath his compliances with artificial society, would dearly like to serve somebody, to test his own reality by making himself useful and indispensable in some quarter? Do you remember the experiences of the war? The noble youths, who were ashamed to be useless, and though friends objected that they were not of the rough timber which war required,—replied, that, if others were rough, there might be the more necessity that those of finer strain should temper them. And to a certain extent, the belief in this fact discredits the enterprize of political reform in England and France.

There is a certain secular progress of opinion which in civil countries reaches everybody. If Christianity cannot look to us as it looked to our fathers, we must thank Christianity for that very enlargement.

You shall not go to the sermons in the churches for the true theology, but talk with artists, naturalists, and other thoughtful men who are interested in verities, and note how the idea of God lies in their minds; not the less, how the sentiment of duty lies in the heart of the "bobbin-woman," of any unspoiled daughter, or matron, in the farmhouse. These are the crucial experiments, these the wells where the coy truth lies hid.

I think, as I go, Life is always rich; spontaneous graces and forces elevate it, in every domestic circle, which are overlooked, whilst we are reading of something less excellent in old authors. I go through the streets; each one of these innumerable houses has its own calendar of domestic saints, its unpublished anecdotes of

26. The Greeks had staged major revolts against the Turkish rulers of Crete in 1821 and 1866.

courage, of patience, of wit, of cheerfulness. For the best, I know, were in the most private corners.

Everything draws to its kind, and frivolous people will not hear of noble traits; but let any good example of this secret virtue come accidentally to air, like Florence Nightingale, and you shall hear of parallel examples in every direction.[27] From the obscurity and casualty of those which I know, I infer the obscurity and casualty of the like balm, and consolation, and immortality in a thousand homes which I do not know, and all 'round the world. Let it lie hid in the shade there from the compliments and praise of foolish society: it is safer so. All it seems to demand, is, that we know it, when we see it.

The action carries all the qualities of the actor, as the egg does of the bird. I am revealed in my face, form, constitution, manners, speaking, writing, expenditure, dress, and dealing. There is a force at work to make the best better, and the worst good.

27. Florence Nightingale, known as the Lady with the Lamp (1820–1910), English nurse and health reformer.

General Index

Index of Emerson's Works

Essays

Journals and Notebooks